# Fodor's

# PROVENCE &
# THE FRENCH
# RIVIERA

# WELCOME TO PROVENCE AND THE FRENCH RIVIERA

Provence's azure skies, brilliant sunlight, and windswept landscapes have inspired artists like Cézanne and Van Gogh, as well as countless travelers. Medieval villages perch on hilltops between rolling vineyards, fragrant lavender fields, and craggy mountains. On the coast, port towns and glamorous resorts are scattered among the French Riviera's sparkling beaches. Savor the civilized pleasures of the region, too: Aix's elegant boulevards, Arles's and Avignon's archaeological treasures, and glorious Marseille's lively restaurants and architectural gems.

## TOP REASONS TO GO

★ **Natural Beauty:** The dazzling Mediterranean and the untamed Camargue beckon.

★ **Food and Wine:** France's regional cuisines pair perfectly with great local vintages.

★ **Lofty Views:** Built to ward off pirates and pillagers, hilltop villages are stunning.

★ **Market Day:** Farmers display the local bounty at markets in every town and village.

★ **Seaside Splendor:** Sunny beaches and glitzy nightlife define the alluring Côte d'Azur.

★ **Modern Art:** Marvelous museums display masterpieces by residents Picasso and Matisse.

# Fodor's PROVENCE & THE FRENCH RIVIERA

**Publisher:** Amanda D'Acierno, *Senior Vice President*

**Editorial:** Arabella Bowen, *Editor in Chief*; Linda Cabasin, *Editorial Director*

**Design:** Fabrizio La Rocca, *Vice President, Creative Director*; Tina Malaney, *Associate Art Director*; Chie Ushio, *Senior Designer*; Ann McBride, *Production Designer*

**Photography:** Melanie Marin, *Associate Director of Photography*; Jessica Parkhill and Jennifer Romains, *Researchers*

**Maps:** Rebecca Baer, *Senior Map Editor*; Mark Stroud (Moon Street Cartography) and David Lindroth *Cartographers*

**Production:** Linda Schmidt, *Managing Editor*; Evangelos Vasilakis, *Associate Managing Editor*; Angela L. McLean, *Senior Production Manager*

**Sales:** Jacqueline Lebow, *Sales Director*

**Marketing & Publicity:** Heather Dalton, *Marketing Director*; Katherine Fleming, *Senior Publicist*

**Business & Operations:** Susan Livingston, *Vice President, Strategic Business Planning*; Sue Daulton, *Vice President, Operations*

**Fodors.com:** Megan Bell, *Executive Director, Revenue & Business Development*; Yasmin Marinaro, *Senior Director, Marketing & Partnerships*

**Editorial Contributors:** Sarah Elizabeth Callaway, Nancy Heslin, Jennifer Ladonne

**Editors:** Debbie Harmsen, Maria Hart, Denise Leto, John Rambow, Mark Sullivan, Caroline Trefler

**Production Editor:** Jennifer DePrima

10th Edition

ISBN 978-0-8041-4212-0

ISSN 1944-2912

## SPECIAL SALES

This book is available at special discounts for bulk purchases for sales promotions or premiums. For more information, e-mail specialmarkets@randomhouse.com

PRINTED IN COLOMBIA

10 9 8 7 6 5 4 3 2 1

# CONTENTS

**Fodor's Features**

# CONTENTS

# ABOUT THIS GUIDE

### Fodor's Recommendations
Everything in this guide is worth doing—we don't cover what isn't—but exceptional sights, hotels, and restaurants are recognized with additional accolades. **Fodor's**Choice★ indicates our top recommendations, and **Best Bets** call attention to notable hotels and restaurants in various categories. Care to nominate a new place? Visit Fodors.com/contact-us.

### Trip Costs
We list prices wherever possible to help you budget well. Hotel and restaurant price categories from **$** to **$$$$** are noted alongside each recommendation. For hotels, we include the lowest cost of a standard double room in high season. For restaurants, we cite the average price of a main course at dinner or, if dinner isn't served, at lunch. For attractions, we always list adult admission fees; discounts are usually available for children, students, and senior citizens.

### Hotels
Our local writers vet every hotel to recommend the best overnights in each price category, from budget to expensive. Unless otherwise specified, you can expect private bath, phone, and TV in your room. For expanded hotel reviews, facilities, and deals visit Fodors.com.

### Restaurants
Unless we state otherwise, restaurants are open for lunch and dinner daily. We mention dress code only when there's a specific requirement and reservations only when they're essential or not accepted. To make restaurant reservations, visit Fodors.com.

### Credit Cards
The hotels and restaurants in this guide typically accept credit cards. If not, we'll say so.

**Top Picks**
★ **Fodor's**Choice

**Listings**
⊠ Address
⊠ Branch address
☎ Telephone
🖶 Fax
⊕ Website
✉ E-mail
🎫 Admission fee
🕓 Open/closed times
Ⓜ Subway
⊹ Directions or Map coordinates

**Hotels & Restaurants**
🖼 Hotel
⤴ Number of rooms
🍽 Meal plans
✕ Restaurant
🍴 Reservations
👔 Dress code
▭ No credit cards
Ⓢ Price

**Other**
⇨ See also
☞ Take note
🏌 Golf facilities

# EXPERIENCE PROVENCE AND THE FRENCH RIVIERA

# PROVENCE TODAY

If you're used to the hustle and bustle of Paris, the tempo of life in Provence and the French Riviera may come as a pleasant surprise. People move at a relaxed pace, businesses still close for a leisurely lunch or for the entire winter, and a "big city" like Nice has a population of around 345,000. But as the rest of France lunges forward into the 21st century, there are also changes big and small in this slow-moving region.

### Eating on the Run

The rule of thumb, according to locals, is that American trends come to Provence and the rest of France about 10 years later. Take fast food, for instance. In 2012 sales jumped 12 percent to more than half of the overall market, beating traditional restaurants for the first time. The French now spend less than 30 minutes eating the average meal, down from 1 hour and 20 minutes in 1975. What's perhaps more striking is that daily bread consumption has fallen from a whole baguette per person 30 years ago to half that in 2012. (In 1900, the daily per capita consumption of baguettes was a belt-busting three a day.) Panicked by this turn of events, the French government has come up with an ad campaign with the slogan "Coucou, tu as pris la pain?" ("Hi, did you pick up the bread?"), inspired by the American "Got Milk?" campaign.

### To Tip or Not to Tip

American travelers may be big tippers (second only to the Germans), but they have a lot of questions about tipping abroad. So let's set the record straight once and for all. French law requires restaurants, cafés, and pubs to include service charges and taxes in the total price the customer is to pay. You'll frequently come across phrases like *service compris* (sevice included) at the bottom of a menu or on a menu board. If service isn't included, you'll see the phrase *service non-compris 15%*, and that percentage will be added to your total bill. Contrary to popular belief, however, this is not the same as tipping (*le pourboire*). Tipping remains discretionary. If the service is exemplary, feel free to leave an extra two or three percent on the table as you leave. Either way, don't expect waiters to go the distance to make your meal the most memorable ever in hopes of getting a juicy tip. Frankly, most feel that they are just doing their paid-by-the-hour job.

### How the Other Half Lives

The Côte d'Azur has once again topped the Prime Enclave Index, which tracks the average prices of luxury properties in some of the world's most desirable destinations. A 2013 report from Savills World Research revealed that a typical five-bedroom luxury property in the south of France will set you back $28.5 million, outshining even fifth-ranked Monaco, where a place of the same size would cost $25 million. (Monaco can comfort itself with the fact that it's soon to be home to the world's most expensive apartment: a five-floor penthouse in the new Odeon Towers, the second-tallest building on the Mediterranean, with a purported sale price expected to exceed $250 million.) Savills concluded that the "sought after" French Riviera "is the ultimate and most expensive leisure enclave for home transactions among the ultrawealthy, attracting buyers from across Europe, North America, and, most actively at present, from the Middle East and Russia." It's no wonder that the not-so-ultra-wealthy locals can't get into the property market on the Riviera, where prices are being pushed up by foreigners buying second residences.

## En Anglais, S'il Vous Plait!

After weeks of struggling with your English-French dictionary or with getting your vowel pronunciation just right, you may find that it's time to let your brain slide back into the peaceful land of complete comprehension with the local English-language media. The FM station 107.7 Radio Traffic has updates in English hourly and can be heard across the coast. Riviera Radio 106.5, which has news, weather, and traffic, has a more limited range. The monthly *Riviera Times* can be found on newsstands, and the *Riviera Reporter*, published since 1987, can be downloaded to your iPad. There are also three English-language bookstores stocking a range of new and secondhand titles, making them great stops before a trip to the beach. They are Heidi's Bookshop, in Antibes; the Cannes English Bookshop; and the English Book Centre, in Valbonne.

## Café Culture Reigns

Although many local traditions are falling by the wayside, café culture is very much alive in the south of France. You will not see the French sipping from an insulated mug in their car or on the bus. Most stop by their local haunt for an unhurried *café* (espresso), which they enjoy sitting or standing at the bar, sipping every last caffeinated drop. So what to order? Get a *café, petit café,* or *un express*, and a tiny shot of coffee will be placed before you. If you prefer to keep your eyes in their sockets, try a *café américain* (also known as a *café allongé*), which is that same espresso diluted with more water and put in a bigger cup.

Sugar will always be served on your saucer (with a biscuit, if you're lucky), but you'll need to ask for milk. *Café au lait* can also be ordered as a *café crème* or *un crème*, and there's also an espresso-size version called a *noisette* (meaning hazelnut). And then there's cappuccino, although the quality ranges from super-creamy on down to that of instant cocoa. Dairy options are limited: don't even bother with figuring out low-fat or no-fat lingo because even if your waiter nods yes, you'll almost certainly still be getting whole milk. For the lactose intolerant, there are only a few places in Nice that serve soy milk, including Starbucks, Emile's Cookies, and the Café Marché. Otherwise, *une tisane* (herbal tea) may be a safer choice. One last piece of coffee advice: it's only tourists who order their evening coffee at the same time as dessert—everyone else orders it afterward. Whether or not you care what your waiter thinks is up to you.

## Time to Celebrate

One thing hasn't changed: people in this region still know how to party. Sometimes it's a glittery affair, such as the world-famous Cannes International Film Festival of the Nice Jazz Festival. But oftentimes the best local celebrations are the ones where there's not a single movie star in attendance. St-Rémy is fond of festivals, borrowing traditions of bull races and ferias from its lowland neighbors and creating a few of its own. Things don't get more traditional than at St-Rémy-de-Provence's Fête de la Transhumance, during which thousands of sheep are led from Provence into the Alps.

# WHAT'S WHERE

*Numbers refer to chapters*

**2 The Alpilles, Arles, and the Camargue.** Between the Rhône River delta and the hills of the Alpilles, this region has been a major crossroads since Roman times. Haunting natural beauty can be found in the Camargue but nearby are the cosmopolitan centers of the feisty Latin Nîmes, chic St-Rémy, and Van Gogh's golden Arles.

**3 The Vaucluse.** Anchored by the medieval city stronghold of Avignon, the Vaucluse spreads luxuriantly north into the Rhône vineyards of Châteauneuf-du-Pape and east along the Lavender Route. Check out the Roman theater in Orange, then head to the Luberon—the quintessential Provençal landscape—set with magical hilltop towns like Gordes and Roussillon.

**4 Aix, Marseille, and the Central Coast.** Famous for its tree-lined boulevards, Aix-en-Provence has a bevy of posh cafés where you can enjoy some perfect people-watching, just as Cézanne used to do. South lies Marseille—France's second-largest city—a Mediterranean melting pot. Studded with the rocky Calanques, the nearby coast has pockets of natural beauty that could pass for an Aegean island.

## 5 The Western Côte d'Azur.

This is where the legend begins: palm trees, parasol pines, and sea improbably blue, all framed against the red-rock Massif de l'Estérel. There's St-Tropez, with its white-sand beaches and its port bars thick with off-duty celebs plus *sportif* resorts like St-Raphaël. Inland, the woolly backcountry of Haute-Provence headlines the Gorges du Verdon.

## 6 Nice and the Eastern Côte d'Azur.

This is the heart of the glamorous Côte d'Azur. Nice has its Old Town's bonbon-color palaces. Eastward lies Cannes, famed for its May film festival, and the zillion-dollar hotels of Cap d'Antibes. The sky may kiss the perched village of Èze, but the rainbow ends in the famous art villages: Renoir's Haut-de-Cagnes, Picasso's Antibes, and Matisse's St-Paul and Vence.

## 7 Monaco.

Take the high-rises of Hong Kong, add the amusement-park feel of Disneyland, and mix in a royal touch, and there you have Monte Carlo—all 473 acres of it. Monaco remains the playground of royalty, wealthy playboys, and glamourous film stars.

# PROVENCE PLANNER

## When to Go?

July and August can be stifling here, not only because of the intense heat but the crowds of tourists and vacationers. June and September are the best months to be in the region, as both are free of midsummer crowds and the weather is balmy. June comes with long daylight hours, although cheaper prices and many warm days, often lasting well into October, make September attractive. Try to avoid the second half of July and all of August, when almost all of France goes on vacation. Don't travel on or around July 14 and August 1, 15, and 31, when every French family is either going on vacation or driving home. Watch out for May, riddled with church holidays—one a week—and the museum closings they entail. Anytime between March and November will offer you a good chance to soak up the sun on the Côte d'Azur. After All Saints (November 1), the whole region begins to shut down for winter, and won't open its main resort hotels until Easter. Still, off-season has its charms—the pétanque games are truly just the town folks' game, the most touristy hill towns are virtually abandoned, and when it's nice out you can bask in direct sun in the cafés.

## Making the Most of Your Time

**A Way of Life as Much as a Region.** Peter Mayle's classic memoir *A Year in Provence* prescribes just that, but even a year might not be long enough to soak up all the charm of this captivating region. In three days you can see three representative (and very different) towns: Arles, Avignon, and St-Rémy; with seven days you can head eastward to the French Riviera to explore Nice, Antibes, and Èze; with 10 days you can head back to check out St-Tropez and Marseille.

But no matter where you head, plan to divide your days between big-city culture, backcountry tours, and waterfront leisure. Be sure to tear yourself away from the coastal *plages* (beaches) on the Riviera to visit the perched villages in Provence's "backcountry."

If you must, you can "do" Provence at a breakneck pace, but its rural roads and tiny villages will amply reward a more leisurely approach. Provence is as much a way of life as a region charged with tourist must-sees, so allow time to savor its old-fashioned pace.

**Where to Begin?** That depends if you're starting with Provence (to the west) or the French Riviera (to the east). Avignon is Provence's gateway city, with fast TGV trains to and from Paris. From here you can access every part of Provence easily, either by train, by bus, or by car. For the French Riviera—the Côte d'Azur region—head to Nice, also with an express TGV train to and from Paris. This colorful city is more than nice for hub-and-spoke explorations thanks to its Marseilles–Ventimille (Ventimiglia) train, which connects with all the coastal towns to the east and west of the city.

**What to Avoid?** Unless you enjoy jacked-up prices, traffic jams, and sardine-style beach crowds, avoid the French Riviera coast in July and August. Many of the better restaurants simply shut down to avoid the coconut-oil crowd, and the Estérel is closed to hikers during this flash-fire season. And remember: Cannes books up early for the film festival in May.

## Transportation Basics

**Getting Here.** Public transport to the South of France is well organized, with most areas accessible by plane, train, bus, or boat. Flying in is a good option, as Nice and Marseille have two of the largest airports in France, and regular flights come in from Paris and London. Although the Aéroport Toulon-Hyères is much smaller, it also has frequent flights in and out. If you prefer the more scenic route, note that the high-speed trains—the fabulous TGVs—go directly to Marseille, Aix-en-Provence, Toulon, and Nice in about the same time as a flight.

**By Train, Bus, and Boat.** A big selection of local and regional trains will take you efficiently to many towns along the Riviera coast. The SNCF train network is excellent, with frequent trains to all the major towns and cities (many of the latter enjoy express TGV service, too)—log on to *www.voyages-sncf.com* and *www.tgv.com* for full information. There is a moderately good network of buses run by several independent bus companies—see the Getting Here sections under town listings to figure out which one operates in the area you wish to travel. Note that buses on Sunday and on holidays run on limited schedules, and in some cases don't run at all. There are also boat services that run from Nice, Cannes, Marseille, and Toulon and out to the Isles de Hyères and the Calanques.

**By Car.** Cars have it easy along the Riviera: parallel roads along the Corniches, plus the A8 main *autoroute* (toll highway), allow for access to many towns, allowing you to zip up and down from Monaco to Fréjus–St-Raphael. Cars are even more useful in Provence, where some of the famous villages have only one bus a day, and some of the best restaurants aren't so easy to access. Try to stick to the National (RN) or District (RD) roads, which are far less scary to drive than the highways. Make sure your car has GPS, as the road signs are often as clear as mud, especially off the main autoroute. (And to ensure that the GPS doesn't take you on a wild goose chase, be sure to enter the full name of your destinations: for instance, use "St-Paul-de-Vence" and not just St-Paul.) Finally, a couple of safety reminders: keep car doors locked at all times while driving, and put purses or bags in the glove compartment or trunk so that nothing is visible to scooters passing by.

## Finding a Place to Stay

Space is at a premium in Provence. June, July, and August are considered to be high season, and it can be particularly difficult to find a place to stay. In the smaller towns, make sure always to email or call ahead at least a month or two in advance as in the off-season many of the smaller hotels close and in the high season they are often full long in advance. Book as far in advance as possible for some of the more popular spots—it's not uncommon to book up to six months to a year in advance. Many return visitors book their next year's stay at the end of this year's visit. If you are having trouble finding a place to stay, check with the local tourism website or office. They may have a list of hotels.

In Marseille, be careful to note where your hotel is located. Even if the hotel is deluxe, it may be near an unsavory neighborhood.

## Information Please

*Contact information for tourist offices and their websites are listed under town names. For the main regional tourist office and their websites see the Planner section in the opening pages of each regional chapter.*

# PROVENCE AND THE FRENCH RIVIERA TOP ATTRACTIONS

## Aix-en-Provence

Hometown of Cézanne and Zola, ritzy and charming Aix is epitomized by its Cours Mirabeau, a tree-lined boulevard with lovely cafés in which a lengthy roster of famous literati once lounged.

## Arles

**(A)** Arles actually manages to live up to the beauty of Van Gogh's swirling renditions, but the town's biggest attractions are the Roman theater and amphitheater, built around 46 BC. Time seems to have stood still since 1888 in pockets of the *Vieille Ville* (Old Town).

## Avignon

**(B)** Once considered the "second Rome," the medieval walled city of Avignon is surprisingly youthful and vibrant. This art-filled spot allows you to spend the day at the famous 14th-century Papal Palace, then attend a 21st-century avant-garde theatrical "happening" in the evening at the summer Festival d'Avignon.

## The Calanques

Probing the tall white cliffs just west of picture-perfect Cassis are the rocky, pine-studded finger coves called the Calanques—be sure to enjoy a plunge into the turquoise waters of these film-set lagoons.

## The Camargue

**(C)** Provence's amazing nature park is set with plains of marsh grass stretching to the sea, interrupted only by explosions of flying flamingos bursting into waves of color or modest stampedes of stocky bulls. Tour the region like a local: on horseback, led by one of the area's *gardiens*, or "cowboys."

## The Lavender Route

**(D)** Like Holland's May tulips, the lavender of Haute-Provence is in its glory only once a year, from the end of June to the first two weeks of July, when for miles the landscape breaks out in saturated shades of purple in the region east of the Rhône and north of the Luberon.

1

## Marseille

(E) Visit the Vieux Port of Marseille, heavily renovated in 2013, and relish in the way the light and the cries of the fishmongers bounce off the anchored sailboats; then bring your wide-angle lens to capture the views of the entire city from the crow's-nest church of Napoléon III's Notre-Dame-de-la-Garde.

## Pont du Gard

No other ancient Roman sight in Provence rivals this 2,000-year-old bridge, the highest the Romans ever built. Magnificent views can be had from the opposite bank and at night, when it is spectacularly illuminated.

## St-Paul-de-Vence

(F) This famous walled hill town is home to La Colombe d'Or, the beloved inn of many artists. Have dinner here under a real Picasso or have coffee and dessert next to the Calder in the garden. It's easy to see why some call this the most beautiful hotel on the French Riviera, perhaps in all of France. Other splendors here include the Fondation Maeght, with a pine-forested park dotted with Giacometti and Miró sculptures.

## St-Rémy-de-Provence

(G) The "Hamptons" of Provence remains a haven for chic urbanites. Dappled with the shade of ancient plane trees, this mellow retreat is surrounded by fields of sunflowers immortalized by Van Gogh.

## St-Tropez

(H) Make a summer pilgrimage to St-Tropez, the town Brigitte Bardot made famous, if only to sit along the port eating ice cream and watching the wildly wealthy or tacky file by. And, darling, don't forget your Tod's espadrilles.

# TOP EXPERIENCES

How will you experience Provence and the French Riviera? Will you while away the hours in the Cours Saleya marketplace of Nice? Or play queen-for-a-stay at the Châteaux de la Chevre d'Or? These suggestions, and the following, await you as memorable experiences for your next trip to the south of France.

## Yes You Cannes

You look fabulous, darling, so be like George or Angelina and climb the stairs of the Cannes Film Festival's Palais des Festivals for a photo-op. Be bold and pop into Louis Vuitton on Boulevard de la Croisette (no matter if you're really going to buy) on the modest Rue d'Antibes. Head farther along to the Carlton Hotel for a glass of champagne on the terrace and watch as envious passersby wonder if you aren't somebody famous behind those sunglasses.

## Lapping Up the Lavender

Don't even think twice about it: a drive through Provence's Routes de la Lavande (⊕ *www.grande-traversee-alpes.com*) is a must in late June through mid-July. Nothing can fully illustrate fields upon fields of the purple blossoms as you cross the Drôme with its 2,000 producers. Descend upon Abbaye Notre-Dame de Sénanque before stopping to breathe in the vistas from the Belvedere in Gordes—you may just hear your artist within calling.

## Avignon On and Off

Imagine watching a Shakespeare production in an open-air theater at the 14th-century Papal Palace among 2,000 other spectators. Since 1947, the palace's Cour d'honneur has been the launching venue for the Festival d'Avignon (⊕ *www. festival-avignon.com*), which runs 300 English and non-English shows through July in various locations around the city. The OFF Festival (⊕ *www.avignonleoff. com*) sprawls across city streets with an additional 1,200 performances.

## I'll Drink to That

Develop your palate for Châteauneuf-du-Pape—the most recognized Côte de Rhône wine—with tastings in the village's vineyards or caves. In the heart of the village, you can visit Christophe Ogier's cave, founded in 1859 (⊕ *www. ogier.fr*); visit the fourth generation of wine experts at Château Mont-Redon (⊕ *www.chateaumontredon.fr*); or try Famille Quiot, winemakers since 1748 (⊕ *www.famillequiot.com*).

## Naturally Salty in the Camargue

Have your camera ready to snap the famous pink flamingos, black bulls, and white horses of the Camargue's natural preserve, and get up close and personal with their fascinating environment—the Salins de Camargue, or salt marshes—with a thrilling four-wheel drive (⊕ *www. visitesalinsdecamargue.com*).

## Stargazing in St-Tropez

Hedonistic St-Tropez in July and August is spring break on stilettos. To better your chance for star-spotting, splurge for a night at Hotel Byblos and lunch at Pampelonne beach's Club 55. When things get too hot, climb aboard the *Brigantin II* (⊕ *www.taxi-bateau.com*) for a one-hour cruise around the Bay of Billionaires to snap celebrity villas and giant yachts. End the night at Les Caves du Roy.

## Confine Yourself to St-Rémy-de-Provence

Vincent van Gogh may be the most beloved painter in the world, and if you want to channel his spirit visit (quietly) the St-Paul-de-Mausolé asylum. This is where he was happiest—at least artistically—because he

created 143 canvases here, reproductions of which are on view at the town's Centre d'Art Présence Van Gogh.

### Easter Antiques Hunt at L'Isle-sur-la-Sorgue
It may not be an organized hunt with baskets and eggs, but this twice-annual international antiques fair and flea market (also in August) may win you a prize in the form of a rare treasure. L'Isle-sur-la-Sorgue is highly recognized for its Sunday markets.

### Cardin in Lacoste
In 2001, Pierre Cardin launched the chic Lacoste Festival (⊕ *www.festivaldelacoste.com*) to present opera and theater performances at the former château of the Marquis de Sade. Cardin shares the marquis's vision of Lacoste as a refuge for thespians and artistes—see it come alive during one week each July.

### Do the "Cézanne Circuit"
Explore the actual countryside that forever altered the map of 20th-century painting with a tour of Cézanne's hometown of Aix-en-Provence. A veritable Cézanne theme park, it is filled with his hangouts: pick up a "Cézanne Circuit" map and then hit his hangout, Café Les Deux Garçons, his Jas de Bouffan home, and his "Les Lauves" studio (⊕ *www.atelier-cezanne.com*), where he painted legendary views of Mont Ste-Victoire from a nearby lookout point.

### Gorging on the Gorges du Verdon
Lace up the hiking shoes, throw on the backpack, and start to climb France's "Grand Canyon," the 2,300-foot-high Gorges du Verdon. Its most notorious trail is the Sentier Martel, a challenging six-hour-plus path, but there are more than 1,500 routes to choose from—at ground level opt for kayaking, rafting, or horseback riding.

### Dining with Picasso in St-Paul-de-Vence
It's rare that a Picasso is hanging on the wall of a restaurant, or a Matisse or a Miró. In fact, the Colombe d'Or (⊕ *www.la-colombe-dor.com*) in St-Paul-de-Vence has been likened to a museum and is usually a must-see for art lovers.

### Mediterranean Mardi Gras
A revitalized Carnival (⊕ *www.nicecarnaval.com*) nicely breaks up winter over the last two weeks of February with France's most famous parades (including the *batailles de fleurs* along the Promenade des Anglais). At night, Place Massena explodes with music and fireworks. Don't miss the burning of the King!

### Sports Spice Is Nice
The Alpes–Maritimes Marathon (⊕ *www.marathon06.com*) in November starts at the Promenade des Anglais in Nice and finishes at the Palais des Festivals in Cannes. The 26.2-mile spectacularly scenic run crosses five coastal towns and is already France's second largest, with more than 10,000 runners.

### The Big Prize in Monaco
On the world's most stunning race course, you can watch the Monaco Formula 1 Grand Prix (⊕ *www.formula1.com*), where drivers accelerate 78 times around a 3.34-km-long circuit. And it's more than just race day: the whole weekend is abuzz with festivities presided over by Prince Albert and Princess Charlene.

# QUINTESSENTIAL PROVENCE AND THE FRENCH RIVIERA

## Pastis and Pétanque

In every village from the Rhône Valley to the Italian border, under every deep-shaded *allée* of plane trees, the theater of Provençal life plays itself out slowly, serenely, and sociably. The café is a way of life in Provence, a cool outdoor living room where friends gather like family and share the ritual of the long, slow drink, the discussion of the weather (hot), and an amble over to the *pétanque* (lawn-bowling) court. The players stand, somber and intense, hands folded behind backs, and watch the intricate play of heavy metal balls rolling and clicking. A knot of onlookers gathers, disperses, is reinforced. In this region of the animated debate, the waving gesture, the forefinger punching to chest, it is a surprisingly quiet pastime.

Just as refined a ritual is the drinking of the requisite pastis. The server arrives with a tray loaded with the appropriate props: a carafe of water emblazoned with "Ricard" or "51"; a bowl with an ice cube or two; a bowl of olives, black as jet; and a stubby glass cradling two fingers of amber liquid redolent of anise and licorice. Plop an ice cube into the liquor, then slowly pour a rope of cool water into the glass, watching for the magic moment when the amber transforms itself to milky white. Sip slowly, mop your forehead, and settle in.

## Dining à la Midi

You'll eat latish in the Midi (south of France), rarely before 1 for lunch, usually after 8 at night. In summer, shops and museums may shut down until 3 or 4, as much to accommodate lazy lunchers as for the crowds taking sun on the beach. But a late lunch works nicely with a late breakfast—and that's another southern luxury. As morning here is the coolest part of the day and the light is at its sweetest, hotels of every class take

pains to make breakfast memorable and whenever possible served outdoors. There may be tables in the garden with sunny-print cloths and a nosegay of flowers, or even a tray on your private balcony table. Accompanied by birdsong and cool morning sun, it's one of the three loveliest meals of the day.

### Yours for the Basking

With their worldwide fame as the earth's most glamorous beaches, they often comes as a shock to first-timers: much of the Côte d'Azur is lined with rock and pebble, and the beaches are narrow swaths backed by city streets or roaring highways. Some beaches are reviled for their famous *galets,* round white stones the size of a fist, heaped along the shoreline, just where the sand should be. Some resorts ship in truckloads of sand or shovel in loads from deep water. There are some natural-sand beaches on the southern French coast—especially

between St-Tropez and Cannes—and some beaches like La Garoupe on Cap d'Antibes enjoy legendary status. Provence's coastline—between the Camargue and St-Tropez—alternates sandy pockets with rocky inlets called *criques* and *calanques,* where you perch on black rocks and ease yourself into turquoise water.

In many of the resort towns along the coast you are charged a fee to use the restaurant/hotel beaches, which usually includes a sun-lounger and a parasol. (Note: you can use many hotel beaches for free if you drink or dine on them.) But free stretches of public beach are available, generally close to the center but not on the main "strip," and you need to bring parasol, sun chair, and towel with you. Be sure to arrive early, as both kinds of beaches are popular with locals as well as tourists.

# IF YOU LIKE

## Being Scott and Zelda

Married new money? Made a stock-market killing? Or just remember the old saw "If you don't travel first class, your heirs will"? Well, the Riviera has been a hard place to practice self-denial ever since F. Scott Fitzgerald arrived with the rest of his Jazz Age literati. So drain that glass of Dom. Enough lollygagging! It's time for a power decision: which luxurious pleasure palace will you treat yourself to? Hey, if you can't be self-indulgent on the French Riviera, where can you be?

**Cap–Eden Roc, Cap d'Antibes.** Where once Hemingway ordered yet another Pernod and Zelda wore her latest Poiret, this famous hotel is today the rendezvous of the film stars. You may find Justin and Jessica in the bar, Harrison behind his iPad, and Beyoncé keeping a low profile under her parasol by the cliff-edge pool. Try to be cool, and focus on the menu.

**Château de la Chevre d'Or, Èze.** Seemingly set just below cloud level, this sky-high aerie occupies some of the choicest real estate in Èze, that magical island-in-the-sky perched 1,500 feet over the sea and St-Jean-Cap-Ferrat. Little wonder the views out your window rival those from space.

**La Colombe d'Or, St-Paul-de-Vence.** Yes, those are real Picassos, Mirós, Braques, and Bonnards over your dinner table. This legendary hotel and restaurant was once the favored hangout of these artists when you could buy one of their daubs for $5. Today, it is super-stylish, utterly elegant, and you can't move without bumping into a Calder mobile—or an off-duty celebrity dining on the enchanting terrace.

## Villages Perchés

Practically defying gravity, the sky-kissing, hilltop-perched villages of Provence and the Riviera are some of the most spectacular sights in France. In the Middle Ages, pirates and Saracens drove villagers to move well above the fray. Thus sprouted these villages from the hilltops, Babel-like towers of canted cubes and blunt cylinders seeming to grow out of the rock. Houses mount several levels; thus freed from obstructing neighbors, their windows take in light and wide-open views. The tiniest of streets weave between rakish building blocks, and the houses seem tied together by arching overpasses and rhythmic arcades. Wells spring up in miniature *placettes* (little squares), the trickling sound echoing loud in the stone enclosure. Succumb to their once-upon-a-timeliness and be sure to visit two or three.

**Èze.** As cute as a Fisher-Price toy village, Èze is so relentlessly picturesque it will practically take the pictures for you.

**Haut-de-Cagnes.** Topped by a Grimaldi castle, once a forgetaway favored by the likes of Renoir, Soutine, and Simone de Beauvoir, this enchanting labyrinth of steep alleys and Renaissance stairways is a magical place where time seems to be holding its breath.

**Oppède-le-Vieux.** Isolated above the Luberon, this village stands alone in the mist, utterly noncommercial and lovingly cared for by its residents.

## Relishing the Riviera

The Côte d'Azur is home to top chefs who are redefining the "new Mediterranean cuisine" in all its costly splendor: "scrambled" sea urchins; herb sausages with chopped truffles and lobster; frogs' legs soup with fresh mint; and poached sea bass flan with crayfish sauce. Grand names like Alain Ducasse still present such delights at showplaces like Monaco's Le Louis XV, but there are any number of young stars on the make. But with access to some of the world's best ingredients, Provençal chefs face a dilemma—do they uphold tradition or go out on a limb? Here are some legends who balance both schools beautifully.

**Le Chantecler, Nice.** At his restaurant inside the historic Hotel Negresco, Jean-Denis Rieubland says he's "inspired by Provence," as is proven by his lightly seared foie gras and truffles, white-wine consommé, and brioche, made with local chestnuts.

**Le Louis XV, Monte Carlo.** Crystal, gilt, and period pomp frame the extraordinary cuisine of Alain Ducasse—truffle-sprinkled artichokes, ember-grilled pigeon breast, and salt-seared foie gras, anyone?

**Le Park 45, Cannes.** Furnished with Swedish teak and facing La Croisette, this sleek spot showcases young chef Sébastien Broda, who stops the show with such wows as his M&M–like balls of foie gras in pea soup.

**Mirazur, Menton.** Argentinean–Italian Mauro Colagreco excels at *la jeune cuisine*, thanks to studying with Bernard Loiseau and Alain Ducasse, then he adds in those much-talked-about modernist "techniques" such as *spuma* (foam).

## Where Art Comes First

Artists have been drawn to the south of France for generations, awed by its luminous colors and crystalline light. Monet, Renoir, Gauguin, and Van Gogh led the way, followed over the years by Léger, Matisse, Picasso, Chagall, and Cocteau. Cézanne had the good fortune to be born in Aix, and he returned to it, and to his beloved country home nearby, throughout his life. The artists left behind a superb legacy of works, utterly individual but all consistently bathed in Mediterranean color and light. That's why a visit to this region can be as culturally rich as a month in Paris and just as intimately allied to the setting that inspired the work. Art museums abound—but don't forget to pay your respects to Cézanne's studio in Aix and Renoir's garden home in Cagnes.

**Fondation Maeght, St-Paul-de-Vence.** With its serene setting in a hilltop woods and its light-flooded displays of modern works, this gallery-museum is the best mixed-artist exhibition space in the south of France.

**Musée de l'Annonciade, St-Tropez.** St-Tropez was the Riviera's first "Greenwich Village" and artists—Signac, Derain, and Matisse, among them—flocked here in the early 20th century. Today, the collection has its share of masterworks.

**Musée Matisse, Nice.** In a superb Italianate villa above Nice, Matisse's family has amassed a wide-ranging collection of the artist's works.

# AN APPETITE FOR PROVENCE
## TOP COOKING SCHOOLS

Ever wondered what it might be like to cook in Julia Child's kitchen? Or look at fresh vegetables with a local's eye? With a food history as richly varied as its produce, Provence is the ideal place to expand your culinary repertoire by signing up for some cooking lessons.

Great chefs and great cooking schools have made Provence and the Riviera into some of the most foodie-friendly places on the planet.

At a time when "fresh" and "seasonal" are the words on every food-lover's lips, Provençal cooking has never looked more modern—even if many of the most popular recipes are centuries old. Vividly colored vegetables and olive oils—tasting of artichokes, almonds, or freshly cut grass—form the basis of most meals, with meat or fish often a secondary ingredient. Most sessions involve several days of classes with accommodation included, but day programs are also available, such as Les Petits Farcis's classes and tours in Nice. However long the program, you will leave with a deeper knowledge of southern French culture and a taste for market-fresh produce that will never fade. No wonder Provençal cooking holidays have never been more popular.

—Rosa Jackson

### MATISSE SHOPPED HERE

Founded in 1861, the Cours Saleya is one of the most atmospheric outdoor markets on the French Riviera. Wander and savor, just like Matisse (whose apartment overlooked the market), such specialties as *pissaladière* (caramelized onion tart) and *socca* (a chickpea-flour pancake). Recognizable by their smaller stalls, farmers sell the freshest local produce.

**1**

## COOKING WITH FRIENDS

If you loved the film *Julie & Julia*, treat yourself to a week of classes in Julia Child's old kitchen under the guidance of Kathie Alex. Weathered copper pots dangle from hooks over the workstation where Alex studied with Simca Beck (famed coauthor of *Mastering the Art of French Cooking*). The course of classic favorites starts with Sunday dinner and ends with Saturday breakfast, with cooking classes in the mornings and free time in the afternoon. (No address listed: too many people drop by to see Julia Child's kitchen.) ☎ *562/221–1417* ⊕ *www.cookingwithfriends.com* ✉ *$2,650 per person* ⊙ *Schedule varies.*

## LES PETITS FARCIS

Longtime food writer Rosa Jackson runs market tours and cooking classes in the heart of Nice's Old Town. Classes begin at a café facing the market, before an informative tour during which Rosa picks up seasonal produce from small farmers for the day's class. Then it's a short walk to her 17th-century apartment, with lessons in traditional Niçoise cooking, which has a strong Italian influence. Each class ends with a convivial lunch that includes a platter of local cheeses. ✉ *7 rue du Jésus, Nice* ☎ *06–81–67–41–22* ⊕ *www.petitsfarcis.com* ✉ *From €195 per person* ⊙ *Year-round.*

## MAS DE CORNUD

Nito Carpita and her personable husband, David, run this cooking school from their home; you can come on a Wednesday for a market tour, cooking class, and lunch or, instead, sign up for several days of cooking lessons. Nito regularly brushes up her skills at professional schools all over the world and her kitchen has 10 well-equipped workstations. The focus is on traditional Provençal cooking, and guest chefs have included the likes of Jacques Pépin. ✉ *7 petite rte. des Baux, St-Rémy-de-Provence* ☎ *04–90–92–39–32* ⊕ *www.mascornud.com* ✉ *From €155 per person* ⊙ *Apr.–early July and Sept.–mid-Oct.*

## PROVENCE COOKS

Madeleine and Erick Vedel run two separate businesses: Madeleine's hiking and biking tours with a focus on food and local artisans, and Erick's one-day cooking classes. Their location in Avignon means that they have access to the finest produce, seafood, and Côtes du Rhône wines. Erick's classes involve three hours of cooking, during which students prepare four to six typically Provençal dishes for lunch or dinner. ✉ *1041 chemin des Vendages, Avignon* ☎ *06–88–50–03–62* ⊕ *www.cuisineprovencale.com* ✉ *From €250 for 1 or 2 people* ⊙ *Year-round.*

# GREAT ITINERARIES

## ONE WEEK IN PROVENCE: AIX, ARLES, AND AVIGNON

### 7 Days

If you want to focus only on the best of Provence—its history, its architecture, its markets, and its cafés, devote your time to the "three As" and the area between them that anchors the heart of Provence.

### Days 1–3: Avignon and St-Rémy

Nowadays the population of Avignon swells most during the extensive midsummer Drama Festival that sees the "gateway city" to Provence at its liveliest. Yet this historic, pretty town, with its protective medieval ring of muscular towers, is seldom dull at any time of year. In the 14th century, this was the center of Christendom, when French-born pope Clement V shifted the papacy from Rome to Avignon's magnificent Palais des Papes (Papal Palace). After viewing the palace, the Pont St-Bénezet ("Sur le pont d'Avignon . . ."), and the Rocher des Doms park, escape into the cobblestoned alleys to see the Avignonnais leading their daily lives. One afternoon make an excursion 25 km (15 miles) west of Avignon to the three-tier stone spectacular that is the Pont du Gard, built in 19 BC as an aqueduct by the ancient Romans and one of the wonders of the classical world. On the third day escape to the "Hamptons of Provence," the picturesque town of St-Rémy-de-Provence, where mellow 18th-century mansions line the streets, the main ones leading to St-Paul-de-Mausolée, the ancient monastery where Vincent van Gogh spent some of his most productive months. ⇨ *Chapters 2 and 3.*

### Days 4–5: Arles and the Camargue

Head 33 km (21 miles) southwest to Arles, which competes with Nîmes for the title "Rome of France," thanks to its famous Roman theater, *arenès* (amphitheater), Alyscamps, and Cryptoporticus. All the main sights are in the small *vieille ville* (Old Town), speckled with pockets where time seems to have stood still since 1888, the year Vincent van Gogh immortalized the town in his paintings. Study reproductions of the best canvases, which have come to define Provence as much as its herbs and traditional costumes, at Arles's Espace van Gogh and see the places he immortalized during the two years he lived here along the town's "Promenade Vincent van Gogh." Arles has a similar beauty and history to Aix-en-Provence but a less aristocratic, more down-to-earth feel to it. Inquire at the tourist office about bus tours to the neighboring Camargue, famed for its pink flamingos, black bulls, white horses, and gardiens—one of the most unique natural preserves in France. ⇨ *Chapter 2.*

### Days 6–7: Aix-en-Provence

The museums and churches in Aix are overshadowed by the town itself, an enchanting beauty with elegant hôtels particuliers (mansions), luxurious fountains gracing every square, and an architectural layout that attests to Aix's prominent past as the 17th-century cultural and political capital of Provence. Walking is not only the easiest way to get around but the best, as the center is a maze of narrow streets and lovely squares (where people and café tables take up every inch). The tree-lined Cours Mirabeau divides old Aix in half, with the Quartier Ancien's medieval streets to the north and the 18th-century mansions

Pont du Gard

Avignon

Arles

St-Rémy-de-Provence

CAMARGUE

Etang de Vaccarès

Etang de Berré

Aix-en-Provence

Golfe de Fos

Villefranche-sur-Mer

St-Paul-de-Vence

Haut-des-Cagnes

Antibes

Cap d'Antibes

Èze

Nice

Beaulieu-sur-Mer

St-Jean-Cap-Ferrat

*Mediterranean Sea*

of the Quartier Mazarin to the south. Connecting most of the dots—including such sightseeing musts as the Musée Granet, the Cathédrale St-Sauveur, and the gorgeous Pavillon de Vendôme—is the Paul Cézanne Trail, which allows you to follow in the footsteps of Aix's most famous native son, from his studio to his Jas de Bouffan home to his favorite hangout, the Café-Brasserie Les Deux Garçons. ⇨ *Chapter 4.*

# ONE WEEK ON THE RIVIERA: CRUISING THE CÔTE D'AZUR

## 7 Days

To hit the highlights of this sun-blessed region and get up close and personal to the tropical glamour of the Côte d'Azur, here's a weeklong itinerary that allows you to get a good feel for what makes the Riviera famous—and wonderful. Make like a movie star and follow the coastline from Antibes to St-Jean-Cap-Ferrat—hitting the best beaches, circling the emerald-green capes, perusing the markets, and making the requisite hill-town stop. Other than St-Paul-de-Vence, all destinations here are on the coast and linked by the wonderful coastal railway.

## Days 1–2: Antibes and St-Paul-de-Vence

Sitting on the western side of the Baie des Anges (Bay of Angels), Antibes is a heavenly place. While a bustling town, it has a waterfront quarter that is so picturesque you'll be tempted to set up an easel—mere photographs don't do it justice—just like Picasso, whose works are on view in the town's Château Grimaldi. The surrounding alleys are a maze of enchantment with the Cours Massena overflowing with charm and flowers at its daily market and Le Safranier, a historic quarter of tiny cobblestone streets and flower-box-filled windowsills. Then enjoy a day of tropical hedonism on the Cap d'Antibes, a rocky promontory (which juts out into the Bay of Millionaires) adorned with Gilded Age mansions, one of which, the Villa Eilenroc, is open to the public. Then, even if you're too sunburned, fit in an excursion by bus up to the pretty perched medieval village of St-Paul to lunch at the Picasso-blessed Colombe d'Or (a must and the highpoint of any trip to the Riviera) and a visit to the Fondation Maeght's Giacomettis. ⇨ *Chapter 6.*

### Day 3: Haut-des-Cagnes

Could this be the most beautiful village in southern France? Part-time residents Renoir, Soutine, Modigliani, and Simone de Beauvoir are just a few who thought so. You will forever dream about this place after leaving: with its tiny medieval streets, array of 15th- and 17th-century houses, corkscrew alleys, and vaulted arches draped with bougainvillea, it is a lovely dip into the Middle Ages. Many of the pretty residences are like dollhouses (especially the hobbit houses on Rue Passebon) but looming over all is the medieval town castle, with a grand Renaissance courtyard and three quirky collections. ⇨ *Chapter 6*.

### Day 4–5: Nice

Just 15 minutes away from Haut-des-Cagnes by train, Nice is the big-city leg of your trip, so immerse yourself in culture: the Matisse and Chagall museums (set in the Cimiez suburb, high over the city), or the cutting-edge modern art museum. Start the day at the magnificent Cours Saleya Market, which shuts down by 1 pm—if you're up early enough, you can watch the chefs squabble over the best produce. Then stroll through the labyrinthine Old Town. A few steps away lies the shoreline, where you can spend an hour or two strolling the famed Promenade des Anglais bordering Nice's vast crescent of beach. Amble toward the port and you'll find La Promenade des 100 Antiquaires, which runs up to Place Garibaldi. ⇨ *Chapter 6*.

### Day 6–7: Villefranche-sur-Mer and St-Jean-Cap-Ferrat

Either of the pretty ports of Villefranche or St-Jean takes you back to the days before the Riviera became the land of pink concrete, and both offer easy access to the tropical glories of Cap Ferrat and the sky-kissing perched village of Èze. First, marvel at Villefranche's deep blue bay, study the hillside estates (one is Paul Allen's Villa Maryland), and visit the town's Chapelle St-Pierre, decorated by Jean Cocteau. Then take the bus or walk over to Cap Ferrat, a favorite getaway of the sunglasses-and-sapphires set. Be sure to tour the art-charged rooms and expansive gardens of the Villa Ephrussi-Rothschild on Cap Ferrat. Then set out to do the half-hour hike along the Promenade Maurice Rouvier (lots of movie stars do their power-walking here) to nearby Beaulieu-sur-Mer, home to the fabulous re-creation of ancient Greece that is the Villa Kerylos. Your final excursion should be to the sky-high village of Èze, an eagle's-nest wonder threaded by stone alleys that lead to the most spectacular vistas of the coast. One step higher and you will be, indeed, in paradise. Take the shuttle back down to the coast and then the train to Nice to get back home. ⇨ *Chapter 6*.

# PROVENCE FESTIVALS

### Aix-en-Provence

**Festival d'Aix-en-Provence.** Every July, you can see world-class opera productions in the courtyard of the Palais de l'Archevêché. It is one of the most important opera festivals in Europe, attracting some 83,000 festival goers, and cutting-edge productions involve the best artists available. The repertoire is varied and often offbeat, featuring works like Britten's *Curlew River* and Bartók's *Bluebeard's Castle* as well as the usual Mozart, Puccini, and Verdi. ✉ *Palais de l'Ancien Archevêché, 28 pl. des Martyrs de la Résistance* ☎ *08–20–92-29–23 0.12€/min* ⊕ *www.festival-aix.com.*

### Antibes

**Antibes Art Fair.** At this antique fair, held for two weeks each April, about 25,000 people from all over the world come to view the treasures on display and pick up a little something for back home; it's one of the largest events of its kind in France. ✉ *Old Port, Antibes* ☎ *04–93-34–65-65.*

**Voiles d'Antibes.** The first week of June, check out the Voiles d'Antibes, a major meeting of beautiful old teak and brass sailing vessels, metric classes, and maxi-cruisers more than 20 meters long. The Match Race regatta sets sail across 23 km of coastline. ✉ *Old Port, Antibes* ☎ *04/93-34–42-47 for information* ⊕ *www.voilesdantibes.com.*

**Festival International Jazz à Juan.** Every July the world-renowned Jazz à Juan festival stages a stellar lineup in a romantic venue under ancient pines. This 50-plus-year-old festival hosted the European debut performances of such stars as Miles Davis and Ray Charles. More recently, it spawned the fringier Jazz Off, with 200 musicians and free street concerts, and the Jazz Club at Les Ambassadeurs beach, where you can enjoy a drink with live music (headliners have been known to pop in for impromptu concerts here). ✉ *Juan-les-Pins* ☎ *04–22-10–60-06 ticket information* ⊕ *www.jazzajuan.com.*

### Arles

**Les Rencontres d'Arles** (*Photography Festival*). In July the famed Les Rencontres d'Arles brings movers and shakers in international photography into the Théâtre Antique for five days of specialized colloquiums and other events. Ordinary folks can profit by attending the 50 exhibitions of mostly unpublished work. These are displayed at various heritage sites in Arles and are open to the public from July to September. Tickets, which range from €2 to €8, can be purchased online or from various locations in Arles, including the festival office. ✉ *Office, 34 rue du Docteur Fanton, Arles* ☎ *04/90-96-76-06* ⊕ *www.rencontres-arles.com.*

### Avignon

**Festival d'Avignon** (*Festival d'Avignon*). Held annually over three weeks in July, the Festival d'Avignon has brought the best of world theater to this ancient city since 1947. Avignon's version of fringe, the OFF Festival (⊕ *www.avignonleoff.com*), is staged at the same time. The two combined host more than 1,500 performances, with the main venue being the Palais des Papes. ■ TIP➔ Tickets go on sale around mid-June and sell out quickly. ✉ *Avignon* ☎ *04/90-14–14-14 tickets and information* ⊕ *www.festival-avignon.com.*

**Les Hivernales.** An annual winter festival, Les Hivernales, celebrates French contemporary dance over one week starting in late February with performances, workshops, and exhibitions at various cultural locations throughout Avignon. Its central venue is the Théâtre du CDC Les Hivernales (at 18 rue Guillaume Puy). ☎ *04/90-82–33-12* ⊕ *www.hivernales-avignon.com.*

## Cannes

**International Cannes Fireworks Festival.** During this festival, which takes place over various nights in August, six countries compete in an amazing 25-minute musical fireworks display that lights up both the water and the sky. The fireworks are set off from barges 400 meters offshore from the Baie of Cannes; you can watch for free beachside amongst the masses of locals who come early. ☎ 04–92–99–33–88 *for information* ⊕ *www.festival-pyrotechnique-cannes.com.*

**Cannes International Film Festival.** The Riviera's cultural calendar is splashy and star-studded, and never more so than during the International Film Festival in May. The film screenings are not open to the public, so unless you have a pass, your stargazing will be on the streets or in restaurants (though if you hang around the back exits of the big hotels around 7 pm, you may bump into a few celebs on their way to the red carpet). *Cinéma de la Plage* shows Cannes Classics and Out of Competition films free at Macé beach at 8:30 pm. In addition, the Cannes Cinéphiles (⊕ *www.cannes-cinema.com*) is a group of public screenings of competition films. You can apply online in February. ⊠ *Cannes* ⊕ *www.festival-cannes.com.*

## Nice

**Nice Carnaval.** During the two weeks leading up to Mardi Gras and Lent, the Niçois let loose in disguise during this carnival, which attracts roughly a million visitors. The parades along the Promenade des Anglais include 30,000 floats made up of some 80,000 flowers, dancers of varying levels of expertise and enthusiasm, and makeup stands for kids. For the best view, it's worth investing in tickets (seats €25; standing €10). ☎ *08–92–70–74–07 0.34€/min* ⊕ *www.nicecarnaval.com.*

**Nice Jazz Festival.** For five days in July, the Nice Jazz Festival draws performers from around the world to Place Masséna and Théâtre de Verdure. Tickets begin around €35 per show and can be purchased online directly or from FNAC and Carrefour. Enter at Place Masséna. ⊠ *Place Masséna and Théâtre de Verdure, Espace Jacques Cotta, Nice* ☎ *08–92–68–36–22* ⊕ *www.nicejazzfestival.fr.*

## St-Rémy-de-Provence

**Fête de la Transhumance.** Held on Pentecost Monday (the end of May), the Fête de la Transhumance celebrates the passage of the sheep from Provence into the Alps. Costumed shepherds lead some 4,000 sheep, goats, and donkeys through the streets. There's an antiques fair and cheese market in the ancient village, as well as other events throughout the day.

**Grande Feria.** The Grande Feria brings the Camargue to St-Rémy-de-Provence for this highly anticipated festival in mid-August. Bullfights and bull runs, Peña flamenco music, DJs, parades, kids' races, and plenty of food are all on offer during its three days. ⊕ *www.saintremy-de-provence.com.*

**La Route des Artistes.** Four or five Sundays a year, from May to October, are devoted to the La Route des Peintres, as 200 amateur artists line the streets of St-Rémy's old town. Each day draws upward of 15,000 art lovers, so try to get there soon after it begins, around 10 am. ⊕ *artistes13210.canalblog.com.*

# THE ALPILLES, ARLES, AND THE CAMARGUE

# WELCOME TO THE ALPILLES, ARLES, AND THE CAMARGUE

## TOP REASONS TO GO

★ **Vincent van Gogh's Arles:** Ever since the fiery Dutchman immortalized Arles in all its chromatic drama, this town has had a starring role in museums around the world.

★ **A dip in the Middle Ages:** Wander the ghostly ruins of the Château des Baux in Les Baux-de-Provence—a tour de force of medieval ambience.

★ **Provence unplugged:** The famous lagoons of the Camargue will swamp you with their charms once you catch sight of their white horses, pink flamingos, and black bulls.

★ **St-Rémy's relentless charm:** Find inspired gourmet cooking, meditate quietly on Greco-Roman antiquity, or browse bustling markets, basket in hand, at this fashionable village enclave.

★ **The Pont du Gard:** This aqueduct of the ancient Roman era is also a spectacular work of art.

**1** Languedoc frontier. The westernmost edge of Provence is highlighted by Nîmes, which competes with Arles and Orange as "the Rome of France" and is home to the Maison Carrée, the best-preserved ancient temple in Provence (Thomas Jefferson admired it so much he used it as a model for the Virginia state capitol). To the north is the Pont du Gard, most awe-inspiring in the early morning light.

**2** The Camargue. A bus ride away from Arles and bracketed by the towns of Aigues-Mortes and Stes-Maries-de-la-Mer, the vast Camargue nature park is one of France's most fascinating areas. Horseback ride across its mysterious marshland, then enjoy home-style cooking at one of the exclusive *mas* (converted-farmhouse) hotels.

## GETTING ORIENTED

Rugged and beautiful, the landscape here is different from everywhere else in the South. Nowhere else will you find the Camargue's hypnotic plane of marshland stretching out to the sea, or the rocky Alpilles that jut upward hiding medieval fortress towns. Yet city folk find joy here, too, in Van Gogh's colorful Arles or in feisty, fiercely independent Nîmes. And if it all gets just a bit too dusty, there is a plethora of options for some pampered R&R.

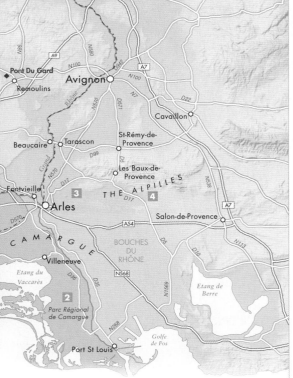

**3 Arles.** Although little is left of the town that Van Gogh once painted, there are spots where you can still channel his spirit. Today, Arles remains fiercely Provençal and is famed for its folklore events.

**4 The Alpilles.** These spiky mountains guard treasures like Les Baux-de-Provence—be bewitched by both its *ville morte* (dead town) and its luxurious L'Oustau de la Baumanière inn. Nearby is ritzy St-Rémy-de-Provence, Van Gogh's famous retreat.

# PROVENCE'S VILLAGE MARKETS
## WHERE TO GET THE GOODS

In Provence, forget about the supermarket and head to the marketplace—an integral part of French culture anywhere in France, but even more so in this region.

Among the most prized gifts are Provençal *santon* figurines (above); less overhead means cheap prices (right, top); gourmet goodies for sale (right, bottom).

Provence is the equivalent of market heaven. Whether foodie, collectibles, antiques, or clothing, there is a (very often famous) street market in every Provençal town. Every marketplace here has an energy of its own and they offer the best way to get to know the natives. So even though you may wonder if you should resist that table-cloth of pink-and-yellow Souleiado fabric, yield to the delight of puttering through a village market. Happily, they are a daily occurrence in Provence, passed from village to town—Sunday is for Isle-sur-la-Sorgue, Saturday for Arles, Wednesday for St-Rémy, Tuesday, Thursday, and Saturday for Aix. Each market transforms itself to reflect something organic and intrinsic to the area itself. But remember to pick the wheat from the chaff. Give wide clearance to the bastard children of legitimate crafts, such as bubble-gum-scented olive-oil soaps and Day-Glo versions of Van Goghs. Provence lovers back home, however, will love those sunflower coasters.

### FEATS OF CLAY

Top gifts are the miniature figures called *santons*, or "little saints." When the French Revolution cracked down on Christmas reenactments, a crafty Marseillais decided to make terra-cotta figurines, which soon upstaged their human counterparts for good. Sold year-round, models include red-cheeked town drunks, lavender-cutters, and, wait, isn't that Gerard Depardieu and Carla Bruni-Sarkozy?

## AIX-EN-PROVENCE

Aix has some delightful street markets. Unlike the more traditional fare of other markets, the one in Aix is more focused on food: you can find rare delicacies side by side with cured sausages bristling with Provençal spices, vats of olives, tapenade, and oils from the Pays d'Aix (Aix region), or bags of orange-spice shuttle-shape *navettes* (cookies). The food market takes place every day in Place Richelème, and just up the street in Place Verdun is a good all-purpose market Tuesday, Thursday, and Saturday morning.

## ARLES AND THE CAMARGUE

Every Saturday morning along the Boulevard des Lices, which flows into Boulevard Clemenceau, Arles hosts one of the best textile markets in the area. Here you can find the famous *boutis* (cotton throws), textured fabrics in all styles and colors, and an endless array of brightly dyed and embroidered tablecloths, children's clothes, and Arlesian costumes. On the first Wednesday of every month, this same spot converts into an antiques and collectibles market—all the more interesting because wares are mostly regional.

## AVIGNON AND THE VAUCLUSE

Avignon has a great mix of French chains and youthful clothing shops, and the Les Halles food stalls are a sight to see. Every Wednesday morning,

St-Rémy-de-Provence hosts one of the most popular markets in France. The Place de la République and the narrow town streets overflow with fresh produce, olives, tapenade by the vat, and a variety of other delicacies. In the Vaucluse area, you can find anything made from lavender, including soaps, oils, creams, perfumes, and little sachets filled with dried lavender to keep your clothes—and your suitcase—fresh.

## MARSEILLE

The main shopping drag lies between La Canebière and the Préfecture, but Marseille offers up a large selection of quirky shops, urban youth boutiques, and brand-name stores all over the city. There are more than 30 street markets, the most renowned of which is the fish market in the port. Probably the most famous item sold, however, is the Savon de Marseille (Marseille soap).

## THE SORGUE VALLEY

The best place to go trolling for time-burnished treasure is the famed antiques market held in lovely L'Isle-sur-la-Sorgue every weekend. Twice a year, around Easter and mid-August, some 350 antiques merchants set up shop over four days for the *Grand Déballage*, or the "Great Unpacking." In August, the rush is such that vendors stay open until 11 pm on Thursday evening.

Updated
by Jennifer
Ladonne

Scoured by the mistral and leveled to prairie flatlands by aeons of earth deposits carried south by the Rhône, this region is Provence in its rawest form. At first glance it is endless space broken only by the occasional gully lined with wildflowers, yet after a few moments it starts to take form as one of the most beautiful and intriguing regions in France.

It is big-sky country here: mysterious, romantic, and colored with a kaleidoscope of lavenders, wheat-yellows, vibrant greens, and burnt reds. Only the giant rock outcrops of the Alpilles interrupt the horizon, dusted with silvery olives and bristling with somber cypress spears. To the west, where the Provençal dialect gives way to Languedoc, the ancient language of the southwest, vineyards swathe the countryside in rows of green and black. Along the southern coast, the Camargue's savage landscape of reeds and cane conceals exotic wildlife—rich-plumed egrets, rare black storks, clownish flamingos—as well as domestic oddities: dappled white horses and lyre-horned bulls descended from ancient, indigenous species.

The scenery is surpassed only by the genuine warmth of the populace and the feisty energy of the cities. In-your-face, tatty Nîmes has a raffish urban lifestyle that surges obliviously through a ramshackle, gritty-chic Old Town and a plethora of Roman architectural marvels. Graceful, artsy Arles, harmonious in Van Gogh hues, mixes culture with a healthy dose of late-night café street life. Chic, luxurious St-Rémy is a gracious retreat for cosmopolitan regulars. Often misleadingly dubbed the Hamptons of Provence, it's not all about luxe, for St-Rémy has an amazingly steady infusion of style, art, and street sass mixed with a love of all things Provençal.

Each of these cities would be fascinating to explore even without its trump card: classical antiquities, superbly preserved, unsurpassed in northern Europe. The Colosseum-like arenas in Nîmes and Arles are virtually intact, solid enough to serve their original purpose as stadiums; they date from the time of Christ. The mausoleum and *Arc Triomphal* outside St-Rémy are still so richly detailed they look like reproductions, but they're signed by the children of Caesar Augustus. And across the street, the vivid high-relief ruins of Glanum trace back to the Hellenism of the 3rd century BC.

Rich in history and legends, the region is as varied as the people who inhabit it. There are precise and perfect miniature fortress towns, like Aigues Mortes and Les Baux-de-Provence—where it is sometimes difficult to distinguish between bedrock and building—or the wide-open marshlands of the Camargue, dotted with hidden natural treasures. Add to these attractions Romanesque châteaux and abbeys, seaside fortresses that launched crusades, and sun-sharpened landscapes seen through the perceptive eyes of Van Gogh and Gauguin, and you have a region not only worth exploring in depth, but worth savoring every minute.

This is the kind of country that inspires a Latin latitude (if not lassitude), so with all the ruins and châteaux to visit, allow yourself time to wander through food markets and to sit on a shady terrace watching the painterly changes in light. When mapping out your itinerary remember that although Nîmes belongs in spirit to the Languedoc, its proximity to the Camargue and Arles makes it a logical travel package with them. With their rugged hills and rich olive groves, the Alpilles are a world apart, but easily accessible from Arles and environs. You can move from site to site, or choose a central base—say, Arles—and explore them all without driving more than an hour to any one attraction. A couple of days passing through the region allows you to see world-class antiquities; five days allows time to wander the Camargue; a week lets you see the principal sites, enjoy a nature tour, and take a break by the sea. And don't forget that the ravishing old city of Avignon (⇨ *Chapter 3*) is an hour's easy run up from Arles.

# PLANNER

## WHEN TO GO
July and August are the high season, especially along the coast, and are best avoided if possible, both because of the crushing crowds and the grilling heat. In winter (from November through February, even into March) you'll find many tourist services closed, including hotels and restaurants, and much of the terrace life driven indoors by rain and wind. Around Easter, the plane trees begin to leaf out and the café tables begin to sprout.

## PLANNING YOUR TIME
The best place to start your trip is either in Arles or Nîmes, because they both have direct train links to most major cities in France. Here you can start the process of slowing down—Provence is all about spending lazy afternoons. From either city you can easily plan trips into the countryside by bus or by car.

## FESTIVALS
Arles hosts its famous Fête des Gardiens ("cowboys") on May 1, when the Queen of Arles is crowned. In May, Nîmes celebrates Pentecost with its Spanish-accented *féria,* a festival of parades, bull races, and *corridas*

(bullfights) in the town's Roman arena. In June, Arles also dusts off traditional costumes for its own *féria,* with bullfights, parades, and races in the town's famous Roman arena. In May, St-Rémy-de-Provence observes Pentecost with another beast—the sheep—through its Fête de la Transhumance, the great migration of the wooly herds; some 4,000 sheep trot through town guided by costumed shepherds. In early October, the Fêtes d'Aigues Mortes sees this Camargue fortress town go wild with bull races and dancing on Place St-Louis.

### GETTING HERE AND AROUND

Public transport is well organized in the Alpilles, Arles, and the Camargue, with most towns accessible by train or bus. It's best to plan on combining the two—often smaller Provençal towns won't have their own train station, but a local bus connection to the train station at the nearest town over. For instance, take a train to Nîmes or Arles and then bus to the smaller towns like Les Baux or St-Remy. Driving is perhaps the best option, since you can travel the National or District roads or brave the speeding highways to go quickly from point to point. But be sure to get a good map—road signs can be confusing—and slow down to enjoy all the scenery.

### AIR TRAVEL

Marseille (an hour drive from Arles) is served by frequent flights from Paris and London and a new direct flight from New York.

Daily flights from Paris arrive at the smaller airport in Nîmes.

In summer, Air France flies direct from New York to Nice, 200 km (124 miles) from Arles.

### BUS TRAVEL

A moderately good network of private bus services links places not served, or badly served, by trains. Arles is one of the largest hubs, serviced out of the *gare routière* (bus station) on Avenue Paulin-Talabot, opposite the train station. Within the city, bus stations are mainly on Boulevard G. Clémenceau.

You can travel from Arles to such stops as Nîmes (Edgard ligne C30, €1.50, one hour, 11 daily) and Avignon (LER ligne 18, €7, one hour, 10 daily). Ten buses daily also head out to Aix-en-Provence (only two run on Sundays).

Popular destinations include the Camargue's Stes-Marie-de-la-Mer (Cartreize 20, €2.70, one hour, three daily), Mas du Pont de Rousty, and Pont de Gau.

There are also stops in the Alpilles area, including Les Baux-des-Provence and St-Rémy-de-Provence (neither have train stations). You can also reach the latter's bus station at Place de la République by frequent buses from Avignon.

From Nîmes's bus station on Rue Ste-Félicité, you can connect to Avignon and Arles, while Edgard runs you into the deep country. As for Pont du Gard, this is a 40-minute ride from Nîmes; you are dropped off 1 km (½ mile) from the bridge at Auberge Blanche.

**Bus Information Edgard** ☏ *08–10–33–42–73* ⊕ *www.edgard-transport.fr.*
**LER** ☏ *08–21–20–22–03* ⊕ *www.info-ler.fr.*

## CAR TRAVEL

The A6/A7 toll expressway (*péage*) channels all traffic from Paris toward the south. It's called the Autoroute du Soleil (Highway of the Sun) and leads directly to Provence. From Orange, A9 (La Languedocienne) heads southwest to Nîmes. Arles is a quick jaunt from Nîmes via A54.

With its swift autoroute network, it's a breeze traveling from city to city by car in this region. But some of the best of Provence is experienced on back roads and byways, including the isolated Camargue and the Alpilles.

Navigating the flatlands of the Camargue can feel unearthly, with roads sailing over terrain uninterrupted by hills or forests. Despite this, roads don't always run as the crow flies and can wander wide of a clean trajectory, so don't expect to make time.

Rocky outcrops and switchbacks keep you a captive audience to the arid scenery in the Alpilles; to hurry—impossible as it is—would be a waste.

## HORSE TRAVEL

The best way to tour the Camargue park is on horseback, although the wild glamour of the ancient race of Camargue horses becomes downright pedestrian when the now-domesticated beauties are saddled en masse. Rent-a-horse stands proliferate along the highways. Much of this land is limited to walkers and riders, so a trip on horseback lets you experience this landscape without getting your feet wet—literally.

## TRAIN TRAVEL

Two Arles-bound TGV (Trains à Grands Vitesses) trains arrive direct from Paris daily; from the Gare Centrale station (*Av. Paulin Talabot*) you can connect to Nîmes (30 minutes, €9.70), Marseille (1 hour, €15), Avignon Center (20 minutes, €8.80), and Aix-en-Provence (1 hour 30 minutes with connection, €28.56).

The Gare Avignon TGV station is a few miles southwest of the city in the district of Courtine (a navette shuttle bus connects with the train station in town); other trains (and a few TGV) use the Gare Avignon Center station at 42 boulevard St-Roch, where you can find trains to destinations like Orange (20 minutes, €5) and Arles (20 minutes, €7.30).

To Nîmes, there are more than a dozen TGV trains daily on the three-hour trip from Paris; frequent trains connect with Avignon Center (30 minutes, €9.40) and Arles (22 minutes, €9.70). To reach the Vieille Ville from the station, walk north on Avenue Fauchères.

**Contacts SNCF** ☎ *36–35 [€0.34 per min]* ⊕ *www.voyages-sncf.com.*
**TGV** ☎ *3635* ⊕ *www.tgv.com/en.*

## HOTELS

Although Arles, Les Baux, and St-Rémy have stylish, competitive hotels with all the requisite comforts and Provençal touches, from wrought iron to *folklorique* cottons, Nîmes doesn't attract—or much merit—the overnight crowds; thus, its hotels, with rare exception, have little in the way of charm. But throughout the region and well outside the towns you can find lovely converted *mas* (farmhouses), blending into the landscape as if they'd been there a thousand years—but offering modern pleasures: gardens, swimming pools, and sophisticated cooking.

**VISITOR INFORMATION**

Regional tourist offices often charge for a phone call (numbers begin with 8, €0.34 per minute) while written inquiries are free. If you prefer calling, be aware there may be an additional charge. The Comité Régional du Tourisme du Languedoc-Roussillon provides information on all towns west of the Rhône. The remainder of towns covered in this chapter are handled by the Comité Regional du Tourisme de Provence-Alpes-Côte d'Azur.

For information on the area around Arles and St-Rémy, contact the Comité Départemental du Tourisme des Bouches-du-Rhône.

**Addresses Comité Départemental du Tourisme des Bouches-du-Rhône**
✉ *13 rue de Brignoles, Marseille* ☎ *04–91–13–84–13* ⊕ *www.visitprovence.com.*
**Comité Regional du Tourisme de Provence-Alpes-Côte d'Azur**
✉ *61 La Canebière, Marseille* ☎ *04–91–56–47–00* ⊕ *www.tourismepaca.fr.*
**Comité Régional du Tourisme du Languedoc-Roussillon** ✉ *20 rue République, Montpellier* ☎ *04–67–20–02–20* ⊕ *www.sunfrance.com.*

**TOURS**

The Arles tourist office offers five individual tours of the town, including visits to the Roman monuments, during the summer season. Dates and times vary depending on demand; check with them regarding English-speaking guides. To learn more about Nîmes's monuments and Old Town, pick up an audio guide at the tourist office.

For about €44, you can tour the town in a taxi for an hour. When you stop in front of a monument, the driver slips in a cassette with commentary in the language of your choice.

For about €60, taxis can take you on a round-trip ride from Nîmes to the Pont du Gard. Ask the taxi to wait while you explore for about 30 minutes.

# THE LANGUEDOC FRONTIER

Nîmes and its famous aqueduct hold forth in Gard, considered more a part of the Languedoc culture than that of Provence. Yet because of its proximity to the heart of Provence and its similar climate, terrain, and architecture, it is included as a kindred southern spirit. Center of gaily printed *indienne* cottons, Camargue-style bullfights, and spectacular Roman ruins, it cannot be isolated from its Provençal neighbors. After all, the *langue d'oc* (language of oc) refers to the ancient southern language Occitane, which evolved from Latin; northern parts developed their own *langue d'oïl*. Their names derive from their manner of saying yes: *oc* in the south and *oïl* in the north. By an edict from Paris, the *oïl*s had it in the 16th century, and *oui* and its northern dialect became standard French. Languedocien and Provençal merely went underground, however, and still crop up in gesticulating disputes at farmers' markets today.

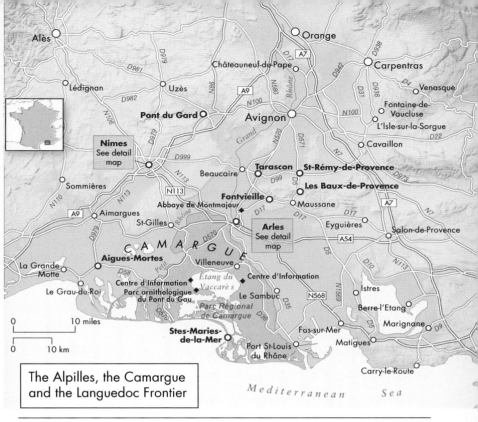

The Alpilles, the Camargue
and the Languedoc Frontier

## PONT DU GARD

Fodor's Choice
★

*24 km (15 miles) northeast of Nîmes; 25 km (15½ miles) north of Arles;
25 km (15½ miles) west of Avignon.*

No other ancient Roman sight in Provence rivals the Pont du Gard, a
mighty, three-tiered aqueduct midway between Nîmes and Avignon and
the highest bridge the Romans ever built. Erected some 2,000 years ago
as part of a 48-km (30-mile) canal supplying water to Roman Nîmes,
it is astonishingly well preserved. You can't walk across it anymore,
but you can get close enough to see the amazing gigantic square blocks
of stone (some weighing up to 6 tons) by traversing the 18th-century
bridge built alongside it. If you come to the Pont du Gard very early in
the morning—before dawn is ideal—you can discover Provence in its
purest blend of natural beauty and antiquity.

### GETTING HERE AND AROUND

The best way to get to Pont du Gard is via Nîmes, which is on the direct
TGV line from Paris and takes about three hours. The Nîmes bus station is right behind the train station, and Edgard runs several buses
daily except Sunday (about 1 hour, €1.50 one way) between Nîmes and
Pont du Gard. If you are coming by car, take the A9 to Nîmes, exit 50;
then take the D979, direction Uzès. Pont du Gard is 14 km (9 miles)
southeast of Uzès on the D981.

### EXPLORING

**Fodor's Choice**
★

**Pont du Gard.** The ancient Roman aqueduct is shockingly noble in its symmetry, the rhythmic repetition of arches resonant with strength, testimony to an engineering concept that was relatively new in the 1st century AD, when the structure was built under Emperor Claudius. And, unsullied by tourists and by the vendors of postcards and Popsicles that dominate the site later in the day, the nature is just as resonant, with the river flowing through its rocky gorge unperturbed by the work of master engineering that straddles it.

You can approach the aqueduct from either side of the Gardon River. If you choose the south side (Rive Droite), the walk to the *pont* (bridge) is shorter and the views arguably better. ⚠ Note there have been reports of break-ins in the parking area, so get a spot close to the booth. Although access to the spectacular walkway along the top of the aqueduct is now off-limits, the sight of the bridge is still a breathtaking experience. ⊠ *400 Route du Pont du Gard, Vers-Pont-du-Gard* ☎ *04–66–37–50–99* ⊕ *www.pontdugard.fr* ⬚ *€18 for up to 5 people, including parking* ☉ *Mar.–May and Oct., daily 9–6; June and Sept., daily 9–7; July and Aug., daily 9–8; Nov.–Feb., daily 9–5.*

**Espaces Culturels.** At the Espaces Culturels, a museum and themed cinema detail the history of the aqueduct; in addition, there is a hands-on children's area and an interactive exhibition about life in Roman times that covers topics such as archaeology, nature, and water. ⊠ *Pont du Gard* ☎ *04–66–37–50–99* ⬚ *Included with entry to Pont du Gard* ☉ *Mar.–May and Oct., daily 9–6; June and Sept., daily 9–7; July–Aug., daily 9–8; Nov.–Feb., daily 9–5*

### WHERE TO STAY

**$$$$**
HOTEL

**Le Vieux Castillon.** A wonderfully romantic getaway just up the road from the Rive Gauche of the Pont du Gard, this medieval retreat is made up of several restored houses and has sweeping views of the Ventoux valley, plus guest rooms styled in a variety of tasteful themes, from Egyptian to Provençal. **Pros:** discreet but warm welcome; food is hearty and good; no charge for pets. **Cons:** only one elevator in the main house, making access to some rooms difficult. $ *Rooms from: €280* ⊠ *10 rue Turion Sabatier, Castillon-du-Gard* ☎ *04–66–37–61–61* ⊕ *www.vieuxcastillon.com* ⬌ *30 rooms, 3 suites* ☉ *Closed Jan.–mid-Feb. Restaurant closed lunch Mon. and Tues.* ⦿ *No meals.*

# NÎMES

*24 km (15 miles) southwest of Pont du Gard; 29 km (18 miles) northwest of Arles.*

If you have come to the south to seek out Roman treasures, you need look no farther than Nîmes (pronounced *neem*), for the Arènes and Maison Carrée are among Continental Europe's best-preserved antiquities. But if you have come to seek out a more modern mythology—of lazy, graceful Provence—give Nîmes a wide berth. It's a feisty, rundown, rat race of a town, with jalopies and Vespas roaring irreverently around the ancient temple and rock bands blasting sound tests into the Arena's wooden stands. Its medieval Old Town has none of the gentrified grace of those in Arles or St-Rémy. Yet its rumpled and rebellious ways trace directly back to its Roman incarnation, when its population swelled with soldiers, arrogant and newly victorious after their conquest of Egypt in 31 BC.

Already anchoring a fiefdom of pre-Roman oppida (elevated fortresses) before ceding to the empire in the 1st century BC, this ancient city bloomed to formidable proportions under the Pax Romana. A 24,000-seat coliseum, a thriving forum with a magnificent temple patterned after Rome's temple of Apollo, and a public water network fed by the Pont du Gard attest to its classical prosperity. Its next golden age bloomed under the

**FROM NÎMES, WITH LOVE**

Blue jeans were first created in Nîmes: the word "denim" is derived from the phrase "de Nîmes" ("from Nîmes"). Originally used by local farmers to make wagon covers and work clothes, denim soon made its way to San Francisco, thanks to Bavarian merchant Levi Strauss. Strauss's durable denim work pants, or jeans (which, incidentally, comes from the American mispronunciation of the Italian port Gênes, from which the fabric was originally shipped), became an instant success with gold miners.

Protestants, who established an anti-Catholic stronghold here and violated iconic architectural treasures—not to mention the papist minority. Their massacre of some 200 Catholic citizens is remembered as the Michelade; many of the victims were priests sheltered in the *évêché* (Bishop's Palace), now the Musée du Vieux Nîmes (Museum of Old Nîmes). Chapels throughout the surrounding countryside were damaged by Calvin's righteous rebels.

Perhaps inspired by the influx of architects who studied its antique treasures, Nîmes has opted against becoming a lazy, atmospheric Provençal market town and has invested in progressive modern architecture. Smack-dab across from the Maison Carrée stands the city's contemporary answer, the modern-art museum dubbed the Carré d'Art (Art Square) after its ruthlessly modernist four-square form—a pillared, symmetrical glass reflection of its ancient twin. Other investments in contemporary art and architecture confirm Nîmes's commitment to modern ways.

If you want to see everything, or a lot of things in Nîmes, then the Visite Ensemble ticket is good value for the money. The ticket costs a mere €10, is valid for three days, and can be purchased at most local monuments and sites.

**GETTING HERE AND AROUND**

On the Paris-Avignon-Montpellier train line, Nîmes has a direct rail link to and from Paris (about a three-hour ride). The Nîmes gare routière (bus station) is just behind the train station. Edgard runs several buses to and from Arles (11 daily Monday–Saturday, two Sunday). STD Gard has several buses (daily except Sunday) between Avignon and Nîmes and Uzès and Nîmes. Some Uzès buses stop at Remoulins for the Pont du Gard and a few continue on to St-Quentin-la-Poterie.

Note that although all the sites in Nîmes are walkable, the useful Tango bus runs a good loop from the station and passes by many of the principal sites along the way for €1.10.

**VISITOR INFORMATION**
**Nîmes Tourist Office** ⊠ *6 rue Auguste* ☏ *04–66–58–38–00* ⊕ *www.nimes-tourisme.com.*

## EXPLORING
### TOP ATTRACTIONS

Fodor'sChoice   **Arènes.** The best-preserved Roman amphitheater in the world is a min-
★   iature of the Colosseum in Rome (note the small carvings of Romulus and Remus—the wrestling gladiators—on the exterior and the intricate bulls' heads etched into the stone over the entrance on the north side). More than 435 feet long and 330 feet wide, it had a seating capacity of 24,000 in its day. Bloody gladiator battles, criminals being thrown to animals, and theatrical wild-boar chases drew crowds to its bleachers—and the vomitoria beneath them. Nowadays the corrida (bullfight) transforms the arena (and all of Nîmes) into a sangria-flushed homage to Spain. Concerts are held here year-round, thanks to a high-tech glass-and-steel structure that covers the arena for winter use. ⊠ *Bd. des Arènes* ☏ *04–66–21–82–56, 04–66–02–80–80 feria box office* ⊕ *www.arenes-nimes.com* ✉*€8.50; €11 joint ticket with Tour Magne and Maison Carrée* ☉ *Mar. and Oct., daily 9–6; Apr., May, and Sept., daily 9–6:30; June, daily 9–7; July and Aug., daily 9–8; Nov.–Feb., daily 9:30–5.*

**Carrée d'Art.** The glass-fronted Carrée d'Art (directly opposite the Maison Carrée) was designed by British architect Sir Norman Foster as its neighbor's stark contemporary mirror. It literally reflects the Maison Carrée's creamy symmetry and figuratively answers it with a featherlight deconstructed colonnade. Homages aside, it looks like an airport terminal. It contains a library, archives, and the **Musée d'Art Contemporain** (Contemporary Art Museum). The permanent collection falls into three categories: French painting and sculpture; English, American, and German works; and Mediterranean styles, all dating from 1960 onward. There are often temporary exhibits of new work, too. But as lovely as the museum is, the facade suffers traffic pollution and could do with a bit of a cleanup. ⊠ *Pl. de la Maison Carrée* ☏ *04–66–76–35–70* ⊕ *carreartmusee.nimes.fr* ✉*€5* ☉ *Tues.–Sun. 10–6.*

**Cathédrale Notre-Dame et St-Castor** (*Nîmes Cathedral*). Destroyed and rebuilt in several stages, Nîmes Cathedral was damaged by Protestants during the 16th-century Wars of Religion but still shows traces of its original construction in 1096. A remarkably preserved Romanesque frieze portrays Adam and Eve cowering in shame, the gory slaughter of Abel, and a flood-wearied Noah. Inside, look for the 4th-century sarcophagus (third chapel on the right) and a magnificent 17th-century chapel in the apse. ⊠ *Pl. aux Herbes* ☏ *04–66–67–27–72* ☉ *Weekdays 8:30–6, Sat. 8:30–noon and 2–6.*

**Maison Carrée** (*Square House*). Lovely and forlorn in the middle of a busy downtown square, this exquisitely preserved temple strikes a timeless balance between symmetry and whimsy, purity of line and

Straddling the Gardon River and built during the rule of Emperor Claudius, the Pont du Gard was an aqueduct that brought water to nearby Nîmes.

richness of decor. Modeled on the Temple to Apollo in Rome, adorned with magnificent marble columns and elegant pediment, the Maison Carrée remains one of the most noble surviving structures of ancient Roman civilization anywhere. Built around 5 BC and dedicated to Caius Caesar and his grandson Lucius, the temple has survived subsequent use as a medieval meeting hall, an Augustine church, a storehouse for Revolutionary archives, and a horse shed. Temporary art and photo exhibitions are held here, and among a permanent display of photos and drawings of ongoing archaeological work is a splendid ancient Roman fresco of Cassandra (being dragged by her hair by a hunter) that was discovered in 1992 and carefully restored. There's even a fun 3-D projection of the heroes of Nîmes. ⊠ *Pl. de la Maison Carrée* ☎ *04–66–21–82–56* ⊕ *www.arenes-nimes.com* ⊠ *€4.80; joint ticket with Tour Magne and Arénes €11* ☽ *June, daily 10–7; July and Aug., daily 10–8; Apr., May, and Sept., daily 10–6:30; Mar. and Oct., daily 10–6; Nov.–Feb., daily 10–1 and 2–4:30.*

**Musée des Beaux-Arts** (*Fine Arts Museum*). The centerpiece of this early 20th-century building, stunningly refurbished by architect Jean-Michel Wilmotte, is a vast ancient mosaic depicting a marriage ceremony that provides intriguing insights into the lifestyle of Roman aristocrats. Also in the varied collection are seven paintings devoted to Cleopatra by 18th-century Nîmes-born painter Natoire Italian, plus some fine Flemish, Dutch, and French works (notably Rubens's *Portrait of a Monk* and Giambono's *The Mystic Marriage of St. Catherine*). ⊠ *23 rue de la Cité Foulc* ☎ *04–66–67–38–21* ⊕ *www.nimes. fr* ⊠ *€5* ☽ *Tues.–Sun. 10–6.*

**CLOSE UP**

## Provence's Tasty Treats

If eating is the national pastime in France, it is a true vocation in Provence. And the pleasure of relaxing in a shady square over a pitcher of local rosé, a bowl of olives, and a regional *plat du jour* is only enhanced in western Provence by quirky local specialties. Consider nibbling tiny *tellines*, salty clams the size of your thumbnail, fresh from the Camargue coast. Or try a crockery bowl of steaming bull stew (*gardianne*), a sinewy daube of lean-and-mean beef from the harsh Camargue prairies, ladled over a scoop of chewy red Camargue rice. The mouthwatering oddity called *brandade* (salt cod pestled with olive oil and milk into a creamy spread) has a peculiar history; cod isn't even native to Nîmes, but was traded, in its leathery salt-dried form, by medieval Breton fishermen in exchange for south-coast salt. The Nîmois mixed in local olive oil and created a regional staple.

It's true that every meal is a culinary event here, but in summer the local cafés and hotels make a special effort to make breakfast memorable. In turn, breakfast is one of the loveliest meals of the day. It's coolest in the morning—the birds chirp, the air is crisp, and the smell of freshly baked croissants is in the air. Stroll to the nearest square to sit under shady plane trees and listen to the relaxing bustle of Provence waking up. Tables are adroitly nestled in gardens or sprawled across freshly swept cobblestones, wrapped in flower-print tablecloths, and sprinkled with nosegays of local flowers. Waiters bustle to and fro calling out friendly greetings while the first gilt-edged cups of espresso are prepared. "Early morning" can be misleading: it could well be 10 or 11 am, but another example of southern charm is the option of a late breakfast. Hey, it makes a great excuse for a long late lunch!

**Musée du Vieux Nîmes** (*Museum of Old Nîmes*). Housed in the 17th-century bishop's palace opposite the cathedral, this museum shows off garments embroidered in the exotic and vibrant style for which Nîmes was once famous. Look for the 14th-century jacket made of blue serge de Nîmes—the famous fabric (now simply called denim) from which Levi Strauss first fashioned blue jeans. ⊠ *Pl. aux Herbes* 🕾 *04–66–76–73–70* ⊕ *www.nimes.fr* 🔁 *Free* ☉ *Tues.–Sun. 10–6.*

**WORTH NOTING**

**Jardins de la Fontaine** (*Fountain Garden*). The Jardins de la Fontaine, an elaborate formal garden, was landscaped on the site of the Roman baths in the 18th century, when the Source de Nemausus, a once-sacred spring, was channeled into pools and a canal. It's a shady haven of mature trees and graceful stonework, and a testimony to the taste of the Age of Reason. It makes for a lovely approach to the Temple of Diana and the Tour Magne. ⊠ *Corner of Quai de la Fontaine and Av. Jean-Jaurès* 🕾 *04–66–58–38–00* 🔁 *Free* ☉ *Mid-Sept.–Mar., daily 7:30–6:30; Apr.–mid-Sept., daily 7:30 am–10 pm.*

**Musée Archéologique et d'Histoire Naturelle** (*Museum of Archaeology and Natural History*). This old Jesuit college houses a wonderful collection of local archaeological finds, including sarcophagi, beautiful pieces of

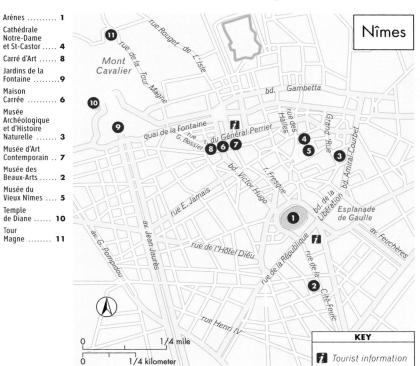

Roman glass, statues, busts, friezes, tools, coins, and pottery. Among the highlights are a rare pre-Roman statue called *The Warrior of Grezan* and the Marbacum Torso, which was dug up at the foot of the Tour Magne. ⊠ *13 bd. Amiral Courbet* ☎ *04–66–76–74–80* ⊕ *www.nimes. fr* ⊠ *Free* ☺ *Tues.–Sun. 10–6.*

**Temple de Diane** (*Temple of Diana*). This shattered Roman ruin dates from the second century BC. The temple's function is unknown, though it's thought to have been part of a larger Roman complex that is still unexcavated. In the Middle Ages Benedictine nuns occupied the building before it was converted into a church. Destruction came during the Wars of Religion. ⊠ *Jardins de la Fontaine.*

**Tour Magne** (*Magne Tower*). At the far end of the Jardins de la Fontaine, you'll find the remains of a tower the emperor Augustus had built on Gallic foundations; it was probably used as a lookout post. Despite losing 30 feet in height over the course of time, the tower still provides fine views of Nîmes for anyone energetic enough to climb the 140 steps. ⊠ *Jardins de la Fontaine, Pl. Guillaume-Apollinaire* ☎ *04–66–21–82–56* ⊠ *€3; joint ticket with Arènes and Maison Carrée €11* ☺ *Nov.–Feb., daily 9:30–1 and 2–4:30; Mar. and Oct., daily 9:30–1 and 2–6; Apr., May, and Sept., daily 9:30–6:30; June, daily 9–7; July and Aug., daily 9–8.*

## WHERE TO EAT

$$$$ MODERN FRENCH 🍴 **Alexandre.** Chef Michel Kayser adds a personal touch to local specialties at this *à la mode* modern restaurant. The menu changes according to the season and the chef's creative whimsy. Golden zucchini flowers with frothy truffle mousseline followed by a rich bull steak, roasted in its own juice and served with pan-roasted potatoes, may not leave room for dessert. The decor is elegantly spare, with stone walls and large bay windows; but the gardens are extensive, and often apricots and peaches plucked from the overhanging branches will appear on your plate, magically transformed into some delicious creation. [$] *Average main: €50* ✉ *2 rue Xavier Tronc, Rte. de l'Aeroport* ☎ *04–66–70–08–99* 🌐 *www.michelkayser.com* ✍ *Reservations essential* ⏲ *Closed Sun. dinner. Closed Mon. and Tues. Sept.–June, and Sun. and Mon. July–Aug. Closed 2 weeks end of Feb. and Aug.*

$$ FRENCH 🍴 **L'Enclos de la Fontaine.** Nîmes's most fashionable post-corrida gathering spot is in the Hotel Impérator, with warm-weather dining in an idyllic garden court. The food is hearty and delicious, with surprisingly Spanish touches. Chef Thierry Plaideau carefully structures his menu, sprinkling in dishes such as almond duck, dried cod stuffed in red peppers, and roasted lamb cooked in wild mint. Have an after-dinner drink in the Bar Hemingway; after all, they named it for him because he loved to drink here. [$] *Average main: €24* ✉ *15 rue Gaston-Boissier* ☎ *04–66–21–90–30* 🌐 *www.hotel-imperator.com* ⏲ *Closed Mon. No lunch Sat., no dinner Sun.*

$$ FRENCH 🍴 **Le Jardin d'Hadrien.** This chic enclave, with its quarried white stone, ancient plank-and-beam ceiling, and open fireplace, would be a culinary haven even without its lovely hidden garden, a shady retreat for summer meals. Chef Christophe Adlin changes menus monthly to bring the freshest seasonal combinations to your palate, so you might be treated to fresh cod and zucchini flowers filled with *brandade* (the creamy, light paste of salt cod and olive oil) or, in winter, sautéed veal and crayfish with saffron potatoes. Two prix-fixe menus served year-round—gourmand and saveur—change every other month. [$] *Average main: €21* ✉ *11 rue Enclos Rey* ☎ *04–66–21–86–65* 🌐 *www.lejardindhadrien.fr* ✍ *Reservations essential* ⏲ *No lunch Mon.–Thurs., no dinner Sun.*

$$ BISTRO 🍴 **Le Passage de Virginie.** It may be a postage stamp–size dining room with an even smaller terrace on a miniscule street, but this typically southern bistro offers oversize pleasures in the form of fresh, well-prepared, and unpretentious cuisine served in a warm and inviting, if slightly funky, atmosphere. Dishes like tiny mussels with spicy aioli and melting lamb shoulder with sweet onion confit enhanced by hearty regional wines—all at a reasonable price (especially the two-course €15 lunch menu)—keep devoted locals coming back. A rare find in the heart of the Old Town. [$] *Average main: €18* ✉ *15 impasse Fresque* ☎ *04–66–38–29–26* ✍ *Reservations essential* ⏲ *Closed Tues. Sept.–Apr.*

$$ BISTRO FAMILY 🍴 **L'Imprevu.** This warm and convivial contemporary dining room—well located near the Museum of Contemporary Art and the Old Town—has become a favorite haunt of locals seeking gourmet dining on a budget. Chef Vincent Gourdier's market-driven cuisine emphasizes local bounty with a Mediterranian flair. Portions are ample for

dishes like grilled scallops and spinach with smoked pumpkin cream and wild rice, or cocotte of slow-cooked veal with sage, fricasseed mushrooms, and macaroni gratin. There are also plenty of vegetarian dishes and a fine children's menu. The inviting outdoor terrace is a relaxing place to enjoy your meal along with a little people watching. Best of all, it's open seven days a week, a rarity in France. [$] *Average main: €22* ✉ *6 place d'Assas* ☎ *04–66–38–99–59* 🌐 *www.l-imprevu.com* ✍ *Reservations essential.*

$ FRENCH 🍴 **Vintage Café.** This popular Old Town wine bar draws a loyal crowd of oenophiles for serious tastings and simple, compatible foods—cod stew, hot lentil salad with smoked haddock, beef stewed with capers and pickles, and a pressed-goat-cheese terrine. The bar still dominates—all the better for bellying up to a glass of *côstières de Nîmes*—but the dining room has expanded to embrace the neighboring building. Bright ceramics and warm lamplight enhance the warm-ocher Mediterranean interior. Summer nights on the terrace are idyllic. [$] *Average main: €14* ✉ *7 rue de Bernis* ☎ *04–66–21–04–45* 🌐 *www.restaurant-levintage-nimes.com* 🕒 *Closed Sun. and Mon.*

$ FRENCH 🍴 **Wine Bar Le Cheval Blanc.** This classic mahogany-and-brass wine bar, owned and managed by a former sommelier, has more than 350 different wines to serve along with their good seafood—including *brandade de morue* (salt-cod paste)—and brasserie classics: foie gras salad, fried calamari, simple steaks. The more adventurous diner will enjoy the superb fried pigs' feet and traditional steak tartar (raw meat). You may opt to dine on the sidewalk terrace, adjacent to the square. Menus start at just €18. [$] *Average main: €15* ✉ *1 place des Arènes* ☎ *04–66–76–19–59* 🌐 *www.winebar-lechevalblanc.com* 🕒 *Closed Sun.*

## WHERE TO STAY

$ HOTEL 🏨 **Amphithéâtre.** Just behind the Arena, this big, solid, old private home has fortunately fallen into the hands of a loving owner, who has stripped 18th-century double doors and fitted rooms with restored-wood details, white-tiled bathrooms, and antique bedroom sets. **Pros:** ideally located; good value for the price. **Cons:** rooms can be small and a bit stuffy; amenities are limited. [$] *Rooms from: €89* ✉ *4 rue des Arènes* ☎ *04–66–67–28–51* 🌐 *hoteldelamphitheatre.com* 🛏 *17 rooms* 🍽 *No meals.*

$$$ B&B/INN 🏨 **La Maison de Sophie.** Far from the hustle of town and yet just five minutes from the arena, this luxurious hôtel particulier has all the charm—especially in its elegant and tranquil guest rooms—that the city itself often lacks. **Pros:** big-city elegance mixes nicely with country charm and quiet nights; warm welcome. **Cons:** often fully booked long in advance; pool is quite small. [$] *Rooms from: €190* ✉ *31 av. Carnot* ☎ *04–66–70–96–10* 🌐 *www.hotel-nimes-gard.com* 🛏 *5 rooms, 2 suites* 🍽 *No meals.*

$$ HOTEL 🏨 **Royal Hôtel.** Jazz, art deco ironwork, and caged birds set the Latin tone at this bohemian, family-run, shabby-chic urban hotel. **Pros:** the hotel is studiously casual; palm-filled lobby and club chairs are a nice touch. **Cons:** rooms can be quite small; some rooms are noisy. [$] *Rooms from: €115* ✉ *3 bd. Alphonse Daudet* ☎ *04–66–58–28–27* 🌐 *www.royalhotel-nimes.com* 🛏 *23 rooms* 🍽 *Breakfast.*

This photo by Mike Tumchewics, a Fodors.com member, captures Nîmes bathed in Provence's extraordinary light.

## SPORTS AND THE OUTDOORS

The *corrida* (bullfight) is a quintessential Nîmes experience, taking place as it does in the ancient Roman Arena. There are usually three bull-fighting times a year, always during the carnival-like citywide *férias* (festivals): in early spring (mid-February), at Pentecost (end of May), and during the wine harvest (end of September). These include parades, a running of the bulls, and gentle Camargue-style bullfights (where competitors pluck a ring from the bull's horns). But the focal point, unfortunately, is a twice-daily Spanish-style bullfight, complete with *l'estocade* (the final killing) and the traditional cutting of the ear. Those with delicate nerves will stay away.

**Aquatropic.** An indoor and an outdoor pool, wave machines, slides, water cannons, and whirlpools add to the fun for kids and adults. Aquatropic is open weekdays 10–8 and weekends 11–7 for €5.50 (€1.95 children under eight). Since it's south of the city, it's best to exit the autoroute at Nîmes Ouest. ⊠ *39 chemin de la Hostellerie* ☎ *04–66–38–31–00* ⊕ *www.aquatropic-equalia.fr.*

## SHOPPING

In Nîmes's Old Town you'll find the expected rash of chain stores mixed with fabulous interior-design boutiques and fabric shops selling the Pro-vençal cottons that used to be produced here en masse (Les Indiennes de Nîmes, Les Olivades, Souleiado). Antiques and collectibles are found in tiny shops throughout the city's backstreets, but there is a concentration of them in the Old Town. The Monday-morning marché that stretches the length of the Boulevard Jean-Jaurès highlights bright regional fabrics, linens, pottery, and brocante (collectibles).

**Les Halles.** This permanent covered market is at the heart of the city and puts on a mouthwatering show of olives, fresh fish, cheeses, and produce. ⊠ *5 Rue des Halles* ☎ *04–66–21–52–49* ⊕ *www.leshallesdenimes. com* ☉ *Daily 8–1.*

**Maison Villaret.** The longtime local favorite boulangerie–patisserie Villaret is the best place to buy Nîmes's other specialty: jaw-breaking *croquants* (roasted almonds in caramelized sugar). ⊠ *13 rue de la Madeleine* ☎ *04–66–67–41–79* ☉ *Daily 7 am–8 pm.*

# THE CAMARGUE

For 570 square miles, the vast alluvial delta of the Rhône River known as the Camargue stretches to the horizon, an austere marshland unrelievedly flat, scoured by the mistral, swarmed over by mosquitoes. Between the endless flow of sediment from the Rhône and the erosive force of the sea, its shape is constantly changing. Even the Provençal poet Frédéric Mistral described it in bleak terms: *"Ni arbre, ni ombre, ni âme"* ("Neither tree, nor shade, nor soul"). Yet its harsh landscape harbors a concentration of exotic wildlife unique in Europe, and its isolation has given birth to an ascetic and ancient way of life that transcends national stereotype. It is a strange region, one worth discovering slowly, either on foot or on horseback—especially as its wildest reaches are inaccessible by car. If people find the Camargue interesting, birds find it irresistible. Its protected marshes lure some 400 species, including more than 160 in migration—little egrets, gray herons, spoonbills, bitterns, cormorants, redshanks, and grebes, and the famous flamingos. All this nature surrounds a few far-flung villages, rich in the region's odd history and all good launching points for forays into the marshlands.

## AIGUES-MORTES

Fodor'sChoice
★
*39 km (24 miles) south of Nîmes; 45 km (28 miles) southwest of Arles.*

Like a tiny illumination in a medieval manuscript, Aigues-Mortes (pronounced ay-guh-*mort*-uh) is a precise and perfect miniature fortress-town, contained within perfectly symmetrical castellated walls, with streets laid out in geometric grids. Now awash in a flat wasteland of sand, salt, and monotonous marsh, it once was a major port town from whence no less than St-Louis himself (Louis IX) set sail to conquer Jerusalem in the 13th century. In 1248 some 35,000 zealous men launched 1,500 ships for Cyprus, engaging the enemy on his own turf and suffering swift defeat; Louis himself was briefly taken prisoner. A second launching in 1270 led to more crushing losses, and then Louis succumbed to typhus in Tunis.

### GETTING HERE AND AROUND

The nearest train station is in Nîmes, and from there several trains a day run to Aigues-Mortes. The trip takes 45 minutes to an hour and costs €7.90. Edgard Transport's C32 bus runs every two hours from Nîmes to Aigues-Mortes. The trip takes an hour and costs €1.50 each way. By car, take the A9 to exit Gallargues (direction Aimargues–St- Laurent-d'Aigouze) and take the D979 directly to Aigues-Mortes.

A striking landmark of Aigues-Mortes, the Tour de Constance presides over Louis IX's spectacular fortress-port, erected during the age of the Crusades.

## VISITOR INFORMATION

**Aigues-Mortes Tourist Office** ✉ *Pl. St. Louis* ☎ *04–66–53–73–00* ⊕ *www.ot-aiguesmortes.fr.*

## EXPLORING

**Fortress-Port.** Louis's state-of-the-art fortress-port is astonishingly well preserved. The stout walls now contain a small Provençal village filled with tourists, but the visit is more than justified by the impressive scale of the original structure. ✉ *Pl. Anatole France, Porte de la Gardette* ☎ *04–66–53–61–55* 🎫 *€7.50* ⊗ *May–Aug., daily 10–7; Sept.–Apr., daily 10–5:30.*

**Place St-Louis.** A 19th-century statue of the father of the fleur-de-lis reigns under shady pollards on this square with a mellow village feel, a welcome retreat from the clutter of souvenir shops on surrounding lanes. The pretty, bare-bones **Église Notre-Dame des Sablons,** on one corner of the square, has a timeless air (the church dates from the 13th century, but the stained glass is modern), and the spectacular Chapelle des Pénitents Blancs and Chapelle des Pénitents Gris are Baroque-era marvels. ☎ *04–66–53–73–00* 🎫 *Free.*

## WHERE TO EAT AND STAY

**$$**
FRENCH
✕ **Chez Bob.** In a smoky, isolated stone farmhouse filled with old posters, you'll taste Camargue cooking at its rustic best. There's only the daily four-course menu (€43), which can include anything from *anchoïade* (crudités with hard-cooked egg—still in the shell—and anchovy vinaigrette), homemade duck pâté thick with peppercorns, and often the pièce de résistance: a thick, sizzling slab of bull steak

grilled in the roaring fireplace. Sprinkle on hand-skimmed sea salt and dig in while listening to the migrating birds pass by. Sunday at lunch, professional musicians add to the already authentic ambience. $ *Average main: €21* ⊠ *Mas Petite Antonelle, Rte. du Sambuc, Villeneuve* ☎ *04–90–97–00–29* ⊕ *www.restaurantbob.fr* ⌂ *Reservations essential* ⊘ *Closed Mon. and Tues. No dinner Sun.*

**THINK PINK**

In the Camargue, ivory-pink flamingos are as common as pigeons on a city square. Their gangly height, dodolike bill, and stilty legs give them a cartoonish air, and their flight style seems comic up close. But the sight of a few thousand of these creatures taking flight in unison is one you won't forget.

**$$**
**BISTRO** ✕ **L'Atelier de Nicolas.** Laid back and unpretentious though it may be, when it comes to the food, chef Nicolas is on his toes, serving up traditional local cuisine with a flair and exuberance that makes this unassuming restaurant one of the best choices in town. Modern decor, an open kitchen, and a chalkboard menu—and a bright outdoor terrace—add to the casual feel, while the warm and friendly service enhances the dining experience. But it's the food that really shines—dishes like a meltingly tender slow-cooked bull (a local specialty) served with wild morels and a puree of root vegetables; or sea bass served with savory herb *pistou* (Provence's answer to pesto) and crisp local vegetables. Desserts like fig crumble or white chocolate mousse are hard to resist. All this washed down with a refreshing local rosé (the locally influenced wine list has plenty of choices by the glass) adds up to an exemplary dining experience that's easy on the wallet. $ *Average main: €18* ⊠ *28 rue A. Lorraine* ☎ *04–34–28–04–84* ⊘ *Closed Wed.*

**$$**
**B&B/INN** ⌂ **Les Arcades.** This beautifully preserved 16th-century house has large, airy guest accommodations, some with tall windows overlooking a green courtyard. **Pros:** rooms overlook lovely courtyard; free parking card provided at check-in. **Cons:** not much English spoken at hotel. $ *Rooms from: €110* ⊠ *23 bd. Gambetta* ☎ *04–66–53–81–13* ⊕ *www. les-arcades.fr* ↘ *9 rooms* ⧀ *No meals.*

**$$**
**HOTEL** ⌂ **Les Templiers.** In a 17th-century residence within the ramparts, this delightful hotel sets the stage with stone, stucco, and terra-cotta floors. **Pros:** the welcome is wonderfully warm; space is charmingly intimate—you'll feel right at home in no time. **Cons:** some rooms are small; amenities are lacking (no minibars). $ *Rooms from: €125* ⊠ *23 rue de la République* ☎ *04–66–53–66–56* ↘ *14 rooms, 2 suites* ⧀ *No meals.*

**$**
**HOTEL** ⌂ **St-Louis.** Within the rampart walls, close to the Tour de Constance and just off Place St-Louis, this homey little hotel warms its medieval construction of cool stone with Provençal charm and comfort. **Pros:** situated in the center of the medieval village, this hotel offers up an authentic visit into Provençal past; the welcome is genuine; great value for money. **Cons:** some rooms are small and can be hot in the summer; no pool. $ *Rooms from: €100* ⊠ *10 rue Amiral Courbet* ☎ *04–66–53–72–68* ⊕ *www.lesaintlouis.fr* ↘ *22 rooms* ⊘ *Closed late Nov.–mid-Mar.* ⧀ *No meals.*

## STES-MARIES-DE-LA-MER

*31 km (19 miles) southeast of Aigues-Mortes; 40 km (25 miles) southwest of Arles.*

The principal town within the confines of the Parc Régional de Camargue, Stes-Maries became a pilgrimage town due to its fascinating history. Provençal legend has it that around AD 45 a band of the first Christians was rounded up and set adrift at sea in a boat without a sail and without provisions. Their stellar ranks included Mary Magdalene, Martha, and Mary Salome, mother of apostles James and John; Mary Jacoby, sister of the Virgin; and Lazarus, risen from the dead (or another Lazarus, depending on whom you ask). Joining them in their fate: a dark-skinned servant girl named Sarah. Miraculously, their boat washed ashore at this ancient site, and the grateful Marys built a chapel in thanks. Martha moved on to Tarascon to tackle dragons, and Lazarus founded the church in Marseille. But Mary Jacoby and Mary Salome remained in their old age, and Sarah stayed with them, begging in the streets to support them in their ministry. The three women died at the same time and were buried together at the site of their chapel.

A cult grew up around this legendary spot, and a church was built around it. When in the 15th century a stone memorial and two female bodies were found under the original chapel, the miracle was for all practical purposes confirmed, and the Romanesque church expanded to receive a new influx of pilgrims. But the pilgrims attracted to Stes-Maries aren't all lighting candles to the two St. Marys: the servant girl Sarah has been adopted as an honorary saint by the Gypsies of the world, who blacken the crypt's domed ceiling with the soot of their votive candles lighted in her honor.

To honor the presiding spirits of Stes-Maries-de-la-Mer, two extraordinary festivals take place every year in Stes-Maries, one May 24–25 and the other on the Sunday nearest to October 22 (⊕ *www. saintesmariesdelamer.com*). On May 24 Gypsy pilgrims gather from across Europe and carry the wooden statue of Sarah from her crypt, through the streets of the village, and down to the sea to be washed. The next day they carry a wooden statue of the two St. Marys, kneeling in their wooden boat, to the sea for their own holy bath. The same ritual is repeated by a less colorful crowd of non-Gypsy pilgrims in October, who carry the two Marys back to the sea.

### GETTING HERE AND AROUND

The nearest train station is in Arles, and from here several buses a day run to Stes-Maries-de-la-Mer. The company serving this area is Cartreize, which runs buses four to seven times a day. The trip takes about 45 minutes and costs €3 one way. By car, take the A54 and at exit 4 take the D570 directly to Stes-Maries-de-la-Mer.

*Continued on page 63*

# DON'T FENCE ME IN: FRANCE'S "WILD WEST"

**TIME: 7:30 AM.** Place: The Camargue reserve, Provence's extraordinary nature park. A flock of flamingos suddenly erupts from a stand of black-green parasol pines. To your left, a group of herons mince through rice paddies. Ahead, a bandanna-wrapped *gardian*—a kind of open-range cowboy—roams the field on a sturdy dappled-white horse, prodding a herd of prong-horned bulls whose bloodlines predate the cave paintings of Lascaux.

Atop your pony, you turn your binoculars to watch the rising sun turn the sky rosy red over the endless savannas. This is why you got up so early: to see the Camargue at dawn, primeval and virgin-pure, the last gasp of the Rhône as it seeps over the delta into the Mediterranean sea. This Edenic preserve, where exotic fauna and flora live in splendor in lagoons and salt marshes, remains France's most distinctive nature wonderland.

# TOURING THE CAMARGUE PARK

Gardians and bull on the Camargue beach.

A land of haunting natural beauty, the Camargue was one of the *oubliettes* (forgotten areas) of France only a few decades ago. Today, it is *à la mode*. No matter that the mosquitoes are large and hungry in the summer, or that the mistral wind whistles furiously over sand and sea in the early spring, when thousands of tenderfeet begin to head here to discover a peculiar ecosystem all its own and a culture—wild, quirky, isolated—just as unique.

With its hypnotic plane of marsh grass stretching to the sea, the Camargue is what the French call a *désert d'eau,* a watery desert. Expanses of saltwort, canals, reedbeds, marshy plains, and *è'tangs* (saltwater lagoons) alternate with vast salt-marsh islands called *sansourire.* Little wonder you can appear to be standing in a body of water—beware: there are treacherous pits of quicksand in places—and sink on flat land. The Camargue is formed by the alluvial deposits of the two arms of the Rhône flowing south to the Mediterranean, and the sea does its best to fight back. So much so that an enormous system of dikes, known as the Digue à la Mer, has been built along a 15-mi stretch of the coast near Stes-Maries-de-la-Mer and is now one of France's most spectacular seaside promenades (and best biking routes).

At the Camargue's heart is the Réserve Nationale Zoologique et Botanique de Camargue, a 30,000-acre area set around the Étang de Vaccarès lagoon—a birdwatcher's paradise famed for its rich sightings of egrets, bee-eaters, avocets, cranes, sandpipers, flamingos, and hundreds of other species. Nature has been left blissfully untouched—almost. Man has only squatters' rights to these eternal tidal flats, yet here and there you'll find isolated *mas* (farmhouses, now sometimes converted to luxurious dude ranches); *manades,* the French style of ranches, where the famous bulls are often corralled; and *cabanes,* white-washed houses with plaited roofs used

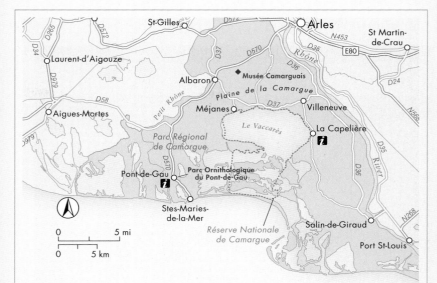

as residences by the gardians. Horses are for rent everywhere, and a gallop across this wide, lonely prairie country will set you apart from the ordinary run of tourists.

As you drive the few roads that crisscross the Camargue, you'll usually be within the boundaries of the **Parc Naturel Régional de Camargue** (⊕ www.parc-camargue.fr). Unlike state and national parks in the United States, this area is privately owned and utilized within rules imposed by the state. The principal owners, the famous *manadiers* (the Camargue equivalent of a small-scale rancher), with the help of their gardians, keep it for grazing their wide-horned bulls and their broad-bellied, dappled-white horses. The strong, heavy-tailed Camargue horse has been traced to the Paleolithic period (though some claim the Moors imported an Arab strain) and is prized for its stolid endurance and tough hooves. The curved-horned bull, if not indigenous, may have been imported by Attila the Hun. When it's not participating in a bloodless bullfight, a bull may well end up in the wine-rich regional stew called *gardianne de taureau,* an acquired taste.

## IN THE PINK

*Les fleurs qui volent* ("the flying flowers"), flamingos are the most spectacular residents of the Camargue. Proving the preserve's success, the indigenous population of the *flamants roses* (pink flamingos) is now a healthy 50,000.

Right, flamingos, Parc Regional de Camargue

## ALL ABOUT THE BIRDS . . .

Purple Heron (Ardea purpurea), Little Camargue, France

Up north a few miles from Stes-Maries-de-la-Mer, the main town in the Camargue, is a private reserve called the ☼ **Parc Ornithologique du Pont-de-Gau** (Ornithological Park of the Pont-de-Gau). On some 150 acres of marsh and salt lands, birds are welcomed and protected; injured birds are treated in large pens and released if and when ready. Boardwalks (including a short, child-friendly inner loop past the easy-viewing stands) snake over the wetlands, the longest leading to a blind where a half hour of silence, binoculars in hand, can reveal unexpected treasures. Near the park entrance is the Hostellerie Pont-de-Gau, which offers hearty meals much favored by local ranchers. ✉ *D570, 5 km (3 miles) north of Saintes Maries de la Mer* ☎ *04–90–97–82–62* ⊕ *www.parcornithologique.com* ✉ *€9* ☉ *Oct.–Mar., daily 10–sunset; Apr.–Sept., daily 9–sunset; Oct.–Mar., daily 10–sunset.*

### DEEP IN THE HEART OF . . . PROVENCE?

Historians now tell us that the American cowboy is actually descended from the French gardian, the Provençal cowboy. "Go West," Horace Greeley once advised, and in the early 19th century, these Camargue ranchers did exactly that: shipping out to the French colony of New Orleans, they then fanned out across America as the first horse-wranglers. Although they traded in their iron trident pole for a lariat, they brought along their black felt hats, string ties, and—to the later gratification of Levi Strauss—*bleus de travail*, or "jeans" (invented in the Provence city of Nîmes). Their festival wear—seen in full glory during the Fête des Gardians in Arles in May—inspired a local homeboy, couturier Christian Lacroix. Today, les gardians are a unique breed, proud of their centuries-old traditions and disdainful of the Hollywood "cowboy."

## THE BEES . . .

Le Vaccarès, the central lagoon of the Camargue preserve

If you're an even more committed nature lover, hike, bike, or horseback ride through the inner sanctum of the Camargue, the **Réserve Nationale de Camargue**. This intensely protected area contains the central pond called **Le Vaccarès**, home to birds, nutria, fish, and rich insect life. Pick up maps and information at the **Centre d'Information du Parc Naturel Régional du Camargue** (✉ D570 ☎ 04–90–97–00–97 ⊕ *www.reserve-camargue.org* ⊘ *Apr.–Sept., daily 10–6; Oct.–Mar., Sat.–Thurs. 9:30–5*).

North past the village of Albaron is the converted sheep-ranch-now-museum, the **Musée de la Camarguais** (✉ *Mas du Pont de Rousty, D570* ☎ *04–90–97–10–82* 💳 *€4.60* ⊘ *Apr.–June, daily 9:15–5:45; July–Aug., 9:15–6:45; Sept., 9:15–5:45; Oct.–Mar., 10:15–4:45*). Focusing on the region's history, produce, and people, it is also a good place to pick up info on nature trails.

### ON THE HORNS OF A DILEMMA

Car, bus, boat, bike, or foot? Actually, the best way to explore the Camargue is by horse. Some 30 places rent them for a *promenade équestre* (horseback tour). The **Association Camarguaise de Tourisme Équestre** publishes a list of names and numbers, available at the **Centre d'Information du Parc Naturel Régional du Camargue** at Pont-du-Gau or at the **Stes-Maries tourist office** (5 av. van Gogh). Stables line the roads throughout the Camargue, so they're easy to find; several are concentrated along D570 north of Stes-Maries as well as along the eastern loop D85. An hour's ride averages between €15 and €30, and a whole day €60 to €90 (with *pique-nique* thrown in). While a *promenade à cheval* can last all day, most are two hours long; accompanied by commentary on such topics as folklore and ecology, these are called *ballades*.

## . . . AND THE BULLS

Camargue herdsmen crossing the swamps with their bulls.

Near the northern shore of the Étang de Vaccarès, one of the larger ranches in the Camargue has been turned into a showplace for all things taurine.

Bullfights, ferrades, horse rides, and *spectacles taurine* (bull-baiting) are just some of the activities offered at the **Domaine de Méjanes Paul Ricard,** 4 km (2½ mi) south of Albaron on D37. You'll learn about the history of the unique regional species of bull-fight, the *cours camarguaise*. In these special combats, bulls are not killed in the arena but simply taunted by *rase-teurs* (runners) who try to pluck off a red cockade and two white tassels mounted on the bull's horns.

Bulls live to enter the arena again and again, and some become such celebrities they have appeared on the covers of French magazines.

At the Domaine, you can also ride a *petit train* for a fun 20-minute tour of the marshlands. ⊠ *D37, on edge of Étang de Vaccarès* ☎ *04–90–97–10–10* ⊕ *www.mejanes.camargue.fr.*

At the easternmost point of the Étang du Vaccarès, another good visitor center is found at La Capelière. The **Centre d'Information de la Réserve Nationale de Camargue** has maps, exhibits on wildlife, and three *sentiers de décou-verte* (discovery trails). ⊠ *5 km (3 mi) south of Villeneuve/Romieu, off D37* ☎ *04–90–97–00–97.*

Man must remove ribbons tied on bull's horns.

### EXPLORING

As you enter this town's mammoth and medieval cathedral, the Église des Stes-Maries, you'll notice an oddity that wrenches you back to this century: a sign on the door forbids visitors to come *torse nu* (topless). For outside its otherworldly role as the pilgrimage center hallowed as the European landfall of the Virgin Mary, Stes-Maries is first and foremost a beach resort, dead-flat, whitewashed, and more than a little tacky. Unless you've made a pilgrimage to the sun and sand, you probably won't want to spend much time in the town center. And if you've chosen Stes-Maries as a base for viewing the Camargue, consider one of the discreet country inns outside the city limits.

**Église des Stes-Maries.** What is most striking to a visitor entering the damp, dark, and forbidding fortress-church Église des Stes-Maries is its novel character. Almost devoid of windows, its tall, barren single nave is cluttered with florid and sentimental ex-votos (tokens of blessings, prayers, and thanks) and primitive artworks depicting the famous trio. Another oddity brings you back to the 21st century: a sign on the door forbids visitors from entering *torse nu* (topless). For €2.50 you can climb up to the terrace for a panoramic view of the Camargue. 🌐 *www.sanctuaire-des-saintesmaries.fr.*

### WHERE TO STAY

$$ B&B/INN 🏨 **Cacharel Hôtel.** A haven for nature lovers, this quiet, laid-back retreat is nestled in the middle of 170 acres of private marshland. **Pros:** screens on windows to keep out mosquitoes; a real taste of the Wild West with silent nights, wind blowing through long grass, animals rustling outside; perfect for those who want to de-urbanize. **Cons:** rooms are very sparse, almost monastery-like; not much to do in the way of socializing. [$] *Rooms from: €136* ✉ *Rte de Cacharel, 4 km (2½ miles) north of town on D85* ☎ *04–90–97–95–44* 🌐 *www.hotel-cacharel.com* 🛏 *16 rooms* 🍴 *No meals.*

$$$$ HOTEL 🏨 **Mas de la Fouque.** With stylish rooms and luxurious balconies that look out over a beautiful lagoon, this upscale converted farmhouse is a perfect escape from the rigors of horseback riding and bird-watching. **Pros:** in the heart of nature. **Cons:** that means mosquitoes. [$] *Rooms from: €330* ✉ *Rte. du Petit Rhône* ☎ *04–90–97–81–02* 🌐 *www.masdelafouque.com* 🛏 *26 rooms* 🕒 *Closed Jan. and Feb.* 🍴 *No meals.*

# ARLES AND NEARBY

## ARLES

*31 km (19 miles) southeast of Nîmes; 40 km (25 miles) northwest of Stes-Maries.*

Reigning over the bleak but evocative landscape of the marshlands of the Camargue, the small city of Arles is fiercely Provençal, nurturing its heritage and parading its culture at every colorful opportunity. Warming the wetlands with its atmosphere, animation, and culture, it is a patch of hot color in a sepia landscape—and an excellent home base for sorties into the raw natural beauty and eccentric villages of the Rhône delta.

If you were obliged to choose just one city to visit in Provence, lovely little Arles would give Avignon and Aix a run for their money. It's too charming to become museumlike yet has a wealth of classical antiquities and Romanesque stonework; quarried-stone edifices and shuttered town houses shading graceful Old Town streets and squares; and pageantry, festivals, and cutting-edge arts events. Its atmospheric restaurants and picturesque small hotels make it the ideal headquarters for forays into the Alpilles and the Camargue.

Yet compared to Avignon and Aix, it's a small town. You can zip into the center in five minutes without crossing a half hour's worth of urban sprawl. And its monuments and pretty old neighborhoods are conveniently concentrated between the main artery Boulevard des Lices and the broad, meandering Rhône.

> **WHISPERS ABOUT VAN GOGH'S EAR**
>
> Ill-received and ostracized in Arles, Van Gogh was packed off to an asylum in nearby St-Rémy after he cut off the lobe of his left ear on December 23, 1888. Theories abound, but historians believe he made the desperate gesture in homage to Gauguin, who had arrived to set up a "Studio of the South." Following the fashion in Provençal bullrings for a matador to present his lady love with an ear from a dispatched bull, Vincent wielded the knife after arguing with Gauguin, whom he had come to idolize.

It wasn't always such a mellow site. A Greek colony since the 6th century BC, little Arles took a giant step forward when Julius Caesar defeated Marseille in the 1st century BC, transforming it into a formidable civilization—by some accounts, the Rome of the north. Fed by aqueducts, canals, and solid roads, it profited from all the Romans' modern conveniences: straight paved streets and sidewalks, sewers and latrines, thermal baths, a forum, a hippodrome, a theater, and an arena. It became an international crossroads by sea and land and a market to the world. The emperor Constantine himself moved to Arles and brought with him Christianity.

The remains of this golden age are reason enough to visit Arles today. Yet its character nowadays is as gracious and low-key as it once was cutting-edge. If you plan to visit many of the monuments and museums in Arles, purchase a *visite générale* ticket for €13.50, which covers admission to all of them.

**GETTING HERE AND AROUND**

If you're arriving by plane, note that Arles is roughly 20 km (12 miles) from the Nîmes-Arles-Camargue airport. The easiest way from the landing strip to Arles is by taxi (about €35). Buses run between Nîmes and Arles 11 times daily on weekdays and four times on Saturday (not at all on Sunday). Four buses run weekdays between Arles and Stes-Maries-de-la-Mer, through Cartreize. The SNCF runs three buses Monday–Saturday from Avignon to Arles. Arles is along the main coastal train route, and you can take the TGV (Trains à Grands Vitesses) to Avignon from Paris and jump on the local connection to Arles. You can also reach Arles directly by train from Marseille.

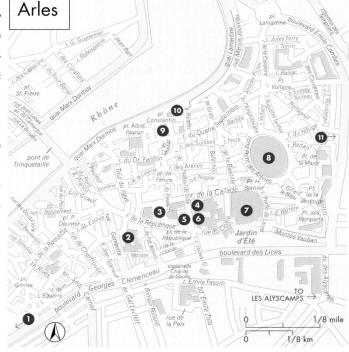

### VISITOR INFORMATION

**Arles Tourist Office** ✉ *Esplanade Charles de Gaulle, Boulevard des Lices*
☎ *04-90-18-41-20* ⊕ *www.arlestourisme.com.*

### EXPLORING

Seated in the shade of Arles's plane trees on the Place du Forum, sunning at the foot of the obelisk on the Place de la République, meditating in the cloister of St-Trophime, or strolling the rampart walkway along the sparkling Rhône, you can see what enchanted Gauguin and drove Van Gogh mad with inspiration. It's the light: intense, vivid, crystalline, setting off planes of color and shadow with prismatic concentration. As a foil to this famous light, multihue Arles—with its red-and-gold ocher, cool gray stone, and blue-black shade—is unsurpassed.

### TOP ATTRACTIONS

Fodor'sChoice **Arènes** (*Arena*). Rivaled only by the even better-preserved version in
★ Nîmes, the arena dominating old Arles was built in the first century AD to seat 21,000 people, with large tunnels through which wild beasts were forced to run into the center. Before being plundered in the Middle Ages, the structure had three stories of 60 arcades each; the four medieval towers are testimony to a transformation from classical sports arena to feudal fortification. Complete restoration began in 1825, and today the arena holds nearly as many people as it once

did. It's primarily a venue for the traditional spectacle of the *corridas* (bullfights), which take place annually during the *féria pascale*, or Easter festival. The less bloodthirsty local variant *Course Carmarguaise* (in which the bull is not killed) also takes place here. Festivities start with the Fête des Gardians on May 1, when the Queen of Arles is crowned, and culminate in early July with the award of the Cocarde d'Or (Golden Rosette) to the most successful bullfighter. Tickets are usually available, but for the more popular fights, it is advisable to book ahead. ⊠ *24 bis, Rond Point des Arènes* ☎ *04–90–18–41–20, 08–91–70–03–70 Courses Carmarguaise* ⊕ *www.arlestourisme.com* ✉ *€8.50 joint ticket with Théâtre Antique* ۞ *May–Sept., daily 9–7; Oct., daily 9–6; Nov.–Feb., daily 10–5; Mar.–Apr., daily 9–6.*

**Cloître St-Trophime** (*St.Trophime Cloister*). This peaceful haven, one of the loveliest cloisters in Provence, is tucked discreetly behind St-Trophime, the notable Romanesque treasure. A sturdy walkway above the Gothic arches offers good views of the town. ⊠ *Off Place de la République* ☎ *04–90–18–41–20* ⊕ *www.arlestourisme.com* ✉ *€3.50* ۞ *May–Sept., daily 9–7; Oct., daily 9–6; Nov.–Feb., daily 10–5; Mar.–Apr., daily 9–6.*

**Église St-Trophime.** Classed as a world treasure by UNESCO, this extraordinary Romanesque church alone would justify a visit to Arles. The side aisles date from the 11th century and the nave from the 12th; the church's austere symmetry and ancient artworks (including a stunning early Christian sarcophagus) are fascinating. But it's the church's superbly preserved Romanesque sculpture on the 12th-century **portal**— the recently renovated entry facade—that earns international respect. Particularly remarkable is the frieze of the Last Judgment, with souls being dragged off to Hell in chains or, on the contrary, being lovingly delivered into the hands of the saints. Christ is flanked by his chroniclers, the evangelists: the eagle (John), the bull (Luke), the angel (Matthew), and the lion (Mark). ⊠ *Pl. de la République* ⊕ *www.arlestourisme.com* ✉ *Free* ۞ *Not open to the public between noon and 2 pm.*

**Fodor's Choice**
★

**Espace Van Gogh.** A strikingly resonant site, this was the hospital to which the tortured artist repaired after cutting off his earlobe. Its courtyard has been impeccably restored and landscaped to match one of Van Gogh's paintings. The cloistered grounds have become something of a shrine for visitors, and there is a photo plaque comparing the renovation to some of the master's paintings, including *Le Jardin de la Maison de Santé*. The exhibition hall is open for temporary exhibitions; the garden is always on view. ■ TIP➔ Also check out shows of contemporary art inspired by the artist at the beautifully restored Fondation Vincent Van Gogh, 5 Place Honoré Clair. ⊠ *Pl. Dr. Félix Rey* ☎ *04–90–18–41–20* ⊕ *www.arlestourisme.com* ✉ *Free.*

**Fondation Vincent Van Gogh.** Van Gogh's 15-month stay in Arles represents a climax in the artist's career. Enchanted with Arles's limpid light, vibrant landscape, and scenic monuments, Van Gogh experienced here what was to be his greatest blossoming in a decade as a painter. The Fondation Vincent Van Gogh, originally conceived in the mid-80s in response to the 100th anniversary of the artist's arrival in Arles, pays homage to Van Gogh's legacy and monumental influence via an

Van Gogh immortalized the courtyard of this former hospital—now the Espace Van Gogh, a center devoted to his works—in several masterpieces.

impressive range of artworks contributed by 90 contemporary artists. Opened in spring 2014 in the beautifully restored 15th-century Hôtel Léautaud de Donines, the Fondation houses a superb collection of contemporary art and provides a vital addition to Arles's cultural life with a revolving series of temporary art exhibitions, performance art, concerts, and happenings. ✉ *5 place Honoré Clair* ☎ *04–90–93–08–08* ⊕ *www. fondation-vincentvangogh-arles.org.*

**Musée Départemental Arles Antiques** (*Museum of Ancient Arles*). Though it's a hike from the center, this state-of-the-art museum is a good place to set the tone and context for your exploration of Arles. You can learn all about the city in its Roman heyday, from the development of its monuments to details of daily life. The bold, modern triangular structure (designed by Henri Ciriani) lies on the site of an enormous Roman *cirque* (chariot-racing stadium), and the permanent collection includes jewelry, mosaics, town plans, and carved 4th-century sarcophagi. ■ TIP→ **A new wing features a rare intact barge dating from AD 50 and a fascinating display illustrating how the boat was meticulously dredged from the nearby Rhône.** The quantity of these treasures gives an idea of the extent of Arles's importance. Seven superb floor mosaics can be viewed from an elevated platform, and you exit via a hall packed tight with magnificently detailed paleo-Christian sarcophagi. As you leave you will see the belt of St-Césaire, the last bishop of Arles, who died in AD 542 when the countryside was overwhelmed by the Franks and the Roman era met its end. Ask for an English-language guidebook. ✉ *Ave de la 1ère Division Française Libre, Presqu'île du Cirque Romain* ☎ *04–13–31–51–03* ⊕ *www.arles-antique.cg13.fr* ✄ *€8, free first Sun. of the month* ☾ *Wed.–Mon. 10–6.*

## CLOSE UP

# A Good Walk

The best of Arles is enclosed in the inner maze of streets and alleyways known as the Old Town, nestled along the Rhône, where you can find noble 18th-century architecture cheek-by-jowl with antiquities. Only Les Alyscamps necropolis lies outside the city center, but it's still within walking distance.

Though it's a hike from the center, a good place to set the tone and context for your exploration of Arles is at the state-of-the-art **Musée Départemental Arles Antiques**. From here, take advantage of the free museum shuttle; there's an adjacent parking lot if you're day-tripping by car. Get off at the Boulevard Clémenceau and arm yourself with literature at the tourist information center just up the road, on Boulevard des Lices. Then walk up Rue du President Wilson, and left to the **Espace Van Gogh**, the hospital where Van Gogh was taken after he severed his ear. Continue

up Rue du President Wilson to the Rue de la République and the broad **Place de la République**, where you can study the Roman obelisk and the extraordinary Romanesque facade of the **Église St-Trophime**. Next door, enter the hidden oasis of the **Cloître St-Trophime**. Continue up Rue du Cloître to the **Théâtre Antique**, now in Byronesque ruins. Just above rears the **Arènes**, site of gladiator battles and modern bullfights.

Now wander down evocative back streets to the river and the **Thermes Constantin**, the ruins of Roman baths. On Rue du Grand Prieuré, stop into the **Musée Réattu**, which glorifies native-son painter Jacques Réattu and 20th-century peers. Not Van Gogh, alas. Pay homage to that painter by walking up Rue du Quatre Septembre and Rue Amédée Pichot to **Place Lamartine**, where the star-crossed artist lived in his famous Maison Jaune, destroyed in World War II.

**Place Lamartine.** Stand on the site of Van Gogh's residence in Arles—the now-famous Maison Jaune (Yellow House), destroyed by bombs in 1944. The artist may have set up his easel on the Quais du Rhône, just off Place Lamartine, to capture the view that he transformed into his legendary *Starry Night*. Eight other sites are included on the city's "Arles and Vincent van Gogh" (⊕ *www.arlestourisme.com*), linking sight to canvas, including the Place du Forum, the Trinquetaille bridge, Rue Mireille, the Summer Garden on the Boulevard des Lices, and the road along the Arles à Bouc canal. A map (*le Circuit Van Gogh*) can be purchased for €1 at the tourist office.

**OFF THE BEATEN PATH**

**Les Alyscamps.** Though the romantically melancholic Roman cemetery lies 1 km (½ mile) southeast of the Vieille Ville, it's worth the hike—certainly Van Gogh thought so, as several of his famous canvases prove. This long necropolis amassed the remains of the dead from antiquity to the Middle Ages. Greek, Roman, and Christian tombs line the shady road that was once the main entry to Arles, the Aurelian Way. The finest of the stone coffins have been plundered over the centuries, thus no single work of surpassing beauty remains here (they're in the Musée Départmental Arles). Next to the ruins rise the Romanesque tower and ruined church of St. Honorat, where (legend has it) St. Trophimus fell to his knees when God spoke to him. ✉ *Allée des Sarcophages* ☎ *04–90–49–36–74* ⊕ *www.arlestourisme.com* 🏷*€3.50* ⊙ *May–Sept., daily 9–7; Oct., daily 9–noon and 2–6; Nov.–Feb., daily 10–noon and 2–5; Mar. and Apr., daily 9–noon and 2–6.*

**Théâtre Antique** (*Ancient Theater*). Directly up Rue de la Calade from Place de la République, you'll find these ruins of a theater built by the Romans under Augustus in the first century BC. It's here that the noted Venus of Arles statue, now in the Louvre, was dug up and identified. The theater was once an entertainment venue that held 10,000 people, and is now a pleasant, parklike retreat. Only two columns of the amphitheater's stage walls and one row of arches remain; the fine local stone was used to build early Christian churches. Only a few vestiges of the original stone benches are left, along with the two great Corinthian columns. Today the ruins are a stage for the Festival d'Arles, in July and August, and site of Les Recontres d'Arles (Photography Festival) from early July to mid-September. ✉ *Rue de la Calade* ☎ *04–90–49–59–05* ⊕ *www.arlestourisme.com* 🏷*€6.50 joint ticket with Arènes* ⊙ *May–Sept., daily 9–7; Oct., daily 9–6; Nov.–Feb., daily 10–5; Mar. and Apr., daily 9–6.*

**WORTH NOTING**

**Cryptoportiques.** Entering through the elegant 17th-century City Hall, you can gain access to these ancient underground passages dating from 30 BC to 20 BC. The horseshoe of vaults and pillars buttressed the ancient forum from below ground. Used as a bomb shelter in World War II, the galleries still have a rather ominous atmosphere. Yet openings let in natural daylight and artworks of considerable merit have been unearthed here, adding to the mystery of the site's original function. ✉ *Rue Balze, Pl. de la République, City Hall* ☎ *04–90–18–41–20* ⊕ *www.arlestourisme.com* 🏷*€3.50* ⊙ *May–Sept., daily 9–noon and 2–7; Oct., daily 9–noon and 2–6; Nov.–Feb., daily 10–noon and 2–5; Mar. and Apr., daily 9–noon and 2–6.*

**Musée Réattu.** Three rooms of this museum, housed in a Knights of Malta priory dating to the 15th century, are dedicated to local painter Jacques Réattu. But the standouts are works by Dufy, Gauguin, and 57 drawings (and two paintings) done by Picasso in 1971—including one delightfully tongue-in-cheek depiction of noted muse and writer Lee Miller in full Arles dress. They were donated to Arles by Picasso himself, to thank the town for amusing him with bullfights. ✉ *10 rue Grand Prieuré* ☎ *04–90–49–37–58* ⊕ *www.museereattu.arles.fr* 🏷*€8* ⊙ *Nov.–Feb., daily 10–5, Mar.–Oct., daily 10–6.*

**Place de la République.** The slender, expressive saints of St-Trophime overlook the wide steps that attract sunners and foot-weary travelers who enjoy the modern perspective over this broad urban square, flanked by the classical symmetry of the 17th-century **Hôtel de Ville.** This noble Italianate landmark is the work of the great 17th-century Parisian architect François Mansart (as in mansard roofs); a passageway allows you to cut through its graceful vestibule from Rue Balze. The **obelisk,** of Turkish marble, used to stand in the Gallo-Roman cirque and was hauled here in the 18th century.

**CLOSE UP**

# Van Gogh in Arles and St-Rémy

It was the light that drew Vincent van Gogh to Arles. For a man raised under the iron-gray skies of the Netherlands and the gaslight pall of Paris, Provence's clean, clear sun was a revelation. In his last years he turned his frenzied efforts to capture the resonance of "...golden tones of every hue: green gold, yellow gold, pink gold, bronze or copper colored gold, and even from the yellow of lemons to the matte, lusterless yellow of threshed grain."

Arles, however, was not drawn to Van Gogh. Though it makes every effort today to make up for its misjudgment, Arles treated the artist badly during the time he passed here near the end of his life—a time when his creativity, productivity, and madness all reached a climax. It was 1888 when he settled in to work in Arles with an intensity and tempestuousness that first drew, then drove away his companion Paul Gauguin, with whom he had dreamed of founding an artists' colony.

Frenziedly productive—he applied a pigment-loaded palette knife to some 200 canvases in that year alone—he nonetheless lived in intense isolation, counting his *sous*, and writing his visions in lengthy letters to his long-suffering, infinitely patient brother Theo. Often drinking heavily, occasionally whoring, Vincent alienated his neighbors, goading them to action. In 1889 the people of Arles circulated a petition to have him evicted, a shock that left him less and less able to cope with life and led to his eventual self-commitment to an asylum in nearby St-Rémy. The houses he lived in are no longer standing, though many of his subjects remain as he saw them. The paintings he daubed and splashed

Vincent van Gogh, Self-Portrait, 1887, Musée d'Orsay, Paris, France.

with such passion have been auctioned elsewhere.

Thus you have to go to Amsterdam or Moscow to view Van Gogh's work. But with a little imagination, you can glean something of Van Gogh's Arles from a tour of the modern town. In fact, the city has provided helpful markers and a numbered itinerary to guide you between landmarks. You can stand on the Place Lamartine, where his famous Maison Jaune stood until it was destroyed by World War II bombs. *Starry Night* may have been painted from the Quai du Rhône just off Place Lamartine, though another was completed at St-Rémy.

The Café La Nuit on Place Forum is an exact match for the terrace platform, scattered with tables and bathed in gaslight under the stars, from the painting *Terrasse de café le soir*; Gauguin and Van Gogh used to drink here. (Current owners have determinedly maintained the Fauve color scheme to keep

Vincent van Gogh, Sunflowers, 1888, National Gallery, London, England.

the atmosphere.) Both the Arènes and Les Alyscamps were featured in paintings, and the hospital where he broke down and cut off his earlobe is now a kind of shrine, its garden reconstructed exactly as it figured in *Le Jardin de l'Hôtel-Dieu*. The drawbridge in *Le pont de Langlois aux Lavandières* has been reconstructed outside of town, at Port-de-Bouc, 3 km (2 miles) south on D35.

About 25 km (15½ miles) away is St-Rémy-de-Provence, where Van Gogh retreated to the asylum St-Paul-de-Mausolée. Here he spent hours in silence, painting the cloisters. On his ventures into town, he painted the dappled lime trees at the intersection of Boulevard Mirabeau and Boulevard Gambetta. And en route between the towns, you'll see the orchards whose spring blooms ignited his joyous explosions of yellow, green, and pink.

**Thermes Constantin** (*Constantine Baths*). Along the riverfront stand the remains of vast and sophisticated Roman baths, luxurious social centers that once included sports facilities and a library—the Barnes & Noble of the 4th century. You can still see the caldarium and bricks of the under-floor heating system. ✉ *Pl. Constantin at the corner of Rue de l'Hôtel de Ville* ☎ *04–90–49–59–05* 🌐 *www.tourisme.ville-arles.fr* 🎫 *€3* 🕒 *Apr.–Sept., daily 9–7; Oct.–Mar., daily 10–6.*

## WHERE TO EAT

$ TAPAS 🍴 **Bodeguita.** This popular institution near Place du Forum is known for excellent tapas at more than reasonable prices. Embrace the bullfighter within and try a range of morsels: spicy stuffed dumplings, roasted Camembert with chorizo bread, or sliced chicken Catalonia-style. Grilled bull steak with creamed garlic sauce and a few other entrées are also available. The warm reception by chef Anthony is matched by the vivid yet simple interior. [$] *Average main: €16* ✉ *49 rue des Arénes* ☎ *04–90–96–68–59* 🕒 *Closed lunch Sun.–Thurs., Nov.–Apr.*

$$ FRENCH 🍴 **Brasserie Nord-Pinus.** With its tile-and-ironwork interior straight out of a design magazine and its Place du Forum terrace packed with all the right people, this cozy-chic retro brasserie highlights light, simple, and purely Provençal cooking in dishes such as roast rack of lamb au jus and pan-fried fillet of beef in a morel-and-cream sauce. The fois gras *cocotte* is simply delicious. Discreet service and a nicely balanced wine list only add to its charm. And wasn't that Christian Lacroix (or Kate Moss or Juliette Binoche) under those Ray-Bans? [$] *Average main: €24* ✉ *Pl. du Forum* ☎ *04–90–93–58–43* 🌐 *www.nord-pinus.com* ✍ *Reservations essential* 🕒 *Closed Sun. and Mon.*

$$$$ FRENCH Fodor's Choice ★ 🍴 **La Chassagnette.** Reputedly the original registered "organic" restaurant in Provence, this sophisticated yet down-home comfortable spot—located 12 km (7½ miles) south of Arles—is fetchingly designed and has a dining area that extends outdoors, where large family-style picnic tables await under a wooden-slate canopy overlooking the extensive gardens. Using ingredients that are grown right on the property, innovative master chef Armand Arnal (who has been awarded a Michelin star) serves prix-fixe menus that are a refreshing, though not inexpensive, mix of modern and classic French-country cuisine—you can expect to pay €85–€125 per person. The à la carte options are equally admirable and much more affordable: picture a fillet of wild sole with roasted asparagus and bottarga for €35. Environmentally conscious oenophiles can wash it all down with a glass of eco-certified wine. [$] *Average main: €37* ✉ *Rte. du Sambuc, D36* ☎ *04–90–97–26–96* 🌐 *www.chassagnette.fr* ✍ *Reservations essential* 🕒 *Closed Feb. May–Oct., closed Tues. and Wed.; Nov.–Apr., closed Mon.–Wed.*

$ FRENCH 🍴 **L'Affenage.** A vast smorgasbord of Provençal hors d'oeuvres draws loyal locals to this former fire-horse shed. They come here for heaping plates of fried eggplant, green tapenade, chickpeas in cumin, and a slab of ham carved off the bone—followed by roasted potatoes and lamb chops grilled in the great stone fireplace. In summer you can opt for just the first-course buffet and go back for thirds; reserve a terrace table out front if you can—in the summer, call at least a week in advance. [$] *Average main: €13* ✉ *4 rue Molière* ☎ *04–90–96–07–67* 🕒 *Closed Sun. and 3 wks in Aug. No lunch Mon.*

**$$** ✕ **La Gueule du Loup.** You reach your table through the kitchen, bustling
FRENCH  with chopping, sizzling, and wafting scents, which is a nice introduction
to what awaits. The cooking is serious—Provençal specialties such as
*rouget* (red mullet) with pureed potatoes, *caillette d'agneau* (lamb baked
in herbs), and crème brûlée with anise; and the four set menus, priced
from €15 (lunch only) to €33, will surely appeal to all appetites. Jazz
music and vintage magic posters bring the old Arles stone-and-beam
interior up to date for a memorably pleasant experience. $ *Average
main: €18* ✉ *39 rue des Arènes* ☎ *04–90–96–96–69* ⚐ *Reservations
essential* ☉ *Closed Sun., Mon. and mid-Jan.–mid-Feb.*

**$$$$** ✕ **L'Atelier de Jean-Luc Rabanel.** Jean-Luc Rabanel is the culinary success
MODERN FRENCH  story of the region, famous for fresh garden-inspired cuisine that he fea-
tures in this stylish restaurant and cooking school, one of the few organic
eateries in France to merit two Michelin stars. A super-chic Japanese-style
reception area, which includes the five elements—water, fire, earth, air,
and spirit—ensures that "guests will come into harmony with their cui-
sine." Menus are prix fixe only; the seven-dish tapas-style lunch (€65)
is a treat not to be missed. Those keeping to a budget should try **A Côté**
(*04–90–47–61–13* ⊕ *www.bistro-acote.com*), a few doors down, where
you can more affordably experience the genius of this super-chef by sam-
pling a tasty selection of upmarket tapas and regional wines. $ *Average
main: €40* ✉ *7 rue des Carmes* ☎ *04–90–91–07–69* ⊕ *www.rabanel.com*
⚐ *Reservations essential* ☉ *Closed Mon. and Tues.*

**$$** ✕ **L'Autruche.** This small contemporary bistro in central Arles pro-
BISTRO  vides cheerful, friendly service and innovative, affordable cuisine with
modern leanings. The menu changes frequently depending on what's
available in the market, but sumptuous dishes that are typical of this
inventive chef's repertoire include fillet of cod with golden turnips,
pumpkin puree, and wild mushrooms sprinkled with fresh chervil;
and creamy risotto with beef bouillon and cheese crisps sprinkled
with hazelnuts. On warm days, the terrace out front is a delightful
place to while away an afternoon over a bottle of regional rosé and
a good-value gourmet lunch. $ *Average main: €22* ✉ *5 rue Dulau*
☎ *04–90–49–73–63* ⚐ *Reservations essential* ☉ *Closed Sun.*

**$** ✕ **Lou Caleu.** In a charming 16th-century building behind the Amphithe-
FRENCH  ater, this popular, unpretentious place serves regional specialties cooked
by the genial owner and chef Christian Gimenez—homemade salt-cod
brandade, *jarret d'agneau* (lamb roasted with black olives), and *bourride* (Provençal soup)—at good prices. The pureed potatoes with truffled olives are a remarkable garnish, and make sure to order one of the
many excellent Rhône Valley whites with the fish. ■TIP➜ **Don't miss
the terrific lunch deals.** $ *Average main: €17* ✉ *27 rue Porte de Laure*
☎ *04–90–49–71–77* ⊕ *www.restaurant-lou-caleu-arles.com* ⚐ *Reservations essential* ☉ *Closed Sun. and Mon.*

**$$$** ✕ **Lou Marquès.** Whether you dine indoors, surrounded by glowing
FRENCH  woodwork and rich Provençal fabrics, or amid the greenery of this
former Carmelite cloister, atmosphere figures large in your evening at
this Arles institution in the Jules César Hotel. Chefs Pascal Renaud
and Joseph Kriz mix classical grandeur with Provençal rusticity: lob-
ster risotto, roast pigeon with porcini, grilled bull steak, salsify with

veal and tomato polenta, and strawberries in a pastry shell with fresh cream. The wine list is as ambitious as Caesar himself. $ *Average main: €30* ⊠ *Jules César Hotel, 9 Bd. des Lices* ☎ *04–90–52–52–52* ⊕ *www. hotel-julescesar.fr* ⚓ *Reservations essential.*

## WHERE TO STAY

**$$$**
HOTEL
Fodor'sChoice
★
 **Grand Hotel Nord-Pinus.** A richly atmospheric stage-set for literati (or literary poseurs), decor-magazine shoots, and people who prize ambience, this scruffy-chic landmark is not for everyone—but if Picasso once felt at home here, perhaps you will too. **Pros:** unique atmosphere transports you to a less complicated time, when bullfighting was not part of the political arena, and people still dressed for dinner; free mineral water in rooms. **Cons:** rooms at front of hotel can be noisy, especially in summer. $ *Rooms from: €185* ⊠ *Pl. du Forum* ☎ *04–90–93–44–44* ⊕ *www.nord-pinus.com* ↝ *25 rooms, 1 apartment* ⋔ *No meals.*

**$$**
HOTEL
 **Hôtel d'Arlatan.** Once home to the counts of Arlatan, this noble 15th-century stone house stands on the site of a 4th-century basilica, and a glass floor reveals the excavated vestiges under the lobby. **Pros:** staying at this hotel is an experience in French hospitality: the pace is slow, the welcome warm and the food good. **Cons:** the pool is quite small; hotel seems crowded in high season. $ *Rooms from: €110* ⊠ *26 rue du Sauvage* ☎ *04–90–93–56–66* ⊕ *www.hotel-arlatan.fr* ↝ *40 rooms, 6 suites* ☾ *Closed Jan.* ⋔ *No meals.*

**$$$**
HOTEL
 **Le Calendal.** In a prime location in Arles's Old Town just steps from the Théâtre Antique, this quaint hotel lacks nothing in the way of charm or service—a more welcoming staff could hardly be imagined. **Pros:** close to everything; welcoming staff; discounted parking for guests. **Cons:** rooms can be dark. $ *Rooms from: €159* ⊠ *5 rue Porte de Laure* ☎ *04–90–96– 11–89* ⊕ *www.lecalendal.com* ↝ *38 rooms* ⋔ *No meals.*

**$$**
HOTEL
 **Le Cloître.** Built as the private home for the provost of the Cloisters, this grand old medieval building has luckily fallen into the hands of a friendly, multilingual couple devoted to making the most of its historic details—with their own bare hands. **Pros:** lovely architecture made apparent with clever use of color; proud owners eager to talk about the history of hotel. **Cons:** rooms can be sparse to the point of being bare; can be noisy during feria season. $ *Rooms from: €110* ⊠ *16 rue du Cloître* ☎ *04–90–96–29–50* ⊕ *www.hotelcloitre.com* ↝ *30 rooms* ☾ *Closed Nov.–Mar.* ⋔ *No meals.*

**$$$$**
HOTEL
Fodor'sChoice
★
 **L'Hôtel Particulier.** Once owned by the Baron of Chartrouse, this extraordinary 18th-century *hôtel particulier* (mansion) is delightfully intimate and decorated in sophisticated yet charming style, with gold-framed mirrors, white-brocade chairs, marble writing desks, artfully hung curtains, and hand-painted wallpaper. **Pros:** quiet and secluded but only a short walk to town; combines historical ambience with modern high-tech conveniences. **Cons:** a 50% nonrefundable deposit is required when booking; the pool is small, which can be difficult in summer when every guest wants to be in the water; optional breakfast steep (€23). $ *Rooms from: €309* ⊠ *4 rue de la Monnaie* ☎ *04–90–52–51–40* ⊕ *www.hotel-particulier.com* ↝ *18* ⋔ *No meals.*

**$$$$**
HOTEL
 **Mas de Peint.** Sitting on roughly 1,250 acres of Camargue ranch land, this exquisite 17th-century farmhouse may just offer the ultimate mas experience. **Pros:** isolated setting makes for a perfect escape—romantic

or otherwise; reception is warm; no detail is missed in service or style. **Cons:** make sure you confirm room has a shower; unheated pool is a tad chilly even in September; not much to do once sun goes down. ⓢ *Rooms from: €260* ⊠ *D36, 20 km (12 miles) south of Arles, Le Sambuc* ☎ *04–90–97–20–62* ⊕ *www.masdepeint.com* ⤳ *8 rooms, 5 suites* ⊗ *Closed mid-Nov.–end of Mar.; open for two weeks at Christmas* ⓞ *No meals.*

$   ⚏ **Muette.** This Old Town option has 12th-century exposed stone

HOTEL   walls, a 15th-century spiral staircase, and weathered wood, plus Provençal prints and fresh sunflowers in every room to add just the right homey touch. **Pros:** excellent value; enthusiastic welcome; generous buffet breakfast (extra). **Cons:** some rooms can be very noisy, especially in the summer; parking can be tricky. ⓢ *Rooms from: €70* ⊠ *15 rue des Suisses* ☎ *04–90–96–15–39* ⊕ *www.hotel-muette.com* ⤳ *18 rooms* ⊗ *Closed mid-Nov.–Feb.* ⓞ *No meals.*

## NIGHTLIFE AND THE ARTS

To find out what's happening in and around Arles (even as far away as Nîmes and Avignon), the free weekly *Le César* lists films, plays, cabaret, jazz, and rock events. It's distributed at the tourist office, in bars, clubs, and cinemas. For information on what's happening locally in Arles and the towns of Provence, including festivals, exhibitions, and leisure activities, the online journal Ferandole is an excellent resource.

**Actes Sud.** This is the large publishing house's arts complex and cinema. ⊠ *Pl. Nina Berberova* ☎ *04–90–99–53–52* ⊕ *www.actes-sud.fr/cinemas-actes-sud.*

**Association du Méjan.** Founded in partnership with Actes Sud and housed in the beautiful Chapelle Saint-Martin du Méjan, this arts organization hosts a year-round program of classical and sacred music; a revolving series of exhibitions featuring painting, sculpture, and photography; and the superb Arles Jazz Festival, held every year in May. ⊠ *Pl. Nina-Berberova* ☎ *04–90–49–56–78* ⊕ *www.lemejan.com.*

**El Patio de Camargue.** Though Arles seems to be one big sidewalk café in warm weather, the place to drink is at the hip bar-restaurant El Patio de Camargue on the banks of the Rhône. They serve great tapas and you can hear Gypsy guitar, song, and dance from Chico and Los Gypsies, led by a founding member of the Gypsy Kings. ⊠ *49 Chemin de Barriol* ☎ *04–90–49–51–76* ⊕ *www.patiodecamargue.com.*

**Le Cargo de Nuit.** This is Arles's main venue for live jazz, reggae, and rock, with a dance floor next to the stage. A meal allows you reduced entry to see the show. ⊠ *7 av. Sadi-Carnot* ☎ *04–90–49–55–99* ⊕ *www.cargodenuit.com.*

## SHOPPING

Despite being chic and popular, Arles hasn't sprouted the rows of designer shops found in Aix-en-Provence and St-Rémy. Its stores remain small and eccentric and contain an overwhelming variety of Provençal goods.

Arles's colorful markets, with produce, regional products, clothes, fabrics, wallets, frying pans, and other miscellaneous items, take place every Saturday morning along the Boulevard des Lices, which flows into the Boulevard Clemenceau.

One of the centers of Provençal folklore, Arles is host to a bevy of parades featuring locals dressed in regional costume.

**Christian Lacroix.** You'll find Lacroix's exuberant scarves, accessories, and colorful sunglasses (Jackie O herself once bought a pair here) and a colorful selection of scented candles, stationery, and glassware in a range of gorgeous jewel colors, as well as some vintage items. ⊠ *52 rue de la République* ☎ *04–90–96–11–16* ⊕ *www.christian-lacroix.com.*

**Les Olivades.** Regional fabric is available at every turn, including a boutique for Les Olivades, Provence's decor central, with tastefully designed curtains, throw pillows, table linens, and a range of their famously luxe upholstery fabrics. ⊠ *4 bd. des Lices* ☎ *04–90–96–37–55* ⊕ *www.lesolivades.fr.*

**L'Occitane.** Having put Provence on the worldwide fragrance map, it's fun to shop close to where it all began. The products here are still made locally (in Manosque) using regional ingredients. ⊠ *58 rue de la République* ☎ *04–90–96–93–62* ⊕ *www.loccitane.com.*

**Marie Couture.** This store is a veritable gold mine for all things Arlési-ennes: beautiful old-fashioned fans, parasols and gloves made of local lace, scarves, jewelry, and accessories to re-create the traditional costume of the region or to wear on their own. There are also some lovely table-clothes and linens, every notion you can imagine, as well as a line of linge-rie. ⊠ *12 rue Jean Lebas* ☎ *04–90–96–61–02* ⊕ *www.mariecouture.net.*

**Pure Lavande.** This boutique specializes in a huge range of pure, plant-based cosmetics from Le Château de Bois, one of Provence's oldest and most venerable producers of fine lavender oil. The range includes face creams, hand and body lotions, toning gels, massage oil, bath milk, hydrosol, and much more, all made with the purest essential oils produced nearby. ⊠ *42 rue de la République* ☎ *04–90–52–01–35* ⊕ *www.lavandeandco.fr.*

**Souleiado.** The principal rival of Les Olivades, Souleiado, has a well-stocked boutique with a good selection of fabrics, linens for the table, and clothes for men and women. ⊠ *10 blvd. des Lices* ☎ *04–90–96–37–55* ⊕ *provence.souleiado.com.*

## ABBAYE DE MONTMAJOUR

Fodor'sChoice  *6 km (4 miles) north of Arles, direction Fontvieille.*

★  Once the spiritual center of the region and a major 12th-century pilgrimage stop (it contained a small relic of the true cross), the haunting ruins of the Abbaye de Montmajour still dominate this romantic windswept landscape.

### GETTING HERE AND AROUND

From Arles by car, take the D17 in the direction of Fontvieille and follow the signs to the Abbaye. Cartreize bus No. 29 runs from Arles 10 times weekdays and twice on weekends (€2).

### EXPLORING

Fodor'sChoice  **Abbaye de Montmajour.** This magnificent Romanesque abbey looming
★  over the marshlands north of Arles stands in partial ruin. Begun in the 10th century by a handful of Benedictine monks, the abbey grew according to an ambitious plan of church, crypt, and cloister and, under the management of worldly lay monks in the 17th century, became more sumptuous. When the Church ejected those monks, they sacked the place, and what remained was eventually sold off as scrap. A 19th-century medieval revival spurred a partial restoration, but portions are still in ruins. What remains is a spare and beautiful piece of Romanesque architecture. The cloister rivals that of St-Trophime in Arles for its balance, elegance, and air of mystical peace: Van Gogh, drawn to its isolation, came often to the abbey to reflect, but the strong mistral winds kept him from painting there. The interior, renovated by contemporary architect Rudy Ricciotti, is used for world-class contemporary art exhibitions, and the Chapelle St-Croix is open for visits—but you need to ask for the keys. ⊠ *On D17 northeast of Arles, rte. de Fontvielle, direction Fontvieille* ☎ *04–90–54–64–17* ⊕ *www.montmajour. monuments-nationaux.fr* ▨ *€7.50* ⊙ *Apr.–June, daily 9:30–6; July–Sept., daily 10–6:30; Oct.–Mar., daily 10–5.*

## TARASCON

*18 km (11 miles) north of Arles; 16 km (10 miles) west of St-Rémy.*

Tarascon's claim to fame is the mythical Tarasque, a monster said to emerge from the Rhône to gobble up children and cattle. Luckily, Saint Martha (Ste-Marthe), who washed up at Stes-Maries-de-la-Mer, tamed the beast with a sprinkle of holy water, after which the natives slashed it to pieces. This dramatic event is celebrated on the last weekend in June with a parade and was immortalized by Alphonse Daudet, who lived in nearby Fontvieille, in his tales of a folk hero known to all French schoolchildren as *Tartarin de Tarascon.* Unfortunately, a saint has not yet been born who can vanquish the fumes that emanate from Tarascon's enormous paper mill, and the hotel industry is suffering for it.

# Those Ubiquitous Provençal Cottons

Vivid medallion prints, soft floral sprigs, assertive paisley borders—they've come to define the Provençal Experience, these brightly patterned fabrics, with their sunny colors, naive prints, and country themes redolent of sunflowers and olive groves. And the southern tourist industry is eager to fulfill that expectation, swagging hotel rooms and restaurant dining rooms with busy Provençal patterns in counterpoint to the cool yellow stucco and burnished terra-cotta tiles. Nowadays, both in Provence and on the coast, it's all about country—back to the land with a vengeance.

These ubiquitous cottons are actually Indian prints (*indiennes*), first shipped into the ports of Marseille from exotic trade routes in the 16th century. Ancient Chinese wax-dyeing techniques—indigo dyes taking hold where the wax wasn't applied—evolved into wood-block stamps, their surfaces painted with mixed colors, then pressed carefully onto bare cotton. The colors were richer, the patterns more varied than any fabrics then available—and, what's more, they were easily reproduced.

They caught on like a wildfire in a mistral, and soon mills in Provence were creating local versions en masse. Too well, it seems. By the end of the 17th century, the popular cottons were competing with royal textile manufacturers. In 1686, under Louis XIV, the manufacture and marketing of Provençal cottons was banned.

All the ban did was contain the industry to Provence, where it developed in Marseille (franchised for local production despite the ban) and in Avignon, where the papal possessions were above royal law. Their rarity and

their prohibition made them all the sexier, and fashionable Parisians—even insiders in the Versailles court—flaunted the coveted contraband. By 1734, Louis XV cracked down on the hypocrisy, and the ban was sustained across France. The people protested. The cottons were affordable, practical, and brought a glimmer of color into the commoners' daily life. The king relented in 1758, and the peasants were free to swath their windows, tables, and hips with a limitless variety of color and print.

But because of the 72-year ban and that brief burgeoning of the southern countermarket, the tight-printed style and vivid colors remained allied in the public consciousness with the name "Provençal," and the region has embraced them as its own. If once they trimmed the windows of basic stone farmhouses and lined the quilted petticoats of peasants to keep off the chill, now the fabrics drape the beveled-glass French doors of the finest hôtels particuliers (private mansions) and grandest Riviera hotels.

Two franchises dominate the market and maintain high-visibility boutiques in all the best southern towns: Souleiado and Les Olivades. Fierce rivals, each claims exclusive authenticity—regional production, original techniques. Yet every tourist thoroughfare presents a hallucinatory array of goods, sewn into every salable form from lavender sachets to place mats to swirling skirts and bolero jackets. There are bread bags and bun warmers, undershorts and toilet kits, even olive-sprigged toilet-paper holders. For their fans around the world, these folkloric cotton fabric prints can't be beat.

**GETTING HERE AND AROUND**
By car, take the D999 (which turns into the D99) from Nîmes or the N570 from Arles. Local trains also stop at Tarascon on the Avignon-Centre-Arles line. Cartreize is an umbrella organization of buses shuttling between Arles and Tarascon (three buses daily except Sunday, €2.80, 30 minutes). Edgard buses also run from Nîmes (€1.50), although this is a longer journey (1¼ hours).

**VISITOR INFORMATION**
**Cartreize** ☎ 08–00–19–94–13 ⊕ www.lepilote.com. **Tarascon Tourist Office** ✉ Av. de la République ☎ 04–90–91–03–52 ⊕ www.tarascon.org.

EXPLORING
**Château.** Despite Tarascon's modern-day drawbacks, with the walls of its formidable Château plunging straight into the roaring Rhône, this ancient city on the river presents a daunting challenge to Beaucaire, its traditional enemy across the water. Begun in the 15th century by the noble Anjou family on the site of a Roman *castellum,* the castle grew through the generations into a splendid structure, crowned with both round and square towers and elegantly furnished. René the Good (1409–80) held court here, entertaining luminaries of the age. Nowadays the castle owes its superb preservation to its use, through the ensuing centuries, as a prison. It first served as such in the 17th century, and released its last prisoner in 1926. Complete with a moat, a drawbridge, and a lovely faceted spiral staircase, it retains its beautiful decorative Renaissance stonework and original cross-mullioned windows. ✉ *D970 at the riverfront, Blvd. du Roi René, direction Beaucaire* ☎ *04–90–91–01–93* ⊕ *chateau.tarascon.fr* ☜ *€7* ☉ *Feb.–May and Oct., daily 9:30–5:30; June–Sept., daily 9:30–6:30; Nov.–Jan., daily 9:30–5.*

# THE ALPILLES

Whether approaching from the damp lowlands of Arles and the Camargue or the pebbled vineyards around Avignon, the countryside changes dramatically as you climb into the arid heights of the low mountain range called the Alpilles (pronounced ahl-*pee*-yuh). A rough-hewn, rocky landscape rises into nearly barren limestone hills, the fields silvered with ranks of twisted olive trees and alleys of gnarled *amandiers* (almond trees). It's the heart of Provence, and is appealing not only for the antiquities in St-Rémy and the feudal ruins in Les Baux, but also for its mellow pace when the day's touring is done. Here, as much as anywhere in the south, is the place to slip into espadrilles, nibble from a bowl of olives, and attempt nothing more taxing than a lazy game of pétanque (lawn bowling). Hence, the countryside around St-Rémy is peppered with gentrified *gîtes* (guesthouses) and mas, and is one of the most sought-after sites for Parisians' (and Londoners') summer homes.

## FONTVIEILLE

*19 km (12 miles) northeast of Arles; 20 km (12½ miles) southeast of Tarascon.*

The village of Fontvieille (pronounced fohn-*vyay*-uh), set among the limestone hills, is best known as the home of 19th-century writer Alphonse Daudet.

### GETTING HERE AND AROUND

The nearest train station is in Arles, and from here Cartreize bus line runs several buses a day to Fontvieille (ligne 29). The direct trip takes about 30 minutes and costs €1.50 each way. By car, take the A54 to RN113, then RN568, direction Fontvieille.

### EXPLORING

**Moulin de Daudet** (*Daudet's Windmill*). Summering in the Château de Montauban, Daudet frequently climbed the windswept, pine-studded hilltop to the rustic old windmill that ground the local grain from 1814 to 1915. There the sweeping views of the Rhône valley and the Alpilles inspired his famous, folkloric short stories called *Lettres de Mon Moulin*. Today you can visit the well-preserved Moulin de Daudet, where there's a small museum devoted to his writings; you can walk upstairs to see the original milling system. ☎ 04–90–54–60–78 ✉ €3 ⊗ Apr.–Oct., daily 9:30–6. Closed Tue. and Nov.–Mar.

## LES BAUX-DE-PROVENCE

Fodor's Choice ★ *9 km (5½ miles) east of Fontvieille; 19 km (12 miles) northeast of Arles.*

When you first search the craggy hilltops for signs of Les Baux-de-Provence (pronounced *boh*), you may not quite be able to distinguish between bedrock and building, so naturally does the ragged skyline of towers and crenellation blend into the sawtooth jags of stone.

It was from this intimidating vantage point that the lords of Baux ruled throughout the 11th and 12th centuries over one of the largest fiefdoms in the south, commanding some 80 towns and villages. Their virtually unchallenged power led to the flourishing of a rich medieval culture: courtly love, troubadour songs, and knightly gallantry; but by the 13th century the lords of Baux had fallen from power, their stronghold destroyed.

Today Les Baux offers two faces to the world: the ghostly ruins of its fortress, once referred to as the ville morte (dead town), and its beautifully preserved Renaissance village. As dramatic in its perched isolation as Mont-St-Michel and St-Paul-de-Vence, this tiny château-village ranks as one of the most visited tourist sites in France. Lovely 16th-century stone houses, even their window frames still intact, shelter the shops, cafés, and galleries that line its car-free main street, overwhelmed by day with the smell of lavender-scented souvenirs. But don't deprive yourself for fear of crowds. Stay late in the day, after the tour buses leave; spend the night in one of its modest hotels; or come off-season, and you can experience its spectacular character—a tour-de-force blend of medieval color and astonishing natural beauty.

Rising up from a calcareous rock valley, the Château des Baux is the most extraordinary landmark of the "dead city" of Les-Baux-de-Provence.

### GETTING HERE AND AROUND

The easiest way to get to Les Baux is by car. Take the A7 until you reach exit 25, then the D99 between Tarascon and Cavaillon. Les Baux is 8 km (5 miles) south of St-Rémy by the D5 and the D27. Otherwise, Cartreize runs a bus between Arles and Les Baux (summer only, €2.30). Local trains stop at Tarascon (☎ *08–36–35–35–35* ⊕ *www.voyages-sncf.com*); from here in summer you can take a Cartrieze bus to St-Rémy and Les Baux (20 minutes, €1).

### VISITOR INFORMATION

**Les Baux-de-Provence Tourist Office** ⊠ *Maison du Roy* ☎ *04–90–54–34–39* ⊕ *www.lesbauxdeprovence.com.*

### EXPLORING

**Carrières de Lumières.** This vast old bauxite quarry has 66-foot-high stone walls that make a dramatic setting for a multimedia show in which thousands of images are projected onto the walls. Exhibitions change periodically, but recent showings have showcased the life and work of Vincent van Gogh, Monet, Renoir, and Chagall. ⊠ *Petite Rte. de Mailliane, D27* ☎ *04–90–54–47–37* ⊕ *www.carrieres-lumieres.com* ▧ *€9.50; €14.50 joint ticket with Château des Baux* ☉ *Apr.–Sept., daily 9:30–7:30; Oct.–Mar., daily 10–6.*

FAMILY **Château des Baux.** High above the Val d'Enfer, the 17-acre cliff-top sprawl of ruins is contained under the umbrella name the Château des Baux. At the entry, the Tour du Brau contains the **Musée d'Histoire des Baux,** a small collection of relics and models, which shelters a permanent music-and-slide show called *Van Gogh, Gauguin, Cézanne au Pays de l'Olivier,* featuring artworks depicting olive orchards in their infinite variety. From April through September there are fascinating medieval exhibitions: people dressed up in authentic costumes, displays of medieval crafts, and even a few jousting tournaments with handsome knights carrying fluttering silk tokens of their beloved ladies. The exit gives access to the wide and varied grounds, where the tiny **Chapelle St-Blaise** and towers mingle with skeletal ruins. ⊠ *Rue du Trencat* ☎ *04–90–54–55–56* ⊕ *chateau-baux-provence. com* 🎧 *€9.50 with audio guide; €14.50 joint ticket with Carrières de Lumières* ☉ *Mar.–May, daily 9:15–7:15; June–Aug., daily 9–8:15; Sept.–Nov., daily 9:30–6; Dec.–Feb., daily 10–5.*

**Hôtel de Manville.** Vestiges of the Renaissance remain in Les Baux, including the pretty Hôtel de Manville, built at the end of the 16th century by a wealthy Protestant family. Step into its inner court to admire the mullioned windows, Renaissance-style stained glass, and vaulted arcades. Today it serves as the *mairie* (town hall). Up and across the street, the striking remains of the 16th-century Protestant temple still bear a quote from Jean Calvin: "post tenebras lux," or "after the shadows, light." ⊠ *Grand Rue Frédéric Mistral.*

**Musée Yves-Brayer** (*Yves Brayer Museum*). In the Hôtel des Porcelet, which dates from the 16th century, the Musée Yves-Brayer shelters this local 20th-century artist's works. Figurative and accessible to the point of naiveté, his paintings highlight Italy, Spain, even Asia, but demonstrate most of all his love of Provence. Brayer's grave lies in the château cemetery. The house at No. 4 on Place de l'Eglise is also decoratred with frescoes by the artist. ⊠ *Pl. F. de Herain* ☎ *04–90–54–34–39* ⊕ *www. yvesbrayer.com* 🎧 *€5* ☉ *Apr.–Sept., daily 10–12:30 and 2–6:30; Oct.–Mar., Wed.–Mon. 10–12:30 and 2–5:30.*

**WHERE TO EAT AND STAY**

$$
MODERN FRENCH

✕ **Le Café des Baux.** For good-value gourmet cuisine, this intimate space in the heart of Les Baux, in view of the château walls, is your place. Well-presented and inventive dishes such as foie gras and sweet onion confit, apple-glazed lamb with crisped potato gratin and chanterelles, and salmon tartare with mango and green apple compare with those of pricier eateries. Don't miss the desserts: the chef's specialty. Popular and petit despite its terrace, you'll want to reserve in advance. $ *Average main: €23* ⊠ *Rue du Trencat* ☎ *04–90–54–52–69* ⊕ *www.cafedesbaux. com* 🍴 *Reservations essential* ☉ *Closed Nov.–Mar.*

$$$
HOTEL

🏨 **La Benvengudo.** With manicured grounds shaded by tall pines, this graceful shuttered mas feels centuries old but was built to look that way some 30 years ago. **Pros:** quiet and secluded; affordable; friendly service. **Cons:** some rooms could do with a face-lift; some rooms do not have refrigerators. $ *Rooms from: €160* ⊠ *Below Les Baux, direction Fontvieille, Vallon de l'Arcoule* ☎ *04–90–54–32–54* ⊕ *www. benvengudo.com* 🛏 *25 rooms, 2 apartments* ☉ *Closed Nov.–Mar.* 🍴 *No meals.*

$$$
HOTEL

🏨 **La Cabro d'Or.** Slightly less haughty (and expensive) than its elegant sister, L'Oustau de la Baumanière, with whom it shares a spa, the splendid five-star La Cabro d'Or maintains a plush farmhouse chic appeal. **Pros:** the best of both worlds: high luxury in the countryside. **Cons:**

it's a walk to the spa (but shuttles are available). *Rooms from: €200 ✉ Mas Carita, Route d'Arles ☎ 04–90–54–33–21 ⊕ www.lacabrodor.com ⇨ 25 rooms ꟾ No meals.*

$ B&B/INN **La Reine Jeanne.** Churchill and Jacques Brel, Sartre and de Beauvoir (who had separate rooms but a shared balcony—and what a balcony) were all happy guests at this modest but majestically placed inn nicely situated to provide rugged views of the château up the street. **Pros:** views are lovely; a *chambre familiale* sleeps four. **Cons:** some rooms are tiny; only two rooms have (small) balconies. *Rooms from: €60 ✉ Grande Rue ☎ 04–90–54–32–06 ⊕ www.la-reinejeanne.com ⇨ 7 rooms, 1 apartment ⊙ Closed Jan. No meals.*

$$ B&B/INN **Le Prince Noir.** Each of the three rooms of this unique bed-and-breakfast is carved right out of the stone face but the semi-troglodyte effect is softened by jute carpets, warm woods, and unbeatable views over the Val d'Enfer. **Pros:** stunning vistas from each window; unbeatable service. **Cons:** rooms are cold in the winter; few amenities. *Rooms from: €110 ✉ Rue de Lorme, Cité Haute ☎ 04–90–54–39–57 ⊕ www.leprincenoir.com ⇨ 1 room, 1 suite, 1 studio ⊙ Closed mid-Jan.–Feb. Breakfast.*

$$$$ HOTEL Fodor's Choice ★ **L'Oustau de la Baumanière.** Spread over three historic buildings just outside the village of Les Baux, guest rooms at this fabled hotel are the last word in Provençal chic—breezy, private, and beautifully furnished with antiques yet done with a contemporary flair. **Pros:** low-key in style and flair with lots of amenities; one of the greatest restaurants in Provence. **Cons:** so low-key, with some rooms bordering on generic, you wonder if it is worth it; can be hit-and-miss with service. *Rooms from: €370 ✉ Val d'Enfer ☎ 04–90–54–33–07 ⊕ www.oustaudebaumaniere.com ⇨ 17 rooms, 13 suites ⊙ Hotel and restaurant closed Jan.–Feb.; restaurant closed Wed. and Thurs. in Mar., and Oct.–mid-Dec. No meals.*

## ST-RÉMY-DE-PROVENCE

Fodor's Choice ★ *11 km (7 miles) northeast of Les Baux; 25 km (15½ miles) northeast of Arles; 24 km (15 miles) south of Avignon.*

There are other towns as pretty as St-Rémy-de-Provence, and others in more dramatic or picturesque settings. Ruins can be found throughout the south, and so can authentic village life. Yet something felicitous has happened in this market town in the heart of the Alpilles—a steady infusion of style, of art, of imagination—all brought by people with a respect for local traditions and a love of Provençal ways. Here, more than anywhere, you can meditate quietly on antiquity, browse redolent markets with basket in hand, peer down the very row of plane trees you remember from a Van Gogh, and also enjoy urbane galleries, cosmopolitan shops, and specialty food boutiques. An abundance of chic choices in restaurants, mas, and even châteaux awaits you; the almond and olive groves conceal dozens of stone-and-terra-cotta gîtes, many with pools. In short, St-Rémy has been gentrified through and through, and is now a sort of arid, southern Martha's Vineyard or, perhaps, the Hamptons of Provence.

St-Rémy has always attracted the right sort of people. First established by an indigenous Celtic-Ligurian people who worshipped the god Glan, the village Glanum was adopted by the Greeks of Marseille in the 2nd and 3rd centuries BC, who brought in sophisticated building techniques. Rome moved in to help ward off Hannibal, and by the 1st century BC Caesar had taken full control. The Romans eventually fell, but the town that grew up next to their ruins came to be an important market town, and wealthy families built fine hôtels (mansions) in its center—among them the family De Sade (whose distant black-sheep relation held forth in the Lubéron at Lacoste). Another famous native son, the eccentric doctor, scholar, and astrologer Michel Nostradamus (1503–66), is credited by some as having predicted much of the modern age.

Perhaps the best known of St-Rémy's visitors was the ill-fated Vincent van Gogh. Shipped unceremoniously out of Arles at the height of his madness (and creativity), he had himself committed to the asylum St-Paul-de-Mausolée and wandered through the ruins of Glanum during the last year of his life.

**GETTING HERE AND AROUND**

Like Les Baux-de-Provence, the easiest way to get to St-Rémy is by car. Take the A7 until you reach exit 25, then the D99 between Tarascon and Cavaillon, direction St-Rémy on the D5. Otherwise, in summer Cartreize runs an Arles–St-Rémy–Les Baux bus service (daily except Sunday, €2.30). Local trains stop at nearby Tarascon, and from here you can take a Cartreize bus to St-Rémy (20 minutes, €1).

**VISITOR INFORMATION**

**St-Rémy Tourist Office** ⊠ *Pl. Jean-Jaurès* 🕾 *04–90–92–05–22* ⊕ *www.saintremy-de-provence.com.*

**EXPLORING**

**Collégiale St-Martin.** St-Rémy is wrapped by a lively commercial boulevard, lined with shops and cafés and anchored by its 19th-century church Collégiale St-Martin. Step inside to see the magnificent 5,000-pipe modern organ, one of the loveliest in Europe. Rebuilt to 18th-century specifications in the early 1980s, it has the flexibility to interpret new and old music with pure French panache; you can listen to it Saturday afternoon at 5:30 from July through September for free. ⊠ *Pl. de la République.*

FAMILY **Glanum.** A slick visitor center prepares you for entry into the ancient village of Glanum, with scale models of the site in its various heydays. A good map and an English brochure guide you stone by stone through the maze of foundations, walls, towers, and columns that spread across a broad field; helpfully, Greek sites are noted by numbers, Roman ones by letters. Glanum is across the street from Les Antiques and set back from the D5, and the only parking is in a dusty roadside lot on the D5 south of town (in the direction of Les Baux). ⊠ *Rte. des Baux de Provence, off the D5, direction Les Baux* 🕾 *04–90–92–23–70* ⊕ *www. glanum.monuments-nationaux.fr* 🖼 *€7.50* ☉ *Apr.–Aug., daily 10–6:30; Sept., Tues.–Sun., 10–6:30; Oct.–Mar., Tues.–Sun. 10–5.*

**Les Antiques.** Two of the most miraculously preserved classical monuments in France are simply called Les Antiques. Dating from 30 BC, the **Mausolée** (mausoleum), a wedding-cake stack of arches and columns, lacks nothing but a finial on top, and is dedicated to a Julian, probably Caesar Augustus. A few yards away stands another marvel: the **Arc Triomphal,** dating from AD 20.

**Musée Estrine Présence Van Gogh.** The 18th-century Hôtel Estrine is now the Musée Estrine Présence Van Gogh and has many reproductions of the artist's work, along with letters to his brother Theo and exhibitions of contemporary art, much of it inspired by Vincent. It also houses temporary exhibitions and a permanent collection dedicated to the father of Cubism, Albert Gleizes, who lived in St-Remy for the last 15 years of his life. ✉ *Hôtel Estrine, 8 rue Lucien Estrine* ☎ *04–90–92–34–72* 🌐 *www.musee-estrine.fr* 🎟 *€4.80* 🕒 *May–Sept., Tues. and Thurs.–Sun. 10–12:30 and 2–7, Wed. 10–7; Mar., Apr., and Oct.–Feb., Tues.–Sun. 10:30–12:30 and 2–6.*

**St-Paul-de-Mausolé.** You can cut across the fields from Glanum to St-Paul-de-Mausolé, the isolated asylum where Van Gogh spent the last year of his life (1889–90). Enter quietly: the hospital shelters psychiatric patients to this day, all of them women. You're free to walk up the beautifully manicured garden path to the church and its jewel-box Romanesque **cloister,** where the artist found womblike peace. ✉ *Chemin Saint-Paul* ☎ *04–90–92–77–00* 🌐 *www.saintpauldemausole.fr* 🎟 *€4.50* 🕒 *Apr.–Sept., daily 9:30–6:45; Oct., Nov., and Mar., daily 10:15–5.*

**Vieille Ville.** Within St-Rémy's fast-moving traffic loop, a labyrinth of narrow streets leads you away from the action and into the slow-moving inner sanctum of the Vieille Ville. Here trendy, high-end shops mingle pleasantly with local life, and the buildings, if gentrified, blend in unobtrusively.

## WHERE TO EAT

$$ BISTRO 🍴 **Bistrot Découverte.** Claude and Dana Douard were happy to collaborate with some of the greatest chefs of our time before getting away from the big city lights to open this bistro-wine bar hotspot in the center of St-Rémy. The wine selection is magnificent, and so is the simple food based on top-notch local ingredients. Try the braised veal in wild-lemon sauce served on fresh tagliatelle pasta, or the made-to-order beef tartare. [$] *Average main: €18* ✉ *19 bd. Victor Hugo* ☎ *04–90–92–34–49* 🌐 *www.bistrotdecouverte.com* ✍ *Reservations essential* 🕒 *Closed Oct.–mid-Mar.*

$$$$ FRENCH 🍴 **Bistrot d'Eygalières.** Belgian chef Wout Bru's understated restaurant near St-Rémy has gained a reputation (and Michelin stars) for light and subtly balanced cuisine like sole with goat cheese, lobster salad with candied tomatoes, and foie gras carpaccio with summer truffles. Gastronomes who have indulged too much can stagger upstairs to the seven chic and comfortable guest rooms. [$] *Average main: €50* ✉ *Rue de la République, 10 km (6 miles) southeast of St-Rémy on D99 and then on D24, Eygalières* ☎ *04–90–90–60–34* 🌐 *www.chezbru.com* ✍ *Reservations essential* 🕒 *No lunch Mon. and Tues. Closed two wks. in Nov. and two wks. in Feb.*

### DID YOU KNOW?

No matter that St-Rémy-de-Provence is called "the Hamptons of Provence" (due to its chic shops and restaurants), the town has succeeded in remaining true to its Provençal roots.

$$ BISTRO 🍴 **L'Aile ou la Cuisse.** A popular place for lunch or dinner, this modern bistro and terrace in the heart of the old village draws a lively mix of locals, expats, and tourists looking for authentic market-driven meals. A small but satisfying menu is generously laced with local delicacies—savory ragout of wild boar, cod with pureed local vegetables and tapenade-laden croutons, and poached-egg cocotte with foie gras cream and turmeric-balsamic toasts. A generous wine list offers plenty of local choices by the glass and the dessert tray in the window—another big draw—features tantalizing concoctions, like a classic chantilly-topped baba al rhum and creamy *tarte au citron*. Service can be slow but it's always friendly. [$] *Average main: €22* ✉ *5 rue de la Commune* ☎ *04–32–62–00–25* ✍ *Reservations essential* ⏲ *Closed Sun. May–Sept.; closed Sun. and Mon. Oct.–Apr.*

$$$$ FRENCH 🍴 **La Maison Jaune.** This 18th-century retreat with a Michelin star in the Vieille Ville draws crowds of summer people to its pretty roof terrace, with accents of sober stone and lively contemporary furniture both indoors and out. The look reflects the cuisine: with vivid flavors and a cool, contained touch, chef François Perraud prepares fresh Mediterranean sea bream, bouillabaisse, grilled lamb from Provence, and other specialties on his seasonally changing menus. [$] *Average main: €36* ✉ *15 rue Carnot* ☎ *04–90–92–56–14* 🌐 *www.lamaisonjaune.info* ✍ *Reservations essential* ⏲ *Closed Sun. and Mon. Mar.–June and Sept.–Feb.*

### WHERE TO STAY

$$$$ B&B/INN 🏨 **Château de Roussan.** Philippe Roussel, a descendant of the 17th-century owners, has filled his château with lovingly polished antique family furniture, buffed the red clay floors to their original shine, and ensured that guest rooms are light and airy and the bathrooms equipped with all the modern trinkets. **Pros:** eager-to-please, house-proud staff are happy to recount the hotel's history; rooms are very quiet. **Cons:** some rooms are small; elevator doesn't provide access to all rooms; restaurant closed three days a week in low season. [$] *Rooms from: €220* ✉ *D99, Rte. de Tarascon* ☎ *04–90–90–79–00* 🌐 *www.chateauderoussan.com* 🛏 *16 rooms, 4 suites* ⏲ *Restaurant closed Sun.–Tues. low season* 🍽 *No meals.*

$$$$ HOTEL Fodor's Choice ★ 🏨 **Château des Alpilles.** Reached via a lane of majestic plane trees and set on eight luxuriant acres of parkland, cypress groves, and gardens, this gracious mas and château date back to medieval times, yet underwent a complete face-lift when the present owners bought the estate in the 1970s. **Pros:** service anticipates your every need; gorgeous Italian designer linens; lovely breakfast on the terrace. **Cons:** outside the city center; some rooms are small and can be stuffy. [$] *Rooms from: €340* ✉ *Route de Rougadou* ☎ *04–90–92–03–33* 🌐 *www.chateaudesalpilles.com* 🛏 *17 rooms, 4 suites* ⏲ *Closed Jan.–mid-Mar.* 🍽 *No meals.*

$$$$ HOTEL 🏨 **Hôtel de l'Image.** Set on a four-acre park with a view of the Alpilles mountain range, this stylish hotel in the heart of St-Rémy offers both city and countryside in one modern package. **Pros:** modern decor; fun and dynamic vibe; gorgeous estate; genuine welcome. **Cons:** public salons seem more photograph galleries than welcoming hotel. [$] *Rooms from: €250* ✉ *36 bd. Victor Hugo* ☎ *04–90–92–51–50* 🌐 *www.hotel-image.fr* 🛏 *25 rooms, 7 suites* ⏲ *Closed Nov.–Mar.* 🍽 *No meals.*

### NIGHTLIFE AND THE ARTS

**Collégiale St-Martin.** At 5:30 every Saturday in July, August, and September, you can hear the magnificent organ of Collégiale St-Martin in a free recital, often featuring the boy wonder *organiste-titulaire* Jean-Pierre Lecaudey. ⊠ *Pl. de la République.*

**Festival A-Part.** For nearly two months of the summer, this Alpilles-wide contemporary arts festival fills nearly 15 venues in several towns, most prominently in St-Rémy. ⊕ *www.festival-apart-2013.com.*

**La Galine.** A very young crowd gathers here (on Friday and Saturday nights only) to eat by the pool and dance into the night. ⊠ *Chemin Cante Perdrix et Galine* ☎ *04–90–92–00–03* ⊕ *www.lagaline.com.*

### SHOPPING

Every Wednesday morning St-Rémy hosts one of the most popular and picturesque markets in Provence, during which the Place de la République and narrow Old Town streets overflow with herbs and spices, olive oil by the vat, and tapenade by the scoop, as well as fabrics and brocante (collectibles). There's a smaller version Saturday morning.

**Christallerie Alban Gaillard.** Colorful, whimsical, elegant—these sculptural creations of handblown glass range from exquisite perfume flacons and decorative paperweights to everything you need to impress at the dining table. ⊠ *1405 Rte. de Maillane* ☎ *04–32–60–10–28* ⊕ *www. cristalleriedart.com.*

**Joël Durand Chocolatier.** Known for his creamy ganaches, Joël Durand carries a range of gourmet chocolates, nut creams, toffee, and marmalades made in Provence from tree-ripened fruit. ⊠ *3 bd. Victor Hugo* ☎ *04–90–92–38–25* ⊕ *www.chocolat-durand.com.*

Fodor'sChoice
★
**Lilamand.** Much more than just a sweet shop, this historical *confiseur* dates back to 1866 and is in its fifth generation of family ownership on the same St-Rémy premises. Makers of the famous Provençal *calisson*, an almond-shaped marzipan confection, as well as a gorgeous array of candied fruits—including everything from cherries and strawberries to kiwis, fennel, and even whole pumpkins—from a recipe credited to Nostradamus (a native son). There are also fruit syrups, jams, chocolates, and regional honey. A tour of the factory and a stop in the beautiful boutique make for a highly pleasurable hour or two. ⊠ *5 av. Albert Schweitzer* ☎ *04–90–92–11–08* ⊕ *www. confiserie-lilamand.com.*

**Souleiado.** The quintessentially Provençal boutique, Souleiado has high-end fashions, fabrics, housewares, and linens, all made in Provence. ⊠ *Pl. de l'Église, 2 av. de la Résistance* ☎ *04–90–92–45–90* ⊕ *www. souleiado.com.*

# THE VAUCLUSE

with Avignon

# WELCOME TO THE VAUCLUSE

## TOP REASONS TO GO

★ **The walled city of Avignon:** While most exciting during the theater festival at the Palais des Popes in July, Avignon is surprisingly youthful and vibrant year-round.

★ **Châteauneuf-du-Pape:** Probably the most evocative Côtes du Rhône vineyard but just one of many villages in this area where you can sample exceptional wines.

★ **Lovely lavender:** Get hip-deep in purple by touring the Lavender Route between the Abbaye de Senanque and the historic towns of Sault and Forcalquier.

★ **The sky's no limit!:** Experience the perched villages of the region, including Gordes and Bonnieux, in a patchwork landscape right out of a medieval Book of Hours.

★ **Seeing red in Roussillon:** With its ocher cliffs that change tones—copper, pink, rust—depending on the time of day, this town is a gigantic ruby embedded in the Vaucluse bedrock.

**1 Avignon.** Avignon's most famous bridge—the subject of a French children's song—now stretches only halfway across the river, so don't make the mistake of trying to drive across it. Take the next bridge to L'Île de la Barthelasse, an amazingly rural setting minutes from the city, where you can ride a bike through vineyards and overnight in lovely auberges.

**2** Haut Vaucluse.

This region' rolling hills and rock-strewn moonscapes, presided over by Mont Ventoux, Provence's highest peak, are a graceful backdrop for vineyards, orchards, fields of purple lavender, perched villages, and some splendid ruins. There's much to see here, so plan to spend some time and do as the natives do—slow down, savor, enjoy.

**3** The Sorgue Valley.

If you're fond of antiques, plan to join the festive hordes trawling for treasures at the famous Sunday flea market in L'Isle-sur-la-Sorgue. After exploring the fancier *antiquaires* (antiques stores) in town, enjoy an idyllic lunch by one of the town watermills, then track down the "source" of the River Sorgue in the famous spring of Fontaine-de-Vaucluse—the fifth largest in the world.

**4** The Luberon. Like so many Luberon villages, Gordes might seem a touch too perfect at first sight. Persist and you can find real charm in its narrow, hilltop streets. To get off the beaten track, head to once-upon-a-time Oppède-le-Vieux, Bonnieux, and Lacoste, or stroll through Apt's colorful Saturday market for a taste of la vraie Provence.

## GETTING ORIENTED

The largest city on the banks of the Rhône after Lyon, Avignon is one of the most interesting places in the South of France: with a feast of medieval streets, crenellated palaces, and sweet museums, it is an ideal gateway to explore the lower Rhône area. Just up the highway are the sun-scorched vineyards of the Côtes du Rhône and the Roman ruins of Vaison-la-Romaine and Orange; just east is the perfectly picturesque Luberon countryside; 20 miles north lie the storybook hilltop villages of the Haut Vaucluse.

Updated
by Jennifer
Ladonne

For many, the Vaucluse is the only true Provence—one vast Cézanne masterpiece, where sun-bleached hills and fields are tapestries of green-and-black grapevines and silver-gray olives, and rolling rows of lavender harmonize with mountains looming purple against an indigo sky. It is here, in his beloved Luberon, that British author Peter Mayle discovered and described the simple pleasures of breakfasting on melons still warm from the sun, buying fresh-dug truffles from furtive farmers in smoke-filled bars, and life without socks. The world shared his epiphany, and vacationers now flock here in search of the same sensual way of life.

As if an invisible hand had drawn lines dividing this region into three, the Vaucluse changes character dramatically from north to south, west to east. East of Avignon, you can find sun-scorched *villages perchés* (perched villages) that lord over the patchwork valleys—Gordes, Bonnieux, Ménerbes, and ocher-tinted Roussillon. Though mass tourism has given them something of a Disney feel, you need only wander off the main shopping drags to get a sense of medieval life in the labyrinthine back alleys and pollard-shaded squares resonant with the splashing of ancient fountains. The otherwise tranquil town of L'Isle-sur-la-Sorgue has become a magnet for international antiques fiends, reaching its peak of activity on Sunday, when the entire town turns into a giant *brocante* (flea market).

Anchored by the magnificent papal stronghold of Avignon, the glories of the Vaucluse region spread luxuriantly eastward of the Rhône. Its famous vineyards seduce connoisseurs, and its Roman ruins in Orange and Vaison-la-Romaine draw scholars and arts lovers. Plains dotted with orchards of olives, apricots, and cherries give way, around formidable Mont Ventoux, to a rich and wild mountainous terrain, then flow into the primeval Luberon, made a household name by Peter Mayle. The antiques market in L'Isle-sur-la-Sorgue makes for a terrific Sunday excursion, as does the nearby Fontaine-de-Vaucluse, a dramatic spring cascade (outside drought season). But the Luberon and its villages perched high up in the hills are a world of their own and worth allowing time for—perhaps even your whole vacation. Note that the Pont du Gard, the superbly preserved Gallo-Roman aqueduct, is a 30-minute drive west of Avignon, and that Arles, Nîmes, and the windswept Camargue are a stone's throw to the south and west.

Just north lies a wine-lover's paradise, as the Côtes du Rhône produce some of the world's most muscular vintages: Châteauneuf-du-Pape and Beaumes-de-Venise are two of the best-known villages, though the names Vacqueyras, Gigondas, and St-Joseph also give wine buffs goose bumps. Despite their renown, this area feels off the beaten track even in midsummer, when it's favored by the French rather than foreign tourists. A brisk wind cools things off in summer, as do the broad-leaved plane trees that shade the sidewalk tables at village restaurants and cafés.

East of here, the countryside grows increasingly dramatic, first with the jaw-droppingly jagged Dentelles de Montmirail, whose landscape is softened by olive groves and orchards, then the surprisingly lush Mont Ventoux, best known as the Tour de France's most difficult stage. Along the way, you'll find villages such as Séguret and Vaison-la-Romaine, where you can sample the slow-paced local lifestyle over a game of pétanque or a lingering apéro. And all this lies a stone's throw from thriving Avignon, its feudal fortifications sheltering a lively arts scene and a culture determinedly young.

No matter what sights are on their lists, vacationers love to retreat to lavishly renovated farmhouses with cypress-shaded pools or to the luxurious inns that cater to people fleeing Avignon's smog. There are budget accommodations, too, in the form of cheerful *chambres d'hôtes* and modest but well-run hotels, which often have good restaurants. Given the intense summer heat and the distance from the sea, swimming pools and air-conditioning are de rigueur, with a few exceptions higher up in the mountains, where there is a refreshing breeze.

Geographically speaking, in fact, Avignon, as well as the Roman centers and papal vineyards to its north, lies in arid lowlands, and getting from point to point through these flats can be uninspiring. It's to the east that the real Vaucluse rises up into the green-studded slopes of Mont Ventoux and the Luberon. Here, the back roads are beautiful—the temptation to abandon your rental car in favor of foot travel is often irresistible. Give in; the combination of the smells of wild thyme, lavender, wet stone, and dry pine can be as heady as a Châteauneuf-du-Pape.

## PLANNER

### WHEN TO GO

High heat and high season hit in July and August with a wallop: this lovely region is anything but undiscovered, thanks in part to Peter Mayle's revelations (he took a break from Provence to avoid the crowds he inspired, then relocated to the quieter south face of the Luberon). June and September are still intense, but better.

Low season falls between mid-November and mid-March, when many restaurants and hotels take two or three months off. That leaves spring and fall: if you arrive after Easter, the flowers are in full bloom, the air cool, and the sun warm, and you'll still be able to book a table on the terrace. The same goes for October and early November, when the hills of the Luberon turn rust and gold, and game and wild mushrooms figure on every menu.

### PLANNING YOUR TIME

The Vaucluse is more refined than its flashy counterpart, the Côte d'Azur, so take advantage of its gastronomic blessings and sign up for a wine tasting or cooking course. Hôtel de la Mirande in Avignon offers a superb roster for 6–12 people, in English, including courses around truffles, pastry, cheese, and wine. Or at La Maison sur la Sorgue, the owners will arrange visits (and be the designated drivers) to several of the local vineyards for a dose of viticulture and tasting. While you're in L'Isle-sur-la-Sorgue, arrange to stay over on a Saturday and wake up to the chatter and clatter of the Sunday antiques vendors. Avignon is almost a never-ending festival: Les Hivernales dance festival (February); Jazz Festival (July and August); Arts Festival (July); Le Off Festival (also July); and the Gastronomy Festival (September). On another musical note for July: Lacoste has a successful arts festival; Orange takes on opera; and noted dance troops take part in Vaison-la-Romaine's Dance Festival, held at the town's Roman theater. But if you want to tiptoe through the best lavender, keep in mind that claims of bizarre weather patterns are now faulted for smaller, less superior crops, so you'll want to drive through the Luberon during July to take in endless rows of glorious lavender before it's too late.

### GETTING HERE AND AROUND

If arriving in Avignon by TGV train (Paris–Avignon, 2 hours 40 minutes; Nice–Avignon, 3 hours 15 minutes), arrange for a rental car prior to arrival. Driving is the best choice, allowing you to control your schedule and not fall slave to a public system that isn't on par with that of the Alpes–Maritimes.

Even anxious drivers can find roads linking one village to the next rather easy (pleasant even!) to handle—the only downside is that the driver won't be able to take in all those breathtaking views, like when driving from Le Barroux down into the Luberon.

Traveling by train in the region can be done from L'Isle-sur-la-Sorgue, Cavaillon, Aix, Arles, Orange, and Avignon; Vaucluse regional buses are few and far between with infrequent schedules. Consult ⊕ *www.tcra.fr* or ⊕ *www.beyond.fr* for up-to-the-minute listings and fares for Avignon, Orange, Vaison, Carpentras, Manosque, Castellane, and other bus routes.

## AIR TRAVEL

Marseille's Marignane airport—known as Marseille Provence or MP—is served by frequent flights from Paris and London; it's about an hour's drive from Avignon.

The smaller Avignon Caumont airport has frequent daily flights from Paris and Clermont Ferrand.

**Air Travel Information** **Avignon Caumont airport** ⊠ *141 allée de la Chartreuse, Montfavet, southeast of Avignon* ☎ *04-90-81-51-51* ⊕ *www.avignon.aeroport.fr.* **Marignane airport** ☎ *04-42-14-14-14* ⊕ *www.marseille.aeroport.fr.*

## BOAT TRAVEL

Cruises Mireio, operating out of Avignon, offers various outings to such local sites as Arles, Tarascon, and Châteauneuf-du-Pape. Trips cost from €8 (for a 45-minute "promenade") to €69, and can include lunch, dinner, and dancing.

New riverboat cruises for two to four people (champagne optional) depart from the Pont d'Avignon.

**Boat Travel Information** **Les Croisières Mireio** ⊠ *Allées de L'Oulle, Avignon* ☎ *04-90-85-62-25* ⊕ *www.mireio.net.*

## BUS TRAVEL

Major bus transport companies carry travelers from surrounding cities into towns not accessible by rail; bus and rail services usually dovetail. Avignon's *gare routière* (bus station) has the heaviest interregional traffic.

A reasonable network of private bus services (called, confusingly enough, *cars*) links places not served or poorly served by trains. Ask for bus schedules at train stations and tourist offices. Avignon has a sizable station, with posted schedules.

TransVaucluse has a booth just outside the Avignon train station, offering daily bus excursions into different regions—for instance, the Luberon, Vaison, and the Alpilles. The main destinations serviced to/from the Avignon bus station (10 to 20 buses daily) are Orange (€3, 45–60 minutes) and Carpentras (€2, 45 minutes). Five or fewer buses daily connect with: Aix-en-Provence (€7.60, 1½ hours), Apt (€5, 1½ hours), Arles (€6.60, 1½ hours), Cavaillon (€2, 1 hour), Nîmes (€1.50, 1½ hours), and Pont du Gard (€1.50, 1 hour).

Bus companies serving the Vaucluse have essentially all merged into TransVaucluse to provide more routes, easier schedules, and cheaper fares. You can access the Luberon villages, Cavaillon, L'Isle-sur-la-Sorge, Aix-en-Provence, and some of the hard-to-reach hilltop villages like Bonnieux from the main Avignon bus station on Avenue Monclar with TransVaucluse buses. Some destinations need a transfer.

**Bus Travel Information** **Cars Lieutaud** ☎ *04-90-86-36-75* ⊕ *www.cars-lieutaud.fr.* **Gare Routière** ⊠ *5 av. Monclar, at Bd. St-Roch, Avignon* ☎ *04-90-82-07-35.* **TransVaucluse** ⊕ *vmobile.vaucluse.fr.*

## CAR TRAVEL

The A6/A7 toll (*péage*) expressway channels all traffic from Paris to the south. Orange A7 splits to the southeast and leads directly to Avignon and D10 (in the direction of Apt), which dives straight east into the Luberon. To reach Vaison and the Mont Ventoux region from Avignon, head northeast toward Carpentras on D942. D36 jags south from D10 and leads you on a gorgeous chase over the backbone of the Luberon, via Bonnieux and Lourmarin; from there it's a straight shot to Aix and Marseille or to the Côte d'Azur. Or you can shoot back west up D973 to Cavaillon and Avignon.

With spokes shooting out in every direction from Avignon and A7, you'll have no problem accessing the Vaucluse. The main *routes nationales* (national routes, or secondary highways) offer fairly direct links via D942 toward Orange and Mont Ventoux and via D10 into the Luberon. Negotiating the roads to L'Isle-sur-la-Sorgue and Fontaine-de-Vaucluse requires a careful mix of map and sign reading, often at high speeds around suburban *giratoires* (rotaries). But by the time you strike out into the hills and the tiny roads—one of the best parts of the Vaucluse—give yourself over to road signs and pure faith. As is the case throughout France, directions are indicated by village name only, with route numbers given as a small-print afterthought. Of course, this means you have to recognize the minor villages en route.

If you have access to the Internet while traveling, Vinci Autoroutes is a good website to consult. It not only gives directions for highways and village roads in southern France, but it also indicates weather conditions and traffic problems. Although it's in French, it's not difficult to follow. Keep in mind that *péages* are toll booths and *aires* are gas and rest stops.

**Car Travel Information Vinci Autoroutes.** ⊕ *www.vinci-autoroutes.com.*

## TRAIN TRAVEL

Trains arrive in Marseille from many main cities, including Paris, Strasbourg, Nantes, and Bordeaux. Those from Paris and Strasbourg pass through Orange and Avignon. The quickest train connection remains the TGV *Méditerranée* line that arrives in Avignon after a 2-hour, 40-minute trip from Paris. These TGV trains then connect with Nîmes (from €8.70, 18 minutes), Marseille (from €15.30, 35 minutes), and Nice (from €30.80, 3 hours). From Avignon's main rail station, the Gare Avignon Centre, connections include Orange (€5.70, 15 minutes), Arles (€7.60, 20 minutes), and L'Isle-sur-la-Sorgue. Another big rail nexus is the city of Orange, but note that the center city is a 10-minute walk from the train station. Also be aware that it costs €0.34 a minute for train information at the SNCF number. After a recorded message, there is a pause. At this moment say the words *Billet Loisir* (pronounced Bee-yay Lwah-zeer); this directs you to a service agent. Ticket prices range according to time of day and season, so look online before speaking with an agent.

**Train Travel Information SNCF** ☎ *3635 France, 33–892–35–35–35 outside France* ⊕ *www.sncf.com.* **TGV** ☎ *3635* ⊕ *www.tgv.com.*

# The Vaucluse

Forcalquier

Manosque

Courbières

La Tour-D'Aigues

Banon

Simiane

Reillanne

Villelaure

Viens

Caseneuve

La Bastide-des-Jourdans

Grambois

Cadenet

Lagarde-d'Apt

Fort de Buoux

Saignon

Lourmarin

Apt

Buoux

Bonnieux

Silvacane

Sault

Mormoiron

Abbaye de Sénanque

Roussillon

Ménerbes

Lacoste

Mont Ventoux

Bédoin

Crillon-le-Brave

Venasque

Fontaine de Vaucluse

Gordes

Coustellet

Oppède-le-Vieux

Notre-Dame du Groseau

Caromb

Pernes-les-Fontaines

Lagnes

Cavaillon

Vaison-la-Romaine

Crestet

Malaucène

Carpentras

L'Isle-sur-la-Sorgue

Séguret

Gigondas

Le Barroux

Beaumes-de-Venise

Velleron

Le Thor

Caumont

Vacqueyras

Bedarrides

Vedène

Sorgues

Orange

Châteauneuf-du-Pape

Avignon *see detail map*

Noves

Châteaurenard

Eyragues

St-Rémy-de-Provence

Maussane-les-Alpilles

Villeneuve-lès-Avignon

Graveson

Les Baux-de-Provence

Fontvieille

Barbentane

Bagnols-sur-Cèze

Tarascon

Beaucaire

Bellegarde

Pont-du-Gard

Remoulins

MONT VENTOUX

PLATEAU DE VAUCLUSE

MONTAGNE DU LUBERON

ALPES DE HAUTE PROVENCE

DRÔME

BOUCHES-DU-RHÔNE

GARD

6 mi

6 km

## VISITOR INFORMATION

The ADT Vaucluse Tourisme accepts written queries and calls; specify your needs by category (lodging or restaurants, for example).

Information **L'ADT Vaucluse Tourisme** ⊠ *12 rue Collège de la Croix, Avignon* ☎ *04–90–80–47–00* ⊕ *www.provenceguide.com.*

## RESTAURANTS

As the cultural capital of the Vaucluse, Avignon might logically be considered the culinary capital, too. Visit during the July theater festival, however, and you'll have the opposite impression. Sunny sidewalk tables spill out temptingly onto the streets, but nearly all serve the kind of food designed for people on tight schedules: salads, pizzas, and charcuterie plates, often of indifferent quality. For more generous and imaginative Provençal food, you will have to seek out Avignon's few culinary gems or scour the countryside, where delightful meals can be had in roadside restaurants, renovated farmhouses, and restaurants with chefs whose talents are as stunning as the hilltop settings where they operate. Be sure to indulge in the sun-drenched local wines from the Luberon, the Côtes du Ventoux, and the Côtes du Rhône (especially its lesser-known vineyards), and if a full bottle seems too much for two people, order one of the 50 cl bottles now popular here (the equivalent of two-thirds of a regular bottle). It pays to do research—too many restaurants, especially in summer, are cynically cashing in on the thriving tourist trade, and prices are generally high.

## HOTELS

One of the most popular vacation regions in France, after the seaside, the Vaucluse has a plethora of sleek and fashionable converted *mas* (farmhouses), landscaped in lavender, cypress, and oil jars full of vivid flowers.

Given the crushing heat in high summer, the majority have swimming pools and, these days, air-conditioning (but it's wise to check ahead if you're counting on it). However, only a few provide *moustiquaires,* mosquito netting put over the bed or window screens to keep out troublesome flies. Reservations are essential most of the year, and many hotels close down altogether in winter.

## MARKETS

Browsing through the *marché couvert* (covered food market) in Avignon is enough to make you renounce dining in the tempting local restaurants.

All the *fantastique* seafood, free-range poultry, olives, and produce cry out to be gathered in a basket and cooked in their purest form.

Village open-air markets are carefully scheduled to cover in turn all the days of the week, including in the yard of the old barracks at Caserne Chabran on Boulevard Limbert on Saturday and a flea market at Place des Carmes on Sunday.

But food plays second fiddle at one of the most famous markets in Provence. L'Isle-sur-la-Sorgue draws crowds of bargain hunters and collectors to its Sunday antiques and *brocante* (collectibles) fair. See our special Spotlight section on this famous marketplace.

## WINERIES AND VINEYARDS

The most serious wine center in the South of France is the southern portion of the Côtes du Rhône, home to the muscular reds of Gigondas, Vacqueyras, Rasteau, Cairanne, and of their more famous neighbor Châteauneuf-du-Pape.

Nearby Beaumes-de-Venise is famous for its sweet, light muscat. Not to be overlooked are the wines of the Côtes du Ventoux and the Côtes du Luberon.

You can visit most vineyards without an appointment. If you find touring vineyards slightly intimidating or impractical, you can still purchase wines from the region: most wine-making towns have a shop where local wines are sold at the producer's price, with no markup.

> **TIRED TOOTSIES?**
>
> Tired feet after too many rocky cobblestone paths? Head over to the Allées de l'Oulle and take a cruise along the river Rhône. For €8 (children under eight free), Le Mireio (⊕ www.mireio.net) runs a year-round 45-minute cruise from Avignon to the Isle of Bathelasse to Villeneuve-lez-Avignon. A lunch cruise around the Popes' Palace or the vineyards near Châteauneuf-du-Pape is also a more civilized way to take in the surrounding sights.

# AVIGNON

*44 km (28 miles) northeast of Nîmes; 70 km (43 miles) northwest of Aix-en-Provence.*

Of all the monuments in France—cathedrals, châteaux, fortresses—the ancient city of Avignon (pronounced ah-veen-*yonh*) is one of the most dramatic. Wrapped in a crenellated wall punctuated by towers and Gothic slit windows, its old center stands distinct from modern extensions, crowned by the Palais des Papes (Popes' Palace), a 14th-century fortress-castle that's nothing short of spectacular. Standing on the Place du Palais under the gaze of the gigantic Virgin that reigns from the cathedral tower, with the palace sprawling to one side, the bishops' Petit Palais to the other, and the long, low bridge of childhood-song fame stretching over the river (*"Sur le pont d'Avignon on y danse tous en rond . . ."*), you can beam yourself briefly into the 14th century, so complete is the context, so evocative the setting.

Yet you'll soon be brought back to the present with a jolt by the skateboarders leaping over the smooth-paved square. Avignon is anything but a museum; it surges with modern ideas and energy and thrives within its ramparts as it did in the heyday of the popes—like those radical church lords, sensual, cultivated, and cosmopolitan, with a taste for lay pleasures. For the French, Avignon is almost synonymous with its theater festival in July—thousands pack the city's hotels to bursting for the official festival and le Festival OFF, the fringe festival with nearly a thousand shows. If your French isn't up to a radical take on Molière, look for the English-language productions, or try the circus and mime—there are plenty of shows for children, and street performers abound.

### GETTING HERE AND AROUND

Avignon is a major rail crossroads and springboard for the Vaucluse and has plenty of car-rental agencies located at the Gare Avignon TGV (best to reserve your car in advance). The quickest train link is the high-speed TGV (Trains à Grande Vitesse) *Méditerranée* line that connects Paris and Avignon (2 hours 40 minutes). Nice to Avignon on the TGV (3 hours) costs €31. Keep in mind that the Gare Avignon TGV is on Chemin du Confluent, a few miles southwest of the city (a *navette* shuttle bus connects with the train station in town every 15 minutes from early morning to late at night). Other trains, such as the Avignon–Orange line (€5.70, 35 minutes) use the Gare Avignon Centre station at 42 boulevard St-Roch; other lines go to Arles, Nîmes, Orange, Toulon, and Carcassonne. Next door at 5 avenue Monclar, you'll find the bus terminal (☎ 04–90–82–07–35); buses run to and from Avignon, Arles (€7.10, 1 hour), Carpentras (€2, 45 minutes), Cavaillon (€2, 1 hour), Nîmes (€1.50, 1½ hours), or farther afield to Orange, Isle/Sorgue, Marseille, Nice, and Cannes. The Avignon–Orange bus runs several times during the day and takes under an hour and is €2 one way. In addition, there are 27 city buses to get you around Avignon itself, run by TCRA (⊕ *www.tcra.fr*).

### VISITOR INFORMATION

**Avignon Tourist Office** ⊠ *41 cours Jean-Jaurès* ☎ *04–32–74–32–74* ⊕ *www.avignon-tourisme.com.*

> ## THE AVIGNON PASSION PASS
>
> A good investment is the *Avignon PASSion*: you pay full price for the first site/monument you visit and thereafter there are various reductions on all the other sites, depending on which of them you visit. The 15-day pass, available for free at the tourist office, as well as participating sites and monuments, gives discounts of 20%–50% on visits to every site in Avignon and Villeneuve-lez-Avignon for you and up to five people.

## EXPLORING

Though it is merely the capital of the Vaucluse these days, Avignon's lively street life, active university, and colorful markets present a year-round spectacle far beyond the thousands of productions on view during the summer Avignon Theater Festival. To add to the allure, many of the landmark buildings and churches have been enhanced with new lighting fixtures that literally light up the nights.

To take it all in, travel the city's steep streets via the tourist train, a type of tram car that resembles a children's party ride. Le Petit Train d'Avignon (⊕ *www.petittrainavignon.fr*) leaves from the Popes' Palace Square daily, March 15 through October 30, every 30 minutes from 10 am to 7 pm ('til 8 pm in July and August) and takes you on a 40-minute ride through the Rocher des Doms gardens, the historic city center, and by major monuments. It costs €7.

Beautiful town squares form the hub of historic Avignon, as seen in this view from the roof of the famed Palais des Papes.

As a city, Avignon boasts one of the most fabled and time-stained histories in France. It was transformed into the "Vatican of the north" when political infighting in the Eternal City drove Pope Clement V to accept Philippe the Good's invitation to start afresh. In 1309 his entourage arrived, preferring digs in nearby priories and châteaux; in 1316 he was replaced by Pope John XXII, who moved into the bishop's palace (today the Petit Palais). It was his successor Pope Benedict XII who undertook construction of the magnificent palace that was to house a series of popes through the 14th century. During this holy reign Avignon evolved into a sophisticated, cosmopolitan capital, attracting artists and thinkers and stylish hangers-on. As the popes' wealth and power expanded, so did their formidable palace. And its sumptuous decor was legendary, inspiring horror and disdain from the poet Petrarch, who wrote of "towers both useless and absurd that our pride may mount skyward, whence it is sure to fall in ruins." The abandoned Italians dubbed Avignon a "second Babylon." Additionally, the University of Avignon, which had been founded in 1303, burgeoned as thousands of the faithful from across Europe came to Avignon on pilgrimage.

After a dispute with the king, Pope Gregory XI packed up for Rome in 1376, but Avignon held its ground. While he was on his death-bed in 1378, the French elected their own pope, Clement VII, and the Great Schism divided the Christian world. Popes and antipopes abused, insulted, and excommunicated each other to no avail, though the real object of dispute was the vast power and wealth of the papacy. When the king himself turned on the last antipope, Avignon lost out to Rome and the extravagant court dispersed.

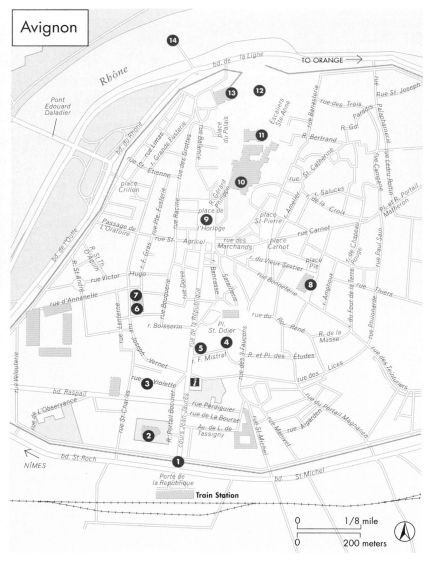

Avignon

## TOP ATTRACTIONS

**Cathédrale    Notre-Dame-des-Doms.** Built in a pure Provençal Romanesque style in the 12th century, this cathedral was soon dwarfed by the extravagant palace that rose beside it. The 14th century saw the addition of a cupola, which promptly collapsed. As rebuilt in 1425, the cathedral is a marvel of stacked arches with a strong Byzantine flavor and is topped with a gargantuan Virgin Mary lantern—a 19th-century afterthought—whose glow can be seen for miles around. Closed for renovation, the museum will reopen in 2015. ✉ *Pl. du Palais* ☎ *04–90–86–81–01* ⊘ *Daily 8–6.*

> ### HOW TO PLAY THE PALACE
>
> The Palais des Papes is one of those grand, must-see monuments that can be overwhelmed by shutter-popping groups of travelers at times. But it should be seen nonetheless; aim for visiting during opening time, lunchtime, or evenings if you are there in the middle of summer.

**Fodor's Choice** ★ **Collection Lambert.** Known for the breadth of its collection as well as the scope of its exhibitions, the Lambert is a must-see for contemporary art lovers. Housed in an elegant 17th-century mansion, this impressive assembly of contemporary artworks came out of the private collection of Paris art dealer Yvon Lambert, who founded the museum in 2000 in honor of Avignon's designation as European Capital of Culture. Comprising more than 1,200 pieces dating from the 1960s to the present, the Lambert Collection also hosts an influential series of exhibitions, cultural events, lectures, and arts eduction programs independently or in conjunction with other arts institutions worldwide. The impressive bookshop carries dozens of original, limited-edition works by artists represented in the collection, including prints by Cy Twombly, Sol Lewitt, and Jenny Holzer, and the breezy courtyard café offers gourmet snacks, beverages, and light lunches under the shade of sleepy plane trees.

Three exhibitions are ✉ *5 rue Violette* ☎ *04–90–16–56–20* ⊕ *www. collectionlambert.fr* ☜ *€15* ⊘ *Daily 11–6, until 7 July–Aug.*

**Le Musée du Petit Palais.** This residence of bishops and cardinals before Pope Benedict built his majestic palace houses a large collection of old-master paintings, the majority of which are Italian works from the early-Renaissance schools of Siena, Florence, and Venice—styles with which the Avignon popes would have been familiar. Later works here include Sandro Botticelli's *Virgin and Child*, and Venetian paintings by Vittore Carpaccio and Giovanni Bellini. ✉ *Pl. du Palais* ☎ *04–90–86–44–58* ⊕ *www.petit-palais.org* ☜ *€6* ⊘ *Wed.–Mon. 10–1 and 2–6.*

**Les Luminessences d'Avignon.** As if the Palais des Papes weren't spectacular enough, twice nightly for six weeks in August and September (9:15, 10:15 pm), the magical Les Luminessences 3-D light show transforms the palace into a gigantic canvas for a magnificent retelling of the history of the Avignon popes in glorious color. It hardly matters that the accompanying narration is in French, the imagery is provocative and arresting enough to stand on its own. A Christmas spectacle in lights is also held in the last weeks of November through December (free admission). ✉ *Place du Palais, 6 rue Pente Rapide* ☎ *04–31–74–32–74* ⊕ *www.lesluminessences-avignon.com* ☜ *€10.*

**Les Remparts** (*The Ramparts*). More than 4 kilometers (2½ miles) long, these protective crenellated walls and towers were built by the popes in the 14th century to keep out rampaging brigands and mercenary armies attracted by legends of papal wealth. It's extraordinarily well preserved, thanks in part to the efforts of architect Viollet-le-Duc, who restored the southern portion in the 19th century. Modern-day Avignon roars around its impervious walls on a noisy ring road that replaced a former moat. ⊠ *Place du Palais.*

**Musée Calvet.** Worth a visit for the beauty and balance of its architecture alone, this fine old museum contains a rich collection of antiquities and classically inspired works. Acquisitions include Neoclassical and Romantic pieces and are almost entirely French, including works by Manet, Daumier, and David. There's also a good modern section, with works by Bonnard, Duffy, and Camille Claudet (note Claudet's piece depicting her brother Paul, who incarcerated her in an insane asylum when her relationship with Rodin caused too much scandalous talk). The main building itself is a Palladian-style jewel in pale Gard stone dating from the 1740s; the garden is so lovely that it may distract you from the art. ⊠ *65 rue Joseph-Vernet* ☎ *04–90–86–33–84* ⊕ *www. musee-calvet-avignon.com* ▨ *€6* ⊙ *Wed.–Mon. 10–1 and 2–6.*

**Palais des Papes.** This colossal palace creates a disconcertingly fortress-like impression, underlined by the austerity of its interior. Most of the original furnishings were returned to Rome with the papacy; others were lost during the French Revolution. Some imagination is required to picture the palace's medieval splendor, awash with color and with worldly clerics enjoying what the 14th-century Italian poet Petrarch called "licentious banquets." On close inspection, two different styles of building emerge at the palace: the severe **Palais Vieux** (Old Palace), built between 1334 and 1342 by Pope Benedict XII, a member of the Cistercian order, which frowned on frivolity, and the more decorative **Palais Nouveau** (New Palace), built in the following decade by the artsy, lavish-living Pope Clement VI. The Great Court, entryway to the complex, links the two.

The main rooms of the Palais Vieux are the **Consistory** (Council Hall), decorated with some excellent 14th-century frescoes by Simone Martini; the **Chapelle St-Jean,** with original frescoes by Matteo Giovanetti; the **Grand Tinel,** or Salle des Festins (Feast Hall), with a majestic vaulted roof and a series of 18th-century Gobelin tapestries; the **Chapelle St-Martial,** with more Giovanetti frescoes; and the **Chambre du Cerf,** with a richly decorated ceiling, murals featuring a stag hunt, and a delightful view of Avignon. The principal attractions of the Palais Nouveau are the **Grande Audience,** a magnificent two-nave hall on the ground floor, and, upstairs, the **Chapelle Clémentine,** where the college of cardinals once gathered to elect the new pope. ⊠ *Pl. du Palais, 6 rue Pente Rapide* ☎ *04–32–74–32–74* ⊕ *www.palais-des-papes.com* ▨ *€11; €13.50, includes tour of Pont St-Béneze; audioguide for the palace €2, free for the bridge.* ⊙ *Mar. daily 9–6:30; Apr.–June and Sept–Oct., daily 9–7; July, daily 9–8; Aug., daily 9–8:30; Nov.–Feb., daily 9:30–5:45.*

**Bouteillerie.** For wine lovers, there's a wine cellar devoted to Côtes du Rhônes at the Bouteillerie of the Popes' Palace, where you can sample and buy regional wines. The selection changes every year. Although it's in the palais, you don't need to pay admission to go to the store. ⊠ *Pl. du Palais* ☎ *04–90–27–50–85* ☽ *Daily, with the midday closure from 1–2.*

**Place de l'Horloge** (*Clock Square*). This square is the social nerve center of Avignon; the concentration of bistros, brasseries, cafés, and restaurants draws swarms of locals to the shade of its plane trees.

**Pont St-Bénezet** (*St. Bénezet Bridge*). "Sur le pont d'Avignon on y danse, on y danse . . . " Unlike London Bridge, this other fragment of childhood song (and UNESCO World Heritage site) still stretches its arches across the river, but only partway. After generations of war and flooding, only half remained by the 17th century. Its first stones allegedly laid with the miraculous strength granted St-Bénezet in the 12th century, it once reached all the way to Villeneuve. It's a bit narrow for dancing "tous en rond" (round and round) though the traditional place for dance and play was under the arches. For a fee, you can rent an audioguide and climb along its high platform for broad views of the Old Town ramparts. ⊠ *Port du Rhône* ☎ *04–32–74–32–74* ⊕ *www. avignon-pont.com* 🖾 *€4.50; €13.50 for combination ticket with Palais des Papes* ☽ *Daily Apr.–June, 9–7; July, 9–8; Aug.–Sept. 14, 9–9; Sept. 15–Nov., 9–7; Dec. 1–Mar. 14, 9:30–5:45; Mar. 15–31, 9:30–6:30.*

Fodor'sChoice
★ **Rocher des Doms** (*Rock of the Domes*). Set on a bluff above town, this lush hilltop garden has grand Mediterranean pines, a man-made lake (complete with camera-ready swans), plus glorious views of the palace, the rooftops of Old Avignon, the Pont St-Bénezet, and formidable Villeneuve across the Rhône. On the horizon loom Mont Ventoux, the Luberon, and Les Alpilles. The garden has lots of history as well: Often called the "cradle of Avignon," its rocky grottoes were among the first human habitations in the area. ⊠ *Montée du Moulin off Pl. du Palais* ☎ *04–32–74–32–74* ⊕ *www.avignon-tourisme.com* ☽ *Dec.–Jan., daily 7–5:30; Feb. and Nov., daily 7:30–6; Mar., daily 7:30–7; Apr.–May, and Sept., daily 7:30–8; June–Aug., daily 7:30–9; Oct., daily 7:30–6:30.*

## WORTH NOTING

**Espace Saint Louis.** This graceful old 17th-century Jesuit cloister has been converted for office use by the well-known Avignon Festival—a performing arts event that lasts most of the month of July. The cloister's symmetrical arches (now partly enclosed as the sleek Hôtel Cloître Saint Louis) are shaded by ancient plane trees. You can wander around the courtyard after you've picked up your festival information. Occasional exhibits are held inside as well. ⊠ *20 rue du Portail Boquier* ☎ *04–90– 27–66–50* ⊕ *www.festival-avignon.com.*

**Les Halles.** By 6 every morning (except Monday) the merchants and artisans have stacked their herbed cheeses and arranged their vine-ripened tomatoes with surgical precision in pyramids and designs that please the eye before they tease the salivary glands. This permanent covered market is as far from a farmers' market as you can get, each booth a designer boutique of *haute de gamme* (top-quality) goods, from

Side-by-side with Avignon's gigantic Palais des Papes is the Byzantine-style Cathédrale Notre-Dame-des-Doms.

jewel-like olives to silvery mackerel to racks of hanging hares worthy of a Flemish still life. Even if you don't have a kitchen to stock, consider enjoying a cup of coffee or a glass of (breakfast) wine while you take in the sights and smells. Tuck into a plate of freshly shucked oysters and a *pichet* of the crisp local white, or, on Saturdays from 11 to noon, September through July, watch Saturday's cooking demonstration, "La Petite Cuisine du Marché," by a well-known Provençal chef. ⊠ *Pl. Pie* ☎ *04–90–27–15–15* ⊕ *www.avignon-leshalles.com* ☾ *Tues.–Sun. 6 am–1:30 pm, until 2 on Wed.*

**Musée Angladon.** This superb collection of major 18th to 20th century paintings and furnishings was assembled by the famous Parisian couturier Jacques Doucet (1853–1929), who counted many of the major painters and writers of his day among his close circle and purchased— or funded—some of the great works of the 20th century (he was the original owner of Picasso's *Desmoiselles d'Avignon*). With an unerring eye, this great appreciator of the arts created a collection that he then housed in this mansion, which he purchased toward the end of his life; it includes works by Degas, Van Gogh, Manet, Cézanne, Modigliani, and Picasso, along with important drawings, sculpture, photography, and furniture. The museum also hosts temporary exhibitions. ⊠ *5 rue Laboureur* ☎ *04–90–82–29–03* ⊕ *www.angladon.fr* 🎟 *€6* ☾ *Nov.–Mar. Wed.–Sun. 1–6; Apr.–Oct. Tues.–Sun. 1–6.*

**Musée Lapidaire.** Housed in a pretty little Jesuit chapel on the main shopping street, this collection of sculpture and stonework is primarily from Gallo-Roman times but also includes Greek and Etruscan works. There are several interesting inscribed slabs, a selection of *shabtis* (small statues buried with the dead to help them get to the afterlife), and a notable depiction of *Tarasque of Noves,* the man-eating monster immortalized by Alphonse Daudet. Most items, unfortunately, are haphazardly labeled and insouciantly scattered throughout the chapel, itself slightly crumbling yet awash with light. ✉ *27 rue de la République* ☎ *04–90–85–75–38* 🌐 *www.musee-calvet-avignon.com* 🎟 *€2* 🕒 *Tues.–Sun.*

**Musée Requien.** Don't bother to rush to this eccentric little natural history museum, but since it's next door to the Calvet Museum, and free, you might want to stop in and check out the petrified palm trunks, the dinosaur skeleton, the handful of local beetles and mammals, and the careful and evocative texts (French only) accompanying them. The museum is named for a local naturalist and functions as an entrance to the massive library of natural history upstairs. ✉ *67 rue Joseph-Vernet* ☎ *04–90–82–43–51* 🌐 *www.museum-avignon.org* 🎟 *Free* 🕒 *Tues.–Sat. 10–1 and 2–6.*

## WHERE TO EAT

$$$ FRENCH Fodor's Choice ★

🍴 **Christian Étienne.** Stellar period decor in a renovated 12th-century mansion makes for an impressive backdrop to innovative and delicious cuisine. Try the pan-roasted medaillon of veal with dried porcini blinis and thinly sliced mushrooms with chervil, or splurge for the whole lobster sautéed in olive oil, muscat grapes, and beurre blanc with verjuice. The seasonal truffle menu may be too rich for some (€150), but a €35 lunch menu offers nice balance for budget-conscious travelers. [$] *Average main: €30* ✉ *10 rue de Mons* ☎ *04–90–86–16–50* 🌐 *www.christian-etienne.fr* ✍ *Reservations essential* 🕒 *Closed Sun.–Mon.*

$$ FRENCH Fodor's Choice ★

🍴 **La Fourchette.** The food here is some of the best in town, as the bevy of locals clamoring to get in proves. It all smells so good that you may be tempted to rip one of the decorative forks off the wall and attack your neighbor's plate. Service is prompt and friendly, and you can dig in to heaping portions of escalope of salmon, chicken cilantro à l'orange, or what is likely the best Provençal daube (served with macaroni gratin) in France. [$] *Average main: €20* ✉ *17 rue Racine* ☎ *04–90–85–20–93* 🌐 *www.la-fourchette.net* ✍ *Reservations essential* 🕒 *Closed Sat.–Sun., and first 3 wks of Aug.*

$$$$ FRENCH

🍴 **La Mirande.** Whether you dine under the 14th-century coffered ceilings, surrounded by Renaissance tapestries, or in the intimate garden under the Popes' Palace walls, the restaurant of the luxurious Hôtel de la Mirande transports you to another time. Chef Julien Allano rediscovers this establishment's roots with authentic organic menus: pan-seared pike perch, crayfish, and artichokes in a ravioli with Nantua-style sauce, and pork in four different ways with mashed potatoes. Foodies, take note: Tuesday and Wednesday dinners are table d'hôtes, and one week every month the restaurant's cooking school, Le Marmiton, invites guest chefs to teach casual, multilingual cooking classes for six to 12 people around the kitchen table, followed by a feast—and there are classes for children, too. [$] *Average main: €40* ✉ *4 pl. de la Mirande* ☎ *04–90–85–93–93* 🌐 *www.la-mirande.fr* ✍ *Reservations essential* 🕒 *Closed Tues.–Wed., and Jan.*

$$$$ FRENCH Fodor's Choice ★ 🍴 **La Vieille Fontaine.** Summer-evening meals around the old fountain and boxwood-filled oil jars in the courtyard of the Hôtel d'Europe would be wonderful with *filet de boeuf* alone, but combine this romantic backdrop with stellar southern French cuisine and you have a special event. Give yourself over to one of the most renowned restaurants in the Vaucluse, complete with the best regional wines and an army of urbane servers—and hope for moonlight. The €37 lunch menu, coffee and parking included, quickly refuels before tackling the afternoon's touring. [$] *Average main: €45* ✉ *12 pl. Crillon* ☎ *04–90–14–76–76* 🌐 *www.heurope.com* ✍ *Reservations essential* ⏲ *Closed Sun.–Mon.; first wk in Jan.; first two wks in Feb.; last 2 wks in Aug.*

3

$ BISTRO 🍴 **Le 9 Restaurant.** Beautiful terrace, amazing view, delicious local fare—this is probably enough, but add a warm welcome and attentive service and you've got Le 9 Restaurant's winning formula. Everything on the small and meat-centric menu is prepared with care, starting with the excellent *fromage de Banon*, a local small-production cheese, served with smoked lamb, followed by local venison with cranberries, or whole-roasted sea trout. For dessert, a plum tart is just the thing. A wine list of local standouts is icing on the cake. [$] *Average main: €14* ✉ *9 av. Jean Giono, Forcalquier* ☎ *04–92–75–03–29* 🌐 *www.le9-forcalquier.fr* ✍ *Reservations essential* ⏲ *Closed Tues. and Wed.*

$$ FRENCH 🍴 **Le Moutardier.** The papal mustard used to be made here, and while some establishments would hide behind such a heavenly pedigree and offer mediocre fare, the Perrin family has successfully married their setting in the Palace Square with the simplicity of Provençal food. Appetizing dishes, such as a tuna fillet with carrot compote flavored with vanilla or steamed asparagus with Parmesan and pistou, are light and uncomplicated, not disguised in heavy sauces, and are presented as objets d'art. The shaded terrace with its white-clothed tables is spectacular yet unpretentious, while the frescoes and chandeliers dazzle alongside the cream and gold interior. More than 80 Vaucluse wines are listed. ■ **TIP→ The €25 lunch menu is available at both meals.** [$] *Average main: €24* ✉ *15 pl. du Palais des Papes* ☎ *04–90–85–34–76* ✍ *Reservations essential.*

$$ FRENCH 🍴 **L'Epicerie.** This restaurant doesn't have great gastronomic pretensions, but the cheerful food, hip waiters, and perfect terrace in the quiet, cobbled Place St-Pierre make it a local favorite. Order a steak with *vraies frites* (real, chunky French fries) and soak up the atmosphere with the help of some well-chosen local wine. [$] *Average main: €21* ✉ *10 pl. St-Pierre* ☎ *04–90–82–74–22* 🌐 *www.restaurantlepicerie.fr* ✍ *Reservations essential* ⏲ *Closed Nov.–Mar.*

$$ FRENCH 🍴 **L'Essentiel.** This chic hot spot is founded on two concepts: a gastronomic restaurant with two set menus (€31 and €43) served in a white tableclothed, Zen-esque atmosphere, and a bar *à tatines* that serves lip-smacking, grilled open-faced sandwiches, pasta pistou, or salad (about €11) in a brighter, slightly less formal room. Trained by Bardet and Senderens, chef-owner Laurent Chouviat makes his experience apparent with dishes like open ravioli with asparagus and small peas in a creamed basil sauce with garlic, or roast cod with confit tomatoes, fresh coriander, and Arborio risotto. The quaint terrace on this side street will allure passersby, but the romantic 17th-century

interior courtyard will keep them coming back. There's a lunch menu for €17 and a glass of wine starts at €5. $ *Average main: €20* ⊠ *2 rue Petite Fusterie* ☎ *04–90–85–87–12* ⊕ *www.restaurantlessentiel.com* ⊙ *Closed Sun. and Mon.*

**$**
BRITISH

× **Simple Simon.** Since the 1970s, this quaint (there is no other word for it) English tearoom—dark wooden beams, teapots on shelves, a table laden with cakes and pies—has catered to homesick expats and locals, who are intrigued by the pieman's tempting wares and the properly brewed teas served in silver pots. Owned from the beginning by a Frenchwoman whose mother was English, Simple Simon is a real ode to British tradition, with cornish salad, bacon, and eggs and hot dishes such as shepherd's pie, cheese-and-onion crumble tart, or turkey hotpot at lunch. During the theater festival, it's also open for dinner. $ *Average main: €15* ⊠ *26 rue Petite Fusterie* ☎ *04–90–86–62–70* ⊙ *Closed Sun.–Mon. and Aug. No dinner (except during festival).*

## WHERE TO STAY

**$$$**
B&B/INN

⌗ **À l'Ombre du Palais.** You will not find a better, unobstructed panoramic rooftop view in such close proximity of the Palais du Papes than this, and accessing it is half the fun. **Pros:** unique rooftop terrace and views; pedestrian exit of Palais des Papes parking is in front. **Cons:** rooms are fitted only with fans, so things could get sticky; owner smokes in house. $ *Rooms from: €145* ⊠ *6 rue de la Vieille Juiverie, Place du Palais du Papes* ☎ *06–23–46–50–95* ⊕ *www.alombredupalais.com* ⇲ *5 rooms* ⊙ *Closed Jan.* ❢⊙❢ *Breakfast.*

**$$$$**
HOTEL

⌗ **Cloître Saint-Louis.** Standing serene and noble within its sturdy 16th-century walls, this sleek hotel encloses a magnificently cloistered courtyard lined with grand old plane trees. **Pros:** exquisite building; heated pool. **Cons:** rooms lack character; some rooms with handheld showers. $ *Rooms from: €300* ⊠ *20 rue du Portail-Boquier* ☎ *04–90–27–55–55* ⊕ *www.cloitre-saint-louis.com* ⇲ *80 rooms* ❢⊙❢ *Breakfast.*

**$$$**
HOTEL

⌗ **Hôtel d'Europe.** This classic vine-covered 16th-century home once hosted Victor Hugo, Napoléon Bonaparte, and Emperor Maximilian; regally discreet, it is notable for its walled, tree-shaded courtyard and an interior filled with Aubusson tapestries, porcelains, and Provençal antiques. **Pros:** authentic historical setting close to everything; perfect as a secluded romantic hideaway. **Cons:** least expensive rooms are small; high season can make for some noisy evenings. $ *Rooms from: €194* ⊠ *12 pl. Crillon* ☎ *04–90–14–76–76* ⊕ *www.heurope.com* ⇲ *39 rooms, 5 suites* ❢⊙❢ *No meals.*

**$$$$**
HOTEL
Fodor's Choice
★

⌗ **Hôtel de la Mirande.** A designer's dream of a hotel, this *petit palais* permits you to step into 18th-century Avignon—enjoy painted coffered ceilings, sumptuous antiques, extraordinary handmade wall coverings, and other superb *grand siècle* touches (those rough sisal mats on the floors were the height of chic back in the Baroque era). **Pros:** spectacular setting of the hotel; free bottled water from minibar during your stay. **Cons:** rooms can be a little stuffy; breakfast is expensive. $ *Rooms from: €450* ⊠ *Pl. de la Mirande* ☎ *04–90–14–20–20* ⊕ *www.la-mirande.fr* ⇲ *25 rooms, 1 suite, 1 apt* ❢⊙❢ *No meals.*

$$ HOTEL **Hôtel de Blauvac.** Just off rue de la République and Place de l'Horloge, this 17th-century nobleman's home turned simple hotel has been divided into 16 guest rooms, many with pristine exposed stonework, and lovely tall windows that look, alas, onto backstreet walls. **Pros:** well-priced for location. **Cons:** smallish rooms; street noise but need to leave windows open as there's no air-conditioning; no elevator. [$] *Rooms from: €100* ✉ *11 rue de la Bancasse* ☎ *04–90–86–34–11* 🌐 *www.hotel-blauvac.com* 🛏 *16 rooms* 🍴 *No meals.*

$$ HOTEL **Hotel du Palais des Papes.** This third-generation family-run institution is a notably solid and comfortable place—all the better for its location just off the Place du Palais. **Pros:** 40% reduction on Palais des Papes parking with hotel stamp; some rooms with double-glazed windows. **Cons:** can be stifling in summer; aspects of decor appear touristy kitch. [$] *Rooms from: €120* ✉ *3 pl. du Palais* ☎ *04–90–86–04–13* 🌐 *www.hotel-palais-des-papes.fr* 🛏 *26 rooms, 2 suites* 🍴 *No meals.*

$$$$ HOTEL **Le Couvent des Minimes.** It makes sense that L'Occitane, the global Provence-based cosmetics and fragrance giant, would situate its newest overnight spa in the heart of lavender country—this is where the company's roots are and they've made it a point of honor to offer their guests an experience worthy of the pedigree. **Pros:** package deals available to save on room prices. **Cons:** spa treatments are expensive on top of the room price; service can be indifferent. [$] *Rooms from: €300* ✉ *Chemin des Jeux de Maï, Mane-en-Provence* ☎ *04–92–74–77–78* 🌐 *www.couventdesminimes-hotelspa.com* 🛏 *42 rooms* 🍴 *No meals.*

$$$ B&B/INN **Le Limas.** Located two minutes from the famous Avignon bridge, this contemporarily decorated B&B offers a rooftop terrace view of the palace but also tranquility away from the noisy palace streets. **Pros:** rooftop terrace fridge stocked with rosé so you can enjoy evening cocktails with a fab view; computer available. **Cons:** only one room can accommodate more than two people. [$] *Rooms from: €155* ✉ *51 rue de Limas* ☎ *04–90–14–67–19* 🌐 *www.le-limas-avignon.com* 🛏 *4 rooms* 🍴 *Breakfast.*

$ HOTEL **Pop Hostel.** Situated in the heart of the city in a magnificent historical building two steps from the Palais des Papes, this updated version of a hostel is fully equipped with a wine bar (with tapas menu), lounge, and boutique. **Pros:** reasonable rates. **Cons:** can be noisy; service perfunctory. [$] *Rooms from: €25* ✉ *17 rue de la République* ☎ *04–32–40–50–60* 🌐 *www.pophostel.fr* 🛏 *22 rooms* 🍴 *No meals.*

## NIGHTLIFE AND THE ARTS

Small though Avignon is, its inspiring art museums, strong university, and 60-some years of saturation in world-class theater have made the city a second satellite for the arts, after Paris.

**FNAC.** For information on events and tickets, stop into this massive book-and-record chain. ✉ *19 rue de la République* ☎ *08–92–68–36–22* 🌐 *www.fnac.com.*

### NIGHTLIFE

Within its fusty old medieval walls, Avignon teems with modern nightlife well into the wee hours.

**Bistrot d'Utopia.** Enjoy drinks in this dark, intimate space just outside the cinema in La Manutention. ⊠ *4 rue des Escaliers Ste-Anne.*

**Le Bakao's.** This funky disco lounge for younger crowds, open Wednesday through Saturday from 10 pm to 5 am, offers its own shuttle-bus navette to get you to and from the party. ⊠ *9 bis Quai St Lazare* ☎ *04–90–82–47–95.*

**Le Delirium.** An über-cool hangout for live music, performance, and entertainment during the Avignon Festival and on weekends, Le Delirium covers its walls with ongoing exhibits to create a truly artsy atmosphere. ⊠ *23 rue de la République* ☎ *04–90–85–44–56* ⊕ *www.ledelirium.net.*

**Le Rouge Gorge.** This is the venue for dinner shows done cabaret-style, with singers and dancers; it also hosts jazz, blues, and rock concerts, theater performances, and special events. ⊠ *10 bis rue Peyrollerie* ☎ *04–90–14–02–54.*

**Les Ambassadeurs.** This club attracts a mature crowd, but don't let the well-dressed revelers here fool you: Les Ambassadeurs is not high priced, but rather drinks are decently priced. Dancing ends around 2, Thursday through Saturday. ⊠ *27 rue Bancasse* ☎ *04–90–86–31–55* ⊕ *www.clublesambassadeurs.fr.*

**Pub Z.** The hot spot for rock, sometimes live, Pub Z has a black-and-white interior that incorporates a zebra theme. ⊠ *58 rue Bonneterie* ☎ *04–90–85–42–84.*

### THE ARTS

Two cinema complexes show first-run, mainstream movies in *v.o.* (*version originale,* meaning in the original language with French subtitles).

**Cinéma Utopia-La Manutention.** This theater shows hard-to-find international independent works. ⊠ *4 rue des Escaliers Ste-Anne* ☎ *04–90–82–65–36* ⊕ *www.cinemas-utopia.org/avignon* 🎟 *€6.50.*

**Cinéma Utopia-République.** This is a popular cinema. ⊠ *5 rue Figuière* ☎ *04–90–82–65–36* ⊕ *www.cinemas-utopia.org/avignon* 🎟 *€6.50.*

**La Manutention.** This cultural complex includes the cinema Utopia-La Manutention; a well-regarded restaurant, La Manutention; and jazz club, Ajmi. ⊠ *4 rue des Escaliers Ste-Anne* ☎ *04–90–86–08–61 Jazz club, 04–90–86–86–77 Restaurant* ⊕ *www.jazzalajmi.com.*

**Opéra-Théâtre d'Avignon.** This theater proves that culture and the arts are not limited to festival season. ⊠ *1 rue Racine* ☎ *04–90–82–42–42* ⊕ *operagrandavignon.fr/en.*

# SHOPPING

Avignon is too big and too resident-oriented to be full of tourist-aimed boutiques; instead, it has a cosmopolitan mix of French chains, youthful clothing shops (it's a college town), and a few plummy dress shops. **Rue des Marchands,** off Place Carnot, is one shopping stretch, but **Rue de la République** is the main artery.

**Cami-li Books & Tea.** If you're hungry for books in English, find Cami-li Books & Tea; in addition to new and used books in English, it has a tearoom, café, and terrace. ⊠ *155 rue Carreterie* ☎ *04–90–27–38–50* ⊕ *www.camili-booksandtea.com.*

**Fusterie Quarter.** If you're into Louis XVI, the Fusterie quarter caters to antique hunters and interior decorators. ⊠ *Rue Petit Fusterie.*

**Jaffier-Parsi.** Fans of fine French cookware should head to Jaffier-Parsi, a professional cooking supply store that has been stocking heavy copper pots, stainless-steel ladles, mortar-and-pestle sets, and great knives since 1902. ⊠ *42 rue des Fourbisseurs* ☏ *04–90–86–08–85.*

**Joseph Vernet Quarter.** The more luxurious shops along rue Joseph-Vernet and St-Agricol in the Joseph Vernet quarter merit some *lèche-vitrine* (window licking, as the French say).

**Les Délices du Luberon.** For those with a taste for all things Provençal, this gourmet épicerie is a treasure trove of the many delicacies you'd find in the best local markets, all neatly packaged and suitcase ready—if they make it that far. There's everything from olive oils, tapenades, herbs, sweet and savory conserves, bottled soups, fruit jams, honey, pastries, lavender-based sweets and cosmetics, and much more. ⊠ *20 rue du Changé* ☏ *04–90–84–03–58* ⊕ *www.delices-du-luberon.fr.*

**Les Olivades.** Goods made from signature printed fabrics can be found at Les Olivades, a competitor of Souleïado's. ⊠ *56 rue Joseph Vernet* ☏ *04–90–86–13–42.*

**Mouret Chapelier.** This shop has a cornucopia of old-fashioned, old-world, and marvelously eccentric hats in a jewel-box setting. ⊠ *20 rue Marchands* ☏ *04–90–85–39–38.*

**Shakespeare.** If you're hungry for books in English, find Shakespeare; in addition to new and used books in English, it has a tearoom, café, and terrace. ⊠ *155 rue Carreterie* ☏ *04/90–27–38–50.*

**Souleïado.** All those famous, gorgeous Provençal fabrics can be found at Souleïado. ⊠ *19 rue Joseph-Vernet* ☏ *04–90–86–32–05* ⊕ *provence. souleiado.com.*

# HAUT VAUCLUSE

Situated north and northeast of Avignon, this land of rolling orchards and vineyards spreads lazily at the foot of Mont Ventoux, redolent of truffles, lavender, and fine wine. Perhaps that's why the Romans so firmly established themselves here, erecting grand arenas and luxurious villas that still in part remain. From Avignon head north into the vineyards, making a brief tour of Châteauneuf-du-Pape, even if you don't stop to drink and buy wine. Orange is just up the highway; though the town isn't the most picturesque, its Roman theater is a must-see. Between Orange and Mont Ventoux are wine centers (Beaumes-de-Venise, Gigondas, Vacqueyras) and picturesque villages such as Crestet, Séguret, Le Barroux, and Malaucène, which the first French pope preferred to Avignon. Visit Vaison-la-Romaine for a strong concentration of Roman ruins.

## VILLENEUVE-LEZ-AVIGNON

*2 km (1 mile) west of Avignon.*

Just across the Rhône from Avignon, this medieval town glowers at its powerful neighbor to the east. In the 14th century, Villeneuve benefited enormously from the migration of the popes into Avignon, as an accompanying flood of wealthy and influential cardinals poured over the river. No fewer than 15 of the status-seeking princes of the church built magnificent homes on this neighboring hilltop—in truth, some simply requisitioned mansions from other owners, giving these "freed" town palaces the unfortunate moniker *livrées cardinalices*. In addition, kings Philip the Fair and Louis VIII built up formidable defenses on the site to keep an eye on the papal territories.

Nowadays its abbey, fortress, and quiet streets offer a pleasant contrast to Avignon's bustle.

### GETTING HERE AND AROUND

The No. 5 from the Avignon "center" train station runs every 20 minutes and costs € 1.30 for the five-minute ride. To drive, it's 4 kilometers (2½ miles) from Avignon; just follow the signs.

### VISITOR INFORMATION

Villeneuve-lez-Avignon ⊠ *1 pl. Charles-David* ☎ *04–90–25–61–33* ⊕ *www.villeneuvelezavignon.fr.*

### EXPLORING

**Abbaye St-André Gardens.** Don't miss the formal Italianate gardens of Fort St-André, littered with remains of the abbey that preceded the fortifications. The gardens are now privately owned. ⊠ *Abbaye St-André, Rue Montée du Fort* ☎ *06–71–42–16–90* 🖾 *€5* ⊘ *Tues.–Sun. 10–12:30 and 2–6 (closes at 5 Oct.–Mar.).*

**Chartreuse du Val-de-Bénédiction.** The bounty and extravagant lifestyles of the cardinals nourished the abbey in Villeneuve-lez-Avignon. Inside the abbey—known as Chartreuse du Val-de-Bénédiction or, literally, the Charterhouse of the Valley of Blessings—are spare cells with panels illuminating monastic life, the vast 14th-century **cloître de cimetière** (cemetery cloister), a smaller Romanesque cloister, and, within the remains of the abbey church, the Gothic tomb of Pope Innocent VI. Theatrical events are staged here during Avignon's annual theater festival. ⊠ *58 rue de la République* ☎ *04–90–15–24–24* ⊕ *www.chartreuse.org* 🖾 *€7.70* ⊘ *Apr.–Sept., daily 9:30–6; Oct.–Mar., daily 9:30–5.*

**Fort St-André.** At the top of the village is the Fort St-André, which once ostensibly protected the town of St-André, now absorbed into Villeneuve. The fortress's true importance was as a show of power for the kingdom of France in the face of the all-too-close Avignon popes. You can explore the fortress grounds and the bare ruined walls of inner chambers (there's a good view from the Notre Dame de Belvézet church within the fort walls), and you can also climb into the twin towers for broad views over Avignon, the Luberon, and Mont Ventoux. ⊠ *Abbaye St-André, Rue Montée du Fort* ☎ *04–90–25–45–35* ⊕ *www.monum.fr* 🖾 *Towers: €5.50* ⊘ *Apr.–Sept., daily 10–1 and 2–6; Oct.–Mar., daily 10–1 and 2–5.*

**Musée Pierre de Luxembourg.** Below the abbey, the Musée Pierre de Luxembourg gives you access to one of the luxurious 14th-century cardinals' manors, which contains a notable collection of art, including the spectacularly colorful and richly detailed *Couronnement de la Vierge* (Coronation of the Virgin), an altarpiece painted in 1453 by Enguerrand Quarton. One of the greatest paintings of the 15th century, it shows rows and rows of

> ### SWIRL. SIP. SAVOR.
>
> Storefront wineries invite tasters of every level of experience to sample their vintages. Feel free to enter and taste; most outlets are happy to let you try a few without pressure to purchase. (Although etiquette dictates that you leave a few euros tip if you've been slurping down glass after glass.)

Avignonnais hieratically sitting around the figures of God the Father and God the Son. Depicted by Quarton—the leading painter of the Avignon School—as identical twins, they bless Mary and hover over a surreal landscape that places Montagne St-Victoire in between Heaven and Hell. ⊠ *2 rue de la République* ☎ *04–90–27–49–66* ⊕ *www.gard-provencal.com/musees/pdluxem.htm* 🎫*€3.20* ⊙ *Apr.–Sept., Tues.–Sun. 10–12:30 and 2–6:30; Oct.–Mar., Tues.–Sun. 10–12 and 2–5.*

## CHÂTEAUNEUF-DU-PAPE

*17 km (10 miles) north of Avignon; 22 km (13½ miles) west of Carpentras.*

The countryside around this famous wine center is a patchwork of rolling vineyards, of green-and-black furrows striping the landscape in endless, retreating perspective. Great gates and grand houses punctuate the scene, as symmetrical and finely detailed as the etching on a wine label, and signs—discreet but insistent—beckon you to follow the omnipresent smell of fermenting grapes to their source. Behind barn doors, under cellar traps, and in chilly caves beneath châteaux, colossal oak vats nurture this noble Rhône red to maturity. The pebbly soil here is particularly suited to the growth of vines: the small stones act like a wool sweater, retaining the heat of the sun's rays and keeping the vines warm and cozy during the night.

Once the source of the table wine of the Avignon popes, who kept a fortified summer house here (hence the name of the town, which means "new castle of the pope"), these vineyards had the good fortune to be wiped out by phylloxera in the 19th century. The wine's revival as a muscular and resilient mix of up to 13 varietals with an almost portlike intensity (it can reach 15% alcohol content) moved it to the forefront of French wines. The whites, though less significant, are also to be reckoned with.

There are *caves de dégustation* (wine-tasting cellars) on nearly every street; get a free map of the caves from the tourist office on Place du Portail. Also head to the discreet *vignobles* (vineyards) at the edge of town. Some of the top Châteauneufs (and the oldest) come from Château la Nerthe, Château de Vaudieu, and Château Fortia, and are priced accordingly. If you're not armed with the names of a few great houses, look for *medaille d'or* (gold medal) ratings from prestigious wine fairs; these are usually indicated by a gold sticker on the bottle.

Châteauneuf-du-Pape is a beautiful hillside town, just a half-hour bus ride from Avignon, that lends its name to some of the world's most renowned wines.

Better yet, for the best selection of wines in one place as well as expertise to match, go with Vinadea *(see Shopping)*, which is the official maison des vins of Châteauneuf.

### GETTING HERE AND AROUND

The Avignon bus (€2)—which is also the local school bus—runs once a day in the early evening and around noon on Wednesday and Saturday and takes 35 minutes. Going the other direction, however, from Châteauneuf-du-Pape to Avignon, the bus leaves in the morning (no buses on Sunday). To/from Orange, the 25-minute journey is €1.50 with several possibilities throughout the day in both directions. Best to drive: take the D225, the D907, and then the D17 direction Orange and follow signs to Châteauneuf (about 30 minutes).

### VISITOR INFORMATION

**Châteauneuf-du-Pape Tourist Office** ☎ *04–90–83–71–08*
⊕ *www.pays-provence.fr.*

### EXPLORING

**Château.** If you're disinclined to spend your holiday sniffing and sipping, climb the hill to the ruins of the château. Though it was destroyed in the Wars of Religion and its remaining *donjon* (keep) blasted by the Germans in World War II, it still commands a magnificent position. From this rise in the rolling vineyards, you can enjoy wraparound views of Avignon, the Luberon, and Mont Ventoux.

**Musée des Outils de Vignerons Père Anselme.** To learn about local wine production, stop in at the Musée des Outils de Vignerons Père Anselme, a private collection of tools and equipment displayed in the *caveau* (wine cellar) of the Brotte family. ⊠ *Ave. St. Pierre de Luxembourg* ☎ *04–90–83–59–44* ⊕ *www.brotte.com* ⊠ *Free* ⊙ *Apr.–Sept., daily 9–1 and 2–7; Oct.–Mar., daily 9–noon and 2–6.*

### WHERE TO EAT AND STAY

$ ✕ **La Maisouneta.** This cozy restaurant with cheerful planters and homey

FRENCH lace curtains is run by a young husband-and-wife team and specializes

FAMILY in pasta dishes and regional French comfort food (from Savoie, Nice, and Provence). Although not exactly gastronomic, dishes like basil-and-cheese ravioli, stuffed peppers, and *crème anchoïade* (anchovy cream) are seasonal, well-prepared, and deeply satisfying. Pair dinner with a glass of the local red and then marvel at the modest check. $ *Average main: €15* ⊠ *6 rue Joseph Ducos* ☎ *04–90–32–55–03* ⚠ *Reservations essential* ⊙ *Closed Jan. No dinner Thurs. Closed Wed.*

$ ✕ **Le Verger des Papes.** It's well worth the slog up the hill to the château

FRENCH simply to linger on the terrace of this long-established restaurant and savor the view over Mont Ventoux, Avignon, the Luberon, and the Rhône—and you can visit the restaurant's well-stocked wine cellar on your way to the top. The Estenevins have lived in Châteauneuf-du-Pape for three generations, and Philippe and Jean-Pierre took over the restaurant from their parents. The specialty here, *tarte à la tomate confite* with goat cheese and iced white cheese, reveals their love for the region's cuisine. $ *Average main: €17* ⊠ *Rue Montée du Château* ☎ *04–90–83–50–40* ⊕ *www. vergerdespapes.com* ⊙ *Closed Mon. No dinner Sun. and Tues.*

$$ ⛺ **L'Espace de L'Hers.** The charming hosts of this serene and scenic coun-

B&B/INN try B&B set among vineyards and forest go to every length to assure that you enjoy a true Provençal experience, from organizing wine tastings and tours to offering cooking classes and allowing guests to assist in the kitchen. **Pros:** gourmet meals are served by advance reservation; price includes breakfast; an 800-square-foot cottage, with kitchen (accommodates up to six), can be rented by the week. **Cons:** fills up quickly. $ *Rooms from: €140* ⊠ *5 chemin de L'Hers* ☎ *06–22–65–41–18* ⊕ *www.espacedelhers.com* ↩ *5 rooms* ⏦ *Breakfast.*

### SHOPPING

**Vinadea.** The official *maison des vins* of Châteauneuf-du-Pape, Vinadea has the town's best selection of wines, along with wine expertise if you have questions. ⊠ *8 rue Maréchal Foch* ☎ *04–90–83–70–69* ⊕ *www. vinadea.com.*

## ORANGE

*12 km (7 miles) north of Châteauneuf-du-Pape; 31 km (19 miles) north of Avignon.*

Cradled in northern Provence in the land of Côte du Rhône vineyards, Orange really isn't very big, but when compared with the sleepy wine villages that surround it, it's a thriving metropolis. In many ways, Orange captures the essence of the region: the Provençal accent here is quite thick, and savory food and wine can be had—for a price. Come to see its two ancient Roman monuments, the Théâtre Antique and the Arc de Triomphe, spectacular vestiges of history that seem transported from a different world.

## GETTING HERE AND AROUND

The Paris TGV at 3 hours 20 minutes serves Orange twice daily, but from Nice to Orange by TGV is more complicated. Take Nice to Marseille and then change trains to Orange; the fare is about €53, but with the stopover it takes about 5 hours 30 minutes. From Orange to Gare Avignon Centre, it costs €6.30 for the 20-minute train. Orange's center is a 10-minute walk from the train station (head from Avenue F. Mistral to Rue de la République, then follow signs). By bus to Avignon's *gare routière* (bus station) there are 10 to 20 buses daily at €3 one way (45 minutes) departing from the train station.

## VISITOR INFORMATION

**Orange Tourist Office** ✉ *5 cours Aristide Briand* ☎ *04–90–34–70–88* ⊕ *www.otorange.fr.*

## EXPLORING

**Arc de Triomphe.** North of the city center is the Arc de Triomphe, which once straddled the Via Agrippa between Lyon and Arles. Three arches support a heavy double attic (horizontal top) floridly decorated with battle scenes and marine symbols, references to Augustus's victories at Actium. The arch, which dates from about 20 BC, is superbly preserved, particularly the north side, but to view it on foot you'll have to cross a roundabout seething with traffic. ✉ *Av. de l'Arc de Triomphe.*

**Musée d'Orange.** Across the street from the theater, the small Musée d'Orange displays antiquities unearthed around Orange, including fragments of three detailed marble *cadastres* (land survey maps) dating from the first century. Upstairs, a vivid series of 18th-century canvases shows local mills producing Provençal fabrics, each aspect illustrated in careful detail. There are also personal objects from local aristocrats and a collection of faience pharmacy jars. ✉ *Rue Madeleine Roch* ☎ *04–90–51–17–60* ⊕ *www.theatre-antique.com* 🎫 *€9, joint ticket with Théâtre Antique* ⊗ *Nov.–Feb., daily 9:45–4:30; Apr., May, and Sept., daily 9:45–6; Mar. and Oct., daily 9:45–5:30 (closed from 12:30–1:30 during these months); June–Aug., daily 9:15–7.*

**Théâtre Antique.** Even less touristy than Nîmes and just as eccentric, the city of Orange (pronounced oh-*rawnzh*) nonetheless draws thousands every year to its spectacular Théâtre Antique, a colossal Roman theater built in the time of Caesar Augustus. The vast stone stage wall, bouncing sound off the facing hillside, climbs four stories high—a massive sandstone screen that Louis XIV once referred to as the "finest wall in my kingdom." The niche at center stage contains the original statue of Augustus, just as it reigned over centuries of productions of classical plays. Today the theater provides a backdrop for world-class theater and opera. ✉ *Pl. des Frères-Mounet* ☎ *04–90–51–17–60* ⊕ *www.theatre-antique.com* 🎫 *€9 joint ticket with the Musée d'Art et d'Histoire* ⊗ *Apr.–May and Sept., daily 9–6; June–Aug., daily 9–7; Mar. and Oct., daily 9:30–5:30; Nov.–Feb., daily 9:30–4:30.*

**Vieil Orange.** This Old Town neighborhood, which you must cross to hike from one Roman monument to the other, carries on peacefully when there's not a blockbuster spectacle in the theater. Lining its broad squares, under heavy-leaved plane trees, are a handful of shops and a few sidewalk cafés.

### WHERE TO EAT AND STAY

**\$\$**  ✕ **Au Petit Patio.** This ultra-popular eatery on the edge of Orange's Old
BISTRO  Town consistently serves fresh, locally sourced cuisine with a price-to-
quality ratio that keeps happy locals coming back. Imaginative dishes
like the house foie gras with teck-fruit sauce, *pot au feu de coquilles
Saint Jacques*, and mussels in saffron broth are ample and served with
flair. The prix-fixe menus at lunchtime (€18, two courses with wine and
coffee) and dinner (€26, €37 for four courses) are a bargain. Choose
between a table on the umbrella-shaded terrace or one in the pleasantly
unpretentious dining room. $ *Average main: €22* ⊠ *58 cours Aristide-
Briand* ☎ *04–90–29–69–27* ⌲ *Reservations essential* ⊗ *No dinner
Thurs. Closed Wed. and Sun.*

**\$\$**  ⊡ **Best Western Hôtel Arene Külm.** On a quiet square in the old center,
HOTEL  this comfortable hotel is filled with a labyrinth of spacious guest rooms
decorated in Provençal yellow and blue with Italian-styled bathrooms
and LCD TVs. **Pros:** ecological rooms available; lots of in-room amenities. **Cons:** can't access rates by Internet. $ *Rooms from: €110* ⊠ *Pl.
de Langes* ☎ *04–90–11–40–40* ⊕ *www.hotel-arene.fr* ⇥ *33 rooms, 2
suites* ⊙⊙ *No meals.*

**\$**  ⊡ **Hôtel Lou Cigaloun.** For price, location, and ambience this central bud-
HOTEL  get hotel is hard to beat. **Pros:** comfortable beds. **Cons:** only two parking
spots (and you have to pay); not the prettiest exterior. $ *Rooms from:
€90* ⊠ *4 rue Caristie* ☎ *04–90–34–10–07* ⊕ *www.hotel-loucigaloun.
com* ⇥ *24 rooms* ⊙⊙ *No meals.*

**\$**  ⊡ **L'Orangerie.** Just 4 kilometers (2½ miles) north of Orange, this 18th-
HOTEL  century auberge has new owners, who spared no corner during renovations. **Pros:** comfortable beds and flat-screen TVs. **Cons:** a drive
from the city center. $ *Rooms from: €98* ⊠ *4 rue de l'Ormeau, Piolenc*
☎ *04–90–29–59–88* ⊕ *www.orangerie.net* ⇥ *6 rooms* ⊗ *Closed one wk
at Christmas* ⊙⊙ *Breakfast.*

### NIGHTLIFE AND THE ARTS

**Les Chorégies d'Orange.** To witness the torches of *Nabucco* or *Aïda* flick-
ering against the 2,000-year-old Roman wall of the Théâtre Antique and
to hear the extraordinary sound play around its semicircle of ancient
seats is one of the great summer festival experiences in Europe. Every
July and the first week in August, Les Chorégies d'Orange echo tradition and amass operatic and classical music spectacles under the summer stars in Orange. Be sure to book tickets well in advance; they go
on sale the previous October. ⊠ *15 Pl. Silvain* ⊕ *www.choregies.com.*

## BEAUMES-DE-VENISE

*23 km (14 miles) east of Orange.*

Just west of the great mass of Mont Ventoux, surrounded by farmland
and vineyards, is Beaumes-de-Venise, where streets of shuttered bour-
geois homes slope steeply into a market center. This is the renowned
source of a delicately sweet muscat wine, but if you're tasting, don't
overlook the local red wine.

Beaumes lies at the foot of the **Dentelles de Montmirail,** a small range
of rocky chalk cliffs eroded to lacy pinnacles—hence the name *dentelles*

(lace). From tiny D21, east of town, you'll find dramatic views north to the ragged peaks and south over lush orchards and vineyards interspersed with olive groves, pine, and yew trees. It's a splendid drive, and if you love nature it would be well worth staying in this area—many of the stone houses have been converted into bed-and-breakfasts.

In the town center you can also buy fruity, unfiltered olive oil produced in the area; it's made in such small quantities that you're unlikely to see it anywhere else.

### GETTING HERE AND AROUND
There is no direct bus service to Beaumes-de-Venise. You can take bus line 5.1 from Avignon to Carpentras, about 10 km (6 miles) away (€2, one hour), and take a taxi the rest of the way for about €20. The best way to get here is by car.

### VISITOR INFORMATION
**Beaumes-de-Venise Tourist Office** ✉ *122 pl. du Marché* ☎ *04–90–62–94–39.*

### EXPLORING
**Domaine des Bernardins.** This vineyard has a tasting cave, where you can sample some of the wines, which include mostly whites but also reds from grapes such as grenache. ✉ *Rte. de Lafare, 138 av. Léon Gambe* ☎ *04–90–62–94–13* ⊕ *www.domaine-des-bernardins.com* ☉ *Mon.–Sat. 8:30–noon and 2–6:30.*

### WHERE TO STAY
**$$$$** **Le Clos Saint Saourde.** Jérôme and Geraldine, both of whom speak
**HOTEL** English, have a winning way of meeting all your needs in this classic yet chic converted farmhouse with stone walls. **Pros:** vineyard views from breakfast terrace and pool; picnic essentials available should you wish to prepare a basket yourself. **Cons:** toiletries not provided; the main terrace is in front of the parking area. $ *Rooms from: €230* ✉ *Rte. de St Véran* ☎ *04–90–37–35–20* ⊕ *www.leclossaintsaourde.com* 🛏 *2 rooms, 2 suites, cabin* ○ *Breakfast.*

## VACQUEYRAS

*5 km (3 miles) northwest of Beaumes-de-Venise.*

Smaller and more picturesque than Beaumes, with stone houses scattered along its gentle slopes, Vacqueyras gives its name to a robust, tannic red wine worthy of its more famous neighbors around Châteauneuf-du-Pape or Gigondas. Wine domaines beckon from the outskirts of town, and the center strikes a mellow balance of plane trees and cascading wisteria, punctuated by discreet tasting shops. Thanks to its consistently rising quality, Vacqueyras was the latest of the Côtes du Rhônes to earn its own appellation—the right to put its village name on the bottle instead of the less prestigious, more generic Côtes-du-Rhône label.

### GETTING HERE AND AROUND
There is no direct bus service to Vacqueyras. The only way to get here is by car.

## GIGONDAS

FodorsChoice    *3 km (2 miles) north of Vacqueyras.*
★

The prettiest of all the Mont Ventoux Côtes-du-Rhône wine villages, Gigondas is little more than a cluster of stone houses stacked gracefully up a hillside overlooking the broad sweep of the valley below. At the top, a false-front Baroque church anchors a ring of medieval ramparts; from here you can take in views as far as the Cévennes.

Its few residents share one vocation: the production of the vigorous Grenache-based red that bears the village name. At the more than 60 *caveaux* (tasting caves) scattered through the village and the surrounding countryside, you're welcome to visit, taste, and buy without ceremony. Pick up a contact list from the tourist office at the village entrance beside the town hall.

### GETTING HERE AND AROUND

There is no direct bus service to Gigondas. The only way to get here is by car.

### WHERE TO EAT AND STAY

$$    ⓘ **Les Florêts.** Winter or summer, Les Florêts makes a romantic hide-
HOTEL    away with its full-on view of the Dentelles de Montmirail and a salon centered around a giant white fireplace and body-hugging red armchairs. **Pros:** "Wine Uncovered" visits can be arranged; breathtaking scenery from charming rooms. **Cons:** mistrals could dampen outings. Ⓢ *Rooms from: €120* ⊠ *Rte. des Dentelles* ☎ *04–90–65–85–01* ⊕ *www.hotel-lesflorets.com* ⤳ *15 rooms* ☉ *Closed Jan. and two wks in Feb. during school holidays* �ⓄⅠ *No meals.*

## SÉGURET

*8 km (5 miles) northeast of Gigondas.*

Nestled into the sharp rake of a rocky hillside and crowned with a ruined medieval castle, Séguret is a picture-book hill village that is only moderately commercialized. Its 14th-century clock tower, Romanesque St-Denis Church, and bubbling Renaissance fountain highlight steep little stone streets and lovely views of the Dentelles de Montmirail cliffs. Here, too, you can find peppery Côtes du Rhône for the tasting.

### GETTING HERE AND AROUND

There is no direct bus service to Séguret. The only way to get here is by car.

### WHERE TO STAY

$    ✕ **Côté Terrasse.** A modern restaurant with a pleasantly shaded terrace
BISTRO    and a view describes dozens of restaurants in Provence, including this one, but the real standouts here are the warm and welcoming service and the consistently good food. The menu features plenty of fresh and inventive salads, like wild salmon with shrimp, melon, and tomato confit, not always easy to find, along with heartier dishes—cod with garlic aioli and grilled vegetables, Iberian pork with chestnuts and whipped potatoes, and a classic roasted duck breast. At €16, the

Picturesquely set on the banks of the Ouvèze River amid vast vineyards, Vaison-la-Romaine is a jumble of architectural styles that reflect the town's Gallo-Roman past.

two-course lunch menu is just the thing. $ *Average main: €18* ⊠ *Les Poternes* ☎ *04–90–28–03–48* ⚑ *Reservations essential* ☉ *Closed Mon. May–Oct. No dinner Nov.–Apr.*

**$**  🛏 **La Bastide Bleue.** Once an idyllic youth hostel, this old stone farmhouse
**HOTEL**  with blue-shuttered windows is now an unpretentious but enchanting country inn set in a pine-shaded garden court. **Pros:** garden-lined pool. **Cons:** proper and clean but not chichi. $ *Rooms from: €85* ⊠ *1 km (½ mile) south of Séguret on D23* ☎ *04–90–46–83–43* ⊕ *www. bastidebleue.com* ⌁ *7 rooms* ☉ *Closed Jan. and Feb.* ⊚ *Breakfast.*

## VAISON-LA-ROMAINE

**Fodor's Choice**  *10 km (6 miles) northeast of Séguret; 27 km (17 miles) northeast*
★  *of Orange.*

In a river valley green with orchards of almonds and apricots, this ancient town thrives as a modern market center. The Provençal market on Tuesday is a major tourist draw (there is also a smaller organic farmers' market on Thursday morning), as is the five-day food festival in early November. Yet it retains an irresistible Provençal charm, with medieval back streets, lively squares lined with cafés and, as its name implies, remains of its Roman past. Vaison's well-established Celtic colony joined forces with Rome in the 2nd century BC and grew to powerful status in the empire's glory days. No gargantuan monuments were raised, yet the luxurious villas surpassed those of Pompeii.

**GETTING HERE AND AROUND**

There's a 40-minute bus (No. 4; €3) running through the day from the Orange SNCF station to Vaison as well as a 45-minute bus (No. 11) from Carpentras (€2). A taxi to Orange is €43 or to Avignon, count on at least €85 during the week (and weekend fares are 50% more).

**EXPLORING**

Fodor'sChoice ★ **Patricia Wells's Cooking Classes.** While Vaison has centuries-old attractions, the most popular for Americans may well now be Patricia Wells's Cooking Classes. A living monument of Provence, the celebrated food critic first made her name known through

**FAST-FORWARD TO THE 1300S**

Take the time to climb up into Vaison's **Haute Ville**, a medieval neighborhood perched high above the river valley. Its 13th- and 14th-century houses owe some of their beauty to stone pillaged from the Roman ruins below, but their charm is from the Middle Ages: a trickling stone fountain, a bell tower with wrought-iron campanile, soft-color shutters, and blooming vines create the feel of a film set of an old town.

posh food columns and *The Food Lover's Guide to France*. First-hand, she now introduces people to the splendors of French cooking in her lovely farmhouse near Vaison through week-long cooking seminars—luxe ($5,000 a student), 12 students only, and set over Madame Wells's own Chanteduc vineyards. The truffle workshop in January is usually sold out, so book early (online only). ⊕ *www.patriciawells.com*.

**Quartier de Puymin.** Like a tiny Roman forum, the Quartier de Puymin spreads over the field and hillside in the heart of town, visible in passing from the city streets. Its skeletal ruins of villas, landscaped gardens, and museum lie below the ancient theater, all of which are accessed by the booth across from the tourist office. Closest to the entrance, the foundations of the **Maison des Messii** (Messii House) retain the outlines of its sumptuous design, complete with a vast gentleman's library, reception rooms, an atrium with a rain-fed pool, a large kitchen (the enormous stone vats are still there), and baths with hot, cold, and warm water. It requires imagination to reconstruct the rooms in your mind (remember all those toga movies from the '50s), but a tiny detail is enough to trigger a vivid image—the thresholds still show the hinge holds and scrape marks of swinging doors. A formal garden echoes a similar landscape of the time; wander under its cypresses and flowering shrubs to the **Musée Archéologique Théo-Desplans.** In this streamlined venue, the accoutrements of Roman life have been amassed and displayed by theme: pottery, weapons, gods and goddesses, jewelry, and, of course, sculpture, including full portraits of the emperor Claudius (1st century) and a strikingly noble nude Hadrian (2nd century). Cross the park behind the museum to climb into the bleachers of the 1st-century **Theater,** which is smaller than Orange's but is still used today for concerts and plays. Across the parking lot is the **Quartier de la Villasse,** where the remains of a lively market town evoke images of main-street shops, public gardens, and grand private homes, complete with floor mosaics. The most evocative image of all is in the *thermes* (baths): a neat row of marble-seat toilets lined up over a raked trough that rinsed waste instantly away. ⊠ *Rue Burrus* ☎ *04–90–36–02–11* 🎫 *Ruins, museum, and cloister, €8* ⊗ *Quartier de Puymin and museum: June–Sept., daily 9:30–6:30; Mar. and Oct., daily 10–12:30 and 2–5:30; Nov.–Feb., daily 10–noon and 2–5; Apr. and May, daily 9:30–6. Quartier de la Villasse: June–Sept., daily 10–noon and 2:30–6:30; Mar. and Oct., daily 10–12:30 and 2–5:30; Nov.–Feb., daily 10–noon and 2–5; Apr. and May, daily 10–noon and 2:30–6.*

### WHERE TO STAY

**$$**
HOTEL

🛏 **Le Beffroi.** Perched on a cliff top in the Old Town, this gracious grouping of 16th-century mansions comes together as a fine hotel. **Pros:** free parking in front; light food available all day. **Cons:** village pool can fill up quickly with kids; very narrow street to reach the hotel. $ *Rooms from: €100* ⊠ *Rue de l'Évêché* ☎ *04–90–36–04–71* ⊕ *www.le-beffroi. com* ⊃ *22 rooms* ⊗ *Closed mid-Jan.–mid-Mar.* ⦿ *No meals.*

## CRESTET

*7 km (4½ miles) south of Vaison-la Romaine.*

Another irresistible, souvenir-free aerie perched on a hilltop at the feet of the Dentelles de Montmirail cliffs and of Mont Ventoux, Crestet has it all—tinkling fountains, shuttered 15th-century houses, an arcaded *place* at the village's center, and a 12th-century castle crowning the lot. Views from its château terrace take in the concentric rings of tiled rooftops below, then the forest greenery and cultivated valleys below that.

### GETTING HERE AND AROUND

You can take the bus to nearby Vaison-la-Romaine, but the best way to get here is by car.

## LE BARROUX

Fodor'sChoice
★

*16 km (10 miles) south of Vaison-la-Romaine.*

Of all the marvelous hilltop villages stretching across the South of France, this tiny ziggurat of a town has a special charm. Le Barroux has more than a whiff of fairy tale in the air, lording over a patchwork landscape as finely drawn as a medieval illumination, as bright as an illustration in a children's book. This aerie has just one small church, one post office, and one tiny old *épicerie* (small grocery store) selling canned goods, yellowed postcards, and today's *Le Provençal.* You are forced, therefore, to look around you and listen to the trickle of the ancient fountains at every labyrinthine turn. Houses, cereal-box slim, seem to grow out of the bedrock, closing in around your suddenly unwieldy car.

### GETTING HERE AND AROUND

There is no direct bus service to Le Barroux. The only way to get here is by car.

### EXPLORING

**Château du Barroux.** With grand vaulted rooms and a chapel dating from the 12th century, this château is Le Barroux's main draw. Some of its halls serve as venues for contemporary art exhibits, and the perfect condition of all the rooms reflects a complete restoration after a World War II fire. ☎ 04–90–62–35–21 ⊕ *www.chateau-du-barroux.com* ✉ €5 ⊙ *Apr. and May, weekends 10–7; June, daily 2:30–7; July–Sept., daily 10–7; Oct., daily 2–6.*

## MONT VENTOUX

*29 km (18 miles) west of La Barroux.*

The tallest mountain in the region, Mont Ventoux has a majestic presence that dominates the sweeping vistas and landscapes of northwestern Provence. The mountain's limestone peaks—often mistaken for snow cover—reach nearly 6,000 feet and harbor a unique wind-buffeted ecosystem recognized by UNESCO and strictly protected by France. Perhaps best known for its foreboding role in the Tour de France bike race, if you can summit the "Beast of Provence" you'll be amply rewarded with some truly breathtaking views.

### GETTING HERE AND AROUND

The mountain is a favorite spot for hikers and cyclists (bike rentals are plentiful in Bédoin and Sault), but unless you're in tip-top shape, you'll need a car to explore the mountain.

### EXPLORING

**Mont Ventoux.** In addition to all the beautiful views *of* Mont Ventoux, there are equally spectacular views *from* Mont Ventoux. From Malaucène or any of the surrounding hill towns you can take an inspiring circle drive along the base and over the crest of the mountain, following the D974. This road winds through the extraordinarily lush south-facing greenery that Mont Ventoux protects from vicious mistral winds. Abundant orchards and olive groves peppered with stone farmhouses make this one of Provence's loveliest landscapes. Stop for a drink in busy **Bédoin,** with its 18th-century Jesuit church at the top of the Old Town maze.

Mont Ventoux was the site of the first recorded attempt at *l'escalade* (mountain climbing), when Italian poet-philosopher Petrarch grunted his way up in 1336. Although people had climbed mountains before, this was the first "do it because it's there" feat. Reaching the summit itself (at 6,263 feet) requires a bit of legwork. From either Chalet Reynard or the tiny ski center Mont Serein, you can leave your car and hike up to the peak's tall observatory tower. The climb is not overly taxing, and when you reach the top you are rewarded with gorgeous panoramic views of the Alps. And to the south, barring the possibility of high-summer haze, you'll take in views of the Rhône Valley, the Luberon, and even Marseille. Hiking maps are available at *maisons de la presse* (newsstands) and tourist offices. Town-to-town treks are also a great way to explore the area; one of the most beautiful trails is from Malaucène to Séguret. In the off-season, lonely Mont Ventoux is plagued with an ungodly reputation due to destructive winds. Attempts at saving its soul are evidenced by the chapels lining its slopes. Whether it's possessed by the devil or not, don't attempt to climb it in inclement weather. From late fall to early spring, in fact, the summit is closed by snow.

### WHERE TO EAT AND STAY

$$$$
B&B/INN
Fodor's Choice
★

**La Bastide de Brurangère.** Set among 12 acres of sun-drenched vineyards in view of Mont Ventoux, this little slice of heaven offers all the luxuries of a grand hotel along with the charm and privacy of a country hideaway—yet it is a good base for many local attractions (if you can tear yourself away from the relaxing options here). **Pros:** some rooms can accommodate more than four people; welcome couldn't be warmer; stay six nights and your seventh is free. **Cons:** closed for three months of the year. $ *Rooms from: €230* ⊠ *137 chemin des Rols* ☎ *06–75–24–59–29* ⊕ *www.labastidedebrurangere.com* ⇥ *4 rooms* ☉ *Closed Nov.–Feb.* ⦿ *Breakfast.*

## SAULT

*43 km (27 miles) southeast of Le Barroux, 41 km (25½ miles) northeast of Carpentras.*

Though at the hub of no fewer than six main roads, Sault remains an utterly isolated market town floating on a stony hilltop in a valley of lavender. Accessed only by circuitous country roads, it remains virtually untouched by tourism. The landscape is traditional Provence at its best—oak-forested hills and long, deep valleys purpled with the curving arcs of lavender. In the town itself, old painted storefronts exude the scent of honey and lavender. The damp church, Église Notre Dame de la Tour, dates from the 12th century; the long, lovely barrel nave was doubled in 1450.

From Sault all routes are scenic. You may head eastward into Haute-Provence, visiting (via D950) tiny **Banon,** source of the famed goat cheese. Wind up D942 to see pretty hilltop Aurel or down D30 to reach perched **Simiane-la-Rotonde.** Or head back toward Carpentras through the spectacular **Gorges de la Nesque,** snaking along narrow cliff-edge roads through dramatic canyons carpeted with wild boxwood and pine. If you're exploring the Lavender Route, head eastward some 48 km (27 miles) to discover the epicenter of Haute-Provence's fabled lavender in the sleepy, dusty town of **Forcalquier.**

### GETTING HERE AND AROUND

There is no direct bus service to Sault. The only way to get here is by car.

### VISITOR INFORMATION

**Sault Tourist Office** ⊠ *Av. de la Promenade* ☎ *04–90–64–01–21* ⊕ *www.saultenprovence.com.*

### FESTIVALS

**Fête de la Lavande.** This day-long festival, usually held around Aug. 15, is entirely dedicated to lavender. Village folk dress in traditional Provençal garb and parade on bicycles, horses leap over barrels of fragrant bundles of hay, and local producers display their wares at the market—all of which culminates in a communal dinner (€20) served with lavender-based products. ⊠ *Along the D950 at the Hippodrome le Defends* ⊕ *www.fetedelalavande.fr.*

### WHERE TO EAT AND STAY

$$$ HOTEL **Hostellerie du Val de Sault.** The feeling of being on a quiet retreat-type vacation infiltrates this former summer camp, where rooms have private decks overlooking the valley. **Pros:** you're 2,600 feet up, so nights are cool for sleeping even after the hottest of days; six-day cycle tours offered. **Cons:** breakfast and dinner demi-pension plan required. [$] *Rooms from: €190* ✉ *Route de St-Trinit* ☎ *04–90–64–01–41* 🌐 *www.valdesault.com* 🛏 *15 rooms, 5 suites* 🕒 *Closed Nov.–Mar.* 🍴 *No meals.*

## FORCALQUIER

*53 km (33 miles) east of Sault; 41 km (25½ miles) northeast of Carpentras.*

As a local center of lavender production, this small town has a lively Monday morning market with many lavender-based products. It's also a great departure point for walks, bike rides, horse rides, or drives into the lavender world that surrounds the town. In the 12th century, Forcalquier was known as the capital city of Haute-Provence and was called the Cité des Quatre Reines ("the City of the Four Queens") since the four daughters of the ruler of this region, Raimond Beranger V (Eleanor of Aquitaine among them), all married royals. Relics of this former glory can be glimpsed in the Vieille Ville of Forcalquier, notably its Cathdédrale Notre-Dame and the Couvent des Cordeliers. However, everyone heads here to marvel at the lavender fields outside town; pick up a lavender calendar at the tourist office. To explore on two wheels, get saddled up on a bicycle for a trip into the countryside at the town's Moulin de Sarret.

#### GETTING HERE AND AROUND

There is no direct bus service to Forcalquier. The only way to get here is by car.

#### VISITOR INFORMATION

**Forcalquier Tourist Office** ✉ *13 pl. Bourguet* ☎ *04–92–79–10–20* 🌐 *www.forcalquier.com.*

### EXPLORING

**France Montgolfière.** The blue-and-purple patchwork of the Luberon's famous lavender fields have never been seen to better effect than while floating freely at 1,500 feet in the air in a hot-air balloon. Adventurous travelers can take in the whole vista of mountains, perched villages, and sprawling lavender fields on an hourlong flight at either dawn or dusk when air currents are calm. For the three-hour event, the company picks you up in the village, gives you breakfast (or snack), takes you up for an hour flight, and brings you to home base. After the balloon is packed away, your courage will be honored with a *flûte de champagne* and the traditional "*toast des aéronautes.*" ✉ *Place du Village, Forcalquier* ☎ *03–80–97–38–61* 🌐 *www.france-balloons.com* 🎟 *€200 per person.*

Fodor's Choice ★ **Jardins de Salagon and Priory.** On a site occupied since the Gallo-Roman period, this picturesque 11th- to 12th-century priory—a rich archaeological site classed as a Historic Monument—presides over 10 acres of

3

themed gardens. The restored priory, with well-preserved Gothic and Romanesque flourishes, now houses an ethnological museum, a testament to the various cultures and peoples of this part of Provence. The garden functions as both a visual delight and a preserve for 2,500 species of plants and flowers native to the region, from ancient times to the present, organized into five themes, like "simple gardens and village plants," which includes field and cultivated plants that were both consumed and used medicinally. There's also a medieval garden, a fragrant garden, with benches under the roses and honeysuckle for maximum sensory effect, and a modern "exotic" garden that crosses five continents. ⊠ *Prieuré de Salagon, Mane-en-Provence* ☎ *04–92–75–70–50* ⊕ *musee-de-salagon.com* ⊗ *May–Sept., daily; Oct.–Dec. 15, Feb. and Apr., Wed.–Mon.*

**L'Occitane.** Nine kilometers (15 miles) south of Forcalquier is Manosque, home to the famed L'Occitane factory, a leading purveyor of lavender magic. Manosque is certainly not a draw on its own, but a trip here is worth it for a visit to the cosmetics and skin care company that is now the town's main employer. Once you make a reservation via the Manosque tourist office, you can take a two-hour tour of the production site, view a documentary film, get a hand massage with oils, then stock up on Occitane products at the company shop. ⊠ *Z. I. St-Maurice, Manosque* ☎ *04–92–78–01–08* ⊕ *www.loccitane.com* ⊗ *Mon.–Sat. 10–7.*

# THE SORGUE VALLEY

This gentle, rolling valley east of Avignon follows the course of the River Sorgue, which wells up from caverns below the arid hills of the Vaucluse plateau, gushes to the surface at Fontaine-de-Vaucluse, and rolls down to turn the mossy waterwheels in picturesque L'Isle-sur-la-Sorgue. It is a region of transition between the urban outskirts of Avignon and the wilds of the Luberon to the east.

## L'ISLE-SUR-LA-SORGUE

FodorsChoice  *30 km (19 miles) east of Avignon.*

★  Crisscrossed with lazy canals and still alive with waterwheels that once drove its silk, wool, and paper mills, this charming valley town retains its gentle appeal—except on Sunday. Then this easygoing old town transforms itself into a Marrakech of marketeers, "the most charming flea market in the world," its streets crammed with antiques and *brocantes*, its cafés swelling with crowds of chic bargain browsers making a day of it. Yves St-Laurent bigwig Pierre Bergé, Viscount Linley (the noted furniture designer and son of Princess Margaret), and interior decorator Jacques Grange all flock here. Even hardcore modernists inured to treasure hunts enjoy the show as urbane couples with sweaters over shoulders squint discerningly through half lenses at monogrammed linen sheets, zinc washstands, *barbotine* ware, china spice sets, Art Deco perfume bottles, tinted engravings, and the paintings of modern almost-masters. For high-style big purchases—furniture,

$5,000 quilts, and the like—head to the town's noted antiques shops (⇨ *Shopping, below*). There are also street musicians, food stands groaning under rustic breads, vats of tapenade, cloth-lined baskets of spices, and miles of café tables offering ringside seats to the spectacle. After London's Portobello district and the flea market at St-Ouen outside Paris, L'Isle-sur-la-Sorgue is reputedly Europe's third-largest antiques market. L'Isle's antiques market ratchets up to high speed twice a year when the town hosts a big antiques show, usually four days around Easter and another in mid-August, nicknamed the *Grand Déballage*—the "Great Unpacking" (⊕ *foire–islesurlasorgue.com*). Prices can be high, and bargains are few, but remember that in many cases dealers expect to bargain.

On a nonmarket day, life returns to its mellow pace. Dealers and clients catch up on gossip at the Place Gambetta fountain and at the Café de France, opposite the church of Notre-Dame-des-Anges. Wander the maze inside the ring to admire a range of architectural styles, from Gothic to Renaissance, with the occasional burst of color where an owner has broken from local tradition to paint an archway indigo blue or a pair of shutters lemon yellow.

The Provençal Venice, L'Isle is dotted with watermills and canals that once drove the wheels of silk, paper, oil, grain, and leather mills. Today, these wheels—14 of them—turn idly, adding to the charm of the winding streets. If you want to explore the vestiges of L'Isle's 18th-century heyday, stop in the tourist office and pick up a brochure called "Vagabondages L'Isle-sur-la-Sorgue" (available in English).

### GETTING HERE AND AROUND

There's a 40-minute bus (No. 6) from the Avignon train station that stops at Place Robert Vasse in Isle-sur-la-Sorgue (where the large Caisse d'Epargne bank is). It's €2 one way or €1, if you return on the same day. By car the distance is 5 km (3 miles). The TER train line links Avignon and L'Isle-sur-la-Sorgue from the L'Isle-Fontaine train station.

### VISITOR INFORMATION

**L'Isle-sur-la-Sorgue Tourist Office** ⊠ *Pl. de la Liberté* ☎ *04–90–38–04–78* ⊕ *www.oti-delasorgue.fr.*

### EXPLORING

**Collégiale Notre-Dame-des-Anges.** L'Isle's 17th-century church, the Collégiale Notre-Dame-des-Anges, is extravagantly decorated with gilt, faux marble, and sentimental frescoes. The double-colonnade facade commands the center of the Vieille Ville. Visiting hours change frequently, so check with the tourist office.

**Hôtel de Campredon–Maison René Char.** One of the finest of L'Isle's mansions, the Hôtel de Campredon–Maison René Char, has been restored and reinvented as a modern-art gallery, mounting temporary exhibitions of modern masters. ⊠ *20 rue du Docteur Tallet* ☎ *04–90–38–17–41* 🖾 *€6* ⊗ *July–Aug., Tues.–Sun. 10–1 and 3–7; Sept.–June, Tues.–Sat. 10–12:30 and 2–5:30.*

## WHERE TO EAT

$$ FRENCH

🍴 **Le Jardin du Quai.** This is where local antiques dealers come to eat, and the place feels so welcoming that it would be easy to linger for hours. Chef Daniel Hébet made his name at La Mirande in Avignon and Le Domaine des Andéols in St-Saturnin-lès-Apt before opening this bistro in his own image—young, jovial, and uncompromising when it comes to quality. Off a noisy street near the train station is the gate to this garden haven, with metal tables under the trees and an airy interior with a vintage tile floor. Hébet offers a single set menu at lunch and another at dinner, and the food is so good that no one is complaining at the lack of choice (though he has been known to substitute meat for fish on request): poached egg with truffles, Saint Pierre with a hint of green onion, lobster in ever-so-delicate pastry, and cherry meringue are all delicious. [$] *Average main: €23* ✉ *91 av. Julien Guigue* ☎ *04–90–20–14–98* 🌐 *www.danielhebet.com* ⏲ *Closed Tues. and Wed.*

$$$ FRENCH Fodor's Choice ★

🍴 **Le Vivier.** Patrick and Céline Fischnaller returned to southern France from London only three years ago and have already won acclaim with this dazzler just outside L'Isle-sur-la-Sorgue's center. Start off with a glass of wine (from €3) on the orange sofa in the Deco lounge before devouring some foie gras and smoked eel terrine, pigeon pie, or strawberry soup with basil and black olives from the €43 menu (or opt to go à la carte). But be sure to leave room for the sublime roast beef with cherry marmalade or roasted cod with stuffed pequillos peppers. The couple's philosophy that wine is equally as important is reflected in an extensive list. Did we mention the Sorgue river runs underneath the terrace? [$] *Average main: €28* ✉ *800 cours Ferande Peyre* ☎ *04–90–38–52–80* 🌐 *www.levivier-restaurant.com* ✍ *Reservations essential* ⏲ *Closed Mon. No lunch Fri.–Sat. No dinner Sun. Closed last wk Feb.–mid-Mar.*

## WHERE TO STAY

$ B&B/INN

🏨 **La Gueulardière.** After a Sunday glut of antiquing along the canals, you can dine and sleep just up the street in a hotel full of collectible finds, from the school posters in the restaurant to the oak armoires and brass beds that furnish the simple lodgings. **Pros:** ideal location for antique hunters to stay; rooms are bright and cheerful. **Cons:** some rooms are noisy; can be stuffy and hot in summer. [$] *Rooms from: €63* ✉ *1 cours René Char* ☎ *04–90–38–10–52* 🌐 *www.gueulardiere.com* 🛏 *5 rooms* ⏲ *Closed mid-Dec.–mid-Jan. Restaurant closed Mon. dinner and Tues. during winter* 🍽 *No meals.*

$$$$ HOTEL Fodor's Choice ★

🏨 **La Maison sur la Sorgue.** This 17th-century home wins guests over as soon as they walk in the door, thanks to its composed elegance and authentic style rarely found in a hotel setting—innkeepers Frédéric and Marie-Claude did their architectural homework before they renovated. **Pros:** all-out treatment plus amenities (shampoos and soaps); courtyard breakfast includes morning surprises beyond the basic croissant and jam fare. **Cons:** moquette carpet (while practical) is rough on the feet; some handheld showers. [$] *Rooms from: €350* ✉ *6 rue Rose Goudard* ☎ *04–90–20–74–86* 🌐 *www.lamaisonsurlasorgue.com* 🛏 *2 rooms, 2 suites* ⏲ *Closed last 2 wks of Nov. and 2 wks Feb.* 🍽 *Breakfast.*

$$$ B&B/INN Fodor's Choice ★ **La Prévôté.** Five beautifully decorated and freshly painted rooms, each styled with exquisite taste in soft colors and Provence chic, offer an ideal respite after a long day of antiques shopping. **Pros:** price includes breakfast; top dining; antiques-bedecked decor. **Cons:** a little tricky to find; parking may be difficult. [$] *Rooms from: €160* ✉ *4 bis rue Jean Jacques Rousseau* ☎ *04–90–38–57–29* 🌐 *www.la-prevote.fr* ✍ *Reservations essential* 🛏 *5 rooms* 🕓 *Closed Feb. and Nov. Restaurant closed Wed. Sept.–June and Tues. year-round* 🍴 *Breakfast.*

**WORD OF MOUTH**

"Sunday is the huge market day in L'Isle. Being able to walk out your hotel door and attend the market sure beats driving around to find parking. This market is every bit as good as the one in Nice. We cannot wait to plan a return visit." —DeeDee_Goose

### SHOPPING

Throughout the pretty backstreets of L'Isle's Old Town (especially between Place de l'Église and Avenue de la Libération), there are boutiques spilling baskets full of tempting goods onto the sidewalk to lure you inside; most concentrate on home design and Provençal goods.

**Passage du Pont.** Of the dozens of antiques shops in L'Isle, one conglomerate—Passage du Pont (formerly L'Isle aux Brocantes)—concentrates some 40 dealers under the same roof. It's open Friday afternoons and all day the rest of the week. ✉ *7 av. des Quatre Otages* ☎ *06–20–10–58–15.*

**Sous un Olivier.** This food boutique is crammed to the ceiling with bottles and jars of tapenade, fancy mustards, candies shaped like olives, and the house olive oil. ✉ *16 rue de la République* ☎ *04–90–20–68–90* 🌐 *sousunolivier.com.*

**Un Jour Ailleurs.** For more than 200 years, this store has been making wool blankets, quilts, and bed accessories—sold alongside Brun de Vian Tiran's cashmere or mohair shawls and scarves. ✉ *Pl. Ferdinand Buisson* ☎ *04–90–38–50–19.*

**Xavier Nicod.** Higher-end antiques are in plentiful supply at the twin shops of Xavier Nicod et Gérard Nicod. ✉ *9 av. des Quatre Otages* ☎ *06–07–85–54–59* 🌐 *www.xaviernicod.com.*

## FONTAINE-DE-VAUCLUSE

*7 km (4½ miles) east of L'Isle-sur-la-Sorgue; 30 km (19 miles) east of Avignon.*

Like the natural attraction for which it is named, this village has welled up and spilled over as a Niagara Falls–type tourist center; the rustic, pretty, and slightly tacky riverside town is full of shops, cafés, and restaurants, all built to serve the pilgrims who flock to its namesake. And neither town nor fountain should be missed if you're either a connoisseur of rushing water or a fan of foreign kitsch.

*Continued on page 141*

Van Gogh may have made the sunflower into the icon of Provence, but it is another flower —one that is unprepossessing, fragrant, and tiny—that draws thousands of travelers every year to Provence. They come to journey the famous "Route de la Lavande " (the Lavender Route), a wide blue-purple swath that connects over 2,000 producers across the south of France.

# BLUE GOLD: THE LAVENDER ROUTE

Once described as the "soul of Haute-Provence," lavender has colored Provence's plains since the days of the ancient Romans. Today it brings prosperity, as consumers are madly buying hundreds of beauty products that use lavender essence. Nostrils flared, they are following this route every summer. To help sate their lavender lust, the following pages present a detail-rich tour of the Lavender Route.

Gorde

**1** Have your Nikon ready for the beautifully preserved Cistercian simplicity of the **Abbaye Notre-Dame de Sénanque**, a perfect foil for the famous waving fields of purple around it.

**2** No shrinking violet, the hilltop village of **Gordes** is famous for its luxe hotels, restaurants, and lavender-stocked shops.

**3** Get a fascinating A to Z tour—from harvesting to distilling to production—at the **Musée de la Lavande** near Coustellet.

**4** If you want to have a peak lavender experience—literally—detour 18 km (10 mi) to the northwest and take a spectacular day's drive up the winding road to the **summit of Mont Ventoux** (follow signs from Sault to see the lavender-filled valleys below).

**5** Even if you miss the biggest blow-out of the year, the Fête de la Lavande in **Sault** (usually on August 15), take in the charming *vieille ville* boutiques or the fabulous lavender fields that surround the hillside town.

**6** The awe-inspiring lavender fields around **Forcalquier** are one step away from perfection, and the Monday morning market is a treasure trove of local products.

**7** Distillerie "Le Coulets" on the outskirts of Apt has been a lavender farm for generations and offers free tours and products for sale at its boutique.

**8** You've bought the famous lavender products of L'Occitane everywhere, so how can you resist a tour of their **Manosque** factory?

Provence is threaded by the "Routes de la Lavande" (the Lavender Routes), a wide blue-purple swath that connects over 2,000 producers across the Drôme, the plateau du Vaucluse, and the Alpes-de-Haute-Provence, but our itinerary is lined with some of the prettiest sights—and smells— of the region. Whether you're shopping for artisanal bottles of the stuff (as with wine, the finest lavender carries its own Appellation d'Origine Contrôlée), spending a session at a lavender spa, or simply wearing hip-deep purple as you walk the

Forcalquier Market

Purple haze

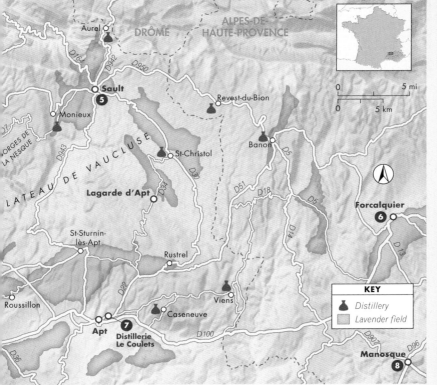

**KEY**

🏺 Distillery

⬜ Lavender field

fields, the most essential aspect on this trip is savoring a magical world of blue, one we usually only encounter on picture postcards.

To join the lavender-happy crowds, you have to go in season, which runs from June to early September. Like Holland's May tulips, the lavender of Haute-Provence is in its true glory only once a year: the last two weeks of July, when the harvesting begins—but fields bloom throughout the summer months for the most part. Below, we wind through the most generous patches of lavender. Drive the colorful gambit southeastward (Coustellet, Gordes, Sault, Forcalquier, and Manosque), which will give you good visiting (and shopping) time in a number of the villages that are *fou de la lavande* (crazy for lavender). And for the complete scoop on the hundreds of sights to see in lavender land, contact **Les Routes de la Lavande** through the association La Grande Traversée des Alpes in Grenoble (☎ *04–76–42–08–31* ⊕ *www.grande-traversee-alpes.com*).

Abbaye Notre-Dame de Sénanque

# DAY 1

## SÉNANQUE
### A Picture-Perfect Abbey

An invisible Master of Ceremonies for the Lavender Route would surely send you first to the greatest spot for lavender worship in the world: the 12th-century Cistercian **Abbaye Notre-Dame de Sénanque**, which in July and August seems to float above a sea of lavender, a setting immortalized in a thousand travel posters. Happily, you'll find it via the D177 only 4 km (2½ miles) north of Gordes, among the most beautiful of Provence's celebrated perched villages. An architecture student's dream of neat cubes, cylinders, and pyramids, its pure Romanesque form alone is worth contemplating in any context. But in this arid, rocky setting the gray stone building seems to have special resonance—ancient, organic, with a bit of the borie about it. Along with the abbeys of Le Thornet and Silvacane, this is one of the trio of "Three Sisters" built by the Cistercian order in this area. Sénanque's **church** is a model of symmetry and balance. Begun in 1150, it has no decoration but still touches the soul with its chaste beauty.

The adjoining **cloister,** from the 12th century, is almost as pure, with barrel-vaulted galleries framing double rows of discreet, abstract pillars. Next door, the enormous vaulted dormitory and the refectory shelter a display on the history of Cistercian abbeys. The few remaining monks here now preside over a cultural center that presents concerts and exhibitions. The bookshop is one of the best in Provence, with a huge collection of Provençaliana (lots in English).

After spending the morning getting acquainted with the little purple flower at Sénanque, drive south along the D2 (or D177) back to **Gordes**, through a

## THE ESSENCE OF THE MATTER

Provence and lavender go hand in hand—but why? The flower is native to the Mediterranean, and grows so well because the pH balance in the soil is naturally perfect for it (pH 6–8). But lavender was really put on the map here when ancient Romans arrived to colonize Provence and used the flower to disinfect their baths and perfume their laundry (the word comes from Latin *lavare*, "to wash"). From a small grass-roots industry, lavender proliferated over the centuries until the first professional distillery opened in Provence in the 1880s to supply oils for southern French apothecaries. After World War I, production boomed to meet the demand of the perfumers of Grasse (the perfume center of the world). Once described as the "soul of Haute-Provence," lavender is now farmed in England, India, and the States, but the harvest in the South of France remains the world's largest.

dry, rocky region mixed with deep valleys and far-reaching plains.

Wild lavender is already omnipresent, growing in large tracts as you reach the entrance of the small, unspoiled hilltop village, making for a patchwork landscape as finely drawn as a medieval illumination. A cluster of houses rises above the valley in painterly hues of honey gold, with cobbled streets winding up to the village's picturesque Renaissance château, making it one of the most beautiful towns in Provence.

Gordes has a great selection of hotels, restaurants, and B&Bs to choose from (see our listings under Gordes). Spend the early afternoon among tasteful shops that sell lovely Provençal crafts and produce, much of it lavender-based, and then after lunch, head out to Coustellet.

### COUSTELLET
#### A Great Lavender Museum

Set 2 miles south of Gordes, Coustellet is noted for its **Musée de la Lavande** (take the D2 southeast to the outskirts of Coustellet). Owned by one of the original lavender families, who have cultivated and distilled the flower here for over five generations, this museum lies on the outskirts of more than 80 acres of prime lavender-cultivated land.

### ON THE CALENDAR

If you plan to be at the Musée de la Lavande between July 1 and August 25 you can work up a sweat cutting your own swath of lavender with a copper scythe, then make your own distillation in the museum's lab.

Not only can you visit the well-organized and interesting museum (note the impressive collection of scythes and distilling apparatus), you can buy up a storm in the boutique, which offers a great selection of lavender-based products at very reasonable prices.

There are four main species. True lavender (*Lavandula angustifolia*) produces the most subtle essential oil and is often used by perfume makers and laboratories. Spike lavender (*Lavandula latifolia*) has wide leaves and long floral stems with several flower spikes. Hybrid lavender (*lavandin*) is obtained from pollination of true lavender and spike lavender, making a hybrid that forms a highly developed large round cluster. French lavender (*Lavendula stoechas*) is wild lavender that grows throughout the region and is collected for the perfume industry. True lavender thrives in the chalky soils and hot, dry climate of higher altitudes of Provence. It was picked systematically until the end of the 19th century and used for most lavender-based products. But as the demand for this remarkable flower grew, so did the need for a larger production base. By the beginning of the 20th century, the demand for the flower was so great that producers planted fields of lavender at lower altitudes, creating the need for a tougher, more resistant plant: the hybrid *lavandin*.

In many towns, Provence's lavender harvest is celebrated with charming folkloric festivals.

# DAY 2

### LAGARDE D'APT
### A Top Distillerie

On the second day of your lavender adventure, begin by enjoying the winding drive 25 km (15 miles) east to the town of **Apt**. Aside from its Provençal market, busy with all the finest food products of the Luberon and Haute Provence, Apt itself is unremarkable (even actively ugly from a distance) but is a perfect place from which to organize your visits to the lavender fields of Caseneuve, Viens, and Lagarde d'Apt.

Caseneuve (east exit from Apt onto the D900 and then northwest on the D35) and Viens (16 km/10 miles east from Apt on the D209) are small but charming places to stop for a quick bite along the magnificent drive through the rows upon rows of lavender, but if you have to choose between the three, go to the minuscule village of Lagarde d'Apt (12 km/7 miles east from Apt on the D209).

Or for a closer look, take the D22 (direction Rustrel) a few kilometres out-side of Apt to **Distillerie "Les Coulets."** From June to September, you can take a free tour of the distillery, visit the farm and browse the gift shop.

### SAULT
### The Biggest Festival

To enjoy a festive overnight, continue northwest from Lagarde d'Apt to the village of **Sault**, 15 km (9 miles) to the northeast. Beautifully perched on a rocky outcrop overlooking the valley that bears its name, Sault is one of the key stops along the Lavender Route.

There are any number of individual distilleries, producers, and fields to visit— to make the most of your visit, ask the Office du Tourisme (☎ *04–90–64–01–21* ⊕ *www.saultenprovence.com*) for a list of events. Make sure to pop into the **Centre de Découverte de la Nature et du Patrimoine Cynégétique** to see the exhibitions on the natural history of the region, including some on lavender. Aim to be in Sault for the not-to-be-missed **Fête de la Lavande**, a day-long festival entirely dedicated to lavender, the best in the region, and usually held around August 15.

Village folk dress in traditional Provençal garb and parade on bicycles, horses leap over barrels of fragrant bundles of hay, and local producers display their wares at the market—all of which culminates in a communal Provençal dinner (€20) served with lavender-based products.

## DAY 3

### FORCALQUIER
### The Liveliest Market

On your third day, the drive from Sault over 53 km (33 miles) east to Forcalquier is truly spectacular.

As you approach the village in late July, you will see endless fields of *Lavandula vera* (true wild lavender) broken only by charming stone farmhouses or discreet distilleries.

The epicenter of Haute-Provence's lavender cultivation, **Forcalquier** boasts a lively Monday morning market with a large emphasis on lavender-based products, and it is a great departure point for walks, bike rides, horse rides, or drives into the lavender world that surrounds the town.

In the 12th century, Forcalquier was known as the capital city of Haute-Provence and was called the *Cité des Quatre Reines* (City of the Four Queens) because the four daughters (Eleanor of Aquitaine among them) of the ruler of this region, Raimond Béranger V, all married royals.

Relics of this former glory can be glimpsed in the Vieille Ville of Forcalquier, notably its Cathédrale Notre-Dame and the Couvent des Cordeliers.

However, everyone heads here to marvel at the lavender fields outside town. Contact Forcalquier's Office du Tourisme (⊠ *13 pl. Bourguet* ☎ *04-92-75-10-02* ⊕ *www.forcalquier.com*) for

## MAKING SCENTS

### BLOOMING

Lavender fields begin blooming in late June, depending on the area and the weather, with fields reaching their peak from the first of July to mid-October. The last two weeks in July are considered the best time to catch the fields in all their glory.

### HARVESTING

Lavender is harvested from July to September, when the hot summer sun brings the essence up into the flower. Harvesting is becoming more and more automated; make an effort to visit some of the older fields with narrow rows—these are still picked by hand. Lavender is then dried for two to three days before being transported to the distillery.

### DISTILLING

Distillation is done in a steam alembic, with the dry lavender steamed in a double boiler. Essential oils are extracted from the lavender by water vapor, which is then passed through the cooling coils of a retort.

information on the lavender calendar, then get saddled up on a bicycle for a trip into the countryside at the town's **Moulin de Sarret**.

Plan on enjoying a fine meal and an overnight stay (reserve way in advance) at the town's most historic establishment, the **Hostellerie des Deux Lions**.

## MANOSQUE
### Love That L'Occitane
About 25 km (15 miles) south of Forcalquier is Manosque, home to the **L'Occitane** factory.

You can get a glimpse of what the Luberon was like before it became so hip—Manosque is certainly not a tourist epicenter—but a trip here is worth it for a visit to the phenomenally successful cosmetics and skin care company that is now the town's main employer.

Once you make a reservation through the Manosque Tourist Office (⊠ *Pl. du Docteur Joubert* ☎ *04–92–72–16–00* ⊕ *www.manosque-tourisme.com*) you can take a two-hour tour of the production site, view a documentary film, get a massage with oils, then rush into the shop where you can stock up on L'Occitane products for very reasonable prices.

**BRINGING IT HOME**

Yes, you've already walked in the pungent-sweet fields, breathing in the ephemeral scent that is uniquely a part of Provence. Visually, there is nothing like the waving fields rising up in a haze of bees. But now it's time to shop! Here are some top places to head to stop and smell the lavender element in local wines, honey, vinegar, soaps, and creams. A fine place to start is 8 km (5 mi) east of Sault at the **Ho! Bouquet de Lavande** (⊠ follow signs on the D189, Ferrassières ☎ 04–75–28–87–52). Take a free guided visit and cut your own lavender bouquet before buying up all the inventory available in the shop.

In Gordes and Sault there are lovely Provençal markets that have a wide range of lavender-based products, from honey to vinegar to creams. A great selection of the finest essential oils is available at **Distillerie du Vallon** (⊠ Rte. des Michouilles, Sault ☎ 04–90–64–14–83). **L'Occitane** (⊠ Z.I. St-Maurice, Manosque ☎ 04–92–70–19–00) is the mother store. In nearby Volx you can hit the **Maison aux Huiles Essentiels** (⊠ Z.I. La Carretière, Volx ☎ 04–92–78–46–77) for aromatherapy in all its glory.

SCENT-SATIONAL

## GETTING HERE AND AROUND

You can take bus line 6 (running eight times daily, twice on Sunday) from Avignon TGV station (€2, 1 hour). Otherwise arriving by car is your best option.

## VISITOR INFORMATION

**Fontaine-de-Vaucluse Tourist Office** ⊠ *Chemin du Gouffre* ☎ *04–90–38–04– 78* ⊕ *www.oti-delasorgue.fr.*

## EXPLORING

**Château.** Fontaine has its own ruined château, perched romantically on a forested hilltop over the town and illuminated at night. First built around the year 1000 and embellished in the 14th century by the bishops of Cavaillon, the castle was destroyed in the 15th century and forms little more than a sawtooth silhouette against the sky.

**Fontaine-de-Vaucluse.** There's no exaggerating the magnificence of the Fontaine-de-Vaucluse, a mysterious spring that gushes from a deep underground source that has been explored to a depth of 1,010 feet— so far. Framed by towering cliffs, a broad, pure pool wells up and spews dramatically over massive rocks down a gorge to the village, where its roar soothes and cools the visitors who crowd the riverfront cafés.

You must pay to park, then run a gauntlet of souvenir shops and tourist traps on your way to the top. But even if you plan to make a beeline past the kitsch, do stop in at the legitimate and informative **Moulin Vallis-Clausa.** A working paper mill, it demonstrates a reconstruction of a 15th-century waterwheel that drives timber crankshafts to mix rag pulp, while artisans roll and dry thick paper *à l'ancienne* (in the old manner). The process is fascinating and free to watch (the guided tour lasts half an hour and must be arranged in advance; minimum 10 people), though it's almost impossible to resist buying note cards, posters, even lamp shades fashioned from the pretty stuff. Fontaine was once a great industrial mill center, but its seven factories were closed by strikes in 1968 and never recovered. All the better for you today, since now you can enjoy this marvelous natural spot in peace. ⊠ *On the riverbank walk up to the spring* ☎ *04–90–20–34–14* ☽ *Daily 10–6.*

**Le Musée-bibliothèque F. Pétrarque.** The great Renaissance poet Petrarch, driven mad with unrequited love for a beautiful married woman named Laura, retreated to this valley to nurse his passion in a cabin with "one dog and only two servants." He had met the woman in the heady social scene at the papal court in Avignon, where she was to die years later of the plague. Sixteen years in this wild isolation didn't ease the pain, but the serene environment inspired him to poetry, and the lyrics of his *Canzoniere* were dedicated to Laura's memory. The small museum, built on the site of his residence, displays prints and engravings of the virtuous lovers, both in Avignon and Fontaine-de-Vaucluse. ⊠ *On the left bank, direction Gordes* ☎ *04–90–20–37–20* ☞ *€3.50* ☽ *Apr.–Nov., Tues.–Sun. 10–12 and 2–6.*

### WHERE TO EAT AND STAY

$ FRENCH 🍴 **Philip-Jardin de Pétrarque.** If you want a truly regional experience, take a seat on the shaded terrace of Restaurant Philip, opened in 1926 by Philip's uncle. Set apart from the other eateries, it's located just before the trail to the spring. Enjoy the river views and dig in to some *cuisses de grenouille* or trout from the Sorgue cooked in white butter sauce or pink trout marinated in olive oil. A three-course menu goes for only €27, and there's a decent regional wine list. Sandwiches, salads, and ice cream can be ordered next door at its Bar Glacier. [$] *Average main: €17* ✉ *Chem. de la Fontaine* ☎ *04–90–20–31–81* ⏲ *Closed Oct.–Mar. No dinner Apr.–June and Sept.*

$$ HOTEL 🏨 **Hotel du Poete.** A river runs through it is no exaggeration at this amiable hotel with breakfast room, pool, terrace, gardens, Jacuzzi, terrace bar, and several guest rooms overlooking (and in some cases atop) the melodious streams that meander from the famous Sorgue *source*, a kilometer away. **Pros:** a short walk from Fontaine-de-Vaucluse and restaurants. **Cons:** some ground floor rooms lack views. [$] *Rooms from: €119* ✉ *Le Village* ☎ *04–90–20–34–05* 🌐 *www.hoteldupoete.com* 🛏 *24 rooms* 🍽 *No meals.*

## THE LUBERON

" 'Have you ever been to the Luberon? Between Avignon and Aix. It's getting a little chichi, specially in August, but it's beautiful—old villages, mountains, no crowds, fantastic light. . . . Leave the autoroute at Cavaillon, and go towards Apt.'. . . Murat poured the red wine and raised his glass. '*Bonnes vacances,* my friend. I'm serious about the Luberon; it's a little special. You should try it.' "

After Peter Mayle typed these words in his first novel, *Hotel Pastis,* the world took a map in hand. They had already taken note when his chronicles *A Year in Provence* and *Toujours Provence* painted a delicious picture of backcountry sunshine, copious feasts, and cartoonishly droll local rustics; now they had directions to get there.

They came. They climbed over Mayle's hedges for autographs. They built pink-and-yellow houses, booked his favorite restaurant tables, traced his footsteps with the book in hand. And not only the English. *A Year in Provence* sold 5 million copies and was translated into 38 languages, including French (where its sequel corrected his grammar to *Provence Toujours*). His name is a household word here (Peet-aire May-eel) and doesn't always bring the oft-described grin and shrug from the locals. Perhaps that's why Mayle took a sabbatical from Provence, relinquishing the home with the famously immovable stone table. He has since returned, putting down roots on the south face of the Luberon, in Lourmarin.

The dust has settled a bit, and despite the occasional Mayle Country bus tour rattling through from Cavaillon, the Luberon has returned to its former way of life. There were always Lacoste shirts here, and converted mas with pools (after all, Mayle's mas was already gentrified when it installed central heating), and sophisticated restaurants catering to seekers of the Simple Life. They're all still here, but so are the extraordinarily beautiful golden perched villages and the countryside, with its sun-bleached rocks and blue-black forests.

The broad mountain called the Luberon is protected nowadays by the Parc Naturel Régional du Luberon, but that doesn't mean you should expect rangers, campsites, and his-and-her outhouses. It has always been and remains private land, though building and forestry are allowed in moderation and hiking trails have been cleared.

The D10, anchored to the west by the market town of Cavaillon and to the east by bustling Apt, parallels the long, looming north face of the Luberon, and from it you can explore the hill towns and valley villages on either side. To its north, the red-ocher terrain around Roussillon, the Romanesque symmetry of the Abbaye de Sénanque, and the fashionable charms of Gordes punctuate a rugged countryside peppered with ancient stone *bories* (drystone huts). To its south lie Oppède-le-Vieux, Ménerbes, Lacoste, and pretty perched Bonnieux. From Bonnieux you can drive over the rugged crest through Lourmarin and explore the less gentrified south flank of the mountain. Although the Luberon is made up of two distinct regions, only the more civilized Petit Luberon, up to Apt, is covered in this chapter. If you're a nature lover, you may want to venture into the wilder Grand Luberon, especially to the summit called Mourre Nègre.

## GORDES

*10 km (6 miles) east of Fontaine-de-Vaucluse; 39 km (24 miles) east of Avignon.*

The famous village perché (hilltop village) of Gordes is only a short distance from Fontaine-de-Vaucluse, but you need to wend your way south, east, and then north on D100A, D100, D2, and D15 to skirt the impassable hillside. It's a lovely drive through dry, rocky country covered with wild lavender and scrub oak and it may tempt you to a picnic or a walk. How surprising, then, to leave such wildness behind and enter resort country. Once a summer retreat favored by modern artists such as André Lhôte, Marc Chagall, and Victor Vasarely, Gordes is now surrounded by luxury vacation homes, modern hotels, restaurants, and B&Bs, much patronized by chic Parisians. No matter. The ancient stone village still rises above the valley in painterly hues of honey gold, and its mosaiclike cobbled streets—lined with boutiques, galleries, and real-estate offices—still wind steep and narrow to its Renaissance château. Gorde's year-round farmers' market (Tuesday 8 to 1) is a grand event, offering more upscale wares than some of its neighbors—truffle-infused olive oil, charcuterie, locally made foie gras, and pretty Provençal linens.

### GETTING HERE AND AROUND
There's no bus service to Gordes, so you'll need a car or taxi: a taxi ride to Avignon is about €75 or to Fontaine-de-Vaucluse, €40.

### VISITOR INFORMATION
**Gordes Tourist Office** ⊠ *Le Chateau* ☎ *04-90-72-02-75*
⊕ *www.gordes-village.com.*

EXPLORING

**Abbaye de Sénanque.** If you've fantasized about Provence's famed lavender fields, head to the wild valley some 4 kilometers (2½ miles) north of Gordes (via D177), where this photogenic 12th-century Romanesque abbey seemingly floats above a redolent sea of lavender (in full bloom late June to August). Begun in 1150 and completed at the dawn of the 13th century, the **church** and adjoining **cloister** are without decoration but still touch the soul with their chaste beauty. Along with the abbeys of Le Thornet and Silvacane, this is one of a trio of "Three Sisters" built by the Cistercian Order in this area. Next door, the enormous vaulted **dormitory** contains an exhibition on Abbaye de Sénanque's construction, and the **refectory** shelters a display on the history of Cistercian abbeys. The few remaining monks here now preside over a cultural center presenting concerts and exhibitions. The bookshop has a huge collection of books about Provence (lots in English). ☎ 04–90–72–05–72 ⊕ *www.senanque.fr* ⊠ *€7* ⊘ *Guided tours (in French) only; see website for hrs* ⊘ *For guided tour hrs, see website and reserve in advance.*

**Belvédère.** From this spot you can overlook the miniature fields and farms below. From this height all those modern vacation homes blend in with the ancient mas—except for the aqua blue pools. Belvédère is just downhill from the château; look for the signs.

**Château de Gordes.** The only way you can get into this château is by paying to see a collection of photo paintings by pop artist Pol Mara, who lived in Gordes. It's worth the price of admission, though, just to look at the fabulously decorated stone fireplace, created in 1541. Unfortunately, opening hours change constantly (afternoon visits are your best bet). ⊠ *Pl. Genty Pantaly* ☎ *04–90–72–02–75* ⊠ *€4* ⊘ *Daily 10–1 and 2–6:30.*

**Musée de la Lavande.** Owned by one of the original lavender families, who have cultivated and distilled the flower here for over five generations, this museum lies on the outskirts of more than 80 acres of prime lavender-cultivated land. Not only can you visit the well-organized and interesting museum (note the impressive collection of scythes and distilling apparatus), but also, if you plan to be there between July 1 and August 25, you can work up a sweat cutting your own swath of lavender with a copper scythe, then make your own distillation in the museum's lab. Less energetic travelers can head to the boutique, which offers a great selection of lavender-based products at reasonable prices. The museum is 3.2 kilometers (2 miles) outside of Gordes (take the D2 southeast to the outskirts of Coustellet). ⊠ *276 rte. de Gordes, Cabrières-d'Avignon* ☎ *04–90–76–91–23* ⊕ *www.museedelalavande. com* ⊠ *€6.80* ⊘ *Feb.–Apr. and Oct.–Dec., daily 9–12:15 and 2–6; May–Sept., daily 9–7.*

**St-Firmin.** The interior of the village's church of St-Fermin is overblown Rococo—all pink and gold. ⊠ *Rue du Belvédère.*

**Village des Bories.** Just outside Gordes, on a lane heading north from D2, you'll see signs leading to the Village des Bories. The bizarre and fascinating little stone hovels called *bories* are found throughout this region of Provence, and here they are concentrated some 20 strong in an ancient community. Their origins are provocatively vague: built as shepherds' shelters with tight-fitting, mortarless stone in a hive-like form, they may date to the Celts, the Ligurians, even the Iron Age—and were inhabited or used for sheep through the 18th century. A photo exhibition shows other structures, similar to bories, in countries around the world. ☎ *04–90–72–03–48* 🌐 *www.gordes-village.com* 🎟 *€6* 🕒 *Daily 9–dusk.*

3

### WHERE TO EAT AND STAY

$$ FRENCH 🍴 **Les Cuisines du Château.** This tiny but deluxe bistro across from the château has daily *aioli,* a smorgasbord of fresh cod and lightly steamed vegetables crowned with the garlic mayonnaise. Evenings are reserved for intimate, formal indoor meals à la carte—roast Luberon lamb, beef with truffle sauce, and the like. The '30s-style bistro tables and architectural lines are a relief from Gordes's ubiquitous rustic-chic, and there is a revolving array of paintings by local artists, many of which are for sale. There are only 26 seats, so book well in advance. [$] *Average main: €20* ✉ *Pl. du Château* ☎ *04–90–72–01–31* ✍ *Reservations essential* 🕒 *Closed Wed. No dinner Tues., Sept.–May and mid-Jan.–mid-Mar. Closed Nov.–mid-Dec. and mid-Jan.–Easter.*

$$$ FRENCH 🍴 **Restaurant l'Estellan.** Just outside of town, this restaurant is worth the journey thanks to such delights as the sea bream with cherry tomatoes and flax seed, the trilogy of goat and ewe cheese with black olive jam, or the pike perch roasted with risotto Arborio—plus from here you get spectacular village views. The bistro-Provençal decor is equally as delicious in detail and the perfect setting for a long, leisurely lunch (whether inside or on the terrace) that any visit to Gordes commands. There are two menus €37 or €49 (lunch for €19 or €25) that will leave you licking your fingers, and many à la carte offerings as well. [$] *Average main: €26* ✉ *Montée de Gordes, Les Imberts* ☎ *04/90–72–04–90* 🌐 *www.restaurant-estellan.com* ✍ *Reservations essential* 🕒 *Closed Mon.–Tues. Oct.–Mar.*

$$$ B&B/INN 🏨 **Domaine de l'Enclos.** Though this cluster of private stone cottages has had a major face-lift (eradicating much patina), antique tiles and faux patinas keep it looking fashionably rustic. **Pros:** ideal for families; dinner available. **Cons:** website doesn't list prices. [$] *Rooms from: €200* ✉ *Rte. de Sénanque* ☎ *06–83–67–89–13* 🌐 *www.domainedelenclos.com* 🛏 *11 rooms, 3 suites* 🍽 *Breakfast.*

$$$$ HOTEL 🏨 **La Bastide de Gordes.** Spectacularly perched on Gordes's hilltop, the smartly renovated 16th-century Bastide houses traditional and comfortable guest rooms, with a few *haut-Provençal* accents, and a superb restaurant with an impressive 800 labels in the wine cellar. **Pros:** views are unmatched in the area; wine cellar is an enthusiast's dream. **Cons:** dress code has become increasingly select; service can be correspondingly pretentious. [$] *Rooms from: €395* ✉ *Le Village, Rue de la Combe* ☎ *04–90–72–12–12* 🌐 *www.bastide-de-gordes.com* 🛏 *33 rooms, 6 suites* 🕒 *Closed Jan.–Feb.* 🍽 *No meals.*

$$ B&B/INN 🏨 **Le Mas des Romarins.** This intimate inn atop a hill—the views are lovely—on the outskirts of Gordes is just a five-minute walk to the village. **Pros:** nights are so quiet you can hear the buzzing of insects in the

fields; convenient location. **Cons:** can be difficult to find; some rooms are small. [$] *Rooms from: €139* ✉ *Rte. de Sénanque* ☎ *04–90–72–12–13* 🌐 *www.masromarins.com* 🛏 *13 rooms* 🕓 *Closed mid-Nov.–mid-Dec., Jan., and Feb.* 🍴 *Breakfast.*

### SHOPPING

**Le Jardin.** If you're shopping for a gift or souvenirs, you'll find tasteful Provençal tableware at Le Jardin, which also has a charming tearoom in its leafy courtyard garden. ✉ *Rte. des Murs* ☎ *04–90–72–12–34.*

## ROUSSILLON

Fodor's Choice ★ *14 km (9 miles) southeast of Gordes; 43 km (27 miles) southeast of Avignon.*

A rich vein of ocher runs through the earth of Roussillon, occasionally breaking the surface in Technicolor displays of russet, deep rose, garnet, and flaming orange. Roussillon is a mineral showcase, perched above a pocket of red-rock canyonlands that are magically reflected in the stuccoes applied on every building in town, where the hilltop cluster of houses blends into the red-ocher cliffs from which their stones were first quarried. The ensemble of buildings and jagged, hand-cut slopes are equally dramatic, and views from the top look over a landscape of artfully eroded bluffs that Georgia O'Keeffe would have loved.

Unlike neighboring hill villages, there's little of historic architectural detail here; the pleasure of a visit lies in the richly varied colors that change with the light of day, and in the views of the contrasting countryside, where dense-shadowed greenery sets off the red stone with Cézannesque severity. There are pleasant *placettes* (tiny squares) to linger in nonetheless, and a Renaissance fortress tower crowned with a clock from the 19th century; just past it, you can take in expansive panoramas of forest and ocher cliffs.

#### GETTING HERE AND AROUND

There is no direct bus service to Roussillon. The only way to get here is by car from the D4.

#### VISITOR INFORMATION

**Roussillon Tourist Office** ✉ *Pl. de la Poste* ☎ *04–90–05–60–25* 🌐 *www.roussillon-provence.com.*

### EXPLORING

**L'Ocrier.** Choose from local flavors such as *calisson d'Aix* (almond candy), *pain d'épice* (gingerbread), and melon at the ice-cream shop and café of L'Ocrier before wandering through the village or taking the *sentier* (hiking path) to explore the cliffs. ✉ *Les Ocres, av. Burlière* ☎ *04–90–05–79–53.*

**Sentier des Ocres** (*Ocher Trail*). The Sentier des Ocres starts out from the town cemetery and allows you to wend your way through a magical, multicolor palette *de pierres* (of rocks) replete with eroded red cliffs and chestnut groves; the circuit takes about 45 minutes. 🎟 *€2.50, €7 joint ticket with Usine Mathieu Roussillon* 🕓 *July and Aug., daily 9–7:30; Sept. and May, daily 9:30–6:30; Oct. daily 10–5:30; Nov. 1–15, daily 10–4:30; Nov. 16–Dec. and Feb. 14–27, daily 11–3:30; Feb. 28–Mar., daily 10–5; Apr., daily 9:30–5:30; June, daily 9–6:30.*

**Usine Mathieu de Roussillon** (*Roussillon's Mathieu Ocher Works*). The area's famous vein of natural ocher, which spreads some 25 kilometers (16 miles) along the foot of the Vaucluse plateau, has been mined for centuries, beginning with the ancient Romans, who used it for their pottery. You can visit the old Usine Mathieu de Roussillon to learn more about ocher's extraction and its modern uses. ✉ *On D104 southeast of town* ☎ *04–90–05–66–69* 🌐 *www.okhra.com* 🎫 *€6.50, €7 joint ticket with Sentier des Ochres* ⏲ *Mar.–June and Sept.–Nov., daily 9–1 and 2–6; Dec. and Feb., Wed.–Sun., 9–1 and 2–6; July–Aug., 9–7. Closed Jan.*

### WHERE TO STAY

$$ HOTEL 🏨 **Le Clos de la Glycine.** This centrally located hotel combines modern comforts (an elevator, air-conditioning) with Provençal tradition, and makes up for in charm what it lacks in size. **Pros:** perfect for sunrise views; easy-walking distance to town. **Cons:** often fully booked far in advance. [$] *Rooms from: €140* ✉ *Pl. de la Poste* ☎ *04–90–05–60–13* 🌐 *www.luberon-hotel.com* 🛏 *9 rooms* 🍴 *No meals.*

## MÉNERBES

*27 km (17 miles) southwest of Roussillon; 30 km (19 miles) southeast of Avignon.*

This picturesque fortified town isn't designated one of the "plus beaux villages du France" for nothing. Perched high on a rocky precipice, Ménerbes's narrow streets, winding passageways, and limitless views have clinched its status as one of most visited villages of the region, along with its fellow most beautiful villages Gordes and Roussillon.

#### GETTING HERE AND AROUND

There is no direct bus service to Ménerbes. The only way to get here is by car.

### EXPLORING

**Castellet.** This 15th-century fortress jets out at the prow of Ménerbes.

**Musée du Tire-Bouchon** (*Corkscrew museum*). Don't miss the quirky Musée du Tire-Bouchon, which has an enormous selection of corkscrews on display and interesting historical detail on various wine-related subjects. ✉ *Domaine de la Citadelle, Rte de Cavaillon* ☎ *04–90–72–41–58* 🌐 *www.domaine-citadelle.com* 🎫 *€4* ⏲ *Apr.–Oct., daily 9–noon and 2–7; Nov.–Mar., Mon.–Sat. 9–noon and 2–7.*

**Place de l'Horloge** (*Clock Square*). A campanile tops the Hôtel de Ville on pretty Place de l'Horloge, where you can admire the delicate stonework on the arched portal and mullioned windows of a Renaissance house. Just past the tower on the right is an overlook taking in views toward Gordes, Roussillon, and Mont Ventoux.

### WHERE TO EAT AND STAY

$$ MODERN FRENCH ✕ **Maison du la Truffe et du Vin.** If wine and truffles are your thing, get thee to this temple of gastronomic bliss in the form of *tuber melanosporum* or *aestivum*, depending on the season. Fresh dishes at this lunch-only restaurant exalt the fungi-perfumed bounty of Provence. Start with a velvety pumpkin *velouté* with truffle butter followed by

CLOSE UP

## Old as the Hills

Since the first cave paintings, man has extracted ocher from the earth, using its extraordinary palette of colors to make the most of nature's play between earth and light. Grounded in these earth-based pigments, the frescoes of Giotto and Michelangelo glow from within, and the houses of Tuscany and Provence seem to draw color from the land itself—and to drink light from the sky. As Barbara Barrois of the Conservatoire des Ocres et Pigments Appliqués at Roussillon puts it, "Ça vibre à l'oeil!" (literally, "It vibrates to your eyes").

The rusty hues of iron hydroxide are the source of all this luminosity, intimately allied with the purest of clays. Extracted from the ground in chunks and washed to separate it from its quartz-sand base, it is ground to fine powder and mixed as a binder with chalk and sand. Applied to the stone walls of Provençal houses, this ancient blend gives the region its quintessential repertoire of warm yellows and golds, brick, sienna, and umber.

In answer to the acrylic imitations slathered on new constructions in garish shades of hot pink and canary yellow (following a Côte d'Azur trend), there is an ocher revival under way, thank goodness.



ravioli stuffed with succulent wild *cêpes* or a truffle-flecked omelet. Even the cheese course (truffled *chèvre chaud*) and desserts (caramelized apple with black truffle) are shroomy. Prices are reasonable, with a two-course €19 lunch menu, and two three-course all-truffle menus for €45 or €57. Wines are a big deal here, too—the lovely 17th-century stone building serves as a school for oenephiles, a wine library, a museum, and a boutique where local wines can be purchased. Tastings and courses on wine and truffles are held daily; check online for details. [$] *Average main: €20* ✉ *Place de l'Horloge* ☎ *04–90–72–38–37* 🌐 *www.vin-truffe-luberon.com* ✍ *Reservations essential* ⏲ *No dinner. Closed Nov. and Dec.*

$$ B&B/INN 🏨 **Hostellerie Le Roy Soleil.** In the imposing shadow of the Luberon, this luxurious 17th-century country inn has pulled out all stops on comfort and decor: witness the marble and granite bathrooms, wrought-iron beds, and coordinated Provençal fabrics. **Pros:** softer-than-clouds beds are marvelous; attractive online rates. **Cons:** some say service can be hit and miss; food sometimes rather ordinary for such a seductive setting. [$] *Rooms from: €110* ✉ *Rte. des Beaumettes, D103* ☎ *04–90–72–25–61* 🌐 *www.roy-soleil.com* 🛏 *10 rooms, 9 suites, 3 apartments* ⏲ *Restaurant closed mid-Nov.–Mar.* 🍴 *No meals.*

$$ B&B/INN 🏨 **Le Mas du Magnolia.** A warm welcome—a little like visiting friends—and a relaxed atmosphere prevail at this small but spectacularly situated bed-and-breakfast close to villages and sites. **Pros:** massages available; convenient location. **Cons:** not for those seeking solitude. [$] *Rooms from: €125* ✉ *D103* ☎ *04–90–72–48–00* 🌐 *www.masmagnolia.com* 🛏 *4 rooms* 🍴 *Breakfast.*

# LACOSTE

*7 km (4½ miles) east of Ménerbes; 37 km (23 miles) southeast of Avignon.*

Like Ménerbes, gentrified hilltop Lacoste owes its fame to an infamous literary resident.

### GETTING HERE AND AROUND

There is no direct bus service to Lacoste. The only way to get here is by car.

### EXPLORING

**Château de Sade.** Little but jagged ruins remain of the once magnificent Château de Sade, where the Marquis de Sade (1740–1814) spent some 30 years of his life, mostly hiding out. Exploits both literary and real, judged obscene by various European courts, kept him in and out of prison despite a series of escapes. His mother-in-law finally turned him in to authorities, and he was locked away in the Paris Bastille, where he passed the time writing stories and plays. Written during his time in the Bastille, *120 journées de Sodome* (*120 Days of Sodom*) featured a Black Forest château suspiciously similar in form and design to his Lacoste home. The once-sumptuous château was destroyed with particular relish in the Revolution but for some years, the wealthy Paris couturier Pierre Cardin has been restoring the castle wall by wall. Under his generous patronage the **Festival Lacoste** takes place here throughout the month of July. A lyric, musical, and theatrical extravaganza, events (and their dates) change yearly, ranging from outdoor poetry recitals to ballet to colorful operettas. Lacoste has a few lodging options, the oldest of which is Le Café de France. ⊠ *Carrière du Château* ☏ *04–90–75–93–12* ⊕ *www.festivaldelacoste.com* 🎫 *Festival performances: €60–€120.*

### WHERE TO STAY

**$$**
**B&B/INN**

🏨 **Domaine de Layaude Basse.** Innkeepers Lydia and Olivier have created a unique and affordable setting, with panoramic views of Gordes, Roussillon, and Mont Ventoux from the sprawling terrace and family antiques sprinkled around the modern and comfortable interior. **Pros:** perfect location at the bottom of village and steps away from Château du Marquis de Sade; room service and fresh towels daily. **Cons:** no credit cards. 🅢 *Rooms from: €91* ⊠ *Chemin de St-Jean* ☏ *04–90–75–90–06* ⊕ *www.domainedelayaude.com* ⟿ *5 rooms* ▭ *No credit cards* ⦿ *Breakfast.*

# BONNIEUX

Fodor'sChoice ★ *5 km (3 miles) southeast of Lacoste; 42 km (26 miles) southeast of Avignon.*

The most impressive of the Luberon's hilltop villages, Bonnieux (pronounced Bun-*yuh*) rises out of the arid hills in a jumble of honey-color cubes that change color subtly as the day progresses. Strewn along D36, the village is wrapped in crumbling ramparts and dug into bedrock and cliff. Most of its sharply raked streets take in wide-angle valley views, though you'll get the best view from the pine-shaded grounds of the 12th-century **Église Vieille du Haut,** reached by stone steps that wend

**3**

past tiny niche houses. Shops, galleries, cafés, and fashionable restaurants abound here, but they don't dominate. It's possible to lose yourself in a back *ruelle* (small street) most of the year. If you have a car, you're in luck—to every point of the compass, there are lovely drives from Bonnieux threading out through Le Petit Luberon. Of the four, the best is the eastward course, along the D943 and D113, which leads to the Romanesque ruins of the Prieuré de St-Symphorien. If you have a car, follow the road above Bonnieux toward Loumarin to the lofty Forêt des Cèdres. Perched on a mountaintop, the unparalleled 360-degree views and cool breezes make it popular spot for a picnic or hike among majestic hundred-year-old cedars.

### GETTING HERE AND AROUND

The TransVaucluse (Avignon–Apt) bus line services Bonnieux. There are seven buses a day, three on Sundays departing from Avignon's Gare Routière (€2, 1 hour 15 minutes). The only other way to get here is by car. With a car, you can explore the nearby ruins and other worthwhile sites.

### VISITOR INFORMATION

**Bonnieux Tourist Office** ⊠ *7 pl. Carnot* ☎ *04–90–75–91–90* ⊕ *www.bonnieux.com.*

### WHERE TO STAY

**$$$**

HOTEL

⛺ **Auberge de l'Aiguebrun.** An anti-perched village experience, this rustic former *relais postale* is set deep in the valley among walking paths and endless greenery. **Pros:** dream for nature lovers; breakfast included for double rooms. **Cons:** toilets in cabins separated by shutters (not in a different room); small towels. ⓢ *Rooms from: €170* ⊠ *Domaine de la Tour, RD 943* ☎ *04–90–04–47–00* ⊕ *www.aubergedelaiguebrun.fr* ⇗ *7 rooms, 4 cabins* ☽ *Closed Nov.–Mar.* ❡⊙❡ *Breakfast.*

**$$$**

B&B/INN

⛺ **Le Clos du Buis.** At this Gîtes de France B&B, whitewash and quarry tiles, lovely tiled baths, and carefully juxtaposed antiques create a regional look in the guest rooms. **Pros:** full access to kitchen to cook or keep stock in fridge; plenty of restaurants within easy walking distance. **Cons:** parking is difficult. ⓢ *Rooms from: €144* ⊠ *Rue Victor Hugo, D3* ☎ *04–90–75–88–48* ⊕ *www.leclosdubuis.com* ⇗ *8 rooms* ☽ *Closed mid-Nov.–Feb.* ❡⊙❡ *Breakfast.*

## BUOUX

*8 km (5 miles) northeast of Bonnieux; 9 km (5½ miles) south of Apt.*

To really get into backcountry Luberon, crawl along serpentine single-lane roads below Apt, past orchards and lavender fields. Deeply ensconced in the countryside, the tiny hamlet of Buoux (pronounced Bu-*ooks*) offers little more than a hotel and a café, sheltered by white brush-carpeted cliffs. If you squint, you can just make out the dozens of rock-climbers dangling, spiderlike, from slender cables along the cliff face.

### GETTING HERE AND AROUND

There is no direct bus service to Buoux. The only way to get here is by car.

### EXPLORING

**Fort de Buoux.** This site contains the ruins of an ancient village and a fortification that for years defended the valley, in both Ligurian and Roman times. Several houses and an entire staircase were chiseled directly into the stone; it's uncertain whether they're prehistoric or medieval. Louis XIV dismantled the ancient fortifications in the 17th century, leaving Turneresque ruins to become overgrown with wild box and ivy. It is a hike up, and it's not kid friendly due to the drop-offs above the ravines. ⊠ *D113* ☎ *04–90–74–25–75* ⊕ *www.buoux-village. com* ☞ *€4* ☉ *Daily sunrise–sunset in good weather.*

### WHERE TO STAY

**$**    🛗 **Auberge des Seguins.** Delve deep into this romantic valley to find this
HOTEL   fabulous hideaway, at the foot of an imposing white-rock cliff, where the *dortoires* (shared public bunk rooms) and simple tile-and-stucco rooms make it a terrific retreat for families, hikers, and rock-climbers. **Pros:** great location for hikers and bikers; French immersion program offered. **Cons:** no à la carte; children's rates are for ages seven and under. **$** *Rooms from: €60* ⊠ *3 km (2 miles) below downtown Buoux* ☎ *04–90–74–16–37* ⊕ *www.aubergedesseguins.com* ⇄ *27 rooms, 20 bunks* ☉ *Closed mid.-Nov.–Feb.* ⎟⊖⎟ *All meals.*

## SAIGNON

*15 km (9 miles) northeast of Buoux; 5 km (3 miles) southeast of Apt.*

Set on the Plateau de Claparédes and draped just below the crest of an arid hillside covered with olive groves, lavender, and stone farms, Saignon is an appealing hill town anchored by a heavyset Romanesque church. Neat cobbled streets wend between flower-festooned stone houses and surround a central *placette* (small square) with a burbling fountain. Yes, it's been gentrified with a few boutiques and restaurants, but the escapist feel hasn't been erased.

### GETTING HERE AND AROUND

There is no direct bus service to Saignon. The only way to get here is by car.

### WHERE TO STAY

**$$$**    🛗 **Le Parfum des Collines.** The "haute" is emphasized in this serene and
B&B/INN   sophisticated *maison d'hôte* (bed-and-breakfast) nestled in the picturesque Luberon countryside—an elegant-modern retreat with all the amenities of an upscale auberge, including pool, billards room, library, a small but reasonably priced roster of spa treatments, and manicured grounds. **Pros:** near the village perché; excellent hiking from the grounds; dining options here are a treat, as breakfasts are plentiful and gourmet dinners are available. **Cons:** pricier than the usual maison d'hôte. **$** *Rooms from: €190* ⊠ *Rte. de Saignon, D48, Auribeau* ☎ *04–32–52–93–46* ⊕ *www.parfum-collines.com* ⇄ *4 rooms* ⎟⊖⎟ *Breakfast.*

## APT

*40 km (25 miles) east of Avignon.*

Actively ugly from a distance, with a rash of modern apartment blocks and industrial buildings, Apt doesn't attract the tourism it deserves. Its central Old Town, with tight, narrow streets shaded with noble stone houses and strings of fluttering laundry, seethes with activity. The best time to visit is Saturday, when the town buzzes with a vibrant Provençal market, selling crafts, clothing, carpets, jewelry, and—not incidentally—all the finest food products of the Luberon and Haute-Provence.



#### GETTING HERE AND AROUND

You can reach Apt by the TransVaucluse bus line 15.1 from Avignon. There are seven buses a day (only three on Sunday) departing from Avignon's Gare Routière (€2, 1½ hours). The only other way to get here is by car.

### EXPLORING

**Distillerie Lavande 1100.** As one of the most important distilleries in the region, this heavenly domain, planted by Maurice Fra at an altitude of 1,100 meters, produces primarily lavender, but also delves into the realms of other aromatic plants. The picture-perfect stone building rises up like a lighthouse surrounded by waves of color; aside from admiring the views, you can tour the distillery about how to cultivate lavender and take your time to browse among the all-natural products that line the shelves of the shop. The distillery is in the minuscule village of Lagarde d'Apt, 12 kilometers (7 miles) east from Apt on the D209; follow signs on the D34. ✉ *D34, Lagarde d'Apt* ☎ *04–90–75–01–42* 🕒 *Daily late July–Aug. Hrs vary.*

EN ROUTE

Between Apt and Lourmarin, the D943 winds dramatically through deep backcountry, offering the only passage over the spine of the Luberon. Bone-dry and bristling with scrub oak, pine, coarse broom, and wild lavender, it's a landscape reminiscent of Greece or Sicily. If you climb into the hills, you won't get views; this is landlocked, isolated terrain, but it's wildly beautiful.

### WHERE TO STAY

$$$$ HOTEL Fodor's Choice ★

🏨 **Le Coquillade.** Set among gentle rolling hills, elegant gardens, and 60 sundrenched acres of vineyards (from which the estate wine is produced), this fabulous upscale hideaway is made up of six historic country houses restored to designer perfection and offering every modern luxury—just as terrific for a relaxing spa getaway as an active weekend of swimming, hiking, and biking on one of the hotel's Swiss-made mountain bikes. **Pros:** your every need has been anticipated; close to the Luberon's best sites. **Cons:** a challenge to tear yourself away. [$] *Rooms from: €310* ✉ *Domaine de la Coquillade, Gargas* ☎ *04–90–74–71–71* 🌐 *www.coquillade.fr* 🛏 *28 rooms* 🍴 *No meals.*

## LOURMARIN

*12 km (7 miles) southeast of Bonnieux; 54 km (33 miles) southeast of Avignon.*

The highly gentrified village of Lourmarin lies low-slung in the hollow of the Luberon's south face, a sprawl of manicured green. Albert Camus loved this place from the moment he discovered it in the 1930s. After he won his Nobel Prize in 1957 he bought a house here and lived in it until his death in 1960 (he is buried in the village cemetery).

### GETTING HERE AND AROUND

There is no direct bus service to Lourmarin. The only way to get here is by car.

### VISITOR INFORMATION

**Lourmarin Tourist Office** ⊠ *9 av. Philippe de Girard* ☎ *04–90–68–10–77* ⊕ *www.lourmarin.com.*

### EXPLORING

**Château.** Loumarin's Renaissance-era château, which was privately restored in the 1920s to appealing near-perfection, is the town's main draw. The "new" wing (begun in 1526 and completed in 1540) is the prettiest, with a broad-ranging art collection, rare old furniture, and ornate stone fireplaces—including one with exotic *vases canopes* (ancient Egyptian figure vases). In summer, the château hosts concerts. ☎ *04–90–68–15–23* ⊕ *www.chateau-de-lourmarin.com* 🎫 *€6.50* ⊙ *May and Sept., daily 10:30–12:30 and 2:30–6; June–Aug., daily 10–6:30; Mar., Apr., and Oct., daily 10:30–12:30 and 2:30–5; Nov., Dec., and Feb., daily 10:30–11:30 and 2:30–4; Jan., weekends 2:30–4:30 (may vary with daylight).*

### WHERE TO STAY

**$**

**B&B/INN**

🖳 **Villa Saint Louis.** In a town as gentrified as Lourmarin, it's surprising to find such a bargain as this B&B set in a 17th-century house replete with antiques and enclosed garden. **Pros:** attractive price includes breakfast; shared fridge. **Cons:** no credit cards; allergy sufferers, be warned—Madame's cat wanders around freely. **$** *Rooms from: €65* ⊠ *35 rue Henri de Savornin* ☎ *04–90–68–39–18* ⊕ *www.villasaintlouis.com* 🛏 *5 rooms* ⊟ *No credit cards* ⊙ *Closed Jan.* ¶⊙¶ *Breakfast.*

4

# AIX, MARSEILLE, AND THE CENTRAL COAST

# WELCOME TO AIX, MARSEILLE, AND THE CENTRAL COAST

## TOP REASONS TO GO

★ **Aix's extraordinary Cours Mirabeau:** The Champs-Elysées of posh Aix-en-Provence, this boulevard is lined with lovely cafés like Les Deux Garçons, where the decor looks pretty much as it did when it opened in 1792.

★ **Go fishing for Marseille's best bouillabaisse:** Order ahead at Chez FonFon and indulge in classic bouillabaisse—this version will practically make your taste buds stand up and sing "La Marseillaise."

★ **Become a Calanques castaway:** Near Cassis, these picturesque coves make you feel like you've stumbled onto a movie set.

★ **Paul Cézanne, superstar:** Tour Cézanne Country in the area around Montaigne Ste-Victoire, outside the artist's hometown of Aix-en-Provence.

★ **Îles d'Hyéres, nature's paradise:** In season the tourists arrive en masse but the sense of pure escape can still be enjoyed on these forested islands.

**1 Aix-en-Provence.** For one day, join all those fashionable folks for whom café-squatting, people-watching, and boutique-hopping are a way of life in Aix-en-Provence, then track the spirit of its most famous native son, Paul Cézanne. Head into the countryside to visit the Jas de Bouffan, his family estate, and Montagne Sainte-Victoire, the main "motif" for this giant of modern art.

**2 Marseille.** France's second-largest city, Marseille is the place to enjoy the colorful sights and smells of a Mediterranean melting pot, where far-flung cultures have mingled ever since the Greeks invaded around 600 BC. Tour its cathedrals and museums, visit its spiffed-up Vieux Port's fabulous new architectural gems, then head east to **Aubagne** to walk its Circuit Pagnol.

**3 The Central Coast.** Stretching along the eastern coastline from Marseille, the famously beautiful calanque (coves) form a sapphire chain of jagged fjordlike coves interspersed with rugged cliffs and lovely harbor towns that conjure up the St-Tropez of the 1940s. Take an excursion boat to these hidden coves, enjoy a picnic and a chilled bottle of Bandol rosé, or take in the view from Cassis's breathtaking heights. Not far from the big-city lights of Toulon are the idyllic Îles d'Hyéres. Porquerolles, the largest, is an idyllic spot with several chic resorts.

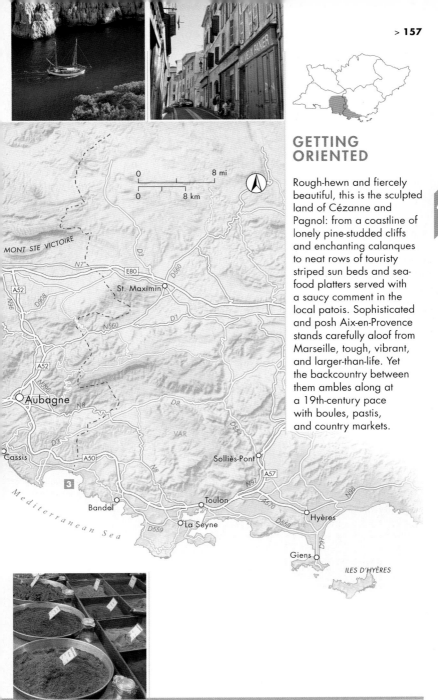

## GETTING ORIENTED

Rough-hewn and fiercely beautiful, this is the sculpted land of Cézanne and Pagnol: from a coastline of lonely pine-studded cliffs and enchanting calanques to neat rows of touristy striped sun beds and seafood platters served with a saucy comment in the local patois. Sophisticated and posh Aix-en-Provence stands carefully aloof from Marseille, tough, vibrant, and larger-than-life. Yet the backcountry between them ambles along at a 19th-century pace with boules, pastis, and country markets.

# PROVENCE'S WINES
## RED, WHITE, AND ROSY

As the world has now discovered, there is a wine that is neither red nor white—a rosé, a versatile wine you can drink with almost anything. Delightfully, light rosés are the perfect summer wines. And, happily, Provence turns out to be the rosé capital of France.

To understand why Provence's wines are becoming more and more in demand around the world, log on to ⊕ *www.provencewineusa.com.*

The Mediterranean embodies a long tradition of making fruity, dry rosés, and Provence has several appellations counting rosé as up to three-quarters of their production. Demand for them has grown greater since people have discovered that rosés are not just for summer: many keep the chilled bite of a dry white wine on a hot day while retaining the fruitiness and body of a red. Still, it came as shocking news to recently learn the French consumed more rosé than white wine. How could the most educated drinkers in the world prefer *pink* wine over a buttery white burgundy? Fingers pointed directly to three main regions that have developed an amazingly cultivated rosé wine culture: the Côtes du Rhône, Côtes de Provence, and Côteaux d'Aix en Provence.

—Sarah Fraser

### LA VIE EN ROSÉ

One sip and you'll agree: rosé wines taste wonderful along the Riviera coast. Some experts even claim that the sea air enhances the aroma (perhaps why a Côtes de Provence rosé loses some of its magic at home). Rosés are usually drunk icy-cold, whether to quench arid thirsts or to hide a less-than-rounded finish. Try a top-rated Bandol at least once but, usually, you can't go wrong with a good local rosé.

While reds and whites are strong in Provence—the most famous red is Châteauneuf-du-Pape, while Cassis is the top white-producing area—more people choose to stop and taste the rosés.

The vast region of **Côtes de Provence** stretches across the Var towards Marseille to the west and Grasse to the east; its scores of vineyards produce everything from cheap plonk to serious vintages. Château Minuty (⊠ *Rte. de Ramatuelle* ☎ *04–94–56–12–09* ⊕ *www.chateauminuty.com*), near St-Tropez, is found on almost every wine list in the area in dry white, fruity rosé and medium-bodied red. Another top vineyard is Château St-Marguerite (⊠ *Le Haut Pansard, La Londe les Maures* ☎ *04–94–00–44–44* ⊕ *www. chateausaintemarguerite.com*), which produces full-bodied reds, lively rosés, and tasty whites.

**Côteaux d'Aix en Provence** spreads out from the Rhône River to the St-Victoire mountain. Rosés from this area are often described as "zingy" or "fruity," while reds and whites range from solid to reasonable. Two names to look for are the classic rosé of Château des Gavelles (⊠ *Chemin Departmental 14C* ☎ *04–42–50–20–19* ⊕ *www.pgadomaines. com)* and the Château Lafoux (⊠ *RN7, near St-Maxime* ☎ *04–94–78–77–86* ⊕ *www.chateaulafoux.com*), with a subtly perfumed white and rosé.

A wine to be reckoned with, **Bandol** rivals Châteauneuf-du-Pape as the region's reigning red. Though pricey, Bandol rosés and whites are luscious and inviting. Domaine Tempier (⊠ *Le Plan de Castellet* ☎ *04–94–98–70–21* ⊕ *www.domainetempier.com*), one of the region's oldest producers, is renowned for its distinctive reds and stunning rosés. **Côtes du Rhône** is along the Rhône delta, and growers tend to focus on organic red wine and rosés. Tops are Domaine Pastouret (☎ *Rte. de Jonquieres, Bellegarde* ☎ *04–66–01–62–29* ⊕ *www.domaine-pastouret. com*) and the Château de Campuget (⊠ *Mas du Campuget, Manduel* ☎ *04–66–20–20–15* ⊕ *www.campuget.com*).

**Châteauneuf-du-Pape** is fondly regarded as the king of reds in Provence. Reds are opulent and warm, and have a high alcohol percentage (up to 14%). Noted names are Domaine Chante Cigale (⊠ *Av. Louis Pasteur* ☎ *04–90–83–702–57* ⊕ *www.chantecigale.com*) and Château Rayas (⊠ *Rte. De Courthezon* ☎ *04–90–83–73–09* ⊕ *www. chateaurayas.fr*).

**Beaumes de Venise** is an appellation that is world-renowned for its Muscat dessert wine, made since the 14th century. The pale-gold wines are sweet and fruity with a high alcohol content (over 15%) and pair well with foie gras.

Updated
by Jennifer
Ladonne

When you cross the imaginary border into Provence for the first time, you may experience a niggling sense of déjà vu. The sun-drenched angular red rooftops, the dagger-narrow cypresses, the picture-perfect port towns, and the brooding massifs fire the imagination in a deep, soul-stirring way. And it's no wonder: some of the world's greatest artists were inspired by the unforgettable landscapes found here.

Cézanne colored his canvases in daubs of russet and black-green, the rough-cut structure of bluff and twisted pine inspiring a building-block approach to painting that for others jelled into Cubism. Marcel Pagnol painted pictures with words: the smells of thyme and rosemary crunching underfoot, the sounds of thunder rumbling behind rain-starved hills, the quiet joy of opening shutters at dawn to a chorus of blackbirds in the olive grove. Both Cézanne and Pagnol were native sons of this region east of the Rhône who were inspired to eloquence by the primordial landscape and its echoes of antiquity. And yet, like most who visit the region, they were equally fascinated with the modern Provençal world and its complex melding of the ancient with the new.

A visit to this region encompasses the best of urban culture, seaside, and arid backcountry. Aix is a small, manageable city with a leisurely pace, studded with stunning architecture and a lively concentration of arts, due in part to its active university life. Marseille offers the yang to Aix's yin. Its brash style, bold monuments, and spectacular sun-washed waterfront center are reminiscent of those of Naples or modern Athens; it is much maligned for its crime rate and big-city energy, and often unfairly neglected by visitors. Up in the dry inland hills, Pagnol's hometown of Aubagne gives a glimpse of local life, with a big farmers' market in the plane tree–lined town center and makers of *santons* (terra-cotta figurines) at every turn. Both the lovely port-village of Cassis and the busy beach town of Bandol allow time to watch the tides come and go, though for the ultimate retreat, take the boat that leaves for the almost tropical Îles d'Hyères. Like most of this region, these islands are a true idyll, but even more so since they are car-free.

That certainly doesn't go for Aix, which lies at a major crossroads of autoroutes: one coming in from Bordeaux and Toulouse, then leading up into the Alps toward Grenoble; the other a direct line from Lyons and Paris. Indeed, Aix is extremely well placed for trips to the Luberon, Avignon, and Arles, and it's a quick half hour from Marseille. When mapping out your itinerary, remember that all the coastal towns hereabouts line up for easy access between Marseille and Toulon, so you can wind up cruising along A50, which follows the coastline, and take in all the sights. Although Marseille is one of the biggest cities in France, it's only a matter of minutes before you're lost in deep backcountry on winding, picturesque roads that lead to Cassis or Aubagne and beyond.

To make the most of your time in this region, plan to divide your days between big-city culture, backcountry tours, and waterfront leisure. You can "do" Marseille in an impressive day or weekend trip, but its backstreets and tiny ports reward a more leisurely approach. Aix is as much a way of life as a city charged with tourist must-sees; allow time to hang out in a Cours Mirabeau café and shop the side streets. Aubagne must be seen on a market day (Tuesday, Saturday, or Sunday) to make the most of its charms. Cassis merits a whole day if you want to explore the Calanques and enjoy a seaside lunch; Bandol is less appealing unless you're committed to beach time. The complete seaside experience, with rocky shoreline, isolated beaches, a picturesque port, and luxurious near-tropical greenery, can be found on the island of Porquerolles, one of the Îles d'Hyères; if your budget and schedule allow, spend a night or two in one of its few hotels and have much of the island to yourself.

# PLANNER

### WHEN TO GO

High season falls between Easter and October, but if you come in winter you may be pampered with warm sun and cool breezes. When the mistral attacks (and it can attack year-round), it channels all its forces down the Rhône Valley and blasts into Marseille like a one-way tornado. But, happily, the assault may last only one day. This is not the day, however, to opt for a boat ride from Cassis or Porquerolles; aim instead for the sheltered streets of Aix.

### PLANNING YOUR TIME

This is an area that moves a little faster than traditional Provence, since the main hubs of Marseille, Aix-en-Provence, and Toulon are large cities, but the average day still includes a two-hour lunch.

Take the time to enjoy an afternoon stroll, a long lunch, a little siesta—because this is, fundamentally, what makes living in Provence so charmingly worthwhile. And even if the cities are, well, cities, you'll note that much of general life comes to a halt between midday and two, so plan accordingly.

Keep your sense of humor intact and learn the Gallic shrug (a typical shoulder movement that can mean anything from "I don't know" to "I really don't care") when you are politely refused service because you are late (or too early); it's a different mentality, one focused on the quality of life for everyone and emphasizing the value of taking the time to dwell on the important things.

To really take advantage of the area, start your trip in a large and vibrant city center like Marseille. From here you can spiral out to Aix, Aubagne, and the coast with ease via train, car, or bus. If you want a stylish and delightful mix of urban chic and country-town beauty, though, Aix-en-Provence can't be beat for a kick-off point.

### GETTING HERE AND AROUND

Public transport in Marseille, Aix, and the Central Coast is well organized, with most areas accessible by plane, train, bus, or boat.

Flying in is a good option, as Marseille has one of the largest airports in France and regular flights come in from Paris and London.

The Toulon-Hyéres airport is much smaller but also has frequent flights.

If you prefer the more scenic route, note that the high-speed TGV trains go directly to Marseille, Aix-en-Provence, and Toulon in about the same time as a flight, and a big selection of local and regional trains will take you to the towns along the Central Coast.

There is a moderately good network of buses run by a large number of independent bus companies, but check with the local tourism offices for the one you need since the "who's who" in the bus world here is confusing.

If driving, get a good map, and make sure you familiarize yourself with the towns and cities along your route first, since those are the signs you'll follow. Don't count on your rental car having GPS.

#### AIR TRAVEL

Marseille has one of the largest airports in France, the Aéroport de Marseille Provence in Marignane, about 20 km (12 miles) northwest of the city center. Regular flights come in daily from Paris and London. In summer Delta Airlines flies direct from New York to Nice (about 190 km [118 miles] from Marseille and about 150 km [93 miles] from Toulon), and XL Airways has two direct flights from New York to Marseille a week. Airport shuttle buses to Marseille center leave every 20 minutes 4:30 am–12:10 am daily (€8). Shuttles to Aix leave hourly 8 am–11:10 pm (€5.40).

**Airport Information Aéroport de Marseille Provence in Marignane** ☎ *04–42–14–14–14* ⊕ *www.marseille.aeroport.fr.*

#### BOAT TRAVEL

If you find yourself without a yacht on this lovely coastline, it's easy to jump on a tourist cruiser, whether you putter from calanque to calanque between Marseille and Cassis or commute to the car-free Îles d'Hyères. Many boats are glass-bottomed for underwater viewing, and most allow you to climb onto the top deck and face the wind as the cruiser bucks the waves.

#### BUS TRAVEL

A good network of private bus services (confusingly called *cars*) strikes out from Marseille's *gare routière* (bus station), adjacent to the Metro Gare St-Charles train station, and carries you to points not served by train. Tickets costs €1.50 and multiple-ticket *carnets* are available.

One look at the flower-filled fields of the Bouches du Rhône region and you'll quickly understand why Van Gogh, Gauguin, and Monet loved Provence.

From Marseille, buses link many destinations, including Aix-en-Provence (€5.40, 1 hour, leaving every 20 minutes), Nice (€32.40, 3 hours, serviced by Phocéens Cars, five buses daily), Cassis (€5.10, 1½ hours, every 20 minutes), Carpentras (€19.70, 2 hours, three buses daily), and Cavaillon (€14.70, 1 hour, three buses daily).

As for Aix-en-Provence, it has a dense network of bus excursions from its station.

To/from destinations include Marseille (€5.40, 1 hour, every 20 minutes), Arles (€9.70, 1½ hours, two to five daily), and Avignon (€17.40, 1½ hours, two to four daily).

Aix-en-Provence has a municipal bus that services the entire town and outlying suburbs (such as Jas de Bouffon). A ticket costs €1, a three-day pass €5.

A *navette* (shuttle bus) connects La Rotonde/Cours Mirabeau with the bus and train station, and one heads out to the TGV station (departing from bus station), which is some 13 km (8 miles) west of town and the Marseille-Provence airport.

**Bus Information Aix-en-Bus** ✉ *Pl. du Général du Gaulle* ☎ *04-42-26-37-28* ⊕ *www.aixenbus.com.* **Aix-en-Provence *gare routière*** (*bus station*) ✉ *Av. de la Europe* ☎ *04-42-91-26-80.* **Lepilote/Cartreize** ☎ *08-10-00-13-26* ⊕ *www.lepilote.com.* **Marseille *gare routière*** (*bus station*) ✉ *3 pl. Victor Hugo, Saint Charles, Marseille* ☎ *3635.* **Phocéens Cars** ☎ *04-93-89-41-45* ⊕ *www.phoceens-cars.com.*

# Paul Cézanne, Superstar

Matisse called him "the father of us all." He helped catapult Picasso into Cubism. And nearly every artist working today owes a huge debt to the man who finally kicked over the traces of traditional art—Paul Cézanne (1839–1906), Aix-en-Provence's most famous native son.

His images of Mont Ste-Victoire and his timeless still lifes are the founding icons of 20th-century painting. With them, he not only invented a new pictorial language but immortalized his Provençal homeland.

Great Cézannes may hang in museums (or appear for sale—including Les Joueurs de Cartes, which at more than $250 million holds the record for the most expensive painting ever sold at auction), but you can't really understand the artist without experiencing his Provence firsthand.

As it turns out, he is everywhere: Aix even has a Cézanne Trail (⊕ www.cezanne-en-provence.com). The route through the town is marked with "C" copper studs.

The two most moving locales, however, are just outside the city. Jas de Bouffan, Cézanne's cherished family home, signaled his father's rise to prominence from hat maker to banker and was a lifetime source of inspiration for the artist, who moved there at the age of 20. Four large decorative panels painted directly on the walls bear the ironic signature "Ingres"—the young artist's rebellious jab at his father, who preferred a more prosaic career for his son. Cézanne remained here until his mother's death, in 1897, left him too brokenhearted to remain and the house was sold. One mile north of Aix's center is "Les Lauves," the studio the artist built in 1901 *(see Atelier Cézanne under Top Attractions),* set in a magically overgrown olive grove. The high point here lies a mile along the Chemin de la Marguerite: the belvedere spot from which the artist painted his last views of Mont Ste-Victoire (indeed, he died shortly after being caught in a storm here).The Mona Lisa of modern art, Cézanne painted self-portraits that were inscrutable.

He was illegitimate; he wound up having a 17-year-long affair with Hortense Piquet; and he hid his own illegitimate son from his father to inherit the family fortune. Indeed, this "painter of peasants" never worked a day in his life. Unless, that is, you consider revolutionizing the art of painting "work."

When he abandoned Aix's art academy for the dramatic landscapes of the surrounding hills, he became smitten with the stark, high-noon light of Provence, rejecting the sugar-almond hues of Impressionism.

4

(opposite) A brooding self-portrait done by Aix's greatest painter. Many of Cézanne's legendary canvases (top) were painted at the artist's charming Les Lauves studio (above, left) and first envisioned at his Jas de Bouffan home (above, right).

Instead of mixing colors to create shadows like Monet, he simply used black. Instead of using translucent haze to create an effect of distance, he focused on ruler-straight Provençal streets (laid out by ancient Romans) to hurtle the eye from foreground to background.

In the end, Cézanne wanted to impose himself on the landscape, not vice versa. So why not do the same? With brochures from the Aix tourist office, head out into Cézanne Country—the roads leading to Le Tholonet and Mont Ste-Victoire.

Walk these shady trails and you'll learn just how Cézanne became the trailblazer of modern art.

### CAR TRAVEL

The A6/A7 toll expressway (*péage*) channels all traffic from Paris toward the south. At Orange, A7 splits to the southeast and leads directly to Aix. From there A51 leads to Marseille. Also at Aix, you can take A52 south via Aubagne to Cassis and A50, the coastal autoroute tollway. The Aix-Marseille-Toulon triangle is well served by a network of autoroutes with a confusing profusion of segmented number-names (A50, A51, A52, A55). Hang on to your map and follow the direction signs. As with any major metropolis, it pays to think hard before driving into Marseille: if you want to visit only the port neighborhoods, it may be easier to make a day trip by train.

However, you'll need to drive to visit the smaller ports and bays outside the center. To approach downtown Marseille, try to aim for the A51 that dovetails down from Aix; it plops you conveniently near the Vieux Port, while A55 crawls through industrial dockside traffic. The autoroute system collapses inconveniently just at Toulon, forcing you to drive right through jammed downtown traffic. Beautiful back roads between Aix, Marseille, and Aubagne carry you through Cézanne and Pagnol country; the N96 between Aix and Aubagne is worth skipping the freeway for. The D559 follows the coast, more or less scenically, from Marseille through Cassis to Hyères.

### TRAIN TRAVEL

The high-speed TGV *Méditerranée* line ushered in a new era in *Trains à Grande Vitesse* (or "Trains at Great Speed") travel in France; the route means that you can travel from Paris's Gare de Lyon to Marseille in a mere three hours. Not only is the idea of Provence as a day trip now possible (though, of course, not advisable), you can even whisk yourself there directly upon arrival at Paris's Charles de Gaulle airport.

After the main line of the TGV divides at Avignon, the southeast-bound link takes in Aix-en-Provence, Marseille, Toulon, and the Côte d'Azur city of Nice. There's also frequent service by daily local trains to other towns in the region from these main TGV stops. With high-speed service now connecting Aix, Nîmes, Avignon, and Marseille, travelers without cars will find a Provence itinerary much easier to pull off. For full information on the TGV *Méditerranée,* log onto the TGV website; you can purchase tickets on this website or through RailEurope, and you should always buy your TGV tickets in advance. It's also easy to take a night train from Paris and wake up in Marseille. From Marseille it's a brief jaunt up to Aix. The main rail line also continues from Marseille to Toulon.

Aix has train routes to Marseille (€7.60, 30 minutes, 44 trains daily), Nice (€38.60, 5½ hours, eight trains daily), and Cannes (€34, 5½ hours, eight trains daily), along with other destinations. Marseille has train routes to Aix-en-Provence (€7.60, 30 minutes, 44 trains daily), Avignon (€19.40, 1 hour, hourly), Nîmes (€27.40, 1½ hours), Arles (€14.10, 1 hour), and Orange (€22.50, 1½ hours). Once in Marseille, you can link up with the coastal train route for connections to all the resort towns lining the coast eastward to Monaco and Menton. You can also catch trains to Cassis, Bandol, Aubagne, and Toulon. One website that provides in-depth info on train travel is ⊕ *www.beyond.fr.* Another is ⊕ *www.voyages-sncf.com.*

Marseille boasts a fine metro system. Most of the two metro lines service the suburbs, but several stops in the city center can help you get around quickly, including the main stop at Gare St-Charles, Colbert, Vieux Port, and Notre-Dame. A ticket costs €1.50, with multiple carnet tickets available.

**Train Information** **Aix-en-Provence** *Gare SNCF* (*train station*) ⊠ *Av. Victor Hugo* ☎ *3635.* **Marseille** *Gare St-Charles* (*train station*) ☎ *04–91–08–16–40.* **SNCF** ☎ *3635* ⊕ *www.ter-sncf.com.* **TGV** ☎ *3635* ⊕ *www.tgv.com.*

## RESTAURANTS

One eats late in Provence: rarely before 1 pm for lunch (and you may find yourself still at the table at 4 pm) and 8 to 9 pm for dinner. Be prepared for somewhat disdainful looks—"tourists!"—and slow responses if you try to come any earlier.

Most restaurants close between lunch and dinner, even in summer, and no matter how much you are willing to spend or how well dressed you are, you will be firmly turned away.

If you are craving an afternoon glass of rosé *bien frais* and a light snack, head to one of the smaller beach or roadside sandwich kiosks, or the local *boulangerie* (bakery), which usually has a selection of fresh bread and treats. In town, cafés serve all day long.

The more intrepid sort can try a slice of Provençal life and brave one of the smoky, lottery-playing, coffee-and-pastis-drinking *tabacs* that line every main street in the south. You'll find they also often have basic fare for a reasonable price.

## HOTELS

Accommodations in the area range from luxury villas to modest city-center hotels. This is no longer just converted *mas* (farmhouse) country. Nonetheless, hotels in this region favor Provençal flavor and aim to provide outdoor space at its loveliest, from gardens where breakfast is served to parasol pine–shaded pools. The bigger cities will always have somewhere to stay, but the good and reputable hotels book up quickly at certain times of the year. June, July, and August are considered to be high season, so reserve ahead of time. In the larger cities, particularly Marseille, be careful to note where your hotel is located because, even if the hotel is deluxe, there are unsavory neighborhoods that can make for an unpleasant, if not downright scary, stay (especially at night).

## VISITOR INFORMATION

The regional tourist office, the Comité Départemental du Tourisme du Var, has extensive documentation on lodging, restaurants, rentals, hikes, and attractions in Var. The same is true for the Comité Départemental du Tourisme des Bouches-du-Rhône.

**Comité Départemental du Tourisme des Bouches-du-Rhône** ⊠ *13 rue de Brignoles, Marseille* ☎ *04–91–13–84–13* ⊕ *www.visitprovence.com.* **Comité Départemental du Tourisme du Var** ⊠ *1 bd. de Strasbourg, Toulon* ☎ *09–63–61–78–70* ⊕ *www.visitvar.fr.* **Comité Regional du Tourisme de Provence-Alpes-Côte d'Azur** ⊠ *12 pl. Joliette, Marseille* ☎ *04–91–56–47–00* ⊕ *www.tourismepaca.fr.*

# AIX-EN-PROVENCE

*32 km (20 miles) north of Marseille; 64 km (40 miles) northwest of Toulon.*

Longtime rival of edgier, more exotic Marseille, the lovely town of Aix-en-Provence (pronounced *ex*) is gracious, cultivated, and made all the more cosmopolitan by the presence of some 40,000 university students. In keeping with its aristocratic heritage, Aix quietly exudes well-bred suavity and elegance—indeed, it is now one of the 10 richest townships in France. The influence and power it once had as the old capital of Provence—fine art, noble architecture, and graceful urban design—remain equally important to the city today. And, although it is true that Aix owns up to a few modern-day eyesores, the overall impression is one of beautifully preserved stone monuments, quietly sophisticated nightlife, leafy plane trees, and gently splashing fountains. With its thriving market, vibrant café life, spectacularly chic shops, and superlative music festival, it's one Provence town that really should not be missed.

The museums and churches in Aix are overshadowed by the city itself, a gorgeously picturesque place thanks to its elegant 18th-century *hôtel particuliers (mansions)*, enchanting marketplace squares, and beautiful fountains. The last bear striking testimony to Aix's ancient past, as the Romans were first drawn here by the area's mild thermal baths.

Under the wise and generous guidance of Good King René in the 15th century, Aix became a center of Renaissance arts and letters. A poet himself and patron of the arts, the king encouraged a veritable army of artists to flourish here. The artists in turn gratefully left a handful of masterpieces, including Nicolas Froment's *Triptyque du Buisson Ardent (Burning Bush Triptych)* in the Cathédrale St-Sauveur. At the height of its political, judicial, and ecclesiastical power in the 17th and 18th centuries, Aix profited from a surge of private building, each *grand hôtel particulier* meant to outdo its neighbor. It was into this exalted elegance that artist Paul Cézanne (1839–1906) was born, though he drew much of his inspiration not from the city itself but from the raw countryside around it, often painting scenes of Montagne Ste-Victoire. A schoolmate of Cézanne's made equal inroads on modern society: the journalist and novelist Émile Zola (1840–1902) attended the Collège Bourbon with Cézanne and described their friendship as well as Aix itself in several of his works. You can sense something of the vibrancy that nurtured these two geniuses in the streets of modern Aix. The city's famous Festival d'Aix (International Opera Festival) has imported and created world-class opera productions as well as related concerts and recitals since 1948. Most of the performances take place in elegant, old Aix settings, and during this time the cafés, restaurants, and hotels spill over with the *beau monde* who've come to Aix especially for the July event.

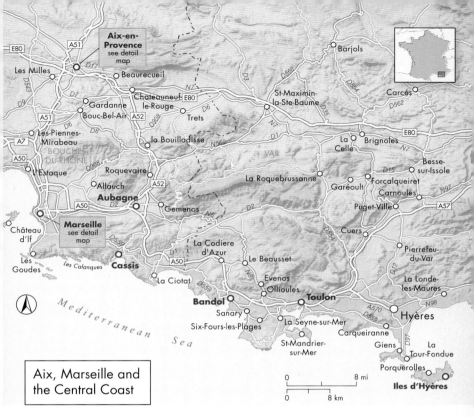

Aix, Marseille and
the Central Coast

### GETTING HERE AND AROUND

The Aix TGV station is 10 km (6 miles) west of the city and is served by regular shuttle buses. The old Aix train station is on the slow Marseille–Sisteron line, with trains arriving roughly every hour from Marseille St-Charles. The center of Aix is best explored by foot, but there is a municipal bus service that serves the entire town and the outlying suburbs. Most leave from La Rotonde in front of the tourism office.

### VISITOR INFORMATION

**Aix-en-Provence Tourist Office** ✉ *Les allées provençales, 300 Ave. Giuseppe Verdi* ☎ *04–42–16–11–61* ⊕ *www.aixenprovencetourism.com.*

### TOURS

Two-hour Aix walking tours in English are organized by the tourist office; tours of the Old Town leave at 10 on Tuesday and Saturday (€8). A tour of Cézanne landmarks (with an optional finish at his Atelier) leaves from the tourist office at 10 Saturday morning (€8); it follows the bronze plaques in the city sidewalks. Reserve ahead with the tourist office.

## EXPLORING

The famous Cours Mirabeau, a broad, shady avenue that stretches from one grand fountain to another, bisects old Aix into two distinct neighborhoods. Below the Cours, the carefully planned Quartier Mazarin is lined with fine 17th- and 18th-century mansions. Above, the Old Town twists and turns from square to fountain square, each turn leading to another row of urban boutiques and another buzzing cluster of café tables. If you turn a blind eye to these enticing distractions, you can see the sights of Aix in a day's tour—but you'll be missing the point. The music of the fountains, the theater of the café crowds, and the painterly shade of the plane trees are what Aix is all about.

### TOP ATTRACTIONS

**Atelier Cézanne** (*Cézanne's Studio*). Just north of the Vieille Ville loop you'll find Cézanne's studio. After the death of his mother forced the sale of the painter's beloved country retreat, Jas de Bouffan, he had this atelier built and some of his finest works, including *Les Grandes Baigneuses* (*The Large Bathers*), were created in the upstairs workspace. But what is most striking is the collection of simple objects that once featured prominently in his portraits and still lifes—redingote, bowler hat, ginger jar—all displayed as if awaiting his return. The atelier is behind an obscure garden gate on the left as you climb the Avenue Paul-Cézanne. ■ TIP➔ **After-dark shows that take place in July and August include movie screenings in the garden.** ⊠ *9 av. Paul-Cézanne* ☎ *04–42–21–06–53* ⊕ *www.atelier-cezanne.com* 🎟€*5.50* ۞ *Apr.–June and Sept., daily 10–noon and 2–6; July and Aug., daily 10–6; Oct.–Mar., daily 10–noon and 2–5. Closed Sun. Dec.–Feb.*

Fodor'sChoice
★ **Café-Brasserie les Deux Garçons.** Cézanne enjoyed his coffee and papers here, as have generations of *beau monde,* intellectuals, and neighborhood *habitués*—Churchill, Sartre, Picasso, Delon, Belmondo, and Cocteau among them—since its founding in 1792. The food is not memorable, but 365 days a year you can savor the linen-decked sidewalk tables that look out to the Cours Mirabeau, where the locals often prefer to take a table, considering it to be *the* place to sit to see and be seen. But if you want to travel back in time to the *époque consulaire,* sit inside: the gold-ivory decor remains exactly as it was when the café opened. ⊠ *53 cours Mirabeau* ☎ *04–42–26–00–51* ⊕ *www. les2garcons.fr.*

**Cathédrale St-Sauveur.** Many eras of architectural history are clearly delineated and preserved here. The cathedral has a double nave—Romanesque and Gothic side by side—and a Merovingian (5th-century) **baptistery,** its colonnade mostly recovered from Roman temples built to honor pagan deities. The deep bath on the floor is a remnant of total-immersion baptism. Shutters hide the ornate 16th-century carvings on the **portals,** opened by a guide on request. The guide can also lead you into the tranquil Romanesque **cloister** next door, with carved pillars and slender columns.

The extraordinary 15th-century *Triptyque du Buisson Ardent* (*Mary and the Burning Bush*) was painted by Nicolas Froment in the heat of inspiration following his travels in Italy and Flanders and depicts the

The museums and churches in Aix-en-Provence are overshadowed by the city itself, with its beautiful fountains, elegant mansions, and charming set pieces like City Hall square.

generous art patrons King René and Queen Jeanne kneeling on either side of the Virgin, who is poised above a burning bush. To avoid light damage, it's rarely opened for viewing; check with the tourist office beforehand. ⊠ *Pl. des Martyrs de la Résistance* ☎ *04–42–23–45–65* ⊕ *www.cathedrale-aix.net.*

**Cours Mirabeau.** Shaded by a double row of tall plane trees, the Cours Mirabeau is one of the most beautiful avenues anywhere, designed so its width and length would be in perfect proportion with the height of the dignified 18th-century *hôtels particuliers* lining it. You can view this lovely assemblage from one of the dozen or so cafés that spill onto the pavement.

**Fontaine d'Eau Chaude** (*Hot Water Fountain*). Deliciously thick with dripping moss, this 18th-century fountain is fed by Sextius's own thermal source. It seems representative of Aix at its artfully negligent best. In sunny Provence, Aix was famous for its shade and its fountains; apropos, James Pope-Hennessy, in his *Aspects of Provence,* compares living in Aix to being at the bottom of an aquarium, thanks to all the fountains' bubbling water and the city's shady streets and boulevards. ⊠ *Cours Mirabeau.*

**Fontaine des Quatre Dauphins** (*Four Dolphins Fountain*). Within a tiny square at a symmetrical crossroads in the Quartier Mazarin, this lovely 17th-century fountain has four graceful dolphins at the foot of a pine cone–topped obelisk. Under the shade of a chestnut tree and framed by broad, shuttered mansions, it makes an elegant ensemble worth contemplating from the park bench. ⊠ *Pl. des Quatre Dauphins.*

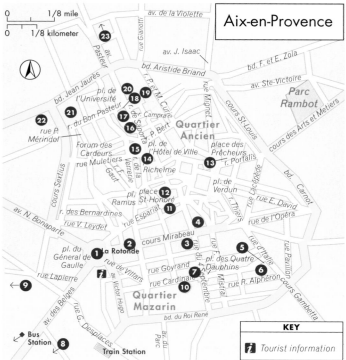

**Hôtel de Ville** (*City Hall*). Built between 1655 and 1678 by Pierre Pavillon, City Hall is fronted by a pebble-encrusted courtyard set off by a wrought-iron gateway. At the back, a double stairway leads to the Salle des Etats de Provences, the old regional assembly room (where taxes were voted on), which is hung with interesting portraits and pictures of mythological characters. From the window, look for the unmistakable 16th-century clock tower with an open ironwork belfry. The tree-lined square in front—where cafés set up tables right into the center of the space—is a popular gathering place. ⊠ *Pl. de L'Hôtel-de-Ville* ☎ *04–42–91–90–00.*

**La Rotonde.** If you've just arrived in Aix's center, this sculpture-fountain is a spectacular introduction to the town's rare mix of elegance and urban bustle. It's a towering mass of 19th-century attitude. That's Agriculture yearning toward Marseille, Art leaning toward Avignon, and Justice looking down on the Cours Mirabeau. But don't study it too intently—you'll likely be sideswiped by a speeding Vespa. ⊠ *Pl. de Gaulle.*

**Musée des Tapisseries.** Housed in the 17th-century **Palais de l'Archevêché** (Archbishop's Palace), this museum showcases a sumptuous collection of tapestries that once decorated the bishops' quarters. There are 17 magnificent hangings from Beauvais and a series on the life of Don Quixote from Compiègne. Temporary exhibitions offer looks at contemporary textile art. The main opera productions of the Festival

d'Aix take place in the broad courtyard. ✉ *28 pl. des Martyrs de la
Resistance* ☎ *04–42–23–09–91*
⊕ *www.aixenprovencetourism.
com* ✉ *€3.50* ☉ *Oct. 16–Apr. 15,
Wed.–Mon. 1:30–5; Apr. 16–Oct.
15, Wed.–Mon. 10–12:20 and
1:30–6. Closed Jan.*

**Musée Estienne de Saint-Jean**
(*Museum of Old Aix*). You'll find
an eclectic assortment of local
treasures inside this 17th-century
mansion, from faïence to santons
(terra-cotta figurines) to ornately
painted furniture. The building
is lovely, too. ✉ *17 rue Gaston
de Saporta* ☎ *04–42–16–11–61*
⊕ *www.aixenprovencetourism.
com* ✉ *Free* ☉ *Feb.–Apr. 14, Wed.–
Mon. 1:30–5; Apr. 15–Oct. 15,
Wed.–Mon. 10–6; Oct. 16–Dec.,
Wed.–Mon.1:30–5. Closed Jan.*

**IT'S AN ILL WIND
THAT BLOWS**

If you come to Provence in late
autumn or early spring, bring your
windbreaker. The infamous mistral
is a bitterly cold, dry wind that
comes sweeping down from the
north whenever a low pressure
weather system develops over the
Mediterranean. The temperature
can drop dramatically in a matter
of minutes. Many roads, fields, and
towns have wind-breaks of closely
planted trees or stone walls to
give some shelter from these
fierce winds, which, some say,
often bring out irritable "mistral
nerves" in the locals—one reason
the Aixois have a reputation for
being snappish.

Fodor'sChoice **Musée Granet.** Once the École de
★ Dessin (Art School) that granted Cézanne a second-place prize in 1856,
the former priory of the Église St-Jean-de-Malte now showcases eight of
Cézanne's paintings, as well as a nice collection of his watercolors and
drawings. Also hanging in the galleries are works by Bonnard, Picasso,
Klee, Rubens, David, and Giacometti. ✉ *Pl. St-Jean-de-Malte* ☎ *04–42–
52–88–32* ⊕ *www.museegranet-aixenprovence.fr* ✉ *€4* ☉ *June–Sept.,
Tues.–Sun. 10–7; Oct.–May, Tues.–Sun. noon–6.*

**Muséum d'Histoire Naturelle** (*Natural History Museum*). An unusual
collection of dinosaur eggs discovered on Mont Ste-Victoire is this
museum's claim to fame. Even if these don't interest you, the 17th-
century Hôtel Boyer d'Eguilles's interiors are magnificent, with ornate
woodwork and sculpture scattered among the fossilized bones. ✉ *6
rue Espariat* ☎ *04–42–27–91–27* ⊕ *www.museum-aix-en-provence.org*
✉ *€3.50* ☉ *Daily 10–noon and 1–5.*

Fodor'sChoice **Pavillon de Vendôme.** This extravagant Baroque villa was built in 1665
★ as a country house for the Duke of Vendome; its position just outside
the city's inner circle allowed the duke to commute discreetly from his
official home on the Cours Mirabeau to this retreat, where his mistress,
La Belle du Canet, was comfortably installed. The villa was expanded
and heightened in the 18th century to draw attention to the classical orders—Ionic, Doric, and Corinthian—on parade in the row of
neo-Grecian columns. Inside the cool, broad chambers you can find a
collection of Provençal furniture and artwork. Note the curious two
giant Atlantes that hold up the interior balcony. ✉ *32 rue Celony* ☎ *04–
42–91–88–75* ⊕ *www.aixenprovence.fr* ✉ *€3.50* ☉ *Oct. 15–Apr. 15,
Wed.–Mon. 1:30–5; Apr. 16–Oct. 14, Wed.–Mon. 10–6. Closed Jan.*

## DID YOU KNOW?

Aix's centre ville (downtown) is a maze of narrow, commercial streets, and it's difficult to keep your sense of direction. Most sights are within central Aix, where walking is the best and most delightful way to get around.

**Place d'Albertas.** Of all the elegant squares in Aix, this one is the most evocative and otherworldly. Set back from the city's fashionable shopping streets, it forms a horseshoe of shuttered mansions, with cobbles radiating from a simple turn-of-the-20th-century fountain. No wonder chamber music concerts are held here in summer. ⊠ *Intersection of Rue Espariat and Rue Aude.*

**Site-Mémorial du Camp des Milles.** Controversial up to its opening in 2012, this museum and memorial is France's only still-intact deportation camp, where 10,000 men, women, and children of 38 nationalities (2,000 of whom were eventually transferred to Auschwitz) were detained over a period of three years, before the structure was repurposed as an armaments factory. Direct contact with internment areas, including sleeping and dining quarters and hiding places, makes for a rare immediacy. Traces of the many artists and intellectuals who were detained here, including surrealist artists Max Ernst and Hans Bellmer and novelist Lion Feuchtwanger, can be found in the many artworks displayed (all made here) and the graffiti still vibrantly intact on the walls. At the conclusion of the visit, museum-goers retrace the deportees' path to a railway wagon parked near the main building, a sobering reminder of a terrible chapter in French history. ⊠ *40 chemin de la Badesse* ☏ *04–42–39–17–11* ⊕ *www.campdesmilles.org* 🎫 *€9.50* ☉ *Daily 10–7.*

**Thermes Sextius** (*Thermal Baths of Sextius*). Warm natural springs first discovered under the leadership of Sextius, the Thermes now house the glass walls of an ultramodern health spa. The small fountain in the interior marks the warm spring of the original 18th-century establishment; today the facility's offerings include a great gym, pressure showers, mud treatments, and underwater massages. ⊠ *55 Ave. des Thermes* ☏ *04–42–22–81–82* ⊕ *www.thermes-sextius.com* ☉ *Weekdays 8:30–7:30, Sat. 8:30–6:30; gym also open Sun. 8:30–7:30.*

**OFF THE BEATEN PATH**

**Jas de Bouffan.** Cézanne's father bought this lovely estate, whose name translates as "the sheepfold," in 1859 to celebrate his rise from hatmaker to banker. The budding artist lived here until 1899 and painted his first images of Mont Ste-Victoire—the founding seeds of 20th-century art—from the grounds. Today the salons are empty but the estate is full of the artist's spirit, especially the Allée des Marronniers out front. The Jas is a mile south of the center of town and can only be visited on tour by booking a minibus seat through the central tourist office, either in person or online. ⊠ *80 rte. de Valcros* ☏ *04–42–16–10–91* ⊕ *www.aixenprovencetourism.com* 🎫 *€5.50* ☉ *Nov.–Mar., Wed. and Sat. 10 am; Apr.–May, Tues., Thurs., and Sat., 10:30, noon, 3:30, in English at 2; June–Sept., daily 10:30, noon, 3:30, in English at 2; Oct., Tues., Thurs., and Sat., 10:30, noon, 3:30, in English at 2.*

## WORTH NOTING

**Ancienne Halle aux Grains** (*Old Grain Market*). Built in 1761, this former grain market serves as a post office today—a rather spectacular building for a prosaic service. The frieze, portraying an allegory of the Rhône and Durance rivers, is the work of Aix sculptor Jean Chaste (1726–93); he also created the fountain out in front. That's a real Roman column at the fountain's top. ⊠ *Pl. Richelme.*

## THE S IS (HARDLY EVER) SILENT

Especially among a people who cut their teeth on the Academie Française, that holy arbiter of the French language, there are variant spins allowed when speaking French in Provence. The rule of thumb here is to pronounce everything, even letters that aren't there. *Pain* becomes "peng" in the south. *Vin* becomes "veng," *enfin* "on feng," and so forth. One of the words caught in the crossfire: *mas*. This old Provençal word for farmhouse is a "mahss"

in the south, but Parisians hold out for a more refined Frenchification: "ma." Cassis is another booby trap. Parisians refer to the blackcurrant liqueur made in Burgundy as "cass-*eess*" but southern French locals refer to the wine from the coastal country east of Marseille as "cass-*ee*." If that weren't confusing enough, Parisians also call the town of Cassis "cass-*eess*," much to the ire of the locals, who insist they live in "cass-ee."

**Collège Royal-Bourbon.** It's within these walls, which now belong to the Lycée Mignet, that Cézanne and his schoolmate Emile Zola discussed their ideas. Cézanne received his baccalauréat *cum laude* here in 1858 and went on to attend a year of law school to please his father. ⊠ *Rue Cardinale at Rue Joseph-Cabassol.*

**Conservatoire de Musique Darius-Milhaud.** Housed in a striking new edifice designed by architect Kengo Kuma in the new Forum Culturel (which includes the Pavillon Noir dance center), the Darius Milhaud Music Conservatory celebrates the music of Marseille's native composer, who spent several years of his childhood in Aix and returned here to die. Milhaud (1892–1974), a member of the group of French composers known as Les Six, created fine-boned, transparent works influenced by jazz and Hebrew chant. Aix has yet to make a museum of his memorabilia. ⊠ *380 av. Mozart* ☎ *04–88–71–84–20.*

**NEED A BREAK?**

**La Brûlerie Richelme.** For an excellent cup of inexpensive, fresh-roast coffee, wander into La Brûlerie Richelme. Comfy chairs and lively student patronage add to the casual ambience, and the light snacks are just the thing. ⊠ *1 Pl. Richelme* ⊕ *www.cafe-the-richelme.com.*

**Église de la Madeleine.** Though the facade now bears 19th-century touches, this small 17th-century church still contains the center panel of the fine 15th-century *Annunciation Triptych,* attributed to the father of Jan Van Eyck, the greatest painter of the Early Netherlandish school. Some say the massive painting on the left side of the transept is a Rubens. The church is used regularly for classical concerts. ⊠ *Pl. des Prêcheurs* ☎ *04–42–38–02–81* ⊙ *Daily 8–11:30 and 3–5:30.*

**Église St-Jean-de-Malte.** This 12th-century church served as a chapel of the Knights of Malta, a medieval order of friars devoted to hospital care. The church was Aix's first attempt at the Gothic style, and it was here that the counts of Provence were buried throughout the 18th century; their tombs (in the upper left) were attacked during the Revolution and have been only partially repaired. ⊠ *Rue Cardinale and Rue d'Italie.*

**Hôtel de Châteaurenard.** Across from a commercial gallery that calls itself the Petit Musée Cézanne (actually more of a tourist trap), this 17th-century mansion once hosted Louis XIV—and now houses government offices. This means that during business hours you can slip in and peek at the fabulous 18th-century stairwell, decorated in flamboyant trompe l'oeil. Pseudo-stone putti and caryatids pop into three dimensions—as does the false balustrade that mirrors the real one in stone. ⊠ *19 rue Gaston de Saporta* ⊘ *Weekdays 9–4.*

**Hôtel Maynier d'Oppède.** This ornately decorated mansion houses the **Institut d'Études Françaises** (Institute of French Studies), where foreign students take French classes. During the July opera Festival d'Aix, the hôtel's courtyard is used for a series of classical concerts. ⊠ *23 rue Gaston de Saporta* ☎ *04–42–21–70–92.*

## WHERE TO EAT

**$$**
FRENCH
╳ **Brasserie Les Deux Garçons.** As you revel in the exquisite gold-ivory decor, which dates from the restaurant's founding in 1792, it's not hard to picture the greats—Churchill, Sartre, Picasso, Delon, Belmondo, and Cocteau among them—enjoying a drink under these mirrors. The food is not memorable, but 365 days a year you can savor the linen-decked sidewalk tables that look out to the Cours Mirabeau. $ *Average main:* €24 ⊠ *53 cours Mirabeau* ☎ *04–42–26–00–51* ⊕ *www.les2garcons.fr.*

**$$**
FRENCH
╳ **La Chimère Café.** Although the decor in this artists' hangout is a bit overdone, there's a sense of playful whimsy in the vertically arranged concoctions of fresh, local ingredients garnished with shaved fennel, spun sugar, or drizzled sauces. The prices are reasonable, the atmosphere is lively, there's an honorable wine selection, and—even better— a Champagne bar—making this an altogether fun place to spend an evening. $ *Average main: €23* ⊠ *15 rue Brueys* ☎ *04–42–38–30–00* ⊕ *www.lachimerecafe.com* ⊘ *Closed Sun. No lunch Sat.*

**$$**
FRENCH FUSION
FAMILY
╳ **Lavault.** Named for its vaulted stone cellar, where you can dine or enjoy your pre-dinner apèro (a better choice decor-wise than the ordinary upstairs), this bistro has a frequently changing menu, but go for the foie gras club if you find it. You can't go wrong with anything on this menu, though: duck ravioli with foie gras and morels, or sea trout with saffron-mussel risotto are equally tempting. For dessert the white chocolate cheesecake or raspberries in lemon cream make for a light finish. A well-rounded wine list, plenty of wines by the glass, and a good children's menu make this a good choice for a family lunch. The three-course menu (€36) is the best deal. $ *Average main: €25* ⊠ *24 rue Felibre Gaut* ☎ *04–42–38–57–28* ⌕ *Reservations essential.*

**$**
FRENCH
╳ **Le Bistro Latin.** With soft tones of orange and yellow and wood-backed chairs, this unpretentious and ultrafriendly little restaurant has only two menus with lots of choice, each combining fresh ingredients and equally fresh ideas. Doing honor to southern cooking, olive oil figures large, as do typical Provençal herbs and spices. Consider mussels and spinach in a saffron sauce, roasted pork loin with honey and garlic, lamb stew, or a subtle terrine of chickpeas and fresh goat cheese with balsamic vinegar. $ *Average main: €16* ⊠ *18 rue de la Couronne* ☎ *04–42–38–22–88* ⊘ *Closed Sun. No lunch Mon. and Wed.*

It's easy to understand why Cézanne painted so many *nature morte* (still-life) paintings once you see the delectable delights on sale in many of the town squares.

**$**   ✕ **L'Épicurien.** The blackboard menu at this small rustic bistro may
BISTRO   seem limited, but that's only because it changes every week according
FAMILY   to what's tempting at the market. Fresh and inventive dishes might
include crispy *poitrine du porc* (pork belly), shrimp in puff pastry with
avocado cream, lobster salad, and passion fruit tiramisu for dessert,
all for a price that's easy on the wallet (two courses at lunch for €19;
€30–€36 at dinner). The kids' menu (€14) is a nice bonus. **$** *Average main: €16* ⊠ *13 pl. des Cardeurs* ☎ *06–89–33–49–83* ⊘ *Closed
Sun. and Mon.*

**$$$$**   ✕ **Le Saint Estève.** A short drive from Aix over scenic Route Cézanne, the
MODERN FRENCH   elegant Le Saint Estève restaurant on the grounds of the Les Lodges
Fodor's Choice   hotel is well worth the trip. Michelin-starred chef Mathias Dandine's
★   spiffed up menu shows a new inspiration—and who wouldn't be
inspired with these breathtaking views of Cézanne's beloved mountain? Dandine doesn't have far to look for the locally sourced products
he favors, either: wild mushrooms for a luscious *velouté de cêpes* (wild
mushroom soup) with ham and spicy Provençal olive oil, or sea bass
with chanterelles and sechuan pepper. Heads turn as virtuosic dishes,
one more beautiful than the next, are flourished at the table. Finish
with tender *fraises des bois* (wild strawberries) in warm strawberry
consommé with a dollop of *fromage frais* ice cream paired with a
sweet local wine. With a shady outdoor terrace overlooking olive
groves and woods, well, what's not to love? **$** *Average main: €45*
⊠ *2500 Route Cézanne, Le Tholonet* ☎ *04–42–27–10–14* ⊕ *www.
leslodgessaintevictoire.com.*

$    ✕ **Sushi Ô Zen.** Don't be put off by the nondescript neighborhood: this
SUSHI    calm and pleasingly unpretentious dining room serves the freshest—
and most reasonably priced—sushi in town, along with hot dishes
(salmon, shrimp, beef) and tuna or salmon tartare. You'll find all the
usual sushi suspects here, too—sashimi, California rolls, and a roster
of classics. There's takeout and delivery service, too. $ *Average main:*
*€12 ✉ 685 rue Albert Einstein ☎ 04–42–65–12–66 ⊕ www.sushiozen.*
*com ☽ Closed weekends. No dinner.*

## WHERE TO STAY

$    ⌂ **Grand Hotel Nègre-Coste.** This 18th-century townhouse lives up to its
HOTEL    prominent Cours Mirabeau position with lavish ground-floor salons,
Provençal decor, and large windows. **Pros:** a perfect location for visiting
Aix; the welcome is warm; affordable. **Cons:** rooms, especially those
near the elevator, can be noisy; some rooms are quite small; not a lot
of sockets for recharging phones, iPads etc. $ *Rooms from: €96 ✉ 33*
*cours Mirabeau ☎ 04–42–27–74–22 ⊕ www.hotelnegrecoste.com ☞ 36*
*rooms, 1 suite* ⦿| *No meals.*

$    ⌂ **Hôtel Cardinal.** In a lovely 18th-century house in the Quartier Maza-
HOTEL    rin, this eccentric and slightly threadbare inn is the antithesis of slick.
Fodor'sChoice    **Pros:** the price for the location is excellent; rooms are clean and bright.
★    **Cons:** rooms can be noisy and hot in summer. $ *Rooms from: €77 ✉ 24*
*rue Cardinale ☎ 04–42–38–32–30 ⊕ www.hotel-cardinal-aix.com ☞ 2*
*rooms, 6 suites* ⦿| *No meals.*

$$$$    ⌂ **Hôtel Cézanne.** Three blocks from Cours Mirabeau and the train sta-
HOTEL    tion, this smart, spiffy, and cozily stylish hotel is a very handy option.
**Pros:** the breakfast buffet is one of the very best around; the honor bar
is a treat. **Cons:** there's no pool; some rooms get street noise. $ *Rooms*
*from: €250 ✉ 40 av. Victor-Hugo ☎ 04–42–91–11–11 ⊕ cezanne.*
*hotelaix.com ☞ 55 rooms, 12 suites* ⦿| *No meals.*

$$$    ⌂ **Hôtel des Augustins.** The best aspect of this Old Town hotel, just a
HOTEL    half block back from Cours Mirabeau, is its reception area: the groin-
vaulted stone, stained glass, and ironwork banister date from the 15th
century, when the house was an Augustinian convent (Martin Luther
was once a guest). **Pros:** you can't beat the location; sincere welcome
is a pleasure. **Cons:** rooms are quite ordinary; some are very small.
$ *Rooms from: €140 ✉ 3 rue de la Masse ☎ 04–42–27–28–59 ⊕ www.*
*hotel-augustins.com ☞ 29 rooms* ⦿| *No meals.*

$$$$    ⌂ **Le Pigonnet.** Cézanne painted Ste-Victoire from what is now the
HOTEL    large flower-filled terrace of this enchanting abode, and you can easily
Fodor'sChoice    imagine former guests Princess Caroline, Iggy Pop, and Clint East-
★    wood swanning their way through the magnificent, pool-adorned,
topiary-accented garden or relaxing in the spacious, light-filled guest
rooms, each a marvel of decoration—and renovated in 2013. **Pros:**
unique garden setting in the center of Aix; welcome is friendly; rooms
all have large French windows. **Cons:** reception area has been called
stuffy and old-fashioned; some of the antiques are a little threadbare;
breakfast is extra (€25). $ *Rooms from: €360 ✉ 5 av. du Pigonnet*
*☎ 04–42–59–02–90 ⊕ www.hotelpigonnet.com ☞ 40 rooms, 4 suites*
⦿| *No meals.*

$$$$ HOTEL Fodor's Choice ★ **Les Lodges Sainte-Victoire.** Set on a picture-perfect 10 acres of woods, olive groves, and vineyards just outside Aix, with Cézanne-immortalized Mont Ste-Victoire as a backdrop, this new hotel raises the bar for lodging in the region. **Pros:** top restaurant Le Saint Estève on the premises. **Cons:** outside the city center. [$] *Rooms from: €315* ✉ *2250 route Cézanne, Le Tholonet* ☎ *04–42–24–80–40* 🌐 *www.leslodgessaintevictoire.com* 🛏 *35 rooms, 4 lodges* 🍴 *No meals.*

$ HOTEL **Quatre Dauphins.** A noble hôtel particulier in the quiet, soigné, and chic Mazarin quarter offers modest but impeccable lodging, with pretty, comfortable little rooms that have been spruced up with *boutis* (Provençal quilts), Les Olivades fabrics, quarry tiles, jute carpets, and hand-painted furniture. **Pros:** ideal center-of-town location; friendly staff; rooms with showers are cheaper than ones with a bath. **Cons:** rooms are small; in summer it is impossible to get a room; breakfast is extra. [$] *Rooms from: €80* ✉ *54 rue Roux-Alphéran* ☎ *04–42–38–16–39* 🌐 *www.lesquatredauphins.fr* 🛏 *13 rooms* 🍴 *No meals.*

$$ HOTEL **St-Christophe.** With so few mid-price *hôtels de charme* in Aix, you might as well opt for this glossy Art Deco–style hotel, where the comfort and services are remarkable for the price. **Pros:** location; price-service ratio. **Cons:** hotel-chain feel; decor lacks charm. [$] *Rooms from: €110* ✉ *2 av. Victor-Hugo* ☎ *04–42–26–01–24* 🌐 *www.hotel-saintchristophe.com* 🛏 *50 rooms, 10 suites* 🍴 *No meals.*

$$$$ HOTEL **Villa Gallici.** Hued in the lavenders, blues, ochers, and oranges of Aix, rooms here swim in the most gorgeous Souleiado and Rubelli fabrics: this all conjures up the swank Provence that used to be colonized by Parisian barons and dukes in the 19th century, far from the usual Provençal farmhouse idyll. **Pros:** rich fabrics and decor create a harmonious look; beautiful environment. **Cons:** no elevator, some showers are handheld; 15-minute walk from town. [$] *Rooms from: €400* ✉ *Av. de la Violette* ☎ *04–42–23–29–23* 🌐 *www.villagallici.com* 🛏 *22 rooms, 4 suites* 🍴 *Breakfast.*

## NIGHTLIFE AND THE ARTS

To find out what's going on in town, pick up a copy of the events calendar *Le Mois à Aix* or the bilingual city guide *Aix la Vivante* at the tourist office.

### NIGHTLIFE

**Casino Aix en Provence.** In between bouts at the roulette tables and slot machines of the Casino Aix en Provence, you can grab a bite at one of five restaurants or take in a floor show. ✉ *21 Av. de l'Europe* ☎ *04–42–59–69–00* 🌐 *www.casinoaix.com.*

**Hot Brass.** A mature crowd comes from the suburbs for live concerts of funk, soul, rock, blues, and Latin bands, mainly local. ✉ *1857 chemin d'Eguilles* ☎ *04–42–23–13–12.*

**Le Mistral.** This established student club has big-name DJs and a strict door policy, so get dressed up and get there early. ✉ *3 rue Frédéric-Mistral* ☎ *04–42–38–16–49* 🌐 *www.mistralclub.fr.*

**Le Scat Club.** This is the place for live soul, funk, reggae, rock, blues, and jazz. ✉ *11 rue de la Verrerie* ☎ *04–42–23–00–23* 🌐 *scatclub.free.fr/scatnet.*

## THE ARTS

**Festival d'Aix.** In late June and July, opera and music lovers descend on Aix for the internationally acclaimed Festival d'Aix to see world-class opera productions in the courtyard of the Palais de l'Archevêché and more of the city's most beautiful venues. The repertoire is varied and often offbeat, featuring works like Britten's *Curlew River* and Bartók's *Bluebeard's Castle* as well as the usual Mozart, Puccini, and Verdi. Most of the singers, however, are not celebrities, but rather an elite group of students who spend the summer with the Academie Européenne de Musique, training and performing under the tutelage of stars like Robert Tear and Yo-Yo Ma. ■ TIP→ Tickets can be purchased online from January. ☎ *04–34–08–02–17* ⊕ *www.festival-aix.com.*

**Le Ballet Preljocaj.** Angelin Preljocaj has created original ballets for the New York City Ballet and the Paris Opera Ballet, and his modern-dance troupe, Ballet Preljocaj, is based at the monolithic Pavillon Noir, designed by architect Rudy Ricciotti. The season runs September to May. The Pavillon hosts an annual series of contemporary ballet and modern dance performances featuring an international roster. ⊠ *530 av. Wolfgang Amadeus Mozart* ☎ *04–42–93–48–00* ⊕ *www.preljocaj.org.*

**Renoir.** Renoir cinemas both show some films in *v.o.* (*version originale,* i.e., not dubbed). ⊠ *24 cours Mirabeau* ☎ *08–36–68–72–70.*

# THE OUTDOORS

Because it's there, in part, and because it looms in striking isolation above the plain east of Aix, its heights catching the sun long after the valley lies in shadow, Cézanne's beloved **Montagne Ste-Victoire** inspires climbers to conquest. The Grande Randonée stretches along its long, rocky crest from the village of Le Bouquet at its western end all the way east to Puyloubier. Its alternate route climbs the milder north slope from Les Cabassols. Along the way it peaks at 3,316 feet at Pic des Mouches, from where the view stretches around the compass. Pick up detailed maps at the tourist office.

# SHOPPING

Aix is a snazzy market town, and unlike the straightforward, country-fair atmosphere of nearby Aubagne, a trip to the market here is filled with rarefied, high-end delicacies shoulder to shoulder with garlic braids. You can find fine olive oils from the Pays d'Aix (Aix region), barrels glistening with olives of every hue and blend, and vats of tapenade (crushed olive, caper, and anchovy paste). Melons, asparagus, and mesclun salad are piled high, and dried sausages bristling with Provençal herbs hang from stands. A **food and produce market** takes place every morning on Place Richelme; just up the street on Place Verdun is a good, high-end *brocante* (collectibles) market Tuesday, Thursday, and Saturday mornings.

In addition to its old-style markets and jewel-box candy shops, Aix is a dazzlingly sophisticated modern shopping town—perhaps the best in Provence. The winding streets of the Vieille Ville above Cours

Mirabeau—focused around **rues Clémenceau, Marius Reinaud, Espariat, Aude, Fabrot**, and **Maréchal Foch**—have a plethora of goods, including high-end designer clothes.

## BOOKS

**Book in Bar.** This cozy English bookshop near Cours Mirabeau is not only a great place to buy and read English-language books, but also to meet other English speakers. ⊠ *4 rue Joseph Cabassol* ☎ *04–42–26–60–07* ⊕ *www.bookinbar.com* ☉ *Mon.–Sat. 9–7.*

## CANDY

A great Aixois delicacy is *calissons*. A blend of almond paste and glazed melon, they are cut into geometric almond shapes and stacked high in *confiserie* windows.

**Béchard.** The most picturesque shop specializing in calissons is the venerable bakery Béchard. ⊠ *12 cours Mirabeau* ☉ *Tues.–Fri. and Sun. 8–7:30, Sat. 8–8.*

**Leonard Parli.** Near the train station, Leonard Parli offers a lovely selection of calissons. ⊠ *35 av. Victor Hugo* ⊕ *www.leonard-parli.com* ☉ *Mon.–Sat. 9–7.*

**Weibel.** An Aix institution since 1954, Weibel is chock-full of sweets that look good enough to immortalize in a still life, let alone eat. Their version of the iconic Provençal calisson is the best around. They make sublime gifts, packaged in lovely lavender boxes. ⊠ *2 rue Chabrier* ☎ *04–42–23–33–21* ⊕ *maisonweibel.fr* ☉ *Weekdays 8–7, Sat. 7:30–7:30, Sun. 7:30–6.*

## CLOTHING

**Catimini.** The French chain Catimini offers an imaginative, jazzy stock of kids' sweaters, jackets, and dresses. ⊠ *9 pl. Chapeliers* ☎ *04–42–27–51–14* ⊕ *www.catimini.com* ☉ *Mon. 2–7, Tues.–Sat. 9:30–1:30 and 2–7.*

**Gago.** On the fashion front, particularly noteworthy is Gago, a fashion leader with stylish designer wear for women including Céline, Balanciaga, and Lanvin. ⊠ *20–24 rue Fabrot* ☎ *04–42–27–60–19* ☉ *Mon.–Sat. 10–7.*

**Gérard Darel.** Contemporary fashions with an emphasis on classic French tailoring, Gérard Darel is known for their chic day-to-evening dresses and sleek trenchcoats; accessories are available, too. ⊠ *13 rue Fabrot* ☎ *04–42–26–38–45* ⊕ *www.gerarddarel.com* ☉ *Weekdays 10–7, Sat. 10–8.*

## CRAFTS

**Les Olivades.** This is one of the last *maisons* that print Provençal fabrics in the traditonal Marseille style. ⊠ *15 rue Marius Reinaud* ☎ *04–42–38–33–66* ⊕ *www.lesolivades.fr* ☉ *Mon.–Sat. 10–7.*

**Santons Fouque.** Aix's most celebrated *santon*, or miniature statue, maker is Santons Fouque. ⊠ *65 cours Gambetta* ☎ *04–42–26–33–38* ⊕ *www.santons-fouque.com* ☉ *Daily 9–noon and 2–6.*

The heart of Marseille is its Vieux Port (Old Port), with its small boats and portside cafés, while the city's soul is hilltop Notre-Dame-de-la-Garde.

## MARSEILLE

*32 km (20 miles) south of Aix; 66 km (41 miles) northwest of Toulon.*

Popular myths and a fishy reputation have led Marseille to be unfairly maligned as dirty urban sprawl plagued with impoverished immigrant neighborhoods and slightly louche politics. It is often given wide berth by travelers in search of a Provençal idyll. A huge mistake. Marseille, even its earliest history, has maintained its contradictions with a kind of fierce and independent pride. Yes, there are scary neighborhoods, some modern eyesores, even a high crime rate—but there is also tremendous beauty and culture. Cubist jumbles of white stone rise up over a picture-book seaport, bathed in light of blinding clarity, crowned by larger-than-life neo-Byzantine churches, and framed by massive fortifications; neighborhoods teem with multiethnic life; souklike African markets reek deliciously of spices and coffees; and the labyrinthine Old Town radiates pastel shades of saffron, marigold, and robin's-egg blue.

Since being designated a European Capital of Culture for 2013, with an estimated €660 million of funding in the bargain, Marseille has been in the throes of an extraordinary transformation, with no fewer than five major new arts centers, a beautifully refurbished port, revitalized neighborhoods, and a slew of new shops and restaurants. Once the underdog, this time-burnished city is now welcoming an influx of weekend tourists who have colonized entire neighborhoods and transformed them into elegant *pieds-à-terre* (or should we say, *mer*). The second-largest city in France, Marseille is one of Europe's most vibrant destinations. Feisty and fond of broad gestures, it is also as complicated and as cosmopolitan now as it was when a band of Phoenician Greeks first sailed into the harbor that is today's Vieux Port in 600 BC.

Legend has it that on that same day a local chieftain's daughter, Gyptis, needed to choose a husband, and her wandering eyes settled on the Greeks' handsome commander Protis. Her dowry brought land near the mouth of the Rhône, where the Greeks founded Massalia, the most important Continental shipping port in antiquity. The port flourished for some 500 years as a typical Greek city, enjoying the full flush of classical culture, its gods, its democratic political system, its sports and theater, and its naval prowess. Caesar changed all that, besieging the city in 49 BC and seizing most of its colonies. In 1214 Marseille was seized again, this time by Charles d'Anjou, and was later annexed to France by Henri IV in 1481, but it was not until Louis XIV took the throne that the biggest transformations of the port began; he pulled down the city walls in 1666 and expanded the port to the Rive Neuve (New Riverbank). The city was devastated by plague in 1720, losing more than half its population. By the time of the Revolution, Marseille was on the rebound once again, with industries of soap manufacturing and oil processing flourishing, encouraging a wave of immigration from Provence and Italy.

With the opening of the Suez Canal in 1869, Marseille became the greatest boomtown in 19th-century Europe. With a large influx of immigrants from areas as exotic as Tangiers, the city quickly acquired the multicultural population it maintains to this day.

### GETTING HERE AND AROUND

The main train station is Gare St-Charles on the TGV line, with frequent trains from Paris, the main coast route (Nice/Italy), and Arles. The gare routière is on Place Victor Hugo. Here you can find Cartreize buses into the Bouches du Rhône and Eurolines coaches between Marseille, Avignon, and Nice via Aix-en-Provence. Marseille has a very good local bus, tram, and métro system (€1.50 for 90 minutes of use), and the César ferry boat (immortalized in Pagnol's 1931 film, *Marius*) crosses the Vieux Port every few minutes and is free of charge.

▧ TIP➔ Le Vélo is Marseille's citywide bicycle network. Grab a bike, take it to your destination, and then pick up another when you're ready to move on. The first 30 minutes are free and a seven-day pass (⊕ *en.levelo-mpm.fr/how-it-works*) costs only €1.

### VISITOR INFORMATION

**Marseille Tourist Office** ✉ *11 la Canebière* ☎ *08–26–50–05–00* *(€0.15 per minute)* ⊕ *www.marseille-tourisme.com.*

### TOURS

The tourist office organizes a variety of walking tours covering the Old Town and port, the Cours Julien and street art, Marseille by night, and many more, and they take place several times a week. Tours start at €9 per person and you can request them in English. Tickets and schedules are available at the tourist office.

# EXPLORING

## THE QUAI DU PORT AND LE PANIER

Though Marseille is the second-largest city in France, it functions as a conglomerate of distinct neighborhoods—almost little villages. One of these microcosms is the Neapolitan-style maze of picturesque lanes, cafés, artist ateliers, and chic boutiques called Le Panier. Site of the first Greek settlements and the oldest neighborhood in France, it merits intimate exploration. Don't miss the striking museum complex of the Vieille Charité. The recently transformed Vieux Port is the most scenic walk in town: from the port's old fish market to the astonishing new Musée des Civilisations de l'Europe et de la Méditerranée (MuCEM), the Villa Méditerranée, and the Musée Regards du Provence, all opened in 2013.

### TOP ATTRACTIONS

**Cathédrale de la Nouvelle Major.** This gargantuan, neo-Byzantine 19th-century fantasy was built under Napoléon III—but not before he'd ordered the partial destruction of the lovely 11th-century original, once a perfect example of the Provençal Romanesque style. You can view the flashy decor (think marble and rich red porphyry inlay) in the newer of the two churches; the medieval one is being restored. ⊠ *Pl. de la Major, Le Panier.*

**Centre de la Vieille Charité** (*Center of the Old Charity*). At the top of the Panier district you'll find this superb ensemble of 17th- and 18th-century architecture designed as a hospice for the homeless by Marseillais artist-architects Pierre and Jean Puget. Even if you don't enter the museums, walk around the inner court, studying the retreating perspective of triple arcades and admiring the Baroque chapel with its novel egg-peaked dome. Of the complex's two museums, the larger is the **Musée d'Archéologie Méditerranéenne** (Museum of Mediterranean Archaeology), with a sizable collection of pottery and statuary from classical Mediterranean civilization, elementally labeled (for example, "pot"). There's also a display on the mysterious Celt-like Ligurians who first peopled the coast, cryptically presented with emphasis on the digs instead of the finds themselves. The best of the lot is the evocatively mounted Egyptian collection—the second-largest in France after the Louvre's. There are mummies, hieroglyphs, and gorgeous sarcophagi in a tomblike setting. Upstairs, the **Musée d'Arts Africains, Océaniens, et Amérindiens** (Museum of African, Oceanic, and American Indian Art) creates a theatrical foil for the works' intrinsic drama: the spectacular masks and sculptures are mounted along a pure black wall, lighted indirectly, with labels across the aisle. ⊠ *2 rue de la Charité, Le Panier* ☎ *04–91–14–58–80* ☎ *€3 per museum* ☉ *Jan.–May., Tues.–Sun. 11–6; June–Sept., Tues.–Sun. 10–6.*

**Le Panier.** This is the heart of old Marseille, a maze of high-shuttered houses looming over narrow cobbled streets, *montées* (stone stairways), and tiny squares. Long decayed and neglected, the quarter is a principal focus of the city's efforts at urban renewal. In the last few years an influx of Bobos (bourgeois-bohemians) and artists have sparked the gentrification process, bringing charming B&Bs, chic boutiques, lively cafés, and artists' ateliers. Wander this picturesque neighborhood of pastel-painted townhouses, steep stairways, and narrow streets at will, making sure to stroll along Rue du Panier, the montée des Accoules, Rue du Petit-Puits, and Rue des Muettes.

# Marseille

Rade
de
Marseille

Bassin
de la
Grande
Joliette

Avant-Port
de la
Joliette

Fort
St-Jean

Jardin
du Pharo

Vieux
Port

Ferry
Boat

Le
Panier

pl.
Daviel
Grand'Rue
pl. Victor
Gelu

quai du Port

bd. Charles    Livon

quai de Rive
Sainte    Nueve
Catherine

rue Sainte

bd. de la Corderie
rue
des Lices

Jardin
P. Puget

cours Pierre Pt

TO ANSES,
PLAGE DU PRADO

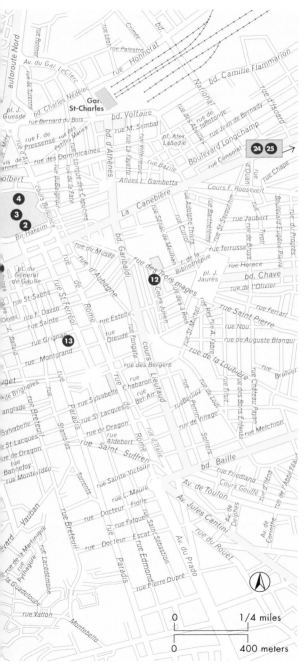

**4**

**Marché aux Poissons** (*Fish Market*). Up and going by 8 am every day, this market—immortalized in Marcel Pagnot's *Fanny* (and Joshua Logan's sublime 1961 film adaptation)—puts on a vivid and aromatic show of waving fists, jostling chefs, and heaps of fish from the night's catch still twitching. You'll hear the thick soup of the Marseillais accent as blue-clad fishermen and silk-clad matrons bicker over prices, and you'll wonder at the rainbow of Mediterranean creatures swimming in plastic vats before you, each uglier than the last: the spiny-headed *rascasse* (scorpion fish), dog-nosed *grondin* (red gurnet), the monstrous *baudroie* or *lotte de mer* (monkfish), and the eel-like *congre*. "Bouillabaisse" as sold here is a mix of fish too tiny to sell otherwise; the only problem with coming for the early morning show is that you have to wait so long for your bouillabaisse lunch. ⊠ *Quai de la Fraternité, Vieux Port* ☉ *Daily 8–1.*

**Musée d'Art Contemporain.** The contemporary arts museum (MAC) houses a permanent collection representative of the major artists and international movements of the later part of the 20th century, including iconic pieces like Chris Burden's *Moonette n.5* and Jean-Michel Basquiat's *King of the Zulus*. The museum also curates ambitious temporary exhibitions of international contemporary artists. The inaugural show, "Le Pont," featured the works of 145 artists on the theme of exchanges between civilizations. The small museum café offers snacks all day and a reasonable €12 menu at lunch. ⊠ *69 av. de Haïfa, Prado* ☎ *04-91-25-01-07* ⊕ *mac.marseille.fr* ⊡ *€5* ☉ *Tues.–Sun. 10–6.*

**Musée des Civilisations de L'Europe et de la Mediterranée.** After a lengthy renovation, the Museum of the Civilizations of Europe and the Mediterranean (MuCEM) opened its doors to great fanfare in the summer of 2013. Made up of three sites designed by Rudy Ricciotti, MuCEM is all about new perspectives on Mediterranean cultures. Themes like "the invention of gods," "the treasures of the spice route," or "at the bazaar of gender" are explored in Ricciotti's virtuosic J4 (named for the esplanade). ■ TIP→ The museum's popular café, bistro, and restaurant (reservations required), overseen by star-chef Gérald Passédat, are great for refreshment and taking in the views. You can access the 12th-century Fort St-Jean, built by Louis XIV with the guns pointing *toward* the city, in order to keep the feisty, rebellious Marseillais under his thumb. If you're not the queasy type, take a suspended footbridge over the sea; it provides spectacular photo-ops and never-been-seen panoramas. On the other side, you can visit a new Mediterranean garden and a folk-art collection. A third building—the Center for Conservation and Resources, near the St-Charles train station—holds the museum's permanent collection of paintings, prints, drawings, photographs, and objects. ⊠ *Quai du Port, Vieux Port* ☎ *04-96-13-80-90* ⊕ *www.mucem.org* ⊡ *€5* ☉ *May–Oct., Wed.–Mon. 11–7; Nov.–Apr., Wed.–Mon. 11–6.*

Fodor'sChoice ★ **Musée d'Histoire de Marseille** (*Marseille History Museum*). With the Port Antique in front, this modern, open-space museum illuminates Massalia's history with a treasure of archaeological finds and miniature models of the city as it appeared in various stages of history. Best by far is the presentation of Marseille's Classical halcyon days. There's a recovered wreck of a Roman cargo boat, its third-century wood amazingly preserved, and the hull of a Greek boat dating from the 4th century BC. The model of the Greek city should be authentic—it's based on an eyewitness description by Aristotle. The museum reopened after a stunning €21 million renovation in the summer of 2013. ⊠ 9 *rue Henri Barbrusse, Vieux Port*

☎ *04–91–90–42–22* ⊕ *musee-histoire-de-marseille.marseille.fr* ⊠ *€5 joint ticket with Jardin des Vestiges* ⊙ *June–Sept., Mon.–Sat. noon–7; Oct.–May., Tues.–Sun. 10–5.*

> **TRIP TIP**
>
> If you plan on visiting many of the museums in Marseille, buy a City Pass (€22 for one day, €29 for two days) at the tourism office or online. It covers the entry fee for all the museums in Marseille as well as public transit.

Fodor's Choice ★

**Navette.** In keeping with the Vieux Port's substantially spiffed-up image, the Marseille regional transport service now offers an efficient public navette ferry service much like its bus or métro services (with free transfers on both for up to 90 minutes). Although free only with a metro pass, the nominal charge of €3 (available only onboard) is well worth it for the fun and convenience of crossing the port by boat. ⊠ *Pl. des Huiles on Quai de Rive Neuve side and Hôtel de Ville on Quai du Port, Vieux Port* ⊠ *€3, free with métro pass.*

**Villa Méditerranée.** Forming a striking black-white contrast with its neighbor MuCEM, the resolutely modernist Villa Méditerranée, designed by Stefano Boeri, suspends a monumental 130-foot cantilevered overhang above a large azure reflecting pool. Part of a far-reaching plan to revitalize the J4 esplanade and the old and new ports, both buildings were financed with funds awarded with the 2013 Capital of Culture designation. The Villa's mission is to encourage cultural exchange through a constantly revolving series of performances, concerts, exhibitions, lectures, and other events that take the Mediterranean as their theme. A recent exhibition, "Beyond the Horizon," examined mobility in the Mediterranean via mass tourism, trade mobility, and legal and illegal immigration. Consult the online calendar for a detailed schedule of events. ⊠ *Esplanade du J4, Rive Neuve* ☎ *04–95–09–42–52* ⊕ *www.villa-mediterranee.org* ⊠ *€7* ⊙ *Tues.–Thurs. noon–7, Fri. noon–10, weekends 10–7.*

**WORTH NOTING**

**Le Centre d'Art MaMo.** Eighteen stories up, atop Le Corbusier's colossal Cité Radieuse—undertaken in 1947–52 to house the displaced of WWII—this sundrenched sculpture center, complete with a theater and garden, replaces an ugly gym, added in 1964, that had obscured Le Corbusier's original tiled rooftop terrace. Conceived by notorious Paris designer (and Marseille native) Ito Morabito, aka Ora-Ito, the roof of the famous building has been restored to its original glory, complete with Charlotte Perriand–designed details, and now hosts a rotating schedule of sculpture exhibitions in the summer months. The building still houses an apartment complex, shops, a hotel, and a well-regarded restaurant. ⊠ *280 bd. Michelet, Prado* ☎ *01–42–46–00–09* ⊕ *mamo.fr* ⊠ *€3* ⊙ *Wed.–Sun. 11–6.*

**Le Port Antique.** This garden in front of the Musée d'Histoire de Marseille stands on the site of the city's classical waterfront and includes remains of the Greek fortifications and loading docks. Newly restored in 2013, the site, with several nearly intact boats (now exhibited in the museum), was discovered in 1967 when roadwork was being done next to the *Bourse* (Stock Exchange). ⊠ *Centre Bourse, Vieux Port* 🕾 *04–91–90–42–22* 🎫 *€5 joint ticket with Musée d'Histoire de Marseille* ⊗ *Mon.–Sat. noon–7.*

**Musée Borély.** After a top-to-bottom renovation for European Capital of Culture 2013, the gracious 18th-century Château Borély became home to the collections of three major museums: Musée des Arts Décoratif (Museum of Decorative Arts), Musée de la Mode (Fashion Museum), and the Musée de la Faïence (Museum of Faïence Ceramics). The bright exhibition rooms feature brilliant lacquered ceilings and installations by French artists and designers, all the better to show off a gorgeous collection of Marseille faïence pottery dating to the early 17th century, tapestries, 18th-century handpainted murals, furniture, and fashions from the 15th to 21st century. The château's large park and café lend themselves to a pleasant afternoon in this lovely part of the city. ⊠ *134 av. Clot Bey, Prado* 🕾 *04–91–55–33–60* ⊕ *www.marseille.fr/siteculture/les-lieux-culturels/musees/musee-borely* 🎫 *€5* ⊗ *Tues.–Sun. 10–6.*

**Musée des Docks Romains** (*Roman Docks Museum*). In 1943 Germans destroyed the neighborhood along the Quai du Port—some 2,000 houses—displacing 20,000 citizens. This act of brutal urban renewal, ironically, laid the ground open for new discoveries. When Marseille began to rebuild in 1947, workers dug up remains of a Roman shipping warehouse full of the terra-cotta jars and amphorae that once lay in the bellies of low-slung ships. The Musée des Docks Romains, which reopened in 2013, was created around the finds and demonstrates the scale of Massalia's shipping prowess. ⊠ *2 pl. de Vivaux, Vieux Port* 🕾 *04–91–91–24–62* ⊕ *musee-des-docks-romains.marseille.fr* 🎫 *€3* ⊗ *Tues.–Sun. 10–6.*

**Musée Regards de Provence.** This beautifully renovated 1948 architectural gem by Fernand Pouillon was once Marseille's *station sanitaire*, where every immigrant entering France was systematically disinfected (deloused, washed, and sprayed with DDT) to guard against epidemic. An absorbing 45-minute film (in English) and the intact machinery tell a fascinating story of Marseille as "gateway to the East." The museum's light-filled second-floor exhibition spaces house a permanent collection of 18th–20th-century paintings depicting Provence and the Mediterranean Sea, as well as a revolving series of temporary exhibitions by contemporary painters. There's also a lovely boutique. ■TIP➔ The museum café (open until 7) has some of the best views of the redeveloped new port and is a great place for a gourmet lunch, a light snack on the terrace, or a restorative beverage. ⊠ *Av. Vaudoyer, Rive Neuve* 🕾 *04–96–17–40–40* ⊕ *www.museeregardsdeprovence. com* 🎫 *€6* ⊗ *Daily 10–6.*

Feisty Marseille flaunts its love of the sea at its famous harbor fish market.

## THE QUAI DE RIVE NEUVE

If in your exploration of Le Panier and the Quai du Port you examined Marseille's history in miniature via myriad museums, this walk will give you the big picture. From either the crow's-nest perspective of Notre-Dame-de-la-Garde or the vast green Jardin du Pharo, you'll take in spectacular Cinemascope views of this great city and its ports and monuments. Wear good walking shoes and bring your wide-angle lens.

### TOP ATTRACTIONS

**Abbaye St-Victor.** Founded in the 4th century by St-Cassien, who sailed into Marseille full of fresh ideas on monasticism that he acquired in Palestine and Egypt, this church grew to formidable proportions. With a Romanesque design, the structure would be as much at home in the Middle East as its founder was. The **crypt,** St-Cassien's original, is buried under the medieval church, and in the evocative nooks and crannies you can find the 5th-century sarcophagus that allegedly holds the martyr's remains. Upstairs, a reliquary contains what's left of St. Victor, who was ground to death between millstones, probably by Romans. There's also a passage into tiny **catacombs** where early Christians worshipped St-Lazarus and Mary Magdalene, said to have washed ashore at Stes-Maries-de-la-Mer. ⊠ *3 rue de l'Abbaye, Rive Neuve* ☎ *04–96– 11–22–60* ⊕ *www.saintvictor.net* ✉ *Crypt €2* ⊙ *Daily 9–7.*

**Bar de la Marine.** Even if you've never read or seen Marcel Pagnol's trilogy of plays and films *Marius, Fanny,* and *César* (think of it as a three-part French *Casablanca*), you can get a sense of its earthy, Old Marseille feeling at the bar it was set in. The walls are blanketed with murals and comfortable café chairs fill the place, all in an effort to faithfully reproduce the bar as it was in the days when the bartender César, his son Marius, and Fanny, the shellfish girl, lived out their salty drama of love, honor, and the call of the sea. ⊠ *15 quai Rive Neuve, Vieux Port* ☎ *04–91–54–95–42* ⊙ *Daily 7 am–midnight.*

**Musée Cantini.** Set in a beautifully restored 17th-century house, this lovely little museum is a must for fans of Fauve and Surrealist art. There are paintings by Signac, Dufy, Léger, Ernst, Arp, and Bacon, as well as Kandinsky and Dubuffet. This is one of the foremost collections in France of the genre. ⊠ *19 rue Grignan, Préfecture* ☎ *04–91–54–77–75* ⊕ *musee-cantini.marseille.fr* ⊡ *€5* ⊙ *Tues.–Sun. 10–6.*

**Notre-Dame-de-la-Garde.** Towering above the city and visible for miles around, this overscaled neo-Byzantine monument was erected in 1853 by Napoléon III. The interior is a Technicolor bonanza of red-and-beige stripes and glittering mosaics, and the gargantuan *Madonna and Child* on the steeple (almost 30 feet high) is covered in real gold leaf. While the panoply of ex-votos, mostly thanking the Virgin for deathbed interventions and shipwreck survivals, is a remarkable sight, most impressive are the views of the seaside city at your feet. ⊠ *Off bd. André Aune, Garde Hill* ⊹ *On foot, climb up Cours Pierre Puget, cross Jardin Pierre Puget, cross bridge to Rue Vauvenargues, and hike up to Pl. Edon. Or catch Bus 60 from Cours Jean-Ballard* ☎ *04–91–13–40–80* ⊙ *May–Sept., daily 7 am–8 pm; Oct.–Apr., daily 7–7.*

## WORTH NOTING

**Jardin du Pharo** (*Pharo Garden*). The Pharo, another larger-than-life edifice built to Napoléon III's epic tastes, was a gift to his wife, Eugénie. It's a conference center now, but its green park has become a magnet for city strollers who want to take in panoramic views of the ports and fortifications. ⊠ *Above Bd. Charles-Livon, Pharo.*

**Les Arcenaulx** (*The Arsenal*). In this broad, elegant stone armory, first built for Louis XIV, a complex of upscale shops and restaurants has given the building—and neighborhood—new life. Its bookstore has a large collection of publications on Marseille (as well as art, photography, history, and rare books), all in French; a boutique sells high-end cooking (and serving) goods with a southern accent; and a book-lined restaurant serves sophisticated cuisine. It's worth a peek to remind yourself that Marseille is not the squalid backwater people continue to expect. ⊠ *25 cours d'Estienne d'Orves, Vieux Port* ☎ *04–91–59–80–30* ⊕ *www.les-arcenaulx.com* ⊙ *Bookstore Mon.–Sat. 10–7; boutique Mon.–Sat., 10 am–11 pm; restaurant Mon.–Sat. noon–11.*

**Place Thiars.** An ensemble of Italianate 18th-century buildings frames this popular center of activity, where one sidewalk café spills into another, and every kind of bouillabaisse is yours for the asking. At night the neighborhood is a fashionable hangout for young professionals on their way to and from the theaters and clubs on Quai de Rive Neuve. ⊠ *Framed by Quai Neuve, Rue Fortia, Rue de la Paix Marcel-Paul, and Cours d'Estienne d'Orves.*

**Théâtre National de Marseille La Criée** (*National Theater of Marseille at "The Fish Auction"*). Behind the floridly decorated facade of this grand old fish-auction house, a prestigious state theater company performs.

Innovative director Jean-Louis Benoit brings an edgy streetwise energy to the season's productions. ✉ *30 quai Rive Neuve, Vieux Port* ☎ *04–96–17–80–00 for reservations* ⊕ *www.theatre-lacriee.com* ✉ *€12–€30* ☾ *Box office Tues.–Sat. 11–6.*

OFF THE BEATEN PATH

**Château d'If.** In the 16th century, François I recognized the strategic advantage of an island fortress surveying the mouth of Marseille's vast harbor and built this imposing edifice. Its effect as a deterrent was so successful that the fortress never saw combat, and was eventually converted into a prison. It was here that Alexandre Dumas locked up his most famous character, the Count of Monte Cristo. Though the count was fictional, the hole through which Dumas had him escape is real enough, on display in the cells. On the other hand, the real-life Man in the Iron Mask, whose cell is also erroneously on display, was not imprisoned here. The IF Frioul Express boat ride (from the Quai des Belges, €10; for information call ☎ *04–96–11–03–50*) and the views from the broad terrace are worth the trip. ☎ *08–26–50–05–00* ⊕ *if.monuments-nationaux.fr/en* ✉ *€5.50* ☾ *Apr.–mid-May, daily 9:30–4:45; mid-May–mid-Sept., daily 9:30–6:10; mid-Sept.–Mar., Tues–Sun. 9:30–4:45.*

## LA CANEBIÈRE

In a direct line east from the Vieux Port, this famous avenue used to serve as the dividing line between those Marseillais who had money and those who did not. In the last hundred years it has lost much of its former glory, and is now dominated by shopping malls and fast-food restaurants. Its architecture and 19th-century wedding-cake facades still make for an interesting walk, and it's a great place from which to make forays through the North African neighborhood along Rue Longue-des-Capucins, to the lively cafés and boutiques of bohemian Cours Julien via Rue d'Aubagne, and on to the Palais Longchamp and its fine-arts and natural-history museums.

### TOP ATTRACTIONS

**Cours Julien.** A center of bohemian *flânerie* (hanging out), this is a lovely place to relax by the fountain, in the shade of plane trees, or under a café umbrella. Its low-key and painterly tableau is framed by graceful 18th-century buildings, and the warrenlike streets surrounding the cours are full of young fashion designers, vintage shops, and hip boutiques. ✉ *La Canebière.*

**Musée Grobet-Labadié.** This lovely and intimate museum houses the private art collection of the wealthy 19th-century couple of the same name. Their 1873 mansion, beautifully renovated, offers an intriguing glimpse into the cultivated art tastes of the time, ranging from 15th- and 16th-century Italian and Flemish paintings to Fragonard and Millet. ✉ *140 bd. Longchamp, La Canebière* ☎ *04–91–62–21–82* ⊕ *musee-grobet-labadie.marseille.fr* ✉ *€5* ☾ *Tues.–Sun. 10–6.*

**Palais de Longchamp.** This recently renovated extravagant and grandiose 19th-century palace, inaugurated in 1869, was built to celebrate the completion of an 84-km (52-mile) aqueduct bringing the water of the Durance river to the open sea. The massive, classical-style building crowns a hill and is splayed with impressive symmetrical grace around a series of fountains with a triumphal arch at its center and museums

### DID YOU KNOW?

A mock-Byzantine extravaganza with Technicolor stripes and mosaics, Marseille's Notre-Dame-de-la-Garde is a cousin to Paris's Sacré-Coeur, thanks to its hilltop perch.

in either wing. In the **Musée des Beaux-Arts** (Fine Arts Museum) are 16th- and 17th-century paintings, including several by Rubens, as well as fine marble sculptures and drawings by the Marseille architect Pierre Puget. There's a delightful group of sculptures by caricaturist Honoré Daumier, and the collection of French 19th-century paintings, including Courbet, Ingres, and David, is strong. In the right wing of the palace is the **Musée d'Histoire Naturelle** (Natural History Museum) with a collection of prehistoric and zoological artifacts, plus a large aquarium with fish from around the world. ⊠ *End of Bd. Longchamp, La Canebière* ☎ *04–91–14–59–30, 04–91–14–59–50* ⊕ *musee-des-beaux-arts.marseille.fr* 🎟 *€5 Musée des Beaux-Arts, €5 Musée d'Histoire Naturelle* ☉ *Tues.–Sun. 10–6.*

**WORTH NOTING**

**La Canebière.** This wide avenue leading from the port, known affectionately as the "Can o' Beer" by American sailors, was once crammed with cafés, theaters, bars, and tempting stores full of zoot suits and swell hats, and figured in popular songs and operettas. It's noisy but dull today, yet you may take pleasure in studying the grand old 19th-century mansions lining it. ⊠ *La Canebière.*

**Rue Longue-des-Capucins/Rue d'Aubagne.** Stepping into this atmospheric neighborhood, you may feel you have suddenly been transported to a Moroccan souk. Shops that serve the needs of Marseille's large and vibrant North African community have open bins of olives, coffee beans, tea, spices, dried beans, chickpeas, couscous, peppers, and salted sardines. Tiny shoebox cafés proffer exotic sweets, and the daily Marché de Noailles in the surrounding maze of streets is the city's most vibrant and colorful market. ⊠ *La Canebière.*

**ANSES: EAST OF TOWN**

Along the coastline east of Marseille's center, a series of pretty little *anses* (ports) leads to the more famous and far-flung Calanques. These miniature inlets are really tiny villages, with pretty, balconied, boxy houses (called *cabanons*) clustered around bright-painted fishing boats. Don't even think about buying a cabanon of your own, however; they are part of the fishing community's heritage and are protected from gentrification by the outside world.

**L'Estaque.** At this famous village north of Marseille, Cézanne led an influx of artists eager to capture its cliff-top views over the harbor. Braque, Derain, and Renoir all put its red rooftops, rugged cliffs, and factory smokestacks on canvas. Pick up the English-language itinerary "L'Estaque and the Painters" from the Marseille tourist office and hunt down the sites and views they immortalized. It's a little seedy these days, but there are cafés and a few fish shops making the most of the nearby Criée (fisherman's auction). This is where the real wholesale auction moved from Marseille's Quai de Rive Neuve. A novel way to see Cézanne's famous scenery is to take a standard SNCF train trip from the Gare St-Charles to Martigue; it follows the L'Estaque waterfront and (with the exception of a few tunnels) offers magnificent views.

## WHERE TO EAT

$$ BISTRO 🍴 **Café des Épices.** This small, unpretentious restaurant (with a large terrace) between the Old Port and Le Panier is a great choice for the kind of fresh, inventive cuisine representative of the best in contemporary bistro cooking. Though the choices are few on the Mediterranean-inspired menu (prix-fixe only), they change daily according to what inspires chef Arnaud Carton de Grammont at the market. Dishes like John Dory with pomegranate, white carrots, and tarragon-flecked mushrooms, or consommé-glazed foie gras with caramelized pear are hearty enough that dessert is optional. Best not to skip it, though. [$] *Average main: €22* ✉ *4 rue du Lacydon, Vieux Port* ☎ *04–91–91–22–69* 🌐 *cafedesepices.com* ✍ *Reservations essential* ⏲ *Closed Sun. and Mon. No dinner Sat.*

$ PIZZA 🍴 **Chez Etienne.** A historic Le Panier hole-in-the-wall, this small pizzeria is filled daily with politicos and young professionals who enjoy the personality of chef Stéphane Cassero, who was famous at one time for having no printed menu and announcing the price of the meal only after he'd had the chance to look you over. Remarkably little has changed over the years, except now there is a posted menu (with prices). Brace yourself for an epic meal, starting with a large anchovy pizza from the wood-burning oven, then dig into fried squid, eggplant gratin, and a slab of rare grilled beef all served with the background of laughter, rich patois, and abuse from the chef. [$] *Average main: €16* ✉ *43 rue de Lorette, Le Panier* ☎ *04–91–54–76–33* ⏲ *Closed Sun.*

$$$$ SEAFOOD 🍴 **Chez Fonfon.** Tucked into the filmlike tiny fishing port Vallon des Auffes, this Marseillais landmark has one of the loveliest settings in greater Marseille. Once presided over by cult chef "Fonfon," it used to be a favorite movie-star hangout. A variety of fresh seafood, impeccably grilled, steamed, or roasted in salt crust, is served in two pretty dining rooms with picture windows overlooking the fishing boats that supply your dinner. Try classic bouillabaisse served with all the bells and whistles—broth, hot-chili rouille, and flamboyant table-side filleting. [$] *Average main: €40* ✉ *140 rue du Vallon des Auffes, Vallon des Auffes* ☎ *04–91–52–14–38* 🌐 *www.chez-fonfon.com* ✍ *Reservations essential* ⏲ *Closed Sun. and Mon. in winter; Sun. and Mon. lunch in summer. Closed first 3 wks in Jan.*

$ PIZZA 🍴 **Chez Jeannot.** This is the poor man's Chez Fonfon, around the port from the prestigious restaurant and run by a member of the same family. It's so popular that it's become something of a theme-restaurant version of itself (plastic menus, wedding-banquet-style dining rooms), but it's a wonderful place to get away from town and enjoy a casual meal in a lovely spot. The pizzas are heavy, and there are towering platters of shellfish still twitching—but you're here for the film-set scenery as much as for the food. Terrace tables overlooking the fishing boats justify taxi fare from the center, but reserve in advance or you'll end up in the dark interior. [$] *Average main: €18* ✉ *129 Vallon des Auffes, Vallon des Auffes* ☎ *04–91–52–11–28* 🌐 *www.pizzeriachezjeannot.net* ⏲ *Closed Mon. No dinner Sun.*

$$$$ BRASSERIE 🍴 **Chez Michel.** This beachside brasserie near the Pharo gardens is considerd the last word in bouillabaisse and draws a knowing local clientele willing to shell out a few extra euros for this authentic classic (€65).

CLOSE UP

# In Search of the Perfect Bouillabaisse

Marseille is a Mediterranean melting pot of people, styles, and, of course—since the city is home to some of the best bouillabaisse on the planet—fish. While some insist that the only true bouillabaisse is the one served to friends in fishermen's cabanons along the rocky coast of Marseille, many others acknowledge Marseille is the true mecca of this fish stew, one that relies on the particular mix of Mediterranean fish found off the Riviera coasts.

According to the bouillabaisse charter—designed to spare unsuspecting diners from poor imitations—this stew should contain at least four of the following once-unappreciated species: scorpion fish, tub gurnard, John Dory, monkfish, weever, and conger. Its robust flavor comes from a combination of tomato, onion, garlic, fennel, orange zest, and saffron, along with plenty of olive oil and sea salt (the fishermen originally used seawater). The brick-red broth is served first, followed by the fish fillets, all of it with plenty of rouille (mayonnaise spiced up with garlic, chili, and saffron).

Before dining, the fish are paraded by your table, then ceremoniously filleted before being served with all the classic accompaniments: a spicy rouille, buttery croutons. Oysters, whole grilled fish (priced by the kilo), and an authentic garlic-steeped bourride are other fine choices—along with a good selection of great local wines. The bouillabaisse is well worth the splurge, but be sure to reserve in advance. $ *Average main: €50* ⊠ *6 rue des Catalans, Vieux Port* ☎ *04-91-52-30-63* ⊕ *www. restaurant-michel-13.fr* ⚑ *Reservations essential.*

$

ITALIAN

✕ **Chez Vincent.** Although it's in the mini-red-light district of the Vieux Port, this little Italian restaurant is all it's cracked up to be. The decor is pure Italian bistro with pristine white tablecloths and copper pots, bunches of dried spices, and flowers on the wall. The spaghetti with tiny clams is excellent, as is the lasagna and the tiramisu. It is jammed with lively night-owl regulars, including singers from the Opéra around the corner, and the happy buzz moves down to a satisfied murmur at the end of the meal. Often full, this spot requires reservations in advance. $ *Average main: €15* ⊠ *25 rue Glandèves, Vieux Port* ☎ *04-91-33-96-78* ☽ *Closed Mon.*

$

BISTRO

**Fodor's** Choice

★

✕ **Le Bistro d'Edouard.** A big part of Marseille's allure is its Mediterranean multiculturalism, which is abundantly expressed at this popular neighborhood tapas restaurant. Red-checked tablecloths and a sunny outdoor terrace add to its low-key Provençal charm, but the food is the real draw here. Simple, flavorful dishes like artichokes drizzled with spicy olive oil, Iberian ham, grilled eggplant, and fresh sardines keep the local crowds coming back. $ *Average main: €14* ⊠ *150 rue Jean Mermoz, Prado* ☎ *04-91-71-16-52* ⚑ *Reservations essential* ☽ *Closed Sun. and Mon.*

$$

BRASSERIE

✕ **Le Malthazar.** This classic Mediterranean brasserie, with brightly tiled floors and a long zinc bar, is the new home of two-star Michelin chef Michel Portos, a native son who threw in the fancy chef's hat in favor of a more relaxed atmosphere and simpler fare. Portos makes spectacular use of the Old Port's fish market a few steps from his door, with dishes like shellfish lasagna with tomato confit; roasted sea bass in spicy fish bouillon with classic rouille; or fillet of sole with wild mushrooms, serrano ham, and hazelnut butter. For dessert the passion fruit baba au rhum is a revelation. A well-priced selection of local wines makes everything go down just right. The three-course (€31) menu for lunch or dinner is an excellent value. [$] *Average main: €22* ✉ *19 rue Fortia, Vieux Port* ☎ *04–91–33–42–46* 🌐 *www.malthazar.com* ✍ *Reservations essential.*

$$$ FRENCH 🍴 **Les Arcenaulx.** At this book-lined, red-wall haven in the stylish book-and-boutique complex of a renovated arsenal, you can have a sophisticated regional lunch and read while you're waiting. If you've had your fill of fish, indulge in the grilled fillet of beef with fried artichokes with sweet onion. The terrace (on the Italian-scale Cours d'Estienne d'Orves) is as pleasant as the interior. [$] *Average main: €25* ✉ *25 cours d'Estienne d'Orves, Vieux Port* ☎ *04–91–59–80–30* 🌐 *www.les-arcenaulx.com* 🕒 *Closed Sun.*

$ FRENCH 🍴 **Mina Kouk.** Armed with her Algerian grandma's recipes and an artist's spirit, Mina Kouk abandoned advanced studies in chemistry to try her hand at something closer to alchemy. Now the smell of mint tea and pastries warm from the oven mingle with the exotic spices of her couscous, spiced chicken tagine, or savory lentil soup that perfume the air at this cozy, bright salon de thé. Everyone is welcomed like a neighbor here and no one leaves without a little pink-and-green box of pastries redolent of pistachio, almond, honey, and rose water. A nonstop stream of regulars, children (Mina's pastry classes for kids are a big draw in the neighborhood), and local hipsters drop in for lunch, tea, a glass of Mina's famous lemonade, or that most ephemeral ingedient of all—love. [$] *Average main: €10* ✉ *21 rue Fontage, Cours Julien* ☎ *04–91–53–54–55* 🌐 *www.minakouk.com* ✍ *Reservations not accepted* 🕒 *Closed Sun.*

$$$$ FRENCH 🍴 **Miramar.** A Marseille institution, this restaurant is justifiably famous for its bouillabaisse, and is one of the best places to sample the city's fabled dish. It maintains a '60s style of red-velvet-and-wood-paneling elegance, but the portside terrace tables cut through the stuffiness. Unlike many seafood restaurants in town, it always has bouillabaisse on the menu, so you don't have to order in advance. Desserts are spectacular, thanks to an innovative pastry chef, and with a chilled bottle of Cassis it is truly a dining event. [$] *Average main: €36* ✉ *12 quai du Port, Vieux Port* ☎ *04–91–91–10–40* 🌐 *lemiramar.fr* ✍ *Reservations essential* 🕒 *Closed Sun., Mon., and 2 wks in Jan.*

$ MODERN FRENCH 🍴 **Regards Café.** Close and yet so far from the hustle and bustle of the Vieux Port and MuCEM's crowded cafés, this luminous dining room in the Musée Regards de Provence has panoramic views over the new port and Marseille's top architectural gems (including the one you're sitting in). Happily, chef Thierry Lennon's cooking lives up to the ambience, with dishes like roasted cod with saffron risotto or tender duck breast with honeyed red cabbage. If you've forgotten to reserve (a must for the lunch-only dining room), don't worry: there's a cafeteria-style buffet with freshly prepared gourmet sandwiches, salads, and desserts to enjoy on one of two terraces. Open until 6, it's a nice place for an afternoon pick-me-up or an apéro before heading off somewhere else for dinner. [$] *Average main: €14* ✉ *Allée Regards de Provence, Rive Neuve* ☎ *04–96–17–40–45* 🌐 *www.museeregardsdeprovence.com* 🕒 *No dinner.*

Continued on page 202

# CUISINE OF THE SUN

Don't be surprised if colors and flavors seem more intense in Provence. It could be the hot, dry climate, which concentrates the essence of fruit and vegetables, or the sun beaming down on market tables overflowing with produce. Or maybe you're seeing the world anew through rosé-tinted wine glasses. Whatever the reason, here's how to savor Provence's *incroyable* flavors and culinary favorites.

Provence's rustic cuisine, based on local tomatoes, garlic, olive oil, anchovies, olives, and native wild herbs—including basil, lavender, mint, rosemary, thyme, and sage—has more in common with other Mediterranean cuisines than it does with most regional French fare. Everywhere you'll find sun-ripened fruit dripping with nectar and vegetables so flavor-packed that meat may seem like a mere accessory.

The natural bounty of the region is ample, united by climate—brilliant sunshine and fierce winds—and divided by dramatically changing landscapes. In the Vaucluse, scorched plains give way to lush, orchard-lined hills and gently sloped vineyards. The wild Calanques of Marseille, source of spiky sea urchins, ease into the tranquil waters of St-Tropez, home to gleaming bream and sea bass. Provence's pantry is overflowing with culinary treasures.

Simple preparations, like grilled vegetables with crusty bread, are best enjoyed with the region's famous rosé wine

# PROVENCE'S TOP REGIONAL DISHES

Ratatouille

Fougasse

### AÏOLI

The name for a deliciously pungent mayonnaise made with generous helpings of garlic, *aïoli* is a popular accompaniment for fish, meat, and vegetable dishes. The mayonnaise version shares its name with "grand aïoli," a recipe featuring salt cod, potatoes, hard-boiled eggs, and vegetables. Both types of aïoli pop up all over Provence, but they seems most beloved in Marseille. In keeping with Catholic practice, some restaurants serve grand aïoli only on Fridays. And it's a good sign if they ask you to place your order at least a day in advance. A grand aïoli is also a traditional component of the Niçois Christmas feast.

### BOUILLABAISSE

Originally a humble fisherman's soup made with the part of the catch that nobody else wanted, bouillabaisse—the famous fish stew—consists of four or five kinds of fish: the villainous-looking *rascasse* (red scorpion fish), *grondin* (sea robin), *baudroie* (monkfish), *congre* (conger eel), and *rouget* (mullet). The fish are simmered in a stock of onions, tomatoes, garlic, olive oil, and saffron, which gives the dish its golden color. When presented properly, the broth is served first, with croutons and *rouille*, a creamy garlic sauce that you spoon in to suit your taste. The fish comes separately, and the ritual is to place pieces into the soup to enjoy after slurping up some of the broth.

### BOURRIDE

This poached fish dish owes its anise kick to pastis and its garlic punch to aïoli. The name comes from the Provençal bourrido, which translates less poetically as "boiled." Monkfish—known as baudroie in Provence and lotte in the rest of France—is a must, but chefs occasionally dress up their bourride with other species and shellfish.

### DAUBE DE BOEUF

To distinguish their prized beef stew from *boeuf bourguignon*, Provençal chefs make a point of not marinating the meat, instead cooking it very slowly in tannic red wine that is often flavored with orange zest. In the Camargue, daube is made with the local taureau (bull's meat), while the Avignon variation uses lamb.

Bourride

Bouillabaisse

## FOUGASSE

The Provençal answer to Italian focaccia, this soft flatbread is distinguished by holes that give it the appearance of a lacy leaf. It can be made savory—flavored with olives, anchovy, bacon, cheese, or anything else the baker has on hand—or sweet, enriched with olive oil and dusted with icing sugar. When in Menton, don't miss the sugary *fougasse mentonnaise*.

## LES PETITS FARCIS

The Niçois specialty called *les petits farcis* are prepared with tiny summer vegetables (usually zucchini, tomatoes, peppers, and onions) that are traditionally stuffed with veal or leftover *daube* (beef stew). Like so many Niçois dishes, they make great picnic food.

## RATATOUILLE

At its best, *ratatouille* is a glorious thing—a riot of eggplant, zucchini, bell peppers, and onions, each sautéed separately in olive oil and then gently combined with sweet summer tomatoes. A well-made ratatouille, to which a pinch of saffron has been added to heighten its flavor, is also delicious served chilled.

## SOUPE AU PISTOU

The Provençal answer to pesto, *pistou* consists of the simplest ingredients—garlic, olive oil, fresh basil, and Parmesan—ideally pounded together by hand in a stone mortar with an olive-wood pestle. Most traditionally it delivers a potent kick to *soupe au pistou*, a kind of French minestrone made with green beans, white beans, potatoes, and zucchini.

## SOCCA

You'll find *socca* vendors from Nice to Menton, but this chickpea pancake cooked on a giant iron platter in a wood-fired oven is really a Niçois phenomenon, born of sheer poverty at a time when wheat flour was scarce. After cooking, it is sliced into finger-lickin' portions with an oyster knife. Enjoy it with a glass of chilled rosé.

## TIAN DE LÉGUMES

A *tian* is both a beautiful earthenware dish and one of many vegetable gratins that might be cooked in it. This thrifty dish makes a complete meal of seasonal vegetables, eggs, and a little cheese.

$
SEAFOOD
✕ **Toinou Dégustation.** You can join the crowd at the outdoor stand and split a few oysters on the hoof. But it's more comfortable settling into a brasserie booth at this landmark shellfish joint where you can get heaps of Cassis urchins, cream-filled *violets* (a kind of monstrous sea slug), clams, mussels, and, of course, oysters. Try the North African hot sauce or opt for the powerful aïoli. $ *Average main: €19* ⊠ *3 Cours St-Louis, Vieux Port* 📷 *04–91–54–08–79* ⊕ *www.toinou.com* ▭ *No credit cards.*

$$$$
SEAFOOD
✕ **Une Table au Sud.** Lionel Lévy left this gorgeously situated eatery with panoramic views of the Old Port in the capable hands of Ludovic Turac—a candidate on TV's *Top Chef 2011.* A Mediterranean menu, with a Michelin-star rating, changes every two months depending on what's in season. A standard is the creamy, fishy Milkshake de Bouille-Abaisse, a one-of-a-kind gourmand delight. $ *Average main: €37* ⊠ *2 quai du Port, Vieux Port* 📷 *04–91–90–63–53* ⊕ *www.unetableausud. com* ⚓ *Reservations essential* ⊗ *Closed Mon. No dinner Sun.*

## WHERE TO STAY

$$
HOTEL
▨ **Alizé.** On the Vieux Port, with front rooms taking in postcard views, this straightforward lodging has been modernized to include tight double-pane windows, slick modular baths, and a laminate-and-all-weather carpeted look. **Pros:** ideal location on the waterfront gives access to shops and sights; friendly service. **Cons:** somewhat generic room decor; Wi-Fi signal may be weak in some rooms; breakfast is extra. $ *Rooms from: €109* ⊠ *35 quai des Belges, Vieux Port* 📷 *04–91–33–66–97* ⊕ *www.alize-hotel.com* ⤳ *39 rooms* ⦿ *No meals.*

$$$
HOTEL
▨ **Grand Hotel Beauvau Vieux Port.** Chopin spent the night and George Sand kept a suite in this historic hotel overlooking the Vieux Port. **Pros:** recent renovations keep all the charm and take away all the inconveniences (noise, etc.); service is excellent. **Cons:** some rooms are small and a bit dark. $ *Rooms from: €155* ⊠ *4 rue Beauvau, Vieux Port* 📷 *04–91–54–91–00* ⊕ *www.accorhotels.com* ⤳ *70 rooms, 2 suites* ⦿ *No meals.*

$
HOTEL
▨ **Hermès.** Although the rooms are rather snug, this modest city hotel is right around the corner from the Quai du Port and is a good value. **Pros:** location and price are excellent value in Marseille. **Cons:** rooms are small and the bathrooms even smaller. $ *Rooms from: €83* ⊠ *2 rue Bonneterie, Vieux Port* 📷 *04–96–11–63–63* ⊕ *www.hotelmarseille.com* ⤳ *29 rooms* ⦿ *No meals.*

$$
HOTEL
▨ **Hotel Peron.** A family-run jewel, this eclectic, rather eccentric hotel features rooms with different decorative themes, from delicate, rather austere Japanese to playful Dutch to colorful Moroccan. **Pros:** price is excellent value, especially for sea views; very friendly service. **Cons:** some rooms need freshening up (new paint); some rooms are quite small. $ *Rooms from: €90* ⊠ *119 corniche J.-F. Kennedy, Endoume* 📷 *04–91–31–01–41* ⊕ *www.hotelperon.com* ⤳ *26 rooms* ⦿ *No meals.*

$$
HOTEL
▨ **Hôtel Saint Ferréol.** Set back from the port in the heart of the shopping district, this cozy, charming little hotel offers a warm reception and a homey breakfast room–cum–bar. **Pros:** cheerful and helpful service; center-of-town location is ideal. **Cons:** some rooms are small; street-facing

rooms can be noisy. $ *Rooms from: €99* ✉ *19 rue Pisançon (at Rue St-Ferréol), Vieux Port* ☎ *04–91–33–12–21* ⊕ *www.hotel-stferreol.com* ☞ *19 rooms* ⦿*No meals.*

$$$$   ⊡**Intercontinental Marseille Hôtel Dieu.** No expense was spared in trans-
HOTEL   forming this graceful edifice, once the city's hospital and a beloved land-
**Fodor's Choice**   mark (built according to plans by Jacques Hardouin-Mansart, architect
★   to Louis XIV), into a gleaming palace. **Pros:** a one-stop luxury spot;
splendid views can be had from the sprawling outdoor terrace bar.
**Cons:** staff is still getting their bearings. $ *Rooms from: €400* ✉ *1 pl. Daviel, Vieux Port* ☎ *04–13–42–42–42* ⊕ *marseille.intercontinental. com* ☞ *192 rooms* ⦿*No meals.*

$$$$   ⊡**Le Petit Nice Passédat.** On a rocky promontory overlooking the sea,
HOTEL   this fantasy villa was bought from a countess in 1917 and converted to
a sleek hotel-restaurant; happily, the Passédat family has been getting it
right ever since, especially in the famous restaurant. **Pros:** a memorable
(if expensive) hotel experience; breathtaking views; good service. **Cons:**
pool is small (though lovely). $ *Rooms from: €290* ✉ *Anse de la Mal-
dormé, Corniche J.-F.-Kennedy, Endoume* ☎ *04–91–59–25–92* ⊕ *www. passedat.fr* ☞ *13 rooms, 3 suites* ☾ *Closed Sun. and Mon. Nov.–Apr. Restaurant closed Sun. and Mon.* ⦿*No meals.*

$   ⊡**Mama Shelter.** Manufacturing hip is this urban chain hotel's claim to
HOTEL   fame (brain child of designer Philippe Starck), and they've got the formula down pat: offbeat (preferably artsy) neighborhood, check; plenty
of graffiti in the decor, check; functional, minimalist rooms, check; sexy
touches, check. **Pros:** breakfasts can't be beat (€19); friendly service.
**Cons:** not always a bargain; miniscule bathrooms; iffy neighborhood.
$ *Rooms from: €99* ✉ *64 rue de la Loubière, Cours Julien* ☎ *04–84–35–20–00* ⊕ *www.mamashelter.com* ☞ *126 rooms* ⦿*No meals.*

$$$   ⊡**New Hotel Vieux Port.** In the heart of things, at the crossroads of the
HOTEL   Quai du Port and the Quai des Belges, this old, urban hotel is being
slicked up a little bit more every month with its ongoing, yet amazingly
quiet, renovations. **Pros:** prompt service; great location. **Cons:** some
rooms are small; some are a bit noisy. $ *Rooms from: €140* ✉ *3 bis rue Reine-Elisabeth, Vieux Port* ☎ *04–91–99–23–23* ⊕ *www.new-hotel. com* ☞ *42 rooms* ⦿*No meals.*

$$$$   ⊡**Pullman Marseille Palm Beach.** Sleek with stunning 360-degree views of
HOTEL   the bay and the islands, this white-on-white modern hotel offers designs
by Starck, Zanotta, and Emu. **Pros:** the view out to sea is truly remark-
able; rooms are large, most with balconies. **Cons:** service lacks warmth;
too many rooms for a personalized welcome. $ *Rooms from: €250* ✉ *200 corniche J.-F. Kennedy, Endoume* ☎ *04–91–16–19–00* ⊕ *www. sofitel.com* ☞ *150 rooms, 10 suites* ⦿*No meals.*

$$$   ⊡**Residence du Vieux Port.** The flat glass-and-concrete facade of this post-
HOTEL   war structure grants all the rooms here broad picture-window views of
**Fodor's Choice**   the Vieux Port all the way to Notre-Dame-de-la-Garde. **Pros:** with so few
★   good value hotels in Marseille, this is a great option with its ideal location; some of the city's best views of the Old Port. **Cons:** terrace views are
semi-obstructed when you're seated by heavy concrete railings. $ *Rooms from: €195* ✉ *18 quai du Port, Vieux Port* ☎ *04–91–91–91–22* ⊕ *www. hotel-residence-marseille.com* ☞ *40 rooms, 8 suites* ⦿*No meals.*

## NIGHTLIFE AND THE ARTS

With a population of 859, 000, Marseille is a big city by French standards, with all the nightlife that entails. Arm yourself with *Marseille L'Hebdo*, a glossy monthly events magazine; *A Nous Marseille*, a hip weekly on theater, art, film, concerts, and shopping in southern Provence; or the monthly *In Situ*, a free guide to music, theater, and galleries. They're all in French.

Marseille's vibrant multicultural mix has evolved a genre of music that fuses all the sounds of Arabic music with rhythms of Provence, Corsica, and southern Italy, and douses it with reggae and rap.

### NIGHTLIFE

**Au Son des Guitares.** The music is passionate and the crowd lively at this fashionable cabaret-bar. ⊠ *18 rue Corneille, Vieux Port* ☏ *04–91–33–11–47.*

**Docks des Suds.** At the vast Docks des Suds, host to the Fiesta des Suds each autumn, you'll find world and Latin music year-round. ⊠ *12 Rue Urbain V, at Bd. de Paris, Vieux Port* ☏ *04–91–99–00–00* ⊕ *www. dock-des-suds.org.*

**Dôme-Zénith.** This is Marseille's big modern venue for international rock acts and various French celebrities. ⊠ *48 av. St-Just, St-Just* ☏ *04–91–47–01–25* ⊕ *dome.marseille.fr.*

**Espace Julien.** Rock, pop, jazz, and reggae concerts, as well as comedy and alternative theater, are held at the Espace Julien. ⊠ *39 cours Julien, Préfecture* ☏ *04–91–24–34–10* ⊕ *www.espace-julien.com.*

**La Dame Noir.** Small and impossibly hip, the louche party crowd gets down to the DJ sounds, electro beats, and live concerts here. It's free, but crowded. ⊠ *30 pl. Notre-Dame du Mont, Vieux Port* ⊕ *ladamenoir.fr.*

**L'Affranchi.** For rap and techno, try L'Affranchi. ⊠ *212 bd. de St-Marcel, La Canebière* ☏ *04–91–35–09–19.*

**L'Intermediaire.** Keep an eye out for the local group Gachempega; they play on occasion at L'Intermediaire, which is the hippest venue in town for jazz, blues, and rock concerts. ⊠ *63 pl. Jean-Jaurès, La Canebière* ☏ *06–87–87–88–21* ⊕ *www.lintermediaire.fr.*

**La Caravelle.** Restaurant by day, bluesy jazz club and tapas bar by night (in the Hotel Belle Vue), La Caravelle harks back to prewar jazz clubs, but without the smoke. There are great views over the port and live jazz two nights a week. ⊠ *34 quai du Port, Vieux Port* ☏ *04–91–90–36–64* ⊕ *www.lacaravelle-marseille.com.*

**La Part des Anges.** Good wines are brought in from all over France and served by the glass or by the bottle here. Open until 2 am daily, it attracts an eclectic crowd, from hip, arty, and trendy to overdressed women and men in bad suits. ⊠ *33 rue Sainte, Vieux Port* ☏ *04–91–33–55–70.*

**Red Lion.** This bar is a mecca for English speakers, who pour onto the sidewalk, pints in hand, pub-style. There's live music, DJs on the weekend, and a lounge for the diehard rugby and football fans who can't go without watching a match. ⊠ *231 av. Pierre Mendès France, Vieux Port* ☏ *04–91–25–17–17* ⊕ *www.pub-redlion.com.*

### THE ARTS

**Abbaye St-Victor.** Classical music concerts are given in the Abbaye St-Victor. ⊠ *3 rue de l'Abbaye, Vieux Port* ☎ *04–91–05–84–48 for information* ⊕ *saintvictor.chez.com.*

**Badaboum Théâtre.** At Badaboum, adventurous, accessible productions for children are performed. ⊠ *16 Quai de Rive Neuve, Vieux Port* ☎ *04–91–54–40–71* ⊕ *www.badaboum-theatre.com.*

**Le Silo.** Marseille's newest performance space in a spanking new building right on the waterfront hosts an impressive series of classic and contemporary concerts, theater, and dance. ⊠ *35 quai du Lazaret, La Canebière* ☎ *04–91–90–00–00* ⊕ *www.silo-marseille.fr.*

**Opéra Municipal de Marseille.** Operas and orchestral concerts are held at the Opéra Municipal. ⊠ *2 rue Molière, Vieux Port* ☎ *04–91–55–11–10* ⊕ *opera.marseille.fr.*

**Théâtre des Marionnettes.** A young audience thrills to entertainment with puppets, dance, and music—occasionally in English. It's by the Gare St-Charles. ⊠ *Theatre Massalia, 41 rue Jobin, La Canebière* ☎ *04–91–11–45–65* ⊕ *www.theatremassalia.com.*

**Théâtre National de Marseille La Criée.** A strong and solid repertoire of classical and contemporary works is performed here. ⊠ *Quai de Rive Neuve, Vieux Port* ☎ *04–91–54–74–54* ⊕ *www.theatre-lacriee.com.*

**Théâtre Off.** This troupe presents alternative productions of classics. ⊠ *2 pl. Francis Chirat, Vieux Port* ☎ *04–91–33–12–92* ⊕ *www.theatreoff.com.*

## SHOPPING

Although you'll want to stock up on savon (soap) de Marseille, the city has lots more to offer in the way of shopping. Offbeat designer clothing, vintage finds, and hip accessories made in Marseille abound around Cours Julien. Nearer the Vieux Port, rues Grignan, Paradis, and Saint form a high-end shopping rectangle, where pricey French designers comingle with chic fashion chains (like Marseille-based Sugar) and edgy-elegant concept stores, like Marianne Cat, where you can also relax over a glass of wine or a cup of tea.

### CLOTHING

**Diable Noir.** Here you'll find glamorous, slightly retro evening dresses in extravagant silk jersey and tulle and colorful accessories. ⊠ *5 rue de la Tour, Cours Julien* ☎ *04–91–55–66–33* ⊕ *www.diablenoir.com* ☉ *Mon. 1:30–7, Tues.–Sat. 10:30–7.*

**Marianne Cat.** Concept store par excellence, at Marianne Cat you'll find a curated choice of offbeat international designer clothing, jewelry, shoes, and accessories for women, along with designer housewares and a charming salon de thé. ⊠ *53 rue Grignan, Belsunce* ☎ *04–91–55–05–25* ☉ *Mon.–Sat. 10–7.*

**Rue de la Tour.** Diable Noir's "downtown" shop anchors the edgy shopping district along Rue de la Tour, across from the Centre Bourse off Place du Général de Gaulle. Dubbed "Rue de la Mode," it parades the earthy creativity of Marseille's fusion-fashion culture. ⊠ *Vieux Port.*

**Sugar.** This Marseille-based chain sells reliably chic sportswear in luscious colors. Mix-and-match separates include everything from sexy pencil skirts to jaunty pea coats and those long French scarves. ⊠ *16 rue Lulli, Vieux Port* ☎ *04–91–33–47–52* ⊕ *www.sugarproduct.com* ⊗ *Mon.–Sat. 10–7.*

### GIFTS AND CRAFTS

**Castaldi.** For every kind of nautical doodad, from brass fittings for your yacht's bathroom to sturdy pea coats and oilskins, head down the quai to Castaldi. ⊠ *25 quai de Rive Neuve, Vieux Port* ☎ *04–91–33–30–49* ⊕ *www.castaldi-decoration-marine.com* ⊗ *Daily 10–6.*

**Galeries Lafayette.** This midrange department store anchors a corner that's one block from the port and the tourist office. ⊠ *28 rue de Bir Hakeim, Vieux Port* ☎ *04–91–56–82–12* ⊕ *www.galerieslafayette.com* ⊗ *Mon.–Sat. 10–7.*

**La Grande Savonnerie.** The newest boutique on Marseille's soap scene, La Grande Savonnerie not only maintains the old ways (notice the statue of St. Florian, patron saint of soapmakers), it's determined to pass them on. Classes in soapmaking are offered every day for a nominal fee. Learn how to make natural cleansing products and cosmetics according to old recipes. Or just stock up on the lusciously scented soaps, in fragrances like lilac, rose, and lily of the valley. There are also cold-pressed beauty oils, handmade rose and orange blossom waters, and a range of Provençal linens. ⊠ *36 Grand Rue, Le Panier* ☎ *09–50–63–80–35* ⊕ *www.lagrandesavonnerie.com* ⊗ *Daily 10–8.*

**Maison Empereur.** If your home is your castle you'll flip at the sheer magnitude of housewares here. Since 1827 this picturesque shop has gathered the best in everything for the home, from French (and European) kitchenware to hardware—including hard-to-find reproductions of classic French door pulls, handles, and light fixures—Staub pots, handmade brushes, savon de Marseille—you name it, they've got it. ⊠ *4 rue des Récolettes, Noailles* ☎ *04–91–54–15–01* ⊕ *www. empereur.fr* ⊗ *Mon.–Sat. 9–7.*

**Savonnerie Marseillaise Licorne.** One of Marseille's oldest traditional manufacturers sells the fragrant *savon* in blocks, ovals, or fanciful shapes. This soapmaker uses the highest olive oil content possible (72%) in the soaps, and only natural essential oils from Provence for the fragrances. Call ahead for a guided tour (in English) of this atmospheric factory—a great way to see the whole process done on traditional machines. ⊠ *34 Cours Julien, Cours Julien* ☎ *04–96–12–00–91* ⊕ *www.savon-de-marseille-licorne.com* ⊗ *Weekdays 9–7, Sat. 10–7.*

### GOURMET GOODIES

**Arax.** For exotic food products shipped into this international port, browse in the Arax, crammed floor to ceiling with Armenian specialties and aromatic goodies from North Africa, China, and the Middle East. ⊠ *27 rue d'Aubagne, La Canebière.*

**Four des Navettes.** This famous bakery, up the street from Notre-Dame-de-la-Garde, makes orange-spice, shuttle-shape *navettes*. These cookies are modeled on the little boat that, it is said, carried Lazarus and the "Three

Marys" (Mary Magdalene, Mary Salome, and Mary Jacobe) to the nearby shore. ✉ *136 rue Sainte, Garde Hill* ☎ *04–91–33–32–12* ⊕ *www. fourdesnavettes.com* ⊘ *Mon.–Sat. 7 am–8 pm, Sun. 9–1 and 3–7:30.*

**La Maison du Pastis.** Specializing in pastis, anisette, and absinthe, this smart little shop offers a dizzying range, but to really savor these unique delights, just head next door to L'Heure Vert, an "absinthe café." ✉ *108 quai du Port, Vieux Port* ☎ *04–91–90–86–77* ⊕ *www. lamaisondupastis.com.*

**Saladin Épices du Monde.** A veritable Ali Baba's cave in the heart of the souklike Arab market, this colorful shop is stuffed to the brim with eye-popping mounds of dried fruit and nuts, exotic condiments, grains, and every spice under the sun. ✉ *10 rue Longue des Capucins, Noailles* ☎ *04–91–33–22–76* ⊕ *www.saladin-epicesdumonde.fr* ⊘ *Daily 7:30–7.*

**Xocoatl Chocolaterie Maino.** The delectable chocolates at this father-and-son enterprise near the Vieux Port are made by hand using only the finest cocoa beans perfumed with Mediterranean spices and flavors—almond, hazelnut, rose, and orange blossom water. ✉ *28 Grand Rue, Vieux Port* ☎ *04–91–90–22–91* ⊘ *Tues.–Sat. 9:30–7.*

# THE CENTRAL COAST

With the floods of vacationers pouring onto the beaches from St-Tropez to Menton every summer, it's surprising that the coast between Marseille and Hyères is often dismissed. Although there are a few industrial pockets around La Ciotat and Toulon, there are just as many sections of magnificent coastline—white cliffs peppered with ragged, wind-twisted pines.

Just inland, in the dry white hills, lies the peaceful market town of **Aubagne**; climb to the top of its outlying hills and you can see the ocean sparkling below. **Cassis** is the jewel of this region, a harbor protected by the formidable Cap Canaille, 1,300 feet high. Between Cassis and Marseille stretch the extraordinary **Calanques,** a series of rocky fjords that probe deep into the coastline, punctuated with pretty seaside towns and the sun-drenched vineyards of picture-perfect **Bandol.** Hub of the region is **Toulon,** an enormous naval base and a tough big city with an interesting Old Town for the intrepid; just east of the city is where you catch the ferry to Porquerolles, the best of the wild and beautiful **Îles d'Hyères.**

## AUBAGNE

*15 km (9 miles) east of Marseille; 10 km (6 miles) north of Cassis.*

This easygoing, plane tree–shaded market town (pronounced oh-*bahn*-yuh) is proud of its native son, the dramatist, filmmaker, and chronicler of all things Provençal, Marcel Pagnol, best known to Anglophones as author of *Jean de Florette, Fanny,* and *Manon des Sources* (*Manon of the Springs*). Here you can spend the morning exploring the animated market or digging through used Pagnol books and collectibles in the Old Town. Make sure you visit Aubagne on a market day (Tuesday, Saturday, or Sunday), when the sleepy center is transformed into a tableau of Provençal life. The Tuesday market is the biggest, where you're sure to find santon figurines, as Aubagne claims the title of santon capital of Provence.

### GETTING HERE AND AROUND

Trains run every 20–30 minutes between Marseille and Aubagne (€3.80, 20 minutes). By bus, line 240 (⊕ *www.lepilote.com*) runs from Marseille every 20–30 minutes (€2.20, 30 minutes). By car, take the A50 from Marseille to exit 6 on the A501.

GUIDED TOURS

Even if you don't choose to hike the 12-km (7-mile) or 20-km (12-mile) loop through the garrigues (scrubland) above Aubagne, there's a bus tour of Marcel Pagnol landmarks that leaves from the tourist office. It takes place in July and August on Wednesday at 3; the cost is €11. Request an English-speaking guide in advance.

### VISITOR INFORMATION

**Aubagne Tourist Office** ⊠ *6 Av. Antide Boyer* ☏ *04–42–03–49–98* ⊕ *www.aubagne.fr.*

### EXPLORING

**Ateliers Thérèse Neveu.** The history of the craft of santon-making and other uses to which the local clay was put—faïence and hand-painted tiles—can be studied at the Ateliers Thérèse Neveu, named for Aubagne's first master *santonière* (santon maker). Also on display are excellent temporary exhibitions about pottery. ⊠ *Chemin Entrecasteaux, at the top of the Old Town hill* ☏ *04–42–03–43–10* ⊠ *Free* ☉ *Tues.–Sun. 10–noon and 2–6.*

**Circuit Pagnol.** Even if you haven't read Pagnol's works or seen his films, you can enjoy the Circuit Pagnol, a hike in the raw-hewn, arid *garrigues* (scrublands) behind Marseille and Aubagne. Here Pagnol spent his idyllic summers, described in his *Souvenirs d'un Enfance* (*Memories of a Childhood*), crunching through the rosemary, thyme, and scrub oak at the foot of his beloved Garlaban. When he grew up to be a famous playwright and filmmaker, he shot some of his best work in these hills, casting his wife, Jacqueline, as the first Manon of the Springs. After Pagnol's death, Claude Berri came back to the Garlaban to find a location for his remake of *Manon des Sources*, but found it so altered by brush fires and power cables that he chose to shoot farther east instead, around Cuges-les-Pine and Riboux. (The lovely village and Manon's well were filmed in Mirabeau, in the Luberon.) Although the trail may no longer shelter the pine-shaded olive orchards of its past, it still gives you the chance to walk through primeval Provençal countryside and rewards you with spectacular views of Marseille and the sea. To access the marked trail by yourself, drive to La Treille northeast of Aubagne and follow the signs. For an accompanied tour with literary commentary, contact the Office du Tourisme.

**Farmers' Market.** Aubagne on a market day is a feast, in more ways than one. Depending on the season, for sale are fresh local asparagus, vine-ripened tomatoes and melons, and mesclun scooped by the gnarled fingers of blue-aproned ladies in from the farm (Tuesday, Thursday,

Thanks to its rich soil, Aubagne is a center of master potters and *santon* artists, many of whom show their wares in the town's marketplace and ceramic festivals.

Saturday, and Sunday). The Friday afternoon market is the biggest, with clothing, purses, tools, and pots and pans spilling onto the esplanade, but the Saturday and Sunday markets make more of regional products; those labeled Pays d'Aubagne must be organically raised. You won't find the social scene you'll see in Aix, but this is a more authentic farmers' market (from 2:30 pm). ⊠ *Cours Voltaire.*

**Le Petit Monde de Marcel Pagnol** (*The Small World of Marcel Pagnol*). You can study miniature dioramas of scenes from Pagnol stories at Le Petit Monde de Marcel Pagnol. The characters are all santons, including superb portraits of a humpback Gerard Dépardieu and Yves Montand, resplendent in mustache, fedora, and velvet vest, just as they were featured in *Jean de Florette.* ⊠ *Esplanade de Gaulle* 🚆 *Free* ⊗ *May–Sept. and Dec.–Mar., daily 9–12:30 and 2:30–6.*

**Musée de la Légion Étrangère** (*Museum of the Foreign Legion*). Another claim to fame for Aubagne: it's the headquarters for the French Foreign Legion. The legion was created in 1831, and accepts recruits from all nations, no questions asked. The discipline and camaraderie instilled among its motley team of adventurers, criminals, and mercenaries have helped the legion forge a reputation for exceptional valor—a reputation romanticized by songs and films in which sweaty deeds of heroism are performed under the desert sun. The Musée de la Légion Étrangère does its best to polish the image by way of medals, uniforms, weapons, and photographs. ⊠ *Caserne Viénot (to get there, take a left off D2 onto D44A just before Aubagne)* 🕾 *04–42–18–12–41* 🚆 *Free* ⊗ *June–Sept., Tues.–Thurs. and weekends 10–noon and 3–7, Fri. 10–noon; Oct.–May, Wed. and weekends 10–noon and 2–6.*

### WHERE TO EAT AND STAY

$ FRENCH 🍴 **La Farandole.** Cosseted here by rustic Provençal lemon-print cloths, lace curtains, and the region's typical bow-legged chairs, you can enjoy good home cooking specializing in seafood and dishes with a Morrocan slant with the regulars who claim the same table every day. They are drawn to the flower-filled terrace with a small fountain, friendly waitresses, and home-baked cakes, all of which enhance the small-town feel. The inexpensive daily menu may contain crisp green salad with foie gras in a raspberry vinaigrette or baked goat cheese; wine is included. [$] *Average main: €15* ✉ *4 rue Martinot(off Cours Maréchal, on a narrow street leading into the Old Town)* ☎ *04–42–03–26–36* 🌐 *www.la-farandole.fr* 🕓 *Closed Mon. No dinner Sun.*

$$ HOTEL 🏨 **Hostellerie de la Source.** Its suburban location 4 km (2 miles) outside of Aubagne, this good-value hotel is a nice option for travelers with a car. **Pros:** quiet and secluded; nice pool; decent restaurant. **Cons:** they cater to conferences and large groups, so you may have to share the space with multitudes. [$] *Rooms from: €115* ✉ *St-Pierre-des-Aubagne* ☎ *04–42–04–09–19* 🌐 *www.hostelleriedelasource.com* 🛏 *26 rooms, 2 apartments* 🍽 *No meals.*

## CASSIS

Fodor's Choice ★ *30 km (19 miles) southeast of Marseille; 10 km (6 miles) north of Aubagne.*

Surrounded by vineyards, flanked by monumental cliffs, guarded by the ruins of a medieval castle, and nestled around a picture-perfect fishing port, Cassis is the prettiest coastal town in Provence. Best known for its delicate white wines and wild Calanques, it is a quiet fishing village out of season and inundated with sun-worshippers in the summer. The pastel houses at rakish angles framing the port and harbor attracted early 20th-century artists including Dufy and Matisse. Even the mild rash of parking-garage architecture in the outer neighborhoods can't spoil the effect of unadulterated charm.

Stylish without being too recherché, Cassis's picture-perfect harbor provides shelter to numerous pleasure-boaters, who restock their galleys at its market, replenish their Saint James nautical duds in its boutiques, and relax with a bottle of local wine and a platter of urchins in one of its numerous waterfront cafés.

### GETTING HERE AND AROUND

Hourly trains between Marseille and Toulon stop at Cassis, but the station is about 3 km (1½ miles) from the center. From the station, there is a local shuttle to the town center that runs every 20 minutes and costs €1. By car, leave the A50 from Marseille and Toulon and take exit 8 for Cassis. The D559 from Marseille to Cassis is dramatically beautiful, continuing along the coast to Toulon, but it might be too curvy for motion-sickness sufferers.

### VISITOR INFORMATION

**Cassis Tourist Office** ✉ *Pl. Baragnon* ☎ *08–92–39–01–03* 🌐 *www.ot-cassis.com.*

# Little Saints with Feet of Clay

They beckon from shop windows in every hill town, these miniatures called *santons,* from the dialect *santouns* for "little saints." But whatever commercial role they may play today, their roots run deep in Provence.

The Christmas crèche has been a part of Provençal tradition since the Middle Ages, when people reenacted the tableau of the birth of Christ, wise men, shepherds, and all. When the Revolution cracked down on these pastoral plays, a Marseillais artisan decided to substitute clay actors. The terra-cotta figures created a new fashion and the santon craze was on.

A Marseille tradition that eventually migrated to Aubagne in the hills above (the clay was better), the delicate doll-like figurines spread throughout Provence, and are displayed every Christmas in church crèches that resemble a rustic back-country hill village as much as they do Bethlehem. Against a miniature background of model stone houses, dried-moss olive groves, and glass creeks, quaint, familiar characters go about their daily tasks—the lumberjack hauling matchstick kindling, the fisherman toting a basket of waxy fish, the red-cheeked town drunk leering drolly at the pretty lavender-cutter whose basket hangs heavy with real dried sprigs. The original cast from

Bethlehem gets second billing to a charming crowd of Gypsies, goatherds, and provincial passersby. And these days there are plenty of Gérard Depardieus, Carla Bruni-Sarkozys, and Yves Montands.

It's a highly competitive craft, and while artisans vie for the souvenir trade, some have raised it to an art form.

Molded, dried, then scraped with sharp tools down to the finest detail—wrinkled foreheads and fingernails—the santons are baked at 1,000°C (1,832°F). Once cool, they are painted with a watchmaker's precision: eyelashes, nostrils, and gnarled knuckles. The larger ones have articulated limbs to allow for dressing; their hand-sewn costumes, Barbie-scaled, are lavished with as much fine detail as the painted features.

Many artisans maintain highly public studios, so you can shop direct. Little santons (about an inch high), without articulated limbs, run about €12; big ones (8 to 10 inches), dressed and painted by the best artists, cost around €50.

But the preferred format is the crèche tableau, and it's easy to get hooked on building a collection of Provençal rustics to be lovingly unwrapped and displayed every Christmas season.

## EXPLORING

**Calanques.** Touring the Calanques, whose fjordlike finger bays probe the rocky coastline, is a must. Either take a sightseeing cruise in a glass-bottom boat that dips into each Calanque in turn (tickets, sold at the eastern end of the port, are €15–€25 depending on how many Calanques you see) or hike across the cliff tops, clambering down the steep sides to these barely accessible retreats. Of the Calanques closest to Cassis, **Port Miou** is the least attractive. It is also the only one fully accessible by car. It was a *pierre de Cassis* (Cassis stone) quarry until 1982 when the Calanques became protected sites, and now has an active leisure and fishing port. **Calanque Port Pin** is prettier, with wind-twisted pines growing at angles from white-rock cliffs. But with its tiny beach and jagged cliffs looming overhead, covered with gnarled pine and scrub and its rock spur known to climbers as the "finger of God," it's **Calanque En Vau** that's a small piece of paradise.

**Château de Cassis.** The imposing Château de Cassis has loomed over the harbor since the invasions of the Saracens in the 7th century, evolving over time into a walled enclosure crowned with stout watchtowers. It's private property today and best viewed from a sunny portside terrace.

**Clos Sainte Magdeleine.** If you're a wine lover, pick up the brochure "Through the Vineyards" from the tourist office. There are 12 domaines open for tasting and buying, but the most spectacularly sited is the Clos Sainte Magdeleine set on the slopes of towering Cap Canaille. This four-generation AOC winery is noted for its delicately balanced whites and an elegant rosé. ✉ *Av. du Revestel* ☎ *04–42–01–70–28* 🌐 *www.clossaintemagdeleine.fr.*

## WHERE TO EAT AND STAY

$$ BISTRO 🍴 **Le Chaudron.** Just off Cassis's picturesque port, locals and visitors alike flock to this welcoming bistro and terrace serving classic Provençal meals on one of the town's charming backstreets. Family-run since 1970, the owners have had plenty of time to perfect their game, and it shows. This being Cassis, fish is a mainstay on the menu; start with gratin of mussels followed by roasted John Dory with Provençal vegetables, or spicy fish soup, all to be savored with the local Cassis wines. [$] *Average main: €22* ✉ *4 rue Adolphe Thiers* ☎ *04–42–01–74–18* ✍ *Reservations essential* ⏲ *No dinner Tues. No lunch Mon.–Sat. Mar.–Nov. No lunch Jul. and Aug.*

$$$ HOTEL 🏨 **Jardin d'Émile.** Just off the waterfront, tucked under massive cliffs and parasol pines, this stylish but homey rose-colored inn stands in a tropical garden and has views of the cape from the restaurant and some rooms. **Pros:** an intimate feel with lots of charm and comfort. **Cons:** often booked in the summer months; reception in high season can be cool. [$] *Rooms from: €139* ✉ *Av. Admiral Ganteaume, Plage du Bestouan* ☎ *04–42–01–80–55* 🌐 *www.lejardindemile.fr* 🛏 *7 rooms* ⏲ *Closed mid-Nov.–mid-Dec. and last wk of Jan.* 🍽 *No meals.*

$$$ HOTEL 🏨 **Les Roches Blanches.** First built as a private home in 1887, this cliffside villa takes in smashing views of the port and the Cap Canaille, both from the best rooms and from the panoramic dining hall. **Pros:** sweeping vistas are captivating; service is quick and friendly; 75% of rooms have balconies. **Cons:** can be hard to find; breakfast is expensive. [$] *Rooms from: €180* ✉ *Rte. des Calanques* ☎ *04–42–01–09–30* 🌐 *www.roches-blanches-cassis.com* 🛏 *19 rooms, 5 suites* ⏲ *Closed Nov.–Mar.* 🍽 *No meals.*

## THE OUTDOORS

**Cassis Calanques Plongée.** The Calanques offer some of the best diving in France. Weather permitting, there are spectacular cave dives daily to view brightly colored coral and abundant fish. Maestro diver Henri Cosquer (famous for discovering one of the oldest caves in the area) runs Cassis Calanques Plongée. ☎ *06–71–52–60–20* 🌐 *www.centrecassidaindeplongee.com* ⏲ *Closed mid-Nov.–mid-Mar.*

With its enchanting harbor and cliffside setting, Cassis beautifully reminds us why so many artists have flocked to the Mediterranean.

## BANDOL

*25 km (16 miles) southeast of Cassis; 15 km (9 miles) west of Toulon.*

Although its name means wine to most of the world, Bandol is also a popular and highly developed seaside resort town. In the 1920s, the glamorous social life of the Riviera stretched this far west, and grand seaside mansions rivaled Cap d'Antibes and Juan-les-Pins for high society and literati. Today its old port is a massive gray parking lot and the Old Town that fronts the quays is lined with seafood snack shops, generic brasseries, and palm trees. Yet westward, toward the Baie de Renecros, are some of the Belle Époque houses that once made Bandol famous. In high season the harbor is filled with yachts, and the waterfront promenade is packed with summer tourist crowds. A portside stroll up the palm-lined Allée Jean Moulin feels downright Côte d'Azur. If you're not a beach lover, pick up an itinerary from the tourist office and visit a few Bandol vineyards just outside of town. After a stroll through Bandol itself, most visitors head to the outskirts to discover several sights around the town that are worth exploring.

### GETTING HERE AND AROUND

Trains run between Marseille and Bandol every 30 minutes (€9.70, 45 minutes). By car, take the A50 towards Toulon to exit 12.

### VISITOR INFORMATION

**Bandol Tourist Office** ⊠ *Pavillon du Tourisme, on the waterfront* ☎ *04-94-29-41-35* ⊕ *www.bandol.fr.*

## EXPLORING

**Cap Sicié.** Head south on the D16 to the D2816 around the cap for a tremendous view across the Bay of Toulon.

**Gorge d'Ollioules.** Head north on D11 to Ollioules; just past the village, follow N8 (in the direction of Le Beausset) through a 5-km (3-mile) route that twists its scenic way beneath the awesome chalky rock faces of the Gorge d'Ollioules.

**Île de Bendor.** Boats leave every half hour to make the 2-km (1.2-mile) trip to Île de Bendor. The island was only a large rock until pastis magnate Paul Ricard bought it in the 1950s and tastefully transformed it into a tourist center with fine beaches, charming cottage shops, an *espace Ricard* showing Paul Ricard's lifetime works, and the Museum of Wine and Spirits. Although the island restaurants offer a surprisingly wide selection, sunny days and scenic views make for a lovely picnic. ☎ *04–94–10–65–20* ⊕ *www.lesilespaulricard.com.*

**Le Castellet.** On the D559 perched high above the Bandol vineyards, the village of Le Castellet has narrow streets, 17th-century stone houses, and (alas!) touristy shops designed for beach lovers on a rainy day.

**Le Gros Cerveau.** For some spectacular views, on the D20 take a left at Ollioules and follow the winding road along the crest of Le Gros Cerveau. You'll be rewarded first with inland mountain views, then an expansive panorama of the coastline.

**Notre-Dame de Pépiole.** Just east of Bandol on the D559, past the smaller resort of Sanary, as you turn left onto the D63 you'll see signs pointing to the small stone chapel of Notre-Dame de Pépiole. It's hemmed in by pines and cypresses and is one of the oldest Christian buildings in France, dating from the 6th century and modeled on early churches in the Middle East. The simple interior has survived the years in remarkably good shape, although the colorful stained glass that fills the tiny windows is modern—composed mainly of broken bottles. ☺ *Most afternoons 3–5.*

FAMILY **Zoa Parc Animalier et Exotique Sanary-Bandol** (*Sanary Bandol's Exotic Garden and Zoo*). Three kilometers (2 miles) north on the D559 is this zoo and garden, where cacti and hundreds of exotic tropical plants grow to remarkable sizes. In a small zoo setting, animals such as flamingos, gibbons, and gazelles frolic in shady gardens. ✉ *131 Av. Pont d'Aran, Sanary-Sur-Mer* ✥ *Exit Bandol from A8, take first right (direction Route de Beausset) and follow the signs to the zoo* ☎ *04–94–29–40–38* ⊕ *zoaparc.com* 🎟 *€9* ☺ *Feb.–Oct., daily 9:30–7; Nov.–Jan., Wed., Sat., and Sun. 9:30–6.*

## WHERE TO EAT AND STAY

$$$$ ✕ **René & Jean-François Bérard.** Chef Jean-François has taken the reins
MODERN FRENCH from his illustrious father, René (who consults on the menu), but the Mediterranean-inspired Provençal cuisine that put this restaurant on the map is as scrumptious as ever, emphasizing local seafood and fresh produce straight from the hotel-restaurant's kitchen garden. Try the ravioli stuffed with goat cheese, sorrel, and Parmesan in a lemon chicken broth; the lightly grilled red mullet wrapped in seaweed and topped with peas and fresh rosemary is another winner. 💲 *Average*

CLOSE UP

## Touring the Calanques

To hike the Calanques, gauge your skills: the GR98 (marked with red-and-white bands) is the most scenic route, but requires ambitious scrambling to get down the sheer walls of En Vau; make sure to stay on approved paths. The alternative is to follow the green markers and approach En Vau from behind. The faded markers could use revision nonetheless. If you're ambitious, you can hike the length of the GR98 between Marseille and Cassis, following the coastline, a distance of roughly 30 km (18 miles). Remember, access in the Calanques is restricted and can be prohibited anytime due to high winds. To check weather conditions, call ☎ *08–11–20–13–13* (€0.06 per minute).

To go on a boat ride to Les Calanques, get to the port around 10 am or 2 pm and look for a boat that's loading passengers. Two of the best choices are the *Notos II* and the *Moby Dick III*—they have huge windows and full commentary (in French only). But a slew of alternative boats won't leave you stranded. Round-trips should include at least three calanques and average €20.



*main: €49 ✉ 7 rue Gabriel-Péri, La Cadiere d'Azur ☎ 04–94–90–11–43 ✍ Reservations essential ⏲ Closed Mon. and Tues. mid-Sept.–mid-July. No lunch Sat.–Tues.*

$$ HOTEL 🏨 **Hostellerie Bérard.** Master Chef René Bérard is as celebrated for his haute cuisine as he is for his elegant country inn with breathtaking views of the countryside and everything required for a pampered weekend on the hotel premises. **Pros:** although a little off the beaten track, the lovely welcome is refreshing; the Bistrôt de Jef is a more casual alternative to the elegant gourmet restaurant. **Cons:** it's easy to get lost in the hotel's sprawling hallways. [$] *Rooms from: €132 ✉ 7 rue Gabriel-Péri, La Cadiere d'Azur ✣ 6 km (4 miles) north of Bandol ☎ 04–94–90–11–43 🌐 hotel-berard.com 🛏 41 rooms, 3 suites ⏲ Closed Jan.–mid-Feb. 🍴 No meals.*

## TOULON

*38 km (24 miles) southeast of Cassis; 67 km (41½ miles) east of Marseille; 29 km (18 miles) northwest of La Tour Fondue (departure point for the Îles d'Hyères).*

Toulon is a city of big contrasts: ugly with crowded postwar high-rises, yet surprisingly beautiful with its tree-lined littoral; a place with some frankly unappealing nightlife and yet by day, charming and colorful with its restaurant scene. Best known for the day in World War II when 75 French ships sank themselves rather than fall into the hands of attacking Germans, Toulon has kept its place as France's leading naval port with a kind of dogged determination. Though you may see nothing but endless traffic and graffiti-covered block-style apartments crossing the city, the **Vieille Ville** (Old Town) and port area have well-kept cafés and a sunny waterfront where yachts and pleasure boats—some available for trips to the Îles d'Hyères or around the bay—add bright splashes of color.

In the heart of Toulon's Old Town, the maze of streets is packed with designer shops and quirkily appealing stretches of ruined medieval houses mixed with lurid neon. Park your car under Place de la Liberté and take Boulevard de Strasbourg, turning right onto Rue Berthelot, which leads into the heart of the pedestrian-only streets of the Vieille Ville. Wander through **Place des Trois Dauphins,** with its mossy and fern-lined fountain, or stop in the café-filled **Place Puget**; Victor Hugo lived in No. 5 when he was researching *Les Misérables*. One block east, the **Cours Lafayette** becomes a wonderfully animated, authentic Provençal morning market (daily except Monday), and the **Hôtel de Ville** has evocative Baroque figures, carved by the Marseillais sculptor Pierre Puget.

Behind the port and the Vieille Ville lies the new town.

### GETTING HERE AND AROUND

Toulon is on the main TGV line from Paris and is served by regional and local trains from Marseille and Nice, so it is easy to navigate your way on the system. Once in Toulon, there is a great network of inner-city buses run by the RMTT (☎ *04–94–03–87–03* ⊕ *www.reseaumistral. com*). No. 23 goes to the beaches at Mourillon, No. 40 to the cable car. By car take the A50 from Marseille in the west and if you are coming from the east, the A57. The coastal D559 goes between Marseille and Toulon via Bandol.

### VISITOR INFORMATION

**Toulon Tourist Office** ⊠ *12 place Louis Blanc* ☎ *04–94–18–53–00* ⊕ *www.toulontourisme.com.*

### EXPLORING

**Mount Faron.** Reach Mount Faron, rising above the town, by the circular Route du Faron in either direction or in six minutes by cable car from Boulevard Admiral Jean-Vence. ☎ *04–94–92–68–25* ⊑ *€7 round-trip* ☉ *July and Aug., Mon. 2:15–7:45, Tues.–Sun. 9:30–7:45; Sept.–June, Tues.–Sun. 9:30–noon and 2:15–6.* ☉ *Closed on windy days.*

**Musée d'Art.** The Musée d'Art shows paintings by Vernet and Fragonard as well as postwar abstract art and the cartoon-influenced Di Rosa brothers. ⊠ *113 bd. Maréchal Leclerc* ☎ *04–94–36–81–01* ⊕ *www. toulon.fr* ⊑ *Free* ☉ *Tues.–Sun. noon–6.*

**Musée National de la Marine** (*Naval Museum*). Avenue de la République, an ugly arrangement of concrete apartment blocks, runs parallel to the waterfront. At the western edge of the gray is the Musée National de la Marine, with large models of ships, figureheads, paintings, and other items related to Toulon's maritime history. Photographs of the World War II sinking bring the sickening story to life. ⊠ *Pl. Monsenergue* ☎ *04–94–02–02–01* ⊕ *www.musee-marine.fr/toulon* ⊑ *€6* ☉ *Wed.–Mon. 10–6.*

**Mémorial du Débarquement.** At Mount Faron's summit are a zoo, a great view, and the Mémorial du Débarquement commemorating the 1944 liberation of Provence. ☎ *04–94–88–08–09* ⊑ *€4* ☉ *Tues.–Sun. 10– noon and 2–4:30.*

**Opera de Toulon.** At Place Victor Hugo, the Opera de Toulon hosts theater, opera, and dance productions. ⊠ *Boulevard de Strasbourg* ☎ *04–94– 92–70–78* ⊕ *www.operadetoulon.fr* ☉ *Box office: weekdays 10–12:30 and 2:30–5:30.*

OFF THE
BEATEN
PATH

**Brignoles.** Although known as the market center for the wines of the Var, Brignoles's largest attraction is still the Abbaye de la Celle, a 12th-century Benedictine abbey that served as a convent until the 17th century. The abbey was abandoned until Maria Fournier, owner of the Îles of Porquerolles, decided to open it as a hotel in 1945. Despite its sudden rise in status with the likes of Charles de Gaulle vacationing here, the town continued to resist change firmly. In fact, the simple Romanesque chapel housing a 14th-century Christ figure largely acclaimed as an anonymous masterpiece still serves today as the parish church. It's here in this historic spot that celebrated chef Alain Ducasse has his culinary hideaway Hostellerie de l'Abbaye de La Celle. ⊠ *45 km (28 miles) north of Toulon, Brignoles.*

## WHERE TO EAT AND STAY

$$$

FRENCH

✕ **Le Gros Ventre.** In a cozy and romantic space enhanced by soft lighting, tasteful decorations, and tables set at discreet distances from each other, you can enjoy some of the best Provençal cooking in Toulon. Specializing in seafood and beef, Chef Nothhelfer brings to the table delights like fillet of beef served with grapes and foie gras, or fish caught daily by the restaurant's personal fisherman. An enormous wine list of more than 5,000 bottles can be a little intimidating, but friendly servers help guide you through it. Ⓢ *Average main: €30* ⊠ *297 Littoral F. Mistral* ☎ *04–94–42–15–42* ⊕ *www.legrosventre.net* ☉ *Closed Wed. and Thurs. No lunch Fri. July–Aug.*

$$$$

B&B/INN

**Fodor's**Choice

★

⊞ **Hostellerie de l'Abbaye de La Celle.** Superchef Alain Ducasse put this beautifully restored 18th-century bastide on the map when he opened a restaurant here in the early 2000s; other draws include guest rooms that mix Louis XVI and regional accents, private gardens, and vineyard views. **Pros:** Michelin-starred eats; lovely view; "standard" category room has lower rates; a true Provençal experience, with all the glamour minus the glitz. **Cons:** some say restaurant service can be slow. Ⓢ *Rooms from: €250* ⊠ *10 Pl. du Général-de-Gaulle, La Celle* ☎ *04–98–05–14–14* ⊕ *www.abbaye-celle.com* ⤶ *10 rooms* ☉ *Restaurant closed Tues. and Wed. mid-Oct–mid Apr.* ⦿*No meals.*

# ÎLES D'HYÈRES

*32 km (20 miles) off coast south of Hyères.*

Strung across the Bay of Hyères and spanning some 32 km (20 miles) is an archipelago of islands reminiscent of a set for a pirate movie. In fact, they have been featured in several, thanks not only to their wild and rocky coastline but also their real pirate history. In the 16th century the islands were seeded with convicts meant to work the land; they promptly ran amok, ambushing and sacking passing ships heading for Toulon. Today the pirates are long gone, replaced by a thriving local population and tourists.

The islands consist of three main bodies: Levant, Port-Cros, and Porquerolles. Eight percent of **Levant** is military property and is kept strictly guarded with barbed-wire fences. The remaining area, Héliopolis, is a nudist colony, where you're welcome if you want to participate, as opposed to simply being curious. **Port-Cros** is a magnificent national park with no cars, no smoking, and no dogs. You can hike on pine-scented trails with spectacular views, or follow the underwater path, snorkeling or diving with fish and aquatic life representative of the Mediterranean. **Porquerolles** (pronounced pork-uh-*rohl*) is the largest and most popular escape from the modern world. The village of Porquerolles was originally used as a retirement colony for Napoleonic officers (the Fort du Petit-Langoustier and the Fort Ste-Agathe, although no longer active, still loom imposingly over the marina), which explains its remarkable resemblance to a military outpost. At the turn of the 20th century a Belgian engineer named François-Joseph Fournier made a killing in the Panama Canal, then bought Porquerolles at auction as a gift for his new bride. It was only in 1970 that France nationalized the island, leaving Fournier's widow with a quarter of her original inheritance; her granddaughter now helps run the luxurious Mas du Langoustier. Off-season it's a castaway idyll of pine forests, sandy beaches, and plunging cliffs over a rocky coastline. Inland, its preserved pine forests and orchards of olives and figs are crisscrossed with dirt roads to be explored on foot or, if you prefer, on bikes rented from one of the numerous rental outfits in both the port and village. In high season (April to October), day-trippers pour off the ferries, running for the beaches and soap boutiques, and T-shirt shops appear out of the woodwork to cater to vacationers' whims.

### GETTING HERE AND AROUND

*To get to the islands, follow the narrow Giens Peninsula to La Tour–Fondue at its tip. Boats (leaving every half hour in summer, every 60 or 90 minutes the rest of year; €18.50 round-trip) make a 20-minute beeline to Porquerolles. For Port-Cros and Levant, depart from Port d'Hyères at Hyères-Plages.*

Ferries run from La Tour Fondu in Giens (every 30 minutes in summer and every 60 to 90 minutes in winter; €18.50 round-trip) for the 20-minute trip to Porquerolles, and from Hyères at Hyères Plages to Port-Cros and Levant (€26.80–€30 round-trip). You can also get to all three islands from Port-de-Miramar or Le Lavandou (35- to 60-minute crossing, €30 round-trip).

### VISITOR INFORMATION

**Îles d'Hyères Tourist Office** ✉ *Rotonde du Park Hôtel, Ave. de Belgique, Hyères* ☎ *04–94–01–84–50* 🌐 *www.hyeres-tourisme.com.*

## WHERE TO STAY

$$$$ RESORT 🏨 **Le Manoir de Port-Cros.** A mix of southern-coast bourgeois and Provençal touches adds a splash of color to the sunlit, airy rooms of this family-owned colonial-style hotel. **Pros:** with a price that can include both your meals and your accommodation, this is a gentle touch of civilization in the isolated wilderness and much in demand. **Cons:** some south-facing rooms are hot in the summer. [$] *Rooms from: €210* ✉ *Isle de Port-Cros, Hyères* ☎ *04–94–05–90–52* 🌐 *www.hotel-lemanoirportcros.com* 🛏 *23 rooms* 🕒 *Closed Nov.–Mar.* 🍴 *No meals.*

$$$$ B&B/INN 🏨 **Les Glycines.** In soft shades of yellow-ocher and sky-blue, this sleekly modernized little bastide has an idyllic enclosed courtyard, as well as some lovely guest rooms with views over a jungle of mimosa and eucalyptus. **Pros:** quiet and simply elegant; set just back from the port in the village

From Cassis, be sure to take an excursion boat to the Calanques, the rocky finger-coves washed by emerald and blue waters.

center. **Cons:** some rooms are small; beds can be creaky. [$] *Rooms from: €340* ✉ *Pl. d'Armes, Île de Porquerolles* ☎ *04–94–58–30–36* 🌐 *www.auberge-glycines.com* 🛏 *8 rooms, 3 suites* 🍴 *Some meals.*

$$$$ HOTEL **Mas du Langoustier.** A fabled getaway, the Langoustier comes with a lobster-orange building, pink bougainvillea, a choice of California-modern- or old-Provençal-style guest rooms, and a secluded location at the westernmost point of the Île de Porquerolles. **Pros:** a bastion of taste; can "upgrade" to dinner at L'Olivier; beach nearby and pool onsite. **Cons:** a hike to get here; no rooms have a sea view. [$] *Rooms from: €210* ✉ *Pointe du Langoustier, 3 km (2 miles) from the harbor, Île de Porquerolles* ☎ *04–94–58–30–09* 🌐 *www.langoustier.com* 🛏 *44 rooms, 5 apartments* ⏲ *Closed Oct.–Apr. Restaurants closed Sun. dinner and Mon., May, June, and Sept.* 🍴 *Some meals.*

## THE OUTDOORS

**Centre Immersion Plongée.** Here you can take a diving class, hire a guide, rent diving equipment, and refill scuba tanks. ✉ *Port Pothuau, 13 ave. des Chalutiers, Hyères* ☎ *04–94–66–39–95* 🌐 *www.immersion-plongee.com.*

**Cycle Porquerollais.** You can rent a mountain bike (*velo tout-terrain*, or VTT) for a day of pedaling the paths and cliff-top trails of Porquerolles. ✉ *1 rue de la Ferme, Île de Porquerolles* ☎ *04–94–58–30–32* 🌐 *www.cycle-porquerollais.com.*

**Locamarine 75.** This shop rents motorboats to anyone interested, whether or not you have a license. ✉ *Port de Porquerolles, Hyères* ☎ *04–94–58–35–84* 🌐 *www.locamarine75.com.*

5

# THE WESTERN CÔTE D'AZUR

including St-Tropez

# WELCOME TO THE WESTERN CÔTE D'AZUR

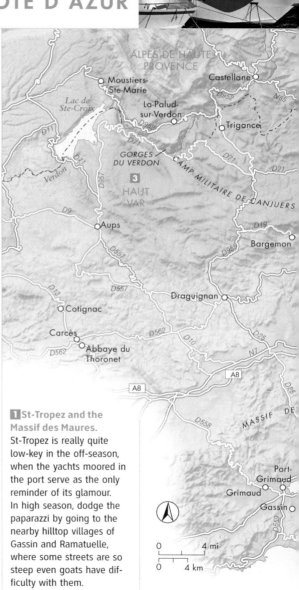

## TOP REASONS TO GO

★ **St-Tropez à go-go:** Brave the world's most outlandish fishing port in high summer and soak up the scene. Just don't forget the fake-tan lotion.

★ **Les Gorges du Verdon:** Peer down into its vertiginous green depths and you'll understand why this is one of the most dramatic natural sites in France.

★ **Picture-perfect Moustiers-Ste-Marie:** Best known for its faience pottery, this town is also worth visiting for the sight of houses clinging to the cliffs—often with entrances on different levels.

★ **A Gothic château extravaganza:** In Mandelieu-La Napoule, discover the most bizarrely extravagant house of the coast—the Château de la Napoule, festooned with tapestries, peacocks, and art students.

★ **The Estérel Corniche:** A mineral showcase, the Estérel coastline is sculpted of rock given to spectacular Technicolor displays of russet, garnet, and flaming orange.

**1 St-Tropez and the Massif des Maures.** St-Tropez is really quite low-key in the off-season, when the yachts moored in the port serve as the only reminder of its glamour. In high season, dodge the paparazzi by going to the nearby hilltop villages of Gassin and Ramatuelle, where some streets are so steep even goats have difficulty with them.

**2 Fréjus, St-Raphaël, and the Estérel Corniche.**
To the east of the twin waterfront resorts of Fréjus and St-Raphaël, the Massif de l'Estérel is pure hiking heaven. Made up of red volcanic rocks and softened by patches of lavender and gorse, its shore is lined with rocky coves and the Corniche de l'Estérel, one of the coast's most spectacular drives.

# GETTING ORIENTED

If it's most often associated with celeb-heavy coastal resorts, particularly St-Tropez, the Western Côte d'Azur is also a nature-lover's paradise. North of the coast, the Massif des Maures and the Massif de l'Estérel remain remarkably wild and unspoiled, while, farther up, the Gorges du Verdon draws hard-core hikers willing to forego the local rosé to keep their wits about them as they tackle France's answer to the Grand Canyon.

**5**

Map showing: Mons, ALPES MARITIMES, Grasse, Seillans, Fayence, Antibes, Mandelieu-La Napoule, Cannes, Golfe Juan, La Napoule, Théoule-sur-Mer, St-Raphael, MASSIF DE L'ESTÉREL, Corniche de l'Estérel, Fréjus, Golfe de Fréjus, MAURES, VAR, Ste-Maxime, Cap des Sardinaux, Cap de St-Tropez, St-Tropez, Ramatuelle. Roads: N95, N85, D2085, D2562, D9, D3, A8, N98, N7, N98, D562, D663, D562, D93. Mediterranean Sea.

**3 Haut Var and the Gorges de Verdon Environs.** Far from the frenzy of the coast, the backcountry hills called the *arrière-pays* remain deeply Provençal. Here, in the region known as the Haut Var, explore Moustiers-Ste-Marie with its faience workshops where you can discover the art of this brightly painted tableware. Not far away is La Palud-sur-Verdon, gateway to the spectacular Gorges du Verdon.

Updated by
Nancy Heslin

The Western Côte d'Azur can supply you with everything your heart desires—and your purse can stand. Home to St-Tropez ("Saint Too Much," as the French call it), the region beckons to both backpackers and billionaires. The former camp out on the stunning Estérel coast, the latter indulge in the mecca of hedonism, splashing out €1,000 a night for a room in the summer. Let's not forget the area is also home to remote hill villages colonized by artists, striking red-rock coves, and scenery gorgeous enough to steal center stage from Deborah Kerr in Hollywood's 1958 Riviera homage, *Bonjour Tristesse*.

For natural beauty the region can't be topped, although the series of picture-book gulfs that scoop into this part of the French Mediterranean coastline remains less famous than its counterparts to the east. Above the coastline of the Var *département* (region), the horizon in all directions is dominated by the rugged red-rock heights of the Massif de l'Estérel and the green-black bulk of the Massif des Maures. Lovely blue-green waters lap at the foot of thriving resort towns—St-Tropez, of course, but also Fréjus, St-Raphaël, and Mandelieu-La-Napoule.

But the biggest pull remains St-Tropez. Like France's perennially popular rock star Johnny Hallyday, St-Trop never fades—it just gets another face-lift and keeps going, brasher than ever. The difficulty reaching its portion of the coast—the train only goes as far as Ste-Maxime—naturally separates the wheat (who swan in by helicopter) from the chaff (who crawl along in midsummer traffic jams, sweaty and miserable). You need to be a little masochistic to visit St-Tropez in August, but the town does have a fair number of budget hotels and sheds most of its pretension in the off-season, becoming simply a small fishing port with very big yachts.

Neighboring resorts can't help but feel lower-key, providing stretches of sandy beach and guaranteed balmy temperatures to sun-starved northerners. In high summer, masses flood the beaches, feast on the fish, fill up the marinas, luxuriate in the spa treatments, and crowd the hotels and cafés. Bored, sunburned, or regarding each other in mutual *snobbisme,* they then take to the hills—the glorious vineyard-lined, village-crowned hills that back the coast as the continent climbs gently toward the Alps and are home to some beautiful *villages perchés* (perched villages) and historic towns.

These destinations make great day trips from the coast, though they're often dominated in high season by busloads of excursion-takers out of Cannes or St-Raphaël. But if you have a car and the time to explore, you can plunge even deeper into the backcountry, past the coastal plateau into the Haut Var. Here the harsh and beautiful countryside—raw rock, pine, and scrub oak—is lightly peppered with little hill villages that are almost boutique-free. You can hear the *pétanque* (lawn bowling) balls thunk, the fountains trickle, and the bells toll within their wrought-iron campaniles. If you like what you see and press on, you'll be rewarded with one of France's most spectacular natural wonders: the Gorges du Verdon, a Grand Canyon–style chasm roaring with milky-green water and edged by one of Europe's most hair-raising drives. Backpacks, hiking boots, and picnics are de rigueur around the Gorges, until you reach lovely Moustiers-Ste-Marie, an atmospheric center for faience, where you can treat yourself to a leisurely meal and take in breathtaking views.

You can visit any spot between St-Tropez and Cannes in an easy day trip, and the hilltop villages and towns on the coastal plateau are just as accessible. Thanks to the efficient A8 highway, you can whisk at high speeds to the exit nearest your destination up or down the coast; thus, even if you like leisurely exploration, you can zoom back to your home base at day's end. Above the autoroute things slow down considerably, and you'll find the winding roads and overlooks between villages an experience in themselves. Venturing farther north, say by the 314-km (195-mile) Route Napoléon, is a bigger commitment and, to be fully enjoyed, should include at least one overnight stop.

# PLANNING

## WHEN TO GO

Summer days are like the film *Groundhog Day*—every day seems exactly the same as the day before with the piercing azure blue sky and sticky sunshine heat. July and August are hot, people move slower and, yes, sweat. By rule of folklore thumb, locals cite August 15 as the beginning of changing weather: clouds tend to roll in frequently and temps become noticeably cooler in the morning and evening. March to April and October to November tend to be the rainier months and, of course, the mistral can come at any time, bringing terrible gusts and nippy drafts. To see the Gorges du Verdon in full fall color, aim for early October, though the odds of rainy days increase as autumn advances.

## PLANNING YOUR TIME

Unless you enjoy jacked-up prices, traffic jams, and sardine-style beach crowds, avoid the coast like the plague in July and August, especially the last week of July and first three weeks of August. Many of the better restaurants simply shut down to avoid the coconut-oil crowd. Another negative about July and August: the Estérel is closed to hikers during this flash-fire season. From Easter through October the café life is in full swing; May is mild and often lovely, but the top restaurants and hotels may be crowded with spillover from the Cannes Film Festival. Planet St-Tropez is really only open for business April through October, and during the warmer months, people-watching in the port and lunching at Pampelonne Beach's Club 55 is a must. Even at the end of the season, there's lots going on: regatta races, the Australian Film Festival, and the annual sale "La Grande Braderie"—held during the last weekend of October—when even you can afford to shop in St-Tropez (okay, so it's last season's stuff, but hey . . .). Moustiers-Ste-Marie celebrates the Fête de la Cité de la Faïence (earthenware) over three days in late spring, (usually) every other year. In February, La Napoule hosts its annual Mimosa festival, complete with competing float parades. Southwest, in Bormes-les-Mimosas, you can visit the president's summer home during the Heritage Day Weekend (Les Journées Européennes du Patrimoine) over the third weekend in September, when many closed-to-the-public establishments open their doors—for free. On the second Sunday in September, Fréjus-St-Aygulf cracks open 13,200 eggs as it celebrates the Giant Omelette Festival. You can work off all that eggcess during a week of guided walks around hilltop villages near St-Raphaël during the Var Rambling Week (Semaine Varoise de la Randonnée) in early October.

## GETTING HERE AND AROUND

Public transportation is not as good here as in other regions of the Riviera and Provence, and some itineraries may require cars. Driving is the best way to village-hop in the Haut Var and take in the spectacular Gorges du Verdon, but be prepared for some challenging bends along the way, like the Route des Crêtes (D23) from La Palud-sur-Verdon (if white knuckles are not for you, opt for the nearby D952).

If traveling by bus, remember that just because you actually found a local bus that stops at the village of choice, it doesn't mean that it's going to drop you in the heart of town. During the summer season, there is no way to avoid the bumper-to-bumper traffic along the N98 Coast route, the Corniche de l'Estérel. Taking a train or bus (for schedules, go to ⊕ *www.varlib.fr*) is much easier here than in the Haut Var, where there are few options. From roughly April to September, ferries to St-Tropez from Nice (2 hours 30 minutes), Cannes (1 hour 15 minutes), and St-Raphaël (1 hour) offer a scenic, hassle-free route.

### BOAT TRAVEL

Considering the congestion that buses and cars confront on the road to St-Tropez, the best way to get to that resort is by train to St-Raphaël, then one of the two Transports Maritimes Ralphaëlois boats each day between April and October (four boats daily during July and August) that leave from the Gare Maritime de St-Raphaël in the Vieux Port. The boat trip takes about an hour and costs €15 one way. Bateaux Verts offers a shuttle boat linking St-Tropez and Ste-Maxime from mid-February to December; tickets are €7.30 one way and the ride is 15 minutes. Once in St-Tropez, from April through September the same company can also take you on a tour around the Calanques de l'Estérel (2–3½ hours; €20) or an hour-long tour of the Baie des Canebiers (nicknamed the "Bay of Stars") to see some celebrity villas (€10–€14.50).

**Boat Information Bateaux Verts** ⊠ *14 Quai Léon Condroyer, Ste-Maxime* ☎ *04–94–96–51–00* ⊕ *www.bateauxverts.com.* **Transport Maritimes Raphaëlois** ⊠ *Gare maritime, Quai Nomy, St-Raphaël* ☎ *04–94–95–17–46* ⊕ *www.bateauxsaintraphael.com.*

### BUS TRAVEL

Local buses cover a network of routes along the coast and stop at many out-of-the-way places that can't be reached by train.

Timetables are available from tourist offices, train stations, and local bus stations (*gares routières*).

Ask for information on commercial bus excursions, too; there are several day-trip tours out of Fréjus and St-Raphaël into the more popular backcountry towns.

St-Tropez's Gare Routière (bus station) is on Avenue du Général de Gaulle (at 5 Quai Avancé) and has bus routes run by VarLib.

These include the popular No. 7601 to/from St-Raphaël (€3, 1½ hours, 12 daily), the town with the nearest railway station; some buses stop in Grimaud and Port Grimaud, Ste-Maxime, and Fréjus (€3, 1 hour) but check the schedule to be sure.

Note that in high season, the traffic jam to St-Tropez can lead to two-plus-hour bus rides, so if you arrive in St-Raphaël, it may be best to hop on one of the shuttle boats that connects the two ports.

Buses link up with Ramatuelle and Gassin (€3, 40 minutes). Buses also connect to Toulon (No. 7801; €3, 2 hours).

St-Raphaël's bus station, at 100 rue Victor Hugo next to the train station, had a €4-million face-lift in 2010. Now offering faster and cheaper service—all routes are €3 except to Nice airport (€20)—local bus companies merged to form VarLib buses.

Service links up with St-Tropez (No. 7601 via Grimaud and Ste-Maxime, €3, 1½ hours), some towns in the Haut Var, and selected stops along the coastal Corniche de l'Estérel.

Fréjus's bus station is on Place Paul-Vernet, but there are no direct buses from here to St-Tropez.

Some Haut Var towns are also serviced by VarLib, departing from the train stations at Les Arcs and Draguignan.

**Bus Information AggloBus Var Esterel Méditerranée** ☎ *04–94–53–78–46* ⊕ *www.agglo-var-esterel-mediterranee.fr/c_transport.htm.* **VarLib.** Included in the 248 routes between Var municipalities are Toulon, Draguignan, Fréjus-St-Raphaël, and St-Tropez, with links to smaller villages in between. ☎ *08–10–00–61–77* ⊕ *www.varlib.fr.*

## CAR TRAVEL

A8 provides swift, easy access to Fréjus and other towns along the coast. To reach resorts along the Estérel, you must follow the coastal highway N98 east. To get to St-Tropez and the resorts at the foot of the Massif des Maures, follow N98 southwest from Fréjus. To explore the hill towns and the Gorges du Verdon, slow and scenic roads lead north and west from Fréjus and Cannes, including the famous Route Napoléon. Sailing from Fréjus and St-Raphaël toward Cannes is a breeze on A8, but N98, which connects you to coastal resorts in between, can be extremely slow, though scenic. To the north and east of this region, you break into the country, and the roads are small, pokey, and pretty. If you want to explore any hill towns in depth and at will, a car is indispensable.

## TRAIN TRAVEL

The main rail crossroads from points north and west are at Fréjus's main station on Rue Martin Bidouré and St-Raphaël's Gare St-Raphaël/Valescure on Rue Waldeck Rousseau, which is the main hub on the coastal TER rail line between Menton and Marseille (it's about one hour and 40 minutes from the latter by rail, with hourly trains costing €25.60). From St-Raphaël/Valescure the train route begins its scenic crawl along the coast to Italy, stopping in La Napoule and Cannes.

The resort port of Mandelieu–La Napoule is on the rail line between St-Raphaël and Cannes. There is no rail access to St-Tropez; St-Raphaël and Fréjus are the nearest stops. The train station nearest the Haut Var and the Gorges du Verdon is at Les Arcs, below Draguignan. From there you have to rent a car or take local buses offered by VarLib into the hills.

**Train Information SNCF** ☎ 3635 €0.34/minute ⊕ www.voyages-sncf.com. **TGV** ☎ 3635 €0.34/minute ⊕ www.tgv.com.

## BEACHES

Following upon their worldwide fame as the earth's most glamorous beaches, the real things often come as a shock to first-time visitors.

Much of the Côte d'Azur is lined with rock and pebble, and the beaches are narrow swaths backed by city streets or roaring highways. Only St-Tropez, on this stretch of the Mediterranean, has the curving bands of sandy waterfront you've come to expect from all those 1950s photographs—and even there, the 3-mile stretch of Pampelonne Beach supports no fewer than some 30 restaurants and private businesses.

Note that there's a range of acceptable behaviors on these beaches: some are topless, some feature nudity, some are favored by gay people. You won't need a diagram to tell you which is which.

## HIKING

Contact local tourist offices for information on hikes in the rugged backcountry of the Massif de l'Estérel. While several *sentiers du littoral* (coastal trails) route around the St-Tropez Peninsula, *grande randonnées* (national hiking trails) GR51, known as the Balcons de la Méditerranée, and GR49 ascend the Estérel heights. The GR49 intersects with France's most spectacular grande randonnée, the GR4, which threads the Gorges du Verdon.

## RESTAURANTS

Restaurants in the coastal resorts are expensive and often a risky investment, as they cater mostly to crowds *en passage*. St-Tropez prices can be higher than prices in Paris. It's a fine town for a (staggeringly expensive) fish feast; however, it is home to one of the country's finest fish markets, just off the port. Inland, you can tap into a culture of cozy auberges (inns) in hilltop villages and have a better chance of finding good home cooking for your money. You can also judge how hard a restaurant is trying to please by the children's menu, which in the better restaurants goes beyond the standard *steak-haché* (bunless hamburger) and frites, sometimes offering gourmet grub such as roast lamb with scalloped potatoes.

In St-Tropez don't forget to try the *tropézienne,* a rich, pastry cream–filled brioche topped with grainy sugar, which provides yet another example of the French Paradox when you see the flawless bodies sprawled on the beach.

Around the Gorges du Verdon, a magnet for hikers and climbers, food becomes less of a priority—expect to find mostly pizzas, salads, and simple hikers' fare.

As a general rule, the curlier the printing on a menu the more pretensions a country auberge has; some of the best post only handwritten chalkboard menus.

## HOTELS

If you've come to this area from other regions in France you'll notice a sudden sharp hike in hotel prices skyrocketing to dizzying heights in summer. St-Tropez's rates vie with those in Monaco. You'll also notice a difference in decor: the look leans toward "le style Côte d'Azur," a slick, neo-Deco pastiche that smacks of Jazz Age glamour.

Up in the hills you can find the charm you'd expect, both in sophisticated inns and in mom-and-pop auberges; the farther north you drive, the lower the prices.

## VISITOR INFORMATION

For information on travel within the Var region—St-Tropez to La Napoule—contact the Tourisme du Var (Agence de Développement Touristique). For Cannes and environs, contact Côte d'Azur Tourisme.

For the Haute-Provence region between Moustiers and Manosque, contact the Agence Développement Touristique des Alpes de Haute-Provence. For the Verdon region, contact Parc Naturel Régional du Verdon.

**Contacts Agence de Développement Touristique des Alpes de Haute-Provence** ⊠ *Immeuble François Mitterand, B.P. 170, 8 rue Bad-Mergentheim, Digne-les-Bains Cedex* ☎ *04–92–31–57–29* ⊕ *www.alpes-haute-provence. com.* **Tourisme du Var** ⊠ *1 bd. de Strasbourg, Toulon* ☎ *09–63–61–78–70* ⊕ *www.visitvar.fr.* **Côte d'Azur Tourisme** ⊠ *455 promenade des Anglais-Horizon, Nice* ☎ *04–93–37–78–78* ⊕ *www.cotedazur-tourisme.com.*

# ST-TROPEZ AND THE MASSIF DES MAURES

Shielded from the mistral by the broad, forested mass of the Massif des Maures, this small expanse of pampered coastline is crowned by the sparkling lights of St-Tropez, itself doubly protected by the hills of the Paillas. A pretty pastel port in winter, in season it becomes glamorous "St-Trop." For day trips you can escape to the simple life in the hill towns of Ramatuelle and Gassin. Ordinary mortals, especially vacationing families on a budget, usually aim for Ste-Maxime, across the bay, where the hyperdevelopment typical of the Riviera begins.

## ST-TROPEZ

*35 km (22 miles) southwest of Fréjus; 66 km (41 miles) northeast of Toulon.*

At first glance, it really doesn't look all that impressive. There's a pretty port with cafés charging €5 for a coffee and a picturesque old town in sugared-almond hues, but there are many prettier in the hills nearby. There are sandy beaches, rare enough on the Riviera, and old-fashioned squares with plane trees and pétanque players, but these are a dime a dozen throughout Provence. So what made St-Tropez an internationally known locale? Two words: Brigitte Bardot. When this *pulpeuse* (voluptuous) teenager showed up in St-Tropez on the arm of Roger Vadim in 1956 to film *And God Created Woman,* the heads of the world snapped around. Neither the gentle descriptions of writer Guy de Maupassant (1850–93), nor the watercolor tones of Impressionist Paul Signac (1863–1935), nor the stream of painters who followed (including Matisse and Bonnard) could focus the world's attention on this seaside hamlet as did this one sensual woman in a scarf, Ray-Bans, and capris.

*Vanity Fair* ran a big article, "Saint Tropez Babylon," detailing the over-the-top petrodollar parties, megayachts, and Beyoncé–d paparazzi. But don't be turned off: the next year, Stewart, Tabori & Chang released an elegant coffee-table book, *Houses of St-Tropez,* packed with photos of supremely tasteful and pretty residences, many occupied by fashion designers, artists, and writers. Once a hangout for Colette, Anaïs Nin, and Françoise Sagan, the town still earns its old moniker, the "Montparnasse of the Mediterranean."

Yet you might be surprised to find that this byword for billionaires is so small and insulated. The lack of train service, casinos, and chain hotels keeps it that way. Yet fame, in a sense, came too fast for St-Trop. Unlike the chic resorts farther east, it didn't have the decades-old reputation of the sort that would attract visitors all year around. For a good reason: its location on the south side of the gulf puts it at the mercy of the terrible mistral winter winds. So, in summer the crowds descend and the prices rise into the stratosphere.

In July and August, you must be carefree about the sordid matter of cash. After all, at the most Dionysian nightclub in town, a glass of tap water goes for $37 and when the mojo really gets going, billionaires think nothing of "champagne-spraying" the partying crowds—think

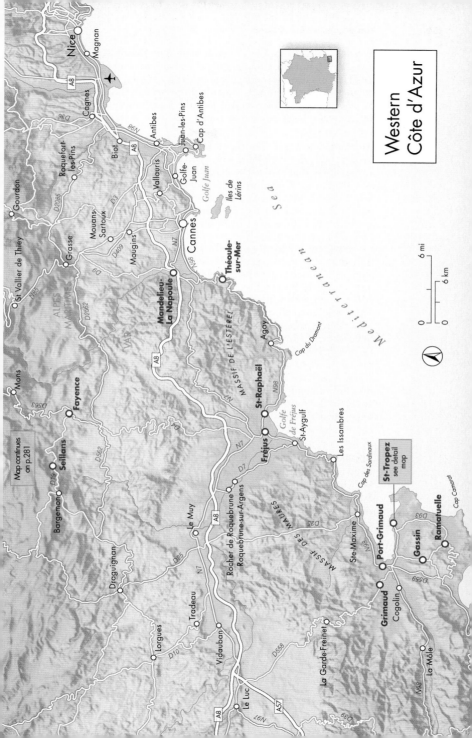

Western
Côte d'Azur

Map continues
on p.281

6 mi

6 km

0

0

Mediterranean Sea

Iles de
Lérins

Golfe Juan

Golfe
de Fréjus

St-Tropez
see detail
map

Nice

Magnan

Cagnes

Roquefort-
les-Pins

Biot

Antibes

Juan-les-Pins

Cap d'Antibes

Vallauris

Golfe-
Juan

Cannes

Théoule-
sur-Mer

Gourdon

St Vallier de Thiey

Grasse

Mouans-
Sartoux

Mougins

Mandelieu-
La Napoule

Agay

Cap du Dramont

St-Raphaël

Mons

Fayence

Seillans

Bargemon

ALPES
MARITIMES

VAR

MASSIF DE L'ESTEREL

Fréjus

St-Aygulf

Les Issambres

Cap des Sardinaux

Port-Grimaud

Gassin

Ramatuelle

Cap Camarat

Draguignan

Le Muy

Rocher de Roquebrune

Roquebrune-sur-Argens

MASSIF DES MAURES

Ste-Maxime

Grimaud

Cogolin

Lorgues

Tradeau

Vidauban

La Garde-Freinet

La Môle

Le Luc

A8

A57

N97

World Series celebrations but with $1,000 bottles of Roederer Cristal instead of Gatorade. Complaining about summer crowds, overpricing, and lack of customer service has become a tourist sport and yet this is what makes St-Tropez—described by the French daily newspaper *Le Figaro* as the place you can see "the greatest number of faces per square meter"—as intriguing as it is seductive. It is, after all, the hajj for hedonists.

Anything associated with the distant past seems almost absurd in St-Tropez. Still, the place has a history that predates the invention of the string bikini, and people have been finding reasons to come here since AD 68, when a Roman soldier from Pisa named Torpes was beheaded for professing his Christian faith in front of Emperor Nero, transforming this spot into a place of pilgrimage. Today, a different sort of celeb is worshipped. Take an early-morning stroll (before a 9 am pétit-dej at Dior des Lices) along the harbor or down the narrow streets—the rest of the town will still be sleeping off the Night Before—and you'll see just how charming St-Tropez is. There's a weekend's worth of boutiques to explore and many cute cafés where you can sit under colorful awnings and watch the spectacle that is St-Trop saunter by. Along medieval streets lined with walled gardens and little squares set with dripping fountains, you can discover historic delights like the Chapelle de la Misericorde, topped by its wrought-iron campanile, and Rue Allard, lined with picturesque houses such as the Maison du Maure. In the evening, everyone (well, at least those less flush) moves from the cafés on the quays to the cafés on the squares, particularly Place des Lices, where a seat at Le Café allows you to watch the *boules* players under the glow of hundreds of electric bulbs (paging Deborah Kerr and David Niven in *Bonjour Tristesse*). In the end, it's not too hard to experience what the artists first found to love and what remain the village's real charms: its soft light, its warm pastels, and the scent of the sea wafting in from the waterfront.

## GETTING HERE AND AROUND

Keep in mind that while St-Tropez can be heaven, getting there can be hellish. Out on a limb, scorned by any train route, you can only get to St-Trop by car, bus, or boat (from nearby ports like St-Raphaël). Driving a car can test anyone's mettle, thanks to the crowds, the narrow roads, and the Parking du Port parking lot (opposite the bus station on Avenue du Général de Gaulle, with shuttle bus into town mid-March to October) or the new Parc des Lices (beneath the Place des Lices) in the center of town. A train-bus connection can be made if you're leaving from Nice center: take the train (direction St-Raphaël) from the Gare SNCF Nice Centre-Ville station (✉ *Av. Thiers* ☎ *3635* ⊕ *www. voyages-sncf.com*), which costs €11.70 one way; from St-Raphaël, there's daily bus service with VarLib (☎ *04–94–24–60–00* ⊕ *www. varlib.fr*), €3 one way. Make sure you get to St-Raphaël's bus station early or you'll be elbowed out of a seat by aggressive bronzed ladies and forced to stand the whole way. Travel time from St-Raphaël to St-Tropez is 1½ hours. The other option is to take a 2½-hour boat from the Nice harbor with Trans Côte d'Azur (☎ *04–92–00–42–30* ⊕ *www. trans-cote-azur.com*), which has daily trips from June to September

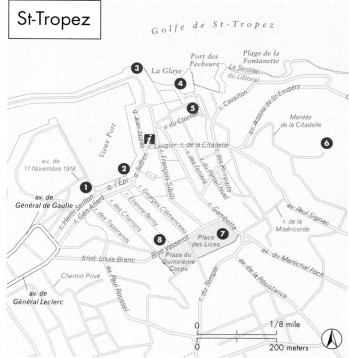

and costs €55 round-trip. If you decide to rent a car, take the N98 coast road, the longest route but also the prettiest, with great picnic stops along the way.

**VISITOR INFORMATION**

**St-Tropez Tourist Office** ✉ *Quai Jean-Jaurès, B.P. 183* ☎ *04–94–97–45–21* ⊕ *www.ot-saint-tropez.com.*

## EXPLORING

### TOP ATTRACTIONS

**Citadelle.** Head up Rue de la Citadelle to these 16th-century ramparts, which stand in a lovely hilltop park offering a fantastic view of the town and the sea. Amid today's bikini-clad sun worshippers it's hard to imagine St-Tropez as a military outpost, but inside the Citadelle's dungeon the modern **Musée de l'histoire maritime tropézienne** (St-Tropez Maritime Museum), which opened in 2013, proves otherwise with its stirring homage to those who served the nation. ✉ *Rue de la Citadelle* ☎ *04–94–97–59–43* 🎟 *Citadelle and/or museum €3* ⊙ *Apr.–Sept., daily 10–6:30; Oct.–Mar., daily 10–12:30 and 1:30–5:30.*

**Musée de l'Annonciade** (*Annunciation Museum*). The legacy of the artists who loved St-Tropez has been carefully preserved in this extraordinary museum, housed in a 14th-century chapel just inland from the southwest corner of the Vieux Port. Cutting-edge temporary exhibitions keep visitors on their toes while works stretching from Pointillists to Fauves to Cubists line the walls. Signac, Matisse, Braque, Dufy, Vuillard, and Rouault are all here, and their work traces the evolution of painting from Impressionism to Expressionism. Temporary exhibits feature local talent and up-and-coming international artists. ⊠ *Quai de l'Épi/Pl. Georges Grammont* ☎ *04–94–17–84–10* 🎫 *€6* ⊙ *Dec.–Oct., Wed.–Mon. 10–1 and 2–6.*

**Place des Lices.** Enjoy a time-out in the the social center of the Old Town, also called the Place Carnot, just off the Montée G.-Ringrave as you descend from the Citadelle. A symmetrical forest of plane trees provides shade to rows of cafés and restaurants, skateboarders, children, and grandfatherly pétanque players. The square becomes a moveable feast (for both eyes and palate) on market days—Tuesday and Saturday— while at night a café seat is as coveted as a quayside seat during the day. Heading back to the Vieux Port area, take in the boutiques lining Rues Sibilli, Clemenceau, or Gambetta to help accessorize your evening look—you never know when that photographer from *Elle* will be snapping away at the trendoisie. ⊠ *Av. Foch and Bd. Vasserot.*

**Vieux Port.** Bordered by Quai de l'Épi, Quai Bouchard, Quai Peri, Quai Suffren, and Quai Jean-Jaurès, Vieux Port is a place for strolling and looking over the shoulders of artists painting their versions of the view on easels set up along the water's edge. Meanwhile, folding director's chairs at the famous portside cafés Le Gorille (named for its late, exceptionally hirsute manager), Café de Paris, and Sénéquier are well placed for observing the cast of St-Tropez's living theater play out its colorful roles.

### WORTH NOTING

FAMILY **La Maison des Papillons.** A block west of Rue Clémenceau, in a pretty house at the end of a typically Tropezien lane, the butterfly museum is a delight for children (and their parents). Sweetly aflutter, the 35,000 specimens can be toured by appointment with the collector, Dany Lartigue. ⊠ *9 rue Étienne Berny* ☎ *04–94–97–63–45* 🎫 *€3* ⊙ *Apr.–Oct., Mon.–Sat. 2:30–6.*

**Quartier de la Ponche.** Past the Quai Suffern—a statue of the Bailli de Suffren, an 18th-century customs official, stands guard—the streets lead by famous cafés to the Mole Jean Réveille, the harbor wall, where, if the wind isn't too strong, you can walk out for a good view of Ste-Maxime across the sparkling bay, the hills of Estérel and, on a clear day, the distant Alps. Retrace your steps along the mole and quayside to the 15th-century **Tour du Portalet** and head past it to the old fishermen's quarter, the Quartier de la Ponche, just east of the Quai Jean-Jaurès. Here you can find the **Port des Pécheurs** (Fishermen's Port), on whose beach Bardot did a star-turn in *And God Created Woman*. Twisting, narrow streets, designed to break the impact of the mistral, open to tiny squares with fountains. Complete with gulfside harbor, St-Tropez's Old Town maze of backstreets and old ramparts is daubed in shades of gold, pink, ocher, and sky-blue. Trellised jasmine and wrought-iron birdcages hang from the shuttered windows, and many of the tiny streets dead-end at the sea. The main drag here,

Problems in paradise? St-Tropez may be a beaut, but it is outrageously priced, has hard-to-reach beaches, and doesn't have much public transportation.

Rue de la Ponche, leads into Place l'Hôtel de Ville, landmarked by a *mairie* (town hall) marked out in typical Tropezienne hues of pink and green. Head up Rue Commandant Guichard to the Baroque **Église de St-Tropez** to pay your respects to the bust and barque of St. Torpes, every day but May 17, when they are carried aloft in the Bravade parade honoring the town's namesake saint.

**Le Sentier du littoral** (*coastal path*). To experience St-Tropez's natural beauty up close, consider walking parts of the *Sentier du littoral* around the peninsula and all the beaches to Cavalaire-sur-Mer. Try the 12½ -km (7-mile) route to Plage de Tahiti and its longish stretches on sand beach, which takes an average of 3½ hours. Leave from the Tour du Portalet or the Tour Vieille at the edge of the Quartier de la Ponche. Follow the footpath from Plage des Graniers along the beaches and cliffs overlooking the water, often with views toward the Estérel or out to the open sea. At Tahiti beach you can walk the 3 km (2 miles, 50 minutes) back to town or continue another 5 km (3 miles, 90 minutes) along the Plage de Pampelonne to Bonne Terasse. From here it gets serious, with another 19 km (12 miles, 6 hours) to Cavalaire to complete the entire trail. But you'll need to plan ahead to catch one of the few buses back to St-Tropez. Otherwise, it's 18 km (11 miles) back to town. ⊠ *Tour du Portalet*.

### BEACHES

Despite the hip-to-hip commerce, piped-in pop music, and 30,000 beachgoers per summer day, the *plages* (beaches) around St-Tropez are the most isolated on the Côte d'Azur, providing one of the rare stretches where your back doesn't lean up against the coastal highway.

**La Bouillabaisse Beach.** This sand public beach as you enter town has free showers and toilets with lifeguard surveillance from mid-June to mid-September. Parking is free and you can rent loungers nearby. **Amenities:** lifeguards; parking (free); showers; toilets. **Best for:** swimming. ⊠ *Quartier La Bouillabaisse, RD98A.*

**New Coco Beach.** At this private beach, you'll spend €23 for a lounger but you should get some pretty awesome views and your feet should feel the spray of the Med as it tempts you to swim—or Jet Ski. **Amenities:** toilets; showers; water sports; food and drink. **Best for:** swimming; sunset; walking. ⊠ *Plage de Pampelonne, Rte. de l'Epi, Ramatuelle* ☎ *04–94–79–83–25* ⊕ *www.newcoco.fr.*

> ## LE LOOK
>
> As the crowds in St-Tropez prove, you can never be too rich, too thin, or too tan. There are still plenty of B.B. wannabes—not all of them female—who strut in skintight leopard skin, toting leopard-collared terriers, often with mates with their own canines on leads (only Golden Retrievers or Dalmatians, please!) and dressed in "Bon chic, bon genre" nautical togs.

**Nikki Beach.** Off the Route des Plages is this most notorious of all the beaches—famous for A-list debauches and a regular clientele of megamovie stars and nymphet wannabes (visualize spring break on stilettos). But Nikki Beach isn't actually on the beach, but rather steps from the beach with a pool and restaurant (with two toilets!). Rent a bed (€35), but you may want to avoid the pool side where champagne showers spare no one. **Amenities:** food and drink; parking (fee and free); showers; toilets. **Best for:** partiers. ⊠ *Rte. de l'Epi, Ramatuelle* ☎ *04–94–79–82–04* ⊕ *www.nikkibeach.com/sttropez.*

**Plage des Graniers.** The closest beach to the town of St-Tropez, at the southern base of the Citadelle and past the cemetery, Graniers beach is easily accessible by foot (it's part of the Sentier du littoral) and the most family-friendly. At the east end, you can rent loungers (€22 plus €7 for an umbrella) from the restaurant. There's free parking but no toilets or showers. **Amenities:** parking (free). **Best for:** swimming. ⊠ *Chemin des Graniers.*

**Plage des Salins.** Situated between Cap des Salins and Point du Capon, this 600-meter public coral beach is the gateway to a stretch of Pampelonne beach. It's lined by huge umbrella pine trees with free showers, toilets, and parking, and you can rent loungers from the beach's private section. Neighboring Crique des Salins is a fine-sand beach, and easier on the feet. **Amenities:** parking (free); showers; toilets. **Best for:** swimming. ⊠ *Route des Salins.*

**Tahiti Beach.** Welcome to Tahiti Plage, the oldest and most famous of St-Trop's private beaches (Bardot filmed along this stretch), with its fine-sand beaches, rentable loungers close to the shoreline, restaurants, and toilets. The crowd is definitely north of 35 but, as they don't act their age, there is lots to see in terms of hardly-there swimwear. **Amenities:** showers: toilets; water sports. **Best for:** swimming; walking. ⊠ *Quartier du Pinet, Ramatuelle* ☎ *04–94–97–18–02* ⊕ *www.tahiti-beach.com.*

## WHERE TO EAT

**$$**
FRENCH

✕ **Dior des Lices.** What could be more fashionable than tucking into cuisine crafted by three-Michelin-star chef Yannick Alléno in an enchanting sheltered garden designed by Peter Wirtz at the House of Dior? Dior des Lices serves a full breakfast, lunch, dinner, and snacks, with a range of reasonable prices, including set menus. Look for lobster and crunchy vegetable salad with garlic broth or linguine with cherry tomatoes, olive oil, and parmesan shavings. Terrifically, the dessert selection is as long the rest of the menu; the D'Choux (cute little round pastries), which come in salted caramel, pistachio, lemon zest, and more flavors, get rave reviews. By day the atmosphere is as playful as the outdoor ice-cream carousel and by sunset this magical oasis is perfect for a glass of champagne. $ *Average main: €24* ⊠ *25 rue François Sibilli* 🕾 *04–98–12–67–65* ⊕ *www.yannick-alleno.com* ⊗ *Closed Oct.–May.*

**$$$**
BISTRO

✕ **La Table du Marché.** This charming bistro, tearoom, and boutique from celebrity chef Christophe Leroy offers up a casual atmosphere, warm service, and a mouth-watering spread of regional specialties alongside a play on the classics: mini goat-cheese burgers, scrambled eggs à la sea urchin, and chocolate spring rolls with spicy caramel sauce. Lunchtime visitors can dive into a nicely balanced set menu or choose from a selection of goods seductively on display. $ *Average main: €29* ⊠ *21 bis rue Allard* 🕾 *04–94–97–01–25* ⊕ *www.christophe-leroy.com* ⊗ *Closed Jan.–Mar.*

**$$$**
BISTRO

✕ **Le Bistrot à la Truffe.** In 2013 "Emperor of the Truffle" Bruno Clément opened this truffle palace over three floors of a typical Provençal house just down the street from the church in St-Tropez. Only Bruno could revolutionize a simple oven-baked dish with cream of Tuber brumale (winter truffle), grated Tuber melanosporum (black truffle), and a dash of olive oil to create a meal of startling decadence. Chef Eric Barbes oversees the kitchen, providing scrumptious truffle feasts on two set menus (€69) and the brumale-melanosporum truffle-combo menu (€115), as well as à la carte options. The wine menu is as fabulous as the truffles; bottles start at €40. $ *Average main: €32* ⊠ *2 rue de l'Église* 🕾 *04–94–43–95–18* ⊕ *www.bistrot-la-truffe.com* ⊗ *No dinner Sun.–Tues. No lunch weekdays. Closed Oct.–Jan. (except Christmas).*

**$$$**
BISTRO

✕ **Le Café.** The busy terrace here often doubles as a stadium for different factions cheering on favorite local pétanque players in the Place des Lices. You, too, can play: just borrow some boules from the friendly bar staff and have your pastis bottle at the ready—you'll need it to properly appreciate the full experience. Hilarious "beginner" pétanque soirees are on tap Saturday nights in spring and summer. The food is not quite as good as the setting but varied (try the Provençal beef stew or traditional fish soup) and there's a well-priced lunch menu. Open daily from 8 am to 3 am, Le Café always seems packed, so reservations are strongly recommended. $ *Average main: €28* ⊠ *5 pl. des Lices* 🕾 *04–94–97–44–69* ⊕ *www.lecafe.fr.*

**$$$$**
SEAFOOD

✕ **Le Girelier.** Fish, fish, and more fish—sea bass, salmon, sole, sardines, monkfish, lobster, crayfish: they're painted on the walls and they fill the boats that pull into the Old Port before finding their way into the hands of chefs David Didelot and Laurent Simon, who've earned two Michelin stars. A buffed and bronzed clientele enjoy the casual

**DID YOU KNOW?**

Many of St-Tropez's charming, narrow streets were designed to break the impact of the fierce mistral winds.

sea-shanty atmosphere and highly visible Vieux Port terrace tables. Grilling (with a little thyme and perhaps a whisper of olive oil and garlic) is the order of the day here, with most fish sold by weight (beware the check), but this is also a stronghold for bouillabaisse. The lunch and set menus are bargains for this town, but otherwise you'll be surprised just how expensive fish per 100g can be. Service can be a little fishy, as everyone is treated like a tourist. [$] *Average main: €34* ✉ *Quai Jean-Jaurès* ☎ *04–94–97–03–87* 🌐 *www.legirelier.fr* 🕓 *Closed Nov.–mid-Mar.*

$$ BRASSERIE 🍴 **Le Sporting.** Be prepared for lively conversations at nearby tables and children not behaving as French children are reputed to, but it's all worth it for a lip-smacking plat du jour for €14.60. Pizza, pasta, burgers, and lamb chops are all served in generous portions and at reasonable prices, every day, all year long. The fixtures are nothing fancy—red awning, metal chairs, and typical café tables—but at least there's a place in St-Tropez that feels a little casual. [$] *Average main: €24* ✉ *42 Pl. des Lices* ☎ *04–94–97–00–65.*

5

$$$$ BISTRO Fodor's Choice ★ 🍴 **Le Suffren Café by Georges.** Too many restaurants in St-Tropez are like the fading celebrities that once made them famous, so the substantial Le Suffren is a welcome departure. Located in the Hotel de Paris St-Tropez, with an unusual interior of black granite slabs and bright yellow cushions and drapes, this dinner-only bistro orchestrated by 3-star Michelin chef Georges Blanc doesn't depend on people-watching in the port to distract you from the quality of the seasonal and market-fresh dishes. On offer are such hits as Côte d'Azur poached egg on gnocchi stuffed with crab and fennel, velvety spinach soup with shellfish and mushrooms, and the Hotel de Paris burger with dry-aged Iberian beef, cheddar cheese, and bacon. [$] *Average main: €39* ✉ *1 Traverse de la Gendarmerie* ☎ *04–83–09–60–00* 🌐 *www.hoteldeparis-sainttropez.com* 🕓 *Closed Jan. and Feb.*

### WHERE TO STAY

$$$ HOTEL 🏨 **Hôtel B. Lodge.** All the small, delicately contemporary rooms of this attractively priced, four-story charmer overlook the Citadelle's green park, some from tiny balconies. **Pros:** good deal for location; rooms without air conditioning are cheaper. **Cons:** minimum stay of four nights in July and August; with only two available parking spots, street parking is a sticky proposition; small rooms. [$] *Rooms from: €165* ✉ *12 rue de l'Aïoli* ☎ *04–94–97–06–57* 🌐 *www.hotel-b-lodge.com* 🛏 *15 rooms* 🕓 *Closed five weeks Nov.–Jan.* 🍽 *Breakfast.*

$$$$ HOTEL Fodor's Choice ★ 🏨 **Hôtel de Paris Saint-Tropez.** The first thing you'll notice when you walk into the lobby of this five-star urban hotel, spread over an entire block near the port, is space—a novelty for this tiny fishing port—and second you'll see a rooftop pool suspended 15 meters in the air, with its glass floor peering down at you. **Pros:** perfectly located; unique rooftop bar and pool with fab 360° views; world-class restaurant; special offer during Grande Braderie (sales) weekend in October. **Cons:** some rooms are small; breakfast needs some fine-tuning. [$] *Rooms from: €640* ✉ *1 Traverse de la Gendarmerie* ☎ *04–83–09–60–00* 🌐 *www.hoteldeparis-sainttropez.com* 🛏 *52 rooms, 38 suites* 🕓 *Closed Jan. and Feb.* 🍽 *No meals.*

$ HOTEL **La Belle Isnarde.** The Robert family has been greeting guests at this villa, just minutes from Place des Lices, since 1965, and while rooms are small, have thin walls, and are as basic as can be, they are clean, with hand-held showers, towels, and shampoo. **Pros:** lots of free parking; cheap rates for St-Tropez; €10 breakfast well priced for St-Trop. **Cons:** a 3-minute taxi to town costs €20; cash only; beds on the soft side. [$] *Rooms from: €100* ✉ *Début Route de la Plage Tahiti, B.P. 39* ☎ *04–94–97–13–64* 🌐 *www.la-belle-isnarde.com* 🛏 *11 rooms* 💳 *No credit cards* 🕒 *Closed Oct. 15–Easter* 🍴 *No meals.*

$$$$ HOTEL **La Résidence de la Pinède.** Perhaps the most opulent of St-Tropez's luxe hangouts, this balustraded white villa and its broad annex sprawl elegantly along a private waterfront, wrapped around an isolated courtyard and a pool shaded by parasol pines. **Pros:** discreet elegance at its best; stunning seascapes (although ground-floor sea-facing rooms may have only partial views); nicely decorated rooms (note the very plump and fluffy pillows). **Cons:** €5 for shuttle one way to town; for the price, some rooms are small. [$] *Rooms from: €1,050* ✉ *Plage de la Bouillabaisse* ☎ *04–94–55–91–00* 🌐 *www.residencepinede.com* 🛏 *32 rooms, 7 suites* 🕒 *Closed Oct.–Apr.* 🍴 *Some meals.*

$$$$ HOTEL **Le Byblos.** Forget five stars: this toy Mediterranean village grouped around courtyards landscaped with palms, olive trees, and lavender and guest rooms *à la provençale* but ultramodern in comfort has obtained "Palace" classification. **Pros:** exquisite service, service, service; the best buffet breakfast you could imagine (but €40). **Cons:** glitz wears thins; some rooms are small for the price. [$] *Rooms from: €855* ✉ *Av. Paul-Signac* ☎ *04–94–56–68–00* 🌐 *www.byblos.com* 🛏 *41 rooms, 50 suites* 🕒 *Closed late-Oct.–Easter* 🍴 *No meals.*

$$ HOTEL Fodor's Choice ★ **Lou Cagnard.** Set inside a lovely garden courtyard, this pretty little villa hotel is owned by an enthusiastic young couple who have fixed it up room by room; recent renovations include satellite TV and Wi-Fi (at no extra charge) in each. **Pros:** fantastic value for your money (try room No. 17); walking distance to everything; free parking. **Cons:** a few of the older rooms share a bathroom. [$] *Rooms from: €108* ✉ *18 av. Paul-Roussel* ☎ *04–94–97–04–24* 🌐 *www.hotel-lou-cagnard.com* 🛏 *19 rooms* 🕒 *Closed Nov.–Feb.* 🍴 *No meals.*

## NIGHTLIFE AND THE ARTS

### NIGHTLIFE

**Kelly's Pub.** This cozy pub is the place to enjoy live music and a pint of cider or Guinness all year long. ✉ *Quartier Frédéric Mistral* ☎ *04–94–54–89–11.*

**Le Papagayo.** Seeking light, action, and music with giddy determination, teens, twentysomethings, and Hollywood Venuses and Tarzans cram into the vast Le Papagayo, which anchors the end of a commercial and residential building called the Résidence du Port. ✉ *Résidence du Port* ☎ *04–94–97–95–95* 🌐 *papagayo-st-tropez.com.*

**Les Caves du Roy.** Costing the devil and often jammed to the scuppers, this disco in the Byblos Hotel is *the* place to see and be seen; it's filled with svelte model types and their wealthy, silver-haired fans. When you hear the theme from *Star Wars*, take comfort while you sip your €27 glass of tap water that someone other than yourself has just spent €35,000 on a Methuselah of Champagne. There's a horrific door policy during high season; don't worry, it's *not you.* ✉ *Av. Paul-Signac* ⊕ *www. lescavesduroy.com* ⊗ *Closed Nov.– Easter. Closed weekdays Apr.–June.*

**VIP Room.** So notorious is the VIP Room for drawing flashy, gilded youths with deep pockets that it spawned a VIP Room Cannes expressly for those that need a dose of film festival before it opens for the summer. ✉ *Residence du Nouveau Port* ☎ *06–38–83–83–83* ⊕ *st-tropez.viproom.fr.*

**ATTENTION: SHOPPERS!**

La Grande Braderie (annual end-of-season sale) takes place in St-Tropez over the last weekend of October, from Friday to Monday. Hit the shops from 9 to 9 with other fashion victims looking for the bargain you couldn't afford *en haute saison*. Be prepared for lots of walking and crowds, but at 50% off, who cares?

### THE ARTS

**Les Nuits du Château de la Moutte.** Every mid-July and August, classical music concerts are given in the gardens of the Château de la Moutte. For ticket information, inquire at the tourist office. ✉ *Chemin de la Moutte* ☎ *04–94–96–96–94 information* ⊕ *www.lesnuitsduchateaudelamoutte. com* ☞ *€45.*

### SPORTS AND THE OUTDOORS

Bicycles are an ideal way to get to the beaches.

**Rolling Bikes.** Rent mountain bikes at €22 for a full 24 hours. ✉ *14 av. Général-Leclerc* ☎ *04–94–97–09–39* ⊕ *www.rolling-bikes.com.*

### SHOPPING

There is something about St-Tropez that makes shopping simply irresistible—unlike Cannes, you'll be welcomed into the stores no matter what you look like or what you're wearing. **Rue Sibilli**, behind the Quai Suffren, is lined with all kinds of trendy boutiques, many carrying those all-important sunglasses. Tuck in behind here to Place de la Garonne for some extra hip purchases.

**La Chemise Tropezienne.** You'll turn more than a few heads wearing one of La Chemise Tropezienne's gorgeous beach kaftans or shirts, in all the colors of a Medterannean rainbow—which for this circa 1960s boutique includes white. ✉ *25 rue Gambetta* ☎ *04–94–79–59–75* ⊕ *lachemisetropezienne.com.*

**La Vieille Mer.** You probably will do more looking than buying here (unless you have a very large suitcase) but "The Old Sea" owner Walter Wolkowicz will put you in a time machine exploring navigational tools, lamps, and antique accoutrements of nautical yesteryear at his 100% marine shop. It's open daily from April to October, 10 am to 1 pm and 5 pm to midnight. ✉ *5 Pl. de l'Ormeau* ☎ *06–74–07–91–46* ⊕ *www. lavieillemer.com* ⊗ *Closed Nov.–Mar.*

**Le Dépot.** If you prefer traditional luxe, Le Dépot stocks castoffs by Chanel, Prada, Gucci, et al. ✉ *Espace des Lices, 7 Bd. Louis-Blanc* ☎ *04–94–97–47–93* ⊕ *leboudoirtropezien.com.*

**Place des Lices.** The aorta of the village, this congregational square overflows with produce and regional foods, as well as clothing and *brocantes* (secondhand items), every Tuesday and Saturday morning. ✉ *Pl. des Lices.*

**Fish Market.** The picturesque little fish market occupies the Place aux Herbes, just past the tourist office, every morning. ✉ *Pl. aux Herbes.*

**Rondini.** You wear those strappy flip-flops back home but are they the real *sandales Tropeziennes*? It's okay, we won't blow your cover, but here's your chance to pick up the real (and handmade) deal at Rodini, St-Tropez's original cobbler, launched in 1927. Did we mention they Fedex to the U.S. (€20)? ✉ *16 rue Clemenceau* ☎ *04–94–97–19–55* ⊕ *www.rondini.fr.*

**Vilebrequin.** In 1971 Fred Prysquel turned his swim trunk designs, sketched on the tablecloth at his favorite St-Tropez café, into Vilebrequin, a brand that now sells in 54 countries. His Golden Turtle designs, 24-carat-gold-embroidered swim trunks, start at $8,000. Each of the four Vilebrequin boutiques in St-Tropez is dedicated to a certain theme (for example, on rue Gambetta, one shop sells only solid colors while the other stocks only patterns), but it's at Place de la Garonne where you can truly hunt for gold. ✉ *1 Pl. de la Garonne* ☎ *04–94–43–33–46* ⊕ *fr.vilebrequin.com* ⊙ *Closed Nov.–Feb.* ✉ *24 rue Gambetta* ☎ *04–94–97–62–04* ✉ *9 rue Jean Mermoz* ☎ *04–94–97–67–12* ✉ *14 rue Gambetta* ☎ *04–94–79–81–30.*

## RAMATUELLE

*12 km (7 miles) southwest of St-Tropez.*

A typical hilltop whorl of red-clay roofs and dense inner streets topped with arches and lined with arcades, this ancient market town was destroyed in the Wars of Religions and rebuilt as a harmonious whole in 1620. Now its souvenir shops and galleries attract day-trippers out of St-Tropez, who enjoy the pretty drive through the vineyards as much as the village itself. After a morning at the beach, cool off at one of the cafés in the town's center. During high season, traffic jams can be spectacular between Ramatuelle and St-Tropez, inflating what should be a short drive into a three-hour crawl. From mid-June to mid-September, a daily courtesy bus (*navette*) will take you from the car parks to the top of the village. At the top of the village you can visit the Moulin de Paillas, on Route du Moulin de Paillas, a windmill restored in the old style with a mechanism made entirely of wood; the site offers a panoramic view of the coastline. Free guided tours of the windmill are held every week—check with the tourist office for times. The town cemetery is the final resting place of Gérard Philipe, an aristocratic heartthrob who died in 1959 after making his mark in such films as *Le Diable au Corps.*

### GETTING HERE AND AROUND

By car from St-Tropez, take the inland D93, then the D61. By bus, there are various routes from St-Tropez through VarLib (€3).

**EN ROUTE** From Ramatuelle, the lovely ride through vineyards and woods full of twisted cork oaks to the hilltop village of Gassin takes you over the highest point of the peninsula (1,070 feet).

### WHERE TO STAY

**$$$$** **Villa Marie.** With its circa-1930s feel, exposed beams, super-chic acid-
HOTEL toned walls, and jewel-colored upholstery, this Italian villa-cum-hotel continues to impress. **Pros:** gorgeous views; tasty food. **Cons:** tubs are in the middle of the rooms; thin walls; €32 breakfast; service doesn't quite match the five-star rating (and prices). $ *Rooms from: €380* ☒ *Route des Plages, Chemin Val de Rian* ☎ *04–94–97–40–22* ⊕ *en.villamarie.fr* 🛏 *45 rooms* ☽ *Closed Nov.–Mar.* ⦿ *No meals.*

## GASSIN

*7 km (4 miles) northwest of Ramatuelle.*

Though not as picturesque as Ramatuelle, this hilltop village gives you spectacular views over the surrounding vineyards and St-Tropez's bay. In winter, before the summer haze drifts in and after the mistral has given the sky a good scrub, you may be able to make out a brilliant-white chain of Alps looming on the horizon. There's less commerce here to distract you; for shops, head to Ramatuelle.

### GETTING HERE AND AROUND

From Ramatuelle, follow Chemin des Moulins de Paillas 5 km (3 miles). Otherwise you can take a VarLib bus (€3).

**EN ROUTE** **Massif des Maures.** The dramatic forest scenery of D558 winding west and northwest of St-Tropez (take the D98 towards Grimaud) merits a drive even if you're not heading up to A8. This is the Massif des Maures, named for the Moors who retreated here from the Battle of Poitiers in 732 and profited from its strong position over the sea. The forest is dark with thick cork oaks, their ancient trunks girdled for cork only every 10 years or so, leaving exposed a broad band of sienna brown. Looming even darker and thicker above are the chestnut trees cultivated for their thick, sweet nuts, which are not allowed to gather from the forest floor, as signs from the growers' cooperative warn. Between wine domaines' vineyards, mushroom-shaped parasol pines, unique to the Mediterranean, crowd the highway.

## GRIMAUD

*10 km (6 miles) west of St-Tropez.*

Once a formidable Grimaldi fiefdom and home to a massive Roman-esque château, the hill-village of Grimaud is merely charming today, though the romantic castle ruins that crown its steep streets still command lordly views over the forests and the coast. The labyrinth of cobbled streets is punctuated by pretty fountains, carved doorways, and artisans' gallery-boutiques. Wander along the Gothic arcades of the Rue des Templiers to see the beautifully proportioned Romanesque **Église St-Michel,** built in the 11th century.

### GETTING HERE AND AROUND

From Gassin follow the D61 for about 11 km (7 miles) to the D14 and take the D98 (which also takes you to St-Tropez). VarLib bus No. 7703 travels here from St-Tropez and Gassin (both €3).

### WHERE TO EAT

$$$ FRENCH 🍴 **Le Magnan.** Just 10 km (6 miles) west of St-Tropez and 4 km (2½ miles) south of Grimaud and the village of Cogolin, this bucolic old farmhouse looms on a hillside over forests dense with cork oak and chestnuts. Whether you eat on the terrace or in the rustic dining room, the food tastes and smells of the surrounding countryside: crispy baked St-Marcelin cheese with honey and nuts or grilled beef tenderloin, fried potatoes, and béarnaise sauce, nicely topped off with chocolate spring rolls and mango sorbet. Add the warm and friendly service and this is your dream French-restaurant experience. Choose from a three-course set menu (€38–€48) or à la carte. [$] *Average main: €26* ✉ *RN 98, 3085 Rte. de Cogolin, Le Môle* ☎ *04–94–49–57–54* 🌐 *www.lemagnan.fr* ⏲ *Closed Jan. No lunch Sun. and Mon. Closed Tues. in Dec.*

## PORT-GRIMAUD

*5 km (3 miles) east of Grimaud; 7 km (4½ miles) west of St-Tropez.*

Although much of the coast has been targeted with new construction of extraordinary ugliness, this, a modern architect's version of a Provençal fishing village, works. A true operetta set and begun only in 1966, it has grown gracefully over the years and offers hope for the pink-concrete-scarred coastal landscape. It's worth parking and wandering up the village's Venice-like canals to admire its Old Mediterranean canal-tile roofs and pastel facades, already patinated with age. Even the church, though resolutely modern, feels Romanesque. There is, however, one modern touch some might appreciate: from March to October small electric tour boats (get them at Place du Marché) that carry you for €5 from bar to shop to restaurant throughout the complex of pretty squares and bridges.

### GETTING HERE AND AROUND

From Gassin follow the D61 for about 11 km (7 miles) to the D14 and take the D98 (which takes you also to St-Tropez). The VarLib bus No. 7702 (€3) runs between Grimaud and the port, and there are other routes. From St-Tropez a Bateaux Vert ferry (€6.50; 20 minutes) to Port Grimaud runs from May to October.

### WHERE TO EAT

$$$ SEAFOOD Fodor's Choice ★ 🍴 **La Table du Mareyeur.** For Ewan and Caroline Scutcher, the honeymoon's definitely not over. The couple hasn't left Port Grimaud since they married here 25 years ago and set up this waterside gem, now reputed as one of the Riviera's finest. In a fun and relaxed atmosphere, they offer the freshest fish and seafood on the coast; certainly the politicians, royalty, and film stars (think Leonardo DiCaprio) who dine portside here amongst the locals don't complain. Selection is simple, uncomplicated, and the lunch menu, wine and coffee included, is a deal. Avoid traffic and ask Le Table to arrange for a water taxi upon reservation. [$] *Average main: €30* ✉ *10/11 place des Artisans* ☎ *04–94–56–06–77* 🌐 *www.mareyeur.com* ⏲ *Closed Dec.–Feb. (except at Christmas).*

## STE-MAXIME

*8 km (5 miles) northeast of Port-Grimaud; 33 km (20 miles) northeast of St-Tropez.*

You may be put off by its heavily built-up waterfront, bristling with parking garage–style apartments and hotels, and its position directly on the waterfront highway, but Ste-Maxime is an affordable family resort with fine, easily accessible, sandy beaches. It even has a sliver of car-free Old Town and a stand of majestic plane trees sheltering the central Place Victor-Hugo. Its main beach, north of town, is the wide and sandy La Nartelle.

#### GETTING HERE AND AROUND

Bateaux Vert ferries connect Ste-Maxime to St-Tropez in 15 minutes. By car, if you're coming from the A8, take the No. 36 exit (Le Muy) and follow the D25. From Fréjus take the RD25. From Grimaud, take the RD558. SNCF trains stop at St-Raphaël where you can connect with a VarLib bus (€3).

5

### WHERE TO EAT

$$$$ FRENCH 🍴 **La Badiane.** Sometimes the best food can be discovered at unpretentious restaurants tucked along a cobblestone lane, and this Michelin-star restaurant is a good example. Pedigreed chef Geoffrey Poësson set up the intimate La Badiane just steps from the local market, Marché Couvert, with only seven tables inside (two extra on the street terrace during summer) and no real views to speak of. All you can do is focus on the food, such as cannelloni with fennel, truffle, and foie gras baked in parmesan, and think about what you'll order next time. There's better value in the prix-fixe menus (€50–€85), as à la carte dishes start at €36 each. The dishes are fresh and the service discreet, but wine will set you back a minimum of €30 a bottle. [$] *Average main: €36* ✉ *6 rue Fernand Bessy* ☎ *04–94–96–53–93* 🕓 *Closed Sun. and most of Jan.–mid-Feb. No lunch.*

$$ FRENCH 🍴 **La Maison Bleue.** Cheerful blue-and-white-checked tablecloths, massive colorful throw-cushions, and a polished wood facade give this "blue house" on the main pedestrian street a welcoming air that matches the straightforward fresh pasta (tagliatelle pistou, ravioli, or gnocchi) and simple grilled fish dishes, accompanied by well-chosen local wines. [$] *Average main: €21* ✉ *48 rue Paul Bert* ☎ *04–94–96–51–92* 🕓 *Closed Nov.–Dec.; Mon. and Tues. Jan.–Mar.; Tues. Apr.–May and Sept.–Oct.*

EN ROUTE As you cling to the coastline on dramatic N98 between Ste-Maxime and Fréjus, you can see a peculiar mix: pretty beaches and fjordlike *calanques* (rocky coves) dipping in and out of view between luxury villas (and their burglar-wired hedges), trailer-park campsites, and the fast-food stands and beach discos that define much of the Riviera. The **Calanque des Louvans** and the **Calanque du Four à Chaux** are especially scenic, with sand beaches and rocks shaded by windblown pines; watch for signs.

# FRÉJUS, ST-RAPHAËL, AND THE ESTÉREL CORNICHE

Though the twin resorts of Fréjus and St-Raphaël have become somewhat overwhelmed by waterfront resort culture, Fréjus still harbors a small but charming enclave that evokes both the Roman and medieval periods. As you then follow the coast east, a massive red-rock wasteland, known as the Massif de l'Estérel, rears up high above the sparkling water. Formed of red volcanic rocks (porphyry) carved by the sea into dreamlike shapes, the harsh landscape is softened by patches of lavender, mimosa, scrub pine, and gorse. At the rocks' base churn azure waters, seething in and out of castaway coves, where a series of gentle resort bays punctuates the coastline. N98 leads to one of the coast's most spectacular drives, the Corniche de l'Estérel. And if you take N7, the mountain route to the north, you can lose yourself in the Estérel's desert landscape, far from the sea. The resorts that cluster at the foot of the Estérel are densely populated pleasure ports, with an agreeable combination of cool sea breezes and escapes into the near-desert behind.

## FRÉJUS

*19 km (12 miles) northeast of Ste-Maxime; 37 km (23 miles) northeast of St-Tropez.*

Turn your back on modern times—the gargantuan, pink, holiday highrises that crowd the Fréjus–St-Raphaël waterfront—and head uphill to Fréjus-Centre with its maze of narrow streets lined with butcher shops, patisseries, and neighborhood stores barely touched by the cult of the lavender sachet.

Fréjus (pronounced fray-*zhooss*) has the honor of having some of the most important historic monuments on the coast. Founded in 49 BC by Julius Caesar himself and named Forum Julii, this quiet town was once a thriving Roman shipbuilding port of 40,000 citizens. In its heyday, Roman Fréjus had a theater, baths, and an enormous aqueduct that brought water all the way from Mons in the mountains, 45 km (28 miles) north of town. Today you can see the remains: a series of detached arches that follow the main Avenue du Quinzième Corps (leading up to the Old Town).

### GETTING HERE AND AROUND

The direct bus from the Nice–Côte d'Azur airport (both Terminal 1 and 2) to Fréjus takes just more than an hour and costs €20. Arriving by train, you'll have to stop at St-Raphaël and take one of the several daily buses (€3; 15 minutes) that heads to Fréjus. A taxi for the same distance runs around €30. Fréjus's bus station is on Place Paul-Vernet and Estérel buses have routes to St-Tropez. By car, you are only 35 minutes from the airport on the A8 highway (take the No. 38 exit Fréjus/St-Raphaël). You can take the N7 or N38 for a more scenic drive but it takes a lot more time, particularly with summer traffic.

**VISITOR INFORMATION**
Fréjus Tourist Office ✉ *Le Florus II, 249 rue Jean-Jaurès* ☎ *04–94–51–83–83* ⊕ *www.frejus.fr.*

## EXPLORING

**Arènes.** The Arènes (often called the Amphithéâtre) is still used for concerts and bullfights, and can still seat up to 5,000. Back down on the coast, a big French naval base occupies the spot where ancient Roman galleys once set out to defeat Cleopatra and Mark Antony at the Battle of Actium. ✉ *Rue Henri Vadon* ☎ *04–94–51–34–31* ▣ *€2* ☉ *Oct.–Mar., Tues. and Thurs.–Sat. 9:30–noon and 2–4:30; Apr.–Sept., Tues.–Sun. 9:30–noon and 2–6.*

**Groupe Épiscopal.** Fréjus is graced with one of the most impressive religious monuments in Provence: The Groupe Épiscopal is made up of an early Gothic **cathedral,** a 5th-century Roman-style **baptistery,** and an early Gothic **cloister,** its gallery painted in sepia and earth tones with a phantasmagoric assortment of animals and biblical characters. Off the entrance and gift shop is a small museum of finds from Roman Fréjus, including a complete mosaic and a sculpture of a two-headed Hermès. ✉ *58 rue de Fleury* ☎ *04–94–51–26–30* ▣ *Cathedral free; cloister, museum, and baptistery €5.50* ☉ *Cathedral daily 8:30–6:30. Cloister, museum, and baptistery June–Sept., daily 10–12:30 and 1:45–6:30; Oct.–May, Tues.–Sun. 10–1 and 2–5.*

> **NEED A BREAK?**
>
> **Bar du Marché.** To drink in the atmosphere of Old Fréjus, settle under the shade of the great plane trees and listen to the sound of the fern-heavy fountain at the Bar du Marché. Here a *croque monsieur* (grilled ham and cheese toast), sundae, or apéritif will buy you time to watch the neighborhood putter through its daily rituals. ✉ *5 pl. Liberté* ☎ *04–94–51–29–09.*

**La Chapelle Notre Dame de Jérusalem.** The eccentric La Chapelle Notre Dame de Jérusalem was designed by Jean Cocteau as part of an artists' colony that never happened. It's an octagon built around a glass atrium and is embellished with stained glass, frescoes depicting the mythology of the first Crusades, and a tongue-in-cheek painting of the apostles above the front door that boasts the famous faces of Coco Chanel, Jean Marais, and poet Max Jacob. ✉ *Av. Nicolaï, La Tour de la Mare, 5 km (2½ miles) north of Fréjus on the RN7* ☎ *04–94–53–27–06* ▣ *€2* ☉ *Apr.–Sept., Tues.–Sun. 9:30–12:30 and 2–6; Oct.–Mar., Tues.–Sun. 9:30–noon and 2–4:30.*

**Théâtre Romain.** Northeast of Old Town and near the Porte de Rome is the Roman theater (circa 1st century); its remaining rows of arches are mostly intact and much of its stage, including the orchestra and substructures, are still visible at its center. Today the site is known as the Philippe Léotard Theatre and hosts Les Nuits Auréliennes every July. ✉ *Rue du Théâtre Romain* ▣ *€2* ☉ *Oct.–Mar., Tues. and Thurs.–Sat. 9:30–noon and 2–4:30; Apr.–Sept., Tues.–Sun. 9:30–noon and 2–6.*

### BEACHES

The urban beaches draped at the foot of Fréjus are backed by a commercial sprawl of brasseries, beach-gear shops, and realtors (for sun-struck visitors who dream of buying a flat on the waterfront). The beaches outside the city, however, are public and wide open, with deep sandy stretches toward St-Aygulf. The calanques just south are particularly wild and pretty, with only tiny sand surfaces. During high season, beaches are cleaned daily and lifeguards are on duty.

**Plage de Fréjus.** This large public sand beach, just east of the port is close to a restaurant where you can rent a lounger. Get here early in the morning to claim your towel space close to the sea; you'll be able to spot the tourists from the locals by the bottoms-only beach wear. **Amenities:** lifeguards; parking (paid); showers; toilets. **Best for:** sunrise; swimming. ⊠ *Bd. Alger.*

### SPORTS AND THE OUTDOORS

**Centre International de Plongée** (*International Diving Center*). Contact the Centre International de Plongée for instruction, equipment rental, and guided outings. ⊠ *Port Fréjus* ☎ *04–94–52–34–99* ⊕ *www.cip-frejus.com.*

## ST-RAPHAËL

*3 km (2 miles) east of Fréjus; 30 km (19 miles) southwest of Cannes.*

Right next door to Fréjus, with almost no division between, spreads St-Raphaël, a sprawling resort city with a busy downtown anchored by a casino. It's also a major sailing center, has five golf courses nearby, and draws the weary and indulgent to its seawater-based thalassotherapy. Along with Fréjus, it serves as a rail crossroads, the two being the closest stops to St-Tropez. The port has a rich history: Napoléon landed at St-Raphaël on his triumphant return from Egypt in 1799; it was also from here in 1814 that he cast off in disgrace for Elba. And it was here, too, that the Allied forces landed in their August 1944 offensive against the Germans.

### GETTING HERE AND AROUND

To take the Nice airport bus from either terminal, it's €20 for the 75-minute journey. If you take a taxi, it'll be around €160. The TGV Paris–St-Raphaël (4 hours 45 minutes; €125) runs throughout the year and there are numerous trains arriving from Nice and Cannes. St-Raphaël is the western terminus of the TER line that runs along the Riviera. To get to towns farther west, you have to take a bus from just behind the train station. If you want a day trip to St-Tropez, from April through October, there's a one-hour ferry ride (€14 one way or €23 round-trip) or a taxi for at least €100. From St-Raphaël's renovated bus station on Avenue Victor-Hugo next to the train station, the 7601 bus links up with St-Tropez (via Grimaud and Ste-Maxime, €3, 1½ hrs), some towns in the Haut Var, and selected stops along the coastal Corniche de l'Estérel. There are daily buses to Fréjus (€3), or take a taxi for about €20. Popular ferries leave from St-Raphaël's Vieux Port for St-Tropez, the Îles-de-Léerins, and the Calanques de l'Estérel.

## VISITOR INFORMATION

**St-Raphaël Tourist Office** ✉ *99 Quai Albert 1er* ☎ *04-94-19-52-52* ⊕ *www.saint-raphael.com.*

## EXPLORING

**Casino Barrière de Saint-Raphaël.** Looking out over the waterfront, catering to the city's many conventioneers, the casino's slot machines operate daily 10 am–3 am (4 am on Saturday), but the table doesn't open for play until 9 pm. ✉ *Sq. de Grand* ☎ *04-98-11-17-77* ⊕ *www.lucienbarriere.com.*

**Église Notre-Dame-de-la-Victoire.** Augmenting the Atlantic City vibe of this modern pleasure port is the gingerbread-and-gilt dome of the neo-Byzantine Église Notre-Dame-de-la-Victoire, which watches over the yachts and cruise boats sliding into the port. ✉ *Bd. Félix-Martin, 19 Rue Jean Aicard.*

**MARK YOUR CALENDARS**

Celebrated since 1984, France's national heritage weekend allows you free access to participating museums and sites that are often closed to the public. "Les Journées du Patrimoine" is usually the third weekend in September—see ⊕ *www.journeesdupatrimoine. culture.fr.* During La Nuit des Musées— ⊕ *www.nuitdesmusees. culture.fr*—usually on the second Saturday in May, hundreds of museums allow free entry from 8 pm to 1 am.

**Église San Rafeu.** Next to the Museum of Archeology in the Vieille Ville (Old Town), the 12th-century Église San Rafeu (also known as St-Pierre-des-Templiers) is a miniature-scale Romanesque church. It was recently discovered that its foundations lie on top of two other churches dating back to the Carolingian era. Climb up the 129 steps of the 13th-century bell tower, the Tour San Rafeu, for its 360-degree panoromic views and snap away. ✉ *Rue des Templiers* ⊙ *Tues.–Sat. 9–noon and 2–6.*

**Musée Archéologique Marin** (*Marine Archaeology Museum*). On the same quiet square as St-Pierre, shaded by an old olive tree, this intimate museum offers a quirky diversion. Its few rooms contain a concise and fascinating collection of ancient amphorae gleaned from the shoals offshore, where centuries' worth of shipwrecks have accumulated; by studying this chronological progression of jars and the accompanying sketches, you can visualize the coast as it was in its heyday as a Greek and Roman shipping center. The science of exploring these shipwrecks was relatively new when French divers began probing the depths; the underwater Leicas from the 1930s and the early scuba gear from the '50s on display are as fascinating as the spoils they helped to unearth. Upstairs, a few objects—jewelry, spearheads, pottery shards, and skulls—illustrate the Neolithic and Paleolithic eras and remind you of the dense population of Celto-Ligurians who claimed this region long before the Greeks and Phoenicians. A few of their dolmens and menhirs are still visible on the Estérel. ■TIP➔ **You can use QR codes throughout the museum as a guide; iPads and iPods can be borrowed from reception.** ✉ *Rue des Templiers* ☎ *04-94-19-25-75* ⊕ *www.musee-saintraphael.com* ⬛ *Free* ⊙ *Tues.–Sat. 9–noon and 2–6.*

Now *this* is what you came to the Riviera for! St-Raphaël has one of the finest beach strands along the coast.

## BEACHES

St-Raphaël's **beaches** form a snaking sliver of sand, starting just east of the port and finally petering out against the red cliffs of the Estérel, covering 8 km (5 miles) toward St-Aygulf, including one of the largest sandy beaches in the Eastern Var surrounded by a dune. Here you'll find a nudist beach (June to September) and an area where dogs on leashes are permitted. From that point on, you can find tiny calanques and *criques* (coves and finger bays) for swimming and basking on the rocks. During high season, beaches are cleaned daily and lifeguards are on duty at Plage du Veillat, Beau-Rivage, Péguière, Plage du Débarquement, Plage d'Agay, and Plage du Lido. Flags indicate the presence of lifeguards or if the water is dangerous for swimming.

**Plage Beau-Rivage.** This is the second public beach in the city center, located between Veillat beach and the port of Santa Lucia. It's divided into two areas, the sandy Handiplage and a large stone pebble beach, and there is a beautiful promenade, shaded by a park with a playground for kids and mini-golf. There are showers and toilets but you can't rent a lounger here. **Amenities:** lifeguards; showers; toilets. **Best for:** sunset; swimming; walking. ⊠ *120 bd. Raymond Poincaré.*

**Plage du Débarquement.** Named after the Allied landings in August 1944, this is a sand-on-top-of-red-stone beach with great views of the private Île d'Or. From town, head toward Agay until Dramont, where you'll see signs for the beach and free parking. **Amenities:** lifeguards; toilets; parking (free). **Best for:** swimming. ⊠ *1300 bd. de la 36ème Division du Texas.*

**Plage du Veillat.** This is the city's main and largest sandy beach, with lifeguard stations during the summer season, when you can also rent a mattress. There are lots of cafés around, and from the Old Port you can take a shuttle to St-Tropez. **Amenities:** lifeguards; parking (fee); showers; toilets. **Best for:** sunset; swimming; walking. ✉ *Corniche Roland Garros and Promenade René Coty.*

## WHERE TO EAT AND STAY

$$ FRENCH 🍴 **La Brasserie.** Chef Philippe Troncy created this authentic eatery with a reputation for being the best in and around town, evident by the capacity crowds. Whether you are seated under the magnolias on the summer terrace or in the newly decorated interior, this affordable fine dining will dazzle your palate. Favorites include poached cod and lobster, zucchini flowers with goat cheese and artichoke oil, and special pork ragout. [$] *Average main: €20* ✉ *6 av. de Valescure, intersection with Rue Marius Allongue* ☎ *04–94–95–25–00* 🌐 *labrasserietg.fr* ✍ *Reservations essential* 🕒 *Closed Sun. Closed mid-Dec.–mid-Jan.*

$$$ FRENCH 🍴 **Le Bouchon Provençal.** *Trés sympa* in decor and ambience, this well-respected local restaurant is a three-minute walk from the main strip to St-Raphaël's Old Town. A few years ago, it was profiled on "Les escapades gourmandes" on French TV, selected for its traditional *terroir* cuisine, as accentuated by the menu: cod crumble in a creamy chorizo sauce, lobster tail stew, and (on Fridays) the aioli façon Pastorel (€28), a famous mayonnaise dip. Lunch (€22) and dinner (€30–€38) menus change often and the wine list is heavy on the—you guessed it—Provençal side. [$] *Average main: €30* ✉ *45 rue de la République* ☎ *04–94–53–89–18* 🌐 *www.bouchon-provencal-st-raphael.fr* ✍ *Reservations essential* 🕒 *Closed Sun. and Mon.*

$$$ HOTEL 🏨 **Excelsior.** This urban hotel combining straightforward comforts and a waterfront position in the center of town attracts a regular clientele. **Pros:** minutes from the sea, train station, and bus station. **Cons:** smallish rooms; €9.10 a day at the public Parking Bonaparte; no amendments or cancellations with "promotional offers" bookings. [$] *Rooms from: €175* ✉ *Promenade du Pres. René Coty* ☎ *04–94–95–02–42* 🌐 *www.excelsior-hotel.com* 🛏 *36 rooms* 🍽 *No meals.*

$ B&B/INN 🏨 **Hôtel Thimothée.** This attractive 19th-century villa offers comfortable, well-priced rooms (the two on the top floor have poster-perfect sea views, worth the extra €29) as well as a lovely garden, where grand palms and pines shade the walk leading to a pretty little swimming pool. **Pros:** familial atmosphere and gentle hospitality; clean rooms and modern bathrooms. **Cons:** beach and waterfront cafés are a 20-minute walk away; really just an affordable place to lay your beach hat. [$] *Rooms from: €70* ✉ *375 bd. Christian-Lafon* ☎ *04–94–40–49–49* 🌐 *www.thimothee.com* 🛏 *12 rooms* 🕒 *Closed mid.-Dec.–first week Feb.* 🍽 *No meals.*

## SPORTS AND THE OUTDOORS

St-Raphaël is a serious sailing and boating center, with nautical complexes at four different sites along the coast: the Vieux Port, Santa Lucia (by Fréjus-Plage), Le Dramont (at the base of a dramatic little cape below the Estérel), and within Agay's quiet harbor.

To explore the wilds of the Estérel on foot, consider a guided hike led by a qualified staffer from the tourist office. Mountain biking is now discouraged in the Estérel for environmental reasons.

**Club Nautique St-Raphaël.** For information on boat rentals, windsurfing, or sailing lessons, contact the Club Nautique St-Raphaël, founded in 1927. ✉ *Av. du Général de Gaulle* ☎ *04–94–95–11–66* 🌐 *www.cnsr.fr.*

## THE CORNICHE DE L'ESTÉREL

Stay on N98 and you'll find yourself careening along a stunning coastal drive, the Corniche de l'Estérel, which whips past tiny calanques and sheer rock faces that plunge down to the sea. At the dramatic Pointe de Cap Roux, an overlook allows you to pull off the narrow two-lane highway (where high-season sightseers can cause bumper-to-bumper traffic) and contemplate the spectacular view up and down the coast. Train travelers have the good fortune to snake along this cliffside for constant panoramas. It's also a hiker's haven. Some 15 trails strike out from designated parking sites along the way, leading up into the jagged rock peaks for extraordinary sea views. (Don't leave valuables in the car, as the sites are littered with glass from break-ins.) For trail maps, ask at the St-Raphaël tourist office across from the train station. There is also a *sentier du littoral* (coastal trail), leaving from St-Raphaël port; you'll see a mix of wild, rocky criques and glamorous villas.

## THÉOULE-SUR-MER

*2 km (1 mile) south of La Napoule.*

Tucked into a tiny bay on the Golfe de Napoule, Théoule seems far removed from the major resorts around it. A sliver of beach, a few shops and villas, and magnificent views toward Cannes make it a pleasant home base for forays along the coast.

### GETTING HERE AND AROUND

By car, take the autoroute to exit No. 40 (Mandelieu-la-Napoule) and continue toward the RD6098 until your reach the sea road (*bord de mer*), then go in the direction of St-Raphaël.

### WHERE TO EAT

$ ITALIAN 🍴 **Nino's.** At the far southeast tip of Théoule's miniature bay, this unpretentious pizzeria serves simple Italian specialties—but, oh, what a setting. A few tables line a wooden "boathouse" porch directly over the lapping water, and at night the whole glittering necklace of Cannes reflects its luxurious glow over the bay. Good wood-oven pizzas, and pastas add superfluous pleasure. [$] *Average main: €16* ✉ *6 chemin Débarcadère* ☎ *04–92–97–61–11* 🌐 *www.pizzanino.fr* 🕒 *Closed Oct.–Easter.*

# MANDELIEU–LA NAPOULE

*32 km (20 miles) northeast of St-Raphaël; 8 km (5 miles) southwest of Cannes.*

La Napoule is the small, old-fashioned port village, Mandelieu the big-fish resort town that devoured it. You can visit Mandelieu for a golf-and-sailing retreat—the town is replete with many sporting facilities and hosts a bevy of sporting events, including sailing regattas, windsurfing contests, and golf championships (there are two major golf courses in Mandelieu right in the center of town by the sea). A yacht-crammed harbor sits under the shadow of some high-rise resort hotels. La Napoule, on the other hand, offers the requisite quaintness, ideal for a portside stroll, casual meal, beach siesta, or visit to its peculiar castle. Unless you're here for the sun and surf, however, these twinned towns mostly serve as a home base for outings to Cannes, Antibes, and the Estérel. In fact, the easternmost beach in Mandelieu dovetails with the first, most democratic beaches of its glamorous neighbor, Cannes.

### GETTING HERE AND AROUND

From Terminal 1 or 2 at Nice airport, take the A8 to exit No. 40 (about 30 minutes) or the 35-minute airport bus (direction St-Raphaël, €20). The closest train stops in Cannes, and you can either take a taxi (about €30 to the city center during the day) or catch the No. 20 bus from Cannes train station, departing frequently throughout the day, for €1.50.

### VISITOR INFORMATION

**Mandelieu–La Napoule Tourist Office** ⊠ *806 av. de Cannes* ☎ *04–92–97–99–27* ⊕ *www.ot-mandelieu.fr.*

### EXPLORING

**Château de la Napoule.** Set on Pointe des Pendus (Hanged Man's Point), the Château de la Napoule looms over the sea and the port and is a spectacularly bizarre hybrid of Romanesque, Gothic, Moroccan, and Hollywood cooked up by the eccentric American sculptor Henry Clews (1876–1937). Working with his architect-wife, Clews transformed the 14th-century bastion into something that suited his personal expectations and then filled the place with his own fantastical sculptures. The couple reside in their tombs in the tower crypt, its windows left slightly ajar to permit their souls to escape and allow them to "return at eventide as sprites and dance upon the windowsill." Today the château's foundation hosts visiting writers and artists, who set to work surrounded by Clews's gargoyle-ish sculptures. ⊠ *Av. Henry Clews* ☎ *04–93–49–95–05* ⊕ *www.chateau-lanapoule.com* ⊠ *€6, gardens only €3.50* ⊙ *Feb.7–Nov 7., daily 10–6, guided visits at 11:30, 2:30, 3:30, and 4:30; Nov 8.–Feb 6., weekdays 2–5, guided visits at 2:30 and 3:30; weekends 10–5, guided visits at 11:30, 2:30, and 3:30.*

### BEACHES

There are three private beaches nestled in between the public beaches, the major difference between public and private being, as it always is, a question of comfort. You can spend the extra euros for a comfortable mattress, access to shade, and the convenience of a nearby restaurant. On the public beach you have to supply your own comforts.

**Le Sweet.** A front-row lounger on the sandy beach at Le Sweet costs €17, which includes an umbrella as well as access to the locker room and shower, and in summer a lifeguard is on-site. There's beach-bar service and a restaurant that specializes in the catch of the day; the prêt-à-porter boutique sells both French and Italian swimwear. **Amenities:** food and drink; lifeguards; showers; toilets. **Best for:** sunset; swimming. ✉ *Av. General du Gaulle (near Av. de la Mer intersection)* ☎ *04–93–49–87–33* 🌐 *www.sweetplage.com.*

**BEATING THE EURO**

Check ahead to see where gas prices are cheapest en route at 🌐 *www.prix-carburants.gouv.fr.* This could save you some euros for that afternoon's village shopping.

## WHERE TO EAT AND STAY

$$$$ MODERN FRENCH 🍴 **L'Oasis.** A culinary landmark with two Michelin stars, this Gothic villa by the sea is home to Stéphane Raimbault—a master of Provençal cuisine who creates unexpected flavor collisions (think medallions of roasted blue lobster in a risotto of spaghetti *à la Puttanesca* or hazelnut venison with a pepper sauce and blueberries). A meal is accented with attentive service plus lots of extras in between courses; and few can quibble with the beauty of the famous garden terrace shadowed by gorgeous palm trees. The €98 menu shouldn't be dismissed. Le Bistro, upstairs, has earned a Michelin BIB designation for "good food at moderate prices" and offers excellent set menus Tuesday to Saturday for both lunch and dinner. Did we mention the cigar collection? [$] *Average main: €80* ✉ *6 Rue Jean Honoré Carle* ☎ *04–93–49–95–52* 🌐 *www.oasis-raimbault.com* ✍ *Reservations essential* ⏲ *Closed Sun. and Mon. Closed mid-Dec.–mid-Jan.*

$$$ SEAFOOD 🍴 **Le Boucanier.** Wraparound plate-glass views of the marina and château make this low-ceilinged room a waterfront favorite. For 30-plus years locals have gathered here for mountains of oysters and whole fish, grilled simply and served with a drizzle of fruity olive oil, a pinch of rock salt, or a brief flambé in pastis. If you're not a fish fan but want to experience the scenery, you'll also find pasta, pizzas, and steak on the menu. [$] *Average main: €26* ✉ *273 av. Henry Clews, Port de La Napoule* ☎ *04–93–49–80–51* 🌐 *www.boucanier.fr* ⏲ *Closed Dec. Closed Thurs. Oct.–Mar.*

$$$$ HOTEL 🏨 **Pullman Cannes Mandelieu Royal Casino.** As much a resort as a hotel, this modern waterfront complex with soundproofed rooms has deluxe comforts on a grand scale, with a broad beach terrace, outdoor pool, casino, restaurant, and access to the Old Course golf club next door. **Pros:** golf course–facing rooms are cheaper; free in-room tea- and coffee-making facilities plus complimentary half bottles of water replaced daily. **Cons:** €30 for a taxi to La Croisette in Cannes; not close to any shops. [$] *Rooms from: €300* ✉ *605 av. Général-de-Gaulle* ☎ *04–92–97–70–00* 🌐 *pullman-mandelieu.com* 🛏 *213 rooms* 🍽 *No meals.*

$ HOTEL 🏨 **Villa Parisiana.** In the residential neighborhood of La Napoule, about 500 feet from the waterfront, this impeccably kept hotel offers simple comforts, chenille bedspreads, and a few updated bathrooms. **Pros:** great value; owners speak English; just a few hundred feet from

Mandelieu–La Napoule train station. **Cons:** could be sticky in the summer months. [$] *Rooms from: €58* ✉ *152 rue de l'Argentière* ☎ *04–93–49–93–02* 🌐 *www.villaparisiana.com* 🛏 *13 rooms* 🕐 *Closed end Nov.–end Dec.* 🍴 *No meals.*

### SPORTS AND THE OUTDOORS

Classified as a *station voile* (sailing resort), Mandelieu–La Napoule is a major water-sports center.

**Centre Nautique Municipal.** For windsurfing and small sailboats, contact Centre Nautique Municipal, next to the restaurant La Plage and open all year round. ✉ *Av. du Général de Gaulle* ☎ *04–92–97–07–70* 🌐 *www.mandelieu.fr.*

**Golf Club de Cannes-Mandelieu.** The Grand Duke Michael of Russia founded the Riviera's first golf course in 1891, known familiarly as The Old Course. Officially it's the International Golf Club Cannes-Mandelieu and has two courses—one with 18 holes (par 71) and one with 9 (par 33), which are the most visually stunning courses in the south of France. The €90 green fee for 18 holes drops nearly 40% if you tee off after 5 pm. ✉ *Rte. du Golf* ☎ *04–92–97–32–00* 🌐 *www.golfoldcourse.com* ⛳ *18-hole course: 5749 meters. Par 71. Green fee: €90. Grand Duke: 9 holes. 2118 meters. Par 33. Green fee: €55.* ☞ *Facilities: Driving range, golf carts, rental clubs, pro-shop, golf academy/lessons, restaurant.*

**Plongée Passion.** Diving off the calanques between Fréjus and Ste-Maxime gives you interesting underwater insight into the marine life lurking in the rocks. Lessons and supplies for scuba diving are available year-round from Armand Ferrand, but you must reserve by phone or email in advance. ✉ *Parking de la Siagne, 606 Av. du Général de Gaulle* ☎ *06–17–94–35–77* 🌐 *www.plongeepassion-mandelieu.com.*

## THE HAUT VAR AND THE GORGES DU VERDON

The hills that back the Côte d'Azur are often called the *arrière-pays,* or backcountry, a catch-all term that applies to the hills and plateaus behind Nice as well. Yet this particular wedge of backcountry—north and west of Fréjus—has a character all its own. If the territory behind Nice has a strong Latin flavor, influenced for centuries by the Grimaldi dynasty and steeped in Italian culture, these westerly hills are deeply, unselfconsciously Provençal: wild lavender and thyme sprout on dry, rocky hillsides; the earth under scrub oaks is snuffled by rooting boars; and hilltop villages are so isolated and quiet you can hear pebbles drop in their mossy fountains.

The rocky swells behind Cannes and Fréjus are known as the Haut Var, the highlands of the département called Var. The untamed, beautiful, and sometimes harsh landscape beyond these hills lies over the threshold of Haute-Provence—itself loosely defined, more a climate and terrain than a region. The author Jean Giono, born in Manosque, evokes its landscape as windswept and often brutal, directly vulnerable to the mistral and the winds whistling down from the Alps.

It's possible to get a small taste of this backcountry on a day trip out of Fréjus or Cannes. On your way north you may choose to trace the steps of Napoléon himself, who followed what is now RN85, today named for him, on his tentative comeback from Elba Island in 1815. But many continue northward to tackle France's "Grand Canyon," the Gorges du Verdon. If you're a "The Sky's *No* Limit!" kind of traveler, you'll want to make the Grand Canyon du Verdon a notch on your own belt.

## FAYENCE

*36 km (23 miles) north of Mandelieu–La Napoule; 27 km (17 miles) west of Grasse; 30 km (19 miles) northwest of Cannes.*

The most touristy of all the hill towns in the Haut Var backcountry (all of which are called Pays de Fayence), Fayence is easiest to reach from the coast and often filled with busloads of day-trippers. Nonetheless, it has a pretty Old Town at the top, magnificent wraparound views from its 18th-century church down to the Massif des Maures and the Estérel, and a plethora of artisans' galleries and boutiques.

### GETTING HERE AND AROUND

There are no trains, but daily buses go from Cannes (No. 3002, 1 hour 20 minutes; €3) and Grasse (No. 3001, 1 hour 10 minutes; €3). It's an hour's drive from Nice airport—take the No. 39 exit (Fayence/Les Adrets) from the A8. A taxi to/from the airport will cost €110 (or €140 at night).

### VISITOR INFORMATION

**Fayence Tourist Office** ✉ *Pl. Léon-Roux* ☎ *04–94–76–20–08* 🌐 *www.paysdefayence.com.*

### WHERE TO EAT AND STAY

$$$ FRENCH 🍴 **Le Temps des Cerises.** Whether under the trellis at the gaily decked café tables or in the elegant, intimate beamed dining room, you'll find your *bonheur* (happiness) in this stylish and popular and centrally located restaurant. Owner/chef Louis Schroder maximizes on blending fresh Mediterranean produce with his Dutch origins. *Tarte tatin* of duck liver with cognac, John Dory with crushed hazelnuts in butter, and rack of lamb with olives are all served with surprising chic for the middle of a tourist town. Too bad about the trucks and motorcycles roaring past. [$] *Average main: €32* ✉ *2 Pl. de la République* ☎ *04–94–76–01–19* 🌐 *www.restaurantletempsdescerises.fr* ⏲ *Closed Tues. and Wed. Oct–Apr. Closed mid-Nov.–mid-Dec.*

$$ HOTEL 🏨 **Moulin de la Camandoule.** On 11 acres of stream-side greenery, this noble old olive mill has been turned into a lovely country inn—complete with beams, the original millwheel, and a *pressoir* (olive press) in the middle of the bar—presenting charming rooms, each uniquely decorated with a touch of Provence, quarry tiles, and Persian rugs. **Pros:** gorgeous viney grounds; outstanding service; minutes from village. **Cons:** try to avoid rooms in the squeaky duplex; three-night minimum stay from June to September; hard to find rates online. [$] *Rooms from: €108* ✉ *Rte. de Notre-Dame-des-Cyprés* ☎ *04–94–76–00–84* 🌐 *www.camandoule.com* 🛏 *9 rooms, 1 apartment* 🍽 *No meals.*

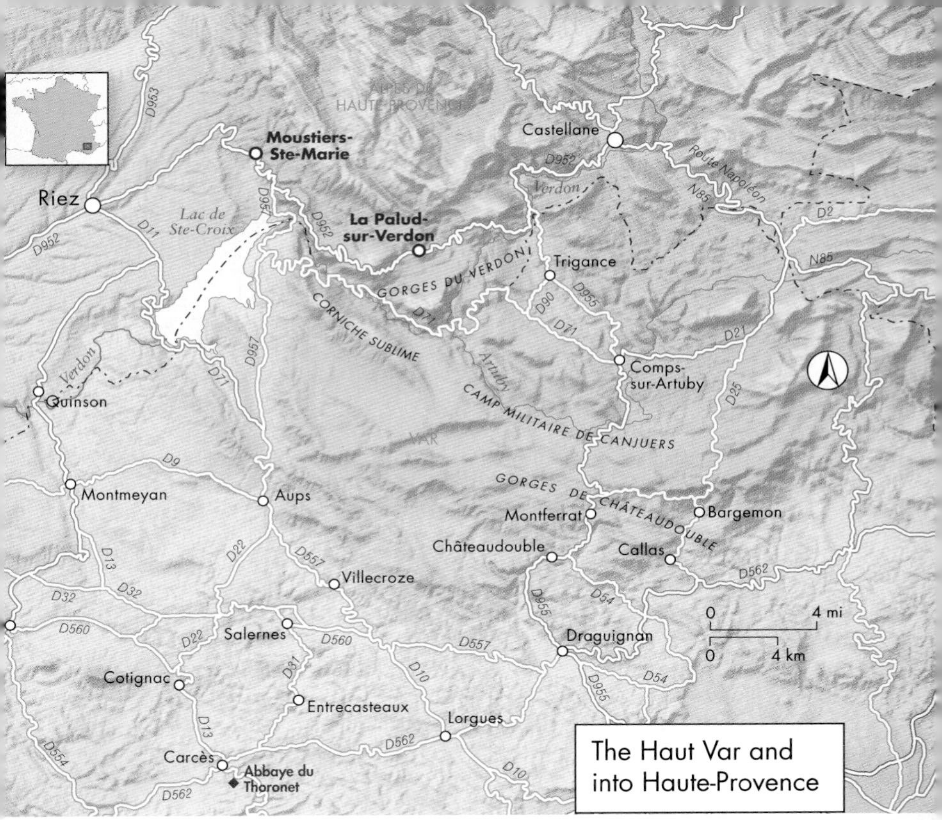


The Haut Var and into Haute-Provence

**$$$$** RESORT FAMILY

🏨 **Terre Blanche.** Keeping in mind this resort (until 2012 operated by Four Seasons) is larger than the Principality of Monaco, it's easy to see how one may be tempted to never leave the grounds: an outdoor 600-square-meter heated infinity pool, indoor ozone pool, 3,200-square-meter spa and fitness center, two golf courses, tennis courts, a kids' club with a home cinema, plus four dining possibilities. **Pros:** free newspapers and tea/coffee in suites; orthopedic or hypoallergenic pillows on request; free Kids' Club (Apr.–Oct.) for ages 2–12 with lots of daytime activities. **Cons:** need car to get here; breakfast not included in standard rate. [$] *Rooms from: €810* ✉ *3100 Rte. de Bagnols en Fôret, Tourrettes* ☎ *04–94–93–90–00* 🌐 *en.terre-blanche.com* 🛏 *90 suites, 21 villas* 🍴 *No meals.*

---

## SEILLANS

Fodor's Choice ★

*7 km (4½ miles) northwest of Fayence; 36 km (22 miles) northwest of Cannes.*

Voted one of "France's most beautiful villages" with its ruined château and ramparts, fountains, flowers, and sunny maze of steeply raked cobblestone streets that suddenly break open over valley views, this is a charming old town that still smacks of yesteryear's Côte d'Azur. Its church—a Renaissance remake of an 11th-century structure—is the best spot from which to admire the panorama; it's worth a pause to take in the musty Latin atmosphere. There are old-style, competitive bakers here, and an active café life on a miniature scale. The French opera composer Gounod and the surrealist Max Ernst were regulars in Seillans; Ernst retired here. Year-round guided tours (€2) of the town start from the tourist office Thursday at 10 and also Tuesday afternoon at 5 during the summer.

### GETTING HERE AND AROUND

From the A8 highway, take the No. 39 Fayence exit and follow the D37/Route du Lac to the D562, then follow the D19 into town. There are a few VarLib buses (€3) that can get you here from Cannes, Grasse, and even St-Raphaël.

### EXPLORING

**Notre-Dame-de-l'Ormeau.** Just east of town on the Route de Fayence is the Romanesque chapel Notre-Dame-de-l'Ormeau, which contains a remarkable altarpiece dating from the 16th century. Sculpted portraits of the wise men and shepherds adoring the Christ child, strikingly real in emotion and gesture, contrast sharply with the simple ex-votos that pepper the walls. Guided visits (€2) take place throughout the year Thursdays at 11:15 and also Tuesdays at 5:15 from mid-June to mid-September. In the winter season, you need to reserve with the tourist office. ⊠ *Rte. de Fayence* ☎ *04–94–76–85–91.*

### WHERE TO EAT AND STAY

$   ✕ **Tilleul Citron.** Stop by this delightful *salon de thé* for a *tarte salée* with
FRENCH   salad (€9) or for owner Pascale Raskin's specialty, panisse with melted goat cheese and figs compote with tomato salad (€12). Try one of their many teas with a yummy dessert or crêpe while you take in the local art on display in this old cork maker's shop. This spot is open for breakfast until 11:30 and right through 7:30 (6 in winter) at night, with a covered terrace and interior seating available. $ *Average main: €12* ⊠ *La Bouchonnerie, Rue de la Capelette* ☎ *04–94–50–47–64* ⊗ *Closed Tues. (and Mon. Mar.–Apr. and Oct.–Dec.). Closed Jan. and Feb.*

$   ⛉ **Hôtel des Deux Rocs.** Picture a tiny square with a trickling fountain,
HOTEL   venerable plane trees, green valley views, and two massive rocks posing, sculpturelike, where they fell aeons ago: a magical place for a hotel. **Pros:** fab old stone house with modern decor; great food. **Cons:** little ventilation in rooms; damp in rainy weather. $ *Rooms from: €80* ⊠ *Pl. Font d'Amont* ☎ *04–94–76–87–32* ⊕ *www.hoteldeuxrocs.com* ⛒ *13 rooms* ⊗ *Closed Jan.–mid-Feb.* ⛘ *No meals.*

## LA PALUD-SUR-VERDON

*48 km (30 miles) northwest of Seillans.*

Though several towns bill themselves as *the* gateway to the Gorges du Verdon, this unassuming village stands in its center, on a plateau just north of the gorge's vertiginous drop (to gain the Gorges's southern flank, enter from the elegant village of Moustiers). It's a hikers' and climbers' town, and—as the Germans and Dutch are more *sportif* than the French—has an international feel. You'll see more beards and

Volkswagen vans here than anywhere in France, and you'll probably share a café terrace with backpackers clad in boots and fleece easing off a load of ropes, picks, and cleats.

### GETTING HERE AND AROUND

Coming by car (your best option) from the coast, take the A8 highway, get off at the Draguignan exit, then follow the D955 north(ish) past Comps-sur-Artuby to the D952, which you can follow west along a demanding drive—keep your eyes on the road.

### VISITOR INFORMATION

**Le Bureau des Guides du Verdon.** Guides can be arranged through Le Bureau des Guides du Verdon. ✉ *Rue Grande* ☎ *04–92–77–30–50* ⊕ *www.escalade-verdon.fr.* **Maison des Gorges du Verdon.** Maps and information on the Gorges are available from the park's tourist office. ✉ *Le Château* ☎ *04–92–77–32–02* ⊕ *www.lapaludsurverdon.com.*

### EXPLORING

**Gorges du Verdon.** You are here for one reason only: to explore the extraordinary Gorges du Verdon, also known as—with only slight exaggeration over another, more famous version—the Grand Canyon. Through the aeons the jewel-green torrent of the Verdon River has chiseled away the limestone plateau and gouged a spectacular gorge lined with steep white cliffs and sloping rock falls carpeted with green forest. The jagged rock bluffs, roaring water, and dense wild boxwood create a savage world of genuinely awe-inspiring beauty, whether viewed from dozens of cliff-top overlooks or explored from the wilderness below.

If you're driving from La Palud, follow the dramatic **Route des Crêtes** circuit (D23), a white-knuckle cliff-hanger not for the faint of heart. When you approach and leave La Palud, you'll do it via D952 between Castellane and Moustiers, with several breathtaking overlooks. The best of these is the **Point Sublime,** at the east end; leave your car by the hotel-restaurant and walk to the edge, holding tight to dogs and children—that's a 2,834-foot drop to the bottom. You can also access the famous drive along D71 called the **Route de la Corniche Sublime** from Moustiers: top lookout points here are the Horserider's Cliff, the Balcon de la Mescla, and the Pont de l'Artuby bridge.

If you want to hike, there are several trails that converge in this prime territory. The most spectacular is the branch of the GR4 that follows the bed of the canyon itself, along the **Sentier Martel.** This dramatic trail, beginning at the Chalet de la Maline and ending at the Point Sublime, was created in the 1930s by the Touring-Club de France and named for one of the gorge's first explorers. Easier circuits leave from the Point Sublime on *sentiers de découverte* (trails with commentary) into the gorge known as Couloir Samson.

### WHERE TO STAY

$ 🍽 **Hotel des Gorges du Verdon.** At an altitude of 3,000 feet, this *logis de France* has panoramas from the breakfast table of La Palud's countryside that will have you chewing mighty fast to head out the door. **Pros:** kid alert: Ping-Pong table, boules, tennis, heated pool; hiking kits with lunch option can be purchased. **Cons:** some rooms are small;

HOTEL
FAMILY

semi-pension option a little expensive at €30 but food is delicious. [$] *Rooms from: €186* ✉ *Rt. de la Maline* ☎ *04–92–77–38–26* 🌐 *www.hotel-des-gorges-du-verdon.fr* 🛏 *27 room, 3 suites* 🕓 *Closed mid-Oct.–Easter* 🍴 *No meals.*

$ B&B/INN 🏨 **Le Perroquet Vert.** In a restored 18th-century house on La Palud's only street, this lovely little sports store-cum-restaurant-cum-B&B complex is run by the charming Christine and Olivier. **Pros:** fine bargain prices; demi-pension for €29 possible. **Cons:** two rooms only; parking in village. [$] *Rooms from: €60* ✉ *Rue Grande* ☎ *04–92–77–33–39* 🌐 *www.leperroquetvert.com* 🛏 *1 room, 1 duplex* 🕓 *Closed Oct.–Apr.* 🍴 *No meals.*

### SPORTS AND THE OUTDOORS

If you're not up to hiking the Sentier Martel, there are other ways of embracing the Gorges.

**Aboard Rafting.** For those interested in rafting in the Gorges du Verdon, excursions run from two to five-plus hours (€33 to €75, respectively). You can also try canoe-rafting or canyoning, and for younger members of the family there's the Adventure Rope Course (3 hours; €25). ✉ *Castellane* ☎ *04–92–83–76–11* 🌐 *www.aboard-rafting.com.*

**La Maison du Canyoning et de l'Escalade.** Want to try canyoning or climbing? Contact La Maison du Canyoning et de l'Escalade from May to September for guided outings, varying from 90 minutes (€35) to full-day excursions (€110). Minimum age participation is 7; you may be asked to bring a lunch. ✉ *04–92–83–39–73* 🌐 *www.maisonducanyoning.fr.*

**Latitude Challenge.** For a completely different perspective of the Verdon, this Marseilles-based outfitter offers bungee jumping (*saut à l'elastique*) all year round starting from €105. ☎ *04–91–09–04–10* 🌐 *www.latitude-challenge.fr.*

**Provisto.** Leave the hassle of driving these hair-raising roads to someone else. Provisto gives a four-hour minibus tour of the region for up to eight people. ☎ *04–92–74–50–53* 🌐 *provisito.fr.*

## MOUSTIERS-STE-MARIE

Fodor's Choice ★ *10 km (7 miles) northwest of La Palud-sur-Verdon.*

At the edge of all this epic wilderness, it's a bit of a shock to find this picture-perfect village tucked into a spectacular cleft in vertical cliffs, its bluffs laced with bridges, draped with medieval stone houses, and crowned with church steeples. The Verdon gushes out of the rock at the village's heart, and between the two massive rocks that tower over the ensemble, a star swings suspended from a chain.

To most, the name *Moustiers* means faience, the fine, glazed earthenware that has been produced here since the 17th century, when a monk brought in the secret of enamel glazes from Faenza in Umbria. Its brilliant white finish caught the world's fancy, especially when the fashionable grotesques of Jean Berain, decorator to Louis XIV, were imitated and produced in exquisite detail. A colony of ceramists still creates Moustiers faience today, from large commercial producers to independent artisans.

**CLOSE UP**

# The Sentier Martel: Trial by Trail

**THE MAIN SHOW**

Threading the Grand Canyon du Verdon is one of France's greatest hiking routes: the Sentier Martel, named in honor of the spelunker-explorer Edouard Martel (1859–1938), who first penetrated the Gorges in 1896 with a canvas canoe, an assistant, and two local trout fishermen. Despite repeated attempts, he didn't manage to negotiate the full canyon's length until 1905.

It was in the 1930s that the Touring Club blasted fire-escape-style ladders and catwalks along the precarious rock walls, and drilled two tunnels through solid stone. They added occasional rope railings and steps, buttressed the trail with rock supports, and one of France's most famous hikes was born.

**MARTEL MUSTS**

It's best to depart from the **Châlet de la Maline** (the Refuge des Malines), striking out on the long descent and then working your way back up gradually to the **Couloir du Samson** and the Point Sublime (D952). Park your car past the Refuge and canteen, 8 km (5 miles) from La Palud-sur-Verdon, and walk 300 yards to the starting point of your descent, just left of the **Refuge des Malines**. Follow the white and red markings along the way (an X indicates the wrong path; an arrow indicates a change in direction).

You'll encounter all types of terrain—pebbles, stone, muddy soil—and sliding down rocks on your buttocks is not out of the question, especially when the alternative is tumbling down, down, and down. Forget about setting a world record and stop to enjoy lunch along the way to take your eyes off your feet

and appreciate the magnificence of the surroundings. Once you exit the tunnels and cross a small bridge, you'll reach the Parking du Couloir Samson but even this is not the final destination. Cross the pavement and continue left to finish the final ascent to **Point Sublime**. Markings here are not as visible but paths are solid soil and you will eventually make it to the top, a rugged terrain where the less daring stop to simply take photos. Have the €3 ready for a nice cold beverage at the only canteen.

**WORDS OF WARNING**

As the Verdon is regulated by two dams, you'll often be confronted with not-so-comforting signs showing a human stick figure running for his life before a tidal wave. This is to warn you to stick to the trail and not linger on the beachlike riverbed when the water is low, as it could rise suddenly at any moment. Remember a flashlight with good batteries; you won't be able to grope your way through the tunnels without it. And be prepared for wet feet—ankle-deep puddles are unavoidable. Dial 112 if you have an emergency.

**WHERE TO PARK?**

A taxi pickup at Point Sublime needs to be arranged the night prior for the 14-km (9-mile) return ride, based on a rough estimate of your own abilities; or leave a car at the final destination and ask a taxi (in advance) to carry you to your takeoff point. The best taxi is **Taxi Verdun** (☎ 06–68–18–13–13). Navettes run only in July and August. With so many other hikers you can also try asking for a lift (*faire du pouce*).

5

While a hot restaurant scene has made Moustiers-Ste-Marie newly fashionable, the town has been a byword for the finest in faience and pottery for centuries.

Every few years (dates are not carved in pottery) the village celebrates the Fete de la Cité de la Faïence over three days in late spring with movies, dancing, walks, faience demonstrations, and, of course, food and apéros.

### GETTING HERE AND AROUND

There's a summer bus from Manosque that takes 90 minutes, but the bigger problem is that there is no shuttle up to the village, so a car is your best bet. From the Côte d'Azur by car take the A8 highway, exit direction "Draguignan," then "Aups, Les Salles" to Moustiers, found just off D952 (a 90-minute drive from Fréjus). There's a bus from Nice to Castellane, and a connecting bus, the LER 27, goes to Moustiers (€7.10; 90 minutes).

### VISITOR INFORMATION

**Moustiers Tourist Office** ⌂ *Place de l'Église, Moustiers* ☎ *04–92–74–67–84* ⊕ *www.moustiers.fr.*

### EXPLORING

**Chapelle Notre-Dame-de-Beauvoir.** Moustiers was founded as a monastery in the 5th century, but it was in the Middle Ages that the Chapelle Notre-Dame-de-Beauvoir (first known as d'Entreroches, or "between rocks") became an important pilgrimage site. You can still climb the steep cobbled switchbacks along with pilgrims, passing modern stations-of-the-cross panels in Moustiers faïence. From the porch of the 12th-century church, remodeled in the 16th century, you can look over the roofs of the village to the green valley, a patchwork of olive groves and red-tiled farmhouse roofs. The forefather of the star that swings in the wind over the village was first hung, it is said, by a crusader grateful for his release from Saracen prison. It takes about 15 minutes to climb the stairs, but remember, what goes up must come down—these worn stone steps yield little traction, so be careful. ✉ *Moustiers.*

**Musée de la Faïence.** The small but excellent Musée de la Faïence has concise audiovisual explanations of the craft and displays a chronology of fine pieces. It is currently housed in a pretty 18th-century *hôtel particulier* (private mansion) with a lovely *salle de mariage* (wedding hall) lined in painted canvas. **TIP→ The museum is currently closed for renovation and scheduled to reopen in 2014.** ✉ *Pl. du Tricentenaire* ☎ *04–92–74–61–64* 🎟 *€3.*

**Route de la Corniche Sublime.** Despite its civilized airs, Moustiers is another gateway to the Gorges du Verdon, providing the best access to the southern bank and the famous drive along D71 called the Route de la Corniche Sublime. (Also, the scenic 23-km [14-mile] route along the northern ridge, Route des Crêtes along the D23, starts at Castellane and has no fewer than 14 belvederes as it cuts through ridges of the canyon.) Breathtaking views over withering drop-offs punctuate this vertiginous road that's just wide enough for two cars if you all hold your breath. The best of the vistas is called the **Balcons de la Mescla,** with viewpoints built into the cliff face overlooking the torrential whirlpool where the Verdon and Artuby combine. ✉ *Moustiers.*

5

## WHERE TO STAY

$ HOTEL 🏨 **Hôtel les Restanques.** Only a five-minute walk from the village, this motel-style building offers excellent value and has spacious, crispy clean rooms, some of which open on to a terrace. **Pros:** beds in fab condition; friendly service; free parking. **Cons:** ask for a room not facing pool. [$] *Rooms from: €104* ✉ *Rte. des Gorges du Verdon* ☎ *04–92–74–93–93* 🌐 *www.hotel-les-restanques.com* 🛏 *18 rooms, 2 suites* 🕒 *Closed Nov. 15–Mar. 15* 🍴 *No meals.*

$$$$ HOTEL Fodor's Choice ★ 🏨 **La Bastide de Moustiers.** Gourmands from around the world flock to this lovely 17th-century *bastide* (country house) transformed by Alain Ducasse into a luxury country retreat surrounded by olive and chestnut trees, cypress, lavender, and trellises filled with the blooms of creeping rose bushes. **Pros:** astronomical bliss; the hotel was completely renovated in 2013. **Cons:** not within easy walking distance of village. [$] *Rooms from: €260* ✉ *Chemin de Quinson* ☎ *04–92–70–47–47* 🌐 *www.bastide-moustiers.com* 🛏 *110 rooms, 1 suites* 🕒 *Closed Jan. and Feb.* 🍴 *No meals.*

$$ B&B/INN 🏨 **La Bouscatière.** Only the most discreet little sign indicates the presence of this exceptional bed-and-breakfast, whose different levels are built down into the rock rather than upwards, offering views of the waterfall and unlikely little terraces (one is accessed through the bathroom). **Pros:** romantic decadence in the heart of a village; you'll feel like part of the family. **Cons:** room access could be a challenge if you have mobility problems. [$] *Rooms from: €140* ✉ *Chemin Marcel Provence* ☎ *04–92–74–67–67* 🌐 *www.labouscatiere.com* 🛏 *4 rooms* 🍴 *No meals.*

## SHOPPING

**L'Atelier Soleil.** At this shop next to the Bastide de Moustiers, second-generation potter Franck Scherer makes custom-made plates for Alain Ducasse's auberges. You can visit the workshop and buy pieces with tiny flaws at a reduced price. ✉ *Chemin de Quinson* ☎ *04–92–74–63–05* ⊕ *www.ateliersoleil.fr.*

**Le Souquet.** Stock up on local olive oils, soaps, fresh herbs, and tea at funky Le Souquet. ✉ *Rue Marcel Provence* ☎ *06–82–68–84–55* ☉ *Closed Oct.–Jan.*

# NICE AND THE EASTERN CÔTE D'AZUR

Cannes, Antibes, and the Hill Towns

# WELCOME TO NICE AND THE EASTERN CÔTE D'AZUR

## TOP REASONS TO GO

★ **Picasso and Company:** Because artists have long loved the Côte d'Azur, it is blessed with superb art museums, including the Fondation Maeght in St-Paul and the Musée Picasso in Antibes.

★ **Èze, island in the sky:** The most perfectly perched of the coast's *villages perchés*, Èze has some of the most breathtaking views this side of a NASA space capsule.

★ **Nice, Queen of the Riviera:** With its bonbon-color palaces, blue Baie des Anges, time-stained Old Town, and Musée Matisse, this is one of France's most colorful cities.

★ **Sun-kissed Cap d'Antibes:** Bordering well-hidden mansions and zillion-dollar hotels, the Sentier Tirepoil is a spectacular footpath along the sea.

**1 Cannes.** Conspicuous consumption, glamorous fanfare, and a host of wannabes characterize the celluloid city of Cannes when its May film fest turns it into a global frat party. But the Louis Vuitton set enjoys this city year-round.

**2 The Pays Grassois.**
A crossbreed of the Alps and Provence, this area has striking hamlets such as Gourdon that cling to a 760-meter (2,500-foot) steep cliff and center around the perfume capital of Grasse. Retrace the steps along Route Napoleon as taken by the Emperor in 1815 on his return from exile crossing Mouans Sartoux to St-Vallier-de-Thiey up to Escragnolles at 1,040 meters (3,412 feet).

**4 The Hill Towns: St-Paul and Vence.** High in the hills overlooking Nice are the medieval walled villages of St-Paul and Vence, invaded by waves of artists in the 20th century. Today, you can hardly turn around without bumping into a Calder mobile, and top sights include the famous inn La Colombe d'Or and Matisse's sublime Chapelle du Rosaire.

**3 Antibes and Environs.**
Antibes is home to one of region's leading yachting ports. When you're done gawking at $475-million yachts in Port Vauban, end-less cobblestone streets beckon you to explore inside the ramparts. The 5-km (3-mile) Sentier Tire-poil bordering the Cap is steps away, as are the sand beaches in Juan-les-Pins.

**5 Nice.** Walking along the seaside Promenade des Anglais is one of the iconic Riviera experiences. Add in top-notch museums, a charming old quarter open till all hours, scads of ethnic restaurants, and an agenda of first-class festivals all year long, and Nice is a must-do.

**6 The Corniche Resorts.**
The sun shines most brightly on the fabled glamour ports of Villefranche-sur-Mer, Beaulieu, and St-Jean-Cap-Ferrat. Also here are Èze and Roquebrune–Cap-Martin. Then there's Menton, an enchanting Italianate resort where winters can be so mild that lemon trees bloom in January.

## GETTING ORIENTED

This region is the real heart of the Côte d'Azur. Its waterfront resorts—Cannes, Antibes, Villefranche-sur-Mer, and Menton—draw energy from the thriving city of Nice, while jut-ting tropical peninsu-las—St-Jean-Cap-Ferrat, Roquebrune–Cap-Martin—frame Monaco. Farther inland, medieval villages mushroom out of the nearby hills, offering refugees escaping from the coastal crowds a token taste of Old Provence. Wherever you head, be it the ooo-la-la opulence of St-Jean-Cap-Ferrat, the palm-tree-lined promenades of Nice, or the art villages of St-Paul and Vence, you'll find this coast to be an intoxicating mix of glamour and relaxation.

Updated by
Nancy Heslin

With the Alps and pre-Alps playing bodyguard against inland winds, and the sultry Mediterranean warming the sea breezes, the eastern slice of the Côte d'Azur is pampered by a nearly tropical climate that sets it apart from the rest of France's southern coast. This is where the real glamour begins: the dreamland of azure waters and indigo sky; white villas with balustrades edging the blue horizon; evening air perfumed with jasmine and mimosa; palm trees and parasol pines silhouetted against sunsets of apricot and gold.

There has been a constant march to this prime slice of the Côte d'Azur, going back to the ancient Greeks, who sailed eastward from Marseilles to market their goods to the indigenes. From the 18th-century English aristocrats, who claimed it as one vast treatment spa, to the 19th-century Russian nobles who transformed Nice into a tropical St. Petersburg, to the 20th-century American tycoons who cast themselves as sheikhs, all have left their mark: Moroccan palaces in Menton, a neo-Greek villa in Beaulieu, the Promenade des Anglais in Nice planted with tropical greenery, to suit English fancies.

The beauty of the coast, however, is merely skin deep—a veneer of luxury backed by a sharp ascent into relatively ascetic heights. Day-trippers seeking contrast head inland behind the Baie des Anges, which has been transfigured into something of a Provençal theme park, filled with historic towns and *villages perchés* (perched villages). Towns such as Mougins, where Picasso spent his last years, and Grasse, with its factories that make perfume from the region's abundant flowers, have transformed themselves to fulfill visitors' dreams of backcountry villages, and galleries, souvenir shops, and snack stands crowd the cobblestones of St-Paul, Vence, and Èze.

But let's recall that most of the earliest inhabitants of this region were fishermen, and peasants who grew wheat and olives, and grapes for wine. This was not one of those lush regions of France where the living was easy. There were no palaces or gracious châteaux, only small villages, with fortifications here and there for use when Celts, Vandals, Ostrogoths, Saracens, and pirates from Algeria's Barbary Coast were on the rampage. It was only in the middle of the 19th century that a troupe of kings and queens (including Victoria and dozens of her relatives), Russian grand dukes, princelings from obscure Balkan countries, English milords, and a rabble of nouveau-riche camp followers began taking prolonged visits here. They had mansions and gardens built; luxury hotels sprang up in imitation of their palaces back home. The newcomers called the coastal strip the French Riviera. The Frenchman Stéphan Liégeard named it *la Côte d'Azur* in 1887, the blue—literally, sky-blue—coast. To the French, "Riviera" refers to the Italian coast farther east and is a word used only by tourists.

All these rich invaders withdrew to the cooler north for the summer months. No person of quality, and above all no lady of quality, would risk getting tanned like those laboring field hands. Until World War I, in fact, many hotels *closed* at the end of May, reopening in October. Up to that time, sea bathing was shunned by all, except as a drastic medical remedy. Then came the fun revolution. In the 1920s and 1930s, people began to like it hot. The peasantry of the West was now pale factory and office workers, and their new badge of leisure and pleasure became the tan that their aristocratic predecessors had so assiduously avoided. Chanel, the famous couturier made tans the chicest of fashion "accessories" in 1923 when she accidentally got scorched on a Mediterranean cruise.

More and more hotels, restaurants, and nightclubs were built. Fun became livelier and more informal. Toplessness, and even bottomlessness, arrived on the beaches. Eleven million passengers passed through Nice–Côte d'Azur airport in 2012 and for many travelers, the Côte remains a demi-paradise.

You could drive from Cannes to the Italian border in two hours and see much of the region, so small is this renowned stretch of Mediterranean coast; the swift A8 autoroute lets you pick and choose your stop-offs, and the three parallel Corniches allow you to explore without retracing your steps too often. But like the artists and nobles who paved the way before you, you will likely be seduced to linger.

# PLANNER

## WHEN TO GO

Southeast France is that magical corner of France where the sun always seems to shine. That's why it holds such a strong attraction for Parisians, who turn the beaches of Nice into one giant rocky bed in summer. If rain is almost unheard of in July and August, the region's short periods of intense rainfall, lasting half a day to a week, are otherwise hard to predict. The most likely periods are October to November and anytime from March to April, while late spring can also be surprisingly wet (locals swear that it always rains on the first day of the Cannes Film Festival). It's no secret that the coast is in its tropical prime July and August. But if you're anxious to enjoy the beaches, aim for June or September. Many hotels and restaurants close from November to Easter, though those in Nice thrive year-round. However, August is the exception: even in Nice, you'll come across popular restaurants who in the height of the tourist season close for the traditional *fermeture annuelle*.

Cannes books early for the film festival in May, so unless you're determined to hover outside the Farfalla with an autograph book, aim for another month. But there are magical times all year on the coast. The eastern Côte d'Azur enjoys a gentle microclimate, protected by the Estérel from the mistral that razors through Fréjus to the west, and from northern winds by the Alps. If you're intent on strolling in shirtsleeves under the palms on a winter day, head for Menton, famous for having one of the mildest climates in France.

## PLANNING YOUR TIME

How you tackle this stretch of the Côte d'Azur will largely depend on the form of transport you have chosen.

With a car, you can base yourself outside a major resort and combine day trips to Nice, Cannes, and Monaco with a taste of more leisurely Provençal life.

If you're dependent on public transport, you might stay in a larger center such as Nice and even find that you don't need to leave it very often, though the great news is that buses and trains will easily take you along the coast and whisk you to such towns as Èze and Antibes.

If sunbathing is a priority, you might prefer the sandy beaches of Cannes to the pebbles of Nice; in the height of summer, aim for the less populated beaches of St-Jean-Cap-Ferrat, Cap d'Ail, Èze, and the Îles de Lérins.

Art is a super-major draw in this area, with must-see museums, such as the Matisse museum in Nice, the Fondation Maeght in St-Paul-de-Vence, the Fernand Léger museum in Biot, and the Picasso museum in Antibes.

There is plenty for music fans, too: Nice and Juan-les-Pins hold major jazz festivals in the summer and Monaco's Printemps des Arts from mid-March to mid-April celebrates music, dance, cinema, and theater. Vence's Nuit du Sud, a world music event which started in 1997, has become so popular that festival-goers on a flight from Paris once asked the pilot to call organizers to say they were late as they didn't want to miss the show.

With so much to see, it's tempting to pack too much into a visit to this area, so be sure to set aside some time for relaxing on café terraces— something that the locals have mastered.

Stroll through a colorful food market, perhaps the Marché Forville in Cannes or the Cours Saleya in Nice, to see how seriously this area takes its fresh produce.

Then visit a good local bistro to taste specialties such as *pissaladière* (caramelized onion tart), *soupe de poissons* (fish soup), and, of course, *salade niçoise* (which in Nice contains neither green beans nor potato).

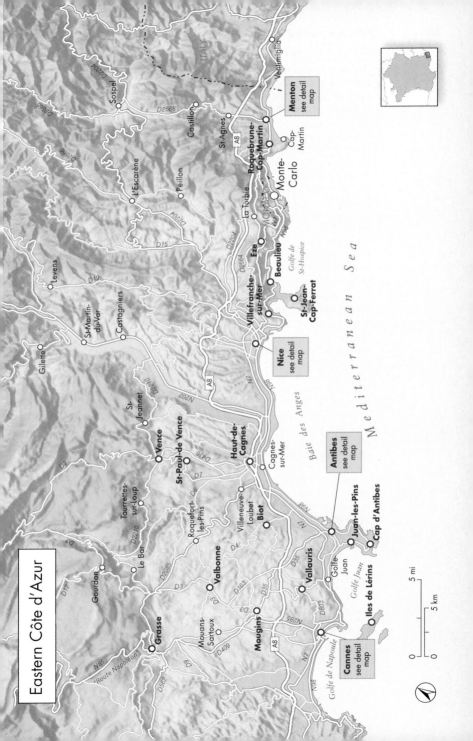

Eastern Côte d'Azur

## GETTING HERE AND AROUND

As home to France's second-busiest airport, Nice is a natural starting point for seeing the area. The airport's location 15 minutes from the town center is particularly convenient, though beware of the high cost of taxis (the airport bus runs every 20 minutes).

East and west of Nice, a train route connects all the main coastal towns—a magic-carpet ride of convenience for travelers. Buses also spider out, but they can take a good two hours between Nice and Cannes (as opposed to 35 minutes on the train). It's a well-kept secret that the Biot train station is a five-minute walk from Marineland, a major attraction near Antibes. Trains also head up into the hills around Grasse.

Surely the biggest bargain in the South of France is the Lignes d'Azur bus ticket (€1.50), valid anywhere between Cannes and Menton. The most scenic line is No. 100, running from Nice to Menton along the Moyenne Corniche. It runs every 15 minutes but can get unpleasantly packed in high season. Buses connect Nice to Èze village (30 minutes), and St-Paul and Vence (at least an hour); be sure to check the schedule, because these buses are not frequent.

■TIP➔ An excellent website to help you calculate your route—bus, tram, train, and boat—across the Riviera is ⊕ *www.ceparou06.fr.*

### AIR TRAVEL

The Nice–Côte d'Azur Airport, the second-busiest in France, sits on a peninsula between Antibes and Nice. There are frequent flights between Paris and Nice on the low-cost airline EasyJet and Air France, as well as direct flights on Delta Airlines from New York. In the off-season, or if you book well in advance, you can find a one-way trip from Paris to Nice for less than €40, which can be cheaper than the train (though extra baggage fees and airport transfers offset this). The flight time between Paris and Nice is about an hour and a half. A taxi from the airport into Nice proper—say, the train station or the Place Masséna—should cost about €25, though unscrupulous drivers sometimes charge much more. You'll be less likely to be ripped off if you tell the driver that you need a receipt ("*reçu*," with the "ç" pronounced like an s). Bus No. 98 makes the run to and from the bus station every 20 minutes Monday through Saturday between 6 am and 9 pm for €6, and the No. 99 goes to and from the train station to the airport. Regular shuttle buses also serve Cannes, Antibes, Monte Carlo, and Menton.

**Airport Information Aéroport Nice–Côte d'Azur** ☎ *08–20–42–33–33* ⊕ *www.nice.aeroport.fr.*

### BOAT TRAVEL

The Côte d'Azur is one of the most beautiful coastlines in the world and there are several companies that allow you to drink it all in via boat and ferry service. Riviera Lines offers routes between Cannes and Monaco and St-Tropez.

Trans Côte d'Azur, with Nice and Cannes departures, has routes including the Corniche de l'Estérel, Monaco, Porquerolles, and St-Tropez, plus specialty excursions that feature nighttime dining and glass-bottom boats. Note that some routes and destinations are available only from June to October.

## BUS TRAVEL

If you're traveling along the coast, the train line is the quickest way to get around. However, to travel to backcountry spots not on the rail line, take a bus out of Cannes, Nice, Antibes, or Menton for a mere €1.50 per ticket (one way). Pick up schedules at tourist offices and at the local *gare routière* (bus station). You must hail a bus to stop; don't presume the driver sees you. Drivers give change and hand you a ticket, which you must get stamped (*composté*) in the ticket validator and keep as proof of payment, as inspectors often board buses to check.

Hook up with buses heading everywhere using the bus station at the Nice airport (next to Terminal 1). Ligne d'Azur Bus No. 100 departs every 15 minutes (between 6 am and 8 pm) from Nice–Ségurane in Place Garibaldi and stops at all the villages between Nice and Menton along the Corniche Inférieure. For the villages set on the Moyenne Corniche, take Bus No. 112, which departs Nice Vauban six times a day (no Sunday service) and ends at the casino in Monte Carlo, or the No. 82, which goes as far as Eze and runs daily. Use Ligne d'Azur No. 116 to get to the few villages on the Grande Corniche, the highest highway. The No. 400 goes from Nice to St-Paul and Vence, stopping first in St-Paul (about 1 hour), and the No. 500 from Albert 1er takes you to Grasse (1 hour 20 minutes).

Nice bus stations are spread across the city, in: Vaubun (north and regional buses to Marseille, Aix); Gare SNCF; Place Blanqui (airport bus); Station J. Bermond (main hub); Cathédrale Vieille Ville; Alberti/Gioffredo and Albert 1er.

In Nice, the Lignes d'Azur operates a modern tram system that's a great way to get from the train station to the Old Town. Tickets cost €1.50 one way and must be purchased before boarding from machines at each stop. You can get information at an office at Place Masséna as well as in front of the train station.

In Cannes, Lignes d'Azur runs routes from in front of the train station, including the 200 to Nice (1½ hours), and the Conseil Général 06 operates routes to Grasse (No. 600 and 610; 45 minutes). Within Cannes, use Bus Azur.

Monaco's buses—Compagnie des Autobus de Monaco—help stitch together the principality's widely dispersed neighborhoods. Antibes bus station is at 1 Place Guynemer and the No. 200 bus connects with Nice and Cannes (€1.50; every 15–20 minutes). Cagnes-sur-Mer is one of the coastal towns served by train. From there it's an easy connection with adjacent St-Paul-de-Vence and Vence using Bus No. 400, which departs every 30 minutes from Cagnes Ville's bus station at Square Bourdet. The No. 200 Nice–Cannes bus stops at the square, too.

Part of the Urban Network of Nice Côte d'Azur's Urban Community, RCA runs express airport buses to Vallauris, Cannes, Monaco, and Menton.

**Bus Information Cannes Gare Routière** ☒ *Place Bernard Cornut Gentille* ☎ *04-93-38-01-41.* **Lignes d'Azur.** ☒ *3 Pl. Masséna, Nice* ☎ *08-10-06-10-06* ⊕ *www.lignesdazur.com.* **Nice Gare Routière.** ☒ *5 bd. Jean-Jaurès, Nice* ☎ *04-93-85-61-81.* **Rapides Côte d'Azur.** ☎ *08-20-48-11-11* ⊕ *www.rca.tm.fr.*

### CAR TRAVEL

A8 flows briskly from Cannes to Antibes to Nice to the resorts on the Grand Corniche; N98 follows the coast more closely along the Corniche Inférieure. The Moyenne Corniche is highway N7. From Paris, the main southbound artery is A6/A7, known as the Autoroute du Soleil; it passes through Provence and joins the eastbound A8 at Aix-en-Provence.

The best way to explore the secondary sights in this region, especially the deep backcountry, is by car. A car also allows you the freedom to zip along A8 between the coastal resorts and to enjoy the tremendous views from the three Corniches that trace the coast from Nice to the Italian border. A car is, of course, a liability in downtown Cannes and Nice, with parking garages expensive and curbside spots virtually nonexistent.

Note: Keep your car doors locked at all times, and keep any bags clear of visibility. Also, this is one of the most dangerous driving regions in Europe, and the speeds and aggressive Grand Prix style of some drivers make it impossible to let your guard down. On the A8 toward Italy, tight curves, hills, tunnels, and construction keep things interesting. For traffic reports tune to 107.7 FM.

### TRAIN TRAVEL

Nice is the major rail crossroads for trains arriving from Paris and other northern cities and from Italy, too. To get from Paris to Nice (with stops in Cannes and other resorts along the coast), you can take the TGV, though it only maintains high speeds to Valence before returning to conventional rails and rates. Night trains arrive at Nice in the morning from Paris, Metz, and Strasbourg.

You can easily move along the coastal towns between Cannes, Nice, and Ventimiglia by train on the slick double-decker Côte d'Azur line, a highly tourist-pleasing branch of SNCF lines, with more than 40 trains running a day. Don't be shocked, though, to see a graffitied clunker pull in.

This line is called Marseille–Vintimille (Ventimiglia, in Italy), heading east to Italy and Vintimille–Marseille in the west direction. Some main stops on this line are: Antibes (€4.40, 30 minutes), Cannes (€6.60, 40 minutes), Menton (€4.40, 30 minutes), and Monaco (€3.70, 20 minutes); other stops include Villefranche-sur-Mer, Beaulieu, Cap Martin, St-Jean-Cap-Ferrat, and Èze-sur-Mer. No trains run to the hill villages, including St-Paul, Vence, and Peillon.

A completely modernized station opened in Cannes in 2014; it included separate arrival and departure points.

**Train Information Gare Cannes Ville.** ⊠ *1 rue Jean-Jaurès, Cannes* ⊕ *www.gares-en-mouvement.com.* **Gare Nice Ville** ⊠ *Av. Thiers, Nice* ☎ *08–36–35–35–35* ⊕ *www.gares-en-mouvement.com.* **SNCF** ☎ *08–36–35–35–35 (€0.34 /minute)* ⊕ *en.voyages-sncf.com.* **TGV** ☎ *284–8633 (€0.34/minute)* ⊕ *www.tgv.com/en.*

## BEACHES

When the French Côte d'Azur starts to sizzle, it's time to beat the heat and hit the beach. Here's how—and where—to savor Provence's greatest liquid assets.

From intimate pebbly stretches to long swaths of golden sand packed with sun worshippers, from nudist beaches to family-friendly ones, the Côte d'Azur is famed for its sunbelievable beaches. Many, however, are reviled for their notorious *galets*, round white stones that can make you feel like a fakir lying on a rounded bed of nails. Sun-loungers then become de rigueur. It's important to note that many beaches are privately operated, renting parasols and mattresses to anyone who pays; if you're a guest at one of the local hotels, you'll get a discount. These beaches also allow you in for free if you are drinking or eating from their menus. The good news is that public beaches (with free toilets during summer and open showers) usually alternate with private *plages*, where you'll pay on average €20 for a mattress, which usually includes a parasol. Happily, the sun is free.

Despite its reputation as a beach paradise, the eastern Côte d'Azur waterfront is mainly surfaced by stretches of smooth, round rocks the size of your fist; from Cagnes-sur-Mer to Menton, you'll spread your beach blanket over these hard lumps instead of nestling into sand. A thin foam mattress can make all the difference, as can a pair of slip-on rubber shoes for negotiating the stones—so consider springing for a lounger on one of those private beaches. ■ TIP→ If lodging inland, leave early for the beach: traffic on N98, which lines the coast, often grinds to a halt.

## HOTELS

In this golden stretch you'll see the prices rise, even beyond those of the Estérel. The atmosphere changes, too. In the coastal resorts the majority of visitors seem to value proximity to the sea over cachet, and you'll often find yourself far from the land of Provençal cottons and cozy country inns. The decor here is a peculiar hybrid—vaguely Jazz Age, a little Hollywood—that falls into a loose category known as Côte d'Azur style. In Cannes the grand hotels are big on prestige (waterfront position, awe-inspiring lobbies, high-price sea views) and weak on swimming pools, which are usually just big enough to dip in; their private beaches are on the other side of the busy street, and you'll have to pay for access, just as non-guests do. Remember that July and August are the busiest months, but plan ahead anytime between May and October. Hotel prices skyrocket in May during the Monaco Grand Prix and the Cannes Film Festival; off-season, there are great deals to be had. The glitziest hotels are in Cannes, Monaco, and the Cap d'Antibes; Nice provides a broader range of prices, while charming family-run hotels can be found around St-Paul and Vence. Renting a rural *gîte* (⊕ *www.gites-de-france.com*) allows you to avoid overpriced breakfasts and make the most of the abundance at the markets. You'll find most hotel rates now include Wi-Fi, but much to the dismay of many travelers, signals can be weak even in the bigger towns or in upscale hotels due to aging infrastructures. ■ TIP→ Don't be surprised at checkout when you see the *taxe de séjour* (usually around €1 to €1.50 per guest per day). This city tax is never included in the price when you book online from travel websites.

# CANNES

*6 km (4 miles) east of Mandelieu-La Napoule; 73 km (45 miles) northeast of St-Tropez; 33 km (20 miles) southwest of Nice.*

Backed by gentle hills and flanked to the south by the heights of the Estérel, warmed by dependable sun but kept bearable in summer by the cool breeze that blows in from the Mediterranean, Cannes is pampered with the luxurious climate that has made it one of the most popular and glamorous resorts in Europe. Its graceful curve of wave-washed sand peppered with chic restaurants and prestigious private beaches, its renowned waterfront promenade strewn with palm trees and poseurs, its status-symbol grand hotels vying for the custom of the Louis Vuitton set—this legend is, to many, the heart and soul of the Côte d'Azur.

A tasteful and expensive breeding ground for the upper-upscale, Cannes has long been a sybaritic heaven further glamorized by the ongoing success of its film festival, as famous as (and, in the trade, more respected than) Hollywood's Academy Awards. About the closest many of us will get to feeling like a film star is a stroll here along the famous La Croisette promenade, lined with fancy boutiques and lorded over by the Carlton hotel, the legendary backdrop to Grace Kelly in *To Catch a Thief*. Nearly 60 years later with life imitating art, a whopping $53 million worth of jewels was stolen from this same hotel, one of many high-profile heists to hit Cannes during the summer of 2013.

Settled first by the Ligurians and then dubbed Cannoïs by the Romans (after the cane that waved in its marshes), Cannes was an important sentinel site for the monks who established themselves on Île St-Honorat in the Middle Ages. Its bay served as nothing more than a fishing port until in 1834 an English aristocrat, Lord Brougham, fell in love with the site during an emergency stopover with a sick daughter. He had a home built here and returned every winter for a sun cure—a ritual quickly picked up by his peers. Between the popularity of Le Train Blue transporting wealthy passengers from Calais, and the introduction in 1936 of France's first paid holidays, Cannes became the destination.

La Croisette, which starts at the western end by the Palais des Festivals and leads over to the Jardin Alexandre III, is precisely the sort of place for which the French invented the verb *flâner* (to dawdle, saunter): from the broad expanse of mostly private beaches to the glamorous shops and luxurious hotels, which these days are filled with the not-so jet set and conventioneers.

### GETTING HERE AND AROUND

Cannes has one central train station, the completely modernized Gare SNCF. All major trains pass through here—check out the SNCF website for times and prices—but many of the trains run the St-Raphaël–Ventimiglia route. You can also take the TGV directly from Paris (5 hours). Cannes's main bus hub is in front of the l'Hôtel-de-Ville by the port and serves all coastal destinations. Rapides Côtes d'Azur runs an express airport shuttle (50 minutes, €20) and Lignes d'Azur runs routes from in front of the train station, including the 200 to Nice (€1.50, 1½ hours). Within Cannes, use Bus Azur (€1.50).

# Cannes

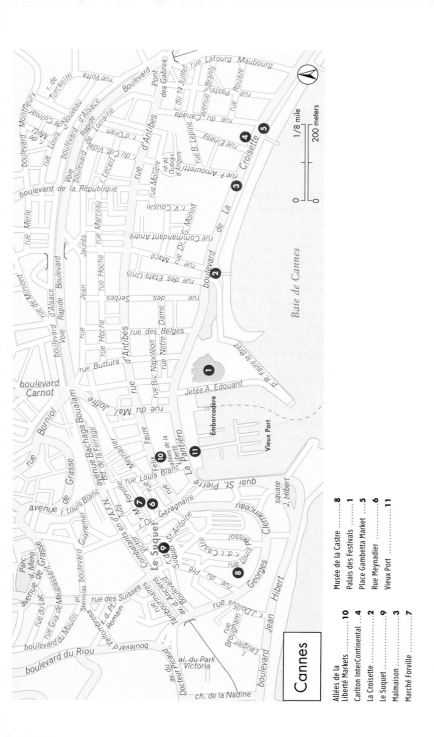

Baie de Cannes

0    1/8 mile
0    200 meters

Bargain-basement ticket fares of €1.50 to all destinations along the coast are a steal (be patient, you may not get a seat), but keep in mind that between Cannes and Nice it's much faster to take the train.

**VISITOR INFORMATION**

**Cannes Tourist Office.** The website for the Cannes Tourist Office provides a wealth of information in English, including how to access the city's free Wi-Fi. Click on "Cannes Practical" and then "Useful Information." ⊠ *1 bd. de la Croisette* ☏ *04–93–39–01–01* ⊕ *www.cannes-destination.com.*

## EXPLORING

### TOP ATTRACTIONS

**Carlton InterContinental.** Built in 1912, this was the first of the grand hotels to stake out the superb stretch of beach and greenery on La Croisette, and thus is the best positioned. It is here that many of the film festival's grand banquets take place. ⊠ *58 bd. de la Croisette* ☏ *04–93–06–40–06* ⊕ *www.intercontinental-carlton-cannes.com.*

**La Croisette.** This is precisely the sort of place for which the verb *flâner* (to dawdle, saunter) was invented. Head to this famous waterfront promenade—which runs for 1.6 kilometers (1 mile) from its western terminus by the Palais des Festivals—and allow the *esprit de Cannes* to take over. Stroll among the palm trees and flowers and crowds of poseurs (fur coats in tropical weather, cell phones on rollerblades, and sunglasses at night). Continue east past the broad expanse of private beaches, glamorous shops, and luxurious hotels (among them the wedding-cake Carlton, famed for its see-and-be-seen terrace-level brasserie). The beaches along here are almost all private, but it's worth forking out the money to get the total Cannes experience. ⊠ *From Palais des Festivals, Bd. de Croisette.*

▌NEED A
BREAK?

**Le 72 Croisette.** Head down Boulevard de la Croisette and fight for a spot at Le 72 Croisette, the most French of all La Croisette bars. It offers great ringside seats for watching the rich and famous enter the Martinez hotel next door. From May to September it's open nearly 24 hours a day (7 am to 4 am) and in off season from 7 am to 9 pm. ⊠ *71 bd. de la Croisette* ☏ *04–93–94–18–30.*

**Le Suquet.** Climb up Rue St-Antoine into the picturesque *vieille ville* neighborhood known as Le Suquet, on the site of the original Roman *castrum*. Shops proffer Provençal goods, and the atmospheric cafés provide a place to catch your breath; the pretty pastel shutters, Gothic stonework, and narrow passageways are lovely distractions. ⊠ *Rue St-Antoine.*

**Malmaison.** If you need a culture fix, check out the modern art and photography exhibitions (admission prices vary) held at the Malmaison, a 19th-century mansion that was once part of the Grand Hotel. ⊠ *47 Blvd. La Croisette, La Croisette* ☏ *04–97–06–44–90* ▨ *€7* ⊙ *Oct.–Apr., Tues.–Sun. 10–1 and 2–6; July–Aug., daily 11–8 (and Fri. to 9); Sept. daily 11–7.*

**Marché Forville** (*Forville market*). Under the permanent shelter that every morning (except Monday) draws the chefs, connoisseurs, and voyeurs of Cannes, you'll see showy displays of still-flipping fish from some 25 local fishing boats alongside glossy vegetables piled high, cheeses

**CLOSE UP**

# The Three Corniches

The lay of the land east of Nice is nearly vertical, as the coastline is one great cliff, a corniche terraced by three parallel highways—the **Corniche Inférieure** (sometimes called the Basse Corniche and N98), the **Moyenne Corniche** (N7), and the **Grande Corniche** (D2564)—that snake along its graduated crests. The lowest (*inférieure*) is the slowest, following the coast and crawling through the main streets of resorts, including downtown Monte Carlo. Villefranche, Cap Ferrat, and Beaulieu are some of the towns along this 20-mile-long highway. The highest (*grande*) is the fastest, but its panoramic views are blocked by villas, and there are few safe overlooks (this is the highway Grace Kelly roared along in *To Catch a Thief*, and some 27 years later, crashed and died on). The middle (*moyenne*) offers views down over the shoreline and villages and passes through a few picturesque cliff-top towns, including Èze.

carried down from the mountains, and sausages, olives, and flower stands. Real farmers sell their fresh local produce down the central aisle—hand-mixed mesclun, fat asparagus, cherries picked yesterday, baby eggplants—but the whole scene gets hosed down by 1 pm, so don't linger too long over breakfast. ⊠ *Rue du Marché Forville.*

**Musée de la Castre.** The hill is topped by an 11th-century château, housing the Musée de la Castre, with its mismatched collection of weaponry, ethnic artifacts, and ceramics amassed by a 19th-century aristocrat. The imposing four-sided **Tour du Suquet** (Suquet Tower) was built in 1385 as a lookout against Saracen-led invasions. ⊠ *Pl. de la Castre, Le Suquet* ☎ *04–93–38–55–26* ☒€6 ⊘ *Oct.–Mar., Tues.–Sun. 10–1 and 2–5; Apr.–June and Sept., Tues.–Sun. 10–1 and 2–6; July and Aug., daily 10–7 (June to Sept. Wed. till 9).*

**Palais des Festivals.** Pick up a map at the tourist office in the Palais des Festivals, the scene of the famous Festival International du Film, otherwise known as the Cannes Film Festival. As you leave the information center, follow the Palais to your right to see the red-carpeted stairs that movie A-listers ascend every year. Set into the surrounding pavement, the **Allée des Étoiles** (Stars' Walk) enshrines some 300 autographed hand imprints—including those of Dépardieu, Streep, and Stallone. ⊠ *Bd. de la Croisette* ⊕ *www.palaisdesfestivals.com.*

**Vieux Port** (*Old Port*). Sparkling at the foot of Le Suquet, this narrow, well-protected port harbors a fascinating lineup of grand luxury yachts and slick little pleasure boats that creak and bob beside weathered-blue fishing barques. From the east corner, off La Pantiéro at the Quai Laubeuf, you can catch a cruise to the Îles de Lérins. The Port as well as Quai St. Pierre, which runs alongside and hosts a plethora of restaurants, was recently made over from its tattered and tired mid-life crisis into a smartly dressed, more energized version of its former self. ⊠ *Vieux Port.*

6

### WORTH NOTING

**Allée de la Liberté Markets.** Shaded by plane trees and sheltering a sandy pétanque field (occupied around the clock by distinctly unglamorous grandfathers inured to the scene on La Croisette), this is a little piece of Provence in a big, glitzy resort town. Every morning but Monday a flower market paints the square in vivid colors, and on the weekend there's a flea market (from 10 am to 6 pm), where you can find almost any item, from moth-eaten uniforms to secondhand gravy boats. ⊠ *Allée de la Liberté*.

**Place Gambetta Market.** Just a couple of blocks east of the train station along rue Jean Jaures, you can pick up fresh fruit and vegetables, as well as clothes, shoes, belts, and bags at this covered market that's a little less upscale than the Marché Forville but with bargains nonetheless. While in the neighborhood you can visit the nearby Asian and kosher shops or stop in for one of the creamiest cappuccinos this side of Italy at Volupté (32 rue Hoche, closed on Sunday). ⊠ *Place Gambetta* ⊘ *Tues.–Sun. 7–7*.

**Rue Meynadier.** You may not notice the pretty 18th-century houses that once formed the main street of Cannes, so distracting are the boutiques they now contain. Here inexpensive and trendy clothes alternate with rarified food and wine shops and some of the best butchers in town. Don't miss the chic patisserie, L'Atelier Jean-Luc Pelé, found at No. 36, whose delicate *macarons* come in flavors such as cassis-violet, Menton lemon, and foie gras–onion confit, and whose ganache-filled chocolates are sublime. At one end of Rue Meynadier is **Rue d'Antibes**, Cannes's main high-end shopping street. ⊠ *Rue Meynadier*.

## BEACHES

Just before tourist season every year, the city of Cannes spends €650,000 to recover sand—some 25,000 cubic meters—that has been swallowed by the sea. They also set up special anti-jellyfish nets until the end of September along Gazagnaire, Mace, and Roubine public beaches so you can swim in peace. Most of the beaches along La Croisette are owned by hotels or restaurants, though this doesn't necessarily mean the hotels or restaurants front the beach. It does mean they own a patch of beachfront bearing their name, from which they rent out chaises, mats, and umbrellas to the public and hotel guests (around €22 per day). One of the most fashionable is the Carlton Hotel's beach. Other beaches where you must pay a fee include Long Beach, Rado Plage, and Zplage, the stretch belonging to the Martinez, which is the largest in Cannes. You can easily recognize public beaches by the crowds; they're interspersed between the color-coordinated private-beach umbrellas, and offer simple open showers and basic toilets (and you can rent a lounger for only €6.70 per day). To be slightly removed from the city traffic and crowds, head west of town where the open stretches of sand run uninterrupted toward Mandelieu. There are a couple of nonsmoking beaches in each sea town across the Riviera. In Cannes, Bijou Plage (also home to Handiplage) and Les Rochers are nonsmoking beaches, and you'll be fined €11 if you're caught lighting up. Plage Macé, near the Palais, runs a beach library from mid-June to August, 10 am to 6 pm. For a €10 deposit readers can sign out books for up to two days; English publications are available.

If you're not a fan of kids at the beach, lay your beach towel far away from the toy-topped poles along Cannes's seafront, which are in place to join up lost children and their parents. **TIP→ If you're at the beach with your children, ask a lifeguard for a bracelet and write your child's name and mobile number on it. Explain to your children to go to the nearest pole if lost.**

**Castel Plage.** At the east end of the Promenade, near Hotel Suisse, there is both a large public beach and a private beach, where you can rent a lounger for about €18, and where the water is calm and clear. The public beach is composed of large stones (*galettes*), which is more comfortable than walking on pebbles. Jellyfish are less of a problem in this corner than on beaches a little farther west along the Promenade, and lifeguards at the neighboring beach are on duty mid-June to mid-September. **Amenities:** none. **Best for:** sunrise; sunset; snorkeling; swimming. ✉ *8 Quai des États-Unis, Nice.*

### "LE TOPLESS"

While some starlets still flaunt their all on St-Tropez's Plage de Tahiti, the French press has now declared that toplessness is *démodé* and old-fashioned. In fact, a 2010 survey titled "Women and Nudity" revealed 37% of younger French women said they were "disturbed by publicly exposed breasts." This generation of demoiselles goes for bikinis or one-pieces, citing feminist concerns, worries about skin cancer, and the *ringard* (tacky) status of the sex goddesses of yore. Scout out a beach first to see if you're on the same *nudiste* vibe as the others.

## WHERE TO EAT

$$$ FRENCH

🍴 **Grill & Wines.** Could it be that Cannes finally has an eatery where good food and friendly service come together? No wonder this place is so busy. You can come for *une verre* on the terrace or a meal in one of two interior rooms, one modern and the other traditional. The steak house offers more than just grilled Argentinean Black Angus steak or Iberian pork caramelized in balsamic vinegar and spices—there are also salmon, seabass, and chicken dishes, while dessert includes tarte citron and an exotic fruit panacotta. **TIP→ A word to the hungry: during convention periods this place should be avoided (and try to overlook the flatscreen TV inside).** [$] *Average main: €25* ✉ *5 rue Notre Dame* ☎ *04–93–38–37–10* 🌐 *www.grillandwines.com* 🕒 *Closed Sun.*

$$$$ FRENCH

🍴 **La Brouette de Grand-mère.** Monsieur Bruno's charming hole-in-the-wall, complete with lace curtains, painted-wood front, fireplace, and old posters, could be a set for one of the Festival's films. Yet it's a true-blue bistro, with a €38 three-course menu that includes both an aperitif and wine. Choose quail roasted in cream, duck glazed in gingerbread and honey, or pork tenderloin in a camembert sauce. It feels especially right in winter. [$] *Average main: €38* ✉ *9 rue d'Oran, Place Lamy* ☎ *04–93–39–12–10* 🌐 *www.labrouettedegrandmere.com* 🕒 *No lunch except Sun. Closed Jan.*

**$$$** ╳ **La Cave.** With walls strewn with Niçois memorabilia, this restaurant
FRENCH (established 1989) is where locals go to satisfy a craving for Provençal
classics. Choosing from the affordable set menu (€34), you might start
with a plate of *farcis* (stuffed seasonal vegetables) before tasting an *aïoli*
(cod with vegetables and garlic mayonnaise) or perhaps veal with black
chanterelles. Desserts, such as crème brûlée or chocolate mousse, are
good, if predictable. As the name suggests, wine plays a starring role
here and you can choose from all the great French regions (including
some worthy Provençal bottles). $ *Average main: €26* ✉ *9 bd. de la
République* ☎ *04–93–99–79–87* ⊕ *lacave-et-fils.com* ⊗ *Closed Sun. and
Aug. No lunch Sat. or Mon.*

**$$$$** ╳ **L'Affable.** When Chef Battaglia decided to set up shop in Cannes, gas-
FRENCH tronomes were delighted—and the chef does not disappoint. The curried
lobster is fantastic, the lamb rack succulent, and the risotto impossibly
creamy. Jammed daily since its opening, reservations are essential. Note
that dinner service is a fixed price with lots of tempting choices. $ *Av-
erage main: €42* ✉ *5 rue Lafontaine, La Croisette* ☎ *04–93–68–02–09*
⊕ *www.restaurant-laffable.fr* ⌂ *Reservations essential* ⊗ *Closed Sat.
lunch, Sun., and Aug.*

**$$$$** ╳ **Le Maschou.** If you're tired of choosing from complicated menus, visit
FRENCH this long-popular restaurant in Le Suquet, where the only thing you'll
have to decide is what kind of meat you want off the grill. Every din-
ner starts with a gigantic basket of whole raw vegetables, to be cut up
and dipped in a selection of sauces. Then come the generous servings of
beef, lamb, or chicken from the restaurant's charcoal grill menu (€48).
With a low beamed ceiling and only a few tables (draped in pink), Le
Maschou (meaning "small pretty house") is best visited in winter, but
it's also a favorite during the Cannes film festival. There's a second €48
menu substituting salmon, eggs, or veggies for meat. $ *Average main:
€48* ✉ *15 rue St-Antoine* ☎ *04–93–39–62–21* ⊕ *www.lemaschou.com*
⌂ *Reservations essential* ⊗ *Closed Nov.–mid-Dec.*

**$$$$** ╳ **Le Park 45.** Set in the chic, retro-'60s Grand Hotel Cannes, this mod-
FRENCH ern spot with sleek plate-glass windows to take in the views is the
Fodor's Choice showcase for chef Sébastien Broda's cooking. The 33-year-old chef of
★ growing fame puts on a real show with some of the most Barnumesque
dishes around: the pea soup with M&M–like balls of foie gras or the
blue lobster with ham shoulder get loud bravos. This local-boy-made-
good (he trained at La Palme d'Or and at Roger Vergé's Mougins land-
mark) has piqued the curiosity of both far-flung foodies and plenty of
trendy Cannoises. $ *Average main: €34* ✉ *45 bd. de la Croisette* ☎ *04–
93–38–15–45* ⊕ *www.grand-hotel-cannes.com* ⊗ *Closed Dec. and Jan.*

**$$$$** ╳ **Mantel.** In a city where style often wins out over substance, food
FRENCH lovers treasure this Suquet address, run by former chef and maître d'
Noël Mantel, who started out at the Negresco before working with
Ducasse at Louis XV in Monaco and then managing Les Muscadins in
Mougins. In 2002 he opened this self-named eatery, now part of the
Relais & Château family, and recently modernized the interior, opt-
ing for a more contemporary setting as appetizing as his cuisine. Find
out for yourself with dishes à la carte or one of the seasonal prix-fixe
menus (€30, €40, €57) drawing on the finest Mediterranean produce

6

to deliver such simple yet eloquent dishes as sea bream served with artichokes, zucchini, and bouillabaisse sauce. $ *Average main: €40* ⊠ *22 rue St-Antoine* ☎ *04–93–39–13–10* ⊕ *www.restaurantmantel. com* ⊘ *No lunch Tues. or Thurs. Closed Wed.*

**$$$$**
FRENCH
✕ **Sea Sens.** This trendy restaurant on the fifth floor of the Five Hotel (long ago it was the town's post office) has a fabulous view over le Suquet. Chef Arnaud Tabarec and world Pastry Champion Jérôme De Oliveira attempt to awaken all your senses through any of the three menus you chose—L'Intemporel (€55), the meat-and-fish Le Terre et Mer (€80), or Le Sensation (€120), a suprise menu for those who live on the gastronomic edge. The selection of very tasty wines can make even a novice appreciate bouquet, taste, and texture. $ *Average main: €55* ⊠ *1 rue Notre-Dame* ☎ *04–63–36–05–05* ⊕ *www.five-seas-hotel-cannes.com* ⊘ *No dinner Mon. Closed most of Feb.*

**$$$$**
FRENCH
✕ **Villa Archange.** Located in the suburb of Le Cannet, this stylish 18th-century villa houses the haute cuisine Villa Archange, headed by Bruno Oger, former chef of the Villa des Lys in Cannes. With an intimate setting seating 26 (terrace tables are seasonal), prix-fixe menus range in price from the €65 lunch to €190 dinner, but along with the à la carte selection, dishes make liberal use of luxury ingredients: typical of his style are the langoustine with Petrossian caviar and veal cooked at low temperature for 24 hours. If this is beyond your means, opt for the three-course, €29 menu at the premise's Le Bistrot des Anges, where dishes are inspired by the Mediterranean and occasionally beyond. While waiting, sink into an armchair and watch the fashion parade at L'Ange Bar. $ *Average main: €67* ⊠ *Rue de l'Ouest, 15 bis rue Notre-Dame-des-Anges, Le Cannet* ☎ *04–92–18–18–28* ⊕ *www.bruno-oger. com* ⊘ *Closed Sun. and Mon. No lunch Tues.–Thurs.*

## WHERE TO STAY

**$**
HOTEL
▾ **Albert Ier.** In a quiet residential area above the Forville market—a 15-minute walk uphill from La Croisette and beaches—this newly renovated neo-deco mansion has tastefully decorated earth-toned rooms (equipped with Wi-Fi) that are both minimal and tidy. **Pros:** great location for price; big cup of coffee with breakfast; free private parking. **Cons:** need to be in reasonable shape for the walk up the hill; no room service. $ *Rooms from: €105* ⊠ *68 av. de Grasse* ☎ *04–93–39–24–04* ⊕ *www.hotel-albert1er-cannes.com* ⤴ *12 rooms* ⦿ *Breakfast.*

**$$$$**
HOTEL
Fodor's Choice
★
▾ **Grand Hotel Cannes.** A two-minute walk from the Palais, this eleven-story, white-brick number with an amazing hotel garden fronting the Croisette is a fun and relaxing place to stay. **Pros:** quieter than some other Croisette properties because it sits back from the road; excellent service; Bulgari toiletries. **Cons:** beach gets crowded. $ *Rooms from: €500* ⊠ *45 bd. de la Croisette, BP 263* ☎ *04–93–38–15–45* ⊕ *www. grand-hotel-cannes.com* ⤴ *70 rooms, 5 suites* ⊘ *Closed Dec. and Jan.* ⦿ *Some meals.*

**$$$$**
HOTEL
▾ **Grand Hyatt Cannes Hotel Martinez.** A Hollywood-style face-lift restored the Art Deco Martinez, part of the Hyatt Group since 2013, to a theatrical version of its original 1930s glamour, and at the extravagant burled-wood and ebony Palme d'Or restaurant overlooking La

Croisette, you'll feel like a celebrity. **Pros:** glamorous setting; excellent service; spacious bathrooms. **Cons:** €40 breakfast so try and book inclusive deal; laundry service expensive but there's a laundromat around the corner. $ *Rooms from: €780 ✉ 73 bd. de la Croisette ☎ 04-92-98-73-00 ⊕ cannesmartinez.grand.hyatt.com ☞ 382 rooms, 27 suites ⎮⊙⎮ Some meals.*

$$$$ 🔲 **Hotel Château de la Tour.** A stay at the 18th-century Château de la
HOTEL Tour—a boutique hotel 10 minutes' drive from Cannes and near a beach—feels like a mini-retreat as guests relax in rooms with views of the sea, the Esterel Massif, or the garden. **Pros:** free in-room coffee and tea; €17 breakfast is the real deal—homemade crepes, eggs, and bacon; can be reached by train with a bit of a hike. **Cons:** some rooms can't facilitate extra cot or bed; located up hill so mobility issues can arise. $ *Rooms from: €285 ✉ 10 av. Font de Veyre, Le Cannet ☎ 04-93-90-52-52 ⊕ www.hotelchateaudelatour.com ☞ 34 rooms ⊗ Closed Feb. ⎮⊙⎮ No meals.*

$$$ 🔲 **Hôtel de Provence.** This hotel has a fabulous location and is affordable, yet the very gracious owners, Julie and Jerry Duburcq, go the
HOTEL extra distance to ensure guests have the service and experience of a much-higher caliber hotel. **Pros:** breakfast from 6 am until noon; five-minute walk from Cannes center; cheaper rates if booking prepaid. **Cons:** only two parking places, so organize ahead of time with owners (street or paid garage otherwise). $ *Rooms from: €169 ✉ 9 rue Molière ☎ 04-93-38-44-35 ⊕ www.hotel-de-provence.com ☞ 30 rooms ⊗ Closed Feb. ⎮⊙⎮ No meals.*

$$$$ 🔲 **InterContinental Carlton Cannes.** Used by Hitchcock as a suitably glamorous frame for Grace Kelly in *To Catch a Thief,* this neoclassical land-
HOTEL mark built in 1911 staked out the best position early on, sitting right on the sidewalk of La Croisette, radiating symmetrically from its figurehead waterfront site—the better for you to be seen on the popular brasserie's terrace. **Pros:** sense of history; great for star-spotting. **Cons:** some rooms are lackluster; outrageous cost of extras, such as in-room Internet for €24. $ *Rooms from: €775 ✉ 58 bd. de la Croisette ☎ 04-93-06-40-06 ⊕ www.intercontinental-carlton-cannes.com ☞ 343 rooms, 39 suites ⎮⊙⎮ Some meals.*

$ 🔲 **Hotel Colette.** Facing the train station, this boutique hotel is suspi-
HOTEL ciously affordable, considering its proximity to the beach, particularly when you book in advance for rooms in the off-season (from mid-October until June). **Pros:** not far from the Palais des Festivals; interior courtyard a bonus; l'Occitane toiletries provided. **Cons:** walls may be a bit thin (but no street noise); local parking is expensive. $ *Rooms from: €71 ✉ 5 pl. de la Gare ☎ 04-93-39-01-17 ⊕ www.hotelcolette.com ☞ 45 rooms ⎮⊙⎮ No meals.*

$$ 🔲 **La Villa Tosca.** Between the train station and the beach, this appar-
HOTEL ently modest little hotel run by a smiling staff has more than its share of charm. **Pros:** helpful staff; excellent value for location. **Cons:** standard rooms are small; don't bother with €13 breakfast–head to Volupté at No. 32 for the best cappuccino in town. $ *Rooms from: €125 ✉ 11 rue Hoche ☎ 04-93-38-34-40 ⊕ www.villa-tosca.com ☞ 22 rooms ⊗ Closed 2 wks in Dec. ⎮⊙⎮ No meals.*

6

$$$ HOTEL **Renoir.** This graceful former mansion on a quiet backstreet in a residential neighborhood behind the city center, within reasonable walking distance of La Croisette, has been transformed into a boutique hotel, with classic decor splashed with modern comforts, complete with a red-carpet entrance and a 1950s Hollywood–style bar. **Pros:** spacious rooms; 15-minute walk to La Croisette; early-booking discounts on hotel's website. **Cons:** noisy sea-view rooms not worth the extra money; late check-in at 3 pm; small elevator and steep steps at the entrance. [$] *Rooms from: €163* ✉ *7 rue Edith Cavell* ☎ *04–92–99–62–62* 🌐 *hotel-renoir.fr* 🛏 *17 rooms, 12 suites* 🕓 *Closed 3 wks in Jan.* 🍴 *No meals.*

$$$ HOTEL **Splendid.** Maintained in simple comfort, this traditional 1873 palace overlooking La Pantiéro and the Old Port offers freshly decorated rooms and up-to-date bathrooms, particularly the recently modernized ones facing the sea—especially a good choice if you covet a waterfront position but can't afford the grand hotels on La Croisette. **Pros:** ideal location; worth the extra price for sea view (request higher floors); last-minute online 20% discount. **Cons:** handheld showers in a bathtub (not walk in showers). [$] *Rooms from: €165* ✉ *Allées de la Liberté, 4–6 rue Félix-Faure* ☎ *04–97–06–22–22* 🌐 *www.splendid-hotel-cannes.fr* 🛏 *60 rooms, 2 apartments* 🍴 *No meals.*

## NIGHTLIFE

As befits a glamorous seaside resort, Cannes has a casino and a lively club.

**Casino Barrière.** The famous Casino Barrière on La Croisette—open 10 am to 3 am—is said to draw more crowds to its slot machines than any other casino in France. ✉ *In Palais des Festivals, 1 La Croisette* ☎ *04–92–98–78–00* 🌐 *www.lucienbarriere.com.*

**Le Bâoli.** The biggest player to date in the Cannes nightlife scene is Le Bâoli, where the likes of Leonardo DiCaprio and Lindsay Lohan have been known to stop by. It's usually packed until dawn even outside of festival time. ✉ *Port Canto, Bd. de la Croisette, La Croisette* ☎ *04–93–43–03–43* 🌐 *www.lebaoli.com* 🕓 *Closed Sun.–Thurs. Nov.–mid-Apr.*

## SPORTS AND THE OUTDOORS

**Club Nautique de la Croisette.** The Centre Nautique Municipal has a private windsurfing base off Île Ste-Marguerite and organizes diving sorties. Kayaks, windsurfers, and catamarans can be rented by the hour from June to October. ✉ *Square de Verdun, 19 av. du Camp Long* ☎ *04–93–47–40–55* 🌐 *www.club-nautique-croisette.fr.*

**Elite Rent a Bike.** This outfitter has three locations in southern France—in Mandelieu, Cannes, and Nice—and rents bikes beginning at €18 a day plus a €150 deposit. For the more daring, you can rent a moped (€35 for the day with a €1,000 deposit) without the need of a special driver's licence. ✉ *19 av. du Maréchal Juin* ☎ *04–93–94–30–34* 🌐 *www.elite-rentabike.com.*

For 12 days each May, the Festival International du Film turns the red carpet at the Palais des Festivals into a display case of the world's most beautiful people.

**Majestic Ski Club** (*Ponton du Majestic*). Go waterskiing or be pulled on a ski-board, an inflatable chair, or up over the water with a parachute from April to September. The owner also runs a water taxi service to Monaco or St-Tropez. ⊠ *Dock at Majestic beach, 10 bd. de la Croisette* ☎ *04–92–98–77–47* ⊕ *majesticskiclub.online.fr.*

**Rivage Croisière Catamaran.** From May to September, climb aboard a 22-meter, three-crew catamaran, destination Lérins Islands. Swim and snorkel (kit provided) as the boat moors between the two islands, or go ashore. The full-day trip (€95) departs at 10 am on Tuesday, Thursday, and Saturday, and returns at 5 pm; it includes lunch on board. The half-day trip (€50; 3 hours, no meal) departs at 9:30 am and 2 pm Wednesday and Friday. Sunset and fireworks cruises are also on the catamaran menu. ⊠ *20 Quai St-Pierre* ☎ *04–92–98–71–31* ⊕ *www. rivage-croisiere.com.*

## SHOPPING

Whether you're window-shopping or splurging on that little Raf Simons number in the Dior window, you'll find some of the best shopping outside Paris on the streets off La Croisette. For stores carrying designer names, try **Rond-point Duboys-d'Angers** off **Rue Amouretti**, **Rue des Serbes**, and **Rue des Belges**, all perpendicular to the waterfront. **Rue d'Antibes** is the town's main shopping drag, home base to every kind of clothing and shoe shop, as well as mouthwatering candy, fabric, and home-design stores. **Rue Meynadier** mixes trendy young clothes with high-end food specialties.

France has only two official sale periods during the year, winter (January) and summer (July) with regional dates set, amazingly, by the government. The event lasts for three weeks with prices further slashed as the sales draw to a close, but a lot of people take the day off work for the first day to get the best selection. It's even said that "retail police" monitor stores to see that prices are legitimately discounted.

## SIDE TRIP FROM CANNES: ÎLES DE LÉRINS

*15–20 minutes by ferry off the coast of Cannes.*

When you're glutted on glamour and tired of dodging limos and the leavings of dyed-to-match poodles, catch a boat from Cannes's Vieux Port to one of two Îles de Lérins (Lérins Islands). On one of these two lovely getaways you can find car-free peace and lose yourself in a tropical landscape of palms, pines, and tidal pools. Ste-Marguerite Island has more in the way of attractions: a ruined prison-fortress, a museum, and a handful of restaurants. Smaller and wilder, St-Honorat Island is dominated by its active monastery and its 10th-century ruins. Allow at least a half day to enjoy either island; you can see both if you get an early start. Although Ste-Marguerite has some restaurants and snack shops, you would be wise to bring along a picnic and drinks; you'll have to do this if you spend the day on the noncommercial St-Honorat.

### GETTING HERE AND AROUND

It's a 20-minute ride to Îles de Lérins from Cannes (€14 round-trip; daily approximately every hour on the hour from 9 am to 5 pm, last boat back at 6 pm; no service on Sundays).

**Horizon Company.** Buy your tickets to Île Ste-Marguerite from one of the ferry companies at the booths on Cannes's Vieux Port; look for the Horizon Company, which operates all year round (€12.50 return/person). ⊠ *Vieux Port, and of parking Laubeuf, Quai Laubeuf* ☎ *04–92–98–71–36* ⊕ *www.horizon-lerins.com.*

**Planaria.** Boats to Île St-Honorat are run by the monks who inhabit the island and tickets must be purchased from their own company, Planaria. Île St-Honorat can be reached in 20 minutes (€14 round-trip) from the Vieux Port at the end of the parking area Laubeuf every hour from 8 to noon and at 2, 3, 4:30, and 5:30 (the last boat back is at 6 pm May to September). ⊠ *Vieux Port, end of parking Laubeuf, Cannes* ☎ *04–92–98–71–38* ⊕ *www.cannes-ilesdelerins.com.*

### WHERE TO EAT

**$$$** ✕ **La Tonnelle.** It's hard to believe that this tranquil island is only 20
**FRENCH** minutes from Cannes by boat, and even more so as you linger under the shade of the trellis at this scenic, 19th-century restaurant run by Brother Marie Pâques from the Île St-Honorat monastery and chef Nathan Laurent. Having preserved a faded charm, La Tonnelle has a St-Tropez feel, thanks to black-and-white pictures of 1950s movie stars who dined here and a private boat that whisks customers directly from their luxury hotels to the restaurant's pier. The menu focuses on the freshest grilled fish, with prices that seem aimed at

modern-day celebrities, but if you desire, you can also have a lighter (and cheaper) meal at the snack bar, open from mid-May to mid-September. ■TIP→ **Take the opportunity to sample the wines, liqueurs, and eaux-de-vie that are produced by the island's busy monks.** [$] *Average main: €29* ⊠ *Abbaye Notre-Dame de Lérins, Ile St-Honorat* ☎ *04–92–99–54–08* ⊕ *www.tonnelle-abbayedelerins.com* ☒ *Reservations essential* ☉ *No dinner.*

# THE PAYS GRASSOIS

Just behind Cannes, the hills that block the mountain winds rise, sun-bleached and jungle-green. From the well-groomed Provençal village-cum-bedroom community of Mougins to the hill-city of Grasse, the hills are tiled with greenhouses that feed the region's perfume factories. Grasse itself supports modern industry and tourist industry with aplomb, offering a dense Italian-style Old Town as well. Beyond, you can head for the hills of the *arrière-pays* on the Route Napoléon.

## MOUGINS

*8 km (5 miles) north of Cannes; 11 km (7 miles) northwest of Antibes; 32 km (20 miles) southwest of Nice.*

Passing through Mougins, a popular residential community convenient to Cannes, Nice, and the big Sophia-Antipolis business park, you may perceive little more than sleek, upscale suburban sprawl. But in 1961 Picasso found more to admire and settled into a mas that became a mecca for artists and art lovers; he died there in 1973. Over the decades, others of note also colonized the town, including Cocteau, Man Ray, Léger, and Christian Dior. Despite overbuilding today, Mougins claims extraordinary views over the coast and an Old Town (which is a *zone piétonne*, or pedestrian zone), on a hilltop above the fray, that has retained a pretty, ultragentrified charm. You'll see quite a few off-duty celebrities here and any number of wealthy Parisians who have chosen to buy a Riviera pied-à-terre here. Where they go, noted chefs follow, and Mougins is now a byword in gourmet circles. If you're not coming here specifically for the food, the town also has plenty of cafés with pleasant terraces.

### GETTING HERE AND AROUND

Getting to Mougins by public transport is time-consuming. The 600 and 630 buses from Cannes stop in Mougins; from there it's a 15-minute walk up the hill to the Vieux Village. Alternatively, you could get off at the Val de Mougins stop and wait for the 650 to take you up to the Vieux Village, but this a weekday service and infrequent at that. If you don't have time to burn, opt for a taxi (around €35). From Nice, the train to Cannes costs €6.60 one way.

### VISITOR INFORMATION

**Mougins Tourist Office** ⊠ *39 pl. des Patriotes* ☎ *04–93–75–87–67* ⊕ *www.mougins.fr/tourisme.*

**EXPLORING**

**Les Étoiles de Mougins.** This festival transformed the medieval village of Mougins into a vast "open-air theater of gastronomy." Each September for three days, hundreds of the greatest chefs from around the globe converge to share their passion for cooking with equally enthusiastic audiences. Demonstrations, workshops, and professional sommeliers and amateur chef competitions dazzle 25,000 spectators. And yes, there are glorious tastings. Park in one of the recognized lots around Mougins and use the free *navette* that shuttles festival-goers to the village. Mougins is about 7 km (4½ miles) north of Cannes. ⊠ *Vieux Village* ☎ *04–93–75–87–67* ⊕ *www.lesetoilesdemougins.com* 🎫 *€5–€15.*

**Musée d'Art Classique de Mougins.** Open for just three years, the Musée d'Art Classique de Mougins has already been consistently nominated for awards, such as European Museum of the Year in 2013. A hidden gem, this museum spread over four floors "highlights the dialogue between the old and the new" with Roman, Greek, and Egyptian art rubbing shoulders with a hundred pieces by Picasso, Matisse, Cézanne, Warhol, and Dali, so expect to come across a sarcophagi alongside a Cocteau or a Hirst sculpture next to an ancient bust. It also houses antique jewelry and the world's largest armory collection. This is as hip as classic will ever be, and not to be missed. ⊠ *32 rue Commandeur* ☎ *04–93–90–00–91* ⊕ *www.mouginsmusee.com* 🎫 *€12* ⊘ *10:30–7 daily June–Sept. and Tues.–Sun. Oct.–May.*

**Musée de la Photographie.** Near Porte Sarrazine, the Musée de la Photographie permanently displays André Villers's portraits of his good friends—Picasso, who gave the French photographer his first camera in 1953, and Dalí, among them. Recommended as one of the world's top 10 free photography museums and attracting 25,000 visitors a year, here the iconic photographer's avant-garde images spread over three floors in a small village house. Temporary exhibits across the year pull in some big names and there's a terrific collection of old cameras. ⊠ *Porte Sarrazine, Mougins village, 67 rue d'Église* ☎ *04–93–75–85–67* ⊘ *May–Sept., daily 10–12:30 and 2–7 (and until 11 on Thurs); Oct.–Apr., daily 10–12:30 and 2–6.*

**Notre-Dame-de-Vie.** You can find Picasso's final home, where he lived for 12 years until 1973, and see why, of all spots in the world, he chose this one, by following D35 2 kilometers (1 mile) south of Mougins to the ancient ecclesiastical site of Notre-Dame-de-Vie. From his room, he could see the 13th-century bell tower and arcaded chapel, a pretty ensemble once immortalized in a painting by Winston Churchill. The chapel, listed as a historical monument since 1927, is said to date back to 1655; it received a face-lift in 2013 thanks to 255 donors who contributed 23% of the needed €247,462. Approached through an *allée* of ancient cypresses, the former priory house Picasso shared with his wife, Jacqueline, overlooks the broad bowl of the countryside (now blighted with modern construction). Unfortunately, his residence was bought by a private investor and is closed to the public. ⊠ *Chemin de la Chapelle.*

## WHERE TO EAT

$$$$ FRENCH 🍴 **La Place de Mougins.** Veteran chef Denis Fétisson (who has worked with Vergé and Ducasse) is in the kitchen to keep an eye on his masterpieces while the masterpieces of Matisse, Warhol, Dufy, and Picasso keep an eye on you in this elegant eatery where the food is as friendly as the service. No wonder it's *la place* to be in Mougins, replacing some of the tired venues that have for too long drawn on dwindling reputations. Each month, Fétisson goes seasonal with *le produit à l'honneur*, which celebrates one particular product—from scallops to chocolate—in a special menu (€55). There's also an à la carte menu, from which you might choose Aveyron lamb with chard gratin, artichokes, fresh almonds, chanterelle mushrooms, and zucchini flowers followed by wild strawberry soufflé with spoon biscuits, strawberry sorbet, and mulled wine de Provence. A sommelier is on hand to guide you through a very impressive selection. [$] *Average main: €35* ✉ *Vieux Village, 41 pl. du Commandant Lamy* ☎ *04–93–90–15–78* 🌐 *www.laplacedemougins.com* ✍ *Reservations essential* 🕒 *Closed Mon., Tues., and most of Nov.*

## WHERE TO STAY

$$$ B&B/INN 🏨 **Le Manoir de l'Etang.** Owner Camilla Richards spent 20 years in London before converting this 19th-century Provençal manor house into an upscale inn, perched over a lotus pond with a spectacular outdoor pool and the Cannes–Mougins golf course a few minutes away. **Pros:** friendly welcome from English-speaking owner and her Beagle Patches; breathtaking setting; exceptional restaurant. **Cons:** stone steps difficult for those with mobility problems; not all rooms equal. [$] *Rooms from: €160* ✉ *Bois de Fond Merle, Rte. d'Antibes, 66 allée du Manoir* ☎ *04–92–28–36–00* 🌐 *www.manoir-de-letang.com* 🛏 *21 rooms* 🕒 *Closed last wk Nov.–1st wk Dec.* 🍽 *Breakfast.*

$$$$ HOTEL 🏨 **Le Mas Candille.** Nestled in a 10-acre private park, this 19th-century *mas* (farmhouse) has been cleverly transformed into an ultraluxurious hotel with antique wallpapers, "reissued" vintage furniture, and many other high-gloss touches that make the place *Elle Decor*–worthy. **Pros:** award-winning service; beautiful views; parking included in price. **Cons:** tricky to find; pay extra for a room with a view. [$] *Rooms from: €470* ✉ *Bd. Clément-Rebuffel* ☎ *04–92–28–43–43* 🌐 *www.lemascandille.com* 🛏 *38 rooms, 7 suites* 🕒 *Closed most of Jan.* 🍽 *Breakfast.*

$$$$ HOTEL 🏨 **Royal Mougins Golf Resort Hotel.** What it lacks in Provençal character, this plush hotel on the green makes up for in modern comforts—each suite, decorated in soothing tones of beige and gray, is an independent apartment with a separate living room and kitchenette. **Pros:** clean and tranquil; higher floors have nicer views; for experienced golfers, the advantage of sleeping across from one of the world's best golf courses is obvious. **Cons:** Wi-Fi can be weak; the resort feels so much like another world that you might never leave the loungers on your private terrace. [$] *Rooms from: €380* ✉ *424 av. du Roi* ☎ *04–92–92–49–69* 🌐 *www.royalmougins.fr* 🛏 *29 suites* 🕒 *Closed Jan. and Feb.* 🍽 *Breakfast.*

## SPORTS AND THE OUTDOORS

**Golf Club de Cannes-Mougins.** Founded in 1923 by members such as Aga Khan and Prince Pierre of Monaco, this course is a stunner. The Club has hosted the European Open of Cannes (Severiano Ballesteros, Ian Woosnam), while the PGA Senior Tour also played here in 2010 and 2011. Nonmembers welcome (maximum handicap 28) and a dress code is enforced (no long-sleeved shirts or denim). ⊠ 1175 ave. du Golf ☎ 04–93–75–79–13 ⊕ www.golfcannesmougins. com ⊡ €100–€120 ⚑ 18 holes, 6902 yards, par 72.

### SCENTS AND SENSIBILITY

It takes 10,000 flowers to produce 2.2 pounds of jasmine petals and nearly 1 ton of petals to distill 1.5 quarts of essence; this helps justify the sky-high cost of perfumes, priced by the proportion of essence their final blend contains.

# GRASSE

*10 km (6 miles) northwest of Mougins; 17 km (10½ miles) northwest of Cannes; 22 km (14 miles) northwest of Antibes; 42 km (26 miles) southwest of Nice.*

Coco Chanel may have first set up shop in Cannes, but when she wanted to create her classic "No. 5" fragrance she headed to Grasse, perfume capital of the world. It's the Côte d'Azur's hothouse climate, nurturing nearly year-round shows of tropical-hue flowers, that has always fostered Grasse's industry. Little wonder: the heady, heavy scent of orange blossoms, pittosporum, roses, lavender, jasmine, and mimosa wraps around you like silk in gardens along the Riviera coast, especially on a sultry night, and since time immemorial people have tried to capture that seductive scent in a bottle. Nowhere else on earth do they do that better than here, as revealed in the town's spectacular perfume museum and the fascinating factory tours on tap.

High on a plateau over the coast, this busy, modern town is usually given wide berth by anyone who isn't interested in its prime tourist industry, the making of perfume. But its unusual art museum featuring works of the 18th-century artist Fragonard and the picturesque back-streets of its very Mediterranean Old Town round out a pleasant day trip from the coast.

In the past, Grasse's legendary perfume-makers laid blossoms face-down in a lard-smeared tray, then soaked the essence away in alcohol; nowadays the scents are condensed in vast copper stills. Only the essential oils are kept, and the water thrown away—except rosewater and orange water, which find their way into delicately perfumed pastries. In Paris and on the outskirts of Grasse, these scents are blended by a professional *nez*, or "nose," who must distinguish some 500 distinct scents and may be able to identify 3,000. The products carry the household names of couturiers like Chanel and Dior, and perfume houses like Guerlain. The laboratories where these great blends are produced are off-limits to visitors, but to accommodate the crowds of inquisitive scent-seekers, Grasse has set up three factories that create

## GREEN FRIENDLY

Golf is the most-played individual sport by the French although, according to the Fédération Française de Golf, only 0.61% of the population practices, not quite on par with the UK (1.9%), Sweden (5.8%), or the United States (9.5%). France will host the 2018 Ryder Cup at Le Golf National on the outskirts of Versailles, making it the second time in the tournament's history that it will take place on the continent.

Grand Duke Michael of Russia founded the Riviera's first golf course—the Old Course in Cannes–Mandelieu—in 1891. This venerated institution now hosts more than 40 competitions a year and, according to *Riviera Golfer* Nick Kent, some 60% of the total rounds are played by English-speakers. Today there are 22 regional golf courses, from Monaco to St-Tropez, and two expat clubs—the Riviera Expatriates Golf Society (REGS) and Landlubbers Golf Club. In September 2013, Cannes Golf Week was introduced in what the city hopes will be a yearly event.

simple blends and demonstrate some of the industry's production techniques. You pass through a boutique of house perfumes on the way back to the bus and—well, you get the idea. You can create your own perfume at Galimard (cost: €45).

For €6 per person, climb aboard **Le Petit Train de Grasse** for a 40-minute tour of the town, including the Vieille Ville and Cathedral. The yellow line departs from the Cours Honoré Cresp from 11 am to 5 pm, April to October (and by reservation during the rest of the year). You may notice a lot of restaurants here are called Lou something-or-other. *Lou* is Provençal for *le* or *la* ("the").

### GETTING HERE AND AROUND
Trains run approximately once an hour from Nice and Cannes to Grasse on the Mandelieu–Ventimiglia line, taking about 75 minutes from Nice (€9.60 one way) and 30 minutes from Cannes (€4.20). Bus No. 500 runs from Albert 1er Jardin in Nice to Grasse on average about every 40 minutes (about 90 minutes). From Cannes, Nos. 600 and 610 run from in front of the SNCF train station (Rue Jean-Jaurès) about every 20 minutes (every hour on Sunday); the 600 is a little faster, reaching Grasse in 45 minutes. All bus tickets in the region cost €1.50.

### VISITOR INFORMATION
**Grasse Tourist Office** ⊠ *Palais des Congrés, 22 cours Honoré Cresp, CS12105* ☎ *04–93–36–66–66* ⊕ *www.grasse.fr.*

### EXPLORING
**Cathédrale Notre-Dame-du-Puy.** On a cliff-top overlook at the Old Town's edge, the Romanesque Cathédrale Notre-Dame-du-Puy contains no fewer than three paintings by Rubens, a triptych by the famed 15th-century Provençal painter Louis Bréa, and *Lavement des Pieds* (*The Washing of the Feet*) by the young Fragonard. ⊠ *Pl. du Petit Puy.*

**Fragonard.** Built in 1782, this perfume factory is open to the public daily for guided tours. ⊠ *20 bd. Fragonard* ☎ *04–93–36–44–65* ⊕ *www.*

*fragonard.com* ✉ *Free* ☉ *Feb.–Oct., Mon.–Sat. 9–6; Nov.–Jan., Mon.–Sat. 9–12:30 and 2–6.*

**Galimard.** Tracing its pedigree back to 1747, Galimard has a factory that is open to visitors. ■ TIP→ **For €45 you can create and name your own perfume in a two-hour workshop at Galimard's Studio des Fragrances around the corner at 5 route de Pegomas.** ✉ *73 rte. de Cannes* ☎ *04–93–09–20–00* ⊕ *www.galimard.com* ✉ *Free* ☉ *Daily 9–6.*

**Molinard.** Established in 1849, Molinard offers an extensive factory tour. ✉ *60 bd. Victor Hugo* ☎ *04–92–42–33–28* ⊕ *www.molinard.com* ✉ *Free* ☉ *Apr.–Sept., daily 9:30–1 and 2–6:30 (open to 7 and with no lunch break in July and Aug.); Oct.–Mar., Mon.–Sat. 9:30–1 and 2–6:30.*

**Musée d'Art et d'Histoire de Provence** (*Museum of the Art and History of Provence*). Just down from the Fragonard perfumery, the Musée d'Art et d'Histoire de Provence has a large collection of *faïence* from the region, including works from the famous pottery towns of Moustiers, Biot, and Vallauris. ✉ *2 rue Mirabeau* ☎ *04–93–36–80–20* ✉ *Free* ☉ *Apr., daily 11–6; May–Sept., daily 10–7; Oct.–Mar., Wed.–Sun. 11–6. Closed three weeks in Nov.*

**Musée International de la Parfumerie** (*International Museum of Perfume*). This is one of the more sleekly spectacular museums along the coast. Housed in a soaring structure of steel, glass, and teak, the museum traces the 3,000-year history of perfume making; highlights include a fascinating collection of 4,000 antique perfume bottles. In the rooftop greenhouse you can breathe in the heady smells of different herbs and flowers, while the expert and amusing guide crushes delicate petals under your nose to better release the scents. ✉ *2 bd. du Jeu de Ballon* ☎ *04–97–05–58–00* ✉ *€3; €4 for temporary expositions* ☉ *Apr., daily 11–6; May–Sept., daily 10–7 and Sat. to 9; Oct.–Mar., Wed.–Mon., 11–6. Closed 3 wks from mid-Nov.*

**Place aux Aires.** Below the central cluster of museums and perfumeries, the picturesque Place aux Aires is lined with 17th- and 18th-century houses and their arcades. Every Saturday morning there's a small market selling produce and spices.

**Vieille Ville** (*Old Town*). Go down the steps to Rue Mirabeau and lose yourself in the dense labyrinth of the Vieille Ville, where steep, narrow streets are thrown into shadow by shuttered houses five and six stories tall. The studio of native Grassois and perfume creator extraordinaire Didier Galgeweski (at 12 rue de l'Oratoire) is steps from the International Perfumery Museum. ✉ *12 rue de l'Oratoire.*

**Villa Musée Fragonard.** This museum headlines the work of Grasse's own Jean-Honoré Fragonard (1732–1806), one of the great French "chocolate-box" artists of his day (these artists were known for their maudlin style that stemmed from the type of artwork found on boxes of chocolate). The lovely villa contains a collection of Fragonard's drawings, engravings, and paintings; also on display are works by his son Alexandre-Evariste and his grandson, Théophile. ✉ *23 bd. Fragonard* ☎ *04–93–36–93–10* ✉ *Free* ☉ *Apr., daily 11–6; May–Sept., daily 10–7; Oct.–Mar., Wed.–Sun. 11–6. Closed last part Nov.*

$$$
FRENCH

✗ **Lou Candeloun.** Nestled in a small quiet street near Place des Aires, Lou Candeloun ("The Chandelier") is so intimate that you might feel as though you're eating at a friend's. And that's a good thing. At 32, chef Alexis Mayroux has spent more than half his life in a kitchen, creating simple dishes with incomparable market freshness. The *cuisine du marché* changes every three weeks, while other options include chicken with fromage frais, and langoustines in shellfish juice with choy cabbage fondue or roasted figs with lavender honey, gingerbread toast, and ginger ice cream. In the summer, there are a couple of tables outside in the lane. $ *Average main: €30* ✉ *5 rue des Fabreries* ☎ *04–93–60–04–49* ⊕ *www.loucandeloun.eresto.net* ⚓ *Reservations essential* ⊗ *Closed Sun. No dinner Mon. Oct.–Apr. No lunch Mon. May–Sept.*

$$$$
B&B/INN

⌂ **La Bastide Saint-Antoine.** This ocher mansion, once the home of an industrialist who hosted the Kennedys and the Rolling Stones, now the domain of celebrated chef Jacques Chibois, welcomes you with old stone walls, shaded walkways, an enormous pool, and guest rooms that glossily mix Louis Seize, Provençal, and high-tech delights. **Pros:** a bastion of culinary excellence; perks like iPod docks, 1,000 TV channels, and coffee/organic tea in each room; deals on Bastide's website. **Cons:** rooms are a touch too Provençal for some tastes; breakfast (€29) not included. $ *Rooms from: €335* ✉ *48 av. Henri-Dunant* ☎ *04–93–70–94–94* ⊕ *www.jacques-chibois.com* ⟿ *9 rooms, 7 suites* ⦿ *No meals.*

# VALBONNE

*18 km (11 miles) north of Cannes; 14 km (9 miles) northwest of Antibes.*

This fiercely Provençal hill town has been adopted by the British and a smorgasbord of other nationalities, who work either at the nearby technology park Sophia-Antipolis (France's Silicon Valley) or commute to, say, London or Geneva during the workweek, thanks to low-cost travel from easyJet. Valbonne exudes a peculiar kind of mixed-country charm, with a plethora of tasteful restorations and restaurants (including Moroccan, Indian, and sushi). Its principal cachet is the novel layout of the Old Town, designed in a grid system in the 16th century by the monks of Lérins. A checkerboard of ruler-straight *ruelles* (little streets) lies within a sturdy rampart of wraparound houses; at the center, a grand place is framed by Renaissance arcades and shady elms, perfect for people-watching at one of the cafés. Most weekends the village hosts a festival of some type (the first Sunday of the month there's an antiques fair), and despite the not-completely French environment, there's something quite captivating about this village.

You'll find upgraded versions of typical gifts to take home at the Friday Provençal market, one of the best in the region, as is the Maison de la Presse Libris newsstand, beside the pharmacy, with its outstanding selection of international press. Memorie de Famille (E18 rue Alexis Julien) has fabulous and affordable housewares that they decoratively wrap for free, while the English Reading Centre, steps from here, is run by an American and could give Amazon a run for its money.

CLOSE UP

# Route Napoléon

One of the most famous and panoramic roads in France is the Route Napoléon, taken by Napoléon Bonaparte in 1815 after his escape from imprisonment on the Mediterranean island of Elba. Napoléon landed at Golfe-Juan, near Cannes, on March 1 and forged northwest to Grasse, then through dramatic, hilly countryside to Castellane, Digne, and Sisteron. Commemorative plaques bearing the imperial eagle stud the route, inspired by Napoléon's remark, "The eagle will fly from steeple to steeple until it reaches the towers of Notre-Dame." Nowadays there are some lavender-honey stands and souvenir shacks, but

they are few and far between. It's the panoramic views as the road winds its way up into the Alps that make this a route worth taking. Roads are curvy but well maintained. The whole 314-kilometer (195-mile) route from Golfe-Juan to Grenoble takes about 14 hours, but you can just do part of it and still take in the lovely scenery. In fact, if you like scenic drives, follow the Route Napoléon to Trigance and on to the spectacular gorge called the Grand Canyon du Verdon. You can then continue on to the heart of the Var and in a mere 30 minutes be swallowed up in the beauty of the spectacular Gorges Country.

6

A few kilometers west of Valbonne is "La Pitchoune," Julia Child's former Provençal home in Plascassier. For more than 20 years American Kathie Alex has run "Cooking with Friends in France" using Julia's kitchen very much as it was.

## GETTING HERE AND AROUND

There are two ways to get to Valbonne: by car (all the parking is free!) or by bus. The Nice–Sophia Antipolis bus No. 230 (75 minutes, €1.50), operates Monday to Friday beginning at 6:30 am with seven buses that go on to Valbonne (although, oddly, a few less for the return), and you can pick it up on the Promenade des Anglais in Nice, near the Negresco hotel. In Cannes, in front of the train station, the daily No. 630 takes about 40 minutes (€1.50) but check that the bus continues to Valbonne after Sophia-Antipolis. And from the bus station in Antibes, the No. 10 accesses Valbonne via Biot (35 minutes, €1.50) and runs seven days a week.

## WHERE TO EAT

**$$$$**
FRENCH
✕ **Daniel Desavie.** Trained for 23 years by Roger Vergé at the famous Moulins de Mougins, Daniel Desavie has built quite a reputation, judging by crowds of regulars at this restaurant that's 10 minutes (7 kilometers or 4½ miles) from Mougins village. His engaging wife, Chantal, who speaks English, makes diners feel very welcome, as does the pristine French Provençal décor. Consider the lobster with tabbouleh and orange-and-mango vinaigrette before digging in to the braised lamb shoulder fricassé. If you want to add wine, there's a sommelier on hand to help you turn your classic meal into a masterful one. Parking is free. $ *Average main: €37* ⊠ *1360 rte. d'Antibes* ✢ *From Mougins village, follow the D3 toward Valbonne, then take a right at the Forum roundabout along the D103* ☎ *04–93–12–29–68* ⊕ *www. restaurantdanieldesavie.fr* ⊘ *Closed Sun. and Mon.*

### SHOPPING

**Galerie Madoura.** Look for the elegant Galerie Madoura, owned by the ceramic house where Picasso worked, which is still run by descendants of his friends Georges and Suzenne Ramié. You can buy good limited-edition reproductions of his ceramics here, but visits are by appointment only (arrange through the tourist office). In the summer, there are tours at 10:30, and some are in English. ⊠ *Rue Suzanne et Georges Ramié, Vallauris* ☏ *04–93–64–66–39.*

# ANTIBES AND NEARBY

The coastline spanning the brief distance from Cannes to Antibes and Nice has a personality all its own, combining some of the most accessible waterfront resorts (Juan-les-Pins, Villeneuve, and Cagnes—which in 2012 was France's fifth most popular beach destination) with one of the most elite (Cap d'Antibes). This is vacationland, with a culture of commercial entertainment that smacks of the worst of Florida in the 1960s. Hot, poky N98, which goes from Antibes to Cagnes, crawls past a jungle of amusement parks, a massive beach disco and casino, and even a horse-race track. The hill towns of Vallauris and Biot cater to souvenir hunters and lunch sorties. Juan-les-Pins is a party town, its cafés and brasseries thriving into the wee hours. And the glass high-rise monstrosities curving over the waterfront below Cagnes and Villeneuve glow unnaturally bright until dawn. Yet minutes away on a peninsula jutting into the sea, the Cap d'Antibes floats aloof, its mansions and manicured gardens turning their backs on the cheaper real estate on the "mainland."

Everyone visiting this little piece of the Côte d'Azur, whether staying in a villa or a concrete cube, is after the same experience: to sit on a balcony, to listen to the waves washing over the sand, and to watch the sun setting over the oil-painted backdrop of the Alpes de Provence. Wherever you base yourself, you are always a 20-minute zip from Cannes or Nice, and you can easily wend your way into the hills to visit the ancient villages of St-Paul, Vence, and beyond.

## VALLAURIS

*6 km (4 miles) northeast of Cannes; 6 km (4 miles) west of Antibes.*

This ancient village in the low hills above the coast, dominated by a blocky Renaissance château, owes its four-square street plan to a form of medieval urban renewal. Ravaged and eventually wiped out by waves of the plague in the 14th century, the village was rebuilt by 70 Genovese families imported by the Abbaye de Lérins in the 16th century to repopulate the abandoned site. They brought with them a taste for Roman planning—hence the grid format in the Old Town—but more important, a knack for pottery making. Their skills and the fine clay of Vallauris were a perfect marriage, and the village thrived as a pottery center for hundreds of years. In the late 1940s Picasso found inspiration in the malleable soil and settled here, giving the flagging industry new life.

Nowadays, Vallauris has a split personality (and a shady reputation, so keep your hands on your purse): the commercial, souvenir-shop tourist section vaunting bins of pottery below, the dense medieval gridwork of the Old Town looming barren and isolated above, with little to see but laundry and cats.

**BRING HOME A PICASSO**

Along **Rue Hoche** and throughout the lower village are shops and galleries crammed with bright pottery and ceramic art.

**GETTING HERE AND AROUND**

The SNCF Golfe–Juan train station is in Place Pierre Sémard in the center of Vallauris–Golfe–Juan. Tickets cost €5.40 one way from Nice and €1.90 from Cannes. Bus 8, part of the Envibus network, runs between the Golfe–Juan train station and Vallauris about every 15 minutes (45 minutes on Sunday). From Place Guynemer in Antibes, Envibus Line 5 goes to Vallauris with frequent departures. Line 200, connecting Nice and Cannes, stops in Golfe–Juan and runs about every 15 minutes. Bus tickets cost €1.50. There's also the Rapides Côte d'Azur No. 250, a daily airport express bus (55 minutes, €10) that stops in Antibes, Juan-les-Pins with Vallauris as its final destination.



## EXPLORING

**Musée National Picasso.** In the late 1940s Picasso settled here in a simple stone house, creating pottery art from the malleable soil with a single-minded passion. But he returned to painting in 1952 to create one of his masterworks in the château's Romanesque chapel, the vast multipanel oil-on-wood composition called *La Guerre et la Paix* (*War and Peace*). The chapel is part of the Musée National Picasso today, where several of Picasso's ceramic pieces are displayed. ✉ *Pl. de la Libération* ☎ *04–93–64–71–83* 🌐 *www.musee-picasso-vallauris.fr* 🎟 *€4* 🕒 *June 16–30 and Sept. 1–15, Wed.–Mon. 10–12:15 and 2–6; Sept. 16–June 15, Wed.–Mon. 10–12:15 and 2–5; July and Aug., daily 10–7.*

## WHERE TO EAT

$ MEDITERRANEAN 🍴 **Café Llorca.** What used to be Café Marianne is now a modern café from one of the "pillars of contemporary Mediterranean cuisine," Alain Llorca. Before taking over from Roger Vergé at the famous Moulins de Mougins, Llorca worked eight years at the acclaimed Negresco. As part of the bistronomomy movement (and one of the best-value eateries in the region), Café Llorca has daily-changing starters from €6 and main courses at around €15, which attract a loyal clientele of locals alongside tourists. The menu mainly sticks to southern classics such as beef cannelloni in a bordelaise sauce and cod with aioli, both served so generously (in pottery dishes from Vallauris) that it's hard to find room for the pastries by Jean-Michel Llorca. [$] *Average main: €15* ✉ *Place Paul Isnard* ☎ *04–93–64–30–42* 🌐 *www.cafellorcavallauris.com.*

*Continued on page 310*

# STROKES *of* GENIUS

*Le Cantique des Cantiques (oil on canvas)*
by Marc Chagall, Musée Chagall

*Fleurs et Fruits* (gouache cutout) by Henri Matisse, Musée Matisse

A kind of artistic Garden of Eden exists in the minds of many painters, a magical place painted in the vivid colors of imagination—a promised land where they can bask in warm sunshine nearly every day of the year, swim in a placid sea of incredible blue, daub flowers so colorful they would challenge even the most riotous palette, and live life as sensually as they sketch it.

This is the dream would-be Adams sought in the late 19th century when, inspired by Impressionist *plein-air* (open-air) painting, artists abandoned the airless studios of Paris for the sunkissed towns of the South of France. By the 1920s, a virtual migration of painters and sculptors heeded the siren call of the Mediterranean muse and began to colonize the Côte d'Azur. Signac made St-Tropez the Riviera's first "Greenwich Village"; Cannes attracted Picasso and Van Dongen; Haut-de-Cagnes and St-Paul-de-Vence lured Renoir, Soutine, and Modigliani; and Matisse and Dufy settled in Nice. A veritable "museum without walls," these locales went on to nurture some of the biggest "isms" in 20th-century art. Creativity was unleashed, cares forgotten, and *le bonheur de vie*—the happiness of life—became a forceful leitmotiv.

The result was an outpouring of art whose exuberance and energy led to the paradise that exists here today: a tightly packed 100-mile stretch of coastline crammed with the houses, gardens, and towns that inspired these artists. Be content to leave their masterpieces to museums scattered around the world, and get ready to savor instead a host of virtual Matisses, 3-D Renoirs, and pop-up Picassos. This rainbow curve of a coast will prove to be an unforgettable road trip through the history of modern art.

# THE MODERN ART ROAD

**MATISSE:** Stroll the stone ramparts of medieval **Vence**, then head out to its New Town to exult in the beauty of Matisse's famous Chapelle du Rosaire, created in 1947. Matisse's last testament is a jewel of stained glass and tiled drawings.

Modigliani

**SIGNAC, MODIGLIANI, BONNARD:** Hilltop **St-Paul-de-Vence** was rediscovered in the 1920s when the artists Signac, Modigliani, and Bonnard met at La Colombe d'Or, an inn whose legendary charm remains intact.

**RENOIR:** At the foot of Haut-de-Cagnes is the Villa "Les Collettes," the last home of Auguste Renoir. He painted his final Impressionist paintings in the two glassed-in studios here, but you can best channel his spirit in the magical garden.

**LÉGER** planned to create a sculpture garden in the medieval village of Biot. In 1960, his widow established instead the Musée National Fernand Léger, whose 350 artworks capture the sparkle of this master of Neo-Plasticism.

**PICASSO** lived or worked on the Riviera for five decades and his presence still resonates through the idyllic backstreets of Old **Antibes**, where he left a striking collection of work at the seaside Château Grimaldi. In **Vallauris**—the "town of a thousand potters"—Picasso's *Man with Sheep* statue anchors the Place du Marché, while nearby is the Musée National Picasso, his vast decorated chapel and "temple of peace" (which rivals *Guernica* for impact). Via the tourist office, arrange a visit to the Galerie Madoura to see the artist's witty ceramic artworks.

## PERIPHERAL VISION

Journey westward to discover three towns where 20th-century art was first incubated: **Arles**, Vincent van Gogh's promised land; **Aix-en-Provence**, Paul Cézanne's hometown; **St-Tropez**, where Matisse discovered abstract color.

*Man with Sheep* statue

### Map labels

Vence
St-Paul-de-Vence
D36
D7
Haut-de-Cagnes
Chateauneuf-Grasse
D2085
D2085
Grasse
D3
Cros-de-Cagnes
Valbonne
D9
Biot
D103
RENOIR
Mougins
D36
Antibes
A8
N285
Vallauris
Léger
Juan-les-Pins
Cannes
N98
Golfe de Napoule
N7
La Napoule
0    4 mi
0    4 km
Miramar
N7
N98

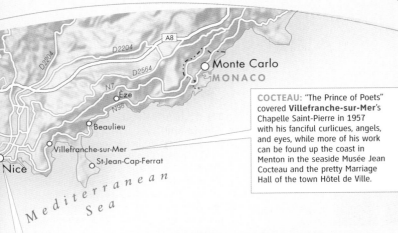

**COCTEAU:** "The Prince of Poets" covered **Villefranche-sur-Mer**'s Chapelle Saint-Pierre in 1957 with his fanciful curlicues, angels, and eyes, while more of his work can be found up the coast in Menton in the seaside Musée Jean Cocteau and the pretty Marriage Hall of the town Hôtel de Ville.

**CHAGALL and MATISSE:** A banquet of museums entices the art lover to **Nice**, including the Musée Matisse, the Musée National Marc Chagall, and the Musée d'Art Moderne, but don't forget to stroll to Matisse's favorite spots—the elegant Promenade des Anglais, Jardin Albert 1er, and enchanting Cours Saleya marketplace.

Marc Chagall Museum

6

**IN FOCUS** STROKES OF GENIUS

"The days follow each other here with a beauty which I would describe as insolent."

—Nietzsche,

writing from Èze, near Beaulieu, 1883

St-Paul-de-Vence                    Chapelle du Rosaire, Vence

**Born:** October 25, 1881, in Málaga, Spain.

**Died:** April 8, 1973, in Mougins, Côte d'Azur.

**Personality Profile:** Genius, philosopher-sage, egoist.

**Claim to Fame:** A one-man history of 20th-century art, Picasso changed styles as often as he did mistresses, but he is best known as the founder of Cubism.

**Picasso Peeking:** Cane fencing has been erected around Picasso's last retreat of Notre-Dame-de-Vie in Mougins by his heirs, and you are obliged to view his majestic Château de Vauvenargues (where he lies buried) through binoculars.

**Picasso Peaking:** The Musée Picasso in Antibes and his War and Peace Chapel in Vallauris are top spots to view his masterworks.

**Best-Known Works:** *Les Demoiselles d'Avignon, Guernica, Au Lapin Agile, Minotauomachy.*

**Quote:** "You see, I have to paint for the both of us now" (on hearing of Matisse's death).

Ceramic Plate by Picasso, Galerie Madoura

## PABLO PICASSO

The "North Pole and South Pole" of 20th-century art (to use Picasso's phrase), the two heavyweights of modernism had a famous push-pull friendship. No matter that Picasso was a structuralist and Matisse a sensualist, or that Picasso was as egocentric as Matisse was self-effacing—the two masters engaged in a decades-long artistic "game of chess," often played out as neighbors on the Côte d'Azur. It was Matisse's mesmerizingly beautiful paintings created in Nice in the 1930s that probably inspired Picasso's move to the South of France in 1946. He wound up painting in Antibes, sculpting in Vallauris, wooing in Golfe-Juan, and seducing in Mougins. But their ventriloquous dialogue began in 1906 when they first met in the Parisian salon of Gertrude Stein (who lost little time in baiting the artists against each other).

Matisse had already created a revolution in color; Picasso, 12 years younger, was about to create one in form with *Les Demoiselles d'Avignon*—the "first" 20th-century painting, whose cubistic structure was inspired by African sculpture—as it turns out, Matisse's African sculpture, since Picasso had studied his collection of Senegalese totems. When Picasso moved to the Midi in 1946, Matisse presented him with a dove, which inspired Picasso to create his famous poster in homage to France's newly won peace.

The same year, Picasso was given the keys to Antibes' Château Grimaldi, where he painted 30 canvases depicting mermaids and minotaurs, all prancing about in direct homage to Matisse's famously joyous paintings, *La Joie de Vie* and *La Danse.*

# HENRI MATISSE

What Tahiti was to Gauguin, Nice was to Matisse. Its flower marketplaces, palaces painted in bonbon pastels, and magnificent palm trees soothed and, together with the constantly changing show of light—so different from the relentless glare of St-Tropez (where, in 1904, he first committed chromatic mayhem with his Fauve "wild beast" masterpiece, *Luxe, Calme, et Volupté*)—inspired him.

By 1919, ailing with bronchitis, he had moved to Nice, where he started to paint images of unrivaled voluptuousness: semi-nude odalisques skimpily clad in harem pantaloons and swathed in Moroccan fabrics. Their popular success allowed Matisse to relocate, in 1921, to a rooftop apartment at 1 Place Charles Félix, which magnificently overlooked Nice's Cours Saleya flower market. To view his art, head for the city's Musée Matisse and the Monastère de Cimiez cemetery, where you'll find his grave.

But to sense his true spirit venture to nearby Vence, where he moved in 1943 when Nice was threatened by World War II. Here he created the sublime Chapelle du Rosaire, his masterpiece ("in spite of all its imperfections") of black-on-white tile drawings and exalted stained-glass windows of emerald, blue, and yellow. The intensely competitive Picasso also saw it, of course, as a challenge. So, in 1952–53 he transformed an empty Romanesque chapel in nearby Vallauris into a "temple of peace" with scenes of La Guerre (war) and La Paix (peace). Unlike Matisse, however, he designed no liturgical gear, chasubles, or altar, since Picasso remained an avowed atheist.

**Born:** December 31, 1869, in Le Cateau, Northern France.

**Died:** November 3, 1954, in Nice, Côte d'Azur.

**Personality Profile:** Buddha, bon vivant, hedonist.

**Claim to Fame:** As father of the Fauves—the phrase "wild beast" described their expressive use of shade and hue—his works simplified design and exalted color.

**Meeting Matisse:** Musée Matisse in Nice, Rosary Chapel in Vence.

**Matisse's muse:** A decade before Sister Jacques-Marie inspired Matisse's Chapelle du Rosaire, she had been a nurse and model to him.

**Best-Known Works:** *Luxe, Calme, et Volupté, The Dance, Jazz, The Red Studio, Pink Nude.*

**Be Matisse:** Rent the Villa Le Rêve, the lovely Vence address he called home for five years. At 261 Avenue Henri Matisse, it is available for €3021 (04-93-58-82-68, www.villalerevevence.com), rented by the week.

**Quote:** "Picasso sees everything."

6

IN FOCUS STROKES OF GENIUS

La danse

# IN LIVING COLOR: LA COLOMBE D'OR

Heading into the hills high above Nice, the road turns and slopes, allowing the full beauty of the rugged coast to be appreciated. A panorama of unexpected charm unfolds upon arriving at St-Paul-de-Vence, a little village perched high on the hills behind its medieval ramparts looking for all the world as if it was a 15th-century Brigadoon. As it turns out, this proved to be one of the cradles of 20th-century art. In the early 1920s, word got out that the owners of its beautiful Colombe d'Or inn would accept paintings and sketches in lieu of payment. Before you knew it, little-known artists were heading to dine and sleep here. The fact that those painters happened to turn out to be Picasso, Matisse, and Braque means that La Colombe d'Or is today one of France's most unique museums—a "museum" you can sleep and dine in. Frankly, if you don't stay or dine here, you simply haven't been to the French Riviera.

Enjoying the pool

**IF THOSE PAINTINGS COULD TALK**
Set just outside the walls of St-Paul—a great location, for summer crowds can easily make you claustrophobic within them—this stone-and-beam auberge occupies a lovely, rose-stone Renaissance-era mansion. Walk into the dining room and you'll do a double take. Yes, those are real Mirós, Bonnards, and Légers on those rustic walls (and yes, they are now nailed down!), indeed given in payment by the artists in hungrier days when this inn was known as the "Café-Restaurant Robinson." It soon became the heart and soul of St-Paul's artistic revival, and the cream of 20th-century France lounged together under its fig trees—Picasso and Chagall, Maeterlinck and Kipling, Yves Montand and Simone Signoret (who met and married here). Off-duty celebs still flock here and it is one of the few places in the world where movie-stars are happy to be recognized.

A "museum" you can sleep and dine in

## UNDER THE FIG TREES

Today, the Colombe is now presided over by François and Danièle Roux, the fourth generation in charge, and the famille Roux's extraordinary sense of style would have delighted Pablo, Georges, and Henri. Give in to the green-shaded loveliness of the restaurant terrace and the gracious manners of the waitstaff. Set under timeless fig trees, a luncheon table here is lorded over by a ceramic Léger mural, while the pool is an idyllic garden bower, complete with a Calder stabile, and there's even a Braque by the fireplace in the bar. Feast on the famous "hors d'oeuvres de la Colombe" (gigantic shrimp, hunks of charcuterie). Segue on to the snail casserole, Sisteron lamb, or

Dining under the fig trees

salmon quenelles, then enjoy the house's signature orange-flavored grappa with dessert while you tune into your neighbor's conversation (". . . the Picasso on my yacht dates from. . . ."). No matter the menu prices are as fabulous as the art collection—a meal here is a must.

## MIND THAT CALDER!

Head upstairs to your room—you'll have to dodge a Calder mobile (painted red with the artist's permission, to offset it from the white walls)—to be bewitched by Louis XIII armoires, medieval fourposters, wood beams, Provençal borders and painted murals; take a look out your window and you might find yourself staring at a roof of tiles painted every shade of the rainbow. While there are two annexes to the main house, all the guest rooms are flawless in taste (note you can enjoy a dinner or drink here without being a hotel guest). Henri Matisse once called La Colombe d'Or "a small paradise"—and who are you to argue? Address: Place Général-de-Gaulle, 06570, St-Paul-de-Vence. Phone: 04-93-32-80-02 Website: www.la-colombe-dor.com. Closed Oct. 26–Dec. 20.

## ANTIBES

Fodor'sChoice
★

*11 km (7 miles) northeast of Cannes; 15 km (9 miles) southeast of Nice.*

Named Antipolis—meaning across from (*anti*) the city (*polis*)—by the Greeks, who founded it in the 4th century BC, Antibes flourished under the Romans' aristocratic rule, with an amphitheater, aqueducts, and baths. The early Christians established their bishopric here, the site of the region's cathedral until the 13th century. It was in the Middle Ages that the kings of France began fortifying this key port town, an effort that culminated in the recognizable star-shaped ramparts designed by Vauban. The young general Napoléon once headed this stronghold, living with his family in a humble house in the Old Town; his mother washed their clothes in a stream. There's still a *lavoir* (public laundry fountain) in the Old Town where locals, not unlike Signora Bonaparte, rinse their clothes and hang them like garlands over the narrow streets.

With its broad stone ramparts scalloping in and out over the waves and backed by blunt medieval towers, it's easy to understand why Antibes (pronounced Awn-*teeb*) inspired Picasso to paint on a panoramic scale. Stroll Promenade Amiral-de-Grasse along the crest of Vauban's sea walls, and watch the sleek yachts purring out to sea. Even more intoxicating, just off the waterfront, is the souklike maze of old streets, its market filled with fresh fish and goat cheese, wild herbs, and exotic spices. This is **Vieil Antibes,** with a nearly Italianate ambience, perhaps no great surprise considering that Antibes' great fort marked the border between Italy and France right up to the 19th century.

Underscoring how picturesque it all is, the town authorities have now set up a "Painters' Trail," complete with stands on the spots where such greats as Picasso, Cross, Boudin, Harpignies, and Monet once set up their easels. Above all, it was Monet who fell in love with the town and his most famous paintings show the fortified Vieil Antibes against the sea. He arrived in January 1888 and expected to stay only a few days; three months later, he had shipped off 39 canvases to be exhibited in Paris at the gallery of Vincent van Gogh's brother. To see Antibes as Monet once did, head to the tourist office for a pamphlet on the Painters' Trail, complete with map or sign up for a guided walk along the trail, every Friday at 10 am (€7).

### GETTING HERE AND AROUND

Antibes has one central train station, the Gare SNCF, which is at the far end of town but still within walking distance of the Vieille Ville and only a block or so from the beach. Local trains are frequent, coming from Nice (20 minutes, €4.40), Juan-les-Pins, Biot, Cannes (10 minutes, €2.80), and almost all other coastal towns.

There are high-speed TGVs (*Trains à Grand Vitesse*) that depart from Antibes. Bus service, available at Antibes' Gare Routière (bus station) (✉ *1 pl. Guynemer*) is supplied by Envibus (☎ *04–89–87–72–00* ⊕ *www.envibus.fr*). For local routes or to get to Cannes, Nice, Cagnes-sur-Mer, Juan-les-Pins, take the Lignes d'Azur No. 200 (☎ *08–10–06–10–06* ⊕ *www.lignedazur.com*), which runs every 15 minutes and costs €1.50.

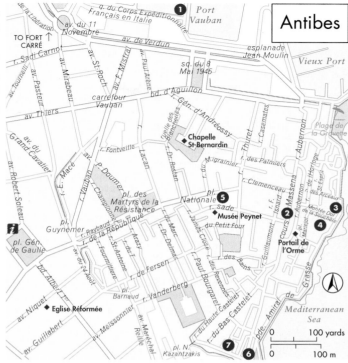

## VISITOR INFORMATION

**Antibes Tourist Office** ✉ *11 pl. de Gaulle, BP 37* ☎ *04-22-10-60-10*
⊕ *antibes-juanlespins.com.* **Gare SNCF.** ✉ *Pl. Pierre-Semard* ⊕ *www.gares-en-mouvement.com.*

## TOURS

The Antibes tourist office offers several guided tours lasting 1 hour and 45 minutes (€7). Themes range from "The Painters Trail" to "Discovering Old Antibes" (in English on Thursday at 10 am from March to October) to "Artists and the Mediterranean." A new addition is the "Gourmet Tour" from June to September. For €12 per person (or €20 a couple) you can taste the town by sampling at three local eateries. Tours must be reserved in advance with the Tourist Office by calling ☎ *04-97-23-11-25.* Or download the tourist office's Monument Tracker app and let it guide you in English through 150 local sites.

## EXPLORING

### TOP ATTRACTIONS

Fodor'sChoice
★ **Commune Libre du Safranier** (*Free Commune of Safranier*). A few blocks south of the Château Grimaldi is the Commune Libre du Safranier, a magical little neighborhood with a character (and mayor) all its own even though it's technically part of Antibes. Not far off the seaside promenade, the Rue de la Touraque is the main street to get here, and you can amble

around the Place du Safranier, where tiny houses hang heavy with flowers and vines, and neighbors carry on conversations from window to window across the stone-stepped Rue du Bas-Castelet. Said to have once been a tiny fishing port, it's now the scene of festivals and quotes of Zorba the Greek, who lived here, including his "I fear nothing, I hope for nothing, I am free." ☒ *Rue du Safranier, Rue du Bas-Castelet.*

**Cours Masséna.** To visit old Antibes, stroll the Cours Masséna, where from 6 am to 1 pm every morning (except Mondays from September to April) a sheltered Provençal market sells lemons, olives, and hand-stuffed sausages, and the vendors take breaks in the shoebox cafés flanking one side. Painters, sculptors, and other artists take over at 3 pm Tuesday through Sunday in the summer, and Friday through Sunday from September to mid-June. From Port Vauban, you'll find the cours by passing through an arched gateway beneath the ramparts and following Rue Aubernon to the old Portail de l'Orme, built of quarried Roman stone and enlarged in the Middle Ages. ☒ *Cours Masséna.*

**Eglise de l'Immaculée-Conception.** This served as the region's cathedral until the bishopric was transferred to Grasse in 1244. The church's 18th-century facade, a marvelously Latin mix of classical symmetry and fantasy, has been restored in stunning shades of ocher and cream. Its stout medieval watchtower was built in the 11th century with stones "mined" from Roman structures. Inside is a Baroque altarpiece painted by the Niçois artist Louis Bréa in 1515. ☒ *Rue du Saint Esprit.*

**Musée Picasso.** Rising high over the water, Musée Picasso is set in the stunning medieval Château Grimaldi. As rulers of Monaco, the Grimaldi family lived here until the revolution; this fine old castle, however, was little more than a monument until its curator offered use of its chambers to Picasso in 1946, when that extraordinary genius was enjoying a period of intense creative energy. The result was a bounty of exhilarating paintings, ceramics, and lithographs inspired by the sea and by Greek mythology—all very Mediterranean. The château, which became the Musée Picasso in 1966, houses some 245 works by the artist, as well as pieces by Miró, Calder, and Léger; the first floor displays more than 100 paintings of Russian-born artist Nicholas de Staël. Even those who are not great Picasso fans should enjoy his vast paintings on wood, canvas, paper, and walls, alive with nymphs, fauns, and centaurs. ☒ *Château Grimaldi, Pl. Mariejol* ☎ *04–92–90–54–20* ⌨ *€6* ☼ *Sept 16–June 15: Tues.–Sun. 10–noon and 2–6; June 16–Sept 15: Tues.–Sun. 10–6.*

**Port Vauban.** Whether you approach the waterfront from the train station or park along the Avenue de Verdun, you'll first confront the awesome expanse of luxury yachts in the Port Vauban, which has a new underground parking lot and attractive new esplanade from which to admire how the other half lives at sea. Swanning back and forth at will between Greece, Saudi Arabia, and other ports of call, some megayachts stretch as long as 500 feet, although in 2011 the 162.5-meter (531-foot) *Eclipse,* with its missile defense system and mini-submarine, was banned from docking here, proving that size does matter. With the tableau of snowy Alps looming in the background and the formidable medieval block towers of the **Fort Carré** (Square Fort) guarding entry to the port, it's difficult to find a more dramatic spot to anchor. This superbly symmetrical island fortress was completed in 1565 and restored in 1967, but can only be admired from afar. Across the Quai Rambaud, which juts into the harbor, a tiny crescent of sand called **La Gravette** beach offers swimmers one of the last soft spots on the coast before the famous Riviera pebble beaches begin as you head east.

### WORTH NOTING

**Musée Archéologique** (*Archaeology Museum*). The Promenade Amiral de Grasse—a marvelous spot for pondering the mountains and tides—leads directly to the Bastion St-André, a squat Vauban fortress that now houses the Musée Archéologique. In its glory days this 17th-century stronghold sheltered a garrison; the bread oven is still visible in the vaulted central hall. The museum collection focuses on Antibes's classical history, displaying amphorae and sculptures found in local digs as well as in shipwrecks from the harbor. ✉ *Av. Général-Maizières* ☎ *04–92–90–56–87* 🎫 *€3* 🕑 *Oct.–May, Tues.–Sun. 10–1 and 2–5; mid-June–mid-Sept., Tues.–Sun. 10–12 and 2–6.*

**Place Nationale.** Not far from the Commune quarter, the Old Town streets invite you to explore the mix of shops, galleries, restaurants, and bakeries. Aim to wind up on Place Nationale, the site of the Roman forum. It's a pleasant place for a drink under the broad plane trees.



## BEACHES

Antibes and Juan-les-Pins together claim 25 km (15½ miles) of coastline and 48 beaches (including Cap d'Antibes). In Antibes you can choose between small sandy inlets, such as **La Gravette,** below the port; the central **Plage du Ponteil; Plage de la Salis** toward the Cap; rocky escarpments around the Old Town; or the vast stretch of sand above the Fort Carré. The Plage de la Salis may be one of the prettiest beach sites on the coast, with the dark pines of the cape on one side and the old stones of Antibes on the other, all against a backdrop of Alpine white. Juan-les-Pins is one big city beach, lined by a boulevard and promenade peppered with cafés and restaurants. If you want to follow in Picasso's footsteps, head to the **Plage de la Garoupe,** halfway down the Cap d'Antibes peninsula and set near the cape's fabulous Sentier Tirepoil footpath: this pretty white-sand crescent is the place locals have always headed to sunbathe and celeb-spot.

## WHERE TO EAT

$$$$
FRENCH
Fodor's Choice ★

🍴 **Le Figuier de Saint-Esprit.** After 18 years performing in the kitchens of others, acclaimed chef Christian Morrisset opened one of the best restaurants in the Old Town of Antibes, on the site of what was formerly La Jarre. It is in a contemporary setting with dark wood tables and is gorgeously shaded by a 40-year-old fig tree and a canopy of vines—the shady street is one of the most picturesque in town. The former chef of Juana has kept his prices democratic at lunchtime, when a meal costs around €20; you can easily spend twice as much at dinner. Typical of his style, which focuses on local ingredients, is a saddle of lamb from the Alpilles cooked in a crust of Vallauris clay with gnocchi and truffles, zucchini, eggplant, and thyme jus. [$] *Average main: €36* ✉ *14 rue Saint-Esprit* ☎ *04–93–34–50–12* 🌐 *www.christianmorisset.fr* 🕑 *Closed Mon. and no lunch Wed. May–Oct. Closed Tues. and Wed. Nov.–Apr. Closed most of Nov.*

$$$ FRENCH 🍴 **Le Nacional.** When you've had enough of the "catch of the day" and need a good old dose of red meat, head to the newly opened Nacional Beef & Wine in old Antibes, where the selection includes Black Angus American, Australian, or Coutancie beef, and various cuts from rump steak to rib to sirloin XXL. You can even read about where your meat (and veal, chicken, and foie gras, also on the menu) was raised, as well as its race, age, and feeding methods. If all of this is too much, you can order pasta. You know where that comes from. Nacional is set among stone walls and has a chic bar-and-grill decor. There's a swanky summer terrace. [$] *Average main: €29* ✉ *61 pl. Nationale, Antibes, France* ☎ *04–93–61–77–30* 🌐 *www.restaurant-nacional-antibes.com* 🕒 *No dinner Sun. No lunch mid-June–Aug. Closed Mon. Sept–mid-June. Closed Jan.*

$$$ FRENCH 🍴 **Taverne le Safranier.** Part of a tiny Old Town enclave determined to resist the press of tourism, this casual tavern is headquarters for the ⇨ *Commune Libre du Safranier.* Tables scattered across the sunny terrace on Place Safranier hold locals and visitors relishing Provençal cuisine, *courgette beignet* (zucchini fritters), Saint Jacques and lobster *cassolette,* thick handmade ravioli, and whole *dorade,* a delicate Mediterranean fish that is unceremoniously split, fried, and garnished with lemon. A laid-back staff shouts your order into the nautical-decor bar. There's a €16 lunch option, and the blackboard specials are homemade and satisfying. [$] *Average main: €28* ✉ *1 pl. Safranier* ☎ *04–93–34–80–50* 🕒 *Closed Mon and Jan.*

## WHERE TO STAY

$$$ HOTEL 🏨 **Le Mas Djoliba.** Tucked into a residential neighborhood on the crest between Antibes and Juan-les-Pins, this cool, cozy inn feels like the private home it once was. **Pros:** peaceful neighborhood; bed-and-breakfast atmosphere; delicious home cooking. **Cons:** parking is limited and tight. [$] *Rooms from: €169* ✉ *29 av. de Provence* ☎ *04–93–34–02–48* 🌐 *www.hotel-djoliba.com* 🛏 *13 rooms* 🕒 *Closed Nov.–mid-Mar.* 🍽 *No meals.*

## NIGHTLIFE

**Blue Lady Pub.** Located next to Geoffrey's British food shop, this pub is frequented by French and foreigners alike (and their kids and dogs). It's a great little spot to recollect your thoughts over a drink after a long day, or to hear live music. It's worth noting that it's more than just a nightlife scene. Beginning at 7:30 am you can grab a latté, smoothie, and even English breakfast (there are newspapers on deck). Or stick around for lunch—homemade burgers or pot pies and fresh salads. Friendly service and free Wi-Fi are bonuses. ✉ *L Galerie du Port, Rue Lacan* ☎ *04–93–34–41–00* 🌐 *www.bluel adypub.com.*

**La Siesta.** This is an enormous summertime entertainment center and the largest beach club in France. The casino has 200 slot machines, four of which are the only of their kind in France, English roulette and blackjack tables, a bistro, and a terrace overlooking the sea. ✉ *Rte. du Bord de Mer* ☎ *04–93–33–31–31* 🌐 *www.joa-casino.com* 🕒 *Disco: Fri. and Sat. June and Sept.; Thurs.–Sat. July and Aug. Casino: 10 am–4 am Sun.–Thurs.; until 5 am Fri. and Sat.*

## SPORTS AND THE OUTDOORS

**Diamond Diving.** Brit Alex Diamond set up his Golfe–Juan Dive Centre shop in 2008 and with his French government-recognized certification he even teaches future French diving instructors "Diving English." ⊠ *Rue des Pêcheurs, Vallauris* ☎ *06–15–30–52–23* ⊕ *www. diamonddiving.net.*

## SHOPPING

In Antibes, two antiques and flea markets occur weekly, both from 7 am to 6 pm: one on Saturday on Place Nationale, and one on Thursday and Saturday at Place Audiberti.

**Old Town.** You can find plenty of eclectic little boutiques and gallery shops in the Old Town, especially along Rue Sade, Rue de la République, and Rue James Close.

# CAP D'ANTIBES

*2 km (1 mile) south of Antibes.*

For the most part extravagantly idyllic, this fabled 4-mile-long peninsula has been carved up into luxurious estates perched high above the water and shaded by thick, tall pines. Since the 19th century its wild greenery and isolation have drawn a glittering assortment of aristocrats, artists, literati, and the merely fabulously wealthy. Among those claiming the prestigious Cap d'Antibes address over the years are: Guy de Maupassant, Anatole France, Claude Monet, the Duke and Duchess of Windsor, the Greek shipping tycoon Stavros Niarchos, and the cream of the Lost Generation, including Ernest Hemingway, Dorothy Parker, Gertrude Stein, and F. Scott Fitzgerald. Now the focal point is the famous Hotel Eden Roc, which is packed with stars during the Cannes Film Festival (not surprisingly, as movie studios always pick up the tab for their favorite celebs). Reserve for lunch here during the festival and be literally surrounded by celebrities to-ing and fro-ing to the pool. Just play it cool, though: keep your sunglasses on at all times and resist taking photos.

### GETTING HERE AND AROUND

Cap d'Antibes doesn't have its own train station; the closest is the SNCF train station in Antibes (Place Pierre Semard). SNCF trains run frequently between Nice and Cannes, stopping in Antibes about halfway (20 minutes from Nice or Cannes). From the bus station at Place Guynemer in Antibes, bus No. 2, operated by Envibus, wends its way around the Cap d'Antibes, leaving about every 40 minutes and taking 15 minutes to reach the other end of the Cap. Stops include Phare du Cap (lighthouse), Fontaine, and Eden Roc (the terminus). Tickets cost €1.

### EXPLORING

**Jardin Thuret** (*Thuret Garden*). To fully experience the Riviera's heady hothouse exoticism, visit the glorious Jardin Thuret, established by botanist Gustave Thuret in 1856 as a testing ground for subtropical plants and trees. Thuret was responsible for the introduction of the palm tree, forever changing the profile of the French Riviera. On his death the property was left to the Ministry of Agriculture, which continues to dabble in the introduction of exotic species. The garden is in the middle of the Cap; from the Port Gallice, head up Chemin du Croûton, turn right on the Boulevard du Cap, then right again on Chemin Raymond. ✉ *90 chemin Raymond* ☎ *04–97–21–25–00* ⊕ *www7.sophia. inra.fr/jardin_thuret* 🖂 *Free* ⊗ *Winter, Mon.–Fri. 8:30–5:30; summer, Mon.–Fri. 8–6.*

Fodor's Choice **Le Sentier du Littoral** (*Sentier Tire-poil*). Bordering the Cap's zillion-
★ dollar hotels and over-the-top estates runs one of the most spectacular footpaths in the world: the Sentier du Littoral (aka Sentier Tire-poil, which mean the wind is so strong it "ruffles the hair"), which was recently extended, bringing the circuit "full circle" around the gardens at Eilenroc over to l'Anse de l'Argent Faux. It now stretches about 5 km (3 miles) along the outermost tip of the peninsula. It begins gently enough at the pretty Plage de la Garoupe (where Cole Porter and Gerald Murphy used to hang out), with a paved walkway and dazzling views over the Baie de la Garoupe and the faraway Alps. Round the far end of the cap, however, and the paved promenade soon gives way to a boulder-studded pathway that picks its way along 50-foot cliffs, dizzying switchbacks, and thundering breakers (*Attention Mort*—"Beware: Death"—read the signs, reminding you this path can be very dangerous in stormy weather). Continue along the new portion of the path to the cove l'Anse de l'Argent Faux, where you can stop and catch your breath before heading up to the entrance of Eilen Roc. Then follow Avenue Beaumont impasse tangent until it touches the Cap's main road RD 2559. On sunny days, with exhilarating winds and spectacular breakers, you'll have company, although for most stretches all signs of civilization completely disappear—except for a yacht or two. The walk is long and takes about two hours to complete, but it may prove to be two of the more unforgettable hours of your trip (especially if you tackle it at sunset). By the way, if you come across locked gates blocking your route it's because storm warnings have been issued and you are not allowed to enter. ■TIP➔ From the bus station in town take the No. 2 bus to the "Fontaine" stop. To return, follow the Plage de la Garoupe until Boulevard de la Garoupe, where you'll make a left to reconnect with the bus.

**Phare de la Garoupe** (*Garoupe Lighthouse*). You can sample a little of what draws famous people to this part of the world by walking up the Chemin de Calvaire from the Plage de la Salis in Antibes—about 1 kilometer (½ mile)—and taking in the extraordinary views from the hill surmounted by the old lighthouse, the Phare de la Garoupe. Next to the lighthouse, the 16th-century double chapel of **Notre-Dame-de-la-Garoupe** contains ex-votos and statues of the Virgin, all in memory and for the protection of sailors. Please note that should renovations begin in January 2014 as planned, the chapel will be closed until mid-2015. ✉ *Chemin de Calvaire* ☎ *04–22–10–60–10* ⊗ *Chapel, Mon. and Fri. 2:30–5:30; mass at 11:30.*

Fodor's Choice **Villa Eilenroc.** The Sentier du Litterol passes along the beach at the
★ Villa Eilenroc, designed by Charles Garnier, who created the Paris Opéra—which should give you some idea of its style. It commands the

tip of the peninsula from a grand and glamorous garden. Over the last decade an eco-museum was completed and a scented garden created at the entrance to the rose garden. On Wednesdays from September to June, visitors are allowed to wander through the reception salons, which retain the Louis Seize-Trianon feel of the noble facade. The Winter Salon still has its 1,001 Nights ceiling mural painted by Jean Dunand, the famed Art Deco designer; display cases are filled with memorabilia donated by Caroline Groult-Flaubert (Antibes resident and goddaughter of the great author); and the boudoir has paneling from the Marquis de Sévigné's Paris mansion. As you leave, be sure to detour to La Rosaerie, the rose garden of the estate—in the distance you can spot the white portico of the Château de la Cröe, another legendary villa (now reputedly owned by a syndicate of Russian billionaires). It has a host of big names attached to it—singer Helene Beaumont built it; and King Leopold II of Belgium, King Farouk of Egypt, Aristotle Onassis, and Greta Garbo all rented here. ✉ *At peninsula's tip, 460 av. L.D. Beaumont* ☎ *04–93–67–74–33* 🌐 *www.antibesjuanlespins.com* 🎟 *Free Oct–Mar.; €2 Apr.–Sept.* ⏲ *Oct.–Mar., Wed. and Sat. 1–4; Apr.–June, Wed. and Sat. 10–5; July–Sept., Wed., Sat., and Sun. 3–7.*

## WHERE TO EAT

$$$$ FRENCH 🍴 **Les Pêcheurs.** In 1954 French resistance hero Camille Rayon built a restaurant on the Cap d'Antibes between two stone fishing huts dating from the early 20th century. It wasn't long before La Maison des Pêcheurs became a fashionable address, though the site was abandoned in the 1990s before being transformed into the Relais & Chateau Cap d'Antibes Beach Hotel in 2009. Although beef dishes are available, fish plays a starring role in chef Philippe Jégo's menu, backed up by vegetables and fruits from the nearby hills; don't miss the stunning desserts (at a whopping €20 each), which will give you an excuse to linger as the sun sets over the Îles de Lérins and the Esterel. [$] *Average main: €50* ✉ *10 bd. Maréchal Juin* ☎ *04–92–93–13–30* 🌐 *www.ca-beachhotel.com* ⏲ *Closed Oct. 20–Apr. 1.*

$$$$ SEAFOOD 🍴 **Restaurant de Bacon.** Since 1948, under the careful watch of the Sordello brothers, this has been *the* spot for seafood on the French Riviera. The catch of the day may be minced in lemon ceviche (€38), floating in a top-of-the-line bouillabaisse (€125), or simply grilled with fennel and crisped with hillside herbs (€80). The dreamy terrace over the Baie des Anges, with views of the Antibes ramparts, justify extravagance, even if the service sometimes falls short of pricey expectations. Many of the à la carte fish dishes are expensive, but there's a €55 lunch menu. (Note that there are very few nonfish alternatives.) [$] *Average main: €80* ✉ *664 bd. de Bacon* ☎ *04–93–61–50–02* 🌐 *www.restaurantdebacon.com* ✍ *Reservations essential* ⏲ *Closed Mon. and Nov.–Feb. No lunch Tues.*

## WHERE TO STAY

$$$$ HOTEL 🏨 **Hôtel du Cap–Eden Roc.** In demand by celebrities from De Niro to Madonna, this extravagantly expensive hotel looking out on 22 acres of immaculate tropical gardens bordered by rocky shoreline has long catered to the world's fantasy of a subtropical idyll on the French Riviera. **Pros:** no other hotel in Southern France has the same reputation

A gigantic unframed painting come to life, Antibes has been immortalized by countless artists, including Monet, Renoir, and Picasso.

or style; specially designed children's summer programs. **Cons:** if you're not a celebrity, tip big to keep the staff interested; don't even try to book a room during the Cannes Film Festival in early May; there *are* prettier hotels on the coast. *$ Rooms from: €570 ⊠ Bd. J.F. Kennedy ☎ 04–93–61–39–01 ⊕ www.edenroc-hotel.fr ⤳ 104 rooms, 14 suites ⊗ Closed Oct.–mid-Apr. ⑩ Breakfast.*

**$$** **Hôtel La Jabotte.** At this adorable guesthouse a few steps from a sandy
HOTEL beach, tastefully decorated and colorful rooms surround a central courtyard, where guests relax over a gorgeous breakfast. **Pros:** very warm welcome is completely unexpected compared with some of the better-known hotels; breakfast with homemade jam is delicious and included in the rate; iPad available at reception. **Cons:** difficult to find, so bring a good map or drive with a GPS; hotel is often full; rooms are small. *$ Rooms from: €120 ⊠ 13 av. Max Maurey ☎ 04–93–61–45–89 ⊕ www.jabotte.com ⤳ 10 rooms ⑩ Breakfast.*

**$$$$** **La Baie Dorée.** Clinging to the waterfront and facing the open sea,
HOTEL this pleasant inn provides private sea-view terraces off every room and a discreet ambience to the point of self-effacing: the reception area is as small as a coat check and when you look out the window, you are reminded that you are paying for location, not sumptuous decor. **Pros:** every room has double glazing and shutters; beach offers water sports; parking and breakfast included. **Cons:** furniture is modest and a throw back to another decade; some rooms are small. *$ Rooms from: €440 ⊠ 579 bd. de la Garoupe ☎ 04–93–67–30–67 ⊕ www.baiedoree.com ⤳ 12 rooms, 3 suites ⑩ All meals.*

**$$**
HOTEL

**La Garoupe-Gardiole.** Cool, simple, and accessible to non–movie stars, this pair of partnered hotels offers a chance to sleep on the hallowed Cap peninsula and bike or walk to the pretty Garoupe beach. **Pros:** location among million-dollar mansions; spacious rooms available for families. **Cons:** breakfast costs extra; some rooms are small. $ *Rooms from: €120* ⊠ *60–74 chemin de la Garoupe* ☎ *04–92–93–33–33* ⊕ *www.hotel-lagaroupe-gardiole.com* ⤳ *37 rooms* ⊙ *Closed mid-Oct–mid-Apr.* ⍁ *No meals.*

### SPORTS AND THE OUTDOORS

**Plage de la Garoupe.** Thanks to the perfect oval bay of La Garoupe, the finest, softest sand on the Riviera, magnificent views that stretch out to Antibes, and relatively calm waters, this northeast-facing beach is a real jewel. The Gucci-clad spill-over from the Hotel du Cap-Eden Roc and other high-end beach clubs gather here. Wannabeseens head to the private Joseph Plage at one end of the beach, where you can rent loungers, while the quieter folk stick to the public middle section. For the weak-walleted, there are also two snack bars (if you dare to be seen at one). There are toilets and showers, and free parking nearby. **Amenities:** showers; toilets. **Best for:** swimming. ⊠ *Chemin de la Garoupe.*

## JUAN-LES-PINS

*5 km (3 miles) southwest of Antibes.*

From Old Antibes you can jump on a bus over the hill to Juan-les-Pins, the jazzy younger-sister resort town that, with Antibes, bracelets the wrist of the Cap d'Antibes. This stretch of beach was "discovered" by the Jazz Age jet set, who adopted it with a vengeance; F. Scott and Zelda Fitzgerald lived in a seaside villa here in the early 1920s, dividing their idylls between what is now the Hôtel Belle Rives and the mansions on the Cap d'Antibes. Here they experimented with the newfangled fad of waterskiing, still practiced from the docks of the Belle Rives today. Ladies with bobbed hair and beach pajamas exposed lily-white skin to the sun, browning themselves like peasants and flaunting bare, tanned arms. American industrialists had swimming pools introduced to the seaside, and the last of the leisure class, weary of stateside bathtub gin, wallowed in Europe's alcoholic delights. Nowadays, the scene along Juan's waterfront is something to behold, with thousands of international sunseekers flowing up and down the promenade or lying flank to flank on its endless stretch of sand.

### GETTING HERE AND AROUND

Regional trains connect the SNCF Juan-les-Pins train station to Nice (€4.20 one way), Cannes (€2.10), and other coastal towns. Antibes–Juan-les-Pins can also be reached by taking the No. 200 bus from the central bus station in Nice to Place Guynemer (1 hour, €1.50). From here, there is a bus connection (No. 3 Envibus) to the Juan-les-Pins train station. Starting at that station, Bus No. 15 loops through Juan-les-Pins, stopping at the public beach. Buses cost €1.

### VISITOR INFORMATION

**Juan-les-Pins Tourist Office** ✉ *60 chem. des Sables, Antibes* ☎ *04–22–10–60–01* 🌐 *www.antibesjuanlespins.com.*

## BEACHES

Antibes and Juan-les-Pins together claim 25 km (15½ miles) of coastline and 48 beaches (including Cap d'Antibes). Juan-les-Pins is one big city beach, lined by a boulevard and promenade peppered with cafés and restaurants.

**Plage d'Antibes les Pins.** This sandy beach west of Juan-les-Pins is popular thanks to its size. You can rent a beach chair from the nearby private beaches that dominate the strip. **Amenities:** toilets; showers. **Best for:** swimming. ✉ *Bd. du Littoral.*

**Port de Crouton Plage.** Covered with fine white sand, this small public beach next to Cap d'Antibes Beach Hotel boasts shallows that slope very slowly, making it ideal for kids. It's a protected bay, so there are no waves, just plenty of shallow water that's bath-water warm in high summer. There are few English tourists, so it is a real *plage à la Française* experience. **Amenities:** parking (pay); toilets. **Best for:** snorkeling; secluded. ✉ *Bd. Marechal Juin.*

6

## WHERE TO STAY

$ HOTEL 🏨 **Hotel des Mimosas.** Situated in an enclosed hilltop garden studded with tall palms, mimosas, and tropical greenery, this is the sort of place where only the quiet buzzing of cicadas interrupts silent nights. **Pros:** nice garden and grounds (worth the extra money for room with terrace); easy 10-minute walk to train station. **Cons:** some rooms are small and dated; breakfast extra (€10); weak Wi-Fi in areas. [$] *Rooms from: €99* ✉ *Rue Pauline* ☎ *04–93–61–04–16* 🌐 *www.hotelmimosas.com* 🛏 *34 rooms* 🕒 *Closed Oct.–Apr.* 🍴 *No meals.*

$$$$ HOTEL 🏨 **Les Belles Rives.** Not far from the onetime villa of Gerald and Sara Murphy—those Roaring Twenties millionaires who devoted their lives to proving the maxim "living well is the best revenge"—the Belles Rives became the home-away-from-home for literary giant F. **Pros:** views are quite spectacular, but ask for a room with a frontal (not lateral) sea view; lots of water sports. **Cons:** restaurant is pricey; some rooms are on the small side. [$] *Rooms from: €450* ✉ *33 bd. Édouard Baudoin* ☎ *04–93–61–02–79* 🌐 *www.bellesrives.com* 🛏 *43 rooms* 🕒 *Closed Jan. and Feb.* 🍴 *Breakfast.*

## NIGHTLIFE AND THE ARTS

### CASINO

**Eden Casino.** The glassed-in complex of the Eden Casino houses slot machines, roulette and blackjack tables, and a panoramic beach restaurant. Texas Hold'em poker is played every night. Players park for free. ✉ *17 bd. Baudoin* ☎ *04–92–93–71–71* 🌐 *www.casinojuanlespins.com* 🕒 *Daily until 4 am (5 am in summer).*

### MUSIC AND DANCE

**Jazz à Juan.** When the Jazz Festival hit the Mediterranean stage in 1960 it was revolutionary, because it put the biggest international names in the business in front of the public—Mingus, Fitzgerald, Coltrane—and

Just add water, and even an overbuilt town like Juan-les-Pins becomes a place worth scrambling for a postage-stamp portion of sun and fun.

they got more out of it than the fans. Now in its 54th year, the event continues over 10 days in July at various venues, including the Jardins de la Pinède. Book online or buy tickets directly from the tourist office in Antibes or Juan-les-Pins. ⊠ *Les Jardins de la Pinède, 10 bd. Ardisson* ☎ *04–22–10–60–06* ⊕ *www.jazzajuan.com.*

**Le Village.** The cavernous Le Village sets the standard for cool in Juan-les-Pins, with thumping music played by the best DJs in town, open from midnight to 5 am every day of the week. ⊠ *1 bd. de la Pinède* ☎ *04–92–93–92–00.*

### SPORTS AND THE OUTDOORS

**Visiobulle.** To study underwater life while circling the cape, contact Visiobulle, which organizes one-hour cruises in tiny, yellow glass-bottom boats. From April to September, boats leave from the Ponton Courbet in Juan-les-Pins four to seven times a day depending on the season; it's best to reserve ahead by phone in summer. ⊠ *Ponton Courbet, Av. Amiral Courbet* ☎ *04–93–67–02–11* ⊕ *www.visiobulle.com* 🎫 *€13.50.*

## BIOT

Fodor's Choice
★ *6 km (4 miles) northeast of Antibes; 15 km (9 miles) northeast of Cannes; 18 km (11 miles) southwest of Nice.*

Rising above a stretch of commercial-industrial quarters along the coast from Antibes, the *village perché* of Biot (pronounced Bee-*otte*) sits neatly on a hilltop, and as some claim, near an ex-volcano. Threaded with cute alleyways and dotted with pretty *placettes* (small squares), the old town is so picturesque it almost demands you pick up brush and palette—mere photographs don't do it justice, especially as it's not on the receiving end of much light. For centuries home to a pottery industry, known for its fine yellow clay that stretched into massive, solid oil jars, Biot has, in recent generations, made a name for itself as a glass-art town. Nowadays its cobblestoned streets are lined with a vast array of boutiques and art galleries, their display windows flashing vividly colored goods.

Despite the new commercialism, traces of old Provence remain in Biot, especially in the evening after the busloads of shoppers leave and the deep-shaded squares under the plane trees fall quiet. Then you can meander around the edges of the Old Town to find the stone arch gates known as the **Porte des Tines** and the **Porte des Migraniers**; they're the last of the 16th-century fortifications that once enclosed Biot. Step into the 15th-century **église**, which contains an early-16th-century altarpiece attributed to Louis Bréa and depicting the Virgin Mary shielding humanity under her cloak; the surrounding portraits are as warmly detailed as the faces and hands in the central panel. Truly Nikon-worthy is centuries-old **Place des Arcades**, the ancient heart of the Old Town which was first colonized by the Knights Templars and then the Hospitallers of St. John of Jerusalem. Found between the tourist office and the church, just behind Rue Barri, it has an otherworldly grace, with its Gothic arcades and tall palm trees. Picturesquely curved and shop-lined, the center of town remains **Rue Saint Sébastien**.

## GETTING HERE AND AROUND

The Biot train station on the coast is 4 kilometers (5 miles) away, but you can jump on Envibus No. 10 from outside the station and arrive in the village in less than 10 minutes (€1). Alternatively, you can telephone Icila d'Envibus (☎ *04–92–19–76–33)* and organize an individual pick-up by mini-bus—still costing only €1. By car, coming up from the D6007, take the CD4 past Marineland and you'll find signage straight to Biot.

## VISITOR INFORMATION

**Biot Tourist Office** ✉ *46 rue St-Sébastien* ☎ *04–93–65–78–00* ⊕ *www.biot-tourisme.com.*

## EXPLORING

**La Verrerie de Biot** (*Biot Glassworks*). On the edge of town, follow the pink signs to La Verrerie de Biot, which has developed into something of a cult industry since its founding in the 1950s. Here you can observe the glassblowers at work, visit the extensive galleries of museum-quality art glass (which is of much better quality than the kitsch you find in the village shop windows), and start a collection of bubbled-glass goblets, cruets, or pitchers, just as Jackie Kennedy did when the rage first caught hold (she liked cobalt blue). Despite the extreme commercialism—there is a souvenir shop, a boutique of home items, audio tours of the glassworks, a bar, and a restaurant—it's a one-of-a-kind artisanal industry, and the product is made before your eyes. ✉ *5 chemin des Combes* ☎ *04–93–65–03–00* ⊕ *www.verreriebiot.com* 🎫 *€3; €6 guided visit* ☉ *May–Sept., Mon.–Sat. 9:30–8, Sun. 10:30–1:30 and 2:30–7:30; Oct.–Apr., Mon.–Sat. 9:30–6, Sun. 10:30–1:30 and 2:30–6:30.*

FAMILY **Marineland** (*Espace Marineland*). Marketed under the umbrella title of Espace Marineland, this extremely commercial amusement complex a short distance from Antibes, and Biot provides parents with bargaining leverage for a day of Picasso and pottery shopping. There's a small Marineland, with lively scripted dolphin shows, dancing killer whales, and a Plexiglass walk-through aquarium, where sharks swim over your head. Animal lovers may wish to avoid this circus and head instead to the surprisingly deep and fascinating collection of old sea paraphernalia in its naval museum. Kid's Island, Adventure Golf, and Aquasplash are also on nearby grounds. A 100-room hotel with a dolphin-shaped swimming pool, provisionally called Hôtel du Lagon, is expected to open on the grounds in May 2015 at a cost of €12 million. ✉ *309 rue Mozart, Antibes* ✣ *From Antibles, take N7 (Departmentale 6007) north, then head left at La Brague onto D4, toward Biot.* ☎ *04–93–33–49–49* 🌐 *www.marineland.fr* 🎫 *€38 adult; €30 children under 12. Joint tickets available for Kid's Island and Adventure Golf.* ⏱ *July and Aug., daily 10 am–11 pm; Oct.–mid-Apr., daily 10–6; mid-Apr.–Jun. and Sept., daily 10–7. Closed Jan.–mid Feb.*

### WHERE TO STAY

$ HOTEL 🏨 **Galerie des Arcades.** Tucked away behind the beauteous palm-lined Place des Arcades in the Old Town, this combination hotel-restaurant–art gallery draws a loyal clientele who come to browse in the gallery, enjoy a weekend in one of the extraordinary guest rooms, or dine on serious, unpretentious, bona fide Provençal food: rabbit sautéed in fresh herbs, stuffed sardines, or a Friday *aïoli* (fish and crudités served with garlic mayonnaise). **Pros:** authentic decor; memorable cuisine; a nearly bargain price. **Cons:** some of the smaller rooms only have showers and not baths; service can be a bit snippy. [$] *Rooms from: €60* ✉ *16 pl. des Arcades* ☎ *04–93–65–01–04* 🌐 *www.hotel-restaurant-les-arcades.com* 🛏 *12 rooms* ⏱ *Restaurant closed mid-Nov.–mid-Dec. and Mon. No dinner Sun.* 🍴 *No meals.*

## VILLENEUVE-LOUBET

*10 km (6 miles) north of Antibes.*

This tiny village, its medieval château heavily restored in the 19th century, is best known for its sprawl of overbuilt beachfront, heavily charged with concrete high-rises and with all the architectural charm of a parking ramp. However, if you're a foodie, you may want to make the pilgrimage to the eccentric Musée de l'Art Culinaire.

### EXPLORING

**Musée de l'Art Culinaire** (*Museum of Culinary Arts*). This is a shrine to the career of the great chef Auguste Escoffier (1846–1935). The epitome of 19th-century culinary extravagance and revered by the French as much as Joan of Arc and de Gaulle, Escoffier was the founding father of the school of haute cuisine Calvin Trillin calls "stuff-stuff-with-heavy," where ingredients are stripped, simmered, stuffed, sauced, and generally intervened with, sometimes beyond recognition. His was the school of food as sculpture—the famous *pièces montées,* wedding-cake spires of spun sugar, and the world of menus of staggering length and complexity. He wowed 'em at the Ritz in Paris and the Savoy and Carlton in London and is a point of reference for every modern chef—if only as a foil for rebellion. In his birthplace you'll view illustrations of his creations and a collection of fantastical menus, including one featuring the meat of zoo animals killed in the war of 1870. ⊠ *3 rue Escoffier* ☎ *04–93–20–80–51* ⊕ *www.fondation-escoffier.org* ⚏ *€5* ⊗ *July–Aug., daily 2–7 (and Mon. and Wed. 10–2); Sept.–June, daily 2–6. Closed Nov.*

## HAUT-DE-CAGNES

**Fodor's**Choice *14 km (9 miles) southwest of Nice; 10 km (6 miles) north of Antibes.*
★

Could this be the most beautiful village in southern France? Part-time residents Renoir, Soutine, Modigliani, and Simone de Beauvoir are a few who thought so. Although from N7 you may be tempted to give wide berth to the seaside town of Cagnes-sur-Mer—with its congested sprawl of freeway overpasses, numerous tourist-oriented stores, beachfront pizzerias, and train station—follow the brown signs inland touting "Bourg Médiéval" and the steep road will lead you up into one of the most heavenly perched villages on the Riviera: Haut-de-Cagnes. Even Alice, of Wonderland fame, would adore this steeply cobbled Old Town, honeycombed as it is with tiny piazzas, return-to-your-starting-point-twice alleys, and winding streets that abruptly change to stairways.

Grab a café seat on the main piazza, watch a pétanque game in progress, admire the looming château across the way, and you'll forget about all those awful headlines back home in a jiffy. Haut-de-Cagnes is a gorgeous dip into the picturesque Middle Ages. You'll find it a total pleasure to wander its old byways, some with cobbled steps, others passing under vaulted arches draped with bougainvillea. Many of the pretty residences are dollhouse-size (especially the hobbit houses on Rue Passebon) and most date from the 14th and 15th centuries. There is nary a shop, so the commercial horrors of Mougins or St-Paul-de-Vence are left far behind. It is little wonder the rich and literate have long kept Haut-de-Cagnes a secret hideaway. Or almost: enough cars now arrive that a garage (Parking du Planastel) has been excavated out of the hillside, while a free *navette* (shuttle bus) links Haut-de-Cagnes with the bus station of Cagnes-sur-Mer (Square Bourdet, about an eight-block walk from the town train station, which lies on the main coastal rail route). Use it to take advantage of Cagnes's 3.5 kilometers (2.2 miles) of coastline along the Promenade, with a path for rollerblading or free Vélo-Bleu bikes. Even better, put your feet up at a waterfront café like Art Beach, which, unlike other beachfront restaurants along the coast, has the luxury of staying open year-round.

### GETTING HERE AND AROUND
Frequent daily trains from Nice or Cannes stop at Cagnes-sur-Mer (get off at Cros-de-Cagnes if you're heading to the beach) from where you take a free shuttle (navette) to Haut-de-Cagnes. The No. 44 runs throughout the day seven days a week. The Lignes d'Azur bus 200 (€1.50) also stops in Cagnes-sur Mer.

By car from Paris or Provence on the A8 highway take the No. 47 Villeneuve–Loubet/Cagnes-sur-Mer exit; if coming from the east (Monaco, Nice), look for exit No. 48, called "Cagnes-sur-Mer."

**VISITOR INFORMATION**

**Cagnes-sur-Mer Tourist Office** ⊠ *6 blvd. Maréchal Juin* ☎ *04–93–20–61–64* ⊕ *www.cagnes-tourisme.com.*

## EXPLORING

**Chapelle Notre-Dame-de-la-Protection.** Nearly hidden in the hillside and entered by an obscure side door, the grand Chapelle Notre-Dame-de-la-Protection, with its Italianate bell tower, was first built in the 14th century after the fortress had been destroyed; as a hedge against further invasion, they placed this plea for Mary's protection at the village edge. In 1936 the *curé* (priest) discovered traces of fresco under the bubbling plaster; a full stripping revealed every inch of the apse to have been decorated in scenes of the life of the Virgin and Jesus, roughly executed late in the 16th century. From the chapel's porch are sweeping sea views. Even if it's closed when you stop by, be sure to note the trompe-l'oeil "shadows" delightfully painted on the bell tower portal. ⊠ *Rue Hippolyte Guis* ☉ *Sat.–Sun. 2–5.*

**Château-Museé de Cagnes.** Crowning Haut-de-Cagnes is the fat, crenellated Château-Museé de Cagnes. Built in 1310 by the Grimaldis and reinforced over the centuries, this imposing fortress lords over the coastline, banners flying from its square watchtower. You are welcomed inside by a grand balustraded stairway and triangular Renaissance courtyard with a triple row of classical arcades infinitely more graceful than the exterior. Filling nearly the entire courtyard is a mammoth, 200-year-old pepper tree—a spectacular sight. Beyond lie vaulted medieval chambers, a vast Renaissance fireplace, and a splendid 17th-century trompe-l'oeil fresco of the fall of Phaëthon from his sun chariot. The château also contains three highly specialized museums: the **Musée de l'Olivier** (Olive Tree Museum), an introduction to the history and cultivation of this Provençal mainstay; the obscure and eccentric **Collection Suzy-Solidor**, a group of portraits of the cabaret chanteuse painted by her artist friends, including Cocteau and Dufy; and the **Musée d'Art Moderne Méditerranéen** (Mediterranean Museum of Modern Art), which contains paintings by some of the 20th-century devotees of the Côte d'Azur, including Chagall, Cocteau, and Dufy. If you've climbed this far, continue to the **tower** and look over the coastline views in the same way that the guards once watched for Saracens. ⊠ *Pl. du Château, Haut de Cagnes* ☎ *04–92–02–47–30* ⊒ *€4; €8 with Renoir Museum* ☉ *Oct.–Mar., Wed.–Tues. 10–noon and 2–5; Apr.–Jun. and Sept., Wed.–Mon. 10–noon and 2–6; July and Aug., Wed.–Mon. 10–1 and 2–6.*

**Musée Renoir.** After staying up and down the coast, Auguste Renoir (1841–1919) settled into a house in Les Collettes, just east of the Vieille Ville, which is now the Musée Renoir. He passed the last 12 years of his life here, painting the landscape around him, working in bronze, and rolling his wheelchair through the luxuriant garden tiered with roses, citrus groves, and some of the most spectacular olive trees along the coast. You can view this sweet and melancholic villa as it

A top pick for France's most beautiful *village perché*, Haut-de-Cagnes is an enchanting place filled with tiny piazzas, winding alleys, and staircase streets.

has been preserved by Renoir's children, and admire 11 of his last paintings. In July 2013, after an 18-month renovation, the museum opened to public view the kitchen and rooms by the garden, which include a set of 17 plaster sculptures donated by Renoir and Guion families, as well as two additional original paintings. Although up a steep hill, Les Collettes is walkable from Place du Général-du-Gaulle in central Cagnes-Ville. ⊠ *Chemin des Collettes* ☎ *04–93–20–61–07* 🖃 *€6; €8 joint ticket with Château-musée Grimaldi* ☉ *Oct.–Mar., Wed.–Mon. 10–noon and 2–5; Apr.–May, Wed.–Mon. 10–noon and 2–6; June–Sept., 10–1 and 2–6.*

### WHERE TO STAY

**$$**
**HOTEL**
**Fodor's Choice**
**★**

🍴 **Château Le Cagnard.** What better way to experience Old Haut-de-Cagnes's grand castle views than to stay in an acclaimed 13th-century manor that is perched on the ramparts of the Grimaldi fortress? **Pros:** free shuttle bus to Cagnes-sur-Mer; service is friendly and prompt; romantic. **Cons:** there's not tons to do in village; better suited if you have a car. 🖄 *Rooms from: €230* ⊠ *54 rue Sous Barri* ☎ *04–93–20–73–21* ⊕ *www.lecagnard.com* ⇶ *12 rooms, 14 suites* ☉ *Closed Nov.–mid-Dec.* 🍽 *No meals.*

**$$**
**HOTEL**

🍴 **Le Grimaldi.** More of a bed-and-breakfast, this little hotel is smack in the middle of the Haut-de-Cagnes' liveliest square, complete with picture-perfect pétanque matches. **Pros:** completely renovated; great views from the rooms; attentive owners speak English. **Cons:** steep stairs in hotel; parking difficult. 🖄 *Rooms from: €135* ⊠ *6 pl. du Château* ☎ *04–93–20–60–24* ⊕ *www.hotelgrimaldi.com* ⇶ *4 rooms, 1 suite* 🍽 *Breakfast.*

# THE HILL TOWNS: ST-PAUL AND VENCE

The hills that back the Côte d'Azur are often called the *arrière-pays*, or backcountry. This particular wedge of backcountry—behind the coast between Cannes and Antibes—has a character all its own: deeply, unself-consciously Provençal, with undulating fields of lavender watched over by villages perched on golden stone. Many of these villages look as if they do not belong to the last century—but they do, since they played the muse to some of modern art's most famous exemplars, notably Pablo Picasso and Henri Matisse.

High in the hills these villages loom, parallel to the sea, smelling fragrantly of wild herbs and medieval history—and soap shops. So hungry have the hordes that flock to the Riviera become for a taste of Picasso that many of the hill towns have been only too happy to oblige. So, in St-Paul, which once hunkered down against the onslaught of Moors, now opens its pale-blue shutters wide to surges of day-trippers. Galleries and boutiques offer everything from neo–Van Gogh sofa art to assembly-line lavender sachets, and everywhere you'll hear the gentle *breet-breet* of mechanical souvenir *cigales* (cicadas). So if you're allergic to souvenir shops, artsy-craftsy boutiques, and middle-brow art galleries, aim to visit off-season or after hours.

## ST-PAUL

*18 km (11 miles) northwest of Nice.*

The medieval village of St-Paul-de-Vence can be seen from afar, standing out like its companion, Vence, against the skyline. In the Middle Ages St-Paul was basically a city-state, and it controlled its own political destiny for centuries. But by the early 20th century St-Paul had faded to oblivion, overshadowed by the growth of Vence and Cagnes—until it was rediscovered in the 1920s when a few penniless artists began paying for their drinks at the local auberge with paintings. Those artists turned out to be Signac, Modigliani, and Bonnard, who met at the **Auberge de la Colombe d'Or** *(Fsee the photo-feature, "Strokes of Genius" in this chapter),* now a sumptuous inn, where the walls are still covered with their ink sketches and daubs.

The most commercially developed of Provence's hilltop villages, St-Paul is a magical place. Artists are still drawn to its light, its pure air, its wraparound views, and its honey-color stone walls, soothingly cool on a hot Provençal afternoon. Get here early in the day to get a jump on the cars and tour buses, which can clog the main D36 highway by noon, or plan on a stay-over.

It won't take you long to "do" St-Paul; a pedestrian circuit leads you inevitably through its Rue-Grande to the *donjon* (fortress tower) and austere Gothic church. The trick is to break away and slip into a few mosaic-cobbled backstreets, little more than alleys; door after door, window after niche spills over with potted flowers and orange trees and they usually lead to an impossibly pretty cul-de-sac. The shuttered stone houses rear up over the streets, so close you could shake hands from window to window.

From St-Paul, there is a scenic hiking path to Vence (next to the Chapelle Ste-Claire); the walk takes an hour and 20 minutes.

### GETTING HERE AND AROUND

It's only 15 minutes from the coast by car; take the Cagnes-sur-Mer highway exit (No. 47 or 48, depending on the direction you're coming from) and look for signs on the RD 436 to La Collle sur Loup/Vence. St Paul is between the two.

There's no train station, but you can get off at Cagnes-sur-Mer and take the 400 bus (€1.50; 15 minutes), which departs directly from Nice or Cannes.

### VISITOR INFORMATION

**St-Paul de Vence Tourist Office** ✉ *2 rue Grande, St-Paul-de-Vence* ☎ *04–93–32–86–95* ⊕ *www.saint-pauldevence.com.*

### LASTING IMPRESSIONS

Famed Impressionist Auguste Renoir spent the final 11 years of his life, from 1907 to 1919, at "Les Colettes." He moved here so the sun could heal his arthritis, then so debilitating he taped paintbrushes to his hands and used a scrollable canvas. Eleven last works on view here radiate a bouillabaisse of red, pink, peach, and crimson hues. To quote Renoir: "Look at the light on the olive trees…it shines like diamonds. It's pink, it's blue. And the sky which plays across them. It drives you mad."

**6**

### EXPLORING

**Café de la Place.** On your way from the overpriced parking garages, you'll pass a Provençal scene played out with cinematic flair yet still authentic: the perpetual game of pétanque outside the Café de la Place. A sun-weathered pack of men (as for the lack of women playing this game anywhere, you're welcome to your own discussions of sexism) in caps, cardigans, and workers' blues—occasionally joined by a passing professional with tie and rolled-up sleeves—gathers under the massive plane trees and stands serene, silent, and intent to toss metal balls across the dusty square. Until his death, Yves Montand made regular appearances here, participating in this ultimate southern scenario. ▦TIP→ Want to give pétanque a go? Order a beverage and the Café de la Place will lend you *boules,* or if you're not thirsty (and want to avoid the boorish service), the Tourist Office rents balls for €2 and you can play for as long as you want. ✉ *Pl. de Gaulle, St-Paul-de-Vence* ☎ *04–93–32–80–03.*

**Chapelle des Pénitents Blanc.** Jean-Michel Folon had a deep affection for the town of St-Paul de Vence, where he befriended artists such as César, so it seems fitting that the decoration of its 17th-century Chapelle des Pénitents Blanc was one of the Belgian artist's last projects before his death in 2005. The overwhelming sensations as you enter the chapel are of peace and clarity: eight oil paintings in pastel colors by Folon collaborator Michel Lefebvre line the walls on either side and four stained-glass windows reinforce the themes of generosity and freedom. Sculptures take the place of the traditional altar and font, and the back wall is covered with a mosaic of the town made up of more than 1 million pieces. Demonstrating the versatility of this artist, the chapel reflects the town's ability to celebrate its past while keeping an eye on the future. Pass by the Tourist Office and arrange for a 45-minute *visite* of the chapel in English (€5). ⊠ *Pl. de l'Eglise, St-Paul-de-Vence* 🕾 *04–93–32–86–95 (tourist office)* ⊕ *www.saint-pauldevence.com* 🎟 *€3* ⊘ *Apr.–Sept., daily 11–1 and 3–6; Oct. and Dec.–Mar., daily 2–5.*

**Fondation Maeght.** Many people come to St-Paul just to visit the Fondation Maeght, founded in 1964 by art dealer Aimé Maeght. High above the medieval town, the small modern art museum attracts 200,000 visitors a year. It's an extraordinary marriage of the arc-and-plane architecture of Josep Sert; the looming sculptures of Miró, Moore, and Giacometti; the mural mosaics of Chagall; and the humbling hilltop setting, complete with pines, vines, and flowing planes of water. On display is an intriguing and ever-varying parade—one of the most important in Europe—of works by modern masters, including Chagall's wise and funny late-life masterpiece *La Vie* (*Life*). On the extensive grounds, fountains and impressive vistas help to beguile even those who aren't into modern art. Café F, should you need time to reflect, is open year round. ⊠ *623 Chem. des Gardettes, St-Paul-de-Vence* 🕾 *04–93–32–81–63* ⊕ *www.fondation-maeght.com* 🎟 *€15* ⊘ *Oct.–June., daily 10–6; July–Sept., daily 10–7.*

### WHERE TO EAT

**$$**
**BISTRO**
⨉ **La Fontaine.** The owners of this St-Paul-de-Vence institution have magically created a contemporary bistro in the center of the old village. There are a few seats on the second-story terrace overlooking the street below. Choose from the plat du jour (€15) or à la carte menu (fried goat cheese salad with potato and arugula, for example), although some say portions are on the small side, so you may want to choose a set menu item (from €35) to fill you up. Half bottles of wine are available, so sit on the terrace (book in advance) with *une verre* and breathe in the views overlooking the fountain square—this may improve your experience if the service is slow. Ⓢ *Average main: €24* ⊠ *10 montée de la Castre, St-Paul-de-Vence* 🕾 *04–93–32–58–01* ⊕ *www.restaurant-lafontaine.fr* ⊘ *Closed mid-Nov.–mid-Dec. and mid-Jan.–mid-Feb.*

**$$$**
**BISTRO**
⨉ **Le Tilleul.** Before you plunge into the dense tangle of ruelles in old St-Paul, stop on the ramparts under the century-old lime tree for a meal or snack at this atmospheric outdoor café, whose breezy terrace looks onto the valley and the Alps. The kitchen makes more of an effort than you might expect, turning out colorful salads (crispy camembert salad with peppered cider dressing) and pastas at lunch and more serious gastronomic fare in the evening. Perhaps the roasted black pork ribs with stuffed potatoes or the gambas in coconut milk with lemongrass, ginger, and red curry will entice. Pop by for the Salon de Thé, daily from 3 pm to 6 pm, which is much more than tea: homemade cakes, crepes, and coffee on a separate menu. Across the street, Le Tilleul sells freshly made sorbets and ice creams to go, with flavors like wild peach or almond milk with sour cherry. Ⓢ *Average main: €29* ⊠ *Pl. du Tilleul, St-Paul-de-Vence* 🕾 *04–93–32–80–36* ⊕ *www.restaurant-letilleul.com.*

**$$$**
**FRENCH**
⨉ **Le Vieux Moulin.** From just outside the walled village, you can see this restaurant that was once a 17th-century oil mill. Though it could be tempting to cater only to tourists, new owner Frédéric Rossi brought on board the young chef Olivier Depardieu, who did his apprenticeship

With masterworks by Mirò, Picasso, Giacometti, and a roomful of Victor Vasaleys (above), the Fondation Maeght in St-Paul-de-Vence is a modern-art treasure house.

at the Colombe d'Or and worked at Château Saint Martin. A mixture of regional dishes—such as fillet of beef in rosemary gravy, *écrasé de Monalisa* and taggiasca olives, or veal in a truffle sauce and pole-fried vegetables with homemade gnocchi—appear on the handwritten menu, which changes with the season. This place is best for a hearty dinner rather than a light lunch, especially since the terrace doesn't get much shade. $ *Average main: €25* ⊠ *Lieu-dit-Ste-Claire, Route de Vence, St-Paul-de-Vence* ☎ *04–93–58–36–76* ⊕ *levieuxmoulin-saintpaul.fr* ⊙ *Closed Nov.–Feb. No dinner Sun. and Wed. Closed Mon.*

## WHERE TO STAY

$

B&B/INN

⬚ **Hostellerie les Remparts.** With original stone walls, coved ceilings, and a perfect location in the center of the Vieille Ville, this small medieval hotel is an uncut gem, even if it's in need of a little polishing. **Pros:** clean; loaded with charm; affordable (most expensive room is €130, breakfast included). **Cons:** must book at least two months in advance for summer stays; village shuts down at night. $ *Rooms from: €105* ⊠ *72 rue Grande, St-Paul-de-Vence* ☎ *04–93–24–10–47* ⊕ *www.hostellerielesremparts.com* ⟿ *9 rooms* ⊙⃝ *Breakfast.*

$$$$

B&B/INN

Fodor's Choice

★

⬚ **La Colombe d'Or.** Often called the most beautiful inn in France, "the golden dove" occupies a rose-stone Renaissance mansion just outside the walls of St-Paul and is so perfect overall that some contend you haven't really been to the French Riviera until you've stayed or dined here. **Pros:** where else can you have an aperitif under a real Picasso? Where else can you wander in the garden, glass of wine in hand, and stare at a real Rodin? **Cons:** some rooms in the adjoining villa have blocked views; menu often outshone by the art; service not always a work of art. $ *Rooms from: €310* ✉ *Pl. Général-de-Gaulle, St-Paul-de-Vence* ☎ *04–93–32–80–02* ⊕ *www.la-colombe-dor.com* ⟿ *13 rooms, 12 suites* ⊘ *Closed Nov.–Christmas* ⏐⊚⏐ *Breakfast.*

**$$**
**B&B/INN**

⏐⏐ **Le Hameau.** Less than a mile below tourist-packed St-Paul, with views of the valley and the village, this lovely little inn is a jumble of terraces, trellises, archways, orange trees, olives, and heavy-scented honeysuckle vines. **Pros:** relaxing setting; old-fashioned charm; walking distance to Maeght Foundation. **Cons:** short uphill walk to St-Paul with no sidewalk; narrow staircase leading to rooms that share building with hotel office. $ *Rooms from: €120* ✉ *528 rte. de la Colle, St-Paul-de-Vence* ☎ *04–93–32–80–24* ⊕ *www.le-hameau.com* ⟿ *17 rooms* ⊘ *Closed mid-Nov.–mid-Feb.* ⏐⊚⏐ *No meals.*

# VENCE

*4 km (2½ miles) north of St-Paul; 22 km (14 miles) north of Nice.*

If you've visited St-Paul first, Vence will come as something of a relief. Just outside the Old Town, its morning food market, though not extensive, attracts genuine producers from the area (look for Tony and his exceptional *socca,* a pancake made with chickpea flour), and the cafés facing this square feel more down-to-earth than anything in St-Paul. Inside the stone walls of the Cité Historique (Historical City), the newly restored Place du Peyra invites you to linger with its restaurant terraces, relatively tasteful shops selling tablecloths or pottery, and a pretty drinking fountain whose water comes directly from the Peyra source. Vence is slightly more conscious of its history than St-Paul—plaques guide you through its historic squares and *portes* (gates). Wander past the pretty Place du Peyra, with its fountains, and Place Clémenceau, with its ocher-color Hôtel-de-Ville (Town Hall), to Place du Frêne, with its ancient ash tree planted in the 16th century, and don't miss the Rue du Marché's old-fashioned food shops, including a butcher, a baker, and a fishmonger.

## GETTING HERE AND AROUND

As with St-Paul-de-Vence, take the Cagnes-sur-Mer highway exit (No. 47 or 48, depending on the direction you're coming from) and look for signs on the RD 436 to La Colle sur Loup/Vence. St Paul is between the two.

There's no train station, but you can get off at Cagnes-sur-Mer and take the 400 bus (€1.50; 15 minutes), which departs directly from Nice or Cannes.

## VISITOR INFORMATION

**Vence Tourist Office** ✉ *8 Pl. du Grand Jardin* ☎ *04–93–58–06–38* ⊕ *www.vence.fr/tourism.*

## EXPLORING

**Cathédrale de la Nativité de la Vierge** (*Cathedral of the Birth of the Virgin, on Place Godeau*). In the center of the Vieille Ville, the Cathédrale de la Nativité de la Vierge was built on the Romans' military drilling field in the 11th and 12th centuries and is a hybrid of Romanesque and Baroque styles. The cathedral has been expanded and altered many times over the centuries. Note the rostrum added in 1499—its choir stalls are carved with particularly vibrant and amusing scenes of daily life in the Middle Ages. In the baptistery is a ceramic mosaic of Moses in the bulrushes by Chagall. ⊕ *vence.fr/ our-lady-of-nativity?lang=fr.*

**Fodor's Choice**
★
**Chapelle du Rosaire** (*Chapel of the Rosary*). On the outskirts of "new" Vence, toward St-Jeannet is the Chapelle du Rosaire, better known to the world-at-large as the Matisse Chapel. The artist decorated it with beguiling simplicity and clarity between 1947 and 1951 as his gift to nuns who had nursed him through illness. It reflects the reductivist style of the era: walls, floor, and ceiling are gleaming white, and the small stained-glass windows are cool greens and blues. "Despite its imperfections I think it is my masterpiece, the result of a lifetime devoted to the search for truth," wrote Matisse, who designed and dedicated the chapel when he was in his 80s and nearly blind. ⊠ 466 *Av. Henri-Matisse* ☎ 04–93–58–03–26 💷 €5 ⊙ *Tues. and Thurs. 10–11:30 and 2–5:30, Mon., Wed. and Sat. 2–5:30; Sun Mass at 10. Closed mid-Nov.–Dec.*

## WHERE TO EAT AND STAY

$
FRENCH
✕ **Le Pigeonnier.** The sight of a lone diner savoring a giant bowl of freshly picked broad beans in their pods sets the tone at this restaurant, which takes pride in its local ingredients. Foie gras terrine, smoked salmon, and fresh pasta are made on the premises, as are the medallions of pork with fig sauce, mashed potatoes, and sautéed zucchini. *Souris d'agneau* (knuckle of lamb) is a specialty. The terrace stretches over a large part of Place du Peyra, and there are dining rooms on two levels indoors. Ⓢ *Average main: €13* ⊠ *5 pl. du Peyra* ☎ 04–93–58–03–00 ⊙ *No dinner Wed. and Sun.*

$$$$
FRENCH
✕ **Les Bacchanales.** Star chef Christophe Dufau's weekly changing menu puts an inventive spin on traditional local ingredients; the suckling pig with onion, fresh walnut, and pumpkin is a must when it's available. Meals are served in a sun-filled, beautifully decorated garden villa, a mere 10 minutes by foot from Vence. In summer, the terrace is an idyllic place to linger over a four-, five- or seven-course set menu. Ⓢ *Average main: €58* ⊠ *247 av. de Provence* ☎ 04–93–24–19–19 ⊕ *www. lesbacchanales.com* ⌂ *Reservations essential* ⊙ *Closed Tues. Closed Wed., Sept.–June.*

$$$$
HOTEL
▪ **Château du Domaine St. Martin.** Occupying the site of an ancient Knights Templar fortress and set amid acres of greenery designed by Jean Mus, this hilltop domain with its noteworthy restaurant, ecological spa, and helicopter pad, welcomes you with light, airy public salons (where afternoon tea and rare champagnes are offered) and luxurious guest quarters that include two- and three-bedroom villas accented with beautiful antiques. **Pros:** stunning views; possible celebrity sightings; Martin's Club for kids in summer. **Cons:** restaurant decor has been labeled old-fashioned; nothing really within walking distance. Ⓢ *Rooms from: €600* ⊠ *2490 av. des Templiers* ☎ 04–93–58–02–02 ⊕ *www. chateau-st-martin.com* ⇥ *40 suites, 6 villas* ⊙ *Closed mid-Oct.–mid-Apr.* ▯◎▯ *Breakfast.*

**6**

Photographs can't do justice to the beauty of St-Paul-de-Vence—one would need to pick up brush and canvas to fully capture its bewitching ambience.

$ B&B/INN 🏨 **L'Auberge des Seigneurs et du Lion d'Or.** Dating to the 17th century and the only hotel set within Vence's old walls, this former stage coach inn has an ambience *à la François Premier*. **Pros:** lovely family atmosphere; parking vouchers available. **Cons:** front rooms with views are noisy (especially in summer) while back rooms are quieter with no view; no air conditioning (but fans). [$] *Rooms from: €90* ✉ *Pl. du Frêne* ☎ *04–93–58–04–24* 🌐 *www.auberge-seigneurs.com* 🛏 *6 rooms* 🕒 *Closed mid-Dec.–mid-Jan.* 🍴 *Some meals.*

$$ B&B/INN 🏨 **Villa Roseraie.** A quick walk up from Old Vence, this 100-year-old house has charming regional details—mix-and-match old furniture, fine local tiles and fabrics, even homemade bath salts and jams—plus there's a giant magnolia outside that spreads its venerable branches over the terrace. **Pros:** clean and spacious rooms; each room on ground floor has private terrace. **Cons:** nearby street noise. [$] *Rooms from: €145* ✉ *128 av. Henri-Giraud* ☎ *04–93–58–02–20* 🌐 *www.villaroseraie.com* 🛏 *10 rooms, 3 suites* 🕒 *Closed mid-Nov.–mid-Feb.* 🍴 *No meals.*

## THE ARTS

**Nuits du Sud.** Since 1997, world music lovers have taken over the Place du Grand Jardin in Vence from mid-July for four weeks, with up to 9,000 revelers a night gyrating to various beats. Even if you don't want to buy concert tickets, come for the atmosphere and share a picnic—the music will find you no matter where you are. ✉ *39 rue de 8 Mai 1945* ☎ *04–93–58–40–17* 🌐 *www.nuitsdusud.com.*

# NICE

*176 km (110 miles) east of Aix-en-Provence; 33 km (20 miles) northeast of Cannes; 20 km (12½ miles) southwest of Monaco.*

United with France only since 1860, Nice has its own history and atmosphere, exemplified by the stark contrast between the openness and modernity of the Promenade des Anglais to the narrow, ocher-tinted streets of the Old Town against the center of town and the sleek tramway whizzing down the main shopping thoroughfare Avenue Jean Médecin. (A second tramway line running to the airport is expected to be operational by 2017.)

It was on Colline du Château (now château-less) and at the Plage des Ponchettes, in front of the Old Town, that the Greeks established a market-port and named it Nikaia. Having already established Marseilles as early as the 4th century BC, they branched out along the coast and founded the city that would become Marseilles' chief coastal rival. The Romans established themselves a little later on the hills of Cimiez (Cemenelum), already previously occupied by Ligurians and Celts, and quickly overshadowed the waterfront port. After falling to the Saracen invasions, Nice regained power as an independent state, becoming an important port in the early Middle Ages.

So cocksure did it become that in 1388, Nice, along with the hill towns behind, effectively seceded from the county of Provence, under Louis d'Anjou, and allied itself with Savoie. Thus began its liaison with the House of Savoy, and through it with Piedmont and Sardinia, it was the Comté de Nice (Nice County). This relationship lasted some 500 years, tinting the culture, architecture, and dialect in rich Italian hues.

By the 19th century Nice was flourishing commercially, locked in rivalry with the neighboring shipping port of Genoa. Another source of income: the dawning of tourism, as first the English, then the Russian nobility discovered its extraordinary climate and superb waterfront position. A parade of fine stone mansions and hotels closed into a nearly solid wall of masonry, separated from the smooth-round rocks of the beach by what was originally named Camin deis Anglés (the English Way), which of course is now the famous Promenade des Anglais, lined by grand hotels; this magnificent crescent is one of the noblest in France.

Many of Nice's most delightful attractions—the Cours Saleya market, the Old Town streets, the Hotel Negresco, and the Palais Masséna—are on or close to Nice's 10-kilometer (6-mile) waterfront, making it the first stop for most visitors. The redevelopment of Nice's port, around the other side of the château, makes it easier for amblers who want to take in the Genoese architecture in this area, or peruse the antiques at the Puces de Nice along Quai Papacino. In September, the port is transformed into an eating adventure (one of the rare occasions you'll witness the French walk and eat simultaneously) during La Fête du Port.

Nice residents by and large support a popular and ambitious mayor, Christian Estrosi, president of France's first metropolis, Metropole Nice Côte d'Azur, created in 2010 with 46 communes. Estrosi has introduced some forward-thinking initiatives that have earned the city two recent honors. First, on the national front, the "Family Plus" label (the airport has free pushchairs, play areas, and restaurants with child-friendly activities) and second, and another first in France, the international "Gay comfort" label from the association IGLTA (Inter-national Gay and Lesbian Travel Association). As a leading destination for gay couples, all Gay Welcoming hotels, restaurants and shops in the Riviera capital display "a natural iridescence" sign. A brochure in English for Family Friendly Nice and Gay Friendly Nice can be downloaded at ⊕ *en.nicetourisme.com (see Discover Nice).*

Estrosi's most ambitious project, however, is to make Nice "the Green City of the Mediterranean," and he's pulled out all the stops. Already he made available rentable bikes and electric cars, but his chef-d'ouevre is the Promenade de Paillon, a 12-hectare park in the middle of town, running from the Théâtre de Verdure (across from McDonald's on the Prom') to the Museum of Modern Art, inaugurated in October 2013.

Nice's population is about 347,000, and they are seeing the changes afoot. Case in point: while there are "Made in France" and "Nissart cuisine" movements on the rise protecting all that is near and dear to the French, the invasion of Starbucks and the Hard Rock Café can't be staved off at sea.

### GETTING HERE AND AROUND

Nice is the main point of entry into the French Riviera region. It's home to the second-largest airport in France, which sits on a peninsula between Antibes and Nice, 6 kilometers (4 miles) southwest of the city. From the airport, you can take a bus to almost anywhere.

There are a few options from the airport: to go to the center of Nice, take the No. 98 bus from either Terminal 1 or 2 (€6), which will take you to the main Gare Routière to Station J. C. Bermond, and from here you can transfer on to a number of lines that spider the city (but you'll have to pay €1.50). If you plan on heading on via train, take the No. 99 bus from the airport (€6) or the backroad No. 23 (from Terminal 1 only; €1.50), both of which will take you to the main Gare SNCF train station (EAv. Thiers). From here you can access all coastal major cities by train.

In Nice, the tram is the fast way to get around the city (€1.50) or you can buy a 24-hour multipass for €5 (7 days for €15). The most popular buses are the 100 (Monaco–Menton), 200 Antibes–Cannes, and 400 St-Paul–Vence, which are cheap (€1.50) but often crowded, especially in the summer. You may find you'll have to wait for the next bus. Also, these are direct buses, which don't make frequent stops so you can't, as an example, take the 200 to the airport.

Hop on one of the city's 900 blue bikes (Vélo Bleu) available at 90 stations across town. There are designated bike paths in the city and along the Promenade as far as Antibes. It's only €1/day or €5/week and you can sign up with any mobile phone (international numbers included). Contact Vélobleu (☏ 04–93–72–06–06; ⊕ *www.velobleu.org).*

Greenrent, France's first electric car rental company, offers competitive rates with the added bonus of delivery and pick up service.

## VISITOR INFORMATION

Greenrent. ✉ *6 bis Meyerbeer* ☎ *09-83-80-98-16* ⊕ *www.greenrent.fr.*

Nice Tourist Office ✉ *5 Promenade des Anglais, BP 4079* ☎ *08-92-70-74-07* ⊕ *www.nicetourism.com.*

## FESTIVAL

**Nice Carnaval.** The world's third-largest Carnaval celebration has free and paid events for all ages in Place Masséna along the Promenade, and includes twenty €30,000 floats over a series of parades. This massive themed event is held for 15 days, culminating on Mardi Gras, with the burning of the King as the finale. ✉ *Office du Tourisme, 5 Promenade des Anglais* ☎ *08-92-70-74-07* ⊕ *www.nicecarnaval.com.*

# EXPLORING

## VIEUX NICE

Framed by the "château"—really a rocky promontory—and Cours Saleya, the Old Town of Nice is its strongest drawing point and, should you only be passing through, the best place to capture the city's historic feeling. Its grid of narrow streets, darkened by houses five and six stories high with bright splashes of laundry fluttering overhead and jewel-box Baroque churches on every other corner, creates a magic that seems utterly removed from the Côte d'Azur fast lane.

## TOP ATTRACTIONS

**Cathédrale Ste-Réparate.** An ensemble of columns, cupolas, and symmetrical ornaments dominates the Vieille Ville, flanked by an 18th-century bell tower and glossy ceramic-tile dome. The cathedral's interior, restored to a bright palette of ocher, golds, and rusts, has elaborate plasterwork and decorative frescoes on every surface. Note that it's usually closed between noon and 2 pm and also on Mondays. ✉ *3 Pl. Rossetti, Vieux Nice* ⊕ *cathedrale-nice.com.*

**Chapelle de la Miséricorde.** A superbly balanced *pièce-montée* (wedding cake) of half-domes and cupolas, this chapel is decorated within an inch of its life with frescoes, faux marble, gilt, and crystal chandeliers. A magnificent altarpiece by Renaissance painter Ludovico Bréa crowns the ensemble. ✉ *7 Cours Saleya, Vieux Nice* ⊙ *Tues. 2:30–5:30.*

**Chapelle Sainte Rita** (*Église de l'Annonciation*). This 17th-century Carmelite chapel, officially known as the Église de l'Annonciation, is a classic example of pure Niçoise Baroque, from its sculpted door to its extravagant marble work and the florid symmetry of its arches and cupolas. ✉ *1 rue de la Poissonerie, Vieux Nice* ⊕ *www.sainte-rita.net* ⊙ *Daily but closes over lunch.*

**Colline du Château** (*Château Hill*). Although nothing remains of this once-massive medieval stronghold but a few ruins left after its 1706 dismantling, the name château still applies to this high plateaulike park, from which you can take in extraordinary views of the Baie des Anges, the length of the Promenade des Anglais, and the red-ocher roofs of the Old Town. Children can let off steam at the playground, while you enjoy a picnic with panoramic views and a bit of shade. You can take the 213 steps up to it, or the free elevator next to the Hotel Suisse; alternatively, ascend the hill slower from the port side, near Place Garibaldi, which is a more gentle climb. ⊠ *At east end of Promenade des Anglais* ⊙ *Daily 8–7 (until 8 in summer; 6 in winter).*

**NEED A BREAK?**

**Glacier Fenocchio.** For fresh, homemade gelato-style ice cream offered in a rainbow of 100 flavors and colors, stop at Glacier Fenocchio from 9 am to midnight any day of the week March through November. There's even a choice of locally grown citrus flavors, including orange, mandarin, and lemon—or try beer! ⊠ *2 Pl. Rossetti, Vieux Nice* ☏ *04-93-62-88-80* ⊕ *www.fenocchio.fr.*

**Cours Saleya.** This long pedestrian thoroughfare—half street, half square—is the nerve center of Old Nice, the heart of the Vieille Ville, and the stage-set for the daily dramas of marketplace and café life. Framed with 18th-century houses and shaded by plane trees, the narrow square bursts into a fireworks-show of color Tuesday through Sunday until 1 pm, when flower-market vendors roll armloads of mimosas, roses, and orange blossoms into *cornets* (paper cones) and thrust them into the arms of shoppers, who then awkwardly continue forward to discover a mix of local farmers and stallholders selling produce (try the fresh figs), spices, olives, and little gift soaps. Cafés and restaurants, all more or less touristy (don't expect friendly service) fill outdoor tables with onlookers who bask in the sun. At the far east end, antiques and *brocantes* (collectibles) draw avid junk-hounds every Monday morning. At this end you can also find Place Charles Félix. From 1921 to 1938, Matisse lived in the imposing yellow stone building at Number 1, and you don't really need to visit the local museum that bears his name to understand this great artist: simply stand in the doorway of his former home and study the Place de l'Ancien Senat 10 feet away—the scene is a classic Matisse.

**Eglise du Gésù.** If Nice's other chapels are jewel boxes, this is a barn. Broad, open, and ringing hollow after the intense concentration of sheer matter in the Miséricorde and Ste-Rita, it seems austere by comparison. That's only because the decoration is spread over a more expansive surface. If it's possible, this 17th-century Baroque chapel is even more theatrical and over the top than its peers. Angels throng in plaster and fresco, pillars spill over with extravagantly sculpted capitals, and from the pulpit (to the right, at the front), the crucifix is supported by a disembodied arm. ⊠ *Corner of Rue Droite and Rue du Jésus.*

**Musée d'Art Moderne.** The assertive contemporary architecture of the Modern Art Museum makes a bold statement regarding Nice's presence in the modern world. The collection inside focuses intently and thoroughly on works from the late 1950s onward, but pride of place is given to sculptor Nikki de Saint Phalle's recent donation of more than 170 exceptional pieces. The rooftop terrace, sprinkled with minimalist sculptures, has stunning views over the city. Guided tours are

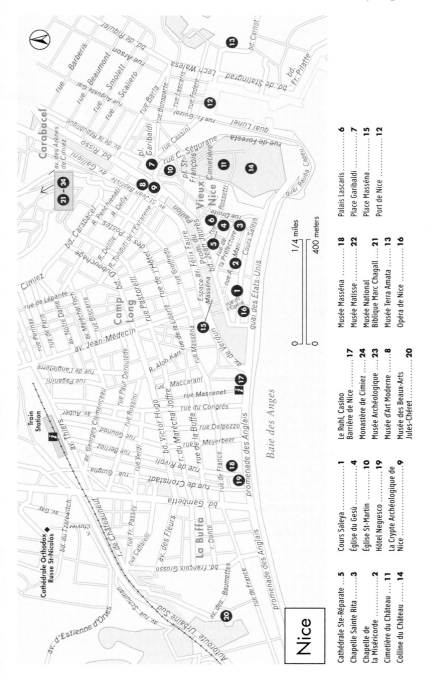

# Nice

1/4 miles

400 meters

6

offered by reservation Wednesdays at 3 pm. ⊠ *Promenade des Arts* ☎ *04–97–13–42–01* ⊕ *www.mamac-nice.org* ⊠ *Free; guide tours €5* ⊙ *Tues.–Sun. 10–6; tours 3 pm Wed. by reservation.*

**Palais Lascaris.** The aristocratic Lascaris Palace was built in 1648 for Jean-Baptiste Lascaris-Vintimille, *marechal* to the duke of Savoy. The magnificent vaulted staircase, with its massive stone balustrade and niches filled with classical gods, is surpassed in grandeur only by the Flemish tapestries (after Rubens) and the extraordinary trompe-l'oeil fresco depicting the fall of Phaëthon. With a little luck, you'll be in time for one of the many classical concerts performed here. ⊠ *15 rue Droite, Vieux Nice* ☎ *04–93–62–72–40* ⊕ *www.palais-lascaris-nice. org* ⊠ *Free* ⊙ *Wed.–Mon. 10–6.*

## WORTH NOTING

**Cimetière du Château** (*Cemetery*). This solemn cluster of white tombs looms prominently over the city below, providing a serene or macabre detail of daily life, depending on your mood. Under Nice's blue skies, the gleaming white marble and Italian mix of melodrama and exuberance in the decorations, dedications, photo portraits, and sculptures are somehow oddly life-affirming. Founded in 1783, there are 2,800 graves here—with prominent names like Jellinek-Mercedes and Leroux—in three sections, to this day segregating Catholics, Protestants, and Jews. ⊠ *Allée François-Aragon.*

**Église St-Martin.** Also known as St-Augustin, this serene Baroque structure at the foot of the château anchors the oldest church-parish in Nice. Built in 1405, it was here that Martin Luther preached in 1510 and Garibaldi was baptized in 1807. ⊠ *Rue Sincaire* ⊙ *Tues.–Sun., with a closure over the lunch period.*

**La crypte archéologique de Nice.** Via steel walkways, explore by tour only an archaeological crypt holding the remains of a 14th-century tower and aqueduct that were hidden underground for centuries. The half-acre underground chamber, located beneath Place Garibaldi, opened in 2012. When Nice's tram system was being built at the beginning of this century, excavators discovered medieval structures that had been razed by Louis XIV in 1706 and promptly forgotten. The Centre du Patrimoine (Heritage Center) offers one-hour guided tours for up to 15 people, but you must reserve with them directly at 75 quai Etats-Unis. The meeting point—place Jacques Toja—is just before Place Garibaldi. ■ TIP→ Bring "sensible shoes," as heels can't be worn in the crypt. ⊠ *Place Jacques Toja* ☎ *3906* ⊠ *€5* ⊙ *Tours Wed.–Sun. at 10, 11, 2, 3, and 4.*

**Musée Terra Amata.** During the digging for the foundation of a building in 1966, the shovels revealed the remains of a temporary settlement once used by elephant hunters thousands of years ago. They were perhaps the oldest known inhabitants of Europe. Now the site is a museum reconstructing the ancient beach-camp known as Terra Amata ("beloved land") as it was, lodgings and all. It incorporates a real human footprint, calcified in the sand. There are recorded commentaries in English; films explain the lifestyle of these earliest Europeans. If you enjoy anthropology, it's worth a stop, but don't expect a blockbuster

No wonder Matisse lived on the top floor of the golden yellow building seen here at the end of the Cours Saleya—this marketplace is one of the most colorful in France.

expo: displays are small scale and mainly limited to tiny models. ✉ 25 bd. Carnot ☎ 04–93–55–59–93 ⊕ *www.musee-terra-amata.org* ✉ *Free* ⊗ *Wed.–Sun., 10–6.*

**Place Garibaldi.** Encircled by grand vaulted arcades stuccoed in rich yellow, the broad pentagon of this square could have been airlifted out of Turin. In the center, the shrinelike fountain sculpture of Garibaldi seems to be surveying you as you stroll under the very attractive arcades and lounge in the surrounding cafés. An antiques market takes over the square on Saturday mornings.

**Port de Nice.** In 1750 the Duke of Savoy ordered a port to be dug into the waterfront to shelter the approach of the freight ships, fishing boats, and yachts that still sail into its safety today. The redevelopement of Nice's port, around the other side of the château, paves an easier way for amblers who want to take in the Genoese architecture in this area, or peruse the antiques at the Puces de Nice along Quai Papacino. From June to mid-October, daily 10 am to 7 pm, the free shuttle *Lou Passagin* ferries you across the port from the Charles Felix dock to Quai d'Entrecasteaux. In early September, keep an eye out for the Fête du Port—a gastronomical explosion outmatched only by fire-eaters and fireworks. ■TIP➔ From the port, you can take the No. 14 bus to visit the 16th-century Fort du Mont-Alban, which has exceptional views of Bordighera, and Saint-Jean-Cap-Ferrat all the way over to Baie des Anges (those crazy circular buildings) and Antibes.

## ALONG THE PROMENADE DES ANGLAIS

Nice takes on a completely different character west of Cours Saleya, with broad city blocks, vast Neoclassical hotels and apartment houses, and a series of inviting parks dense with palm trees, greenery, and splashing fountains. From the Jardin Albert Ier, once the delta of the Paillon River, the famous Promenade des Anglais stretches the length of the city's waterfront.

The original promenade was the brainchild of Lewis Way, an English minister in the growing community of British refugees drawn to Nice's climate. They needed a proper walkway on which to take the sea air, and pooled resources to build a 6½-foot-wide road meandering through an alley of shade trees. Nowadays it's a wide, multilane boulevard thick with traffic—in fact, it's the last gasp of the coastal highway N98. Beside it runs its charming parallel, the wide, sun-washed pedestrian walkway with intermittent steps leading down to the smooth-rock beach; its foundation is a seawall that keeps all but the wildest storms from sloshing waves over the promenade. A daily parade of *promeneurs*, rollerbladers, joggers, and sun-baskers strolls its broad pavement, looking out over the hypnotic blue expanse of the sea. Only in the wee hours is it possible to enjoy the waterfront stroll as the cream of Nice's international society did, when there were nothing more than hoof beats to compete with the roar of the waves.

A few years back, the city launched the extremely popular Prom'Party. These free-to-the public nights are scattered over July and August and transform the Promenade to a bustling dance floor with rolling stages and Cirque du Soleil–type street performers.

■TIP→ The French Riviera Pass is your ticket to museums, gardens, and transportation in Nice; included are guided tours, wine tasting, as well as seven attractions in nearby towns like the oceanography museum in Monaco, the exotic gardens in Èze, and the Ephrussi de Rothschild villa and garden on Saint-Jean-Cap-Ferrat. The passes are available for 24 hours (€26), 48 hours (€38), or 72 hours (€56) and can be purchased at the tourist office or online from their website.

### TOP ATTRACTIONS

**Jardin Albert Ier** (*Albert I Garden*). Along the Promenade des Anglais, this luxurious garden stands over the delta of the River Paillon, underground since 1882. Every kind of flower and palm tree grows here, thrown into exotic relief by night illumination. Home base for many city festivals with its Théâtre de Verdure and also Ciné Prom in the summer (screenings of box office hits at 9:30 pm), the garden is the starting point for Nice's Promenade du Paillon—a 12-hectare park running right through the city, from here up to the Museum of Modern Art. ⊠ 2–16 av. de Verdun.

**Musée des Beaux-Arts** (*Jules-Chéret Fine Arts Museum*). Originally built for a member of Nice's Old Russian community, the Princess Kotschoubey, this Italianate mansion is a Belle Époque wedding cake, replete with one of the grandest staircases on the coast. After the *richissime* American James Thompson took over and the last glittering ball was held here, the villa was bought by the municipality as a museum

Like the Rio of France, Nice is lined with a gigantic crescent beach whose prime spot, the Promenade des Anglais, is home to many palace-hotels.

in the 1920s. Unfortunately, much of the period decor was sold; but in its place are paintings by Degas, Boudin, Monet, Sisley, Dufy, and Jules Chéret, whose posters of winking *damselles* distill all the *joie* of the Belle Époque. From the Negresco Hotel area the museum is about a 15-minute walk up a gentle hill. ⊠ *33 av. des Baumettes, Centre Ville* ☎ *04–92–15–28–28* ⊕ *www.musee-beaux-arts-nice.org* ✉ *Free; guided tours €5 (in French only Wed. & Thurs. 3 pm; reservations required)* ☉ *Tues.–Sun., 10–6.*

**Musée Masséna** (*Masséna Palace*). This spectacular Belle Époque villa houses the **Musée d'Art et d'Histoire** (Museum of Art and History), where familiar paintings from French, Italian, and Dutch masters line the walls. A visit to the palace gardens set with towering palm trees, a marble bust of the handsome General Masséna, and backdropped by the ornate trim of the Hôtel Negresco, is a delight; this is one of Nice's most imposing oases. ⊠ *Entrance at 65 rue de France, Centre Ville* ☎ *04–93–91–19–10* ✉ *Free* ☉ *Wed.–Mon. 10–6.*

**Opéra de Nice.** A half-block west of the Cours Saleya stands a flamboyant Italian-style theater designed by Charles Garnier, architect of the Paris Opéra. It's home today to the Opéra de Nice, with a permanent chorus, orchestra, and ballet corps. The season runs from mid-November to mid-June, and tickets cost anywhere from €8 to €85. ⊠ *4 rue St-François-de-Paule, Vieux Nice* ☎ *04–92–17–40–00* ⊕ *www.opera-nice.org.*

**Place Masséna.** As Cours Saleya is the heart of the Vieille Ville, so this impressive and broad square is the heart of the entire city. It's framed by early 17th-century, Italian-style arcaded buildings, their facades stuccoed in rich red ocher. On the west flank sits the city's Belle Époque icon, the Hôtel Negresco. This enticing space hosts an event at least once a month, from Carnaval to the Christmas market; the new Promenade du Paillon, a 12-hectare park running from the Museum of Modern Art (MAMAC) to the Théâtre de Verdure, runs through the square.

**WORTH NOTING**

**Le Ruhl Casino Barrière Nice.** Renovated to the tune of €5 million by the Barrière group, Le Ruhl now lures in the summer vacationers and the winter convention crowd with vivid colors and fiber-optic lighting. Some sign into the hushed gaming room for roulette and blackjack, others try their luck at one of the 300-some slot machines. ⊠ *1 promenade des Anglais* ☎ *04–97–03–12–22* ⊕ *www.lucienbarriere.com* ☉ *Daily 9 am to 4 am (and until 5 am in the summer).*

**OFF THE BEATEN PATH**

**Cathédrale Orthodoxe Russe St-Nicolas.** This magnificent Russian Orthodox cathedral was built in 1896 to accommodate the sizable population of Russian aristocrats who had adopted Nice as their winter home. This Byzantine fantasy is the largest of its kind outside the motherland. The church has no fewer than six gold-leaf onion domes, rich ceramic mosaics on its facade, and extraordinary icons framed in silver and jewels. The benefactor was Nicholas II himself, whose family attended the inauguration in 1912. For six years the church was challenged over ownership, but in 2013 the French courts rejected a final appeal by ACOR, a *niçois* religious association that managed the property for 80 years. The Russian Archpriest rejoiced: "This ruling shows that it is history that has triumphed." ⊠ *Av. Nicolas II* ⚓ *From the Promenade, hop Bus 7 up Boulevard Gambetta and get off at either the Thiers-Gambetta or Parc Imperial stop, or walk 15 minutes west from the train station.* ☎ *04–93–96–88–02* ⊕ *www. cathedrale-russe-nice.fr* ☉ *Tues.–Sun., 9–noon and 2–6.*

## CIMIEZ

Once the site of the powerful Roman settlement Cemenelum, the hilltop neighborhood of Cimiez—4 km (2½ miles) north of Cours Saleya—is Nice's most luxurious quarter. Villas seem in competition to outdo each other in opulence, and the combination of important art museums, Roman ruins, and a historic monastery make it worth a day's exploration. To visit Cimiez and nearby museums, you need to combine a bus pass or taxi fare with strong legs and comfortable shoes. If you brave the route by car, arm yourself with a map and a navigator. Bus 15 from Place Masséna or Avenue Jean-Médecin takes you to both the Chagall and Matisse museums; from the latter you can visit the ruins and monastery.

**TOP ATTRACTIONS**

**Monastère de Cimiez.** This fully functioning monastery is worth the pilgrimage. You can find a lovely **garden,** replanted along the lines of the original 16th-century layout; the **Musée Franciscain,** a didactic museum tracing the history of the Franciscan order; and a 15th-century **church** containing three works of remarkable power and elegance by Bréa. ⊠ *Pl. du Monastère, Cimiez* ☎ *04–93–81–00–04*

✉ *Free* ⊙ *Church Thurs.–Tues. 8–6:30 and Sun. 2:30–8:30; museum Mon.–Sat. 10–noon and 3–5:30.*

Fodor's Choice ★ **Musée Matisse.** In the '60s the city of Nice bought this lovely, light-bathed 17th-century villa, surrounded by the ruins of Roman civilization, and restored it to house a large collection of Henri Matisse's works. Matisse settled along Nice's waterfront in 1917, seeking a sun cure after a bout with pneumonia, and remained here until his death in 1954. During his years on the French Riviera, Matisse maintained intense friendships and artistic liaisons with Renoir, who lived in Cagnes, and with Picasso, who lived in Mougins and Antibes. He eventually moved up to the rarefied isolation of Cimiez and took an apartment in the Hôtel Regina (now an apartment building, just across from the museum), where he lived out the rest of his life. Matisse walked often in the parklands around the Roman remains and was buried in an olive grove outside the Cimiez cemetery. The collection of artworks includes several pieces the artist donated to the city before his death; the rest were donated by his family. In every medium and context—paintings, gouache cutouts, engravings, and book illustrations—the collection represents the evolution of his art, from Cézanne-like still lifes to exuberant dancing paper dolls. Even the furniture and accessories speak of Matisse, from the Chinese vases to the bold-printed fabrics with which he surrounded himself. A series of black-and-white photographs captures the artist at work, surrounded by personal—and telling—details. ✉ *164 av. des Arènes-de-Cimiez, Cimiez* ☎ *04–93–81–08–08* ⊕ *www.musee-matisse-nice.org* ✉ *Free* ⊙ *Wed.–Mon. 10–6.*

**Musée National Marc Chagall** (*Marc Chagall Museum of Biblical Themes*). Having just celebrated its 40th anniversary in 2013, this museum has one of the finest permanent collections of Chagall's late works (1887–1985). Superbly displayed, 17 vast canvases depict biblical themes, each in emphatic, joyous colors. Chamber music and classical concert series also take place here, though admission fees may apply. The No. 15 and 22 buses stop at the museum. ✉ *Av. du Dr-Ménard, Cimiez* ☎ *04–93–53–87–20* ⊕ *www.musee-chagall.fr* ✉ *€8–€9.50* ⊙ *May–Oct., Wed.–Mon. 10–6; Nov.–Apr., Wed.–Mon. 10–5.*

**WORTH NOTING**

**Musée Archéologique** (*Archaeology Museum*). This museum, next to the Musée Matisse, has a dense collection of objects extracted from digs around the Roman city of Cemenelum, which flourished from the 1st to the 5th century. Among the fascinating ruins are an amphitheatre, frigidarium, gymnasium, baths, and sewage trenches, some dating back to the 3rd century. ■TIP➜ It's best to avoid midday visits on warm days. ✉ *160 av. des Arènes-de-Cimiez, Cimiez* ☎ *04–93–81–59–57* ⊕ *www.musee-archeologique-nice.org* ✉ *Free; €5 guided tour* ⊙ *Wed.–Mon. 10–6.*

## BEACHES

Nice's beaches extend all along the Baie des Anges, backed full-length by the Promenade des Anglais and a thriving and sophisticated downtown. This leads to the peculiar phenomenon of seeing power-suited executives and secretaries stripping down to a band of Lycra, tanning over the lunch hour, then suiting back up for the afternoon's work a block or two away. The absence of sand (there's nothing but those famous Riviera pebbles) helps maintain that dress-for-success look. The downside of the location: the otherwise stylish streets downtown tend to fill up with underdressed, sunburned tourists caked with salt during beach season.

Posh private beaches have full restaurants and bar service, color-coordinated mattresses and beach umbrellas, and ranks of tanners with phones glued to their ears. Several of the beaches lure clients with waterskiing, parasailing, windsurfing, and Jet-Skiing; if you're looking for a particular sport, check the signs posted at the entrance with the restaurant menus. In summer, lifeguards are posted near the Ruhl beach; check the flags to see if it's safe to swim on a windy day.

Fees for private beaches average €17–€22 for a dressing room and mattress and some charge up to €4 for a parasol. Private beaches alternate with open stretches of public frontage served by free toilets and open "showers" (a cold elevated faucet for rinsing off salt). Enterprising vendors cruise the waterfront, hawking ice cream, slabs of melon, coffee, ice-cold sodas, and beer. An excellent beachside read is *They Eat Horses Don't They: The Truth about the French*, by Piu Marie Eatwell. This in-depth look at French myths gives you the skinny on French women, sex and infidelity, music, and month-long August holidays, among other captivating subjects.

**Beau Rivage Beach.** Across from the Cours Saleya, Beau Rivage Plage claims to be the Riviera's largest private beach and has a split personality. On the Zen side, topless sunseekers can rent a cushy lounge chair with umbrella for €19, while at the more sceney Trend zone, bathers enjoy cocktails and tapas, and spending €115 buys the VIP treatment: a king-size beach mattress, fruit bowl, and champagne. The beach is stone, which means water shoes are advisable and if there are jellyfish sightings, you'll see a written warning of "*méduse*" on a beach board. Ditto for strong winds. **Amenities:** food and drink; toilets; showers. **Best for:** swimming; sunset; service; scene. ✉ *107 Quai des États-Unis* ☎ *04–92–00–46–80* ⊕ *www.plagenicebeaurivage.com.*

**Castel Plage.** At the east end of the Promenade, near Hotel Suisse, there is both a large public beach and a private beach, where you can rent a lounger for about €18, and where the water is calm and clear. The public beach is composed of large stones (*galettes*), which is more comfortable than walking on pebbles. Jellyfish are less of a problem in this corner than on beaches a little farther west along the Promenade, and lifeguards at the neighboring beach are on duty mid-June to mid-September. **Amenities:** none. **Best for:** sunrise; sunset; snorkeling; swimming. ✉ *8 Quai des États-Unis.*

Far from the center city, the Musée Matisse draws thousands of art lovers every month to take the long bus ride up the hill to the Cimiez suburb.

**Coco Beach.** East of the port and past La Réserve, just a few steps down from street level, lies one of the quieter beaches in Nice with very clear water, few tourists, and hardly any jellyfish. The catch? The beach is more slabs of rock than sand—this is where locals spread their towels for the day—forming a small crest along the coastline that is exposed to wind. Combine this with the fact that there are no lifeguards and you have the directive to be extra careful. Many fish move about below, making this an excellent place for snorkeling. There's a snack bar on the other side of La Réserve and street parking. **Amenities:** none. **Best for:** swimming; snorkeling; solitude. ⊠ *Av. Jean Lorrain.*

FAMILY  **Hi Beach.** This is the funkiest of the Nice private beaches and pro-green, with designs by Philippe Starck protégé Matali Crasset. A stone beach with packed rows of loungers (one with an umbrella will set you back €22 for the day), Hi Beach appeals to a young and family clientele here—but expect to see breasts all the same. Three Zones target any beachgoer: Hi Energy, Hi Relax, and, for the kids, Hi Play (€69 for a four-person Family House). Offerings include drinks, a full menu (with burgers and sushi, too), Hi Body for those in need of a massage, and beach yoga in English on summer mornings. If there are any water warnings—jellyfish or strong winds—sign boards will keep you informed. **Amenities:** food and drink; showers; toilets. **Best for:** swimming; sunrise; sunset. ⊠ *47 Promenade des Anglais* ☎ *04–97–14–00–83* ⊕ *www.hi-beach.net.*

**Lenval and Magnan beaches.** Locals come early and with umbrellas, chairs, and coolers in tow to these two sizable public beaches around the halfway point of the Promenade. Both beaches are stone and there's the occasional *méduse* (jellyfish), so water shoes are best for getting in and out of the sea. Lenval is a non-smoking beach and during the summer has a massive inflatable pool for kids and adult classes. There are pay underground hot showers, toilets, and lockers, as well as portable toilets in the summer; there are no lifeguards nor a first aid station (but there is next door at Magnan, which is wider and lower than street level). This area is less tourist-dense, so expect to see many (too many) bare torsos. **TIP→ When the winds pick up, this area can be dangerous, so watch for the wind-warning flags (and avoid the beach for 24 hours after storms).** **Amenities:** lifeguards; toilets; showers. **Best for:** sunrise; swimming. ✉ *Promenade des Anglais.*

**Ponchettes beach.** Almost at the end of the Promenade and in front of the Old Town, this basic stony stretch is a popular spot in the summer with a melange of tourists and locals (they're the topless ones) of all ages all day. In the summer are sand-beach volleyball courts, portable toilets, and lifeguards with a first aid station. Keep an eye out for jellyfish. **Amenities:** toilets. **Best for:** swimming; snorkeling; sunrise; sunset. ✉ *Quai des États-Unis.*

## WHERE TO EAT

$ CAFÉ 🍴 **Café Marché.** This quaint café, behind Cours Saleya, doesn't have views of the market, but the creamy café au lait and homemade baked goods more than compensate for its people-watching limitations. If you want more than a snack, you can order from one of the day's three choices (including one that's vegan). [$] *Average main: €12* ✉ *2 rue Barillerie, Vieux Nice* ☎ *09–81–84–92–49* 🌐 *www.cafe-marche.fr* 🕒 *Closed Sat. Oct.–Apr.*

$ BISTRO 🍴 **Carré Llorca.** Young Spanish chef Gabriela Stockler Martinez once worked for celebrated chef Alain Llorca as well as at starred eateries in England and Spain—and now, since July 2013, she has her own digs. Her open kitchen overlooks the central room at Carré Llorca. Designed by Paul Valet, the exposed stone walls and simple wooden tables are both bright and inviting, and from the main floor there's an angled view of the Neoclassical Palais de Justice. Diners are tickled about the sublimely Mediterranean cuisine—*pan bagnat* revisited (€7) or marinated salmon and seasonal veggies (€13)—as much as the reasonable prices. [$] *Average main: €16* ✉ *3 rue de la Préfecture, Vieux Nice, Nice, France* ☎ *04–93–92–95–86* 🌐 *www.carrellorca.com* ✍ *Reservations essential* 🕒 *Closed Sun.*

$$$$ MEDITERRANEAN 🍴 **Chantecler.** Long a showplace for Riviera luxury, the Negresco is replete with Régence-fashion salons decked out with 18th-century wood *boiserie* and Aubusson carpets. Its main dining room has been playing musical chefs for the past few years and currently features Chef Jean-Denis Rieubland, who worked in many of the French Riviera's top restaurants before restoring the Chantecler to its former glory. Rieubland is not afraid to challenge local traditions with lusty dishes inspired by his native southwest France: typical of his style are roasted duckling with flat peaches, hazelnuts, and turnips glazed with honey, braised thighs flavored with verbena, or crab-and-mango cannelloni, citrus fruit

marmalade, caviar, and combava-flavored cream. In the cave, there are 15,000 bottles (if you're counting). **TIP→ If you're watching your centimes, try the *menu plaisir* at Sunday lunch for €58.** [$] *Average main: €67* ✉ *Hôtel Negresco, 37 Promenade des Anglais* ☎ *04–93–16–64–00* 🌐 *www.hotel-negresco-nice.com* ✍ *Reservations essential* ⏲ *Closed Mon. and Tues. Closed Jan. No lunch Wed.–Sat.*

$ FRENCH Fodor's Choice ★ 🍴 **Chez Pipo Socca.** There are plenty of places where you can sample socca in the Old Town, but if you want to understand why so much fuss is made in Nice over this chickpea pancake, this out-of-the-way café behind the Port is the place to go. As normal for making this recipe, a batter of chickpea flour, water, olive oil, and salt is baked in giant copper tins in a wood-fired oven, but here, the cook expertly scrapes the surface of the nearly cooked dough with a metal spatula so that it comes out extra crispy. It's hard to explain why, but this is socca you can eat in large quantities even if you're not hungry: proof is the line on weekend nights, when people are willing to wait an hour or more for their petite or grande plates. **TIP→ For a shorter (or no) wait, show up around 5:30, when Pipo first opens.** [$] *Average main: €13* ✉ *13 rue Bavastro, Old Town/Port* ☎ *04–93–55–88–82* 🌐 *www.chezpipo.fr* 💳 *No credit cards* ⏲ *Closed Mon. No lunch Sun.*

$ FRENCH 🍴 **Co-t-Café.** This brightly colored and vibrant local café, one block from the Promenade and Hotel Negresco, has the best coffee in Nice. Expect creamy lattés, iced coffees, cappuccinos, plus teas and smoothies, in all sizes, to stay or to go. Sandwiches, salads, and wraps—superbly priced and made fresh each morning—are perfect for the beach (look for Winestar, wine in a can, also ideal for a beach picnic). [$] *Average main: €8* ✉ *11 bis rue Meyerbeer, New Town* ☎ *04–93–16–09–84* ⏲ *Closed Dec.–Feb.*

$$ MODERN FRENCH 🍴 **Flaveur.** Run by a young threesome (two chefs and a maître d') with an haute cuisine background, this modern bistro is perpetually packed—which means, plan on booking at least a week ahead for dinner and several days for lunch. The key to the trio's success is the heart that goes into the cooking: the limited menu changes often, and the chefs like to experiment with historical recipes such as *petits farcis* (stuffed vegetables) from a 19th-century cookbook. The hand-cut steak tartare with chickpea fries and thick gazpacho has become a classic. For €28 at lunch, you can sample the *plat du jour* with a glass of wine and coffee. [$] *Average main: €20* ✉ *25 rue Gubernatis, New Town* ☎ *04–93–62–53–95* 🌐 *www.flaveur.net* ✍ *Reservations essential* ⏲ *Closed Sun. and Mon. No lunch Sat.*

$$$$ MODERN FRENCH 🍴 **L'Aromate.** Ambitious young chef Mickäel Gracieux has garnered acclaim with this chic modern bistro in green, black, and stone near the Notre Dame cathedral. The menu draws on seasonal ingredients, but it isn't a place with any Provençal clichés—instead, the waiter might whisk off a cubic "cloche" to reveal a goldfish bowl containing crab in ginger jelly with a tart cream sauce and a fennel emulsion (being from Brittany, the chef is not afraid to be generous with the crème fraîche). The visuals won't disappoint; evening menus are pricey but worth it at €60 or €80. [$] *Average main: €60* ✉ *20 av. Maréchal Foch, New Town* ☎ *04–93–62–98–24* 🌐 *www.laromate.fr* ⏲ *Closed Sun. and Mon.*

$$$ FRENCH 🍴 **La Merenda.** The back-to-bistro boom climaxed here when Dominique Le Stanc retired his crown at the Negresco to take over this tiny, unpretentious landmark of Provençal cuisine. Now he works in the miniature open kitchen creating ultimate versions of stuffed sardines, tagliatelle with pistou, slow-simmered daubes (beef stews), and the quintessential stockfish (the local lutefisk), while his wife whisks the dishes into the dining room. Stop by in person to reserve entry to the inner sanctum (there are two sittings at both lunch and dinner), as there's no phone. [$] *Average main: €25* ✉ *4 rue Raoul Bosio, Vieux Nice* 💳 *No credit cards* 🕒 *Closed weekends, 1st 2 wks in Aug., and holidays.*

$ FRENCH 🍴 **La Part des Anges.** This wine shop with a few tables and chairs at the back is really about *vins naturels*—unfiltered, unsulfured, hand-harvested wines from small producers—but the often-simple food also happens to be excellent. Whether you choose a charcuterie or cheese plate or one of the handful of hot dishes such as spaghetti with razor clams or octopus daube (cooked with red wine), you can expect it to be generous and fresh. No corkage fee is charged for wines off the shelf, a rarity for a wine bar. Reservations are best for Friday and Saturday nights and it's worth noting that bilingual owner Olivier opened a second wine bistrot, La Mise en Verre, at 17 rue Pastorelli. [$] *Average main: €18* ✉ *17 rue Gubernatis, New Town* ☎ *04–93–62–69–80* 🌐 *www.la-part-des-anges-nice.fr* 🕒 *Closed Sun.*

$$$$ FRENCH 🍴 **La Réserve de Nice.** Thirty-one-year-old chef Sébastien Mahuet knows what it takes to earn restaurant acclaim, and his originality and detail are reflected in his creations like millefeuille of foie gras caramelized with maple syrup, fig marmalade flavoured with port wine, cranberry, and red currant jelly; and the coated cod fillet cooked in frothy butter, shallots, and cocoa beans stewed with bacon in a fine truffle bouillon. Price—it's easy to run up a bill of more than €150 per couple with drinks—and quality may not always meet halfway, but the panoramic views, especially upstairs, from this Art Deco building jutting over the sea cannot be faulted; also here is one of the city's most stylish bars. Before coming to La Réserve, the chef worked at La Bastide Saint-Antoine and Château de la Chèvre 'Or. [$] *Average main: €40* ✉ *60 bd. Frank Pilatte, Mont Boron* ☎ *04–97–08–29–98* 🌐 *www.lareservedenice.com* 🕒 *Closed most of Nov. No dinner Sun.*

$ BISTRO 🍴 **Le Bistrot d'Antoine.** You will not find any "concept" cooking here, just pure French bistro fare at its finest—beef salad with anchovy dressing, butter risotto with truffles, sliced leg of lamb, and traditional pork casserole. Leave room for the day's dessert, such as the wonderfully warm peach-and-frangipane tart. The prices here are as appealing as the menu. If you can't score a reservation here, you can try another option: chef Antoine Crespo opened a second eatery, the Comptoir du Marché (at 8 rue du Marché), where he masterfully balances fresh market cuisine at reasonable prices. [$] *Average main: €13* ✉ *27 rue de la Préfecture, Vieux Nice* ☎ *04–93–85–29–57* ✍ *Reservations essential* 🕒 *Closed Sun., Mon., and most of Aug.*

$$$ BISTRO 🍴 **Le Bistrot Gourmand.** Chef David Vaqué received the Maître Cuisinier title in 2013 for his preservation of French cuisine at Le Bistrot Gourmand, a local favorite since it opened in 2011. The setting is convenient—just

A magnificent wedding-cake extravaganza, the Hotel Negresco was the haunt of the Beatles and the Burtons, and still remains the icon of Nice.

steps away from the Hotel Beau Rivage and with an outdoor terrace—but the focus is on the food and the wine. Menu options include black risotto, pan-fried European lobster and Iberian chorizo, and a cappuccino of peppers and ginger, plus a soufflé that may actually leave you *à bout de souffle* (breathless). The sommelier amazingly seems to know your order before you do; a bottle will set you back around €55. Don't expect a warm and cheery interior; while the service is friendly enough, the stark white setting with a few dashes of color is meant to keep your eye on the plate. Even so, take a look around to observe what goes on behind the scenes at an acclaimed restaurant. One can only hope that the prices stay as humble as the staff. [$] *Average main: €30* ✉ *3 rue Desboutin, Vieux Nice* ☎ *04–92–14–55–55* 🌐 *www.lebistrogourmand.fr.*

$$ FRENCH 🍴 **Le Safari.** The Cours Saleya's desirable terrace tables provide an excuse for many of the restaurants along this strip to get away with culinary murder. That's not the case at Le Safari, at No. 1, which pays more attention than most to ingredients and presentation (even if you shouldn't expect miracles). Choose from traditional Niçois dishes—the fish soup served with croutons, spicy mayonnaise, and cheese is particularly good—and Italian-inspired fare such as creamy risotto. Inside the colorful dining room is where the locals eat, and some even claim the food is a notch better there. **TIP→ Wherever you sit, it's a good idea to reserve.** [$] *Average main: €24* ✉ *1 cours Saleya, Old Town/Port* ☎ *04–93–80–18–44* 🌐 *www.restaurantsafari.fr.*

$$$ FRENCH 🍴 **Luc Salsedo.** Young chef Luc Salsedo, who trained at the Louis XV in Monaco, has a hit on his hands with this little ocher-walled bistro. His brief menu, which changes completely every three weeks, often involves modern twists on traditional Niçois dishes, such as socca (a

chickpea flour pancake) wrapped around stir-fried spring vegetables, or delicious desserts like the *pain perdu aux pommes* (french toast with apples and cinnamon served with salted caramel ice cream). Servings are generous—expect a big appetizer plate in addition to the three copious course menu (€45)—and the dining room staff, led by Luc's wife, Christine, is stellar. It's best to reserve because the word has gotten out that this place is "a must." [$] *Average main: €26* ✉ *14 rue Maccarani* ☎ *04–93–82–24–12* 🌐 *www.restaurant-salsedo.com* ⏲ *Closed Wed. No lunch.*

$ FRENCH 🍴 **Lycée Hotellier Paul Augier.** Popular with both locals and expats, the three restaurants at the Paul Augier Hospitality and Tourism School, attended by 1,200 pupils and apprentices, serve lunch Monday through Friday. The food is prepared by aspiring young chefs. The most sophisticated of the three, the Baie des Anges gourmet restaurant, is on the 5th floor. [$] *Average main: €15* ✉ *163 bd. René Cassin* ✥ *Take bus No. 59 along the Promenade and get off at Les Sagnes* ☎ *04–93–72–77–77* 🌐 *www.lycee-paul-augier.com* ⏲ *Closed weekends. No dinner.*

$$$ ECLECTIC 🍴 **Sapore.** Chef Anthony Riou has found a winning formula with his generous five-course tapas menu, which changes frequently to keep the locals coming back to this sleek red-and-gray-walled dining room with ancient wooden beams and an open kitchen. The key to his cooking is his use of simple, bold flavors, as in a thick crab velouté, goat cheese, and very thin bacon slices on toast, deboned duck confit on potato purée, and chocolate cake with mango. Choose from Spanish and French wines to complete this Spanish-accented experience, which attracts a young and fashionable French crowd. [$] *Average main: €32* ✉ *19 rue Bonaparte, Place du Pin, Old Town/Port* ☎ *04–92–04–22–09* 🌐 *www.restaurant-sapore.com* ⏲ *Closed Sun. and Mon.*

## WHERE TO STAY

$$$$ HOTEL 🏨 **Boscolo Hotel Exedra Nizza.** The top-notch features of this Belle Époque extravaganza—Louis Quinze armchairs, minimal mod tables, soaring skylights (including a redo of one originally fashioned by Gustave Eiffel), acres of teakwood walls, 1950s kidney-shape sofas, and some of the biggest black-and-white Murano chandeliers in the world—make this a supermodel of a hotel. **Pros:** five blocks from the beach; near shops and restaurants. **Cons:** service can be hit and miss; €24 breakfast (but lots of cafés close by). [$] *Rooms from: €280* ✉ *12 bd. Victor Hugo, New Town* ☎ *04–93–16–75–70* 🌐 *www.boscolohotels.com* 🛏 *104 rooms, 9 suites* 🍽 *Breakfast.*

$ HOTEL 🏨 **Hotel Felix Beach.** This practical hotel sits a block from the beach on popular Rue Masséna—and, if you choose one of the four rooms that feature a tiny balcony, you'll have a ringside seat over the pedestrian thoroughfare. **Pros:** prime location of hotel makes perfect touring sense; owners are so nice that you feel right at home. **Cons:** rooms can be noisy, especially those facing the street; there's no elevator and rooms are on upper floors. [$] *Rooms from: €90* ✉ *41 rue Masséna, Place Masséna* ☎ *04–93–88–67–73* 🌐 *www.hotel-felix.com* 🛏 *14 rooms* 🍽 *No meals.*

$$$$ HOTEL Fodor's Choice ★ **Hôtel Negresco.** This white-stucco slice of old-fashioned Riviera extravagance remains the icon of Nice today, accommodating well-heeled guests in elegant, uniquely decorated guest rooms replete with swagged drapes and fine antiques (plus a few unfortunate "with-it" touches like those plastic-glitter bathtubs). **Pros:** like staying in a museum; attention and service from the moment you arrive; food at the famous Chantecler is formidable. **Cons:** medicore breakfast is expensive (€30) so head to Caffe Vergnano 1882 in the pietonne. [$] *Rooms from: €330* ✉ *37 promenade des Anglais* ☎ *04–93–16–64–00* 🌐 *www.hotel-negresco-nice.com* 🛏 *96 rooms, 21 suites* ⏲ *Restaurant closed in Jan.* 🍴 *No meals.*

$$ HOTEL **Hôtel Suisse.** Charging modest prices for a spectacular view from the top end of the seafront, where the promenade winds around to the port, the acclaimed Hôtel Suisse far outclasses most other hotels in this price range. **Pros:** balconies with breathtaking sea views; clean, modern rooms; accessible prices in low season. **Cons:** tiny elevator; pricey breakfast at €18 when you can walk to Cours Saleya. [$] *Rooms from: €139* ✉ *15 quai Raubà Capéù, Old Town/Port* ☎ *04–92–17–39–00* 🌐 *www.hotel-nice-suisse.com* 🛏 *38 rooms, 1 suite* 🍴 *No meals.*

$$ HOTEL **La Fontaine.** A block from the waterfront and the Negresco, this immaculate and newly designed hotel on a bustling shopping street offers a friendly welcome from its house-proud owners—for a great price. **Pros:** helpful staff; leafy courtyard; antiallergy flooring and pillows. **Cons:** rooms overlooking the street can be noisy; €12 breakfast expensive but lots of cafés around. [$] *Rooms from: €135* ✉ *49 rue de France, New Town* ☎ *04–93–88–30–38* 🌐 *www.hotel-fontaine.com* 🛏 *29 rooms* ⏲ *Closed 2 wks in Dec. and Jan.* 🍴 *No meals.*

$$$$ HOTEL **La Perouse.** Just past the Vieille Ville, at the foot of the town's château, this hotel is a secret treasure cut into the cliff (an elevator takes you up to reception). **Pros:** discreet elegance steps from the Old Town and the Promenade; very good service. **Cons:** some windows face a stone wall; not good for those with mobility issues; best to get to breakfast (€24) before 10 am as supplies may run low. [$] *Rooms from: €345* ✉ *11 quai Rauba Capeu, Le Château* ☎ *04–93–62–34–63* 🌐 *www.hotel-la-perouse.com* 🛏 *57 rooms* 🍴 *No meals.*

$ HOTEL **Nice Garden Hotel.** It's hard to believe that this gem of a little hotel, with its own courtyard garden, is smack in the middle of Nice, next to the pedestrian shopping streets and a five-minute walk from the Old Town. **Pros:** breakfast (extra) with homemade jam in the garden; extremely helpful owner; check-in from 2–9 pm. **Cons:** breakfast leans on the healthy side (where are the *pain au chocolats*?). [$] *Rooms from: €90* ✉ *11 rue du Congrès, New Town* ☎ *04–93–87–35–62* 🌐 *www.nicegardenhotel.com* 🛏 *9 rooms* 🍴 *No meals.*

$ HOTEL **Solara.** One block from the beach and two from Place Masséna, this tiny budget hotel perches on the 4th and 5th floors, high above the main shopping street. **Pros:** location near the beach; top-floor terraces overlooking pedestrian street; sound-proof windows. **Cons:** unattractive street entrance. [$] *Rooms from: €70* ✉ *7 rue de France, New Town* ☎ *04–93–88–09–96* 🌐 *www.hotelsolara.com* 🛏 *12 rooms* 🍴 *No meals.*

**$$**  ☐ **Villa les Cygnes.** The Baumettes neighborhood is not normally
**B&B/INN**  explored by tourists other than those visiting the Musée de Beaux-
Arts, but it's an area worth getting to know if simply for the sake of
staying in this hotel, which is only a five-minute walk to the beach and
is really more like a luxury bed-and-breakfast. **Pros:** warm and welcom-
ing owners; generous breakfast (extra); big bathrooms. **Cons:** a little
far (30-minute walk) from the tourist center of Nice. $ *Rooms from:
€145* ✉ *6 av. du Château de la Tour, New Town* ☎ *04–97–03–23–35*
⊕ *www.villalescygnes.com* ↘ *6 rooms* ⦿ *No meals.*

**$$**  ☐ **Villa Rivoli.** You'll find this Belle Époque hotel, built in 1890, in the
**HOTEL**  chic Quartier des Musiciens, excellently located a couple of blocks
up from the beach but with very affordable prices. **Pros:** friendly and
helpful service; authentic-period French feel. **Cons:** cost for breakfast
and parking; "Lower Ground Floor" category rooms can be musky.
$ *Rooms from: €156* ✉ *10 rue de Rivoli, New Town* ☎ *04–93–88–80–
25* ⊕ *www.villa-rivoli.com* ↘ *24 rooms* ⦿ *No meals.*

**$$**  ☐ **Windsor.** This is a memorably eccentric hotel—most of its white-on-
**HOTEL**  white rooms either have frescoes of mythological themes or are works
of artists' whimsy—but the real draw at this otherworldly place is its
astonishing city-center garden, a tropical oasis of lemon, magnolia, and
palm trees, only outdone by the excellent service. **Pros:** private pool
and garden in heart of city; enthusiastic welcome; you can print your
boarding pass for free in the lobby. **Cons:** artist-inspired decor is not
for everyone (look online before booking!); street rooms can be noisy;
Ultra-Violet elevator is cool the first time but annoying by the end of
the week. $ *Rooms from: €135* ✉ *11 rue Dalpozzo* ☎ *04–93–88–59–35*
⊕ *www.hotelwindsornice.com* ↘ *57 rooms* ⦿ *No meals.*

## NIGHTLIFE AND THE ARTS

### NIGHTLIFE

Nightlife in Nice for most part ends after a late dinner. There is a
smattering of clubs in the Old Nice–Port district and the pietonne has
developed a lively reputation, with bars around Rue de France and
Rue Halèvy, including Rue Commandant Rafalli, which now houses
less-blatantly tourist bistros.

### BARS

**Bar Le Relais.** If you're all dressed up and have just won big, invest in
a drink in the intimate walnut-and-velour Bar Le Relais in the iconic
Hôtel Negresco. It's worth the price just to get a peek at the wash-
rooms (just don't trip over the owner's lounging cat, Carmen). Jazz
plays beginning at 7:30 pm Sunday through Tuesday. ✉ *37 prome-
nade des Anglais, Promenade Nice* ☎ *04–93–16–64–00* ⊕ *www.hotel-
negresco-nice.com.*

**Seven Blue Bar.** Don't forget your camera when heading up to this
panoramic bar on the 7th floor of the Clarion Grand Aston Hotel.
The views of old Nice and the new Promenade du Paillon across to
the airport are spectacular, and drink prices are more than reason-
able. In the summer, the bar moves to the rooftop, where there's a
pool (for guests) and 360-degree view of France's fifth largest city.

During the famous annual Carnaval, gargantuan sculptures and the famous *grosses têtes*—literally, "fat heads"—fill the streets of old Nice with fantasy.

Note that there are 23 steps from the hotel lobby to the bar's elevator. ✉ *12 av. Felix Faure, Centre Ville* ☏ *04–93–17–53–00* ⊕ *www.hotel-aston.com.*

### DANCE CLUBS

**Glam.** The hottest gay club in Nice, Glam has DJs that oblige you to dance with the the best mixes around. It is open to all clubbers in the know, with only one criterion: be cool. ✉ *6 rue Eugène Emmanuel* ☏ *06–60–55–26–61* ⊕ *www.leglam.org* ☽ *Thurs.–Sun. 11 pm–5 am.*

**High Club.** Nice was a sleepy city until High came around (just ask the neighbors). Tables at this newly decorated club come with a bottle: €120 for four people; €400 for a VIP magnum above the €20 at the door. Don't show up unless you're here to take advantage of strobe lights across three floors. ✉ *45 promenade des Anglais, New Town* ☏ *06–16–95–75–87* ⊕ *www.highclub.fr* ☽ *Fri.–Sun. 11:45 pm–6 am.*

### JAZZ MUSIC

**Théâtre de Verdure.** Built in 1945, the Théâtre de Verdure can seat 1,850 people or provide standing room for 3,200. It's a great spot for concerts and theater. Keep an eye on the summer calendar for the Ciné Prom, when you can watch big-screen movies (€2) here. ✉ *Jardin Albert Ier, Espace Jacques Cotta* ⊕ *www.tdv-nice.org.*

## THE ARTS

### CONCERTS

**Acropolis.** Classical music, ballet performances, and traditional French pop concerts take place at Nice's convention center, the Acropolis. ✉ *Palais des Congrès, Esplanade John F. Kennedy* ☏ *04–93–92–83–00* ⊕ *www.nice-acropolis.com.*

**Conservatoire National.** The regional conservatory in Cimiez has a mixed calendar of events, from classical concerts to dance. ✉ *127 av. de Brancolar, Cimiez* ✛ *Take bus No. 15 to the Cdt. Gérôme stop.* ☎ *04–97– 13–50– 00* ⊕ *www.cnr-nice.org.*

**Nice Jazz Festival.** For five days in July, the Nice Jazz Festival draws performers from around the world to Place Masséna and Théâtre de Verdure. Tickets begin around €35 per show and can be purchased online directly or from FNAC and Carrefour. Enter at Place Masséna. ✉ *Place Masséna and Théâtre de Verdure, Espace Jacques Cotta* ☎ *08– 92–68–36–22* ⊕ *www.nicejazzfestival.fr.*

### FILM AND THEATER

**Cinéma Rialto.** Don't expect to find popcorn and concession stands here, but the Rialto has the city's only selection of foreign- and English-language films. ✉ *4 rue de Rivoli, Cimiez* ⊕ *lerialto.cine.allocine.fr.*

**Théâtre National de Nice.** Headed by Daniel Benoin, the Théâtre National de Nice plays host to 40 productions from all over Europe as part of a new initiative to become a center for innovative European theater. Tickets range from €12 to €40. ✉ *Promenade des Arts* ☎ *04–93–13– 90–90* ⊕ *www.tnn.fr.*

### SPORTS AND THE OUTDOORS

Nice itself is like a playing field for *les sportifs,* and it's not uncommon to see the current mayor, Christian Estrosi, running on the Promenade as he trains for the Nice–Cannes marathon. With his Olympic-hosting vision, Estrosi was behind the construction of the Allianz Riviera, Nice's new 35,000-capacity soccer stadium, completed in September 2013 to the tune of €245 million. But it's not just soccer. One of the world's major sporting events, the Ironman Nice triathlon (⊕ *www. ironmannice.com),* is held every June, with a 70% foreigner participation rate made up of more than 60 nationalities, all testing their physical endurance in one the world's most challenging events.

**Glisse Evasion.** If the idea of parasailing seems a bit terrifying, note that these guys get nothing but smiles from satisfied customers. Parasailing is €65 for two or €30 for "Slydsit" (sitting in a group in an inflatable dinghy). ✉ *In front of Hôtel Negresco, 29 Promenade des Anglais* ☎ *06–10–27–03–91* ⊕ *www.glisse-evasion.com.*

# SHOPPING

Nice's main shopping street, **Avenue Jean-Médecin,** runs inland from Place Masséna; all needs and most tastes are catered to in its big department stores (Galeries Lafayette, Monoprix, and the split-level Étoile mall). The tramway, launched in late 2007, has made this mini Champs-Elysées all the more accessible, so expect crowds on Saturday (the majority of shops are still closed on Sunday). Luxury boutiques, such as Emporio Armani, Kenzo, Chanel, and Sonia Rykiel, line Rue du Paradis, while Rue de France and the Old Town have more accessible shops.

**Confiserie Florian.** A good source for crystallized fruit (and chocolate) is the Confiserie du Florian, known since its opening in 1994 as Confiserie du Vieux-Nice. On the west side of the port, it is open every day except Christmas. ⊠ *14 quai Papacino* ☏ *04–93–55–43–50* ⊕ *www. confiserieflorian.com.*

**Fish market.** Seafood of all kinds is sold at the fish market every day (except Monday) from 6 am to 1 pm. ⊠ *Pl. St-François, Vieux Nice.*

**Henri Auer.** The venerable Henri Auer has sold crystallized fruit since 1820. ⊠ *7 rue St-François de Paule, Vieux Nice* ⊕ *www.maison-auer. com* ⊘ *Closed Sun.–Mon.*

**La Promenade des 100 Antiquaires.** France's third largest *regroupment* of antique collectors form a triangle from Place Garibaldi to the port (Quai Papacino) and along rue Catherine Ségruane at the bottom of the Château (shops are closed on Sunday). There's a helpful map on the website, which includes side streets like Rue Antoine Gautier and Rue Emmanuel Philibert. Make sure to visit Les Puces de Nice with 30 stalls under one roof in Quai Lunel, and on the third Saturday of the month Place Garibaldi hosts an antique market in the morning. ⊠ *Pl. Robilante, Vieux Nice* ⊕ *nice-antic.com.*

**Mademoiselle.** You have to hand it to the French; they even do second-hand fashion right. Steps away from the Hôtel Negresco, Mademoiselle has quickly become a must-stop shop in Nice: Chanel, Dior, Louis Vuitton, Hermès—you name it, the gang's all here, at least in vintage terms. You'll find lots of luxury brand clothes, shoes, bags, and belts to rummage through—all of it excellently priced and gorgeously displayed. Open every day, don't be surprised to walk by at 10 pm on a summer's evening to find owners Jeremy and Sephora sipping champagne with clients. ⊠ *41 rue de France, New Town.*

**Oliviera.** Come here for the best selection of Provençal olive oils in town. Oliviera is run by the passionate Nadim Beyrouti in the Old Town, who also serves Mediterranean dishes made with the finest local ingredients. ⊠ *8 bis rue du Collet* ☏ *04–93–13–06–45* ⊕ *www.oliviera.com* ⊘ *Closed Tues.*

**Star Dog Boutique.** For the jet-set pet, Star Dog Boutique has iPawds (plush toy with FaceBark, DogTube, and Bark Street Journal apps), Doggle sunglasses, and Oh My Dog! cologne to get Fido's tail wagging. It's one of the most fun shops in Nice to browse or at the very least window shop. ⊠ *40 rue de France, New Town* ☏ *04–97–03–27–40* ⊕ *jophicotedazur.com.*

# THE CORNICHES RESORTS

Purists and hard-core regional historians insist that this final sunny sliver of coast—from Cap Ferrat to the Italian border—is the one and only, true Côte d'Azur. It is certainly the most dramatically endowed, backed by forested mountains and crystalline Alps, with Mediterranean breezes relieving the summer heat and radiant light soothing midwinter days. Banana trees, date palms, cactus, and figs luxuriate in the climate, and the hills, bristling with wind-twisted parasol pines, are paved with hothouses, where roses and carnations profit from the year-round sun.

Terraced by three parallel, panoramic highways—the Basse Corniche, the Moyenne Corniche, and the Grande Corniche—that snake along its graduated crests, this stretch of the coast is studded with fabled resorts, their names as evocative of luxury and glamour as haute-couture logos: Cap Ferrat, Beaulieu, and Monte Carlo.

Yet it must be said: these pockets of elegance have long since over-flowed, and it's a rare stretch of cliffside that hasn't sprouted a cluster of concrete cubes in cloying hues of pineapple, apricot, and Pepto-Bismol pink. The traffic along the corniche routes—especially the Corniche Inférieure that follows the coast—is appalling in peak season (so spare yourself and visit May, June, September, or October, or even in the temperate winter, the fashionable season during the 19th century), exacerbated by the manic Italian driving style and self-absorbed luxury roadsters that turn the pavement into a bumper-car battle.

But there are moments. Wrench your car out of the flow, pull over at a rare overlook on the Haute Corniche, and walk to the extremity. Like the ancient Ligurians, who first built their settlements here, you can hang over the infinite expanse of teal-blue sea and glittering waves and survey the resorts draped gracefully along the curves of the coast. It was from these cliffs that for 2,500 years castles and towers held watch over the waters, braced against the influx of new peoples—first the Greeks, then the Romans, the Saracens, trade ships from Genoa, battleships under Napoléon, Edwardian cruise ships on the Grand Tour, and the Allies in the Second World War. The influx continues today, of course, in the great waves of vacationers who storm the coast, spring to early fall.

## VILLEFRANCHE-SUR-MER

*10 km (6 miles) east of Nice.*

Nestled discreetly along the deep scoop of harbor between Nice and Cap Ferrat, this pretty watercolor of a fishing port seems surreal, flanked as it is by the big city of Nice and the assertive wealth of Monaco. The town is a stage set of brightly colored houses—the sort of place where Pagnol's *Fanny* could have been filmed. Genuine fishermen skim up to the docks here in weathered-blue *barques,* and the streets of the Vieille Ville flow directly to the waterfront, much as they did in the 13th century. Some of the prettiest spots in town are around Place de la Paix, Rue du Poilu, and Place du Conseil, which looks out over the water. The deep harbor, in the caldera of a volcano, was once preferred by the likes of Onassis and Niarchos and the royals on their yachts. But the character of the place was subtly shaped by the artists and authors who gathered at the **Hôtel Welcome**—Diaghilev and Stravinsky, taking a break from the Ballet Russe in Monaco; Somerset Maugham and Evelyn Waugh; and, above all, Jean Cocteau, who came here to recover from the excesses of Paris life. Nowadays, its population consists mainly of wealthy retired people, though families do head here to enjoy its sandy (well, gravelly) beach. The only fly in the ointment is Villefranche's popularity: between the endless stream of cruise ships sending their passengers ashore in very, very large numbers and a flood of new construction so villas now virtually elbow each other out of the way up the hillsides, the towns' physical beauty has become more challenging to appreciate on a grand scale or peacefully. Still and all, quaint alleyways and the heavenly panoramas of the town from on high nicely remind you why everyone headed here in the first place.

**GETTING HERE AND AROUND**

Villefranche is a major stop on the Marseilles–Ventimiglia coastal train route, with more than 40 arrivals every day from Nice (6 minutes). Buses connect with Nice and Monaco via Lignes d'Azur No. 100 or from Nice, Nos. 80, 81, or 84 (€1.50). Most public parking is paid during the day (€1.10/hour) and can be tricky to find.

**VISITOR INFORMATION**

**Villefranche-sur-Mer Tourist Office.** This tourist office operates at Place Wilson from May through September. ✉ *Jardin François Binon* ☎ *04–93–01–73–68* ⊕ *www.villefranche-sur-mer.fr.*

## EXPLORING

**Chapelle St-Pierre.** So enamored was Jean Cocteau of this painterly fishing port that he decorated the 14th-century Chapelle St-Pierre with images from the life of St. Peter and dedicated it to the village's fishermen. ✉ *Quai de l'Amiral Courbet Courbet* ☎ *04–93–76–90–70* 💲 *€3* ☉ *Spring and summer, Wed.–Mon. 10–noon and 3–7; fall and winter.–Apr., Wed.–Mon. 10–noon and 2–6.*

**Citadelle St-Elme.** Open year-round, the stalwart 16th-century Citadelle St-Elme, restored to perfect condition, anchors the harbor with its broad, sloping stone walls. Beyond its drawbridge lie the city's administrative offices and a group of minor gallery-museums, with a scattering of works by Picasso and Miró. Whether or not you stop into these private collections of local art (all free of charge), you're welcome to stroll around the inner grounds and circle the imposing exterior. ✉ *Harbor* 💲 *Free* ☉ *Museums: June–Sept., Tues.–Sat. 10–noon and 3–6:30, Sun. 3–6:30; Oct.–Nov. and Jan.–May, Tues.–Sat. 10–noon and 2–5:30, Sun 2–5:30.*

**Église St-Michel.** The modest Baroque Église St-Michel, above Rue Obscure, contains a movingly realistic sculpture of Christ carved in fig wood by an anonymous 17th-century convict. ✉ *Pl. Poullan.*

**Rue Obscure.** Running parallel to the waterfront, the extraordinary 14th-century Rue Obscure (literally, "Dark Street") is entirely covered by vaulted arcades; it sheltered the people of Villefranche when the Germans fired their parting shots—an artillery bombardment—near the end of World War II.

## BEACHES

**Plage des Marinières.** To the east of the port, southwest-facing Plage des Marinères is the biggest beach you'll find in Villefranche, but it's only about a kilometer long. Popular because the shoreline is protected from winds, this beach has coarse sand and lifeguards in the summer. Note that the SNCF train line runs parallel, so the noise factor is a consideration. There are shower and toilet facilities, but no loungers, and jellyfish can be a problem in the warmer months. **Amenities:** none. **Best for:** snorkeling; swimming; sunrise. ✉ *Promenade des Marinières, Villefranche.*

## DID YOU KNOW?

Home to some of the biggest megayachts (and the occasional battleship), the harbor of Villefranche-sur-Mer surrounds one of the deepest and most beautiful bays on the Riviera.

## WHERE TO EAT

**$$$**
MEDITERRANEAN

✕ **Cosmo Bar.** Once you've discovered Cosmo, it's a place you're likely to come back to again and again. Facing the Cocteau chapel with an enviable view of the sea from its terrace, this modern brasserie could easily get away with being merely mediocre. Instead, it serves fresh, colorful Mediterranean food ranging from an addictive *anchoïade*— crudités with anchovy dip—to Moroccan-inspired monkfish tagine. It's a favorite of English-speaking expats in Villefranche and it's easy to understand why, since it brings together all the ingredients that make for a casual yet memorable meal on the French Riviera. Call ahead to be sure of securing a coveted terrace table. $ *Average main: €28* ✉ *11 pl. Amélie Pollonnais* ☎ *04–93–01–84–05* ✍ *Reservations essential* ⊗ *Closed mid-Nov.–mid-Dec.*

**$$$$**
FRENCH

✕ **La Mère Germaine.** This is the ideal eatery to linger over warm lobster salad or sole meuniere in butter with almonds while watching the world go by. The seaside restaurant opened in 1938, and proprietor Germaine Halap soon became a second mother to American naval officers and sailors who came into port. A movie has been made about "Mère Germaine," and excerpts from the book *Mother of the Sixth Fleet* were published in *Readers Digest*. People come here for the location. The food is tasty, but the fabulous setting in this veritable institution is absorbed in the price. The €42 menu is a better value. Valet parking is available from April to October. $ *Average main: €45* ✉ *Quai Corbert* ☎ *04–93–01–71–39* ⊕ *www.meregermaine.com* ⊗ *Closed late Nov.–Christmas.*

**$**
FRENCH

✕ **Le Serre.** It might look like just another pizzeria, but Le Serre is a family-run restaurant where everything from the pizzas to the local specialties is prepared with care. The warm welcome ensures that the restaurant attracts plenty of locals who have learned to tread carefully around tourist traps. Daube, the Provençal beef-and-wine stew with herbs, is served all year; the chef starts its preparation at midnight for the next day. $ *Average main: €17* ✉ *16 rue de May* ☎ *04–93–76–79–91* ⊗ *Closed Mon.–Tues., Jan.–Mar. Closed mid-Nov.–Dec.*

## WHERE TO STAY

**$**
HOTEL

▦ **Hôtel de la Darse.** Who needs luxury fittings and fabrics when you have a view like this one overlooking the old harbor of Villefranche? **Pros:** the views over the Old Port. **Cons:** there is a lot of walking involved both to and within this hotel; it's a little outside the center of town. $ *Rooms from: €82* ✉ *32 av. Général de Gaulle, Villefranche* ☎ *04–93–01–72–54* ⊕ *www.hoteldeladarse.com* ⇱ *21 rooms* ⊗ *Closed mid-Nov.–mid-Feb.* ⦿ *No meals.*

**$**
HOTEL

▦ **Hôtel Provençal.** Within walking distance of the port, this inexpensive hotel may not look like much from the outside but is friendly and accommodating. **Pros:** balconies with sea view (ask for this when booking); breakfast (€11), served on the terrace, is high quality. **Cons:** modest room decor and bathrooms. $ *Rooms from: €90* ✉ *4 av. Maréchal Joffre* ☎ *04–93–76–53–53* ⊕ *www.hotelleprovencal.fr* ⇱ *45 rooms* ⊗ *Closed Nov.–mid-Mar.* ⦿ *No meals.*

$$$$ HOTEL **Hôtel Welcome.** Somerset Maugham holed up in one of the tiny crow's-nest rooms at the top, Jean Cocteau lived here while writing *Orphée*, and Elizabeth Taylor and Richard Burton used to tie one on in the bar (now nicely renovated) at this waterfront landmark—which remains a comfortable and noteworthy retreat. **Pros:** excellent service; credit card payments in American dollars; artistic heritage makes for a nostalgic trip into the Roaring Twenties. **Cons:** decor, especially on the top floor, is distinctly nautical in flavor; some rooms are oddly shaped—narrow and long—so they feel smaller. [$] *Rooms from: €227* ✉ *3 Quai Amiral Courbet* ☎ *04–93–76–27–62* 🌐 *www.welcomehotel.com* 🛏 *32 rooms, 3 suites* 🕒 *Closed mid-Nov.–Christmas* 🍴 *Breakfast.*

## BEAULIEU-SUR-MER

*4 km (2½ miles) east of Villefranche; 14 km (9 miles) east of Nice.*

With its back pressed hard against the cliffs of the corniche and sheltered between the peninsulas of Cap Ferrat and Cap Roux, this once-grand resort basks in a tropical microclimate that earned its central neighborhood the name "Petite Afrique." The town was the pet of 19th-century society, and its grand hotels welcomed Empress Eugénie, the Prince of Wales, and Russian nobles.

### GETTING HERE AND AROUND

With frequent arrivals and departures, Beaulieu is a main stop on the Marseille–Ventimiglia coastal train line. From Beaulieu's train station hourly buses, No. 81 (€1.50), connect with neighboring St-Jean-Cap-Ferrat. Bus No. 100 takes you to/from Nice/Monaco, while No. 84 goes to Nice via Villefranche.

### VISITOR INFORMATION

**Beaulieu Tourist Office** ✉ *Pl. Georges Clemenceau* ☎ *04–93–01–02–21* 🌐 *www.beaulieusurmer.fr.*

### EXPLORING

**Promenade Maurice-Rouvier.** Today Beaulieu is usually spoken of in the past tense and has taken on a rather stuffy ambience, though its small beach attracts families with children. But on the Promenade Maurice-Rouvier, a paved pedestrian path that begins not far from the Villa Kerylos, you can stroll the waterfront, past grand villas and their tropical gardens, all the way to St-Jean-Cap-Ferrat. The 30-minute-walk winds seaside along the Baie des Fourmis (Bay of Ants), whose name alludes to the black rocks "crawling" up from the sea. The name doesn't quite fit, but the walk will give you great views of the sparkling Mediterranean and surrounding mountains.

Fodor's Choice ★ **Villa Kerylos.** One manifestation of Beaulieu's Belle Époque excess is the eye-knocking Villa Kerylos, a 1902 mansion built in the style of classical Greece (to be exact, of the villas that existed on the island of Delos in the 2nd century BC). It was the dream house of amateur archaeologist Théodore Reinach, who hailed from a wealthy German family, helped the French in their excavations at Delphi, and became an authority on ancient Greek music. He commissioned an Italian architect from Nice, Emmanuel Pontremoli, to surround him with

Grecian delights: cool Carrara marble, rare fruitwoods, and a dining salon where guests reclined to eat *à la grecque*. Don't miss this—it's one of the most unusual houses in the south of France. Not far away is the **Promenade Maurice Rouvier,** an enchanting coastal path that leads to St-Jean-Cap-Ferrat. **TIP→ A combination ticket allows you to also visit Villa Ephrussi del Rothschild in nearby St-Jean-Cap-Ferrat in the same week.** ✉ *Impasse Gustave-Eiffel* ☎ *04–93–01–01–44* 🌐 *www.villa-kerylos.com* 🎫 *€11; €19 for both villas* 🕒 *Mid-Feb.–June and Sept.–Oct., daily 10–6; July and Aug., daily 10–7; Nov.–mid-Feb., Mon.–Fri. 2–6, Sat.–Sun. 10–6.*

### WHERE TO EAT AND STAY

$$$$ MEDITERRANEAN

🍴 **La Reserve.** The first impression of old-world grandeur given by the beautiful pink building is carried through to every opulent corner of La Reserve. Its restaurant has been a crown jewel of the Mediterranean since it opened in 1880. The Restaurant des Rois is a marvel of light and color, with a chandelier-bedecked salon lined with bay windows that offer views of a watery nirvana. Chef Romain Corbiere creates original recipes from fresh Mediterranean products, and rarely disappoints: duckling cooked "a la broche," picholines olives, turnip stuffed with baby spinach, and duck thighs pie baked with foie gras. For the price, go for the menu fixe for €115 or €205. To save a few euros (barely, spaghetti is €46) on lunch, head to Vent Debout, perched over the pool. Reserve well in advance during the summer season. [$] *Average main: €80* ✉ *5 bd. General Leclerc* ☎ *04–93–01–00–01* 🌐 *www.reservebeaulieu.com* 🛏 *0* 🕒 *Closed Nov.–mid-Dec.; No lunch May–Oct.*

$$ HOTEL

🏨 **Hôtel Riviera.** If you want to play at being rich without spending the money, book a room at this discreet little hotel in the heart of millionaire country, a five-minute walk from the beach. **Pros:** great value for money; proximity to the beach and bus stop. **Cons:** "petitit chambre economique" is small. [$] *Rooms from: €79* ✉ *6 rue Paul-Doumer* ☎ *04–93–01–04–92* 🌐 *www.hotel-riviera.fr* 🛏 *14 rooms* 🕒 *Closed mid-Oct.–Dec.* 🍽 *No meals.*

## ST-JEAN-CAP-FERRAT

*2 km (1 mile) south of Beaulieu on D25.*

One of the most exclusive addresses in the world, the peninsula of Cap Ferrat is moored by the luxuriously sited pleasure port of St-Jean; from its portside walkways and crescent of beach you can look over the sparkling blue harbor to the graceful green bulk of the corniches. Yachts purr in and out of port, and their passengers scuttle into cafés for take-out drinks to enjoy on their private decks. On shore, the billionaires come and go, and trade gossip about town resident Paul Allen, wondering if he will play host again to Brad, Angelina, and their brood at his fabled Villa Maryland, the great historic residence that lords it over one of the hilltops here. Another local tale involves Villa Leopold, sold in 2008 for a whopping world record price of $750 million to a Russian who then tried to get out of the deal. But forget about celeb-hunting here: the residents of Cap Ferrat fiercely protect it from curious tourists; its grand old villas are hidden for the most part in the depths of tropical gardens. You can nonetheless try to catch peeks of them from the coastline promenade if you strike out from the port. From the Place du Centenaire walk to the main street and take a left on Avenue Claude Vignon, and follow Chemin de la Carrière (meaning "rock quarry") until below the Grand Cap Hôtel du Cap, just before Pointe Malalongue and the lighthouse (phare). It's a bit tricky and uneven here, but follow the little path to the left (otherwise you'll head toward the Cap's middle) until you get to the beach Passable (you should see Villefranche from here) and turn left to take Chemin de Passable. At the tourist office turn right on Avenue Denis Séméria to get back to the village. The 7-kilometer (4-mile) walk passes through rich tropical flora and, on the west side, over white cliffs buffeted by waves.

Two other footpath maps can be found at the Tourist Office at 59 avenue Denis-Séméria: the shorter loop takes you from town out to the Pointe de St-Hospice, much of the walk shaded by wind-twisted pines. From the port, climb Avenue Jean Mermoz to Place Paloma and follow the path closest to the waterfront or the Promenade Maurice Rouvier, which runs along the eastern edge of the peninsula. You'll stumble on reasonably priced cafés, pizzerias, and ice-cream parlors on the promenade of the Plage de St-Jean. The best swimming is a bit farther south, past the port, at Plage Paloma. Keep trekking around the wooded area, where a beautiful path (*sentier pédestre*) leads along the outermost edge of Cap Ferrat. Other than the occasional yacht, all traces of civilization disappear, and the water is a dizzying blue.

### GETTING HERE AND AROUND

The humor is not lost that a bus fare of €1.50 brings you to one of the most exclusive pieces of land on the planet; the No. 81 accesses the cape from Nice.

### VISITOR INFORMATION

**St-Jean-Cap-Ferrat Tourist Office.** There are two tourist offices: one at the entrance to the village and a second near Place Clémenceau. ⊠ *5 & 59 av. Denis Semeria, St-Jean-Cap-Ferrat* ☎ *04-93-76-08-90* ⊕ *www.saintjeancapferrat.fr/tourisme.*

### EXPLORING

**Villa Ephrussi de Rothschild.** Between the port and the mainland, the floridly beautiful Villa Ephrussi de Rothschild bears witness to the wealth and worldly flair of the baroness who had it built. Constructed in 1905 in neo-Venetian style (its flamingo-pink facade was thought not to be in the best of taste by the local gentry), the house was baptized "Île-de-France" in homage to the Baroness Bétrice de Rothschild's favorite ocean liner. In keeping with that theme, her staff used to wear sailing costumes and her ship travel kit is on view in her bedroom. Precious artworks, tapestries, and furniture adorn the salons—in typical Rothschildian fashion, each is given over to a different 18th-century "époque." Upstairs are the private apartments of Madame la Baronne, which can only be seen on a guided tour offered around noon. The grounds are landscaped with no fewer than seven gardens and topped off with a Temple of Diana. Be sure to allow yourself time to wander here, as this is one of the few places on the coast where you'll be

Baroness Ephrussi de Rothschild spared no expense—a garden full of roses, a house full of Renaissance treasures—in creating her dream house above the sea in St-Jean-Cap-Ferrat.

allowed to experience the lavish pleasures characteristic of the Belle Époque Côte d'Azur. Tea and light lunches, served in a glassed-in porch overlooking the grounds and spectacular coastline, encourage you to linger. ■ TIP→ **A combination ticket allows you to also visit Villa Kerylos in nearby Beaulieu in the same week.** ⊠ *Av. Ephrussi, St-Jean-Cap-Ferrat* ☎ *04-93-01-33-09* ⊕ *www.villa-ephrussi.com* ⊠ *€12.50; €19 for both villas* ☉ *Mid-Feb.–Nov., daily 10–6; July and Aug., daily 10–7; Nov.–mid-Feb., Mon.–Fri. 2–6, Sat.–Sun. 10–6.*

### BEACHES

**Paloma Plage.** Ideally located on one of Europe's most expensive pieces of real estate, this lovely shade-dappled stretch of sand is at the bottom of a steep hill only five minutes away on foot from the glamorous village of Saint-Jean. The beach draws families, thanks to the shallow bay, soft sand, and some of the Riviera's clearest water. An added bonus is that you can swim out 100 meters and gaze in awe at the palatial villas above the beach. High-rollers head to the private Paloma Beach club (you can rent loungers for €24 and Jet Skis also), but if your aim is to not see-and-be-seen, go to the public section. **Amenities:** watersports; lifeguards; showers; toilets. **Best for:** swimming; snorkeling; sunrise. ⊠ *Av. Jean Mermoz, St-Jean-Cap-Ferrat.*

### WHERE TO EAT AND STAY

$$$

SEAFOOD

✕ **Le Sloop.** This sleek portside restaurant caters to the yachting crowd and sailors who cruise into dock for lunch. The focus is fish, of course: *soupe de poisson* (fish soup), *St-Pierre* (John Dory) steamed with asparagus, and roasted whole sea bass. Outdoor tables surround a tiny "garden" of potted palms. Chef Alain Therlicocq has manned the kitchen for 29 years and his five-course fixed menu, including a fish and meat dish, is one of the best values on the coast. Reservations are necessary in the summer, but if you arrive without, ask with a smile for a table and Alain's wife, Regine, will find you *une p'tite place.* [$] *Average main: €25* ✉ *Port de St Jean Cap Ferrat, St-Jean-Cap-Ferrat* ☎ *04–93–01–48–63* 🌐 *www.restaurantsloop.com* ⏲ *Closed Wed. in winter. No lunch Wed. in summer. Closed mid-Nov.–mid-Dec.*

$$$ HOTEL **Brise Marine.** With a glowing Provençal-yellow facade, bright blue shutters, balustraded sea terrace, and pretty pastel guest rooms, Brise Marine fulfills most desires for that perfect, picturesque Cap Ferrat hotel. **Pros:** nighttime quiet interrupted only by gently breaking waves; excellent value for location; close walking distance to beach. **Cons:** some rooms are small; only seven available parking spots (paid), and they must be reserved in advance. [$] *Rooms from: €178* ✉ *58 av. Jean Mermoz, St-Jean-Cap-Ferrat* ☎ *04–93–76–04–36* 🌐 *www.hotel-brisemarine.com* 🛏 *16 rooms* ⏲ *Closed Nov.–Feb.* 🍴 *No meals.*

$$$$ HOTEL **Royal Riviera.** Completely revamped by Parisian designer guru Grace Leo Andrieu, this former *residence hôtelière* for British aristocrats now invites visitors on an intimate voyage into neo-Hellenic style, complete with an admiring wink at the nearby Villa Kerylos. **Pros:** excellent service and concierge; gorgeous property; free parking. **Cons:** noise from rooms facing railway, which is near hotel. [$] *Rooms from: €415* ✉ *3 av. Jean Monnet, St-Jean-Cap-Ferrat* ☎ *04–93–76–31–00* 🌐 *www.royal-riviera.com* 🛏 *96 rooms, 3 suites* ⏲ *Closed mid.-Nov.–mid-Jan.* 🍴 *No meals.*

## ÈZE

Fodor's Choice ★ *2 km (1 mile) east of Beaulieu; 12 km (7 miles) east of Nice; 7 km (4½ miles) west of Monte Carlo.*

Medieval and magnificent, towering like an eagle's nest above the coast and crowned with ramparts and the ruins of a medieval château, Èze (pronounced *ehz*) is unfortunately the most accessible of all the perched villages. So even during off-season its streets flood with tourists, some not-so-fresh from the beach, and it was one of the first towns to post pictorial warnings that say, in effect, "No Shoes, No Shirt, No Service." It is, nonetheless, the most spectacularly sited; if you can manage to shake the crowds and duck off to a quiet overlook, the village casts an extraordinary spell. Its streets are steep and, in places, only for the flamboyantly fit; its time-stained stone houses huddle together in storybook fashion, and its history is remarkable. No wonder U2 frontman Bono and guitarist The Edge have beachside villas here.

Colonized millennia ago by the Romans (who may have built a temple here to the Egyptian goddess, Isis—hence the town name), the mountain peak aerie that is Èze was much coveted by locals fleeing from pirating Saracens. By the 19th century, only peasants were left, but when the Riviera became fashionable, Èze's splendid views up and down the coast became one of the draws that lured fabled visitors—lots of crowned heads, Georges Sand, Friedrich Nietzsche, and Consuelo Vanderbilt, who, when she was tired of being Duchess of

Marlborough, traded in Blenheim Palace for a custom-built house in Èze. Remember that if you choose to stay here, it gets very quiet at night, even in high season.

### GETTING HERE AND AROUND

By car, you should arrive using the Moyenne Corniche, which deposits you near the gateway to Èze Village; buses Nos. 112 and 82 from Nice also use this road, but No. 100 (to Monaco) goes by the sea while No. 116 heads up the Grande Corniche from Nice (each fare €1.50). By train, you'll arrive at the station in Èze-sur-Mer, where a daily navette shuttle bus (€1.50) takes you up to hilltop Èze, a trip that, with its 1,001 switchbacks up the steep mountainside, takes a full 15 minutes (keep this in mind if you're hiring a taxi to "rush" you down to the train station). Or you could walk from the train station up the Nietzsche Path to the village (90 minutes at least): high heels not allowed and the trek isn't advised in the dark.

### VISITOR INFORMATION

**Èze Tourist Office** ✉ *Pl. du Général de Gaulle, Èze* ☎ *04–93–41–26–00* 🌐 *www.eze-tourisme.com.*



## EXPLORING

**Jardin Exotique** (*Tropical Garden*). From the crest-top Jardin Exotique, full of rare succulents, you can pan your videocam all the way around the hills and waterfront (and then, just a few feet from the entrance, take a time-out lunch at the Nid d'Aigle, an inexpensive eaterie featuring focaccias and salads, quaintly set on stone levels rising up around a tall tree). But if you want a prayer of a chance of enjoying the magnificence of the village's arched passages, stone alleyways, and ancient fountains, come at dawn or after sunset—or (if you have the means) stay the night—but spend the midday elsewhere. The church of **Notre-Dame,** consecrated in 1772, glitters inside with Baroque retables and altarpieces. Èze's tourist office, on Place du Général-de-Gaulle, can direct you to the numerous footpaths—the most famous being the **Sentier Friedrich Nietzsche**—that thread Èze with the coast's three corniche highways (you can walk it from the train station to the village in 90 minutes, but you need proper footware). Èze Village is the famous hilltop destination, but Èze extends down to the coastal beach and the township of Èze-sur-Mer; on either side a vast **Grande Corniche Parc** keeps things green and verdant. ✉ *20 rue du Château, Èze* ☎ *04–93–41–10–30* 🎟 *€6* ⏲ *Open daily Oct., 9–5:30; Nov.–Jan., 9–4:30; Feb. and Mar., 9–5; Apr. and May, 9–6; June and Sept., 9–7; July and Aug., 9–7:30.*

## WHERE TO EAT AND STAY

$$$$ FRENCH 🍴 **Troubadour.** Amid the clutter and clatter of the nearby coast, Troubadour is a wonderful find (and has been for more than 30 years) with high ratings for charm and decor. This old family house provides pleasant service and excellent dishes like roasted scallops with chicken broth and squab with citrus zest and beef broth. [$] *Average main: €40* ✉ *4 rue du Brec, Èze* ☎ *04–93–41–19–03* ⏲ *Closed Sun., Mon., and mid-Nov.–mid-Dec.*

$$$$ FRENCH 🍴 **La Table de Patrick Raingeard.** For more than 50 years celebs holidayed and dined at Cap Estel in Èze, a private 2-hectare peninsula with all-encompassing views of the Med. And now, with chef Patrick Raingeard, whose produce comes directly from the hotel's garden, the dining here can't get any better. Start with the asparagus salad with creamy cauliflower and wild truffles, followed by the Charolais beef fillet *à la Parillada* in a "Los Lobos" red-wine sauce served with a potato-and-truffle cake. Finish it off with a banana soufflé. Vegetarian options are also available. **TIP→ Lunch set menus are a good value.** [$] *Average main: €45* ✉ *1312 av. Raymond-Poincaré, Èze* ☎ *04–93–76–29– 29* 🌐 *www.capestel.com* 🕓 *Closed Jan. and Feb.*

$$$$ HOTEL Fodor's Choice ★ 🏨 **Château de la Chèvre d'Or.** The "Château of the Golden Goat" is actually an entire stretch of the village, streets and all, bordered by gardens that hang from the mountainside in nearly Babylonian style, and offering some of the most breathtaking Mediterranean views—at a price. **Pros:** unique setting; fabulous infinity pool; faultless service. **Cons:** one-night deposit required for all bookings; no elevator; bit of cobblestone walking involved to reach hotel. [$] *Rooms from: €400* ✉ *Rue du Barri, Èze* ☎ *04–92–10–66–66* 🌐 *www.chevredor.com* 🛏 *30 rooms, 8 suites* 🕓 *Closed Dec.–Feb.* 🍽 *No meals.*

## ROQUEBRUNE–CAP-MARTIN

*5 km (3 miles) east of Monaco.*

Amid the frenzy of overbuilding that defines this last gasp of the coast before Italy, two twinned havens have survived, each in its own way: the perched Vieille Ville of Roquebrune, which gives its name to the greater area, and Cap-Martin—luxurious, isolated, exclusive, and the once-favored retreat of the Empress Eugénie and Winston Churchill. With its lovely tumble of raked tile roofs and twisting streets, fountains, archways, and quiet squares, Roquebrune retains many of the charms of a hilltop village, although it has become heavily gentrified and commercialized. Rue Moncollet is lined with arcaded passageways and a number of medieval houses. Somerset Maugham—who once memorably described these environs as a "sunny place for shady people"—resided in the town's famous Villa Mauresque (still private) for many years.

### GETTING HERE AND AROUND

Regional trains run direct between Cannes (70 minutes; €10) or Nice to Carnolès, a stop closer to Menton. From the Roquebrune–Cap-Martin train station, it's a one-hour hike up to the perched village or a €20 taxi ride. The Nice–Menton bus No. 100, which runs from the bus station in Nice every 15 minutes (€1.50), also stops in the lower part of Roquebrune.

### VISITOR INFORMATION

**Roquebrune-Cap-Martin Tourist Office** ✉ *218 ave. Aristide Briand, Roquebrune–Cap-Martin* ☎ *04–93–35–62–87* 🌐 *www.roquebrune-cap-martin.com.*

The "eagle's-nest" village of the Riviera, Èze perches 1,300 feet above the sea; travelers never fail to marvel at the dramatic setting.

## BEACHES

**Plage de la Buse.** The entirely public Plage de la Buse is a wonderfully small, fine-pebble beach, with few star-chasers and strutting high heels. It's lovely to be protected from the elements by the curved south-facing wall of a huge villa (whose gardens add a lovely tropical feel). Access is just down a few steps from Le Corbusier trail, but it's completely BIY: bring a towel, umbrella, lunch, and water/drinks (there's no toilet or shower). It's great for novice swimmers. **Amenities:** none. **Best for:** solitude; swimming. ✉ *Sentier du Corbusier, Roquebrune–Cap-Martin.*

## WHERE TO STAY

$ B&B/INN 🏨 **Les Deux Frères.** Magnificently situated and oozing with charm (almost as much as the owner), this whitewashed 1854 schoolhouse has been transformed into an inn overlooking the sea. **Pros:** Dutch owner Willem is worth the stay alone; clean and excellently priced; Fraise & Chocolat café next door. **Cons:** small rooms; breakfast is an extra charge. [$] *Rooms from: €75* ✉ *1 pl. des Deux Frères (with GPS 1 av. Raymond Pointcarré)* ☎ *04–93–28–99–00* 🌐 *www.lesdeuxfreres.com* 🛏 *10 rooms* 🕒 *Restaurant: Closed mid-Nov.–mid-Dec. Closed Mon. No dinner Sun. No lunch Tues.* 🍴 *No meals.*

# MENTON

*1 km (½ mile) east of Roquebrune; 9 km (5½ miles) east of Monaco.*

The most Mediterranean of the French resort towns, Menton rubs shoulders with the Italian border and owes some of its balmy climate to the protective curve of the Ligurian shore. Its Cubist skew of terra-cotta roofs and yellow-ocher houses, Baroque arabesques capping the church facades, and ceramic tiles glistening on their steeples, all evoke the villages of the Italian coast. Yet there's a whiff of influence from Spain, too, in its fantastical villas, exotic gardens, and whimsical patches of ceramic color, and a soupçon of Morocco, Corsica, and Greece. It is, in fact, the best of all Mediterranean worlds—and humble to boot: Menton is the least pretentious of the Côte d'Azur resorts, and all the more alluring for its modesty (though it can be quite a sleepy place compared to Nice, Antibes, or Cannes).

Its near-tropical climate and 316 days of sunshine a year nurture orange and lemon trees that hang heavy with fruit in winter. There's another Florida parallel: the warmth attracts flocks of senior citizens who warm their bones far from northern fog and ice. Thus a large population of elderly visitors basks on its waterfront benches and browses its downtown shops. But Menton has a livelier, younger side, too (there's even a tango festival every July), and the farther you penetrate toward the east, the more intriguing and colorful it becomes.

## GETTING HERE AND AROUND

Trains run all day from Nice and Monaco. There are a couple of bus options: Lignes d'Azur No. 100 from Menton to Nice ($1.50; 1 hour) or the No. 110 airport express (stopping at Monte-Carlo Casino) is an hour and costs €20 one way. To get to Monaco via Roquebrune it's Zest Ligne 21 or if passing through Beausoleil, take Zest No. 18 (also €1.50).

## VISITOR INFORMATION

**Menton Tourist Office** ⊠ *Le Palais de l'Europe, 8 Av. Boyer* ☎ *04-92-41-76-76* ⊕ *www.tourisme-menton.fr.*

## TOURS

**Heritage Tours.** Menton acquaints you with is rich architectural heritage by offering regular *visites due patrimoine* (heritage tours) to its gardens, cemetery, museums, and villas; tours start at €6. Details on each visit (including points and time of departure) can be found at the Menton tourist office or the **Maison du Patrimonie.** ⊠ *24 rue St.-Michel* ☎ *04-92-10-97-10* ⊕ *www.tourisme-menton.fr.*

## EXPLORING

The Côte d'Azur was famed for its panoply of grand villas and even grander gardens built by Victorian dukes, Spanish exiles, Belgian royals, and American blue bloods. Although its hothouse crescent blooms everywhere with palm and lemon trees and jungle flowers, nowhere else does it bloom so extravagantly than in Menton, famous for its temperate climes and 24-karat sun.

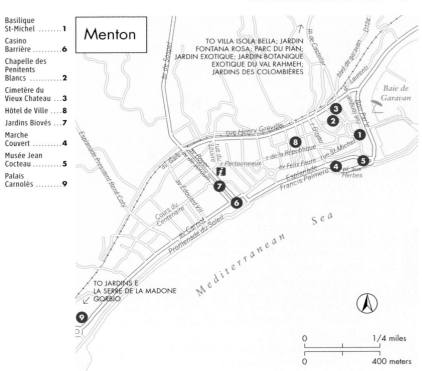

## TOP ATTRACTIONS

**Basilique St-Michel.** This majestic basilica, in particular its bell tower, dominates the skyline of Menton. Beyond the beautifully proportioned facade—a 19th-century addition—the richly frescoed nave and chapels contain several works by Genovese artists plus a splendid 17th-century organ. Volunteers man the doors here, so you may have to wait for the church to open before visiting. ⊠ *Parvis St-Michel, 22 rue St-Michel* ⊙ *weekdays 10–noon and 2–5.*

**Chapelle de Pénitents Blancs.** Just above the Basilique St-Michel, the smaller Chapelle de Pénitents Blancs answers with its own pure Baroque beauty, dating from 1687. Between 3 and 5 pm you can slip in to see the graceful trompe l'oeil over the altar and the ornate gilt lanterns the penitents carried in processions. ⊠ *Place de la Conception.*

**Jardins Biovès** (*Biovès Gardens*). Directly in front of the tourist office, the broad tropical Jardins Biovès stretch 800 meters (2,600 feet) across the breadth of the center, sandwiched between two avenues. Its symmetrical flower beds, exotic trees, sculptures, and fountains representing the spiritual heart of town are free to visit, except during the Lemon Festival, when they display giant sculptures constructed out of 15 tons of citrus fruit. ⊠ *8 av. Boyer.*

**Marché Couvert** (*Covered Market*). Between the lively pedestrian Rue St-Michel and the waterfront, the marvelous Marché Couvert (Les Halles) sums up Menton style with its Belle Époque facade decorated in jewel-tone ceramics. It's equally appealing inside, with merchants selling chewy bread and mountains of cheeses, oils, fruit, and Italian delicacies daily in Caravaggesque disarray (and clothes on Saturdays). ⊠ *Quai de Monléon.*

**Musée Jean Cocteau.** On the waterfront opposite the market, a squat medieval bastion crowned with four tiny watchtowers houses the extraordinary Musée Jean Cocteau, France's memorial to the eponymous artist-poet-filmmaker (1889–1963). Cocteau spotted the fortress, built in 1636 to defend the port, as the perfect site for a group of his works. While the museum has nearly 1,800 *ouevres graphic*, about 990 are original Cocteaus, a donation from the late California businessman and Holocaust survivor Severin Wunderman's personal collection. This is a must-see. ⊠ *2 Quai Monléon, Vieux Port* ☎ *04–89–81–52–50* ⊕ *museecocteaumenton.fr* ⊠ *€8* ⊙ *Daily 10–6.*

**Palais Carnolès** (*Musée de Beaux-Arts*). At the far west end of town stands the 18th-century Palais Carnolès in vast gardens luxuriant with orange, lemon, and grapefruit trees. This was once the summer retreat of the princes of Monaco; nowadays it contains a sizable collection of European paintings from the Renaissance to the present day, plus some interesting temporary exhibits. ⊠ *3 av. de la Madone* ☎ *04–93–35–49–71* ⊠ *Free* ⊙ *Wed.–Mon. 10–12 and 2–6; July and Aug., Wed.–Mon., 10–12 and 3–7.*

**Place aux Herbes.** Right by the market, the pretty little Place aux Herbes is a picturesque spot for a pause on a park bench, a drink, or a meal in the deep shade of the plane trees.

**Serre de la Madone.** With a temperate microclimate created by its southeastern and sunny exposure (the Alps were a natural buffer against cold winds), Menton attracted a great share of wealthy hobbyists, including an American, Major Lawrence Johnston, a gentleman gardener best known for his Cotswolds wonderland, Hidcote Manor.

Fair-haired and blue-eyed, Johnston wound up buying a choice estate in the village of Gorbio—one of the loveliest of all perched seaside villages, set 10 kilometers (6 miles) west of Menton—and spent the 1920s and 1930s making the Serre de la Madone one of the horticultural masterpieces of the coast. He brought back exotica from his many trips to South Africa, Mexico, and China, and planted them in a series of terraces, accented by little pools, vistas, and stone steps. While most of his creeping plumbago, pink belladona, and night-flowering cacti are now gone, his garden has been reopened by the municipality. It is best to call for a reservation at the Serre de la Madone. The garden can be reached from Menton via bus No. 7 (get off at Serre de la Madone stop). ⊠ *74 rte. de Gorbio* ☎ *04–93–57–73–90* ⊕ *www.serredelamadone.com* ⊠ *€8* ⊙ *Apr.–Oct., Tues.–Sun. 10–6; Nov.–Mar., Tues.–Sun. 10–5.*

Not far from the Italian border, Menton enjoys one of the sunniest climates in France and is home to an amazing array of fabulous gardens open to the public.

**WORTH NOTING**

**Cimetière du Vieux-Château** (*Old Château Cemetery*). High above the Parvis St-Michel, the Cimetière du Vieux-Château lies on the terraced plateau where once stood a medieval castle. The Victorian graves here are arranged by nationality, with an entire section of Russian royalty. The birth and death dates often attest to the ugly truth: even Menton's balmy climate couldn't reverse the ravages of tuberculosis.

**Hôtel de Ville.** The 19th-century Italianate Hôtel de Ville conceals a treasure by painter Jean Cocteau: he decorated the **Salle des Mariages** (Marriage Room) with vibrant allegorical scenes; today it is used for civil marriages. ⊠ *17 av. de la République* 🖃 *€1.50* ⊙ *Mon.–Fri. 8:30–12:30 and 1:30–5.*

**Parvis St-Michel.** Up a set of grand tiered stairs that lead from the Quai Bonaparte, the Parvis St-Michel is a broad plaza paved in round white and gray stones patterned in the coat of arms of the Grimaldi family. The plaza was created in the 17th century by Prince Honoré II; the letter H is mingled into the design as a kind of signature at the base of his great gift to the city.

**Promenade du Soleil.** Stroll the length of Menton's famous beachfront along the Promenade du Soleil, broad, white, and studded with palm trees.

**Quai Napoléon III.** To get a feel for the territory, start your exploration at the far-east end of the Vieille Ville and walk out to the end of the Quai Napoléon III, jutting far out into the water. Above the masts of pleasure boats, all of Menton spreads over the hills, and the mountains of Italy loom behind.

**Rue St-Michel.** Serving as the main commercial artery of the Vieille Ville, Rue St-Michel is lined with shops, cafés, and orange trees.

### WHERE TO EAT AND STAY

$$$$ MODERN FRENCH 🍴 **Mirazur.** Avant-garde French cuisine by an Argentinian-Italian chef? Why not, if you're perched on the border of France and Italy, like this restaurant overlooking a cascading tropical garden and the sea on the outer edge of Menton. Mauro Colagreco learned his craft in Latin America before acquiring a solid French base with the likes of Bernard Loiseau in Burgundy, and both Alain Passard and Alain Ducasse in Paris. Today in Menton, he is a perfect example of the wave of young chefs whose style has been dubbed "la jeune cuisine"; for him, the plate is a palette and each ingredient has its precise place and significance. His airy dining room overlooking the sea makes the perfect setting for this expressive cooking, which makes liberal use of those much-talked-about Spanish "techniques," such as *spuma* (foam). Set menus start at €45 at lunch and go up to €135. [$] *Average main: €39* ✉ *30 av. Aristide Briand* ☎ *04–92–41–86–86* 🌐 *www.mirazur.fr* ✍ *Reservations essential* ⏲ *Closed Mon. and Tues. mid-Feb.–Oct.; closed Mon. and no lunch Tues. and Wed. mid-July–Aug.*

$ HOTEL 🏨 **Hôtel Lemon.** Subtropical gardens and 19th-century architecture are two of Menton's main attractions, and this hotel a few minutes' walk from the train station gives you a taste of both. **Pros:** plenty of charm at rock-bottom prices; a few blocks from the sea. **Cons:** street parking can be difficult; street can be noisy; no air conditioning. [$] *Rooms from: €69* ✉ *10 rue Albert 1er* ☎ *04–93–28–63–63* 🌐 *www.hotel-lemon.com* 🛏 *18 rooms* 🍽 *No meals.*

$$$$ HOTEL 🏨 **Napoléon.** This elegantly modern hotel in Garavan—east of the town center toward Italy—is hard to beat when it comes to value for money. **Pros:** warm and efficient service; sea and mountain views from rooms on upper floors worth the price; great rates off season (and less traffic). **Cons:** a bit of a walk from the town center; parking can be difficult in high season. [$] *Rooms from: €275* ✉ *29 porte de France* ☎ *04–93–35–89–50* 🌐 *www.napoleon-menton.com* 🛏 *43 rooms, 2 suites* 🍽 *All meals.*

# MONACO

# WELCOME TO MONACO

## TOP REASONS TO GO

★ **High stakes and high style:** Even if you aren't a gambler, the gold leaf and over-the-top Rococo in the casino are definitely worth a long look.

★ **Princess for a day:** Follow in Grace Kelly's footsteps with a visit to the Palais Princier, the official residence of the royal family.

★ **Walk in the park:** Yes, Virginia, you can afford to visit Monte Carlo—that is, if you head to its magnificent Jardin Exotique de Monaco.

★ **The Undersea World:** One of the world's best oceanography museums, the Musée Océanographique is an architectural masterpiece in its own right.

★ **Hit the Beach:** The chicest spot on the entire French Riviera, Monte Carlo is well known for its underwater diving and its people-watching.

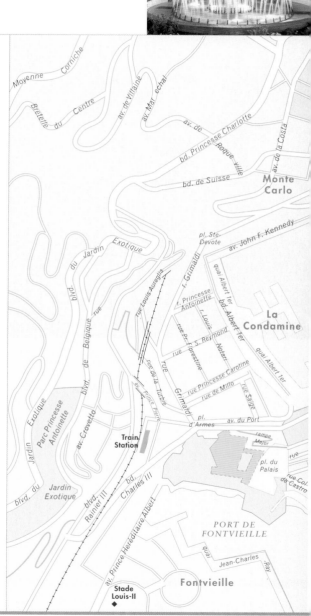

**1 Monaco.** The principality's exceptional position on the Mediterranean seduces the rich and famous, and those who want to see how the other 1% lives. It bristles with gleaming glass-and-concrete corncob-towers 20 and 30 stories high and with vast apartment complexes, their terraces, landscaped like miniature gardens, jutting over the sea.

av. de la Madone

Jardins du Casino

des Spélugues

allée des Boulingrins

pl. du Casino

bd. Louis II

sq. Beaumarchaise

av. de Monte Carlo

◆ Auditorium Rainier-III

av. d'Ostende

bd. du Larvotto

quai des États-Unis

*PORT HERCULE*

quai Antoine 1er

av. de la Quarantaine

av. de la Porte Neuve

rue des Remparts

av. des Pins

ch. des Pêcheurs

Basse

rue Émile de Loth

av. St-Martin

*Jardins St-Martin*

*The Rock (Le Rocher)*

0     1/8 mile

0     200 meters

## GETTING ORIENTED

Monaco covers just 473 acres and would fit comfortably inside New York's Central Park. (That said, it also reaches a height of 528 feet, so bring some walking shoes.) Despite its compact nature, everybody drives here, whether from the Palais Princier perched on the Rock down to the port or up to Casino Gardens at the eastern tip.

**7**

Updated by
Nancy Heslin

On one of the best stretches of the Mediterranean, this classic luxury destination is one of the most sought-after addresses in the world. With all the high-rise towers you have to look hard to find the Belle Époque grace of yesteryear. But if you head to the town's great 1864 landmark Hôtel de Paris—still a veritable crossroads of the buffed and befurred Euro-gentry—or enjoy a grand *bouffe* at its famous Louis XV restaurant, or attend the opera, or visit the ballrooms of the casino, you may still be able to conjure up Monaco's elegant past.

Prince Albert II, a political science graduate from Amherst College, traces his ancestry to Otto Canella, who was born in 1070. The Grimaldi dynasty began with Otto's great-great-great-grandson, Francesco Grimaldi, also known as Frank the Rogue. Expelled from Genoa, Frank and his cronies disguised themselves as monks and in 1297 seized the fortified medieval town known today as Le Rocher (the Rock). Except for a short break under Napoléon, the Grimaldis have been here ever since, which makes them the oldest reigning family in Europe.

In the 1850s a Grimaldi named Charles III made a decision that turned the Rock into a giant blue chip. Needing revenue but not wanting to impose additional taxes on his subjects, he contracted with a company to open a gambling facility. The first spin of the roulette wheel was on December 14, 1856. There was no easy way to reach Monaco then—no carriage roads or railroads—so no one came. Between March 15 and March 20, 1857, one person entered the casino—and won two francs. In 1868, however, the railroad reached Monaco, and it was filled with Englishmen who came to escape the London fog. The effects were immediate. Profits were so great that Charles eventually abolished all direct taxes. Almost overnight, a threadbare principality became an elegant watering hole for European society. Dukes (and their mistresses) and duchesses (and their gigolos) danced and dined their way through a world of spinning roulette wheels and bubbling champagne—preening themselves for nights at the opera, where such artists as Vaslav Nijinsky, Sarah Bernhardt, and Enrico Caruso came to perform.

Along with the tax system, its sensational position on a broad, steep peninsula that bulges into the Mediterranean—its harbor sparkling with luxury cruisers, its posh mansions angling awnings toward the nearly perpetual sun—continues to draw the rich and famous. One of the latest French celebrities to declare himself "Monégasque," thus giving up his French passport, is superchef Alain Ducasse, who said that he made the choice out of affection for Monaco rather than tax reasons.

The Monacans themselves add to the sense of flossy, flashy self-contentment. Nearly everything is dyed-to-match here, even the lap dog in the Vuitton bag, and fur coats flourish from September through May. Doormen and policemen dress in ice-cream–colored uniforms worthy of an operetta, and along the port yacht clubs host exclusive birthday parties for little-rich-girls in couture party dresses. Pleasure boats vie with luxury cruisers in their brash beauty and Titanic scale, and teams of handsome young men—themselves dyed blond and tanned to match—scour and polish every gleaming surface.

As you might expect, all this glitz doesn't come cheap. Eating is expensive, and even the most modest hotels cost more here than in nearby Nice or Menton. As for taxis, they don't even have meters so you are completely at the driver's mercy (with prices skyrocketing during events such as the Grand Prix). For the frugal, Monaco is the ultimate day-trip, although parking is as coveted as a room with a view. At the very least you can afford a coffee at Starbucks.

The harbor district, known as La Condamine, connects the new quarter, officially known as Monte Carlo with Monaco-Ville (or Le Rocher), a medieval town on the Rock, topped by the palace, the cathedral, and the Oceanography Museum. Have no fear that you'll need to climb countless steps to get to Monaco-Ville, as there are plenty of elevators and escalators climbing the steep cliffs. But shuttling between the lovely casino grounds of Monte Carlo and Old Monaco, separated by a vast port, is a daunting proposition for ordinary mortals without wings, so hop on the No. 1 bus from the Jardin Exotique and the No. 2, which stops at Place du Casino—both come up to Monaco Ville (€2).

# PLANNING

### WHEN TO GO

The area is at its hottest in July and August, and the beaches are at their best in June or September.

**Printemps des Arts.** Monte Carlo's month-long spring arts festival, Printemps des Arts, brings together the world's top ballet, operatic, symphonic, and chamber-music performers at venues across Monaco (Opéra de Monte-Carlo, Oceanography Museum, Hôtel de Paris) as well as in Cap d'Ail and Beaulieu. ✉ *Monaco* ☎ *377/98–06–28–28* ⊕ *www.printempsdesarts.com.*

**Top Marques Monaco.** What can you say about a four-day exhibition where you could buy anything from an AgustaWestland helicopter to a Rolex Submariner to a $55,000 bed? So much more than just exclusive cars, Top Marques takes place in the third week of April at Grimaldi Forum. ✉ *10 av. Princesse Grace, Monaco* ☏ *377/97–70–12–77* ⊕ *www. topmarquesmonaco.com* 🎫 *€50.*

## GETTING HERE AND AROUND

From Nice's train station, Monaco is serviced by regular trains along the Cannes–Ventimiglia line; from Nice the journey costs €3.70 one way and takes 20 minutes. A taxi from Nice will cost around €100, depending on the season and the time of day.

### BUS TRAVEL

Compagnie des Autobus de Monaco operates a bus line that threads the avenues of Monaco. Purchase your ticket on board for €2; or save 50 cents a ticket by buying in advance from an agent, a machine, or online. They also operate a solar electric boat from Quai des États-Unis to the casino (there's an elevator at Parking du Pécheurs); it runs daily from 8 to 8 (€2).

The Conseil Général has an express bus that connects Place des Moulins in Monaco with Vauban station in Nice (past the Palais des Expositions); tickets for the 100X (express bus) cost €4, but run only Monday to Friday. The Lignes d'Azur 100 bus costs €1.50 and leaves from the Ségurane stop at Place Garibaldi in Nice—but be prepared for a long ride, as it takes about two hours. A very popular mode of transport to the Principality, the 100 is often full, so it's best to take it directly from Nice or Monaco; otherwise it will drive right by you, no matter how frantically you wave. Info for both can be found on the same website.

**Bus Information Compagnie des Autobus de Monaco.** ☏ *377/97–70–22–22* ⊕ *www.cam.mc.***Lignes d'Azur.** ☏ *04–93–85–64–44* ⊕ *www.lignesdazur.com.*

## HOTELS

Hotel prices skyrocket during the Monaco Grand Prix, so reserve as far ahead as possible. That goes for festivals like the Printemps des Arts as well.

## VISITOR INFORMATION

**Monaco Tourist Office.** Before starting off, arm yourself with a map and a bus schedule or an excellent pair of walking shoes and start at the tourist office, just north of the casino gardens. ✉ *2a bd. des Moulins, Monte Carlo, Monaco* ☏ *377/92–16–61–16* ⊕ *www.visitmonaco.com.*

---

**GRACE'S KINGDOM**

Thanks in part to the pervasive odor of money-to-burn, Monaco remains the playground of royalty, wealthy playboys, and glamorous film stars. One of the loveliest of the latter, Hollywood darling Grace Kelly, became Monaco's princess when she married Prince Rainier in 1956; their wedding, marriage, and her tragic death in a car accident—eerily presaged in scenes filmed in Alfred Hitchcock's *To Catch a Thief*—have only added to the mythology of this fairy-tale mini-principality.

# EXPLORING MONACO

## TOP ATTRACTIONS

**Casino Monte-Carlo.** Place du Casino is the center of Monte Carlo and a must-see, even if you don't like to bet. Into the gold-leaf splendor of the casino, the hopeful descend from tour buses to tempt fate beneath the gilt-edge Rococo ceiling—and some spend much more than planned here, as did the French actress Sarah Bernhardt, who lost 100,000 francs. Jacket and tie are required in the back rooms, which open at 3 pm. Bring your passport (under-18s not admitted). Note that there are special admission fees to get into any of the period gaming rooms. For €10 you can also visit the casino daily in the off hours, from 9 am to 12:30 am, with access to all rooms. ⊠ *Pl. du Casino, Monte Carlo, Monaco* ☎ *377/98–06–20–12* ⊕ *www.casinomontecarlo.com* ⊗ *Daily 2 pm–4 am.*

**Les Thermes Marins de Monte-Carlo** (*Sea Baths of Monte-Carlo*). Added to the city in the 1990s, this seawater-therapy treatment center stretches between the landmark Hôtel de Paris and its sister, the Hermitage, and can be accessed directly from either hotel. Within its sleek, multilevel complex you can pursue every creature comfort, from underwater massage to seaweed body wraps to light, elegant spa-style lunches, in one of the 37 treatment rooms—almost all with views over the port. After all that walking in the principality, you may need the Monte-Carlo Foot Cocooning Massage (50 minutes; €135) or a Sea-Peel for €150 (45 minutes). ⊠ *2 ave. de Monte-Carlo, Monaco* ☎ *377/98–06–69–00* ⊕ *www.thermesmarinsmontecarlo.com* ⊗ *Daily 8–8.*

**Monaco Cathedral.** Follow the crowds down the last remaining streets of medieval Monaco to the 19th-century Cathédrale de l'Immaculée-Conception, which contains the tomb of Princess Grace and Prince Rainier III, as well as a magnificent altarpiece, painted in 1500 by Louis Bréa. It's best to call ahead to check on opening hours; they tend to vary, although you can usually visit daily until 6 pm. ⊠ *Av. St-Martin, Monaco* ☎ *377/93–30–87–70* ⊕ *www.cathedrale.mc.*

FAMILY
Fodor's Choice
★

**Musée Océanographique** (*Oceanography Museum*). Perched dramatically on a cliff, this museum is a splendid Edwardian structure, built under Prince Albert I to house specimens collected on amateur explorations. Jacques Cousteau (1910–97) led the missions from 1957 to 1988. The main floor displays skeletons and taxidermy of enormous sea creatures; early submarines and diving gear dating from the Middle Ages; and a few interactive science displays. The main draw is the famous **aquarium**, a vast complex of backlighted tanks containing countless species of fish, crab, and eel. Make time to visit this *musée;* if possible, take in one of the remarkable exhibitions, like Shark Lagoon and its 450,000-liter aquarium, running until 2015. ⊠ *Av. St-Martin, Monaco* ☎ *377/93–15–36–00* ⊕ *www.oceano.mc* ⊡ *€14* ⊗ *Apr.–June and Sept., daily 10–7; July and Aug., daily 10–8:30; Oct.–Mar., daily 10–6.*

**Opéra de Monte-Carlo.** In the true spirit of the town, it seems that the Salle Garnier Opera House, with its 18-ton gilt-bronze chandelier and extravagant frescoes, is part of the casino complex. The designer, Charles Garnier, also built the Paris Opéra, so we are talking one fabulous jewel-box. On show are some of the coast's most significant performances of dance, opera, and orchestral music. ⊠ *Pl. du Casino, Monaco* ☎ *377/98–06–28–28* ⊕ *www.opera.mc* ☉ *Ticket office Tues.– Sat. 10–5:30.*

**Palais Princier.** The famous Rock, crowned by the palace where the royal family resides, stands west of Monte Carlo. An audio guide leading you through this sumptuous chunk of history, first built in the 13th century and expanded and enhanced over the centuries, reveals an extravagance of 16th- and 17th-century frescoes, as well as tapestries, gilt furniture, and paintings on a grand scale. Note that the **Relève de la Garde** (Changing of the Guard) is held outside the front entrance of the palace most days promptly at 11:55 am. Les Grands Appartements are open to the public from late March through October, and you can buy a joint ticket with the Muséé Océanographique. Across several dates over three weeks from mid-July a summer concert series can be enjoyed at 9:30 pm in the glory of the courtyard. Tickets can be purchased through the Orchestre Philharmonique de Monte-Carlo (www.opmc.com). ⊠ *Pl. du Palais, Monaco* ☎ *377/93–25–18–31* ⊕ *www.palais.mc* ☑ *€8 (includes audio guide); €19 joint ticket with Oceanographic Museum* ☉ *Mar. 29.–Oct. 31., daily 10–6. Closed Nov.–Mar.*

**Port.** It's a hike or a ride on bus No. 6 from Monte Carlo to the port along Boulevard Albert Ier, where pleasure boats of every shape flash white and blue. It's here that they erect the stands for fans of the Grand Prix. And it's from the far corner of the port that the Institut Océanographique launches research boats to study aquatic life in the Mediterranean, as its late director Jacques Cousteau did for some 30 years. ⊠ *Monaco.*

**The Rock.** On the broad plateau known as Le Rocher, or the Rock, the majority of Monaco's touristic sights are concentrated with tidy, self-conscious charm. This is the medieval heart of Monaco, and where its cathedral, palace, and the Oceanography Museum can be found. You can either climb up the Rampe Majeur from the Place d'Armes, behind the right corner of the port, or approach it by elevator from the seafront at the port's farthest end (past Stars'n'Bars). ⊠ *Monaco.*

## WORTH NOTING

FAMILY **Collection des Voitures Anciennes** (*Collection of Vintage Cars*). In this impressive assemblage of Prince Rainier's vintage cars, you'll find everything from a De Dion Bouton to a Lamborghini Countach. Also on the Terrasses de Fontvieille is the **Jardin Animalier** (Animal Garden), a mini-zoo housing the Grimaldi family's animal collection—an astonishing array of wild beasts that includes monkeys and exotic birds. ⊠ *Terrasses de Fontvieille, Monaco* ☎ *377/92–05–28–56, 377/93–25–18–31* ☑ *€6 voitures; €5 animalier* ☉ *Museum: Daily, 10–6. Garden: Oct.–Feb. daily 10–12 and 2–5; Mar.–May, daily 10–12 and 2–6; June–Sept., daily 9–12 and 2–7.*

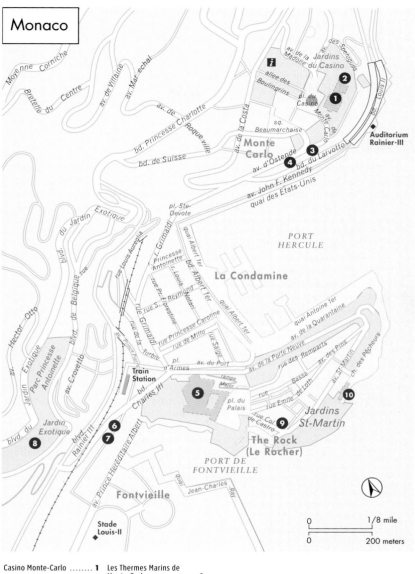

# Monaco

**Nouveau Musée National de Monaco.** To get here take the elevator down from Place des Moulins. NMNM houses two museums, each of which hosts two exhibitions a year. One of the surviving buildings from the Belle Époque, Villa Sauber, with its rose garden, is in the Larvotto Beach complex, which has been artfully created with imported sand. The Villa Paloma (next door to the Jardin Exotique) was recently restored with fabulous stained-glass windows. ⊠ *Villa Sauber, 17 av. Princesse Grace, Monaco* ☎ *377/98–98–91–26* ⊕ *www.nmnm.mc* ⊠ *€6* ⊗ *June–Sept., daily 11–7; Oct.–May, daily 10–6.*

# WHERE TO EAT

**$$$$**
BRASSERIE

✕ **Café de Paris.** The landmark Belle Époque "La Brasserie 1900"—better known as Café de Paris—offers the usual classics (shellfish, steak tartare, matchstick frites, and fish boned table-side). Supercilious, super-pro waiters fawn gracefully over titled preeners, jet-setters, and tourists alike. Open daily beginning at 8 am, there's good hot food until 2 am. ■TIP➔ To claim "I've been there," grab a chair outside in the Place du Casino, order an €8 coke or €15 sundae and sit back to watch the show. Ⓢ *Average main: €34* ⊠ *Pl. du Casino, Monaco* ☎ *377/98–06–76–23* ⊕ *www.casinocafedeparis.com.*

**$$**
MODERN FRENCH

✕ **Explorers Pub.** This gastropub "devoted to adventurers" has stone walls lined with photos of intrepid folks (including Prince Albert II), plus a year-round terrace perfect for sampling roast pig or lamb shank. Wash your meal down with one of the 150 well-priced beers. Premium spirits, world wines, and Café de Monaco freshly roasted on-site, are also available. For your late-night munchies, the pub serves food until 5:30 am on Friday and Saturday in summer. Ⓢ *Average main: €25* ⊠ *Port of Monaco, Monaco* ☎ *377/97–98–70–70* ⊕ *www.explorers-pub.com.*

**$$$$**
FRENCH

✕ **Hostellerie Jérôme.** Prince Albert's country home Roc Angel is located about 10 kilometers (6 miles) behind Monaco in La Turbie, so it's no wonder a top-notch dinner restaurant (read: expensive, expensive, expensive) is situated here as well. The prix-fixe five-course menu is €75, while the famous 13-course menu is €130. Chef Bruno Cirino's scampi Mediterranean in an almond crust with dates or roasted white local figs, sugared black olives, and buffalo milk sherbet has become a signature dish for a reason. Too rich for your blood? Try Cirino's bistro next door, Le Café de la Fontaine, open all year round for lunch and dinner with €15 main courses. Ⓢ *Average main: €75* ⊠ *20 rte. Comte de Cessole, La Turbie, Monaco* ☎ *04–92–41–51–51* ⊕ *www. hostelleriejerome.com* ⊗ *No lunch. Closed Mon. and Tues. Oct. and mid-Feb.–Apr. Closed Nov.–mid-Feb.*

**$$$$**
FRENCH

✕ **La Trattoria.** Set in the entertainment complex Le Sporting d'Été (an expensive cab ride from the center of town), La Trattoria restaurant overlooks Jimmyz and the Med, and is only open during summer months, but an Alain Ducasse window of opportunity must never be overlooked. Take the advice of the enthusiastic waiters and order the purple artichoke risotto or the roasted chicken breast with macaroni gratin—either of which could prove as much of a revelation as the

Monaco's Belle Époque opulence is epitomized by its Opéra House Monte Carlo, designed in 1879 by Garnier.

conversation at the next table (you may overhear something like: "I have 52 million in my bank account"). $ *Average main: €40* ✉ *Le Sporting, Av. Princesse Grace, Monaco* ☎ *377/98–06–71–71* ⊕ *www. alain-ducasse.com* ⬤ *Reservations essential* ☉ *Closed mid-Sept.–mid-May. No lunch.*

**$$$$**
FRENCH
Fodor'sChoice
★

✕ **Le Louis XV.** This extravagantly showy restaurant stuns with neo-Baroque details, yet it manages to be upstaged by its product: the superb cuisine of Alain Ducasse, one of the world's most respected chefs. He leaves the Louis XV kitchen, for the most part, in the more-than-capable hands of Chef Franck Cerutti, who draws much of his inspiration from the Cours Saleya market in Nice. Glamorous iced lobster with chestnuts and Alba white truffles slum happily with stockfish (stewed salt cod) and tripe. The decor is magnificent—a surfeit of gilt, mirrors, and chandeliers—and the waitstaff seignorial as they proffer a footstool for madame's handbag. In Ducasse fashion, the Baroque clock on the wall is stopped just before 12—Cinderella should have no fears. If your wallet is a chubby one, this is a must. The 400,000 bottles in the wine cellar should offer you enough of a choice. $ *Average main: €100* ✉ *Hôtel de Paris, Pl. du Casino, Monaco* ☎ *377/98–06–88–64* ⊕ *www. alain-ducasse.com* ⬤ *Reservations essential* 🎩 *Jacket required* ☉ *Closed Tues. and Wed. (but open Wed. dinner mid-June–Aug.) Closed 3 wks. mid-Feb. Closed exceptionally Nov.–mid-Dec. 2014.*

**$$$**
FRENCH

✕ **Quai des Artistes.** Packing well-heeled diners shoulder-to-shoulder at banquettes lined up for maximum people-watching, this warehouse-scale neo-Deco bistro on the port is the chicest of the chic with Monégasque residents. Rich brasserie classics (lamb shank on the bone, potato purée with rosemary, spicy gravy) are counterbalanced with high-flavor international experiments (salmon served sushi-rare with warm potatoes, pickled ginger, wasabi sauce). There's a fabulous terrace with a palatial view. $ *Average main: €32* ✉ *4 quai Antoine Ier, Monaco* ☎ *377/97–97–97–77* ⊕ *www.quaidesartistes.com* ⚓ *Reservations essential.*

**$$** ✕ **Stars'n'Bars.** This American-style port-side bar/restaurant/entertainment center is like the Monégasque version of a sport-themed Hard
AMERICAN Rock Café. Jerseys and photos hang on the wall, while fat and juicy burgers, cookie sundaes, real ice tea in thick glasses, and (gasp!) pitchers of ice water draw in homesick expats and quesadilla-starved backpackers (so much so that they're willing to pay €12 for onion rings or €23 for a Big Star cheeseburger). $ *Average main: €20* ✉ *6 quai Antoine I, Monaco* ⊕ *www.starsnbars.com.*

# WHERE TO STAY

**$$$$** ⛉ **Hermitage.** They've all been here—kings, queens, Pavarotti in jeans—
HOTEL among the riot of frescoes and plaster flourishes embellished with gleaming brass in this landmark yet relatively low-profile 1900 hotel set back a block from the casino scene. **Pros:** terraces overlooking casino; outstanding everything. **Cons:** public spaces not very lively; rooms on street side may have some traffic noise; watch out for €35 breakfast and €36/day parking charges. $ *Rooms from: €575* ✉ *Sq. Beaumarchais, Monaco* ☎ *377/98–06–40–00* ⊕ *www.hotelhermitagemontecarlo.com* ⤴ *278 rooms, 86 suites* ⃤◯⃥ *Some meals.*

**$$$$** ⛉ **Hôtel Métropole.** The 2013 winner for both the Prix Villégiature
HOTEL for Best Hotel Floral Decoration in Europe and Fodor's 100 Hotels
Fodor's Choice Award "Culinary Gem," this Belle Époque hotel, set on land that once
★ belonged to Pope Leon XIII, has pulled out all the stops in its decoration—famed Paris designer Jacques Garcia has given the rooms his signature hyper-aristocratic look and Karl Lagerfield is the architect behind The Odyssey pool and lounge. **Pros:** flawless and attentive service; "Lifestage" spa treatment; unlike other Monaco hotels, this one has an extended entrance off the street you so feel secluded even in the heart of the city. **Cons:** the food is so superb you won't want to get out and eat anywhere else. $ *Rooms from: €700* ✉ *4 av. de la Madone, Monaco* ☎ *377/93–15–15–15* ⊕ *www.metropole.com* ⤴ *69 rooms, 64 suites* ⃤◯⃥ *Some meals.*

**$$$$** ⛉ **Monte-Carlo Bay Hotel.** Perched on a 10-acre peninsula, with 75%
HOTEL of its rooms offering sea views, this highly acclaimed luxury resort—which immodestly bills itself as "a natural Eden reinvented"—seeks to evoke the Côte d'Azur's 1920s heyday with its neoclassical columns and arches, exotic gardens, lagoon swimming pool, casino, and concert hall. **Pros:** ultraluxurious, with so much to do that there is no need to leave the hotel; sofas on balconies. **Cons:** late check-in time of 4 pm; pool and poolside can become crowded. $ *Rooms from: €1,040* ✉ *40 av. Princesse Grace, Monaco* ☎ *377/98–06–25–25* ⊕ *www.montecarlobay. com* ⤴ *312 rooms, 22 suites* ⃤◯⃥ *No meals.*

# NIGHTLIFE AND THE ARTS

There's no need to go to bed before dawn in Monte Carlo when you can go to the grand casinos or Jimmyz.

## CASINOS

**Casino de Monte-Carlo.** The bastion and landmark of Monte Carlo gambling is, of course, the gorgeously ornate Casino de Monte-Carlo. The main gambling hall is the **Salle Européene** (European Room), where you can play roulette, craps, or blackjack, while the slot machines stand apart in the **Salle des Amériques** and the **Salon Renaissance**. Like these rooms, the **Salons Touzet** (Trente et Quarante and Texas Hold'em poker) also opens at 2 pm, but it has a €10 admission fee (whereas the others are free). Bring your passport (under-18s not admitted). Private areas like the Salle Médecin are for lucky holders of the Cercle Monte-Carlo card, but you can still sneak a peek: €10 will get you an inside look at the closed Casino rooms from 9 am to 12:30 pm daily. ⊠ *Pl. du Casino, Monaco* ☎ *377/98–06–21–21* ⊕ *www.casinomontecarlo.com* ⊗ *2 pm–noon.*

**Salle des Etoiles.** SBM's Le Sporting, a summer-only entertainment complex on the waterfront, has a roof that opens up to the stars and fireworks, perhaps justifying the €150 ticket for the Monte-Carlo Sporting Summer Festival or the €1,000 Red Cross Gala—although the celebs are also part of the draw. Where else can you see Rihanna, Elton John, Rod Stewart, or Duran Duran in a sit-down dinner venue for 700 people with valet parking? The Salles des Etoiles is open year-round, but hosts music and events May through September. ⊠ *Le Sporting, Av. Princesse Grace, Monaco* ☎ *377/92–16–21–25* ⊕ *en.sportingsummerfestival.com.*

**Sun Casino.** Described as the "most American" of all the casinos in the Principality thanks to a more extensive range of gaming tables, the Sun Casino is part of the Fairmont Monte-Carlo. While you can't hit the tables until 5 pm, slot machines open daily from noon and entry is free (you must be over 18). Don't be surprised to cross paths with women's poker champion Isabelle Mercier, a true fan of Sun Casino. ⊠ *12 av. des Spélugues, Monaco* ☎ *377/92–16–21–23* ⊕ *www.montecarlosuncasino.com.*

## DANCE CLUBS

**Jimmyz.** Dominating the club scene, Jimmyz boasts an edgy reputation that reaches far beyond Monaco. The legendary disco at Sporting Monte-Carlo is not for lightweights: the partying is as serious as the need to be seen, so if surgically enhanced faces and body parts upset you, then stay at your hotel. Jimmyz takes up winter residence at Place du Casino, which has a retro dance floor and bohemian bar. ⊠ *Sporting Monte-Carlo, Av. Princesse Grace, Monaco* ☎ *377/98–06–70–68* ⊕ *fr.jimmyzmontecarlo.com* ⊗ *Closed mid-Sept.–mid-Oct.*

**Life Club.** The only club on the Riviera with seafront access, hanging out at the timber-decked Life is like being aboard a private yacht: have a drink, a bite to eat, or just shake what you must on the waterfront dance floor until the early hours when your feet land back on shore. ✉ *35 bd. Louis II, Monaco* ☎ *377/97–98–77–77* ⊕ *www.life-monaco. com* ✉ *€20 entry* ⊙ *Daily 11 pm–5 am.*

### THEATER

**Théâtre Princesse Grace.** During the Spring Arts Festival, the Théâtre Princesse Grace stages a number of plays; the season runs from October to May. ✉ *12 av. d'Ostende, Monaco* ☎ *377/93–25–32–27* ⊕ *www. tpgmonaco.mc.*

# SPORTS AND THE OUTDOORS

## AUTO RACING

**Grand Prix de Monaco.** When the tennis stops, the auto racing begins: the Grand Prix de Monaco takes place the last Sunday of the Cannes Film Festival in May. To watch live, it's €10,000 a person to stand on a balcony overlooking the course. If that's more than you want to spend but you still want to watch action on the same track, two weeks earlier is the Historic Grand Prix of Monaco (but only every other even year); tickets range from €25 to €55. ✉ *Monaco* ☎ *377/93–15–26–00 for information* ⊕ *www.grand-prix-monaco.com.*

## BEACHES

FAMILY **La Note Bleu.** Probably the best of the private beaches is La Note Bleu, which has something for everyone with activities for kids, jazz concerts, and an excellent beach restaurant serving Mediterranean-Asian food (and a lounge with Wi-Fi, if you must!). It's also a jellyfish-free zone, with nets that keep their tentacles at bay. **Amenities:** food and drink; toilets; showers. **Best for:** swimming; sunrise. ✉ *Plage du Larvotto, Av. Princesse Grace, Monaco* ☎ *377/93–50–05–02* ⊕ *www. lanotebleue.mc* ⊙ *Closed Dec.–Mar.*

FAMILY **Larvotto Beach.** The sandy Larvotto Beach just off Avenue Princess Grace, said to be the world's most costly street to live on, is the only free public beach in Monaco, and it has the added bonus of being protected by jellyfish nets. Access by the number 4 or 6 bus, you can rent loungers or just bring your own umbrella. There's a mini-club for kids; dogs are not permitted but that doesn't stop some owners. ■TIP➔ **SkiVol operates from the Larvotto public beach during the summer season with a great range of water sports including wake boarding, donuts, and flyfishing. Amenities:** water sports; lifeguards; toilets; showers. **Best for:** swimming. ✉ *Right side of pier, Av. Princesse Grace, Monaco.*

**Plage Mala.** This lovely stretch of sandy, shaded land is easily one of the most stylish of the Riviera beaches, and despite its proximity to Monaco—half an hour by foot—Plage Mala's public area never gets crowded. Another upside is that the coves under the impressive cliffs produce the best area for snorkeling along the coast. The downside:

there are numerous bare tops. Private beach restaurants are close by where you can rent loungers. The 3.5-kilometer (2.2-mile) Mala footpath that stretches to Plage Marquet in Fontvieille in Monaco is relatively easy to walk, with the most challenging leg being the access to Mala beach itself. Walking to Monte Carlo generally take less than an hour, however, avoid the path during stormy conditions. **Amenities:** none. **Best for:** snorkeling; swimming; walking. ⊠ *Av. Raymond Gramaglia, Cap d'Ail.*

## TENNIS

**Monte Carlo Tennis Open.** This annual event is held in late April on the clay courts of the Monte Carlo Country Club, which lies on the outskirts of Monaco in the French commune of Roquebrune–Cap-Martin. Spaniard Rafael Nadal won the title straight from 2005 until he was defeated in 2012 by Serbian Noval Djokovic. ⊠ *155 Av. Princesse Grace, Roquebrune–Cap-Martin* ☎ *377/04–93–41–30–15 for information* ⊕ *www.montecarlotennismasters.com.*

# FRENCH VOCABULARY

| ENGLISH | FRENCH | PRONUNCIATION |
|---|---|---|

## BASICS

| | | |
|---|---|---|
| Yes/no | Oui/non | wee/nohn |
| Please | S'il vous plaît | seel voo play |
| Thank you | Merci | mair-**see** |
| You're welcome | De rien | deh ree-**ehn** |
| Excuse me, sorry | Pardon | pahr-**don** |
| Good morning/afternoon | Bonjour | bohn-**zhoor** |
| Good evening | Bonsoir | bohn-**swahr** |
| Good-bye | Au revoir | o ruh-**vwahr** |
| Mr. (Sir) | Monsieur | muh-**syuh** |
| Mrs. (Ma'am) | Madame | ma-**dam** |
| Miss | Mademoiselle | mad-mwa-**zel** |
| Pleased to meet you | Enchanté(e) | ohn-shahn-**tay** |
| How are you? | Comment allez-vous? | kuh-mahn-tahl-ay **voo** |
| Very well, thanks | Très bien, merci | tray bee-ehn, mair-**see** |
| And you? | Et vous? | ay voo? |

## NUMBERS

| | | |
|---|---|---|
| one | un | uhn |
| two | deux | deuh |
| three | trois | twah |
| four | quatre | **kaht**-ruh |
| five | cinq | sank |
| six | six | seess |
| seven | sept | set |
| eight | huit | wheat |
| nine | neuf | nuf |
| ten | dix | deess |
| eleven | onze | ohnz |
| twelve | douze | dooz |
| thirteen | treize | trehz |
| fourteen | quatorze | kah-torz |

| fifteen | quinze | kanz |
| --- | --- | --- |
| sixteen | seize | sez |
| seventeen | dix-sept | deez-**set** |
| eighteen | dix-huit | deez-**wheat** |
| nineteen | dix-neuf | deez-**nuf** |
| twenty | vingt | vehn |
| twenty-one | vingt-et-un | vehnt-ay-**uhn** |
| thirty | trente | trahnt |
| forty | quarante | ka-**rahnt** |
| fifty | cinquante | sang-**kahnt** |
| sixty | soixante | swa-**sahnt** |
| seventy | soixante-dix | swa-sahnt-**deess** |
| eighty | quatre-vingts | kaht-ruh-**vehn** |
| ninety | quatre-vingt-dix | kaht-ruh-vehn-**deess** |
| one hundred | cent | sahn |
| one thousand | mille | meel |

## COLORS

| black | noir | nwahr |
| --- | --- | --- |
| blue | bleu | bleuh |
| brown | brun/marron | bruhn/mar-**rohn** |
| green | vert | vair |
| orange | orange | o-**rahnj** |
| pink | rose | rose |
| red | rouge | rouge |
| violet | violette | vee-o-**let** |
| white | blanc | blahnk |
| yellow | jaune | zhone |

## DAYS OF THE WEEK

| Sunday | dimanche | dee-**mahnsh** |
| --- | --- | --- |
| Monday | lundi | luhn-**dee** |
| Tuesday | mardi | mahr-**dee** |
| Wednesday | mercredi | mair-kruh-**dee** |

| Thursday | jeudi | zhuh-**dee** |
| Friday | vendredi | vawn-druh-**dee** |
| Saturday | samedi | sahm-**dee** |

## MONTHS

| January | janvier | zhahn-vee-**ay** |
| February | février | feh-vree-**ay** |
| March | mars | marce |
| April | avril | a-**vreel** |
| May | mai | meh |
| June | juin | zhwehn |
| July | juillet | zhwee-**ay** |
| August | août | ah-**oo** |
| September | septembre | sep-**tahm**-bruh |
| October | octobre | awk-**to**-bruh |
| November | novembre | no-**vahm**-bruh |
| December | décembre | day-**sahm**-bruh |

## USEFUL PHRASES

| Do you speak English? | Parlez-vous anglais? | par-lay **voo ahn**-glay |
| I don't speak . . . | Je ne parle pas . . . | zhuh nuh parl pah |
| French | français | frahn-**say** |
| I don't understand | Je ne comprends pas | zhuh nuh kohm-**prahn** pah |
| I understand | Je comprends | zhuh kohm-**prahn** |
| I don't know | Je ne sais pas | zhuh nuh say **pah** |
| I'm American/ British | Je suis américain/ anglais | a-may-ree-**kehn**/ ahn-**glay** |
| What's your name? | Comment vous appelez-vous? | ko-mahn voo za-pell-ay-**voo** |
| My name is . . . | Je m'appelle . . . | zhuh ma-**pell** . . . |
| What time is it? | Quelle heure est-il? | kel air eh-**teel** |
| How? | Comment? | ko-**mahn** |
| When? | Quand? | kahn |
| Yesterday | Hier | yair |

| Today | Aujourd'hui | o-zhoor-**dwee** |
|---|---|---|
| Tomorrow | Demain | duh-**mehn** |
| Tonight | Ce soir | suh **swahr** |
| What? | Quoi? | kwah |
| What is it? | Qu'est-ce que c'est? | kess-kuh-**say** |
| Why? | Pourquoi? | **poor**-kwa |
| Who? | Qui? | kee |
| Where is . . . | Où est . . . | oo ay |
| the train station? | la gare? | la gar |
| the subway station? | la station de métro? | la sta-**syon** duh may-**tro** |
| the bus stop? | l'arrêt de bus? | la-**ray** duh **booss** |
| the post office? | la poste? | la post |
| the bank? | la banque? | la bahnk |
| the . . . hotel? | l'hôtel . . .? | lo-**tel** |
| the store? | le magasin? | luh ma-ga-**zehn** |
| the cashier? | la caisse? | la **kess** |
| the . . . museum? | le musée . . .? | luh mew-**zay** |
| the hospital? | l'hôpital? | lo-pee-**tahl** |
| the elevator? | l'ascenseur? | la-sahn-**seuhr** |
| the telephone? | le téléphone? | luh tay-lay-**phone** |
| Where are the restrooms? | Où sont les toilettes? | oo sohn lay twah-**let** |
| (men/women) | (hommes/femmes) | (**oh**-mm/**fah**-mm) |
| Here/there | Ici/là | ee-**see**/la |
| Left/right | A gauche/à droite | a goash/a draht |
| Straight ahead | Tout droit | too drwah |
| Is it near/far? | C'est près/loin? | say pray/lwehn |
| I'd like . . . | Je voudrais . . . | zhuh voo-**dray** |
| a room | une chambre | ewn **shahm**-bruh |
| the key | la clé | la clay |
| a newspaper | un journal | uhn zhoor-**nahl** |
| a stamp | un timbre | uhn **tam**-bruh |
| I'd like to buy . . . | Je voudrais acheter . . . | zhuh voo-**dray** **ahsh**-tay |
| cigarettes | des cigarettes | day see-ga-**ret** |

| | | |
|---|---|---|
| matches | des allumettes | days a-loo-**met** |
| soap | du savon | dew sah-**vohn** |
| city map | un plan de ville | uhn plahn de **veel** |
| road map | une carte routière | ewn cart roo-tee-**air** |
| magazine | une revue | ewn reh-**vu** |
| envelopes | des enveloppes | dayz ahn-veh-**lope** |
| writing paper | du papier à lettres | dew pa-pee-**ay** a **let**-ruh |
| postcard | une carte postale | ewn cart pos-**tal** |
| How much is it? | C'est combien? | say comb-bee-**ehn** |
| A little/a lot | Un peu/beaucoup | uhn peuh/bo-**koo** |
| More/less | Plus/moins | plu/mwehn |
| Enough/too (much) | Assez/trop | a-say/tro |
| I am ill/sick | Je suis malade | zhuh swee ma-**lahd** |
| Call a . . . | Appelez un . . . | a-play uhn |
| doctor | Docteur | dohk-**tehr** |
| Help! | Au secours! | o suh-**koor** |
| Stop! | Arrêtez! | a-reh-**tay** |
| Fire! | Au feu! | o fuh |
| Caution!/Look out! | Attention! | a-tahn-see-**ohn** |

# TRAVEL SMART
# PROVENCE AND
# THE FRENCH RIVIERA

# GETTING HERE AND AROUND

The "Getting Here" sections listed under towns in the regional chapters of this book provide detailed information about bus and train routes; in many cases, prices, transport companies, and schedules to and from the towns are listed. It's possible to see the entire region just by taking the train: there are comprehensive connections all the way from Montpellier to Avignon to Marseille and on to the full length of the Italian coast. There are good regional bus networks, too, that connect out of train stations; they may not be the best thing for quick village-hopping and multistop sightseeing (their schedules rarely intersect with yours), but they can prove highly useful. When in doubt, just ask the tourist office or your hotel concierge for more information.

## ■ AIR TRAVEL

Flying time to Paris is 75 minutes from London, 7½ hours from New York, 8 hours and 20 minutes from Chicago, and 11 hours from Los Angeles. A direct flight from New York to Nice is 8 hours. Scheduled flying time between Paris to either Marseille or Nice is approximately 1½ hours. Given the possibility of strikes in France, it's a good idea to confirm your flight online the day before.

**Airlines and Airports Airline and Airport Links.com** ⊕ www.airlineandairportlinks.com.

**Airline Security Issues Transportation Security Administration** ⊕ www.tsa.gov.

### AIRPORTS

The major gateways to France are Paris's Orly and Charles de Gaulle airports. Nice, Marseille, and Montpellier's airports are also served by frequent flights from Paris and London, and daily connections from Paris arrive at the smaller airports in Avignon and Nîmes.

FODORS.COM CONNECTION

Before your trip, be sure to check out what other travelers are saying in the forums on www.fodors.com.

**Airport Information Charles de Gaulle** (CDG). ☎ 0033/1–70–36–39–50 outside of France ⊕ www.adp.fr. **Marseille–Provence** ☎ 04–42–14–14–14 ⊕ www.marseille.aeroport. fr. **Montpellier–Meditérranée** ☎ 04–67–20–85–85, 04–67–20–85–00 flight information ⊕ www.montpellier.aeroport.fr. **Nice–Côte d'Azur** ☎ 04–89–88–98–28, 08–20–42–33–33 flight information ⊕ www.nice.aeroport.fr. **Nîmes–Arles–Camargue** ☎ 04–66–70–49–49. **Orly** ☎ 39–50 in France [€.04 per min] ⊕ www.aeroportsdeparis.fr. **Toulon Hyères** ☎ 08–25–01–83–87.

### FLIGHTS

Most major airlines fly to Paris and have connecting flights to the South of France on domestic airlines. The one exception is Delta, which flies nonstop to Nice from New York. From the United Kingdom, EasyJet offers inexpensive nonstop service to Nice and Marseille; British Airways has direct flights to Nice and Marseille; low-cost Ryanair flies to Nîmes, Marseille, and Montpellier.

Within France, Air France flies frequently from Paris to Marseille, Nice, Montpellier, and Toulon. EasyJet has flights from both Paris airports to Nice.

## ■ BUS TRAVEL

Long-distance buses are rare; regional buses are found mainly where train service is spotty. The weakest rail links in the south lie in the Luberon region of the Vaucluse, in the Alpilles, and in the backcountry of the Haut Var, Haute-Provence, and the pre-Alpes behind Nice. To explore these regions, you must work closely with a bus schedule (available at most train stations) and plan connections carefully. Don't plan on too much multistop sightseeing if you're limited to bus connections, as they rarely dovetail with your plans. To visit the popular hill towns just behind the Côte d'Azur—Grasse, St-Paul, Vence, and Biot—you can catch a regional bus or watch for commercial bus excursions advertised in the bigger coastal resorts. Tourist offices provide information on accompanied excursions. Excursions and bus holidays are organized by the SNCF and a plethora of private tour companies. Ask for more information from the local tourism office.

Buses from the United Kingdom generally depart from London, traveling via hovercraft or ferry from London to Paris. The most direct bus route to the south is from London to Avignon; Eurolines' weekly nonstop service takes 17½ hours and costs £89 round-trip—although check the website before booking as there are often deals that allow you to travel for much less.

If you're planning to travel extensively through Europe, you may wish to purchase a Eurolines Europass, valid for unlimited bus travel between 90 European cities (London, Paris, and Marseille included) for up to 60 days.

**Within France Le Pilote** ⊕ www.lepilote.com. **SNCF** ☎ 36–35 in France [€0.34 per min] ⊕ www.sncf.com.

**Discount Passes Eurolines France** ☎ 08–92–89–90–91 in France [€0.34 per min] ⊕ www.eurolines.fr.

## ▌ CAR TRAVEL

Car travel is the best way to see Provence, especially because buses go to the famous hilltop villages only once a day. However, a car may not be the fastest or most economical way to get to Provence: consider flying into Paris, connecting via a smaller airline to Nice or Marseille, and then renting your car in the south. Or purchase a rail-drive pass, available from the SNCF

(French national rail company) or one of the larger car-rental companies. This will allow a few days' rail travel—say, from Paris to Nice—and a block of car-rental time. By using the train to cover the long distances, then exploring the region in depth by car, you can make the most of both modes of transit.

France's roads are classified into three types and prefixed A, N, or D. For the fastest roads between two points, look for roads marked A for *autoroutes*. A *péage* (toll) must be paid on most expressways: the rate varies but can be steep. Sample toll charges are €61.70 from Paris to Nice; €14.30 from Nice to Aix-en-Provence. At your first toll stop you will simply retrieve a ticket, and at the next toll you will pay. You may pay by credit card; Visa and American Express are accepted at most toll booths. The main toll roads through Provence are the A6 and A7, which connect Paris to Marseille via Lyon, Avignon, and Aix; and the east–west A8, which traverses the region from the Italian border to Aix via Nice.

The N (Route Nationale) roads, which are sometimes divided highways, are the route of choice for heavy freight trucks, and are often lined with industry and large chain stores. More scenic, though less trafficked than the Ns are the D (Route Départementale) roads, often also wide and fast.

Though routes are numbered, the French generally guide themselves from city to city and town to town by destination name. When reading a map, keep one eye on the next big city toward your destination as well as the next small town; most snap decisions will have to be based on town names, not road numbers.

Negotiating the back roads requires a careful mix of map and sign reading, often at high speeds around suburban *giratoires* (rotaries, also known as roundabouts). But once you head out into the hills and the tiny roads, which are one of the best parts of Provence and the Côte d'Azur, give yourself over to road signs and pure faith. Directions are indicated by village name only, with route numbers given as a small-print afterthought. Of course, this means you have to recognize the names of minor villages en route.

To leave Paris by car, figure out which of the *portes* (gates) corresponds to the direction you are going. Major highways connect to Paris at these points, and directions are indicated by major cities. For instance, heading south out of the city, look for Porte d'Orléans (direction Lyons and Bordeaux); after Lyons, follow Avignon, and after Avignon follow Nice and/or Marseille. It's best to steer clear of rush hours (7–9:30 am and 4:30–7:30 pm), although this is only a real concern between Aix and Marseille and around Nice.

### GASOLINE

Gas is expensive, especially on expressways and in rural areas. When possible, buy gas before you get on the expressway and keep an eye on pump prices as you go. These are roughly €1.60 per liter, or about $7.70 a gallon. The cheapest gas can be found at *hypermarchés* (very large supermarkets), but be ready for long lines. It is possible to go for many miles in the country without passing a gas station—don't let your tank get too low in rural areas. Many gas stations are closed on Sunday but, they often have automatic gas distributors that allow you to pay with credit cards that have chips, as long as you enter the card's PIN. If you are worried about your budget, ask for a diesel car; diesel fuel at gas pumps can be labeled as *diesel, gasoil,* or *gazole.* Unleaded gas will be labeled as *sans plomb* (SP95 for regular unleaded and SP98 for super unleaded). Be careful, as many gas stations still sell leaded gas.

### PARKING

Parking can be difficult in large towns; your best option (especially in a metropolis like Nice or Marseille) is to duck into the parking garage nearest the neighborhood you want to visit. Carry the ticket with you, and pay at the vending-machine-style ticket dispenser before you go back to your car. On the street, ticket machines (pay and display) are common and work

with *cartes de stationnements* (parking cards), which are like credit cards and come in three denominations: €10, €20, and €30. Parking cards are available at any café posting the red Tabac sign. Insert your card into the nearest meter, choose the approximate amount of time you expect to stay, and you'll receive a green receipt, which must be clearly visible to the meter patrol; place it on the dashboard on the inside of the front window on the passenger side. Be sure to check the signs before you park, as rules vary.

Be careful when parking your car overnight, especially in towns and village squares; if your car is still there in the early morning on a market day, it will be towed. In smaller towns, parking may be permitted on one side of the street only—alternating every two weeks—so pay attention to signs.

The coastal area of Provence—especially the Camargue and the Calanques—as well as overlooks along the Côte d'Azur are extremely vulnerable to car break-ins, and the parking lots are often littered with broken windshield glass. It's important that you never leave valuables visible in the car, and think twice about leaving them in the trunk. Any theft should be reported formally to the police.

### ROAD CONDITIONS

Road conditions in Provence are above average and potholes are rare, especially on highways. Check with the regional information center or listen to FM107.7 (the traffic station) to find out whether there's anything you should know before setting off.

### ROADSIDE EMERGENCIES

If your car breaks down on an expressway, go to a roadside emergency telephone (yellow or blue boxes), which you'll find every 10 km, and call for assistance. If you have a breakdown anywhere else, find the nearest garage or contact the police. If there is an injury, call the SAMU (ambulance service) or fire brigade.

**Emergency Services Ambulance** ☎ *15*.
**Fire Department** ☎ *18*. **General Emergencies** ☎ *112*. **Police** ☎ *17*.

## RULES OF THE ROAD

In France, you may use your own driver's license, but it must be accompanied by an official translation. You must also be able to prove you have third-party insurance. In 2012, a law was passed requiring all drivers to carry a breathalyzer, but as of this writing there is no fine for failure to do so. Drive on the right and yield to drivers coming from streets to the right. However, this rule does not necessarily apply at roundabouts, where you are obligated to yield to those already within (to your left)— but you should watch out for just about everyone. You must wear your seat belt, and children under 10 may not travel in the front seat. French speed limits vary depending on weather conditions, and are lower in rural areas. The limits in dry weather are 130 kph (80 mph) on freeways, 110 kph (70 mph) on divided highways, 90 kph (55 mph) on other roads, 50 kph (30 mph) in towns, and 30 mph (15 mph) in school zones. French drivers break these limits often, but police also hand out hefty on-the-spot fines.

**Contacts Autoroute Information**
⊕ *www.autoroutes.fr.*

## RENTAL CARS

When you reserve a car, ask about cancellation penalties, taxes, drop-off charges (if you're planning to pick up the car in one city and leave it in another), and surcharges (for being under or over a certain age, for additional drivers, or for driving across state or country borders or beyond a specific distance from your point of rental). All these things can add substantially to your costs. Request car seats and extras such as GPS when you book.

Rates are sometimes—but not always— better if you book in advance or reserve through a rental agency's website. There are other reasons to book ahead, though: for popular destinations, during busy times of the year, or to ensure that you get certain types of cars (vans, SUVs, exotic sports cars).

■ TIP➔ **Make sure that a confirmed reservation guarantees you a car. Agencies sometimes overbook, particularly for busy weekends and holiday periods.**

Though renting a car in France is expensive—up to twice as much as in the United States—and the cost of gas is very high as well, it may pay off if you are traveling with two or more people. And of course renting a car gives you the freedom to move around at your own pace. Rates begin at about €30 a day and €220 to €265 per week for an economy car with a manual transmission (an automatic transmission will cost more). Mileage is extra, but there are often multiday packages or weekly rates including some number of kilometers. Be careful to check whether the price includes the 19.6% V.A.T. tax or, if you pick it up from the airport, the airport tax.

Also, price local car-rental companies—whose prices may be lower still, although their service and maintenance may not be as good as those of major rental agencies—and research rates on the Internet. ADA, a French-owned rental company, has offices in towns, train stations, and airports throughout Provence. The Renault Eurodrive program avoids usual car-rental taxes by offering short-term leases to customers. Offices are in Marseille, Montpellier, and Nice; cars must be rented for longer than 20 days.

In France your own driver's license is acceptable, provided you have a notarized translation. You don't need an International Driver's Permit, unless you are planning on a long-term stay; you can get one from the American or Canadian automobile association, and, in the United Kingdom, from the Automobile Association or Royal Automobile Club.

# ▌ TRAIN TRAVEL

The SNCF is recognized as Europe's best national rail service: it's fast, punctual, comfortable, and comprehensive. You can get to Provence and the coast from all points west, north, and east, though lines out of Paris are by far the most direct. There are various options: local trains, overnight trains with sleeping accommodations, and the high-speed TGV, the *Trains à Grande Vitesse* (high-speed trains).

France is rightly proud of its TGV high-speed rail lines, which zoom along at 300 kpm (186 mph). The LGV Méditerranée connects Paris to Avignon and Aix-en-Provence. With the hassles of airport check-in and transfer, you may find train travel the most efficient way to get from Paris to Provence.

In 2013, SCNF introduced Ouigo, a new line of high-speed low-fare trains traveling between a suburb of Paris and Provence. Note that Ouigo has fewer amenities and more restrictions than TGV, including the stipulation that tickets can only be bought online or through a mobile app at least four hours in advance. You'll also need to provide a French phone number and postal code.

All TGV trains to Provence leave from Paris's Gare de Lyon, and Ouigo trains leave from Marne-la-Vallée–Chessy. Travel time from Paris is 2 hours and 40 minutes to Avignon; 3 hours to Nîmes, Marseille, and Aix-en-Provence; 3¼ hours to Montpellier; 4 hours to Toulon; and 5½ hours to Nice.

Certain models of the TGV, called "train duplex," offer luxurious comfort, with double-decker seating and panoramic views. When one of these passes along the coast—especially from Nice to Menton—it makes for a dramatic sightseeing excursion, though it pokes along at a local-train snail's pace. Ask about duplex trains when you're connecting from one coastal city to another (Marseille–Toulon–Fréjus–Cannes–Nice–Menton).

Traveling first class can cost about 50% more than second class, but, with the exception of wider seats, you won't get many more amenities. You'll still need to buy your own food, although in first class you can order a hot meal, served on china, if you're willing to pay a high price for it.

### BOARDING THE TRAIN

Before boarding, you must punch your ticket (but not Eurail Pass) in one of the orange machines at the entrance to the platforms, or else you risk a €10–€15 fine. If you board your train on the run and don't have time to punch it, look for a conductor (contrôleur) as soon as possible and get him to sign it.

If you are traveling from Paris or any other terminus, get to the station half an hour before departure to ensure that you'll have a good seat.

### RAIL PASSES

France is one of 24 countries in which you can use Eurail Passes, which provide unlimited first-class rail travel, in all of the participating countries, for the duration of the pass. If you plan to rack up the miles, the passes can be a good deal. They are available for 15 days (€585), 21 days (€754), one month (€929), two months (€1,309), and three months (€1,616). If your plans call for only limited train travel, use the Rail Europe Pass Finder to help find the least expensive way to reach the countries on your itinerary.

For two to five adults traveling together, the France Rail Pass Saver allows three to nine days of unlimited train travel (and a discount on Eurostar) in a one-month period. Prices begin at €153 each in second class, and €189 each in first class. For solo travelers, the France Rail Pass allows one to nine days of unlimited travel in a month, starting at €117 for first class and €83 for second class for one day of travel. Additional days may be added for €30 a day in either class. Another option is the France Rail 'n Drive Pass, which combines the cost of rail travel and a rental car.

Don't assume that your rail pass guarantees you a seat on the train you wish to ride. You need to book seats ahead even if you are using a rail pass. You must always make a seat reservation for the TGV—easily obtained at the ticket window or from an automatic machine. Seat reservations are reassuring but seldom necessary on other main-line French trains, except at busy holiday times (as during the summer), particularly on popular routes. You will also need a reservation for sleeping accommodations.

SNCF offers a number of discount rail passes, which are available only for purchase in France. You can get a reduced fare if you are over 60 with the SNCF's Carte Sénior, which costs €50 and entitles the bearer to deep discounts on rail and TGV travel for a year. There are also passes for young people and those traveling with small children.

**Information Eurail** ⊕ *www.eurail.com.* **Eurostar** ☎ *0843–218–6186 in U.K., 08–92–35–35–39 in France [€0.34 per min]* ⊕ *www.eurostar.com.* **Rail Europe** ☎ *800/622– 8600 in U.S. (toll-free)* ⊕ *www.raileurope.com.* **TGV** ⊕ *www.tgv.com.*

# ESSENTIALS

## ■ ACCOMMODATIONS

Consider the kind of vacation you want to spend—going native in a country *gîte* (rental house), being pampered in a luxury penthouse overlooking the Mediterranean in Cannes, or getting to know the locals in a cozy B&B or a converted *mas* (farmhouse). Then check the Fodor's recommendations in each chapter, or contact the local tourist offices for more specific information.

The lodgings we list are the cream of the crop in each price category. Properties are assigned price categories based on a standard double room in high season (excluding holidays).

### APARTMENT AND HOUSE RENTALS

The national rental network, the Fédération Nationale des Gîtes de France, rents rural homes with regional flavor, often restored farmhouses or village row houses in pretty country settings. The system grew out of a subsidized movement to salvage wonderful old houses falling to ruin. Gîtes-de-France are nearly always maintained by on-site owners, who greet you on your arrival and provide information on groceries and nearby attractions.

Individual tourist offices often publish lists of *locations meublés* (furnished rentals); these are often inspected by the tourist office and rated by comfort standards. Usually they are booked directly through the individual owner, which generally requires some knowledge of French. Rentals that are not classified or rated by the tourist office should be undertaken with care, and can fall well below your minimum standard of comfort.

Vacation rentals in France always book from Saturday to Saturday (with some offering weekend rates off-season). Most do not include bed linens and towels, but make them available for an additional fee. Always check on policies on pets and children, and specify if you need an enclosed garden for toddlers, a washing machine, a fireplace, and so on. If you plan to have overnight guests during your stay, let the owner know; there may be additional charges. Insurance restrictions prohibit occupation beyond the specified capacity.

The French Government Tourist Office is another source for information about vacation rentals.

**Local Agents Fédération Nationale des Gîtes de France** ☎ 01/49-70-75-75 ⊕ www.gites-de-france.com. **Nice Properties** ⊕ www.nice-properties.fr.

### BED-AND-BREAKFASTS

Bed-and-breakfasts, known in France as *chambres d'hôtes,* are common in rural Provence, but less so along the Côte d'Azur. Check local tourist offices for details or contact Gîtes de France, and organization that lists thousands of B&Bs all over the country, from rustic to more luxurious. Often *table d'hôte* dinners (meals cooked by and eaten with the owners) can be arranged for an extra, fairly nominal fee. Note that in B&Bs, unlike hotels, it is more likely that the owners will speak only French. Staying in one, however, may give you more of an opportunity to meet French people.

**Reservation Services Chambres Hôtes France** ⊕ www.chambres-hotes-france.org.

### GÎTES (VACATION RENTALS)

Gîtes de France is a nationwide organization that rents vacation housing by the week, in the countryside, by the sea, or in the mountains. Houses and apartments are classified on a scale of one to five, according to comfort. Housing is strictly supervised, with an on-site welcome center from either a representative or the owners of the gîtes themselves. Some gîtes can be quite posh, with swimming pool and all the amenities—these go quickly, so be sure to reserve well in advance if this is what you want. Gîtes de France also has a list of regional bed-and-breakfast sites, and regional farms that open their doors and their dining rooms, where amazing dinners can be arranged. Just about everything served at these tables d'hôte comes from the farm itself; these dinners are growing in popularity and run from the simple to the very high-end. Gîtes de France also organizes a variety of tours: hiking tours, canyoning with certified instructors, biking tours with all-terrain bikes, tours for the wine lover with a certified enologist. Note that if you plan on traveling in July or August, you must do as the French do and organize well in advance. Each town's tourist office usually publishes lists of independent rentals (locations meublés), many of them inspected and classified by the tourist office itself.

The region west of Nîmes, including some parts of the Camargue, lies in the département of Hérault. Gîtes de France offices for this department are based in Montpellier. Nîmes itself and environs are processed by the Gard office. For Arles and the Alpilles, contact the Bouches-du-Rhône office.

**Contact Information Gîtes de France**
⊕ *www.gites-de-france.com.*

## HOTELS

Hotels are classified by the French government from one star to four-star deluxe. Prices must, by law, be posted at the hotel entrance and should include taxes and service. Rates are always by room, not per person. Remember that in France the first floor is one floor up (what Americans call the second floor), and the higher up you go the quieter the street noise will be.

You should always check what bathroom facilities the price includes, if any. Because replumbing drains is often very expensive, if not impossible, old hotels may have added bathrooms—often with *douches* (showers), not *baignoires* (tubs)—to the guest rooms, but not toilets. If you want a private bathroom, state your preference for shower or tub—the latter always costs more. Unless otherwise noted, lodging listings in this book include a private bathroom with a shower *or* tub.

When making your reservation, ask for a *grand lit* if you want a double bed. The quality of accommodations, particularly in older properties and even in luxury hotels, can vary greatly from room to room, as hotels are often renovated floor by floor; if you don't like the room you're given, ask to see another.

If you're counting on air-conditioning, you should make sure, in advance, that your hotel room is *climatisé* (air-conditioned). Air-conditioning is not a given, even at hotels in inland Provence, far from sea breezes. And when you throw open the windows, don't expect screens (*moustiquaires*). Nowhere in Europe are they standard equipment, and the only exceptions are found occasionally in the Camargue marshlands, where mosquitoes are a problem.

Breakfast is not always included in the price, but you are sometimes expected to have it and are occasionally charged for it regardless. Make sure to inform the hotel if you are not going to be breakfasting there. In smaller rural hotels you may be expected to have your evening meal at the hotel, too.

It's always a good idea to make hotel reservations as far in advance as possible, especially in late spring, summer, or fall. If you arrive without a reservation, however, the tourist office may be able to help.

# ■ COMMUNICATIONS

## INTERNET

Getting online in major cities in the south of France shouldn't be difficult. Most hotels have Wi-Fi access. Most laptops are dual-voltage, but you will need an adapter.

## PHONES

The good news is that you can now make a direct-dial telephone call from virtually any point on earth. The bad news? You can't always do so cheaply. Calling from a hotel is almost always the most expensive option; hotels usually add huge surcharges to all calls, particularly international ones. In some parts of France you can phone from call centers or even the post office. Calling cards usually keep costs to a minimum, but only if you purchase them locally.

The country code for France is 33. All phone numbers in France have a two-digit prefix determined by zone: Paris and the Île-de-France, 01; the northwest, 02; the northeast, 03; the southeast, 04; and the southwest, 05. Numbers beginning with 08 followed by an 00 are toll-free, but those beginning with 08–36 are toll calls (with an additional charge on top of making the call). Numbers beginning with 06 are mobile phones.

Note that when dialing France from abroad, drop the initial 0 from the number. For instance, to call a telephone number in Paris from the United States, dial 011–33 plus the phone number minus the initial 0 (phone numbers in this book are listed with the full 10 digits, which you use to make local calls). To call France from the United Kingdom, dial 00–33, then dial the number in France minus the initial 0. Note that toll-free numbers won't work outside of France.

## CALLING CARDS

Most French pay phones are operated by *télécartes* (phone cards), which you can buy from post offices, métro stations, and *tabacs* (tobacco shops). There are almost no coin-operated pay phones left, but phone cards are accepted everywhere. There are a seemingly infinite number of phone card brands; the safest bet is the *télécartes international*, which cost about €14 for 50 units. You can also use your own credit card, but you'll get charged a minimum of €20: the credit expires after 30 days.

## CALLING WITHIN FRANCE

To call anywhere in France while in France, dial the full 10-digit number, including the initial zero.

To find a number in France, dial 3912 for information. For international inquiries, dial 00–33–12 (–11 for the United States, –44 for the United Kingdom).

With the rise of mobile phones, phone booths are increasingly rare. Look for them in airports, train stations, post offices, and subway stations.

## CALLING OUTSIDE FRANCE

To call out of France, dial 00 and wait for the tone, then dial the country code (1 for the United States and Canada, 44 for the United Kingdom, 61 for Australia, 64 for New Zealand) and the area code (minus any initial 0) and number. Expect to be overcharged if you call from your hotel.

■ TIP➔ If you travel internationally frequently, save one of your old mobile phones or buy a cheap one on the Internet; ask your cell phone company to unlock it for you, and take it with you as a travel phone, buying a new SIM card with pay-as-you-go service in each destination.

## MOBILE PHONES

If you have a multiband phone (some countries use different frequencies than what's used in the United States) and your service provider uses the world-standard GSM network (as do T-Mobile, Cingular, and Verizon), you can probably use your phone abroad. Roaming fees can be steep, however: 99¢ a minute is considered reasonable. And overseas you normally pay the toll charges for incoming calls. It's cheaper to send a text message than to make a call, but be aware that text fees vary greatly (from 15¢ to 75¢ and up), and you'll usually pay for incoming messages as well.

If you just want to make local calls, consider buying a new SIM card (note that your provider may have to unlock your phone for you to use a different SIM card) and a prepaid service plan in the destination. You'll then have a local number and can make local calls at local rates. If your trip is extensive, you could also simply buy a new cell phone in your destination, as the initial cost will be offset over time.

## CUSTOMS AND DUTIES

You're always allowed to bring goods of a certain value back home without having to pay any duty or import tax. But there's a limit on the amount of tobacco and liquor you can bring back duty-free, and some countries have separate limits for perfumes; for exact figures, check with your customs department. The values of so-called "duty-free" goods are included in these amounts. When you shop abroad, save all your receipts, as customs inspectors may ask to see them as well as the items you purchased. If the total value of your goods is more than the duty-free limit, you'll have to pay a tax (most often a flat percentage) on the value of everything beyond that limit.

If you're coming from outside the European Union (EU), you may import the following duty-free: (1) 200 cigarettes or 100 cigarillos or 50 cigars or 250 grams of tobacco; (2) 2 liters of table wine and, in addition, (a) 1 liter of alcohol over 22% volume (most spirits) or (b) 2 liters of alcohol under 22% volume (fortified or sparkling wine) or (c) 4 more liters of table wine; (3) 50 milliliters of perfume and 250 milliliters of watered de toilette; (4) 200 grams of coffee, 100 grams of tea; and (5) other goods to the value of €175 (€90 for those under 15).

## EATING OUT

The sooner you relax and go with the French flow, the more you'll enjoy your stay. Expect to spend at least two hours for lunch in a restaurant, savoring three courses and talking over the wine; dinner lasts even longer. If you keep one eye on your watch and the other on the waiter, you'll miss the point and spoil your own fun.

You may benefit from a few pointers on French dining etiquette. Diners in France don't negotiate their orders much, so don't expect serene smiles when you ask for sauce on the side. Order your coffee after dessert, not with it. When you're ready for the check, ask for it. No professional waiter would dare put a bill on your table while you're still enjoying the last sip of coffee. And don't ask for a doggy bag; it's just not done.

Also a word on the great mineral-water war: the French usually drink wine or mineral water—not soda or coffee—with their food. You may ask for a carafe of tap water, *une carafe d'eau*. In general, diners order mineral water if they don't order wine. It's not that the tap water is unsafe; it's usually fine—just not as tasty as Evian or slightly fizzy Badoit. To order flat mineral water ask for *eau naturelle*; fizzy is *eau gazeuse*.

Restaurants along the coast are generally more expensive than those inland; basic regional fixed-price menus average about €17 to €22, though the high end of this figure represents the usual cost of seafood so often featured on restaurant menus. In high summer reserve at popular restaurants, especially if you want a coveted outdoor table.

### MEALS AND MEALTIMES

If you're antsy to get to the next museum, or if you plan to spend the evening dining in grand style, consider lunch in a brasserie, where quick, one-plate lunches and full salads are available. Cafés often serve *casse croûtes* (snacks), including sandwiches, which are simply baguettes lightly filled with ham or cheese; or *croques monsieurs,* grilled ham and cheese open-face sandwiches with a rich layer of béchamel. Bakeries and *traiteurs* (delis) often sell savory items like quiches, tiny pizzas, or pastries filled with pâté. On the Côte d'Azur there's a wealth of street food, from the chickpea-based crepes called *socca* to *pissaladière* (onion-olive pizza) and *pan bagnat* (a tuna-and-egg-stuffed pita-style bun).

One of the wonderful aspects of breakfast in Provence and on the Côte d'Azur is eating outdoors, whether on the restaurant terrace or on your own tiny balcony. Breakfasts are light, consisting of croissants and bread, jam and butter, and coffee. Many hotels also serve yogurt, fruit juice, cereal, cheese, and eggs on request.

You'll notice here more than anywhere in France that the lunch hour begins after 1; some places don't even open before that. If you don't mind being a gauche foreigner, eating at noon is one way to get into those sought-after restaurants that do open at noon. If you want to really do as the locals do, reserve for a lunch at 1 or 1:30.

Breakfast is usually served from 7:30 to 10:30; if you want it earlier, arrange a time the night before. Dinner is usually eaten after 8, and most restaurants do not open for dinner before 7:30.

Unless otherwise noted, the restaurants listed in this guide are open daily for lunch and dinner.

# ▮ ELECTRICITY

The electrical current in France is 220 volts, 50 cycles alternating current (AC). French electrical outlets have two round holes, a "female" and a "male" ground; your appliances must either have a slender, two-prong plug that bypasses that ground, or a plug with two round prongs and a hole.

Consider buying a universal adapter, which has several types of plugs in one lightweight, compact unit. Most laptops and mobile phone chargers are dual voltage (i.e., they operate equally well on 110 and 220 volts), so require only an adapter. These days the same is often true of small appliances, such as hair dryers. Always check labels and manufacturer instructions to be sure. Don't use 110-volt outlets marked "FOR SHAVERS ONLY" for high-wattage appliances such as hair-dryers.

**Contacts Steve Kropla's Help for World Travelers.** The site has information on electrical and telephone plugs around the world. ⊕ *www.kropla.com.*

# ▮ EMERGENCIES

France's emergency services are streamlined and universal, so no matter where you are in the country, you can dial the same phone numbers, listed below. Every town and village has a *médecin de garde* (on-duty doctor) for flus, sprains, tetanus shots, and so on. To find out who's on any given evening, call any *généraliste* (general practitioner) and a recording will refer you. If you need an x-ray or emergency treatment, call the ambulance number and you'll be taken to the hospital of your choice—or the nearest one. Note that outside of Paris it may be difficult to find English-speaking doctors.

In case of fire, hotels are required to post emergency exit maps inside every room door and multilingual instructions.

If you need assistance in an emergency, you can go to your country's embassy or consulate. Proof of identity and citizenship are generally required to enter. If your passport has been stolen, get a police report, and then contact your embassy for assistance.

## OVER-THE-COUNTER REMEDIES

For a headache *(mal à la tête)* ask the pharmacist for *aspirine* (aspirin) or *doliprane* (Tylenol). For gas pains, ask for smecta, and for menstrual cramps you will be given *spasfon*. For car and boat sickness, *primperan*. For cuts, scrapes, and other minor "ouchies," which the French call "bobos," you will be given a disinfectant spray called Bétadine. Gel d'Apis treats mosquito bites (you may need this if you are traveling in the Camargue). Sore throats are treated with lozenges called *pastilles*, and cough syrup is *sirop*. Diarrhea *(diarrhée)* is treated with Immodium.

## HOLIDAYS

With 11 national *jours feriés* (holidays) and five weeks of paid vacation, the French have their share of repose. In May, there is a holiday nearly every week, so be prepared for stores, banks, and museums to shut their doors for days at a time. Be sure to call museums, restaurants, and hotels in advance to make sure they will be open.

Some holidays to keep in mind: January 1, New Year's Day; early to mid-April, Easter and Easter Monday; May 1, Labor Day; May 8, VE Day; mid- to late May, Ascension; late May to early June, Pentecost Monday; July 14, Bastille Day; August 15, Assumption; November 1, All Saints; November 11, Armistice; December 25, Christmas. Tourist sites are especially likely to be closed on New Year's, Labor Day, and Christmas.

France's school vacations tend to unleash hordes of families and *classes de mer* (school trips to the coast) on museums, castles, and family hotels. School vacations are divided by region and are spread out over about three weeks in late October–November, Christmas–New Year's, again in February, and finally in April. Provence and the Côte d'Azur are the most crowded during the summer holidays, usually the last week of July and all of August.

## HOURS OF OPERATION

Bank hours vary from branch to branch, but are generally weekdays 8:30 to 4. Most take a one-hour, or even a 90-minute, lunch break around noon.

Gas stations on the autoroutes are generally open 24 hours. In towns, gas stations close at 8 pm, with the occasional station staying open until 10 pm. Outside the city centers, most stations are closed on Sunday.

Museum hours are somewhat lax in the south, with seasonal variations and a tendency to change slightly and often. Usual opening times are from 9:30 or 10 to 5 or 6, but many close for lunch (noon–2). To allow for long terrace lunches and an afternoon lag in business due to beach time, the lunch hour may be even longer in summer, with some later evening hours to compensate. Most museums are closed one day a week (generally Monday or Tuesday) and on national holidays: check museum hours before you go.

Large stores in big towns in the South of France are open from 9 or 9:30 until 7 or 8. Smaller shops often open earlier (8 am) and close later (8 pm) but take a lengthy lunch break (1 to 4 or 4:30). Corner groceries frequently stay open until around 10 pm. Market days vary from town to town, but stalls generally close by about 1 pm.

## MAIL

Letters and postcards to the United States and Canada cost €0.95 (about $1.30) for 20 grams (about 0.7 ounces). Letters and postcards within France and the rest of Europe (including the United Kingdom) cost €0.63 (about 86 cents) for up to 20 grams. Stamps can be bought in post offices *(bureaux de poste)* and cafés displaying a red TABAC sign outside.

If you're uncertain where you'll be staying, have mail sent to the local post office, addressed as "poste restante," (there's an €0.85 service charge). Bring your passport along to collect your mail.

# ▌ MONEY

The following prices are to give you an idea of costs. Note that it is less expensive to eat or drink standing at a café or bar counter than it is to sit at a table, so two prices are listed, *au comptoir* (at the counter) and *à salle* (at a table). Coffee in a bar: €1 to €2.50 (standing), €1.50 to €5 (seated); beer in a bar: €2 (standing), €3 to €6 (seated); Coca-Cola: €2 to €4 a can; ham sandwich: €3 to €5; one-mile taxi ride: €6; movie: €7.50 to €9.50 (sometimes less expensive for screenings before noon); foreign newspaper: €1.50 to €4; museum admission: €1.50 to €9.

Prices throughout this guide are given for adults. Substantially reduced fees are almost always available for children, students, and senior citizens.

▌TIP→ Banks never have every foreign currency on hand, and it may take as long as a week to order. If you're planning to exchange funds before leaving home, don't wait until the last minute.

## ATMS AND BANKS

Your own bank will probably charge a fee for using ATMs abroad; the foreign bank you use may also charge a fee. Nevertheless, you'll usually get a better rate of exchange at an ATM than you will at a currency-exchange office or even when changing money in a bank. And extracting funds as you need them is a safer option than carrying around a large amount of cash.

▌TIP→ PINs with more than four digits are not recognized at ATMs in many countries. If yours has five or more, remember to change it before you leave.

ATMs (*distributeurs de billets*) are common in major cities and larger towns and are one of the easiest ways to get cash; you'll find one in almost any but the very smallest towns. Banks usually offer excellent, wholesale exchange rates through ATMs.

To get cash at ATMs in France, your PIN must be four digits long. You may have more luck with ATMs if you are using a credit card or a debit card that is also a Visa or MasterCard, rather than just your bank card. Note, too, that you may be charged by your bank for using ATMs overseas; inquire at your bank about charges.

Before you go, it's a good idea to get a list of ATM locations that you can use in France from your bank. Failing that, you can always ask a passerby on the street for the nearest *distributeur de billets*.

## CREDIT CARDS

It's a good idea to inform your credit-card company before you travel, especially if you're going abroad and don't travel internationally very often. Otherwise, the credit-card company might put a hold on your card owing to unusual activity—not a good thing halfway through your trip. Record all your credit-card numbers—as well as the phone numbers to call if your cards are lost or stolen—in a safe place, so you're prepared should something go wrong. Both MasterCard and Visa have general numbers you can call (collect if you're abroad) if your card is lost, but you're better off calling the number of your issuing bank, since MasterCard and Visa usually just transfer you to your bank; your bank's number is usually printed on your card.

If you plan to use your credit card for cash advances, you'll need to apply for a PIN at least two weeks before your trip. Although it's usually cheaper (and safer) to use a credit card abroad for large purchases (so you can cancel payments or be reimbursed if there's a problem), note that some credit-card companies *and* the banks that issue them add substantial percentages to all foreign transactions, whether they're in a foreign currency or not. Check on these fees before leaving home, so there won't be any surprises when you get the bill.

▌TIP→ Before you charge something, ask the merchant whether or not he or she plans to do a dynamic currency conversion (DCC). In such a transaction the merchant (shop, restaurant, or hotel, not Visa or MasterCard) converts the currency and charges you in dollars. In most cases you'll pay the merchant a 3% fee for this service in addition to any credit-card company and issuing-bank foreign-transaction surcharges.

Merchants who participate in them are supposed to ask whether you want to be charged in dollars or the local currency, but they don't always do so. And even if they do offer you a choice, they may well avoid mentioning the additional surcharges. The good news is that you *do* have a choice. And if this practice really gets your goat, you can avoid it using American Express; with its cards, DCC isn't an option.

Many restaurants and stores take both credit and debit cards, though there is often a €10 or €15 minimum.

## CURRENCY AND EXCHANGE

Under the euro system, there are seven notes: 5, 10, 20, 50, 100, 200, and 500 euros. Notes are the same for all countries. There are eight coins: 1 and 2 euros, plus 1, 2, 5, 10, 20, and 50 cents. On all coins, one side has the value of the euro on it and the other side has the national symbol of one of the countries participating in monetary union.

■TIP➔ Even if a currency-exchange booth has a sign promising no commission, rest assured that there's some kind of huge, hidden fee. (Oh . . . that's right. The sign didn't say no fee). And as for rates, you're almost always better off getting foreign currency at an ATM or exchanging money at a bank.

## PACKING

Although you'll usually have no trouble finding a baggage cart at the airport, luggage restrictions on international flights are tight and baggage carts at railroad stations are not always available, so pack light. Even hotel staffs are becoming less and less tolerant of heavy suitcases and heaps of luggage worthy of a *Queen Mary* crossing. If you simply must have every item on your list, you can opt to send your luggage on ahead with a number of different companies, but be prepared to organize shipment at least two weeks in advance.

Over the years, casual dress has become more acceptable, although the resorts along the Côte d'Azur and in the Luberon and Aix-en-Provence are still synonymous with smart dressers and fashion plates.

Jeans are common, though they, too, are worn stylishly, with a nice button-down shirt, polo, or T-shirt without writing. Shorts are a popular item for the younger crowd in most cities. More and more people are wearing sneakers, although you may still stand out as a tourist with them on, especially if you wear them when you go out at night.

There is no need to wear a tie and jacket at most restaurants, even fancy ones, though you should still try to look nice. Most casinos and upscale nightclubs along the Côte d'Azur, however, require jackets and ties, and certainly no jeans allowed.

For beach resorts, take a decent cover-up; wearing your bathing suit on the street is frowned on, even if topless when actually on the beach is commonly accepted.

Most of France is hot in summer, cool in winter. Since it rains all year round, bring a raincoat and umbrella. You'll need a sweater or warm jacket for the Mediterranean in winter, and you should also bring hats, scarves, and gloves.

If you are staying in budget hotels, take along soap. Many hotels either do not provide it or give you a limited amount. You might also want to bring a washcloth.

Lighters, even empty ones, may also be confiscated at check-in.

# ▌ SAFETY

Car break-ins have become part of daily life in the south, especially in the isolated parking lots where hikers set off to explore for the day. Be especially careful around the marshes of the Camargue, the departure point for the Îles d'Hyères ferries, the rocky Esterel between Fréjus and Cannes, and the coastal path around St-Tropez: take valuables with you and, if possible, leave your luggage at your hotel.

Also beware of petty theft—purse snatching and pickpocketing. Use common sense: avoid pulling out a lot of money in public, and wear a handbag with long straps that you can sling across your body, bandolier-style, with a zippered compartment for your money and passport. It's also a good idea to wear a money belt. Men should keep their wallets up front, as safely tucked away as possible. At airports and train stations, never leave your luggage trolley unattended.

Although cities in Provence are safe during the day, take caution at night, especially in port towns such as Marseille, Nice, and Toulon. Marseille is particularly known for its drug-related crime, although in general tourists are not targeted. Avignon also has a high crime rate, and tourists should be alert and walk purposefully through town at night.

▌TIP→ Distribute your cash, credit cards, IDs, and other valuables between a deep front pocket, an inside jacket or vest pocket, and a hidden money pouch. Don't reach for the money pouch once you're in public.

# ▌ TAXES

All taxes must be included in posted prices in France. The initials TTC (*toutes taxes comprises*—taxes included) sometimes appear on price lists but taxes are included whether they are or not. By law, restaurant and hotel prices must also include the tax, and hotels charge a daily habitation tax that usually runs between €1.20 to €2.30 per day (depending on the size of the room you are in).

A number of shops participating in the Tax-Free Shopping program (you'll see a sticker in the shop window) offer V.A.T. refunds to foreign shoppers—under very limited circumstances. To qualify for the refund, you must be a national of a non-EU country, at least 15 years old at the time of purchase, and visiting France for less than six months. If you qualify, you are entitled to an export discount of up to 20%, depending on the item purchased, and only on purchases of at least €175 in a single store.

French retailers are required to provide a computer-generated refund form to travelers, in a system called PABLO. Instead of submitting your form at the customs window, you must now scan your receipts at one of the blue PABLO self-service machines located in airports. As of this writing, there were no PABLO machines at train stations, so if you're leaving France by the rails you'll want to stop off at the airport on your way.

If you leave France without getting your V.A.T refunded, getting the rebate is even more complicated. You'll have to present your receipt and the merchandise at the French consulate in the U.S. in order to obtain a "visa," which you'll then have to submit by mail within six months of the purchase date. The process can take quite a while, and it's not guaranteed to be approved. It's simpler to use the PABLO machines.

**V.A.T. Refunds** V.A.T. Refund Information ⊕ *www.consulfrance-newyork.org/ The-VAT-Refund.*

# ▌ TIME

The time difference between New York and France is six hours; when it's 1 pm in New York, it's 7 pm in France. France is seven hours ahead of Chicago and nine hours ahead of Los Angeles. France is one hour ahead of London. The time difference between France and Sydney is eight to nine hours, depending on when daylight saving time is or is not in effect.

# TIPPING

The French have a clear idea of when they should be tipped. Bills in bars and restaurants include a 15% service fee, but it is customary to round out your bill with some small change unless you're dissatisfied. The amount of this varies: anywhere from €0.10 if you've merely bought a beer, to €2 to €3 after a meal. Tip taxi drivers and hairdressers about 15%. In some theaters and hotels, coat check attendants may expect nothing if there is a sign saying "*pourboire interdit*" (tips forbidden); otherwise give them €1. The same goes for washroom attendants, unless another sum is posted.

If you stay in a hotel for more than two or three days, it is customary to leave something for the chambermaid—about €1.50 per day. In expensive hotels you may well call on the services of a baggage porter (bell boy) and hotel porter and possibly the telephone receptionist. All expect a tip: plan on about €1.50 per item for the baggage boy, but the other tips will depend on how much you've used their services—common sense must guide you here. In hotels that provide room service, give €1 to €2 to the waiter (this does not apply to breakfast served in your room). If the chambermaid does some pressing or laundering for you, give her €1 to €2 on top of the charge made.

Gas-station attendants get nothing for gas or oil, but about €1 for checking tires. Train and airport porters get a fixed €1 to €1.50 per bag, but you're better off getting your own baggage cart if you can.

| TIPPING GUIDELINES FOR PROVENCE | |
|---|---|
| Bartender | €1 to €5 per round of drinks, depending on the number of drinks |
| Bellhop | €1 to €5 per bag, depending on the level of the hotel |
| Hotel Concierge | €5 or more, if he or she performs a service for you |
| Hotel Doorman | €1–€2 if he helps you get a cab |
| Hotel Maid | €1–€3 a day (either daily or at the end of your stay, in cash) |
| Hotel Room-Service Waiter | €1 to €2 per delivery, even if a service charge has been added |
| Porter at Airport or Train Station | €1 per bag |
| Skycap at Airport | €1 to €3 per bag checked |
| Taxi Driver | 15%, but round up the fare to the next euro |
| Tour Guide | 10% of the cost of the tour |
| Valet Parking Attendant | €1–€2, but only when you get your car |
| Waiter | 15%–20%, with 20% being the norm at high-end restaurants; some pocket change if a service charge is added to the bill |
| Other | Restroom attendants in more expensive restaurants expect some small change or €1. Tip coat-check personnel at least €1–€2 per item checked unless there is a fee, then nothing. |

# TOURS

Guided tours are a good option when you don't want to do it all yourself. You travel along with a group (sometimes large, sometimes small), stay in prebooked hotels, eat with your fellow travelers (the cost of meals is sometimes included in the price of your tour, sometimes not), and follow a schedule.

A knowledgeable guide can take you places that you might never discover on your own, and you may be pushed to see more than you would have otherwise. Tours aren't for everyone, but they can be just the thing for trips to places where making travel arrangements is difficult or time-consuming (particularly when you don't speak the language).

Whenever you book a guided tour, find out what's included and what isn't. A "land-only" tour includes all your travel (by bus, in most cases) in the destination, but not necessarily your flights to and from or even within it. Also, in most cases prices in tour brochures don't include fees and taxes. And remember that you'll be expected to tip your guide (in cash) at the end of the tour.

The French tourist office publishes many brochures on theme trips in France, including "In the Footsteps of the Painters of Light in Provence" and "France for the Jewish Traveler."

**Information Tours of Provence** ☎ 06–22–85–64–61 ⊕ www.toursofprovence.com.

# ▮ VISITOR INFORMATION

**Information Comité Régional du Tourisme** (*CRT PACA*). ✉ *61 La Canebière, Marseille, France* ☎ *04–91–56–47–00* ⊕ *www.tourismepaca.fr.* **Côte d'Azur Tourist Office** ⊕ *www.cotedazur-tourisme.com.* **France Guide.** France Guide is the official website of the national Tourist Office. ⊕ *us.franceguide.com.* **French Government Tourist Office.** ⊕ *francetourism.com.* **Provence Tourist Office** ⊕ *www.visitprovence.com.* **Avignon Caumont Airport** ✉ *141 allée de la Chartreuse, Montfavet, southeast of Avignon, France* ☎ *04–90–81–51–51* ⊕ *www.avignon.aeroport.fr.*

# INDEX

## PHOTO CREDITS